WORLD CRUISING DESTINATIONS

JIMMY CORNELL

OTHER BOOKS BY JIMMY CORNELL

World Cruising Routes
Covering all the sailing routes of the world
ISBN: 978-0-07-159289-5

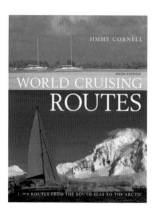

Long established as the bible for long-distance cruisers and a bestseller since its first publication, *World Cruising Routes* is a comprehensive guide to over 1,000 sailing routes covering all the oceans of the world from the tropical South Seas to the high latitudes of the Arctic and Antarctic, geared specifically to the needs of cruising sailors. It contains information on the winds, currents, regional and seasonal weather, as well as suggestions about optimum times for individual routes. This 6th edition assesses the effects of global warming on cruising routes and provides over 6,000 waypoints to assist skippers in planning individual routes. It is the perfect one-stop reference for planning a cruise anywhere in the world.

'The most important book for long-distance voyagers to come along in decades.'
Cruising World

A Passion for the Sea
Reflections on three circumnavigations
ISBN: 978-1-4081-2268-6

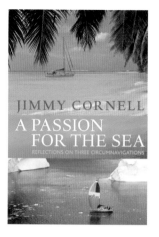

'What Jimmy Cornell doesn't know about cruising isn't worth knowing.'
Yachting World

One of the most influential cruising yachtsmen writing today, Jimmy Cornell has sailed over 200,000 miles in more than thirty years on the oceans, including three circumnavigations and voyages to the Arctic and Antarctic. In this new book, Jimmy tells the story of his own travels in great detail. Decades of offshore sailing experience are distilled into this colourful account, packed with valuable observations, spiced up with entertaining anecdotes, and illustrated with brilliant photos from along the way.

Much more than just an exciting report of his adventures, Jimmy draws on his experiences to share practical tips for anyone inspired to follow his example, along with important technical information.

World Cruising Essentials
An overview of boats, gear, and life on board
ISBN: 0-07-141425-8

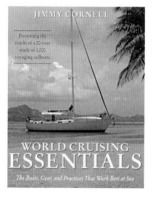

World Cruising Essentials is a unique book that presents a comprehensive overview of the current world cruising scene. *World Cruising Essentials* includes a wealth of practical advice and information for all long-distance cruisers and will be welcomed by the cruising community for its invaluable insight.

Where do the boats go? World movement and distribution of cruising yachts
The cruising boat today: Size, material, rig, equipment, breakages
Life afloat: Provisioning, refrigeration, watermakers, engines and fuel, energy consumption, generation, self-steering gear, anchors, tenders, watchkeeping, weather, pets
The ideal cruising boat: Improvements and comforts
Safety: Piracy, firearms, personal safety, collisions, abandoning ship
Practical aspects of cruising: Formalities and restrictions, cost, communications, tourism, long term planning
Psychological aspects of the cruising life: Crew, expectations, seasickness, the female point of view
The future: Significant incidents and lessons

WORLD CRUISING DESTINATIONS

JIMMY CORNELL

INTERNATIONAL MARINE • McGRAW-HILL
Camden, Maine • New York • Chicago • San Francisco
• Lisbon • London • Madrid • Mexico City • Milan • New
Delhi • San Juan • Seoul • Singapore • Sydney • Toronto

To Gwenda – for everything

The **McGraw-Hill** Companies

www.internationalmarine.com

Copyright © Jimmy Cornell 2010

First edition published 2010

ISBN 978-0-07-163824-1
MHID 0-07-163824-5

A CIP catalog record for this book is available from the Library of Congress.

This book is produced using paper that is made from wood grown in managed, sustainable forests. It is natural, renewable and recyclable. The logging and manufacturing processes conform to the environmental regulations of the country of origin.

Typeset in Haarlemmer MT 8.75pt on 11.5pt
Printed and bound in India by Replika Press Pvt. Ltd.

Originally published by Adlard Coles Nautical.

CONTENTS

INTRODUCTION

At the end of my first circumnavigation I decided to write the kind of book that I wished I had had myself both during the planning of that voyage and the six years that it took us to complete it. Soon after its publication, I realized that while *World Cruising Routes* could help sailors plan the best route to reach their chosen destination, they would still need some additional information on their actual landfall, as in those days there were few cruising guides, and those that were available only covered popular areas such as the Mediterranean and Caribbean. *World Cruising Handbook* tried to put that right by including in one volume all maritime nations of the world and providing the reader both with essential planning data and basic practical and background information on each individual nation. The two books complemented each other well and for a while it looked like mission accomplished. I used both books extensively during my second circumnavigation, but the arrival of the internet and email during that period made me realize that there was now a third dimension that could not be ignored. Thus *World Cruising Handbook* mutated naturally into www.noonsite.com, which since its launch in 2000 has become the most popular source of information for cruising sailors worldwide. The internet is a wonderful tool for the dissemination of knowledge, and noonsite.com has both benefited from it and contributed to it.

Twenty years after the publication of the *Handbook* and ten years after the birth of noonsite.com, it became apparent that even the internet has its limitations, and *World Cruising Destinations* attempts to address some of these. While continuing *World Cruising Handbook*'s primary role as a voyage planner by including practical information for each of the 184 countries covered, this book attempts to add a dash of spice to such factual data by describing in more detail every country's main attractions and, hopefully, whets the reader's appetite to sail there. On a practical level, the book attempts to give an idea of what preparations are needed in the way of visas, cruising permits or guides, as well as what is available locally in terms of repair facilities and services, fuel and provisions, or charter opportunities. As there are no individual cruising guides available for at least half of the countries covered, the following pages contain all the essential information you may need if an unforeseen emergency stop has to be made in a country that is not covered by any other publication.

I am writing these lines while anchored in a small bay on the island of Skyros in the Aegean. Last night Gwenda and I took the dinghy to the nearby harbour of Linaria, a typical Greek port with fishermen mending their nets on the dockside, dazzling-white houses with balconies overflowing with brightly coloured flowers lining the quay, old men chatting over a glass of ouzo, tavernas displaying the catch of the day, and the sleepy place suddenly coming alive with the arrival of the evening ferry. Watching this scene unfold before my eyes, I realized with a pang of joy that in spite of all that has changed in the world since I started cruising, much has remained the same, and that a boat can still take you to places that have remained virtually untouched. Having sailed to over half the countries described in the following pages, and having been fortunate in being able to see so many beautiful places, I hope that this book will inspire many of its readers to cast off the lines and grasp the opportunity to enjoy this wonderful planet of ours.

Aventura, Linares Bay, Skyros, Northern Aegean
June 2009

Twenty years from now you will be more disappointed by the things that you didn't do than by the ones you did. So throw off the bowlines. Sail away from the safe harbour. Catch the trade winds in your sails. Explore. Dream. Discover.
Mark Twain

ABOUT THIS BOOK

ALL COUNTRIES OR ISLAND GROUPS that are visited by cruising yachts, even if only very rarely, are included in this book. It aims to give all the essential information you need to decide if a particular country is worth visiting, to know what to expect once there, and to make the necessary preparations concerning visas, cruising permits or other requirements.

✦ CLIMATE

Weather conditions should be the first factor to be considered when planning a voyage anywhere in the world and the section on climate gives a brief outline of what can be expected. Wherever they occur tropical storm seasons are also mentioned, as certain areas are best avoided at such times. This is a summary of tropical storm seasons throughout the world:

AREA	SEASON	HIGHEST FREQUENCY
Caribbean Sea	June to November	September
North East Pacific	May to November	July–September
North West Pacific	All year	July–October
Bay of Bengal	May to December	October–November
Arabian Sea	April to December	April–May; October–November
South Indian Ocean	November to May	December to March
South Pacific Ocean	November to April	January–March

One of the noticeable effects of climate change is that the weather is even less predictable than it used to be, and this trend has already been seen in the behaviour of tropical storms. Some very violent hurricanes have occurred in recent years, and the actual seasons as well as the affected areas are less well defined than in the past. In both the South Atlantic and the Eastern North Atlantic tropical storms have occurred where they have never been recorded before, and this is perhaps a strong indication that world climate is indeed changing.

✦ PORTS OF ENTRY

Wherever possible, all official ports of entry for each country have been listed. The exceptions are countries where arriving yachts may clear into any major port or where specific phone numbers are listed to call, either to inform the authorities of your impending arrival or to be given instructions as to where to proceed.

✦ FORMALITIES

Clearance formalities vary greatly from country to country – being extremely simple in some, and unnecessarily complicated in others. The complexity of formalities is often a reflection of the nature of the regime in power and it normally can be assumed that the less liberal a country, the more complicated its entry formalities. There are, though, some notable exceptions to this as formalities in Australia and the USA are among the most complex and stringent in the world. On the other hand, in many places regularly frequented by yachts, formalities have been simplified and countries are co-operating in the introduction of a unified system – whether that be completing a pre-arrival form on the internet for some East Caribbean islands; issuing visas that are valid for several countries in Europe or Central America; or abolishing formalities altogether between countries in the EU.

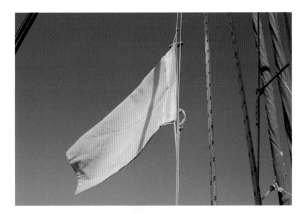

Several countries now insist that the relevant authorities are informed well in advance of a yacht's arrival. Australia was the first to introduce this requirement, which is now being applied by other countries too. Many captains, who have ignored this requirement or infringed other regulations, have been fined and, in a few extreme cases, had their yachts impounded. This is why it must be stressed that however easy or complicated they may appear to be, formalities should always be taken seriously, and even what look like arbitrary restrictions should be complied with. Moreover, however lax or strict a country may be, entry formalities must be completed as soon as possible, and the intention to do so must be indicated immediately you enter that country's territorial waters by flying the Q flag, the country's courtesy flag, and contacting the relevant authorities by radio. Although 12 miles is the international accepted limit of territorial waters, some countries have unilaterally extended these limits and such exceptions are mentioned in the text.

It is also important to know that even countries that do not permit or encourage visits by foreign yachts are obliged by international law to assist a vessel in distress in case of a serious emergency. Should such an emergency occur, the authorities should be contacted at the earliest opportunity and you should insist on being treated in accordance with the provisions of international maritime law.

There are strict regulations concerning firearms and pets in all countries and, as both need to be declared on arrival at the first port of entry, this requirement is not repeated in the text for each individual destination. In some countries, firearms may be confined on board if there is a suitable locker, otherwise they must be deposited ashore and only retrieved, under supervision, when the boat is ready to leave the country – something that can be not only inconvenient, but also very expensive if the port of departure is not the same as the one of arrival and the firearm has to be taken to that port by a customs officer. Restrictions imposed on visiting animals are just as severe, and information on the requirements for individual countries should be ascertained before arrival by consulting an internet source such as noonsite.com.

Quarantine regulations in some countries are very strict and the importation of fresh produce as well as a wide range of foodstuffs is prohibited. In such places it is advisable to arrive with few such stores. Occasionally, one may be allowed to consume such food on board, but in most cases these items are confiscated on arrival and destroyed. In some countries duty-free stores, whether spirits, wine or beer, may be sealed on board, but in most places they must be declared and duty paid on any excess.

Documents

The most common documents needed when clearing in are the ship's registration papers, radio licence, passports and vaccination certificates. Clearance papers from the last country visited may also be requested. Some officials may want to see the vessel's original insurance policy and a certificate of competence for the captain. If firearms are carried, these should be licensed in the country of origin, as this licence will be requested in most places. Similarly, pets must have international health certificates and their anti-rabies and other vaccinations should be kept up to date. Those who carry scuba diving equipment on board may be asked to show their diving qualification certificates before getting tanks filled. Finally, a prescription or a letter from a doctor should accompany any personal medication needed – specifying the medicine and why it is taken, especially those used on a regular basis, such as heart and blood pressure medication, diuretics, tranquillizers, antidepressants, stimulants or sleeping pills.

A radio operator's licence, whether for VHF, HF or amateur radio, is required in most countries, although this is rarely checked. In some places amateur radios can only be used legally if the operator is in possession of a reciprocal licence issued by the country concerned. In a few countries there are restrictions on the use of any radio equipment while in port, while in others, such as Thailand and New Zealand, the use of portable marine VHF radios on land is forbidden.

Although some forms have to be filled in on the spot, considerable time can be saved by having some papers prepared beforehand. It is always a good idea to have photocopies of the ship's registration papers as well as plenty of crew lists, with such details as first name, surname, date of birth, nationality, passport number and date of expiry as well as details of the boat itself: name of vessel, flag, type (sailing yacht), official registration number, gross and net tonnage, LOA (in feet and metres), call sign, name and address of registered owner. A ship's stamp is greatly appreciated in many countries where, for some strange reason, a rubber stamp has a certain authority.

Visas

One aspect that this book tries to clear up is the subject of visa requirements. While in some countries these require-ments are quite clear, in others the situation concerning visiting yachts is confusing. Foreign nationals arriving on a yacht can be treated basically in three different ways by the immigration authorities:

- Sailors are regarded as being the same as ordinary tourists arriving by other means, in which case the usual visa requirements apply.
- Special visa requirements are applied to those arriving by yacht. This may mean that some countries that normally grant visas on arrival to tourists coming by air will insist that anyone arriving on a yacht must have obtained their visa in advance. This is often because tourists coming by air must have an onward ticket to be given a visa, while arriving on a yacht is not always regarded as a guarantee of your ability to depart by the same means.
- Sailors are sometimes given special treatment by being allowed to enter a country without a visa, unlike tourists arriving by other means. At times visas are granted on arrival, and occasionally are dispensed with altogether and a shore pass issued instead. However, in these cases such

special concessions are often given only for a limited time and may be restricted to the duration of the yacht's stay in port or while cruising certain areas. Usually it will be necessary to obtain an ordinary tourist visa to visit other parts of the country or leave by means other than by yacht.

Passports should have a validity that is well in excess of the intended period of travel. A number of countries insist that passports are valid for at least six months beyond the intended stay in that country. In many Arab or Muslim states, an Israeli stamp in your passport may result in you being turned away or experiencing difficulties, so anyone who visits Israel should insist that their passport is not stamped. In some countries, police, the army or security forces do spot-checks, so you should always carry some form of identification when ashore, even if only a photocopy of the relevant passport pages.

For countries where a visa is required, this should be obtained well in advance, although you should make sure that the visa will still be valid when you arrive in the respective country as some places stipulate that entry must take place within a certain time after the date of issue. It is also a good idea to obtain a visa in advance for difficult countries, even if it is stated that visas can be issued on arrival. Obtaining a multiple-entry visa may be advisable if visiting countries that have overseas territories or dependencies, such as France (Martinique, Guadeloupe, French Polynesia, New Caledonia, Reunion, Mayotte), Australia (Norfolk Island, Christmas Island, Cocos Keeling) or the USA (Virgin Islands, Puerto Rico, Hawaii, Guam).

Obtaining a visa on arrival for crew joining a yacht without being in possession of a return ticket is not always easy, and for this reason captains are urged to meet such crew at the airport so as to be able to explain the special circumstances to immigration. Also, in order to pre-empt any problems for crew arriving on a single ticket, the captain should send such crew a letter stating that this person is joining a yacht and will also be leaving the country that way. Such a letter may be acceptable, although some airlines refuse to allow a person to board a flight if not in possession of a return ticket. If all else fails, whether at the airport of departure or arrival, the crew may need to buy a return ticket to his or her country of residence, and if this is a standard ticket and remains unused, its cost can be refunded later in full.

Something that must be borne in mind when cruising is that visa regulations do change and often without warning. You should always try to find out the latest situation before sailing to a certain country. As most places maintain diplo-matic missions in neighbouring countries, these are the best ones to ask about changes and to apply for any necessary visas.

Cruising permits

In some countries, cruising boats are subjected to special regulations or restrictions concerning their movement. In most places, if a cruising permit or transit log is required, it is issued at the first port of entry, so it is not necessary to make any preparations in advance. Any restrictions on the freedom of movement of yachts, which do not require a cruising permit to be obtained in advance, are mentioned in the section of that country. Also mentioned are the few countries where such permits must be secured in advance. There are various reasons why restrictions on the movement of cruising boats are imposed, the main ones being the protection of remote communities from intrusion, the preservation of marine parks and nature reserves, or the wish of authorities to keep foreign sailors away from sensitive military areas or detention centres. Restrictions are also increasingly imposed on genuine cruising boats because of the fear by local authorities that a boat chartering illegally might slip through their net. In some places any crew changes are regarded with deep suspicion and boat owners have occasionally been asked to prove that those joining them were not charter guests. After many years of tolerance or ignorance, the authorities in most countries frequented by charter boats are now aware of what is happening and are trying to get the charter operators to make some contribution to the economy of the country whose beauty they so readily exploit. It is unfortunate that genuine cruising boats have been caught up in this situation, but sailors should try to understand that some of these countries have few resources apart from their picturesque scenery, so their attempts to recoup some of the revenue that others are making out of it should not be condemned too harshly. The same line of thought should be applied to the fees sometimes charged for cruising permits. These fees, which give access to some of the most beautiful and unspoilt areas of the world, are rarely more than one would pay for two or three nights in a marina anywhere in Europe or North America.

Arrival procedure

Most countries show little tolerance towards those who infringe their rules and cruising sailors have faced stiff fines, and even prison sentences, for ignoring local laws and regulations. A basic requirement of every country is that vessels arriving from a foreign destination must proceed directly to an official port of entry. The local port authority has to be contacted at the earliest opportunity on Channel 16 unless otherwise stated (such as a different channel or different name of the authority to be contacted). Arrival procedure is given only for major or more frequented ports, and if landfall is made at a port that has no individual description, Channel 16 is the normal one to call.

There are special regulations for the EU that differ between EU and non-EU-flagged vessels. EU-flagged vessels with only EU nationals on board arriving in an EU port directly from another EU port do not have to complete any formalities, except in Greece. Immigration must be contacted if there are non-EU citizens aboard. Customs must be notified if there is anything to declare, such as firearms. Both EU and non-EU-flagged yachts that arrive in an EU port from a non-EU port must fly the Q flag when entering the 12-mile limit. Customs and immigration must be contacted on arrival. These regulations also apply to vessels arriving from an EU country in offshore island groups such as Madeira, the Canaries or Azores as these vessels are considered to have left the EU and to have arrived from a non-EU destination.

Non-EU nationals must be in possession of a Schengen visa when arriving in an EU country that has signed the Schengen Agreement (see below). The exception is Greece where both EU and non-EU vessels must clear in on arrival and obtain a transit log, wherever they are arriving from.

Departure procedure

In most countries, vessels departing for a foreign destination must complete clearing out formalities and be issued with a departure certificate (known as *zarpe* in Spanish-speaking countries). It is imperative to obtain this document as it is usually requested when clearing into the next country.

On departure from an EU port to a non-EU destination, customs and immigration must be notified by both EU and non-EU vessels.

The European Union (EU)

On 1 January 1993 all countries belonging to the EU became a single market by enforcing the Single European Act and merging into a common customs and Value Added Tax (VAT) zone. VAT is a special tax applied to both goods and services. Because of the lifting of customs controls within the EU, the flying of the Q flag is no longer obligatory if you sail from one EU country to another.

The importation of duty-free goods from one EU country into another is no longer permitted. Where the single market has made a great difference is in lifting all restrictions on the importation of duty-paid goods. In the case of goods bought in normal shops or supermarkets, there are practically no limits, provided the goods are purchased for your own consumption, although for larger quantities you may have to prove this. Especially in some of the Nordic countries, there are severe restrictions on the importation of alcoholic drinks, even from another EU country.

There are 27 countries in the EU, with Croatia and Iceland expected to join in 2010. The maritime nations among them are: Belgium, Bulgaria, Cyprus, Denmark, Estonia, Finland, France, Germany, Greece, Ireland, Italy, Latvia, Lithuania, Malta, the Netherlands, Poland, Portugal, Romania, Slovenia, Spain, Sweden and the UK. Island groups belonging to some of those countries, such as the Azores, Madeira, Canaries, Channel Islands or Åland, have a special status and this will be explained in the relevant section. Different regulations also apply in dependent territories, such as Gibraltar or Greenland.

A vessel owned by a resident of the EU has the right to free movement throughout the EU, provided VAT has been paid on that vessel in one of the EU countries. Although there is no legal time limit on the length of time a EU-registered boat can spend in any EU country, some occasionally enforce local regulations once the boat has been in that country for over six months, as happened in Spain in 2009.

Customs regulations have been largely harmonized and non-EU-flagged vessels may now spend a period of 18 months within the EU, whether in one EU country or several. Non-EU-flagged vessels remaining inside the EU for over 18 months, and being used by the owner or the crew during this period, must be imported and VAT paid on the value of the boat. The preferred way to overcome this restriction by those who wish to have longer in the EU is to leave just before the expiry of the 18-month period and spend some time in a non-EU country, with the clock being restarted on the return to the EU.

The Schengen Agreement

The commitment of European states to the free movement of persons led to the creation of the Schengen Agreement, which was signed by Belgium, France, Germany, Luxembourg and the Netherlands in June 1990. By 2009, a total of 28 countries, including all European Union countries (except Ireland and the United Kingdom) and three non-EU countries (Iceland, Norway and Switzerland) had signed the Schengen Agreement. It must be stressed that Schengen visa holders are not allowed to live permanently or work in the European Union.

The removal of internal borders between the participating states in the Schengen Agreement means that the criteria for who is allowed across the external borders of Schengen countries is of crucial importance. The Schengen countries have therefore committed themselves to abide by a common policy on issuing visas that are valid for the entire Schengen area. Nationals of the following countries do not require a Schengen visa: members of the European Union, Australia, Canada, Iceland, Japan, Liechtenstein, Monaco, New Zealand, Norway, South Korea and the USA.

Citizens of non-EU countries who do not require a visa to visit a Schengen country are still usually (but not always) subject to a 90 day limit on the length of their stay in any 6 month period. This 6 month period starts on the first day of entry into a Schengen Area country. In principle, a new stay of 90 days can be restarted at the end of such a new 6 month period.

Nationals of the following countries do not require a Schengen visa for stays of up to 90 days: Andorra, Argentina, Brazil, Brunei, Chile, Costa Rica, El Salvador, Guatemala, Honduras, Israel, Malaysia, Mexico, Nicaragua, Panama, Paraguay, San Marino, Singapore, Uruguay, Vatican City and Venezuela.

✦ FACILITIES

The section on facilities in this book only gives a general idea of what standard and range of services are available. For important destinations that are also well covered by cruising guides, such information is by force succinct, whereas the information is more detailed for places that are less frequented by yachts and are not covered by a cruising guide. Similarly, individual marinas or yacht clubs are only mentioned in less frequented places. A useful website that lists marinas worldwide is www.marinas.com.

In most parts of the world local yacht clubs welcome visiting sailors and allow them to use their facilities either on a reciprocal basis if the visitor's home yacht club has such an arrangement for its members, or for a fee in case of longer stays. Yacht club staff and their members are often the best source of information on local conditions, repair and other facilities, as well as giving tips on sightseeing. It is always advisable to contact such yacht clubs in advance, and ideally to have your own club send a letter of recommendation directly to the host club.

The use of local agents is mentioned in several instances, whether to complete arrival formalities, arrange a transit of the Panama or Suez Canals, or obtain a cruising permit. As individual agents often change, existing ones are not listed, but they can be found easily by consulting the relevant country's page on noonsite.com or by doing an internet search. It is advisable to agree any fees with such agents in advance and also obtain a written list of services included in the agreed fee, as well as any additional charges that may have to be paid on top of the agency fee. This precaution also applies to any work being done on the boat, where a written estimate should always be requested in advance.

✦ CHARTER

The section on charter lists only established companies operating their own yachts. Wherever bareboats are available, these are mentioned in preference to skippered or crewed yachts. It is always advisable to deal with charter

operators directly and, if possible, avoid the use of agents or intermediaries. If in any doubt, it is strongly recommended to ask the person or company making the offer if it has its own fleet in the country concerned, and insist that details of its base are given, so as to check if this is indeed correct. It is just as important to choose the location carefully, especially in areas with consistent prevailing winds, such as the Caribbean or Aegean, so as not to end up at the end of a charter far downwind of the base where the boat needs to be returned to.

✦ CRUISING GUIDES

All cruising guides listed were in print when this book was written (June 2009), but it should be borne in mind that a more recent edition may now be available or perhaps a new and more up-to-date publication. Also mentioned are a number of cruising guides that can be downloaded from the internet, either free or at a cost. At the end of the book, all cruising guides are listed again arranged by region.

✦ WEBSITES

The listed websites are usually the official tourist board sites of that country or websites that are particularly useful to visitors.

There are several websites that list general cruising information. These are not mentioned under specific countries, but should be consulted to check or update some of the information given in this book. There are also various international cruising associations that publish valuable cruising information, such as the Seven Seas Cruising Association, which anyone is welcome to join. The British Cruising Association and Royal Cruising Club (RCC) have informative websites featuring reports from their widely travelled members. The RCC is the custodian of the Pilotage

Foundation, a charitable project that supports the publication of cruising guides for less frequented areas that may not be commercially viable.

> www.noonsite.com
> www.sail-world.com
> www.cruising.org.uk
> www.rcc.org.uk
> www.ssca.org
> www.cruiser.co.za

✦ USEFUL INFORMATION

The practical data box contains basic emergency information for that particular destination. If there is no telephone number for a diplomatic mission listed, the entry in one of the larger neighbouring countries should be consulted as, for example, most major countries have a diplomatic mission in Fiji, but are not represented in any of the smaller island nations. Similarly, in the Caribbean only the numbers of diplomatic missions that are actually based on the island are listed. In an emergency it would be necessary to contact your diplomatic mission in the larger islands of Trinidad, Barbados or Jamaica. Wherever available, the contact numbers of the diplomatic missions of the main English-speaking countries of the USA, UK, Australia, Canada, New Zealand and South Africa are listed. Where these countries are not represented, a British mission might assist anyone from a Commonwealth country, and similarly Canadian missions also will help Australians or New Zealanders.

The international direct dialling code (IDD) is listed for each country and also the local access code (IAC) to make international calls from that country. When dialling most countries, after the IDD the initial zero should be dropped from the national number with the notable exception of Italy, where the zero must be dialled. For countries where local numbers do not start with a zero (USA, Spain, Greece), the entire number should be dialled after the IDD.

✦ FLAG ETIQUETTE

The yellow Q flag should be flown as soon as the yacht has entered the nation's territorial waters to signal the intention of requesting pratique. This is an old term used by an incoming vessel to state that it was free of contagious diseases, and asking to be permitted to enter a port. Such a vessel would fly a yellow flag, which eventually became the international code flag for the letter Q, signifying quarantine. By showing your intention in this way, you cannot be accused of trying to slip in unnoticed, and in fact in some countries yachts have got into trouble for not hoisting the Q flag until they were in port.

The courtesy flag should also be flown once the boat enters a nation's territorial waters. This flag should be flown from the starboard spreader in a position above any other flag. The courtesy flag should be in a good state and of reasonable size as some officials take offence at yachts that fly a torn or tiny flag. In a number of dependencies or autonomous regions, such as the Canaries, Azores, French Polynesia or Corsica, it is appreciated if the regional flag is also flown, but below that of the metropolitan power. Burgees, house flags and courtesy flags, as well as ensigns, should be lowered at sunset or 2100 hours, whichever is earlier, and hoisted at 0800 in summer and 0900 in winter. It is particularly important to observe this in Scandinavian countries, where people are extremely flag conscious.

✦ ENVIRONMENT PROTECTION

Few other sports or activities depend so much on the environment as sailing and it is therefore in our best interest to do everything possible to protect it from further destruction. There are several ways in which cruising yachts have had a negative impact on the environment, rarely deliberately and usually out of ignorance, but now that so much more is known about the fragility of ecosystems such actions should be avoided whenever possible. Anchoring in vulnerable areas can cause great damage, especially in the tropics, where the anchor and chain will cause irreversible destruction to live coral. Several countries are now imposing restrictions on anchoring in coral and, to avoid further destruction, have laid mooring buoys for the use of visiting yachts in nature reserves, protected areas or popular anchorages. In some places, such moorings may need to be booked in advance and the usage time is limited. In any vulnerable area one should attempt to anchor only on a sand or muddy bottom.

The disposal of garbage is another aspect that should be approached in a responsible manner and only biodegradable waste should be disposed of at sea. All other garbage should be collected in bags and disposed of carefully when returning

to land. It should be noted that not all organic matter is easily degradable and, for example, orange peel or avocado skin can take many years to disintegrate.

Pumping out waste, especially in anchorages or inshore waters, is yet another area that can no longer be simply ignored. Although the use of holding tanks is not yet compulsory throughout the world, in more and more countries the pumping overboard of any waste is prohibited. Holding tanks are now compulsory on many inland waterways and throughout the Baltic, while some Mediterranean countries are following suit. In many ports and marinas, pumping out toilets will result in heavy fines. In the USA, even vessels with holding tanks have been fined for not having the valve handle in the closed position.

Although many cruising boats are not fitted with holding tanks, these should be installed as a matter of priority. As pumping-out stations are not yet widely available, in the absence of another alternative the tanks should only be emptied when well away from a port or marina. In some countries, tanks may not be pumped out when within 6 miles of the coast.

Also in order to protect their environment, many countries are now prohibiting the taking of any live or dead corals or marine life, collecting of shells, spearing fish or fishing without a licence, catching lobsters or coconut crabs, taking eggs, disturbing nests, and even landing on cays or islets during the breeding season. Also prohibited in many areas is the taking of the heart of palm. A thoughtful visitor to that Mecca of cruising sailors, Suwarrow Atoll in the South Pacific, had pinned a notice to a palm tree on Anchorage Island urging his followers to this pristine spot to 'take but nothing, leave but footprints'.

✦ THE RIGHT ATTITUDE

Sailors often complain about the frustration of lengthy formalities or the occasional unfriendly or suspicious attitude of officials, but few seem prepared to admit or even consider that they themselves may also bear some blame. Unless the captain is prepared or able to handle formalities through an agent, unpleasant experiences in dealing with officials can usually be avoided by a right attitude. The first impression of a visiting sailor's behaviour can determine how he or she is treated from the start, and you should not be surprised if local officials do not treat you with respect if your attitude shows an obvious disrespect for them, their position, customs, language, religion or colour of skin. Often such an attitude is caused by ignorance, and it is hoped that the information contained in this book will help dispel some of this. Just as often, such an attitude is caused by an innate feeling of superiority, which a few sailors from developed countries occasionally display towards those in developing countries. Such an air of superiority is not always deliberate – on the contrary, it is often unnoticed by the person who displays it – but it can create an immediate antagonism in the local people that individual deals with, who are so well attuned to this condition that they can sense it as soon as people step into their office. It certainly pays to show a little humility. What you would not do at home, you should not do abroad either. You would not behave in a condescending manner towards a US or British customs official, so why behave differently towards a Sri Lankan, Tahitian or Sudanese? I have witnessed many incidents when a small dose of politeness and respect would have resolved matters on the spot without any further aggravation.

An even bigger factor in provoking antagonism is the way some sailors dress, or rather undress, when visiting other countries. It probably does not even occur to them that the way they dress is not only a sign of disrespect for local customs, but can be downright offensive. Particularly when visiting government offices, men should not go barefoot or in rubber thonged sandals, in shorts or singlets. In some countries, such as Brazil, access to government offices is only permitted if properly attired. In many Arab, Caribbean, Asian and Latin American countries, shorts are never worn by men in public, being considered acceptable only for small boys or on a beach. Therefore you should not be offended if officials do not treat you with the respect due to the captain of a yacht if attired in this way. Generally, a tidy appearance denotes respect for the authorities of the host country and will ensure that you are treated accordingly. The same rules apply when visiting local yacht clubs, where dress rules are often strictly enforced. It is also a good idea to make sure that the boat is tidied up after a long passage, so as to look presentable on arrival, especially in those countries where the yacht is boarded immediately you arrive. Everywhere in the world it is the first impression that counts and it might just be the factor that makes local officials decide whether to conduct a search of the yacht or to take your word that you are not carrying anything illegal.

Dress etiquette is a difficult matter as it varies so much from country to country. In some, a foreign woman's scanty dress can be interpreted as an indication of her morals, which can lead to sexual harassment and even rape. In most Pacific islands, it is more provocative for a woman to bare her thighs than her breasts, so very skimpy shorts should be avoided. In Greece, women should always cover bare shoulders when entering a church, and sometimes their heads too. In Arab countries, it is wise for women to wear trousers or long skirts. Footwear should be removed before entering a Buddhist shrine, and although it is permissible to photograph Buddha statues, one should not pose beside them. Shoes should be removed when visiting Asian homes

and when visiting mosques. There are also certain taboos for using one's hands and feet in a manner that can cause serious offence in some countries. For example, gestures that should be avoided are touching someone's head (which includes patting a child); pointing at people; pointing one's bare soles towards another person; and never using the left hand to handle food or give things to someone. Taking photographs of people without their permission can also cause serious offence.

In strict Islamic states, access to mosques is forbidden to non-believers. Because the consumption of alcohol is against Muslim belief, alcoholic drinks must not be consumed in public, which may include the cockpit if berthed in a port. Nor should food be eaten in public before sunset during Ramadan. Dogs are considered unclean in Muslim countries, so pets are best kept on board. Friday is the day of rest in Islamic countries, when everything is closed. Sunday is observed very religiously in some Pacific countries, particularly Tonga and Fiji, where sporting events are among the activities forbidden on Sundays.

An important rule is not to bribe local officials. Although this might ease matters temporarily for one person, it will certainly make life more difficult for those who follow. There are corrupt officials in many countries and often they attempt to procure a bribe, but if this is firmly resisted, or a detailed official receipt is asked for in exchange for any money demanded, they may give up. When the boat is inspected, if you feel like offering the boarding officers a drink, there is no reason why you should not do so, although it is preferable to stick to non-alcoholic beverages, particularly in Muslim countries. Generally it is not advisable to give presents, except perhaps the small token gifts some yachts carry with their logo or name on. It can be difficult to refuse if an official asks for a gift or money, but it should be avoided as politely as possible so as not to set a precedent. Occasionally, however, a small gift is virtually impossible to avoid and, in spite of my reluctance to do so, even I have had to break my own rules and give a tip to a very insistent official.

When clearing in, it is extremely foolish to try to hide anything, because the penalties for possessing undeclared firearms, pets or drugs can be severe. If in doubt, it is better to declare more than necessary, especially in those countries where moveable items of value – such as cameras, laptops and radios – have to be listed on a declaration. Everything should be declared including prescription drugs, such as strong painkillers, and the relevant prescription or doctor's letter may have to be shown.

The official attitude towards illegal drugs is extremely strict everywhere and many countries operate zero tolerance, so if any illegal drugs are found, you risk paying a heavy fine, going to prison, possibly losing the boat – or even your life, as in some countries drug dealing carries the death sentence. You should therefore be very careful about crew picked up casually and what they might have in their possession. This subject should be discussed very seriously with all crew members as the boat could be confiscated if drugs are found on board, and ignorance on the part of the owner or captain is not accepted as an excuse. If a yacht is searched, either the captain or a crew member should accompany the searching officer to prevent anything being planted, which is known to have happened. If anything is found, it should not be touched, so as not to leave fingerprints. You should also take a photograph of the official holding the incriminating item where it was found. If arrested, you should alert any other yachts in the vicinity immediately, so they can keep an eye on the yacht and also inform their embassy or consulate. In a few countries, sailors have been wrongly arrested, kept for 24 hours, and then released, only to find on their return that their boat has been ransacked and everything of value taken. Foreign visitors are subject to the laws of the place they are visiting, and sailors on cruising boats are not exempt. The powers of your country's ambassador or consul are limited, and although they may be able to assist those faced with an emergency, they can rarely help someone who has contravened the laws of the country, except to ensure that they receive fair treatment.

✦ SAFETY AND PIRACY

Personal safety has become a major concern among cruising sailors in recent years. In spite of some well-publicized cases, attacks on cruising yachts are still relatively rare, although it must be stressed that violent robberies involving sailors have increased and are affecting areas where such incidents were unheard of in the past. Yet in spite of the widespread concern over violent robberies and piracy, sailors are often more vulnerable when sightseeing on land or travelling as ordinary tourists than on their own boats. While ashore, the precautions to be taken are the same as if arriving in a foreign country by plane or car.

The most serious concern is the possibility of a piracy attack, and as such areas are well known they should be avoided if at all possible. Piracy has been an ongoing phenomenon in the Gulf of Aden and around the Horn of Africa since time immemorial, but it has flared up considerably since the collapse of Somalia's government. Anyone planning to sail through that area should monitor the situation carefully and visit the website of international organizations involved in piracy control – such as the International Maritime Organization.

Noonsite.com has kept a record of all reported incidents for the last ten years and has also been instrumental in assisting those who intend to put together a convoy to sail through a critical area in company with other yachts. Indeed, this is an alternative for those who cannot alter their plans to sail a route that avoids a doubtful area.

✦ CRUISING RALLIES

The number of international offshore rallies has greatly increased since the launch of the Atlantic Rally for Cruisers (ARC), the first event of this kind, in 1986. There are now similar rallies all over the world that provide an attractive alternative for those who do not always want to sail alone. Besides the obvious safety factor of sailing in company, some of these rallies also provide the opportunity to go to places that are otherwise off limits or unsafe to visit on your own, and are often sponsored by government organizations so that certain restrictions are lifted. Formalities, such as cruising permits or clearance procedures, as well as docking arrangements, are taken care of by the organizers, who also arrange a programme of events in all ports of call.

Round the World Rally yachts in Tahiti.

HEALTH PRECAUTIONS WORLDWIDE

SAILING IS ONE OF THE HEALTHIEST OF ACTIVITIES and sailors are generally a robust lot. While for those sailing in home waters or within reach of medical facilities a standard first aid kit is quite sufficient, offshore cruising boats should carry a comprehensive medical kit so they can deal with a wide range of accidents and possible illnesses, as help in an emergency on the ocean or in remote places may not be available and, as with every other aspect of offshore cruising, you should try to be as self-sufficient as possible. Most medical problems that occur on board are caused by accidents and are usually relatively easy to deal with. Fortunately, infectious or contagious diseases are not a risk while at sea, but these become a hazard when ashore in many parts of the world.

The two greatest health hazards are mosquitoes and unsafe drinking water or food. These can be guarded against in several ways. Malaria, yellow fever, dengue fever and filariasis are among the diseases that are mosquito-borne and the best precaution is to avoid being bitten in the first place. If cruising for any length of time in the tropics it is wise to have mosquito screens fitted over hatches and portholes, or mosquito netting that can be rigged over bunks. You should keep as much of the body covered as possible at sunset and use insect repellents, sprays or burn coils.

Not all vaccinations give total protection against food and water-borne diseases, so you should be scrupulous about checking water supplies, treating the water where necessary, or drinking bottled water in dubious areas. Also you should avoid raw vegetables, salads, unpeeled fruit, raw shellfish, raw eggs, ice cream, cream and ice cubes in drinks in risk areas, unless you yourself have thoroughly washed or prepared them.

It is highly recommended that supplies of sterilized and sealed items such as syringes, needles, sutures, dressings and infusion cannulae are carried. These sterile packs are available in kits for travellers and can be given to medical staff if seeking treatment abroad where properly sterilized or disposable equipment is not used or available. This is a precaution to be taken for all countries where there is a risk of hepatitis B or HIV/AIDS from contaminated equipment, blood or blood products. If an accident or emergency needs a blood transfusion in countries where donated blood is not screened or checked properly, it is advisable to contact your embassy or consulate, as in some countries a list of vetted donors is kept.

Many countries give reciprocal free treatment in an emergency, but this is only on the same terms as that received by nationals of the foreign country concerned. This usually applies to state healthcare systems, which leave much to be desired in some places. For members of the EU, there is a special EU health card which entitles the person to emergency medical care throughout the EU. The procedure may vary from country to country, but emergency assistance is always assured. For anyone cruising extensively, it is highly recommended that worldwide medical insurance is taken out to cover any treatment required, especially if sailing to destinations where medical care is expensive, such as the USA, Canada or Australia. This insurance should provide also for a seriously ill person to be flown home for treatment, which is a wise option if the emergency occurs in a country with poor medical facilities.

A comprehensive health check should be carried out before setting off on a long voyage and your own doctor is the best person with whom to discuss your cruising plans and vaccinations. Your doctor may also be prepared to prescribe not only any personal medication, but also items for the onboard pharmacy that are not available over the counter. Before setting off, a pharmacist should also be consulted as he or she is usually the best informed as to what prophylactic medicines or vaccinations are recommended for particular countries. Sufficient time before departure should be allowed for any vaccinations, as some cannot be given at the same time as others.

◆ DISEASES AND VACCINATIONS

Details on vaccinations required and precautions against specific diseases are summarized below:

HIV/AIDS

The Acquired Immune Deficiency Syndrome, commonly called AIDS (SIDA in Latin languages), is caused by a virus called HIV. Not everyone infected with the HIV virus develops the disease, although they are likely to remain infected and infectious for much of their lives. There is no way to tell if a person is infected without taking an HIV test. The disease is present worldwide, but in certain countries it is endemic in the general population. The two main ways of contracting the HIV virus is through sexual contact or by contaminated blood getting into the body via a transfusion, injection or poorly sterilized medical equipment. The virus cannot be caught by everyday contact, crockery, food, swimming pools or mosquito bites. The obvious precautions are to avoid casual sexual contacts and to use a condom. You should always carry sterile medical supplies for emergencies that might result in you needing an injection or vaccination. If at all possible, you should also avoid medical or dental treatment involving surgery in destinations where there is a risk of contracting the HIV virus. In many less developed countries, blood for transfusion is not properly screened or treated, but there may be ways of obtaining screened blood and your diplomatic mission may be able to advise on this.

Hepatitis B

This is transmitted in a similar way to HIV, by contact with an infected person or through infected blood or needles. Hepatitis B is found worldwide. There is a vaccination that gives protection, but the course takes up to six months to come to full protection. The best precautions are the same as those described for HIV.

Hepatitis A

This is sometimes called infectious hepatitis and is caught from contaminated food or water, and is prevalent in most parts of the world where there is poor sanitation and hygiene. A full course of three injections of the Havrix vaccine gives protection for ten years, which is ideal for long-term cruising worldwide. The immunoglobulin injection (HNIG) containing antibodies to hepatitis A gives protection for six weeks and is an alternative for short visits to vulnerable areas. Otherwise, the main precaution is to take scrupulous care over what you eat and drink as outlined earlier.

For over twenty years, singlehander Pierre Ribes supplied to West Africa medication and medical equipment donated by French hospitals.

Tetanus

This dangerous disease is found everywhere in the world and results from the tetanus spores entering the body via even a slight scratch or wound. This can easily happen on any dockside, so it is essential that everyone keeps their tetanus vaccination up to date. Fortunately, this vaccination is safe and very effective, and if you had a full course as a child, as most people have, a booster is only necessary every ten years. If someone has failed to keep this up to date and tetanus develops, it can be treated if the patient is taken immediately to somewhere with proper medical facilities. However, these may not be available in remote areas.

Tuberculosis

Tuberculosis is on the increase again in certain areas of Africa, Asia, Central and South America and the Pacific. If you have been vaccinated against it in the past, revaccination is not necessary. Vaccination is only necessary if you are living or working closely with the indigenous population in vulnerable areas. It is unlikely that any cruising sailors would need this vaccination.

Measles

Those born after 1957 should consider a second dose of measles vaccine before travelling abroad. It is essential that children have this vaccination at an early age when usually it is administered as a triple MMR vaccine (against measles, mumps and rubella).

Typhoid

Typhoid occurs almost everywhere except Australia, New Zealand, Europe and North America, and is found especially in conditions of poor hygiene and sanitation. It is caught from contaminated food, water or milk. Sensible precautions are to take care over food and drink, but vaccination against typhoid is recommended for all those sailing outside of the above mentioned areas. There are now two types of typhoid vaccine: an injectible single-dose vaccine giving protection for three years, or a live vaccine taken orally as capsules in three doses on alternate days, giving protection for one year.

Poliomyelitis

This disease is found everywhere except Australia, New Zealand, Europe and North America, and anyone cruising outside of these areas should ensure that their vaccination against polio is kept up to date. To commence vaccination, a course of three doses of oral vaccine are given, normally when you are a child. Reinforcing doses should be taken every ten years to continue protection against this disease. Polio is transmitted by direct contact with an infected person and sometimes by contaminated water or food. An extra booster dose of the vaccine should be received by those aged over 18 travelling to Africa, East and South East Asia, the Middle East, the Indian subcontinent and all countries of the former Soviet Union.

Meningococcal meningitis

This serious disease, which is transmitted by direct contact or airborne infection, has had a rising incidence worldwide. There is a particularly high risk in some parts of Sub-Sahara Africa. Vaccination against meningococcal infection is available for meningitis A and C and gives protection for three years.

Cholera

Cholera is found in some parts of Africa, Asia, South America, South East Asia and the Middle East, and especially in areas of primitive sanitation. The disease is transmitted through contaminated water and food. The cholera vaccine used in the past never worked well and is no longer recommended. Scrupulous hygiene is paramount in endemic areas.

Malaria

This is one of the biggest health risks that will be encountered by cruising sailors, and some forms of malaria are particularly virulent and can even be fatal. Malaria is prevalent in many parts of Africa, Asia, Central and South America and the Western Pacific. The disease is transmitted by mosquitoes, so the first precaution is to avoid getting bitten, as outlined earlier.

Prophylactic treatment is available and anti-malarial tablets should be taken two weeks before entering a malarial area, and continued throughout your stay and for four weeks after departure. The problem has increased because some strains of malaria have become resistant to the drugs in use and therefore different tablets are recommended for particular areas. Although anti-malarial tablets are available over the counter in pharmacies, it is wise to check with a doctor or a centre for tropical diseases as to which are the recommended drugs and doses. The tablets are usually taken once a week and it is essential to take them after food. Children take a dose proportionate to their weight. Advice on malaria prophylaxis changes frequently and no regimen is 100 per cent protective, so it is essential to seek up-to-date advice if cruising in an endemic area.

Areas particularly important for cruising sailors to take precautions in are Vanuatu, the Solomons and Papua New Guinea in the Western Pacific, Guyana, French Guiana in South America, Indonesia, the Philippines in South East Asia, and Sri Lanka, Comoros and East African countries in the Indian Ocean.

There is a diagnostic kit that can confirm whether or not someone has contracted falciparum malaria. The test kit (which needs to be refrigerated) is available from various sources, such as TMVC (Travellers Medical and Vaccination Centre) in Australia. TMVC have a highly informative website dealing with an entire range of tropical and infectious diseases (www.tmvc.com.au).

Yellow fever

This disease is only found in some parts of Africa and South America, and is transmitted by the bite of an infected mosquito. Vaccination against yellow fever gives protection for ten years. Although yellow fever is found mainly in tropical forest areas and therefore sailors are unlikely to encounter it, the vaccination is compulsory for travel to some countries, even if only visiting coastal areas or main ports. A vaccination certificate may be required in subsequent ports if arriving from countries where yellow fever is present. If not possessing a certificate, you may have to be vaccinated on the spot – another reason for carrying those sterile needles and syringes.

Rabies

Rabies is endemic virtually worldwide and is usually fatal if not treated immediately, hence the precautions against admitting animals imposed by countries that are rabies-free. The disease is caught if you are bitten, scratched or even licked by an infected animal such as a dog, cat, bat or monkey. Therefore you should not approach or touch any unknown animal. If you are bitten or scratched by an animal, you should wash and disinfect the wound thoroughly and get medical attention as soon as possible. There is a rabies vaccination, which is a course of injections, which should be started immediately – it can have quite unpleasant side effects. It is not normally recommended to be vaccinated beforehand against rabies unless you are travelling across country in remote parts where treatment is not available.

Bilharzia

This is also called schistosomiasis and is a deadly disease caught from parasites that live in minute snails found in fresh water. Thus swimming in freshwater lakes, rivers or streams should be avoided in much of South America, Africa, Asia and the Caribbean. Bilharzia cannot be caught from swimming in the sea or salt-water estuaries.

Filariasis

This is an infectious tropical disease carried by blood-sucking insects such as mosquitoes or flies. The illness is caused by thread-like filarial worms that enter the lymphatic system, including the lymph nodes, or the serous cavity of the

14

abdomen. Filariasis, which has various forms, is present throughout the tropics. The most spectacular symptom of lymphatic filariasis is elephantiasis, and was the first disease discovered to be transmitted by a mosquito bite.

Diphtheria

Diphtheria is a highly contagious disease that is contracted by inhaling bacteria from an infected person. Thought to have been eliminated through an extensive immunization programme, an upsurge in diphtheria is giving cause for concern. The disease is still common in many countries that include parts of Africa, Eastern Europe, Central America, the Caribbean, the former Soviet Republics, and Asia. Symptoms begin very like a common cold, usually two to five days after transmission, but can progress quickly. The infection can lead to heart failure and paralysis and, in rare cases, to coma or even death in as little as a week. A vaccine is available for adults, and children are normally vaccinated at an early age.

Encephalitis B

This rare, but often fatal, insect-borne infection, also known as Japanese B encephalitis, is found in Asia from India and Sri Lanka throughout South East Asia as far as Japan and the Philippines, including Indonesia. Vaccination is effective for two years and is recommended for stays of more than one month in rural areas during the period June to September.

Ciguatera

This fish poisoning is caught by eating toxic fish from certain reef areas. Fish feeding on coral such as parrot or surgeon fish, or larger carnivorous fish like groupers or barracuda, are the most likely carriers of the toxin. Local knowledge should be sought as to whether fish from a certain coral reef area or island are likely to be affected. Fish caught by trolling in the open ocean are not likely to be toxic. You should avoid large fish such as barracuda caught in reef areas, and repeated meals from reef fish, as the toxin is cumulative. Fish should always be gutted very carefully, and the head, roe or internal organs should never be eaten. The symptoms are very unpleasant, commonly diarrhoea and nausea occurring within a few hours. Typical are tingling feelings in fingers, toes and around the mouth and the alteration of the sensations of hot and cold. Other symptoms may include extreme lethargy, muscle and joint pain, weakened pulse and falling blood pressure, and in rare severe cases respiratory paralysis.

There is a test capable of identifying the presence of ciguatoxin in fish flesh. Cigua-Check™ will test ciguatoxin at levels generally below the level that can cause clinical symptoms in humans. The test kit is available from the Ciguatera Hotline in Hawaii (www.cigua.com).

◆ REEFWALKING AND DIVING HAZARDS

Many of these hazards can be avoided by wearing footwear when walking on reefs and by looking carefully before touching anything while diving or reefwalking.

The stone fish is an ugly creature that looks just like a stone but that gives a poisonous sting if stepped on. If stung, you should keep fairly immobile to delay the spread of poison, flush the puncture with vinegar, and put the foot in hot water. Wrap a bandage immediately above the wound and seek medical assistance. Cone shells have a dart that they launch in defence, and in a few species this can be deadly. You should avoid picking up live cone shells, but if you are stung, you should treat it like snake venom and seek medical advice.

If stung by the jellyfish called Portuguese man-of-war, it is important not to rub the sting, but to detoxify it with alcohol of some sort. The sting should then be rinsed gently with warm water.

Jellyfish stings should similarly be bathed with vinegar and hot water. If sea urchin spikes are trod on or get into the flesh, you must try to remove all the spikes, sucking them out if necessary. The affected area should be soaked in hot water and treated with antibiotic cream or powder. All coral cuts, bites and rashes caused by marine life should be washed well with hot water and disinfected to prevent infection. Similarly, any scratches, however sustained, should be disinfected and treated promptly as they tend to get easily infected in the tropics and can take a long time to heal, especially if they are not kept dry – so swimming should be avoided.

◆ THE SUN

This is one of the most serious dangers encountered by sailors and the power of the sun should never be underestimated. Sunburn should be avoided by using sunblock on exposed skin and covering the head and body until a tan has been acquired. The eyes are particularly vulnerable and should be protected by good sunglasses. The long-term effects on the skin, especially the face, can be quite devastating. While at sea, it is advisable to use a dodger or bimini, and when at anchor to rig up a cockpit awning.

Not only can the sun burn your skin, causing severe pain, but it can also result in the body overheating. When sailing in very hot climates, particularly in equatorial regions or in the Red Sea, you should drink plenty of non-alcoholic fluids and also slightly increase your salt intake to counteract salt loss through sweating.

Heat exhaustion

In very hot temperatures, any fatigue, dizziness, headache or muscle cramps should be taken seriously. The person should be cooled by sponging with tepid water, or by using a fan, and

Good sun protection is essential in the tropics.

given salt and fruit juice or a sugar solution (1 teaspoonful of salt and 4 teaspoonfuls of sugar to 1 litre of water).

Heatstroke

This is characterized by a sudden dramatic rise in temperature, absence of sweat, and odd behaviour. Plenty of water should be given and the skin cooled with water and fans. Medical help will be needed, especially if the person loses consciousness.

Skin cancer

While the above are immediate problems, one of the most serious effects of the sun is the danger of skin cancer. This is caused by prolonged exposure to the sun and may not show up for many years, but it has afflicted many cruising sailors. The risk of developing skin cancer increases as people grow older, but it is important to prevent overexposure to the sun in children and young people as this is a cumulative risk. Chronic exposure to the sun's rays is the main cause of skin cancer, and the carcinomas usually appear on exposed parts of the body, such as face, scalp, hands, arms and legs. The people at highest risk are those with fair skin, light-coloured hair and light-coloured eyes. Also more at risk are those who burn easily and tan with difficulty. Prevention is the most impor-

tant factor, so you should avoid prolonged exposure, use high-factor sunblocks and cover exposed areas of the body.

◆ HEALTH ON THE INTERNET

Health matters are more widely covered on the internet than almost any other subject, so only a few sites that have a direct relevance to anyone sailing to remote places are mentioned. The UK National Health Network and Centre has a detailed and up-to-date travel advice site.

Equally informative and regularly updated is the website of the US-based Center for Disease Control and Prevention. The World Health Organization publishes up-to-date news on health matters and critical areas. Highly recommended is the website of Australian-based TMVC (Travellers Medical and Vaccination Centre). TMVC runs an informative website dealing with an entire range of tropical and infectious diseases.

www.nathnac.org/travel/index.htm
www.cdc.gov/travel
www.who.int/ith/en/
www.tmvc.com.au

MEDITERRANEAN AND BLACK SEA

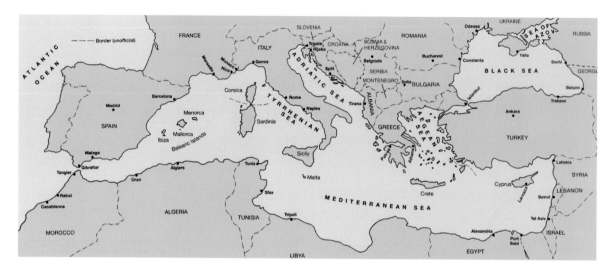

THE MEDITERRANEAN'S REPUTATION as the cradle of Western civilization is undisputed and the beauty of its scenery, as well as the wealth of things to see and do ashore, more than make up for the less than exhilarating sailing conditions. From the pyramids of Egypt to the Minoan remains on Crete, from the treasures of Asia Minor to the wonders of ancient Rome, from the Lycian tombs carved into the cliffs of southern Turkey to the medieval ramparts of Valletta's Grand Harbour, the shores and islands abound in history and many historical sites are close to the sea. The people of the Mediterranean have always looked to the sea for inspiration and you never have far to go to get a taste of the fascinating world that has existed for millennia along these shores.

In most parts of the Mediterranean, the sailing season extends from April until October, but is best enjoyed in late spring and early autumn when the ports are not crowded and the weather is also more pleasant than at the height of summer. It is possible to sail in winter, but a careful eye has to be kept on the weather as violent storms can occur with little warning. A complete season is the least anyone should plan on spending in the Mediterranean, as distances are deceptive and it is more than 2,000 miles from Gibraltar to the Eastern Mediterranean shores.

The ocean routes that lead to the Mediterranean have been sailed for centuries and converge in the funnel-shaped strait overlooked by the Rock of Gibraltar. Sailing to the Mediterranean from northern Europe is relatively straightforward, but as it entails a crossing of the Bay of Biscay, passages should be planned for late spring or early summer when favourable conditions can be expected. The alternative is to take the inland route via the extensive European waterway system and reach the Mediterranean through the French rivers and canals, or by the even longer detour via the Danube and Black Sea.

Eastbound voyages across the Atlantic, whether from the USA or Caribbean, will also benefit from best weather conditions in late spring or early summer, before the start of the hurricane season. Once through the Straits of Gibraltar, those planning to spend only one season in the Mediterranean ought to cover the longer distances first and head straight for the Adriatic or Aegean. Regardless of the length of time spent in that area, if an Atlantic crossing is planned at the end of the season, the Eastern Mediterranean should be left by early August so as to be able to cruise leisurely westward and be on your way to Madeira or the Canaries by late September or early October, as autumn weather can be unreliable and it is not uncommon to be delayed in Gibraltar by unrelenting westerly winds.

Forward planning is easier if arriving from the Red Sea, which normally means a spring arrival. As many Mediterranean ports and marinas get very crowded in July and

August, one should try to avoid the most popular areas such as the French Riviera, Corsica, the Balearics, Croatia or the Greek Cyclades during this time. As places in the Western and Central Mediterranean have been getting more crowded, cruising boats have migrated east, mostly to Turkey and its south coast, now a popular destination that may soon share the fate of other similar victims of their own success.

The Black Sea has a shorter season and the winters can be extremely cold, so cruises there should be planned strictly for the summer. With the opening of this area to cruising, yachts are now sailing to Ukraine, Georgia, Romania and Bulgaria. Except for the interest in visiting these formerly closed countries, cruising attractions in the Black Sea are rather limited, perhaps with the exception of the Georgian coast, where the scenery is more dramatic. Another interesting destination is the Ukraine, whose Crimean peninsula has a pleasant subtropical climate and yachting is well developed by local standards. A cruise to the Black Sea has the added reward of sailing through the Dardanelles, Bosporus and Istanbul, a unique experience which in itself may justify the entire trip.

Yachting facilities are well developed in most parts of the Mediterranean, and even countries with no yachting tradition, such as Tunisia or Turkey, have developed excellent facilities in recent years and there are now marinas and boatyards with good repair services spread all over the Mediterranean.

The benign Mediterranean winters attract many sailors to spend the off season in one of the many marinas, the southern and eastern shores being generally warmer and having a better winter climate. As some countries have restrictions on the time a foreign vessel can spend in their waters, it is essential to make sure that the maximum period is not exceeded. The maximum 18-month stay in the EU applied to non-EU boats is forcing the owners of such vessels to spend some time in a non-EU country before returning to the EU to start the clock again.

Although the climate makes it possible to live on board and even sail for most of the year, for the more adventurous there is the alternative of heading south at the end of the summer season. From the Western Mediterranean, the obvious destinations are the Canaries and Madeira, while the northern Red Sea beckons to those in the Eastern Mediterranean.

View of the Côte d'Azur looking west from the Italian border towards Menton.

ALBANIA

AFTER MANY YEARS OF ISOLATION, Albania has now opened its doors to foreign tourists and the number of visiting yachts is steadily increasing. The legacy of one of the most dogmatic communist regimes in Eastern Europe is still palpable under the surface, and cruising yachts, while warmly welcomed, are still treated with some suspicion by officials.

Cruising along the coast offers many possibilities, although permission to do so must be obtained when clearing in. The scenic, sparsely populated coast described as the Albanian Riviera has wide sandy beaches backed by a chain of massive mountains. One of the most attractive spots is the well-sheltered Porto Palermo, where a small peninsula in the centre of the bay is crowned by the striking Tepelena castle built by Ali Pasha, a ruthless despot who is still remembered with awe in this part of the world. This is a restricted military area and a patrol boat is usually docked in a pen carved into the cliff face that also sheltered submarines during Albania's communist era. Concrete pillboxes still litter all beaches, a silent testimony to a paranoid past.

Albania's most visited attraction is the Greco-Roman city at Butrint, easily accessible from the port of Saranda across the narrow straits from Corfu. The famous ancient site has a well-preserved third-century BCE amphitheatre, a temple, and remains of a spa dedicated to Asclepius, the Greek god of medicine. In Valona Bay, close to the commercial port of Vlorë, an Italian company has built the first marina in Albania. Orikum Marina's main attraction is that it is a safe place to leave the boat to visit the interior, possibly taking the long drive to the capital, Tirana.

As a cruising destination Albania has a long way to go, and for the time being anyone interested in getting a taste of this once forbidden country would do best to stop only at Saranda and perhaps Orikum.

✦ COUNTRY PROFILE

The Illyrians, ancestors of today's Albanians, settled in this region around 2000 BCE, and have been under foreign rule throughout most of their history. In 1920 Albania was finally recognized as a sovereign state, but for much of the Second World War it was occupied by Italy. After the war, Albania was ruled by a strict Stalinist regime, which discouraged any contact with the outside world. The collapse of communism, though, has brought radical changes and Albania now has a democratic government.

The population is 3.6 million and is about 70 per cent Muslim. Greeks and Macedonians are the largest ethnic minorities as well as Vlachs and Roma.

The Albanian Riviera.

✦ CLIMATE

The climate is typically Mediterranean with mild, wet winters and warm, sunny and dry summers. Summer and early autumn have the most settled weather, with a regular pattern of sea and land breezes. The winds in summer are mostly onshore, stronger in the afternoons and dying away at night. Unpredictable thunderstorms that occasionally can generate violent gusts are a feature of the summer period. The warmest months are July and August with an average temperature of 24°C/75°F, and the coolest is January, with an average 6°C/43°F.

✦ FORMALITIES

PORTS OF ENTRY

Saranda	39°53′N 20°00′E	Vlorë	40°26′N 19°30′E
Durrës	41°19′N 19°27′E	Shëngjin	41°49′N 19°36′E

The Albanian Coast Guard frequency Channel 11 should be monitored while in Albanian waters. The Port Authority requires an agent to be used for entry and exit formalities, and there are agents used to dealing with yachts in all ports. They hold the ship's papers until departure, when a clearance document is issued, a procedure repeated at every port. Stopping anywhere outside one of the ports of entry is only allowed if this has been cleared previously with customs.

Saranda: Matters are greatly simplified if you have contacted a local agent in advance who will make all necessary arrangements and meet the yacht on arrival. Visiting yachts are normally asked to dock at the guarded customs quay.
Orikum Marina: 40°20′N 19°28′E. The marina should be contacted on Channel 15 to ask if the authorities will allow formalities to be completed there rather than the commercial port of Vlorë.

Most nationalities do not need to obtain a visa in advance, which is granted for a fee at the first port of call and is valid for the whole of Albania. Visiting sailors may be issued with a shore pass instead of a visa.

✦ FACILITIES

Repair facilities are only available in the larger commercial ports, but even there repairs for yachts are limited. Some repairs are possible in Saranda, while Orikum Marina has the usual marina facilities but few other services.

Cruising Guides
Adriatic Pilot
Ionian
Ionian Cruising Companion
Mediterranean Almanac
Dove Navigare Bolina (details of ports and marinas in Italian)

Websites
www.albaniantourism.com
www.orikum.it

Local time	UTC +1
Buoyage	IALA A
Currency	Leke (ALL)
Electricity	220V, 50Hz

Diplomatic missions	
UK	4 234973
USA	4 247285
Canada	4 257274

Communications	
IDD 355	IAC 00

Emergency numbers
112   Ambulance 17   Police 19

ALGERIA

THE 700 MILE LONG ALGERIAN COAST has few indentations, there are no natural harbours, and all the ports are man-made. With very few exceptions, the ports are crowded and polluted, which is one reason why cruising yachts seldom visit Algeria. The exception is Sidi Fredj, where a tourist development surrounds the harbour, part of which has been converted into a marina. Another reason is the long drawn-out conflict between government forces and the fundamentalist resistance movement, which has made the country unsafe for foreign travellers. The situation has shown some improvement, but as Algeria has few attractions as a cruising destination and touring the interior is still considered unsafe, planning a visit there should only be done when things return to normal throughout the country. If forced to make an emergency stop, you should try to do so in one of the larger ports.

COUNTRY PROFILE

Algeria has been invaded often – from the Phoenicians, Carthaginians and Romans to the Vandals and Byzantines. Arabs brought Islam to the country and under Ottoman rule the port of Algiers became a haven for pirates. The original inhabitants, the Berbers, withdrew to the mountains whenever invaders came and are still a sizeable part of the population.

In the nineteenth century Algeria was incorporated into France. The Algerian nationalist movement grew and in 1954 a rebellion started a long and bitter conflict in which over one million Algerians died and resulted in independence in 1962. In 1991, elections were won by Islamic fundamentalists, but the ruling government cancelled the results and declared a state of emergency. A violent situation followed with the fundamentalists targeting both the government and foreign interests. The situation has been slowly returning to normal.

The population is 34 million, mainly Arab and Berber as most settlers of European origin have left. Arabic is the official language, but French is also spoken.

CLIMATE

Algeria has a typical Mediterranean climate with dry summers and most rainfall occurring in winter. From May to September the weather is generally settled. During the rest of the year it is more changeable, with warm sunny days alternating with cool nights. Prevailing summer winds are easterly, while in winter the winds are either from the west or north.

FORMALITIES

Most ports monitor Channels 12 or 14, but apart from Arabic, only French is usually understood. Yachts must clear in and out of each harbour. Sidi Fredj Marina is the best port of entry as the officials are more accustomed to yachts.

All nationals require visas which should be obtained in advance and will not be issued on arrival.

FACILITIES

Only basic facilities are available and provisioning is limited. There are some repair services in Sidi Fredj Marina, and a 16-ton travelift and fuel.

Cruising Guides	Website
North Africa	www.algeria.com
Mediterranean Cruising	
Mediterranean Almanac	

Local time	UTC +1	Currency	Algerian Dinar (DZD)
Buoyage	IALA A	Electricity	230V, 50Hz

Diplomatic missions			
UK	21 230068	Canada	21 914951
USA	21 691255	South Africa	21 230384

Communications		Emergency numbers	
IDD 213 IAC 00		112	Police 17

PORTS OF ENTRY

Sidi Fredj	36°46′N 2°51′E	Ghazaouet	35°06′N 1°52′W	Oran	35°43′N 0°39′W	Mostaganem	35°56′N 0°04′E
Ténes	36°31′N 1°19′E	Algiers	36°47′N 3°04′E	Tamenfoust	36°49′N 3°14′E	Dellys	36°55′N 3°55′E
Bejaia	36°45′N 5°06′E	Skikda	36°53′N 6°54′E	Annaba	36°54′N 7°45′E	Beni-Saf	35°18′N 1°23′W
Bouharoun	36°38′N 2°40′W	Collo	37°00′N 6°34′E				

BULGARIA

THE BULGARIAN COAST is lined with a succession of small fishing ports, tourist resorts, and a couple of larger commercial harbours. Cruising along the coast is permitted after having cleared in, but there are some restrictions, such as access to the military port of Sozopol. Burgas, the nearest port of entry to the Turkish border, is a convenient first port of call as it has a new marina at the nearby resort of Nessebar. Varna has the best facilities and formalities are relatively easy to complete here as there is a small marina, and visiting sailors have always been warmly welcomed by the local sailing community. Farther north, the small port of Balchik, close to the Romanian border, has a small marina surrounded by a busy tourist resort.

◆ COUNTRY PROFILE

Of Asiatic origin, the Bulgars crossed the Danube in the seventh century and established the Bulgarian kingdom, which was later incorporated into the Byzantine Empire. After being conquered by the Ottoman Turks in 1396, the country did not regain its independence until 1908. An ally of Germany in the Second World War, Bulgaria was occupied in 1944 by the Red Army and a pro-Soviet government was formed. Communist domination ended in 1990, when Bulgaria began the process of moving towards democracy which led to the country joining the EU in 2007. The population is 7.2 million and the capital is Sofia.

◆ CLIMATE

The climate is temperate with very hot summers and cold winters. The warmest month is July, with an average temperature of 24°C/75°F, although day temperatures of 35°C/95°F or higher are not uncommon. The prevailing winds of summer are northeast, although there is a daily alternation of land and sea breezes.

◆ FORMALITIES

PORTS OF ENTRY

Burgas	42°30´N 27°29´E	Varna	43°12´N 27°55´E

Port Control should be called on Channel 77 in Varna or 11 in Burgas. Officials will visit the yacht and the crew must remain on board until cleared. If intending to visit other ports, a cruising permit should be requested; otherwise, yachts must clear in and out of each port.

Visas are not required for EU, US, Australian, Canadian and New Zealand nationals for a stay up to 90 days.

◆ FACILITIES

Facilities on the coast are constantly improving. Varna Yacht Club, Balchik Marina and Golden Sands Marina welcome visitors, have good facilities, and can help with formalities. The new marina at Nessebar is also planned to have good facilities; and the Burgas Yacht Club, the oldest in Bulgaria, welcomes visiting sailors, and is keen to attract more of them to its annual spring regatta. Provisioning is reasonable and fuel is available in all ports. Best repair services are in Varna, while Balchik Marina has a travelift.

◆ CHARTER

The local company Venid has a fleet of both sailing and power yachts that they offer both as bareboat and skippered charters.

www.venidyachtcharter.com

Cruising Guides	Websites
Cruising Bulgaria and Romania	www.bulgariatravel.org
RYA Foreign Cruising Vol 2	www.visitbulgaria.com

Local time	UTC +2
	Summer time: last Sunday in March to last Sunday in October
Buoyage	IALA
Currency	Leva (BGN)
Electricity	220V, 50Hz

Diplomatic missions			
UK	2 9339222	Canada	2 9433704
USA	2 9375100	South Africa	2 9816682

Communications		Emergency number
IDD 359	IAC 00	112

CROATIA

AFTER BEING OVERSHADOWED FOR MANY YEARS by the Greek islands, in recent years Croatia has become the most popular cruising destination in the Mediterranean. From Dubrovnik in the south to the Istria Peninsula in the north, Croatia has an extensive coastline indented with innumerable bays, deep inlets, hundreds of islands and countless attractive ports. As part of a determined drive to develop their tourism industry, the Croatian authorities have initiated a wide-ranging programme of infrastructure development. There is now a network of marinas, most with their own repair yards, and every port has an area set aside for visiting boats. There is a profusion of charter companies, offering a wide range of boats, from bare monohulls and catamarans to large motor yachts as well as the ubiquitous flotilla fleets. As a result, during the peak summer months of July and August, ports, marinas and popular bays are full of boats, although the situation is much better earlier or later in the season, which lasts from late April to early October. Fortunately, there is such a wealth of ports and anchorages that it is usually possible to find a sheltered place within a reasonable distance. Aware of the damage that can be done to the environment by the large influx of pleasure craft, some of the most attractive anchorages and islands have been incorporated into national parks or nature reserves, and in many bays mooring buoys are provided. One of the most popular destinations is the Kornati Islands, a small archipelago of uninhabited islands surrounded by crystal-clear waters. The nearby Luka Telascica on Dugi Otok (Long Island) boasts not only the best protected anchorages in the area, but also one of the best restaurants. Such establishments, usually providing docking facilities and catering primarily for visiting sailors, have sprung up in many popular spots and are a highly appreciated feature. Another nature reserve at Luka Polace on Mljet Island encompasses a perfectly protected anchorage that is overlooked by the massive ruins of a Roman castle. One of Croatia's most popular sites, the Krka Nature Reserve, lies some 30 miles inland and can easily be reached on the navigable Krka river. Its centrepiece is a series of spectacular waterfalls.

The port of Hvar overlooks the Pakleni Islands.

Compared to other former communist countries, Croatia has been fortunate in that most of its ancient towns and buildings have survived intact both communism and the more recent hostilities, and even those that were damaged during the war of independence have been carefully restored. Due to its long association with Rome and later Venice, the Adriatic coast is a treasure trove of beautifully preserved ancient monuments and medieval cities. Foremost among them is Dubrovnik, formerly known as Ragusa, an independent republic and vibrant mercantile centre whose trading ships reached ports as far apart as Istanbul and Lisbon. At the peak of its power, in the sixteenth and seventeenth centuries, Ragusa had a fleet of nearly two hundred ships and the reputation of the Dalmatian captains and seamen was unsurpassed. Almost unique for that period, Ragusa had a democratic system of government, and its pharmacy, orphanage, old people's home and city sewage works were among the first in medieval Europe.

Besides Dubrovnik, many of the ports along the Dalmatian coast and the offshore islands date from medieval or even Roman times – places such as Trogir, Hvar, Pula, Zadar, Split and others. Of special interest is Korcula, the birthplace of Marco Polo. The parental home of this most famous of medieval travellers still stands in a narrow street and is now a museum. Like many others in Croatia, the main port of Korcula, Hvar or Vis, shares its name with that of the island. Due to their perceived strategic importance, some of former Yugoslavia's offshore islands used to be off limits to foreign visitors and still bristle with rusting military installations: well-concealed submarine pens, gun emplacements and pill boxes. Vis was one of those prohibited islands and is now a much frequented place by both charter and cruising yachts. One of Croatia's main attractions are such ports where the town quay has been turned over to visiting yachts, with restaurants, bars and shops lining the welcoming waterfront. As yachts start arriving in late afternoon, enterprising farmers set up their stalls on the quay to sell locally grown fruit and vegetables.

After being ruled for more than forty years by a communist regime as part of Yugoslavia, whose long-term leader Tito was a Croat, Croatia has undergone an amazing change in the relatively short time since it became independent. Private enterprise has flourished, and guesthouses, small hotels and restaurants have mushroomed everywhere.

◆ COUNTRY PROFILE

The region was settled by Slavs in the sixth century, and later a Croat kingdom was established. Following a dynastic union with Hungary at the end of the eleventh century, most of Croatia remained under Hungarian rule until the First World War. In 1918 Croatia became part of the new Kingdom of

Serbs, Croats and Slovenes, renamed Yugoslavia in 1929. After the Second World War Croatia became one of the six republics making up the Yugoslav Federation. In 1990 a referendum backed full independence for Croatia. This was rejected by the Serb minority in Croatia who wished to remain united with Serbia. A bloody conflict broke out in 1991, but the arrival of a UN peacekeeping mission in 1992 brought peace and the international recognition of Croatian independence. By the late 1990s the situation had stabilized and in 2008 Croatia entered the final stage towards EU accession.

The population numbers 4.5 million, of which the majority are Croatian, most Serbs having left the country. The Croatian language is a variant of Serbo-Croat. The capital is Zagreb.

Dubrovnik

24

◆ CLIMATE

The coastal region enjoys a Mediterranean climate with hot dry summers and relatively mild winters. The warmest months are July and August, with averages of 25°C/77°F and day temperatures often well over 30°C/90°F. In summer there is a daily alternation of land and sea breezes. A local northerly wind, the bora, can affect the weather, especially in winter, with prolonged bouts of strong and bitterly cold winds. Violent thunderstorms with strong gusts are an unpleasant feature of the summer months and can be dangerous to vessels caught in the open or in unprotected anchorages.

◆ FORMALITIES

The ports quoted below are open all year round. There are also a number of seasonal ports open from 1 April to 30 October: Umag Marina, Novigrad, Kanegra, Sali, Soline, Kremik, Ravni Zakan, Vela Luka, Ubli (Lastovo) and Vis.

Boats arriving from outside Croatia must proceed to an official port of entry. Some of the busier ports have a special area reserved for clearance and the captain will be told the order in which to visit the various offices. In marinas, the staff will call the relevant officials. Crew must remain on board until formalities are complete.

Cavtat: For boats arriving from the south, this is the best port to clear in as Dubrovnik (Gruz) is a busy commercial harbour and the priority for the officials is to deal with cruise ships. Yachts should come to the main quay or, if there is no space, anchor in the vicinity. All offices are in the port area.
Dubrovnik: Boats are directed into Gruz harbour to complete formalities, where they must come alongside the quay in front of customs, marked by the Q flag. Yachts cannot clear in at Dubrovnik Marina.
Porec: This is an attractive and convenient port to clear in, especially if coming from Venice. Arriving yachts normally tie up at the clearance dock. The immigration office is on the dock; the port authority is two blocks away. Once cleared, the boat can pick up a visitors' mooring inside the harbour or move to one of the marinas.

Citizens of all EU countries, with the exception of Greece, do not need a visa. All other nationals require visas, which are usually granted on arrival.

A cruising vignette must be purchased in local currency. This permit is valid for one year and the yacht is then free to enter any Croatian port without any further formalities. Restricted areas are usually indicated on the permit, which

PORTS OF ENTRY

Umag	45°26´N 13°31´E	Porec	45°13´N 13°36´E	Rovinj	45°05´N 13°38´E
Pula	44°53´N 13°50´E	Rasa	45°02´N 14°04´E	Rijeka	45°19´N 14°26´E
Mali Losinj	44°32´N 14°28´E	Senj	45°00´N 15°14´E	Maslenica	44°3´N 15°32´E
Zadar	44°07´N 15°14´E	Hvar	43°10´N 16°50´E	Sibenik	43°44´N 15°54´E
Primosten	43°35´N 15°56´E	Split	43°30´N 16°27´E	Ploce	43°02´N 17°25´E
Metkovic	43°06´N 17°33´E	Korcula	42°48´N 17°27´E	Dubrovnik (Gruz)	42°38´N 18°07´E
Cavtat	42°34.8´N 18°13.5´E	Murter	43°49´N 15°36´E	Biograd	43°55´N 15°25´E

Porec in Northern Croatia.

is normally required to be surrendered to a marina office and retrieved when fees are paid before departure. Documents needed for clearance are the vessel's registration certificate, proof of ownership of the vessel or an authority from the actual owner, captain's licence or certificate of competence, third party insurance certificate, and crew lists. The crew will be listed on the permit and any subsequent changes must be made at one of the harbour offices.

Boats leaving Croatia must obtain clearance from the harbourmaster at a port of entry. The vessel must leave Croatian territorial waters immediately and by the shortest route.

The Roman arena in Pula.

✦ FACILITIES

As a result of the presence of large charter fleets as well as the influx of cruising boats, repair and haulout facilities are of a good standard. There are some forty marinas along the coast and on the major islands. Some of the larger marinas have their own yards with travelifts, chandleries and areas of hard standing. As a minimum, marinas have a 10-ton crane and the necessary frame to lift boats up to that weight. There are travelifts with a minimum capacity of 30 tons at Umag, Cres, Sukosan, Hramina, Murter, Bettina, Mali Losinj, Kremik, Vodice and Dubrovnik. Most marinas provide fuel, and provisions are available everywhere. The standard of service is good and most yards can undertake a wide range of service and repair to engines, spars, sails, hulls as well as electronic and electrical work. Marine equipment is available, but in a limited range and at higher prices than in other Mediterranean countries.

✦ CHARTER

Croatia probably has the largest number of charter operators in the Mediterranean, offering a choice of all types of vessels from their bases in Dubrovnik, Split, Biograd, Murter, Pula, Šibenik, Kremik, Trogir, Zadar, Krvavica and Agana.

www.sunsail.com
www.moorings.com
www.kiriacoulis.com
www.cosmosyachting.com

Cruising Guides
Adriatic Pilot
Croatia, Slovenia and Montenegro, 777 Harbours and Anchorages
Croatia Cruising Companion
Dove Navigare Bolina (details of ports and marinas in Italian)

Websites
www.htz.hr (National Tourist Board)
www.aci-club.hr (details of publicly owned marinas)
www.about-croatia.com/croatia-marina.php (details of private marinas)

Local time	UTC +1
	Summer time: last Sunday in March to last Sunday in October
Buoyage	IALA A
Currency	Kuna (HRK)
Electricity	220V, 50Hz

Diplomatic missions

UK	1 6009100
USA	1 6612200
Australia	1 4891200
Canada	1 4881200
South Africa	1 4894111
New Zealand	1 4612060

Communications
IDD 385   IAC 00

Emergency numbers
112   Ambulance 94   Police 92

CYPRUS

A LARGE ISLAND tucked into the eastern corner of the Mediterranean, Cyprus has a strategic position, being within close range of Turkey, Syria, Lebanon and Israel. Ironically, it is further from Greece, with which it traditionally had the closest ties. The invasion by Turkish troops in 1974 of Northern Cyprus, which is home to the island's Turkish minority, resulted in the declaration of that area as the separate entity of the Turkish Republic of Northern Cyprus. Recognized only by Turkey, this part of Cyprus has remained under Turkish occupation to this day. The Republic of Cyprus, which claims jurisdiction over the entire island, in effect only administers the southern part which contains the larger Greek community. There was a marked amelioration in the ongoing crisis in 2009, and some travel restrictions between the two areas have been eased or lifted.

Cyprus is an attractive island with a pleasant climate, beautiful mountainous landscape and interesting archaeological sites. According to legend, Aphrodite, the Greek goddess of love, emerged from the sea at Paphos. From the scenic point of view, Northern Cyprus is the more attractive area and, in spite of the restrictions imposed by the Republic of Cyprus, visiting yachts continue to stop there. The medieval port of Girne (Kyrenia) is one of the most impressive sites in the Mediterranean. Lacking natural harbours and anchorages, Cyprus has always been an island to visit from its ports, rather than to cruise around.

✦ COUNTRY PROFILE

The ancient name of Cyprus was Alasia, meaning 'belonging to the sea'. The current name Kypros originates from the Greek word for copper. In ancient times the copper deposits brought considerable wealth to the island and many people

The ancient port of Kyrenia (Girne).

came to settle from the Greek mainland. As a result of its position, Cyprus experienced many invasions and different rulers over the centuries. At various historical periods it has been claimed by the Assyrians, Egyptians, Persians and Romans. Later the island became part of the Byzantine Empire, then the Ottoman Empire, and finally in 1914 it became British. Following four years of fighting against the British troops by the Greek Cypriots, the independent Republic of Cyprus was established in 1960. Immediately afterwards, fighting broke out between the Greek and the Turkish Cypriots over the terms of the independence agreement. The Republic of Cyprus, which controls 60 per cent of the island, is internationally recognized as the government of Cyprus and joined the EU in 2004.

The population of the island is 798,000 and is made up of 78 per cent Greek Cypriot, 18 per cent Turkish Cypriot, and the rest other minorities. Greek is the main language in the south, while Turkish is spoken in the north. English is widely spoken. Nicosia is the capital.

✦ CLIMATE

Although the climate is typically Mediterranean, the proximity to the Asian landmass to the east and north makes Cyprus one of the hottest places in the Mediterranean. Apart from being very hot, the summer is occasionally humid with temperatures of up to 40°C/104°F. The remainder of the year is more pleasant, with short spells of stormy wet weather in winter. July and August are the warmest months, with average temperatures of 23°C/73°F, and January the coolest, 5°C/41°F. September to early November is usually the best time for cruising as the weather is settled and pleasant.

✦ FORMALITIES

PORTS OF ENTRY	
Republic of Cyprus: Larnaca	34°55′N 33°38′E
Limassol	34°40′N 33°03′E
Paphos	34°45′N 32°25′E

Cyprus Radio maintains continuous watch on Channels 16 and 26. The Cypriot courtesy flag must be flown when entering Cypriot waters. In the past, boats that had stopped first in Northern Cyprus faced serious difficulties with the authorities in Southern Cyprus, but this may change.

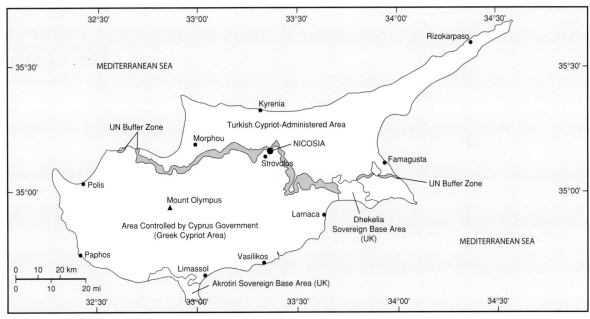

No visas are required by nationals of the EU, USA, Australia, Canada and New Zealand for stays of up to three months. There are no longer any restrictions for crossing the land border from one side to the other.

Northern Cyprus: Girne (Kyrenia)	35°20′ N 33°19′ E

There are no restrictions imposed by North Cyprus authorities for those who wish to visit a port in the north after having visited a port in the south.

◆ CHARTER
Both Cyprus Yachts and Yacht Sun are based in Larnaca Marina and operate a fleet of sailing yachts for bareboat charter. Gold Line Charters (Yachting Cyprus) is based in St Raphael Marina and offers both skippered and bareboat charters.

www.cyprusyachts.com
www.yachtsun.com
www.yachtingcyprus.com

◆ FACILITIES
Republic of Cyprus
As a favourite place for spending the winter, facilities have greatly improved over the years. In Larnaca there are several workshops, which can deal with a wide range of repairs. There is also a boatyard with a travelift. St Raphael Marina (ex-Sheraton Marina) operates in the northern part of the bay of Limassol, with a full range of services including a boatyard and 60-ton travelift. Fuel, some marine equipment and provisions are available in all ports.

Northern Cyprus
Girne is always crowded with local boats, so a better alternative is Delta Marina to the east. There are some repair facilities in Girne as well as at Delta Marina.

Cruising Guides
Turkish Waters and Cyprus Pilot
Mediterranean Almanac
Mediterranean Cruising
Mediterranean Islands

Websites
www.visitcyprus.com
www.northcyprus.cc
www.all-about-cyprus-yachting.com (yachting information)

Local time	UTC +2
	Summer time: last Sunday in March to last Sunday in October
Buoyage	IALA A
Currency	Euro (EUR) in the Republic of Cyprus
	Turkish Lira (TL) in Northern Cyprus
Electricity	240V, 50Hz

Diplomatic missions Republic of Cyprus:
UK	22 861100
USA	22 393939
Australia	22 676739

Communications
Republic of Cyprus:	IDD 357	IAC 00
Northern Cyprus:	IDD 90 392	IAC 00

Emergency numbers
112 (both areas)   Northern Cyprus: Police 155

EGYPT

THE PYRAMIDS AND THE SPHINX AT GIZA, the temples of Luxor and Karnak, and the Valleys of the Kings and Queens are some of the places that make Egypt a major tourist destination, and most visiting sailors try to see at least some of these ancient sites. Cairo and its many treasures are best visited from Port Said, Ismailia or Suez, all of which have yacht clubs where the boat can be left unattended. The sites on the Upper Nile are within a convenient distance from one of the marinas in the Hurghada area.

The Suez Canal has dominated Egypt's modern history. The 87.5 mile long canal links the Mediterranean to the Red Sea by way of several lakes and without any locks. The opening of the canal in 1869 had an enormous impact on international shipping as it halved the distance between Europe and the Middle East. Its importance has grown over the years and most of the Middle East oil today reaches Europe via the Suez Canal. Currently the canal is transited on average by 50 ships every day and work is in progress to both widen and deepen the canal. In its long history it was closed only twice, both times as a result of hostilities – first in 1956, when it was closed for one year, and in 1967, for seven years.

Vessels under 300 tons are allowed to use the canal free of charge, although there are some fees that need to be paid by all craft, including yachts.

A canal of some kind has existed in this area since antiquity and in the time of the early Pharaohs the River Nile was connected to the Red Sea. The canal allowed direct trade with the land of Punt, and bas-reliefs of five ships returning from an expedition undertaken in the reign of Queen Hatshepsut in the fifteenth century BCE seem to confirm this. The Greek historian Herodotus, who lived in the fifth century BCE, was so impressed by the pyramids that he wrote, in his major work *The Histories*, these immortal words: 'Man fears time, time fears the pyramids'. He also confirmed

The port of Alexandria.

the existence of a waterway between the Mediterranean and the Red Sea.

Over the next thousand years, the canal was successively modified, destroyed and rebuilt, until finally it was put out of commission by Caliph al-Mansur in 750 CE. Traces of the old canal were discovered in the nineteenth century, and in 1856 the Frenchman Ferdinand de Lesseps obtained a concession from the viceroy of Egypt to construct a canal open to ships of all nations. The excavation took 11 years, using 30,000 people, the majority of whom were forced labour.

The Mediterranean coast of Egypt is bereft of any cruising opportunities and most sailors come to know the country through transiting the Suez Canal. Even those who intend to see more of the Egyptian coast other than Port Said only have as an alternative the ancient port of Alexandria. Occasionally shallow drafted yachts manage to obtain a permit to sail up the Nile, which is a fascinating way to see Egypt, although most certainly not the easiest. The Red Sea area of Egypt is described on page 387.

◆ COUNTRY PROFILE

Egypt has 5,000 years of recorded history and one of the earliest civilizations in the world. In 3188 BCE the Pharaoh Menes united the Upper and Lower Kingdoms with Memphis as the capital, and the pyramids were built during this period. After this came the Middle Kingdom, with its centre at Thebes, which is present-day Luxor. The New Kingdom, which was the era of Queen Nefertiti and Tutankhamun, established a large empire in the sixteenth to the fourteenth centuries BCE. Invasions from Libya, Nubia, Ethiopia and Assyria brought about the empire's decline. The era of the Pharaohs finally ended with the arrival of Alexander the Great in 332 BCE. Alexandria became the new capital, a sophisticated city that was a centre of Greek culture and civilization. Queen Cleopatra's death in 30 BCE marked the end of independence. Rome and Byzantium dominated until Arab invasions swept across Egypt from the seventh to the tenth centuries and the capital moved to present-day Cairo. In the early sixteenth century the Ottoman Turks gained control and Egypt became a mere province of their vast empire.

In 1798 Napoleon's conquest of Egypt opened it up to modern European influence. France's subsequent withdrawal created a power struggle, until the Albanian Muhammed Ali became Sultan. Efforts were made to modernize the country, and in 1869 the Suez Canal was opened. Britain occupied Egypt in 1882, but nationalist feelings grew among the Egyptians and in 1922 Egypt was recognized as an independent country. Amid growing dissatisfaction with Egypt's status and the monarchy, in 1952 a nationalist revolution led by Gamal Abdel Nasser established a republic. Nasser nationalized the Suez Canal, which provoked the Suez Crisis of 1956, and the military intervention of Israel, France and Britain. Anwar Sadat succeeded Nasser in 1970, establishing better links with the West, and ending the ongoing state of war with Israel in 1979. Sadat was assassinated in 1981, and under President Mubarak relations both with the West and Israel have improved considerably.

The rapidly rising population now numbers 83 million, comprising Egyptians, Bedouins, Nubians, Arabs and some smaller communities. About 7 million are Copts, who claim to be descendants of the original inhabitants, a Hamitic people who lived along the Nile. Islam is the religion of the majority, although the Copts are Christian, and the Coptic Church is one of the oldest in existence. There is also a small Jewish community. Arabic is the official language, and the capital is Cairo – the largest city in Africa.

✦ CLIMATE

The summers are very hot with high temperatures, while winters are mild with little rain. The hottest months are July and August, with average temperatures of 27°C/81°F and day temperatures that often reach 40°C/104°F. January is the coolest month, with an average temperature of 15°C/59°F. The prevailing winds are northerly. Occasionally the *khamsin*, a hot dry wind, blows off the land; this wind is laden with dust and sand, thus reducing visibility. Along the Mediterranean coast there are daily alternating land and sea breezes.

✦ FORMALITIES

PORTS OF ENTRY

Alexandria	31°11´N 29°52´E	Port Said	31°15´N 32°18´E

Port Said: Because of the high density of shipping traffic and the difficult approaches to Port Said, the harbour should not be entered at night. Yachts are normally met by a pilot launch and directed to the Port Fouad Yacht Club on the eastern side of the harbour. It is usually easier if contact has been made in advance with a local agent who will obtain permission to proceed directly to the yacht club. If the yacht is transiting the canal, immigration formalities are simple and no visas will be issued. Those who wish to stay longer and visit other parts of Egypt need to go through the normal entry procedure.

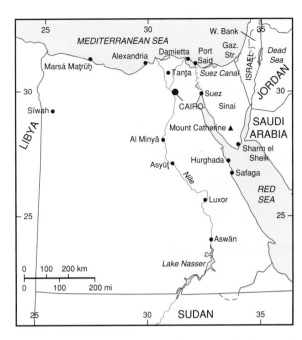

Alexandria: Yachts must go to the eastern harbour and anchor off the Yacht Club of Egypt, whose staff will help with formalities.

If transiting the canal, and not stopping anywhere else after the transit, outward clearance can be obtained while doing the transit formalities. Yachts may then proceed as soon as they have completed the transit and dropped the pilot. Vessels that have obtained outward clearance must leave within 24 hours, or request another clearance.

Visas are not needed by anyone travelling on a yacht transiting the Suez Canal and remaining in the port areas. At all points of entry, visas valid for one month are granted on arrival. Visas can be extended by the police.

Coast Guard cruising permits are no longer available; the permits that are currently issued are monthly cruising permits that are valid for all marinas.

✦ SUEZ CANAL

The captain of yachts intending to transit the canal will be informed at the yacht club either by a club official, or an official of the Canal Authority, on the correct procedure to follow. Although time consuming, the formalities can be carried out by the captain alone, but the service of an agent is highly recommended. The captain has to visit the Small Craft Department in the main building of the Canal Authority in Port Said to be instructed as to the various formalities to be carried out and the payments to be made. These payments include the transiting fee, insurance policy, ports and lights fee. The captain must then arrange for a technical inspection of the yacht. Following this, a transit permit will be issued and a time arranged for the pilot to come on board. On the day of the transit the pilot will arrive early in the morning to guide the yacht as far as Ismailia in the northwest corner of Lake Timsah, where the yacht must spend the night as yachts are not allowed to transit at night. The crew are not allowed to go ashore. Early the following morning, either the same pilot or another one will continue the transit to Suez. Normally yachts stop at the Suez Yacht Club before continuing into the Red Sea.

✦ RIVER NILE

To navigate the river, a security permit has to be obtained from the Coast Guard as well as permission from the Ministry of Foreign Affairs. Navigation is restricted to daytime only. There are several bridges and locks, which open at certain times of the day or on request. The maximum draft must not exceed 5ft (1.5m). Navigation is only possible during winter, from October to May, when the level of water is higher. The river depth falls considerably during the summer months.

✦ FACILITIES

In both Port Said and Suez, cruising yachts normally berth at the local yacht club, which charges a daily fee. Provisioning is somewhat better in Port Said, which is a duty-free port, and stores can be ordered and delivered to the yacht club. There are daily fresh produce markets in both ports. The yacht club

The Suez Canal.

in Alexandria will help with advice as there are various workshops that can undertake engine, electrical and some electronic repairs, as well as fibreglass, metalwork and carpentry. There are slipways at Alexandria, Port Said and Suez.

Arrangements can be made at any of the clubs to leave the boat while visiting the interior, and a local watchman should be employed in such a case. Suez is probably the best place to leave the boat unattended, whether to visit Egypt's interior or go overland to Israel and Jordan.

For those transiting the Suez Canal, Ismailia is a convenient place to leave the boat, the yacht club is well run, the staff are helpful and friendly, and the town itself is well worth a visit.

✦ RESTRICTIONS

All military zones are prohibited areas.

Egypt is very environmentally conscious about the Red Sea: spearfishing, the taking of reef fish, and the collecting of coral, shells and marine animals are all forbidden. There are now national park boundaries on most islands and reefs, and anchoring in coral is prohibited. Mooring buoys are provided on most dive sites.

Cruising Guides	
Red Sea Pilot	
Mediterranean Almanac	
Websites	
www.suezcanal.gov.eg	
www.egypt.travel	

Local time	UTC +2
	Summer time: late April to late August
Buoyage	IALA A
Currency	Egyptian Pound (EGP)
Electricity	220V, 50Hz
Diplomatic missions	
UK	2 27916000
USA	2 27973300
Australia	2 25750444
Canada	2 27978700
South Africa	2 3594365
New Zealand	2 24616000
Communications	
IDD 20	IAC 00
Emergency numbers	
Ambulance 123	Police 122	Tourist police 126

FRANCE

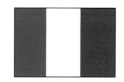

HAVING BOTH A MEDITERRANEAN and an Atlantic coastline, France probably has more variety to offer the cruising sailor than any other European country, from the chic ports of the Côte d'Azur to the tidal creeks and shallow estuaries of Brittany, and the stark beauty of the island of Corsica. For the visiting sailor, each side of France has its special attractions as well as challenges. The Atlantic coast calls for more attentive navigation, but brings its rewards in the many natural harbours and inlets. Mediterranean France is probably more suited to those who prefer to find their pleasures ashore. Sailing into such glittering places as St Tropez, Cannes or Antibes is a special experience and is probably worth the long detour just to spend some time rubbing fenders with some of the most beautiful yachts in the world.

France is one of the leading sailing nations and its top sailors are as well known to the general French public as its best soccer players. The booming French boatbuilding industry, which was the first to put well-designed cruising boats into mass production, has been instrumental in bringing cruising within reach of a wider market. A sustained construction programme has resulted in a string of marinas along the entire Mediterranean coast to cater for a thriving sailing community. The one drawback is that marinas are invariably full and visiting yachts often have difficulty finding a vacant space. This can be a real problem along the Côte d'Azur where there are very few protected anchorages and there is often no alternative to docking in a marina.

There are, however, two groups of offshore islands, where it is easier to find a place to anchor. The Iles de Lérins are close to Cannes, the more famous of the two small islands being Ile Saint Marguerite, dominated by a massive fort whose most notorious prisoner was the legendary man in the iron mask. Away from the Côte d'Azur, a short distance past the other fashionable landmark, St Tropez, lie the three Iles d'Or: Porquerolles, Port Cros and Ile du Levant. Compared to the busy mainland, they are a haven of tranquillity, and the first two have been declared nature reserves. A gem not to be missed on Porquerolles is the Oceanographic Museum. Housed in the fourteenth-century Fort Sainte Agathe, it displays a fascinating array of objects retrieved by divers from the countless trading ships that have perished in these waters since ancient times.

As you sail west, the coast becomes increasingly spectacular as the high cliffs are dissected by fjord-like calanques. A prime attraction in this area is the colourful

Marseille's inner harbour is now almost entirely occupied by yachts.

inner harbour of Marseille, which has been in continuous use since its foundation as the Greek colony of Massilia in the seventh century BCE. On a small rocky islet outside the entrance to the port stands the massive Chateau d'If, the setting for Alexandre Dumas's *The Count of Monte Cristo*.

One of Europe's mighty rivers, the Rhône, reaches the sea close to Marseille and offers the intrepid sailor the opportunity to reach the North or Baltic Seas via the intricate river and canals systems that criss-cross the European continent. The attractive port of Sète, described as the Venice of Languedoc, is the starting point of the Canal du Midi, which provides a shortcut to the Bay of Biscay and the Atlantic. The Atlantic coast of France is covered on page 118.

The Languedoc Roussillon region stretches all the way to the Spanish border, with old ports being interspersed with modern resorts, each incorporating its own marina. Their main advantage is that they provide convenient shelter along a coast that was once mostly barren and dangerous.

Corsica lies only 100 miles off the mainland coast and this large island is different in almost every way from metropolitan France. Massive granite mountains drop steeply into the sea, their slopes covered in impenetrable vegetation while their serrated summits reach for the sky. This savage nature gives the island its special character and explains the fiercely independent nature of its inhabitants for whom compromise is never a solution. The most famous Corsican of them all, Napoleon Bonaparte, fitted this description in every respect.

His birthplace, the port of Ajaccio, is the island's capital and main port and incorporates two marinas. Where nature

has not provided a natural harbour, man has made up for it by building marinas at convenient distances all around the coast. In between the marinas and older ports are a few anchorages, but none provides all-round protection.

Some of the medieval ports are among the most attractive anywhere in the Mediterranean, such as Ajaccio, Bastia and Porto Vecchio, all of which date back to at least the sixteenth century. Going back much further is Bonifacio, which is believed to be the port mentioned in the *Odyssey* as the home of the Laestrogonians, the giants who ate one of Ulysses' crew and bombarded the others with boulders from the top of the high cliffs. The deep fjord-like inlet is now considered safe and provides excellent shelter in any kind of weather in a most attractive setting. Close by, the current-swept Bonifacio straits separate Corsica from Sardinia. Two small islands on the French side of the demarcation line, Cavallo and Lavezzi, have several interesting anchorages, but the maze of rocks and reefs that surround them makes navigation tricky, so they should only be visited in absolutely settled weather.

◆ COUNTRY PROFILE

Remains of the earliest prehistoric human settlements have been found in France and the exquisite cave paintings at Lascaux were created over 30,000 years ago. In historic times, the first settlers were of Ligurian and Iberian stock, followed in the sixth century BCE by the arrival of the Gauls, a Celtic people. Gaul was conquered by the Romans, and from the resulting Gallo-Roman civilization the French language and institutions developed.

The Middle Ages saw a consolidation of royal power against a background of ongoing conflicts with England. In 1789 the Revolution overthrew the old order and the First Republic was established. Napoleon Bonaparte rose to power, becoming Emperor and embarking on a series of military campaigns until his ultimate defeat and exile. During the nineteenth century France expanded as a major colonial power. The First World War, in which France suffered heavy losses, was followed by a period of political instability. In 1940 France was invaded by Germany and a hastily arranged government under Marshal Pétain signed an armistice with the occupying forces. Charles de Gaulle, leader of the Free French, came to power after the war. The following years saw the start of the disintegration of the French colonial empire, first with the war in Indochina, then the Algerian war. France was one of the six founding members of the Common Market, which eventually became the European Union.

The population numbers 62 million, mainly French, but there are also Arab and African minorities in some cities. French is the main language, and regional languages such as Basque, Breton, Corsican or Provençal are only spoken by a few.

Porquerolles is the largest island in the Bay of Hyères.

✦ CLIMATE

Southern France enjoys a Mediterranean climate, with hot dry summers and mild winters. The occasional summer rains are often heavy and associated with thunder. Winds along the Mediterranean coast and Corsica are variable, the strongest wind being the northwesterly mistral, which occurs regularly and often reaches gale force. The warmest months are July and August, with average temperatures of 23°C/73°F and day temperatures often well over 30°C/90°F. January is the coldest month, with an average temperature of 6°C/43°F. Summers in Corsica are equally hot, but winters are milder, with average temperatures of 8°C/46°F in the coolest month of January.

✦ FORMALITIES

As France is a member of the EU and signatory to the Schengen Agreement, those regulations apply. Boats with EU nationals on board coming from a Schengen country do not need to report. If coming from outside of the Schengen area, non-EU boats, or those with non-EU nationals on board, should report to customs at a port of entry. French officials occasionally ask to see proof that VAT has been paid on an EU-flagged vessel. Non-EU vessels may be asked to show proof of their first entry into EU waters.

✦ INLAND WATERWAYS

France has the best inland waterway system in Europe that is

PORTS OF ENTRY

Mainland coast:

Port Vendres	42°31′N 3°07′E	Port la Nouvelle	43°01′N 3°04′E	Sète	43°24′N 3°42′E
Marseilles	43°20′N 5°21′E	Port St Louis du Rhône	43°23′N 4°49′E	Port de Bouc	43°24′N 4°59′E
Toulon-la Seyne	43°07′N 5°55′E	Bandol	43°08′N 5°45′E	Cassis	43°13′N 5°32′E
Hyères	43°04′N 6°22′E	La Ciotat	43°10′N 5°36′E	Le Lavandou	43°08′N 6°22′E
Sanary	43°07′N 5°48′E	St Mandrier	43°05′N 5°55′E	St Tropez	43°16′N 6°38′E
St Maxime	43°18′N 6°38′E	Fréjus-Saint Raphael	43°25′N 6°46′E	Cannes	43°33′N 7°01′E
Antibes	43°35′N 7°09′E	Nice	43°42′N 7°17′E	Menton-Garavan	43°46′N 7°30′E
Corsica:					
Ajaccio	41°55′N 8°44′E	Bastia	42°42′N 9°27′E	Porto-Vecchio	41°36′N 9°17′E
Propriano	41°40′N 8°54′E	Calvi	42°35′N 8°48′E	Ile Rousse	42°39′N 8°56′E
Bonifacio	41°23′N 9°06′E				

still used by commercial traffic as well as yachts. The Atlantic and Mediterranean are connected by a canal and river route of 314 miles with 139 locks, from Bordeaux on the River Garonne to Sète in the Mediterranean. Other canals and river systems go into the heart of Brittany, through the centre of Paris, the eastern part of France, and the Rhône river to the Mediterranean. Yachts must unstep their masts, which can be done at the seaports before entry into the canals, there being facilities that specialize in this operation. There are certain maximum restrictions, the most important being the draft, which is normally 1.80m (6ft), while the maximum air clearance is 3.50m (11ft) and in some places as little as 2.50m (8ft). All vessels using the inland waterways and canals must be in possession of a valid VNF sticker (Voies Navigables de France), which can be bought for a whole year or shorter periods.

✦ FACILITIES

With the most developed yacht-building industry in Europe, yachting facilities are of a high standard. Marinas have been built along the entire Mediterranean coast, and in many places, particularly in the older ports, special docking arrangements have been made for yachts. Chandlery and repair facilities are widely available and small repairs can be undertaken in most ports. For more complex jobs it is best to go to one of the major centres, where there are established boatyards and specialist companies offering a complete range of repair facilities. The best facilities are at Antibes, in the St Tropez–Cogolin area, Hyères, Marseille and Cap d'Agde. In Corsica, the main port of Ajaccio has the best facilities on the west coast, and Bastia on the east coast.

France prides itself on having the best cuisine in the world and the quality of food is excellent everywhere. Supplies are easily obtained, and on the outskirts of every town there are huge hypermarkets. You can purchase fuel in all ports and most marinas have their own fuelling dock. LPG is widely available, but for longer stays it may be advisable to change over to the French system of tanks.

The perfectly protected port of Bonifacio on the south coast of Corsica.

✦ CHARTER

The Côte d'Azur is home to the most beautiful and luxurious yachts in the world, some of which are even available for charter. For those with more modest requirements, there are charter companies operating all along the Riviera and beyond. In spite of its scenic beauty this coast is not particularly amenable to cruising, so this should be borne in mind when choosing your location. In this respect, a port like Hyères has a certain advantage as it is only a short sail to some attractive islands as well as to St Tropez. Charter companies based in Nice, Antibes and Cannes, all within easy reach of Nice airport, see many of their clients head offshore for Corsica with its rich cruising opportunities. The alternative is to charter a boat in Corsica itself, where the main bases are at Ajaccio, Bonifacio and Macinaggio.

> www.cote-dazur-charter.com (Hyères)
> www.moorings.com (Nice and Ajaccio)
> www.kiriacoulis.com (Bormes les Mimosas)
> www.dreamyachtcharter.com (Macinaggio)
> www.lilebleue.com (Antibes and Bonifacio)

Cruising Guides
Mediterranean France and Corsica
Cruising Almanac
Corsica and North Sardinia
Mediterranean Cruising
Mediterranean Almanac
Mediterranean Islands
Inland Waterways of France
Through the French Canals

Websites
www.franceguide.com
www.1yachtua.com/Medit-marinas/France/frmarinas.asp
  (Mediterranean marinas)

Local time	UTC +1
	Summer time: last Sunday in March to last Sunday in October
Buoyage	IALA A
Currency	Euro (EUR)
Electricity	220/240V, 50Hz

Diplomatic missions

UK	01 44513100
USA	01 43122222
Australia	01 40593300
Canada	01 44432900
South Africa	01 53592323
New Zealand	01 45014343

Communications		Emergency number
IDD 33	IAC 00	112

GEORGIA

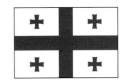

THE MOST SPECTACULAR SCENERY in the Black Sea and some of the best resorts in the former Soviet Union can now be found in this mountainous country bordering the eastern shore of the Black Sea. Ethnic strife and economic problems, which have bedevilled other former Soviet republics, have also left their mark on Georgia. There has been an ongoing conflict in the two autonomous republics within Georgia, Abkhazia and Ajaria, as well as the autonomous region of South Ossetia, seeking greater independence from Georgia. This culminated in Georgia's military action in South Ossetia in August 2008, which led to a Russian response that ended in Russia unilaterally recognizing the independence of Abkhazia and South Ossetia, both of which have de facto separated from Georgia. While the situation continues to be uncertain in this part of the Black Sea, a voyage to Georgia should only be contemplated once it is deemed safe to travel in that part of the world.

The port of Poti lies at the mouth of the River Rhioni that leads to the Bronze Age sites reputed to be associated with the Golden Fleece legend. The coastal area south of Poti all the way to Batumi and the Turkish border is considered to be the most beautiful cruising area in the Black Sea and has not been affected by the troubles further north.

◆ COUNTRY PROFILE

The Georgian Republic is part of the Caucasus region, whose mountains stretch from the Black Sea to the Caspian Sea. Present-day Georgia was the site of Colchis, from where Jason and the Argonauts stole the Golden Fleece. The ancient Greeks and Romans colonized the area, followed by Arab and Mongolian invasions. Later, Georgia put itself under the protection of Russia, who annexed it in 1801. In 1918 an independent republic was proclaimed, but in 1922 Georgia became part of the USSR. Independence was declared in 1991, when the USSR disintegrated into its constituent parts. The population is 4.6 million, of which Georgians comprise over 80 per cent. The Georgian language has its own script. The capital is Tbilisi.

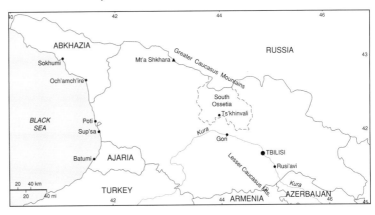

◆ CLIMATE

Protected by the Caucasian mountains, the region's climate is pleasant and mild. In summer the climate is almost tropical, with hot and humid days. Winters are mild and wet.

◆ FORMALITIES

PORTS OF ENTRY

Batumi 41°39´N 41°39.4´E   Poti 42°09´N 41°39´E

Batumi is a busy commercial port, while Poti is Georgia's main naval base, so access may be restricted.

Nationals of the EU, Canada and the USA do not need a visa for a stay of up to 90 days. Nationals of Australia, New Zealand, South Africa, and many other nationals, need a visa, which can be obtained on arrival for a fee.

◆ FACILITIES

While yachting facilities are still modest by international standards, most emergency repairs can be done locally. For any help it is best to contact the local yacht club in Poti. Kvariati Yacht Club has a small new marina in the Kvariati resort, close to Batumi. Provisioning is good and diesel fuel is available.

Websites
www.georgia-tbilisi.info (Georgian Tourism Association)
www.potiseaport.com (Poti Port site)
www.bagebeycity.com/Eng/Projects/Kvariati/ (Kvariati Yacht Club and Marina)

Local time	UTC +4	Currency	Lari (GEL)
Buoyage	IALA A	Electricity	220V, 50Hz

Diplomatic missions			
UK	32 274747	USA	32 277000

Communications		Emergency number	
IDD 995	IAC 810	022	

GIBRALTAR

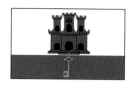

AT THE CROSSROADS of two seas and two continents, Gibraltar's unique position as the gateway to the Mediterranean has given it an importance far exceeding its small size and population. Only 2½ miles long, barely 1 mile wide, the peninsula drops precipitously from a height of 427m (1,397ft) down to the sea. The rock is made of limestone and riddled with caves, a feature used by its inhabitants throughout the ages.

Gibraltar is undergoing a wide-ranging makeover and there is lots of building going on, with every one of its marinas having been refurbished. The biggest change has been the complete rebuilding of the old Sheppard's Marina into a residential complex under the new name of Ocean Village. The number of marinas is now reduced to only two: Marina Bay, near the airport, and Queensway, near the centre.

Very few yachts on their way to or from the Mediterranean fail to stop in this historic port, which is one of the most frequented sailing centres in the world. Although some yachts spend a considerable time in Gibraltar, its main function continues to be that of a transit port, a role that the Rock has fulfilled throughout its colourful and often turbulent history. The movement of yachts is virtually continuous, although there are clearly defined peak periods. Spring and early summer sees boats arriving from across the Atlantic or Northern Europe bound for the Mediterranean. The autumn months see a large movement in the opposite direction as yachts leave the Mediterranean, usually bound for Madeira and the Canaries en route to the Caribbean. Although a convenient place for repairs and reprovisioning with some of the best repair facilities in the area, Gibraltar is also a good place to relax and its cosmopolitan make-up serves this function well.

Dawn over Gibraltar.

✦ COUNTRY PROFILE

Geologically part of Africa, Gibraltar is known to have been settled since prehistoric times. One of the two Pillars of Hercules, Gibraltar marked the limit of the civilized world, beyond which early sailors dared not venture. It was only in the eighth century, with the Moorish expansion into Europe, that people settled here. The Rock was named after the Moorish leader Tarik-ibn-Zeyad, Gebel Tarik (Tarik's mountain), with the name later evolving into Gibraltar.

Ceded to Great Britain by Spain in 1713, the Rock has continued to be claimed by Spain, but repeated referendums have resulted in Gibraltarians voting overwhelmingly to remain a British dependency. An agreement was reached in 2006, with Gibraltar becoming self-governing, while the UK retains responsibility for defence and foreign relations. In 2009 Spain decided unilaterally to extend its territorial waters to include those surrounding Gibraltar. The reason given was the protection of the environment, and Spanish patrol boats made several incursions into what Gibraltarians insisted were their own territorial waters to inspect fishing boats to ensure that they were acting within the law. Such disputes occur from time to time but do not affect the movement of pleasure craft.

An unmistakable presence on the Rock is a colony of Barbary apes. It is said that as long as the apes continue to be around, Gibraltar will remain British; when faced with a rapid decline in their numbers during the Second World War, Winston Churchill ordered a new batch to be brought over from Morocco.

The population of Gibraltar is 28,000. Gibraltarians are a mixture of many nationalities, mainly Spanish and British, with Jewish and Moroccan minorities. English is the official language, but Spanish is widely spoken.

✦ CLIMATE

The tall rock attracts its own weather, often being covered by low cloud. Such mist usually foretells the imminent arrival of the *Levanter*, a strong easterly wind. Normally caused by an approaching Atlantic low, it can reach gale force rapidly, lasting for several days. About 80 per cent of the winds blow either from the east or west. *Poniente* is the name of the westerly wind, which is preceded by low cloud, and occasionally can set in for several days, making life difficult for anyone waiting to reach the Atlantic. With the Atlantic Ocean so near, Gibraltar's weather is not entirely Mediterranean.

However, it is generally a pleasant climate with warm summers and mild winters. Summers are hot, with July the warmest, average temperature 24°C/75°F, and January the coolest, 13°C/55°F.

✦ FORMALITIES

PORT OF ENTRY

Gibraltar   36°08´N 5°22´W

The Port Authority should be contacted on Channels 12 or 16 on arrival to inform the radio officer of the vessel's plans to proceed to one of the marinas or to anchor near the runway. Clearance is conducted at the two marinas: Queensway Quay Marina or Marina Bay Marina. Those who anchor will have to visit the Port Authority office. Yachts are no longer allowed to anchor in the area to the east of 'E' head without prior permission. Larger vessels should contact the harbourmaster for instructions.

Nationals of the EU, Australia, Canada, New Zealand and the USA do not require a visa. Gibraltar enjoys a special status within the EU, but visa requirements are as per the Schengen Agreement. Non-EU nationals who may need to prove that they had left the EU VAT area by spending some time in Gibraltar will need to obtain a form stating this, called *pratique*, which is issued by the Port Authority.

✦ FACILITIES

Gibraltar's yachting facilities are of a good standard and there are haulout facilities up to several hundred tons. If spare parts are not available locally, they can be ordered from the UK from where there are daily flights. Duty-free stores have attractive prices, while provisioning and fresh produce are good.

An aerial view showing Queensway Marina on the left and Marina Bay Marina next to the runway.

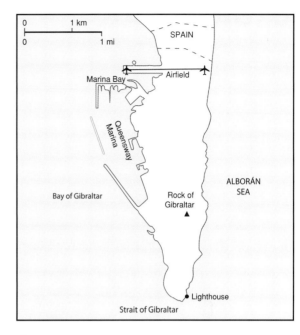

✦ CHARTER

Several companies offer tuition on both power and sail yachts, and some also provide crewed or bareboat charters.

www.atlanticcharters.co.uk
www.straits-sail.com
www.sailing-gibraltar.co.uk

Cruising Guides
Straits Sailing Handbook
Cruising Almanac
North Africa

Websites
www.gibraltar.gov.gi
www.gibraltarport.com
www.yachtscene.gi

Local time	UTC +1
	Summer time: last Sunday in March to last Sunday in October
Buoyage	IALA A
Currency	Gibraltar Pound (GIP)
Electricity	230V, 50Hz

Diplomatic missions
UK   20045440

Communications
IDD 350 IAC 00

Emergency number
999

GREECE

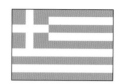

IF SOMEONE WERE TO GRADE the top ten cruising destinations in the world according to such criteria as scenic beauty, weather conditions and variety of ports and anchorages, Greece would definitely be among them. If you also took into account the wealth of things to be seen ashore, as well as that most important ingredient – a pleasant waterfront restaurant or café to while away the balmy evening after a hard day's sail – Greece would probably be close to the top of the list.

The Aegean in particular seems to have been tailor-made for cruising and, after a relatively slow start, in the last 30 years yachting in Greece has taken off at great speed and facilities are constantly improving. Although the more popular places are quite crowded, especially during the high season, the situation is not as bad as it may appear from a distance. There are still plenty of less frequented places dotted around the Aegean and some of the more remote islands rarely see more than a handful of yachts. The crowds are also seasonal and it certainly pays to cruise Greece outside of the peak summer months, ideally around Easter, which is the main holiday in the Greek Orthodox calendar, although it may still be cold on the water around this time. The autumn months are just as attractive; both winds and weather are more pleasant then than in the meltemi-swept months of high summer.

Besides the pleasant weather and picturesque ports, what makes Greece such a special place is the profusion of historical sites, most of which are within a short distance of the sea. The Greeks have always had an affinity with the sea and nothing they ever built was far from it. Among the sites that should not be missed are those on the mainland, the Acropolis of Athens and the temple at Delphi. On the northern shore of the Peloponnese is ancient Corinth, while not far inland is the magnificent amphitheatre at Epidavros, the remains of Olympia and the impressive fortifications of Mycenae that go back over three thousand years. The islands also abound in sites, and it is a great thrill to anchor close to such immortal places as Delos, the birthplace of Apollo and Artemis, visit the palace and labyrinth of the legendary King Minos at Knossos on Crete, the mysterious lion hidden on a hillside on Kea, or climb to the temple of Poseidon on Cape Sounion. Closer to modern times are some magnificent churches and monasteries such as those on Patmos, Symi or Chios. St John dwelt in a cave on Patmos where he wrote the Book of Revelations. The monks at the nearby medieval monastery enact the washing of the feet ceremony every Easter, a unique and unforgettable performance that should not be missed.

Delos, once a sacred city and the focus of the Hellenic Confederacy, is encircled by the Cyclades, 19 mostly small

Easter ceremony on the island of Patmos.

in Europe and Asia, stretching as far as Persia. Greece's time of greatness came to an end with the rise of Rome and its eventual incorporation into the Byzantine Empire. The Ottoman Empire ruled Greece from the fourteenth century until independence was finally achieved in 1829. Despite a desire to remain neutral in the Second World War, Greece was invaded by Italy and Germany. A period of instability followed the war, the King was deposed, and a republic proclaimed in 1973. Greece became a member of the EU in 1981.

The population of Greece is 10.7 million, one-third of whom live in the capital, Athens.

◆ CLIMATE

Spring and autumn weather is the most pleasant, while summers in the Aegean are hot, windy and dry. Weather conditions in the Ionian are generally more benign. Winters are mild in Crete and Rhodes, and cooler as you move north. The prevailing northerly wind of summer, called *etesian* in Greek because of its seasonal character, but better known by its Turkish name *meltemi*, sets in about May or June and lasts until early September. It blows at its strongest in July and August when it can reach force 7 and even 8. Violent storms occur only in winter, February being a particularly bad month, but overall the weather is pleasant and extreme conditions are rare.

In the Central Aegean, the warmest months are July and August, with average temperatures of 25°C/77°F and day temperatures often well in excess of 30°C/90°F. January is the coolest month, with an average temperature of 13°C/55°F. The wettest months are December and January, and the driest are July and August.

◆ FORMALITIES

Although a member of the EU, formalities in Greece (even for EU boats) are more complicated than anywhere else in the EU. All boats must purchase a transit log which will be stamped on entering and leaving each commercial port. The document is valid for 50 ports, after which a new one must be purchased. A new tax to be imposed on pleasure craft was announced in 2009 and may also affect foreign vessels spending longer periods in Greece.

Greece is a signatory to the Schengen Agreement and visa regulations apply accordingly. On arrival in Greece all boats, both EU and non-EU, must clear with the port authority, immigration and customs. Non-EU vessels will be issued with a transit log valid for six months, which is extendable for up to a year. All vessels must have an original insurance certificate and a Greek translation showing third party insurance. For EU boats, proof of VAT status may also be required.

The Greek Coast Guard does not monitor Channel 16. Those who need assistance should call them on Channel 12.

islands – each different in character to its neighbour. All have one common feature: the dazzling-white cubes of their houses. The main settlement, called the chora, is usually inland and fortified against the pirates that once roamed these waters. Totally different in every respect are the Dodecanese, the 12 mountainous islands that lie close to the Turkish mainland. Their indented coastline and well-sheltered harbours make them an ideal cruising ground.

While the Central Aegean tends to overshadow the rest of Greece, there are other attractive island groups that are often overlooked, such as the Sporades in the Northern Aegean and the Ionian islands in Western Greece. Among the latter, Corfu and the islands to its south offer one of the best cruising grounds anywhere in Greece. Here, the island of Ithaka was the home of the legendary Odysseus, one of the most adventuresome sailors of all times, and whose daring deeds in the face of all adversity continue to inspire sailors to this day.

◆ COUNTRY PROFILE

The oldest state in Europe existed on the island of Crete from about 3000 until 1450 BCE. Meanwhile, on the mainland, people moved down from the north and settled on the shores of the Aegean, developing other states and kingdoms. The events that Homer wrote about later were probably based on fact. In this legendary time, Greece was divided into many kingdoms, but these came together under Agamemnon, King of Mycenae, to besiege Troy high above the Dardanelles for nine years. In the fifth century BCE the city of Athens grew in power and its hegemony spread over a wide area. Later, Alexander the Great established the greatest empire yet seen

PORTS OF ENTRY

Mainland:					
Alexandroupolis	40°51´N 25°57´E	Vouliagmeni	37°48´N 23°46´E	Glifada	37°52´N 23°44´E
Itea	38°26´N 22°25´E	Kavala	40°55´N 24°25´E	Lavrion	37°42´N 24°04´E
Piraeus (Zea)	37°56´N 23°38´E	Preveza	38°57´N 20°45´E	Volos	39°21´N 22°56´E
Thessaloniki	40°38´N 22°56´E				
Peloponnese:					
Kalamata	37°00´N 22°07´E	Katakolon	37°39´N 21°20´E	Nafplion	37°40´N 22°48´E
Patras	38°15´N 21°44´E	Pilos	36°55´N 21°42´E		
Ionian Islands:					
Argostoli (Kefalonia)	38°12´N 20°29´E	Corfu Port	39°37´N 19°57´E	Zakinthos	37°47´N 20°54´E
Aegean Islands:					
Chios	38°23´N 26°09´E	Kos	36°53´N 27°19´E	Lesvos (Mitilini)	39°06´N 26°05´E
Limnos (Mirina)	39°52´N 25°04´E	Rhodos (Mandraki)	36°27´N 28°14´E	Samos (Pithagorion)	37°45´N 27°00´E
Siros	37°26´N 24°57´E				
Crete:					
Iraklion	35°16´N 25°09´E	Hania	35°31´N 24°01´E	Agios Nikolaos	35°11´N 25°43´E

✦ CANALS

The Corinth Canal

Linking the Aegean with the Ionian and Adriatic Seas is the Corinth Canal, a historic shortcut that continues to be as useful now as in days gone by. The current canal was opened to traffic in 1893, although an earlier attempt to build a canal was undertaken under the Roman emperor Nero in the first century.

The canal connects the Gulf of Corinth with the Aegean by cutting through the narrow Isthmus of Corinth which separates the Greek mainland from the Peloponnese. The canal is of a greater advantage to boats coming from the west as it provides a shortcut that saves about 200 miles circumnavigating the Peloponnese. It also avoids a hard beat into the strong northerly winds of summer for those planning to head for the Cyclades or the islands of the Dodecanese. For boats leaving the Aegean for points west, the main advantage is a more direct route, especially if heading for the Adriatic Sea. At all other times the longer but less frequented route around the Peloponnese holds a great attraction as it gives the opportunity to call at several historic ports from the days when this area was administered by Venice; two well-preserved ports from that era, Koroni and Methoni, bear the epithet 'eyes of the Venetian Republic' due to their strategic importance.

Euripos Canal

This 8km (5nm) long canal, in reality just a narrow channel, runs between Euboea (Evia) Island and the mainland. It is traversed by the Halkis Bridge which only opens at slack tide or when vessels can pass with a following tide, as there is a very strong current at other times. The captain should visit the port police office on the east (Evia) side of the bridge to make arrangements for the transit and pay the fee. The narrow channel is used by those heading for the northern Aegean and wishing to avoid the strong wind and contrary current that can occur in the Kafireas Strait between Andros and Euboea Islands.

The Corinth Canal.

Lefkas Canal

The Lefkas Canal, separating the island of Lefkas from the mainland, has existed since ancient times. It is used as a shortcut to the Ionian Islands. It has been dredged to a minimum depth of 4.5m (15ft). The canal opens on the hour from 0800 to 2200.

◆ FACILITIES

The expansion in yachting has been accompanied by a parallel development in facilities. Although some of those who know Greece from earlier years may not regard this expansion as a blessing, their alarm is unfounded, as none of the picturesque ports have been ruined by construction inside the centuries-old harbours. Most new marinas have been built inside newly built breakwaters or reclaimed land, and in most islands yachts still either come stern-to the existing quay or stay at anchor. The greatest concentration of facilities is in the Athens–Piraeus area, where there are several boatyards with haulout facilities and a full range of repair services. Most marinas are on the mainland, and this is also where the best repair facilities are, but the islands are rapidly catching up, with good amenities in Rhodes, Crete, Corfu, Kea, Leros and Skiathos – and any other islands that are charter bases. Diesel fuel is widely available in marinas and most ports. Marine stores are available in all places visited by large numbers of yachts, and whatever is not available locally can be ordered from the importer and delivered within 24 hours. Provisioning is generally good and locally grown produce is available everywhere. The cost of labour and services has increased considerably and an estimate should always be requested before commissioning any work.

◆ CHARTER

Other countries may equal Greece's appeal as a cruising destination, but its attraction as a sailing holiday choice continues unabated. There are now bareboat bases all over the islands as well as on the mainland, with potential customers spoilt for choice. Main bases on the mainland: Lavrion; in the Ionian: Corfu, Lefkas; in the Aegean: Kos, Skiathos, Skyros, Rhodes, Paros, Poros.

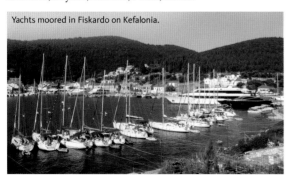
Yachts moored in Fiskardo on Kefalonia.

Old Venetian lighthouse overlooking the Ithaka Channel.

While the Ionian has the more benign sailing conditions, the strong northerly winds of the Aegean summer should be taken into account when choosing a route so as not to end up too far downwind when you need to return to base at the end of the charter.

www.kiriacoulis.com
www.sunsail.com
www.cosmosyachting.com
www.moorings.com
www.olympicyachtcharters.com

Cruising Guides
East Aegean
Greek Waters Pilot
Ionian
Ionian Cruising Companion
Mediterranean Almanac
Mediterranean Cruising
Mediterranean Islands
West Aegean
West Aegean Cruising Companion

Websites
www.greece-yachting.com   www.visitgreece.gr

Local time	UTC +2
	Summer time: last Sunday in March to last Sunday in October
Buoyage	IALA A
Currency	Euro (EUR)
Electricity	230V, 50Hz

Diplomatic missions

UK	210 7272600	Canada	210 7273400
USA	210 7212951	South Africa	210 6106645
Australia	210 8704000	New Zealand	210 6924136

Communications		Emergency numbers	
IDD 30	IAC 00	112/121	Tourist police 171

ISRAEL

ISRAEL HAS COASTLINES on both the Eastern Mediterranean and the Gulf of Aqaba in the Red Sea. A symbol for three of the world's major religions, this corner of the Middle East has been hotly disputed for centuries and the rest of the world is still waiting for the time when lasting peace will finally descend on this troubled corner of the Mediterranean. The coast is low with no natural harbours or anchorages, and visiting yachts have the choice of only a few marinas and ports. The unexciting coastline, stringent security controls and recurring internal problems have kept most cruising craft away from this interesting country, although yachting facilities have been steadily improving to cater for an expanding resident boating community. The few foreign yachts that are not daunted by the difficulties associated with a visit to Israel are rewarded with the opportunity to visit some of the biblical sites, and perhaps also to understand why peace between the Jewish and Palestinian communities continues to be so elusive. For those sailing in the Red Sea, a detour into the Gulf of Aqaba provides the opportunity to call at Eilat, a busy holiday resort with a good marina.

✦ COUNTRY PROFILE

Inhabited from earliest times, the region known in antiquity as the Land of Canaan has seen many peoples move back and forth across it throughout its history. As Palestine it was part of the Roman and Byzantine Empires, then Arab rule was followed by the Ottomans. After the First World War, Britain administered the area under a League of Nations mandate.

Following increasing attacks by Zionist guerillas, Britain withdrew its forces and the state of Israel was unilaterally declared in 1948. Many Palestinians fled to neighbouring countries and since then there has been extensive immigration by Jews from Eastern Europe, North Africa and the Middle East. After defeat in the war of 1967 of Egypt, Syria and Jordan, Israel occupied additional territory and, although it withdrew its forces from Sinai in 1982, Southern Lebanon in 2000, and from Gaza in 2005, it still occupies parts of the West Bank and continues to isolate Gaza. Most of the international community is in favour of a two-state solution that would ensure the safety of Israel and give the Palestinians the statehood and stability they have been denied for over six decades.

The population of Israel is 7.4 million, about 75 per cent of which are Jews of mixed cultures and origins. The rest are mainly Palestinian. Hebrew is the national language and Arabic is spoken by the Palestinians. The Israeli authorities insist that Jerusalem is their capital, but this is not recognized by the United Nations, as a result of which diplomatic missions are located in Tel Aviv.

✦ CLIMATE

The Mediterranean coast has a pleasant climate with warm dry summers and mild winters. The hot summer days are tempered by the alternating land and sea breezes. July and August are the warmest months, with average temperatures of 24°C/75°F, and January the coolest, 6°C/43°F. Winters are cool and rainy, with December being the wettest month.

The port of Eilat in the Gulf of Aqaba.

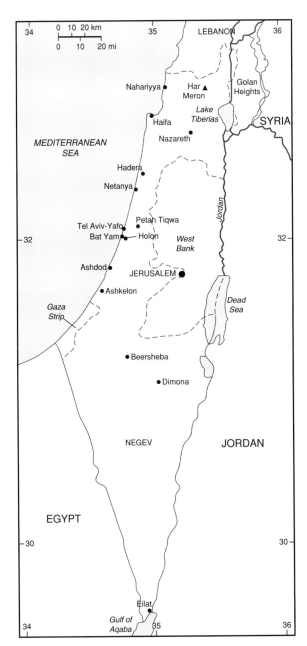

Haifa	32°49′N 35°00′E
Ashdod	31°49′N 34°38′E
Tel Aviv Marina	32°05′N 34°46′E
Ashkelon	31°41′N 34°33′E
Herzliya	32°10′N 34°48′E
Eilat	29°33′N 34°57′E

Nationals of the EU, Australia, Canada, New Zealand, South Africa and the USA do not require visas, or will have them issued on arrival, usually for 90 days. To avoid future complications, you should request that the passport is not stamped.

There is a gas platform off the coast of Israel which must be avoided as it has an 8-mile security zone around it.

✦ FACILITIES

Israel's yachting facilities are of a good standard and there are several marinas along the Mediterranean coast as well as one at Eilat. Some of the best repair and haulout facilities are at Ashkelon Marina. Provisioning is good, especially with fresh produce.

Cruising Guides
Mediterranean Cruising
Red Sea Pilot

Website
www.goisrael.com

Local time	UTC +2
	Summer time: end of March to early October
Buoyage	IALA A
Currency	Israeli Shekel (ILS)
Electricity	230V, 50Hz

Diplomatic missions
UK	3 7251222
USA	3 5197575
Australia	3 6935000
Canada	3 6363300
South Africa	3 5252566
New Zealand	3 6956622

Communications
IDD 972	IAC 00

Emergency numbers
112	Ambulance 101	Police 100

The climate at Eilat on the Gulf of Aqaba is warmer and drier, with an average temperature of 26°C/79°F in July and August, and 10°C/50°F in January.

✦ FORMALITIES

Vessels should report to the Israeli Navy on Channel 16 with their position and yacht details when 40nm from the coast. Detailed instructions will be given and yachts may be approached by a patrol boat, and possibly boarded. A daylight arrival is recommended.

ITALY

WHEN MARK TWAIN PROPOSED THAT 'The Creator made Italy from designs by Michelangelo' he may not have meant the scenery. Yet many sailors are surprised to find that for unspoilt and attractive anchorages, they do not need to go to Croatia, Greece or Turkey as these can also be found in Italy – and especially in her offshore islands. Italy's 5,000 mile long coastline is bathed by the Tyrrhenian, Adriatic, Ligurian and Ionian Seas and is of a great variety, being mountainous in some areas and low lying in others. The smaller islands off Italy's west coast form relatively compact groups: the Aegadean, Lipari (or Aeolian) and the Pontine Islands, while the better-known Capri and Ischia nestle in the Gulf of Naples close to Vesuvius and its victim Pompeii. A favourite destination among local sailors is the beautiful island of Elba and its small archipelago, chosen by Napoleon as his place of exile when he still had a say in such matters.

The larger islands of Sardinia and Sicily are distinctive entities with their own traditions, attitudes and even languages. Although Sardinia embarked on a massive marina building programme that has resulted in the island now being encircled by a chain of marinas, there are a few areas where it is still possible to anchor in natural surroundings. One such area is the northern shore facing the Straits of Bonifacio. In contrast, many of Sicily's attractions lie inland, where you can find some of the best-preserved Greek temples, Roman mosaics and Romanesque cathedrals. Close to the Straits of

Dawn on the Grand Canal in Venice.

Messina you can anchor in the shadow of Stromboli, within sight of Mount Etna, or dock on the elegant waterfront at Syracuse. Every island, large or small, is different, and thousands of years of history have left their indelible mark everywhere.

The east coast of Italy has been less endowed by nature, and even local sailors often prefer to cruise in neighbouring Croatia. There is one notable exception: Venice Lagoon. The long detour is well justified as no sailor can fail to be overcome by the excitement of sailing through the heart of one of the most beautiful cities in the world. At the height of its power during the Middle Ages, the Serene Republic spread its trading tentacles far and wide, and a visit to the Naval History Museum is a perfect opportunity to learn more about the sailing craft that made all this possible.

Once the undisputed domain of powerboating, many Italians have now discovered the beauty of sailing, and to cope with an insatiable demand many marinas have been built that provide facilities of the highest standard. Everywhere in Italy there is a lot to see ashore, and the proximity of ports or marinas to all tourist attractions makes it easy to visit the major points of interest without leaving the boat for more than a few hours.

✦ COUNTRY PROFILE

The Italian peninsula's earliest inhabitants were Ligurian and Illyrian peoples, and later Etruscans, Greeks and Gauls settled there. From the middle of the fourth century BCE, Rome dominated the peninsula, and expanded to form an empire that at its height stretched all around the Mediterranean to the Black Sea and north as far as England. This empire declined after the second century CE and Rome itself fell under waves of barbarian invasions from the fifth century onwards. A confused period followed and, by the fifteenth century, five main states had emerged: the duchy of Milan, the republics of Florence and Venice, the Papal States, and the Kingdom of Naples. Rivalry between the small Italian states was intensified by the interference of France, Spain and Austria. Italian nationalism and the idea of unification grew until in 1861 the kingdom of Italy was proclaimed. The First World War was followed by the fascist government of Benito Mussolini, and Italy entered the Second World War on the side of Germany. Mussolini was overthrown in 1943 and an armistice was signed with the Allies. After the war, a republic replaced the monarchy and for many years the

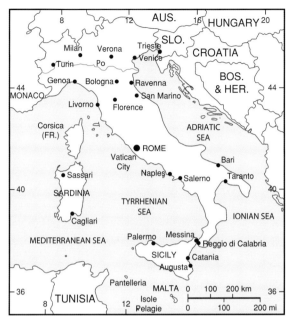

✦ CLIMATE

Generally the coastal areas have a Mediterranean climate, but with distinct regional variations. The climate varies not only from north to south, but also between the various islands. The north can have cold winters, while the south can be extremely hot in summer. The warmest months are July and August, with average temperatures of 25°C/77°F, and day temperatures often in excess of 30°C/90°F. January is the coldest month, with an average temperature of 8°C/46°F in the Rome area and a much milder 12°C/54°F in Sicily. The prevailing winds of summer are northwest, although in many areas there is a daily pattern that alternates between land and sea breezes. The strongest winds are the northerly bora, which occurs mostly in winter and affects the Adriatic, and the mistral (*maestrale*), a northwesterly wind that can occur at any time of year and affects Western Italy and Sardinia.

✦ FORMALITIES

As Italy is a member of the EU, vessels arriving from another EU country, with only EU nationals on board, are not required to complete any formalities. Both EU and non-EU boats arriving from a country outside the EU must contact customs at the first Italian port. On arrival in a port of entry, boats from non-EU countries must clear with the port captain, customs and immigration. The Schengen Agreement applies to visa requirements and non-EU vessels that have called first at other Schengen countries must be able to prove this.

political scene was beset by instability and frequent changes of government. As a founder member of the EU, Italy is now a stable democracy.

The population is 60 million and the language is Italian, which nowadays is spoken by everyone as the regional dialects are slowly being abandoned. The capital is Rome, where the Roman Catholic Church has its own headquarters in the Vatican City, an autonomous state.

PORTS OF ENTRY

As there is such a large number of ports and marinas both on the mainland and in the offlying islands, only those where foreign yachts normally clear in have been listed.

Mainland:

Ancona	43°36´N 13°31´E	Anzio	41°27´N 12°38´E	Bari	41°07.6´N 16°53´E
Brindisi	40°39´N 17°59´E	Chioggia	45°13´N 12°17´E	Civitavecchia	42°04´N 11°48.6´E
Fiumicino	41°46´N 12°14´E	Genoa	44°25´N 8°55´E	Imperia	43°53´N 8°02´E
La Spezia	44°07´N 9°50´E	Naples	40°51´N 14°16´E	Ravenna	44°25´N 12°27´E
Reggio di Calabria	38°07´N 15°39´E	Salerno	40°41´N 14°46´E	San Remo	43°49´N 7°47´E
Taranto	40°27´N 17°12´E	Trieste	45°39´N 13°48´E	Venice	45°26´N 12°20´E

Sardinia:

Alghero	40°34´N 8°19´E	Arbatax	39°56´N 9°42´E	Cagliari	39°12´N 9°05´E
Carloforte	39°09´N 8°19´E	Olbia	40°55´N 9°34´E	Porto Cervo	41°08´N 9°34´E

Elba:

Porto Azzuro	42°46´N 10°24´E	

Sicily:

Catania	37°31´N 15°06´E	Gela	37°04´N 14°15´E	Marsala	37°48´N 12°26´E
Messina	38°12´N 15°34´E	Palermo	38°07´N 13°22´E	Porto Empedocle	37°17´N 13°32´E
Siracusa	37°03´N 15°18´E	Trapani	38°02´N 12°31´E		

All boats must have a valid third party insurance certificate on board. The captain may be asked to show a certificate of competence which is also needed for water scooters and water skiing.

The controversial tax imposed on visiting yachts in Sardinia in 2006 was repealed in 2008 as it had led to a drastic reduction in the number of yachts stopping at the island.

✦ FACILITIES

With a large resident boating population and a considerable boatbuilding industry of its own, yachting facilities in Italy are of a high standard. The best repair facilities are in the northwest of the country where many marinas are concentrated. There are boatyards all around Italy's coasts, and for any repair or haulout one is never too far away from help. Repair facilities in Sicily and Sardinia are best in the main centres, such as Palermo, Cagliari and Porto Cervo, and only adequate in most other places.

Provisioning is good everywhere and most towns have a fresh produce market with a wide selection of fruit and vegetables. Italy is a popular wintering place among American sailors who seem to prefer the marinas in the vicinity of Rome. Weather forecasts are broadcast on Channel 68 in Italian and English 24 hours a day.

Roman remains at Tharros in Sardinia's Bay of Oristano.

✦ CHARTER

All major companies have bases in Italy and there are also several smaller local firms. Virtually all operations are located in the Tyrrhenian Sea. Italy Yacht Charters has over a dozen bases throughout Italy, both mainland and islands, as do Cosmos Yachting and Kiriacoulis. Sunsail has two bases, both in the south, at Palermo and Tropea, while Moorings has bases there as well as at Cannigione and Procida. Based in Trapani, in Sicily, are Sail Adventures, which offers both bareboat and crewed charters.

www.cosmosyachting.com
www.kiriacoulis.com
www.italyyachtcharters.com
www.sunsail.com
www.moorings.com
www.sailadventures.com

Cruising Guides
Adriatic Pilot
Corsica and North Sardinia
Dove Navigare Bolina (details of ports and marinas in Italian)
Italian Waters Pilot
Mediterranean Almanac
Mediterranean Cruising
Mediterranean Islands

Website
www.enit.it (Italian Tourist Board)

Local time	UTC +1
	Summer time: last Sunday in March to last Sunday in October
Buoyage	IALA A
Currency	Euro (EUR)
Electricity	230V, 50Hz

Diplomatic missions

UK	06 42200001
USA	06 46741
Australia	06 852721
Canada	06 854441
South Africa	06 852541
New Zealand	06 8537501

Communications
IDD 39   IAC 00
Note: When calling from abroad, the 'o' should not be dropped after '39'.

Emergency numbers
112   Ambulance 118   Police 113
Coast Guard (Guardia Costiera) 1530

LEBANON

'THITHER CAME PHOENICIANS, men famed for their ships...bringing countless trinkets in their black ships,' wrote Homer in his immortal *Odyssey*. Indeed, the greatest sailors of antiquity hailed from these shores and their swift ships reached the furthest corners of the Mediterranean. This small country has suffered a long and turbulent history, but by the 1970s it had become a popular tourist destination in the eastern Mediterranean. Lebanon was also popular with cruising sailors and there used to be a regular movement of yachts between Cyprus and Lebanon. A prolonged civil war put an end to all that, but with the return of peace, cruising boats are rediscovering Lebanon's attractions. To visit the many sites in the interior such as Baalbek, Byblos or some of the well-preserved Crusader castles, the boat can be left in safety at the marina at Jounieh. This is also a convenient base from which to visit Damascus and the southern part of Syria, which are closer and easier to reach from here than from one of the Syrian ports.

✦ COUNTRY PROFILE

The modern state of Lebanon emerged out of the Ottoman Empire at the end of the First World War. It was ruled under a French mandate, but this was resisted by both Christian and Muslim communities and the country finally gained full independence in 1943. An important commercial centre, Lebanon had a stable government for many years, but the Muslims, who make up 60 per cent of the population, felt excluded as it was the Christians who held the power. Adding to the tension was the arrival of many Palestinian refugees displaced from Israel. In the mid-1970s civil war broke out, exacerbated by the intervention of Syrian and Israeli forces. An uneasy peace has returned after withdrawal of Israeli forces following their invasion of Southern Lebanon in 2006, but the fate of Lebanon continues to depend on forces that are mostly beyond its control.

Aerial view of Beirut.

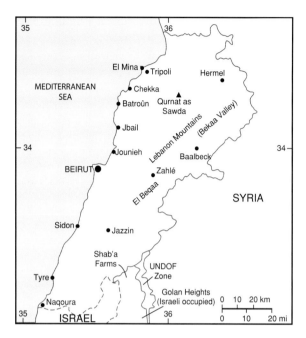

The Arabic-speaking population is about 4 million. English and French are widely spoken. There are both Muslim and Christian communities and the population is divided along religious lines. The capital is Beirut.

✦ CLIMATE

The pleasant climate is Lebanon's main attraction as the weather is mostly sunny. The summers are hot and dry, while the winters are cool and occasionally rainy. Summers can be very humid at night, although days are made more pleasant by the afternoon sea breeze. Winters are mild with rainy spells. December and January are the wettest months. In early and late summer the weather can be affected by spells of the hot, dry khamsin that sweeps in from Arabia and can last several days. July and August are the warmest months, with average temperatures of 23°C/73°F, and January is the coolest, 5°C/41°F.

✦ FORMALITIES

PORTS OF ENTRY

Beirut	33°54´N 35°31´E
Jounieh	33°59´N 35°39´E
Tripoli	34°28´N 35°50´E

The Lebanese Navy (call sign Oscar Charlie) should be contacted on entering territorial waters at 12 miles offshore and again on reaching a point 6 miles distant from the intended port of arrival. Jounieh Marina is reported to be an easy place to clear in as immigration and customs will come to the boat, but marinas in the Beirut area may also help with formalities. All crew should remain on board until cleared.

Visitors from the EU, Australia, Canada, New Zealand and the USA can obtain visas on arrival. Shore passes will be issued. Boats that have stopped in Israel before, or intend to sail there, may be refused entry.

✦ FACILITIES

There is an active local boating community served by several marinas. Yachting facilities are of a good standard and there is a wide range of repair services. Jounieh Marina is run by the Lebanese Automobile Club and its facilities are available to visiting yachts.

✦ CHARTER

Sailing Plus has a fleet of mostly sailing yachts and is based at Marina Joseph Khouri, north of Beirut, but it is also active in some of the other marinas.

www.sailingplus.net

Cruising Guides
Mediterranean Almanac
Mediterranean Cruising

Websites
www.destinationlebanon.com (Ministry of Tourism)
www.atcl.org.lb/english/yacht_index.asp (Jounieh Marina)

Local time	UTC +2
	Summer time: last Sunday in March to last Sunday in October
Buoyage	IALA A
Currency	Lebanese Pound (LBP)
Electricity	230V, 50Hz

Diplomatic missions

UK	1 990400
USA	4 542600
Australia	1 974030
Canada	1 713900

Communications

IDD 972	IAC 00

Emergency number
112

LIBYA

LIBYA HAS A LONG STRETCH OF COASTLINE on the southern shore of the Mediterranean between Egypt and Tunisia. After many years of isolation, Libya is slowly opening up to foreign tourists who must observe certain rules and restrictions. A few cruising yachts have visited the country recently and although the formalities are complex, they can be overcome with the help of a local agent. As there are no natural harbours and coastal cruising is in any case prohibited, the only solution is to be based at one of the main ports and from there visit the various inland attractions. These include some major Roman remains, among which Leptis Magna is reputed to be the best-preserved site from this period. There are other sites and mosaics from the same times, when three Roman provinces flourished in this area. More prosaic, but no less exciting, is the opportunity to join a tour deep into the Sahara.

✦ COUNTRY PROFILE

The Phoenicians were the first to establish trading posts on this coast. After the fall of Rome, Libya was conquered in 655 and incorporated in the Ummayad Caliphate. In the sixteenth century it became part of the Ottoman Empire. In modern times it was an Italian colony and after the Second World War it finally declared its independence as a kingdom under the rule of King Idris. He was overthrown in 1969 by a small group of military officers led by Muammar al-Gaddafi. The revolution established a regime based on Arab socialism under the absolute rule of Colonel Gaddafi. Massive oil resources have brought the country great wealth. The official name of Libya is the Socialist People's Libyan Arab Jamahariya, meaning the state of the masses. The population is 6.3 million, made up almost entirely of Berbers and Arabs, with only a few small minorities.

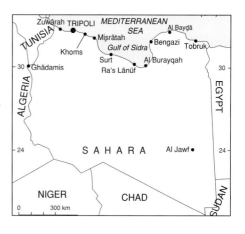

✦ CLIMATE

The summers are very hot with extremely high temperatures. Winters are mild with little rain. The warmest months are July and August, with average temperatures of 26°C/79°F and day temperatures that often exceed 40°C/100°F. January is the coolest month, with an average temperature of 12°C/54°F. The coastal area is affected from March to June by hot, dusty sirocco winds from the desert, which bring very high temperatures – often exceeding 50°C/122°F. They are known locally as *ghibli*.

✦ FORMALITIES

PORTS OF ENTRY

Tripoli	32°54′ N 13°11′ E	Tobruk	32°04′ N 24°00′ E
Khoms	32°39′ N 14°16′ E	Bengazi	32°07′ N 20°03′ E

Yachts should not arrive unannounced, but in an emergency you should try to contact the authorities on Channel 16 as soon as you enter Libyan territorial waters.

Arrangements to visit Libya by yacht must be made in advance with the assistance of a local agent, who will advise on all formalities including visa requirements. Those travelling to Libya must have their passports translated into Arabic and legalized by the local Libyan Embassy. Each person, including children, must have a minimum of US$1,000 in cash and may be required to show this on entry. It does not have to be changed into Libyan currency.

✦ FACILITIES

These are limited and yachts will be docked in commercial harbours. Provisions and fuel are available in all ports.

Local time	UTC +2		
Buoyage	IALA A		
Currency	Libyan Dinar (LYD)		
Electricity	230V, 50Hz		

Diplomatic missions			
UK	21 3403644	Canada	21 3351633
USA	21 3794560	South Africa	21 3337006
Australia	21 3351468		

Communications		Emergency number
IDD 218	IAC 00	193

MALTA

THIS SMALL ARCHIPELAGO in the middle of the Mediterranean consists of three islands, the largest, Malta, being the economic and administrative centre and most heavily populated. Gozo is smaller and picturesque, while Comino is a small islet between the two. All three islands are dry, mostly treeless, with rocky coasts and steep cliffs. Maltese culture is a mixture of European and Arab with strong British influences, due to Malta's long association with Britain. The Knights of St John were based here for 200 years and their distinctive cross became Malta's emblem.

Malta was an important yachting centre before the Balearics, Greece and Croatia became such popular cruising destinations. Its convenient location, excellent harbours and good range of repair facilities continue to attract yachts to its shores, with the mild and pleasant winters making Malta a good wintering spot. Its strategic position in the centre of the Mediterranean also makes it an ideal jumping-off point for other cruising destinations, and for this reason many yachts make their base on the island. Fortunately, there is more to Malta than just its docking, repair and maintenance facilities, as besides the impressive Grand Harbour or Gozo's 5,500-year-old temple of Ggantija, there are several attractive anchorages around the islands.

✦ COUNTRY PROFILE

Malta was inhabited from early times, first by the Phoenicians and Greeks, then it was ruled over by Carthage until the third century BCE, when it became part of the Roman Empire. St Paul and St Luke were shipwrecked there when on their way to Rome in the year 58. After the decline of the Roman Empire, Malta was ruled by Byzantium, the Arabs, and then the Normans. The population remained Muslim until the mid-thirteenth century, when non-Christians were expelled and the Arab presence eliminated.

In the sixteenth century Malta became the home of the Knights of the Order of St John of Jerusalem. The Knights resisted all attempts by the Turks to conquer the island, notably in the Great Siege of 1562. The Knights ruled Malta until 1814 when it was annexed by Britain. Malta was badly bombed during the Second World War when the islands were used as a British naval base. Full independence came in 1964, and in 2004 Malta joined the EU.

The Maltese population is 360,000. The main language is Maltese, which is a Semitic language in origin. English is widely spoken, as is Italian. The capital is Valletta.

Yachts sailing past Valletta.

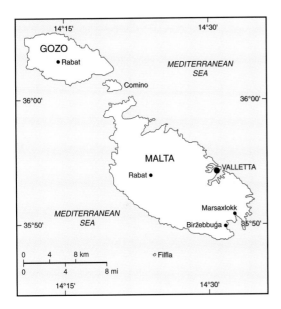

CLIMATE

The climate is similar to North Africa, with hot, dry summers and mild winters. The warmest months are July and August, with average temperatures of 26°C/79°F and day temperatures often well above 30°C/90°F. January is the coldest month, with an average temperature of 7°C/43°F. Prevailing winds throughout the year are northwesterlies. When the hot sirocco wind blows from the south, it comes laden with dust and sand and the weather is sultry and oppressive.

FORMALITIES

PORTS OF ENTRY

Marsamxett Harbour (Msida Marina)	35°53.8´N 14°30.3´E
Grand Harbour	35°53.6´N 14°30.6´E
Gozo (Mgarr Marina)	36°01.5´N 14°18´E

Valletta Port Control must be contacted on Channels 12 or 16 before entering the harbour. During office hours, yachts are normally directed to the reception dock in Msida Marina. Outside office hours, clearance is done in the commercial port, Grand Harbour. It is not advisable to enter Marsamxett Harbour at night.

Msida: The guest berth is located on the Breakwater Quay at the opening into Msida Creek. All formalities are completed here.
Grand Harbour: The Customs House is on Lascaris Wharf. It is possible to come alongside or in the new marina.

Gozo: Yachts are advised to tie up at a vacant slip in Mgarr Marina and visit the offices on the quay.

Malta is a signatory to the Schengen Agreement whose visa regulations apply.

A diving permit from the Department of Health must be obtained if planning to scuba dive in Maltese waters.

✦ FACILITIES

Malta has one of the best natural harbours in the Mediterranean and the decline of its traditional role as a naval base and shipping centre has led to the development of its yachting facilities, which are among the best in the region. The main marine facilities are in the creeks leading off Marsamxett Harbour. Most repair facilities and shipyards are situated on Manoel Island. There is a good selection of marine supplies, with all major manufacturers of marine equipment being represented locally.

✦ CHARTER

There are several local companies offering bareboat charters. Malta Yacht Charters has a fleet of sailing yachts, which can be chartered both as bareboat or crewed. As an associate of Malta Sailing Academy, it also offers sailing tuition. Malta Boat Charter has a mixture of power and sailing yachts.

www.maltayachtcharters.com
www.maltaboatcharter.com
www.maltacharters.com

Cruising Guides
North Africa
Mediterranean Cruising
Italian Waters Pilot (includes section on Malta)
Mediterranean Islands

Websites
www.visitmalta.com
www.mma.gov.mt (Malta Maritime Authority)

Local time	UTC +1
	Summer time: last Sunday in March to last Sunday in October
Buoyage	IALA A
Currency	Euro (EUR)
Electricity	230V, 50Hz

Diplomatic missions

UK	2323 0000	Australia	2133 8201
USA	2561 4000	New Zealand	214 35025

Communications		**Emergency number**
IDD 356	IAC 00	112

MONACO

MONACO is a small independent principality lying on the French Riviera, and is best known for Formula 1 Grand Prix racing and the Monte Carlo casino. But its lasting popularity is due to its status as a tax-free enclave favoured by sporting celebrities and the super-rich, whose yachts usually adorn Monaco's port overlooked by the royal palace.

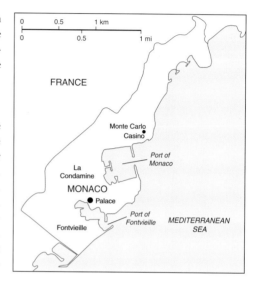

✦ COUNTRY PROFILE

The Grimaldi family have ruled Monaco since the thirteenth century, the principality's independence being recognized by France in 1512. Unlike other small countries in Europe, Monaco was not absorbed by a larger state, although it always remained within the French sphere of influence. A customs union was created between Monaco and France in 1865. Prince Rainier III ruled Monaco for over fifty years until his death in 2005. He was responsible for reforms to Monaco's constitution and for expanding the principality's economy beyond its traditional gambling base. Monaco is a prosperous tourist and business centre, with low taxes and no income tax. Of the 33,000 inhabitants, only around 20 per cent are Monégasques. French is the official language, but English is widely spoken.

✦ CLIMATE

Monaco enjoys a Mediterranean climate with hot dry summers and mild sunny winters. The warmest months are July and August, with average temperatures of 24°C/75°F, while January is the coolest month, with an average temperature of 10°C/50°F.

✦ FORMALITIES

PORTS OF ENTRY

Port de Monaco (Port de la Condamine)	43°44′N 7°26′E
Fontvieille	43°43.7′N 7°25.4′E

Fontvieille: The marina should be contacted on Channel 9. Visiting yachts are directed to the reception dock and should clear formalities at the nearby port captain's office (Capitainerie). Immigration regulations are similar to France. No formalities are needed by EU nationals nor for those of non-EU countries who have already cleared into France. Schengen regulations apply. Nationals of South Africa require a Schengen visa to enter Monaco.

✦ FACILITIES

The main port is always crowded, and finding a space is so difficult that arriving boats are strongly advised to go directly to Fontvieille, less than half a mile southwest. Fontvieille is a fully equipped marina with good services and repair facilities.

A full range of services is available in and around the main port, where several workshops are located on its south side. The fuel dock is in the main port. The latter is geared more to dealing with superyachts, so cruising boats will find Fontvieille more appropriate.

✦ CHARTER

There are several operators offering for charter anything that floats – up to the largest superyachts. The busiest time is during the Grand Prix when yachts docked in the main harbour have a grandstand view of the cars speeding past.

Cruising Guide	
Mediterranean France and Corsica Pilot	
Websites	
www.visitmonaco.com	www.ports-monaco.com
Local time	UTC +1
	Summer time: last Sunday in March to last Sunday in October
Buoyage	IALA A
Currency	Euro (EUR)
Electricity	230V, 50Hz
Diplomatic missions	
UK	93509954
Communications	**Emergency number**
IDD 377 IAC 00	112

MONTENEGRO

THE LATEST OF THE REPUBLICS of former Yugoslavia to take its destiny in its own hands, Montenegro is also the smallest. Endowed with a beautiful coastline and scenic interior, Montenegro's economy depends heavily on tourism, and as sailing plays a major part in it, visiting boats are warmly welcomed.

The coastline is backed by the serrated ridges of the high Black Mountains which gave their name to the country. One of its most attractive ports is Budva, a delightful small town with a medieval citadel at its core enclosed by massive walls. Another attractive place is the medieval town of Kotor, lying in the innermost part of the scenic Bay of Kotor. This spectacular area of enclosed water is dwarfed by high mountains and is surrounded by picturesque ports, one of the most interesting being Perast, whose waterfront is lined with substantial stone houses built by prosperous sea captains in the seventeenth century. Early maritime history is present everywhere in this part of the world, where some of Europe's best navigators hailed from. Local seafarers ranged far and wide over the Mediterranean and were taught in the nautical school that was founded in Perast in the sixteenth century.

✦ COUNTRY PROFILE

At the end of the First World War, out of the ruins of the Ottoman and Austro-Hungarian empires, the Kingdom of Serbs, Croats and Slovenes was formed, being renamed Yugoslavia in 1929. In 1945 a communist government set up a federal republic along communist lines that comprised the six republics of Bosnia-Hercegovina, Croatia, Macedonia, Montenegro, Serbia and Slovenia. However, starting in 1988, dormant inter-ethnic tensions began to worsen as the economic, political and social situation also deteriorated. When Yugoslavia dissolved in 1992, Montenegro federated with Serbia. Following a referendum in 2006, Montenegro declared its independence and separated from Serbia.

The population of Montenegro is 672,000. Apart from Montenegrins, who form the majority, and a large Serb

The Black Mountains tower over the medieval town of Budva.

even if only visiting one port. This vignette must be displayed in a visible position.

No visas are needed for members of the EU, and those from Australia, Canada, New Zealand and the USA do not need a visa for stays up to 90 days. South Africans need a visa in advance.

✦ FACILITIES

There are marinas at Bar, Budva, Kotor, Tivat and Ulcinj with the usual facilities. Repair facilities are adequate, while provisioning is good. Duty-free fuel is available in Bar. A major project is planned for the Bay of Kotor, with a large new marina aimed at superyachts, and extensive developments ashore that threaten to turn one of the most beautiful corners of the Mediterranean into an artificial alien creation of little use or merit.

✦ CHARTER

Several companies offer both crewed and bareboat yachts for charter, some maintaining their bases in neighbouring Croatia.

www.montenegro-yachtcharter.com
www.montenegro-yacht-charter.com
www.montenegro-yacht-charters.eu

Cruising Guides
Adriatic Pilot
Croatia, Slovenia and Montenegro, 777 Harbours and
   Anchorages

Website
www.visit-montenegro.com

Local time	UTC +1
	Summer time: last Sunday in March to last Sunday in October
Buoyage	IALA A
Currency	Euro (EUR)
Electricity	230V, 50Hz

Diplomatic missions	
UK	20 618010
USA	20 225417
Australia	Serbia +381 11 3303400
Canada	Serbia +381 11 3063000

| Communications | |
| IDD 382 | IAC 00 |

| Emergency numbers | |
| 112 | Police 122 |

community, there are also a number of smaller ethnic minorities. The capital is Podgorica.

✦ CLIMATE

The coastal areas enjoy a Mediterranean climate with hot dry summers and mild winters. The warmest months are July and August, with average temperatures of 25°C/77°F, and day temperatures often well over 30°C/90°F. January is the coldest month, with an average temperature of 6°C/43°F. A northerly wind, the bora, occurs mostly in winter with strong and bitterly cold winds. Violent thunderstorms with strong gusts are an unpleasant feature of the summer months.

✦ FORMALITIES

PORTS OF ENTRY

All year:

Bar	42°06´N 19°05´E	Budva	42°17´N 18°51´E
Kotor	42°25´N 18°46´E	Zelenika	42°26.4´N 18°34.5´E

Seasonal:

Ulcinj	41°55´N 19°12´E	Herceg Novi	42°27´N 18°32´E
Risan	42°31´N 18°42´E		

VHF Channel 16 should be monitored permanently in Montenegro waters and details of the yacht given if requested. On arrival at any port, the port captain should be called. A yacht must purchase a cruising permit (vignette)

ROMANIA

SITUATED IN EASTERN EUROPE with a small outlet to the Black Sea, and the River Danube separating it from the Balkans, Romania has always been at the crossroads of east and west, its critical location having dictated its destiny. As the only Latin people in Eastern Europe, Romanians have always regarded themselves as different from their neighbours. The profound changes that followed the collapse of the communist regime have allowed Romania to escape from the stranglehold of its mighty eastern neighbour and look once again for guidance and inspiration to Western Europe, as it has done throughout its modern history.

The Black Sea coast is flat and lacks natural harbours and anchorages. From the cruising point of view, Romania's main attraction is the Danube Delta, one of the largest migratory bird sanctuaries in Europe. Boats coming from the Black Sea should enter the Danube at Sulina, from where a dredged branch of the river leads to Tulcea, 40 miles upriver, with no bridges on the way. The Danube itself is navigable along most of its length and yachts have successfully cruised down the Danube from Austria passing through Slovakia, Hungary, Serbia and Bulgaria to reach Romania and the Black Sea. Sailing the river in the opposite direction is difficult and slow because of the strong current. The opening of the Main–Danube Canal has made it possible to sail across the entire continent of Europe, from the mouth of the Rhine, on the North Sea, to the mouth of the Danube, on the Black Sea. Those who wish to reach the Mediterranean this way and are not daunted by the length of the 3,506 km (2,179 mile) waterway can do it in boats drawing not more than 2.5m (8ft) and with an air clearance of 6m (19.5ft), so as to be able to pass under the many bridges.

The most important of the inland attractions are the painted monasteries of Bucovina, in Northern Romania. The outside of several churches from the fifteenth and sixteenth centuries are covered in exquisite frescoes of biblical scenes.

✦ COUNTRY PROFILE

The state of Dacia was conquered by the Romans and remained for two centuries under Roman rule, to be followed by waves of invaders from the east until eventually coming under the Ottoman Empire. The three regions of Romania were briefly united at the turn of the sixteenth century under Michael the Brave, but in 1691 Austro-Hungary annexed Transylvania, and the Turks hardened their grip over the rest of the region. Moldavia and Wallachia were united as Romania in 1861, but only in 1878 was Romania recognized as an independent kingdom. Romania joined the Allies in the First World War, after which it acquired Transylvania where Romanians have always been in the majority. After the Second World War the communists came to power and the king was forced to abdicate. The communist leader Nicolae Ceauçescu was overthrown by a revolution in 1989 and executed. With the fall of communism, democracy was gradually restored and Romania joined the EU in 2007.

The population is around 22 million, the majority being Romanian, but with just under 2 million Hungarians living mainly in Transylvania. There is also a sizeable Roma community. The capital is Bucharest.

✦ CLIMATE

The climate is temperate with hot summers and cold winters. The warmest months are July and August, with average temperatures of 23°C/73°F, and day temperatures often well over 30°C/90°F. The winds along the coast are influenced by the surrounding landmass and in summer there is a daily pattern of land and sea breezes. An onshore breeze comes up around midday and usually dies by dusk to be followed by a land breeze during the night.

Swans in the Danube Delta.

✦ FORMALITIES

PORTS OF ENTRY

Tomis (Constantza)	44°09´N 28°39´E
Sulina	45°09´N 29°39´E
Mangalia	43°48´N 28°35´E

Port Tomis (Constantza): Arriving yachts should proceed directly to the small boat harbour about half a mile north of the main commercial harbour of Constantza. The marina office should be contacted on Channel 67. The boat will be visited by customs and immigration, after which the captain may have to go into the main harbour and clear with the Port Authority.

Mangalia: The port captain should be contacted before proceeding directly to the customs dock, identified by three round storage tanks.

Sulina: It is possible to clear in at the port of Sulina, at the mouth of the Danube. Yachts can tie up to the main wharf to clear with customs in the nearby administration building. Navigating in the river can be very difficult because of the strong current.

Yachts must clear in and out of each port.

EU nationals, as well as those of Canada, the USA, Australia and New Zealand, do not need a visa for stays of up to 90 days.

✦ DANUBE–BLACK SEA CANAL

Cruising yachts may use this canal, which starts near Constantza and bypasses the Danube Delta. Most craft will have to lower their masts before entering.

✦ FACILITIES

As sailing is becoming more popular, new marinas have opened or are being planned. The best docking facilities are at the new marina, Ana Yacht Club, which now operates at Eforie Nord (44° 03.8´N 28° 38.5´E), a resort 7 miles south of Constantza. It has the best repair and haulout facilities and

is also recommended as a safe place to leave the boat unattended. Docking facilities at Mangalia are poor, but are adequate at the small port of Tomis next to Constantza. Being adjacent to the commercial harbour of Constantza, Tomis has access to a better range of repair services. Only simple repairs are possible in Mangalia or Sulina.

Cruising Guides
Cruising Bulgaria and Romania
RYA Foreign Cruising Vol 2

Websites
www.romaniatourism.com
www.anayachtclub.ro (Ana Yacht Club)

Local time	UTC +2
	Summer time: last Sunday in March to last Sunday in October
Buoyage	IALA A
Currency	New Leu (RON)
Electricity	230V, 50Hz

Diplomatic missions

UK	21 2017200	Australia	21 2003300
USA	21 3167558	Canada	21 3075000

Communications		**Emergency number**
IDD 40	IAC 00	112

Port Tomis

RUSSIA

THE BREAK-UP OF THE SOVIET UNION has radically altered the cruising scene in both the Baltic and Black Seas. While the former Soviet countries have themselves undergone a profound process of liberalization, by contrast the rules affecting the movement of foreign vessels have seen only a limited relaxation. In this respect Russia is the worst example, and formalities for visiting yachts are just as cumbersome as in the past. Foreign vessels, and their crews, continue to be viewed with a high degree of suspicion and the officials can be just as difficult and unpleasant as their Soviet predecessors. Russia has four main outlets to the sea: to the Black Sea via the Sea of Azov, the Baltic outlets at St Petersburg and Kaliningrad, the Arctic ports east of Norway, and the ports in the North West Pacific.

Russia's Black Sea coast has been very much diminished following the independence of Georgia and Ukraine, which also includes the Crimea. Russia's access to the Black Sea is via the Azov Sea and the Kerch Canal. The landlocked Azov Sea is a highly polluted area and a continuing source of dispute with neighbouring Ukraine. Russia's 200 mile long stretch of coastline in the northeast corner of the Black Sea has little cruising appeal as there are only three ports and two anchorages suitable for yachts. The only port of any interest to a cruising yacht is the attractive resort of Sochi, lying close to the border with Georgia.

After an initial outburst of interest, the number of cruising boats visiting Russia has levelled off as sailors realize that visiting Russia on their own boat is perhaps not worth the effort. Similarly, it may be a long time before foreign yachts are given access to Russia's extensive inland waterway system, which would make it possible to take a yacht from the Baltic to the Black Sea through the heart of this interesting country. At the cost of thousands of lives of forced labourers, the Soviet regime created a network in Western Russia that connects the White Sea to the Baltic and the Black Seas by linking two lakes, six artificial inland seas, several rivers and canals. The Russian Inland Waterways Act, passed by Stalin in 1936, prevents all foreign vessels from using these waterways. Access to them will only be possible after this law is repealed. Any request to take a yacht through the extensive inland waterway system is normally turned down.

The Far East is too remote and also less accessible to visiting yachts as several sensitive areas are closed to foreign vessels. The Baltic coast is dealt with on pages 97–98.

✦ COUNTRY PROFILE

Tsar Peter the Great embarked on a wide-ranging programme of modernization of a backward feudal country, a process that continued under Catherine the Great when Russia became a leading European power. Rapid industrialization at the end of the nineteenth century was followed by the rise of revolutionary movements. Following the revolution of 1917, the Union of Soviet Socialist Republics was officially established in 1922. An era of ruthless dictatorship under Stalin was marked by the deportation, and eventual death, of hundreds of thousands of political dissidents, the displacement of entire ethnic communities, the prosecution, sham trials and execution of the old communist guard, as well as the entire leadership of the armed forces. Entirely unprepared for war, Germany's attack in 1941 nearly led to defeat as the front reached the gates of Moscow and Leningrad, but the Red Army managed miraculously to turn the tide. At the cost of millions of lost lives, Russia went on the offensive and thus made a major contribution to the Allied victory over Nazi Germany. The war brought the Soviet Union huge rewards, foremost among them being complete control over most countries in Eastern Europe. The late 1980s saw the collapse of communist rule throughout Eastern Europe that led to major changes in the Soviet Union itself. By 1991 the USSR had splintered into Russia and 14 other independent republics, all of which declared independence as sovereign states in their own right.

The population is 140 million, of which 80 per cent are Russians, the rest being made up of many small minorities. The capital is Moscow.

✦ CLIMATE

The climate varies greatly in this vast country, from the subtropical in the southern areas bordering on the Black Sea to arctic conditions in the northern and eastern regions.

Sochi Yacht Club.

58

Conditions along the coasts are less harsh: winters along the Black Sea coast are milder, and the summers are very hot. As the Black Sea is virtually landlocked, the winds alternate between land and sea breezes.

✦ FORMALITIES

PORTS OF ENTRY

Foreign vessels are only allowed to visit ports listed on the visa or official invitation. The most important ports of entry are listed below:

Black Sea:	Novorossiysk 44°44´N 37°47´E	
Sochi	43°35´N 39°43´E	Tuapse 44°06´N 39°05´E
Taganrog	47°12´N 38°57´E	

Sochi: Arriving yachts must proceed into the commercial harbour to clear formalities before being allowed to go to the yacht club.

Landfall should be made at one of the ports specified in the visa, and no one should leave the boat until formalities have been completed. Yachts must clear in and out of each port, and the authorities must be given notice 24 hours in advance of departure.

All nationalities must obtain a visa in advance. An official invitation is necessary and may be obtained from an accredited Russian travel company, a yacht club or privately through an individual. The visa is a separate document, which lists the dates and ports for which permission has been granted to stop. It has been recommended that sailors apply for a business visa as this allows for greater flexibility in the timing of a yacht's arrival.

✦ FACILITIES

The yacht harbour near Sochi's commercial harbour has basic facilities and the staff are reported as being helpful. Provisioning is very good at the open air market. Repair facilities are good as local mechanics are used to improvising when spares are not available.

Websites
www.visitrussia.org.uk
www.russia-travel.com
www.yacht-club.sochi.net

Local time	UTC +3
	Summer time: last Sunday in March to last Sunday in October
Buoyage	IALA A
Currency	Russian Rouble (RUB)
Electricity	230V, 50Hz

Diplomatic missions
UK	495 9567200
USA	495 7285000
Australia	495 9566070
Canada	495 9256000
South Africa	495 5401177
New Zealand	495 9563579

Communications	Emergency number
IDD 7 IAC 810	112

SLOVENIA

SITUATED BETWEEN ITALY AND CROATIA, Slovenia has a small stretch of coast on the Istrian Peninsula. Although lacking the range of yachting facilities available along the Croatian coast, Slovenia's few ports and marinas are well equipped, and most ports are attractive old towns. Piran, Koper and Izola are some of the best-preserved medieval seaports in the Adriatic, while Portoroz is a popular holiday resort that benefits from Slovenia's ideal location for visitors from the landlocked countries of Central Europe.

✦ COUNTRY PROFILE

During the sixth century Slovene tribes settled in the region. In 788 they were incorporated into Charlemagne's empire and in 1278 came under Hapsburg rule. After Austro-Hungary's defeat in 1918, Slovenia became part of the new Kingdom of Serbs, Croats and Slovenes, later renamed Yugoslavia. After the Second World War, Slovenia was one of the six republics of the Yugoslav Federation. Following the fall of communism, in 1991 Slovenia declared its independence from Yugoslavia. Historical ties to neighbouring countries, a strong economy and stable democracy all assisted in Slovenia's transformation. Slovenia acceded to the EU in 2004. The population of 2 million consists mainly of Slovenes. The capital is Ljubljana.

✦ CLIMATE

The climate is Mediterranean, with hot summers and relatively mild winters. The warmest months are July and August, with average temperatures of 22°C/77°F, but day temperatures often exceed 30°C/90°F. A northerly wind, the bora, occurs mostly in winter; the winds at this time can be bitterly cold.

✦ FORMALITIES

PORTS OF ENTRY

Koper	45°33´N 13°44´E	Izola	45°33´N 13°40´E
Piran	45°32´N 13°34´E	Portoroz	45°30´N 13°36´E

Officials will come to the yacht for clearance. In marinas, the staff will call the relevant officials. If no official arrives, the captain should report to the police for passport control, as well as customs and port captain. The crew must remain on board until formalities have been completed.

Among the documents needed are a certificate of competence, insurance certificate and radio licence. When clearance is complete, a cruising permit will be issued.

Slovenia is a signatory to the Schengen Agreement and those visa regulations apply.

✦ FACILITIES

All marinas are of a good standard. They are located in Koper, Portoroz and Izola. Koper has a chandlery, haulout and repair facilities. Piran is a small marina and handy for checking in, but it rarely has any vacant spaces.

✦ CHARTER

Cosmos Yachting operates out of Portoroz, while Adria Service operates in Izola and has a fleet of sailing monohulls and multihulls as well as powerboats. Buring Club has a base at Biograd, in Croatia, as do other Slovenian operators who maintain their yachts closer to the popular cruising grounds.

www.cosmosyachting.com
www.adriaservice-yachting.com
www.burin-club.com

Cruising Guides
Adriatic Pilot
Croatia, Slovenia and Montenegro, 777 Harbours and Anchorages
Dove Navigare Bolina (details of ports and marinas in Italian)

Website
www.slovenia.info (tourist and yachting information)

Local time UTC +1
Summer time: last Sunday in March to last Sunday in October
Buoyage IALA A
Currency Euro (EUR)
Electricity 230V, 50Hz

Diplomatic missions

UK	1 2003910	Canada	1 2006300
USA	1 2005500	South Africa	1 2524444
Australia	1 4254252	New Zealand	1 5803055

Communications		**Emergency number**
IDD 386	IAC 00	112

SPAIN

WITH COASTS ON BOTH THE ATLANTIC and the Mediterranean, Spain contains five distinctive maritime areas, each with its own character and all very different from a sailor's point of view. The Mediterranean coast stretches the length of the Iberian Peninsula from Gibraltar to the French border, with the Balearic Islands forming a separate offshore group. The Atlantic coast is divided into two sections on either side of Portugal, the northwest coast bordering the Bay of Biscay and the southwest coast of Andalucia covering the area from the Portuguese border to the Straits of Gibraltar. The fifth entity is the Canary Islands (page 109) lying off the coast of Africa and sharing many features with the neighbouring continent. The most attractive cruising areas of Spain are situated at its extremes, with the Balearics, one of the Mediterranean's prime yachting centres, at one end, and the Rias Baixas and Rias Altas of Galicia at the other. The Atlantic coast of Spain is described on page 130.

As nature has been less generous in creating sheltered natural harbours along Spain's Mediterranean coast compared to its Atlantic shores, man had to make his own contribution by building several ports, some of which date

Tossa del Mar on the Costa Brava.

back to medieval times or even earlier. In more recent years, the distinctive coastal areas, Costa del Sol, Costa Blanca, Costa del Azahar, Costa Dorada and Costa Brava, have seen a massive development in yachting facilities with new marinas being built everywhere. There are now marinas placed at convenient intervals all along the mainland coast, so that you are never more than a few hours' sail from the next port. Initially the development was needed to cope with the demands of foreign sailors, many of whose yachts were based permanently in Spain. With the exception of a few traditional sailing centres, such as Palma de Mallorca, Barcelona and Cadiz, until not so long ago there was little interest in yachting, but this attitude has seen a great change as increasing numbers of Spaniards are discovering the joy of sailing, both cruising and racing. This is shown by such prestigious international events as the America's Cup being based in Valencia or the Volvo Ocean race starting from Alicante. An important yachting centre is Barcelona, a vibrant city with excellent facilities which attracts many cruising sailors who use it not only as a base for visiting the rest of Spain, but also to spend the winter.

Cruising opportunities along the mainland coast are rather disappointing mainly due to the absence of natural

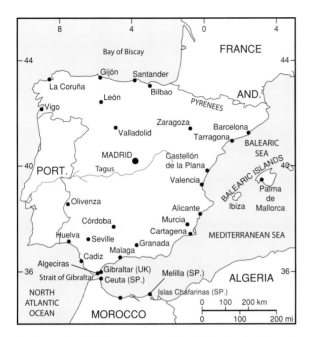

slowly eroded and she gradually lost all her colonies. In the twentieth century, the growth of republicanism resulted in the overthrow of the Bourbon monarchy in 1931, but the new republic was faced with strong opposition from the Church and landowners. Civil war broke out in 1936 when the Falangists under General Franco rose against the government. In 1939 Franco established a dictatorship, which only came to an end with his death in 1975. King Juan Carlos I restored the monarchy and gradually the country returned to democracy. Although formally Spain is a monarchy, practically it is a federal state made up of 17 autonomous communities, each with its own parliament, government and president. Spain joined the EU in 1986.

The population numbers 46 million. Although everyone speaks Spanish (Castilian), which is the national official language, regional languages are officially used in some of the autonomous communities. Catalan is the second major language and is spoken in the Catalonia region centred on Barcelona. The Galician and Basque languages are in common use in those regions. The capital is Madrid.

✦ CLIMATE

The coastal areas and offshore islands enjoy a truly Mediterranean climate, with hot summers and mild winters. Alternating sea and land breezes are a daily feature in summer. The Costa Brava and the Balearics are occasionally affected by the mistral, a northerly wind that can rapidly reach gale force. While summers are hot and often humid, the afternoon heat is tempered by a sea breeze. Occasionally conditions along the south coast can become unpleasant when a hot dry wind (*lebeche*) blows from North Africa. July and August are the hottest months on the mainland coast, with average temperatures of 24°C/75°F and day temperatures that can reach well above 30°C/90°F. January is the coolest month, with an average temperature of 12°C/54°F. In the Balearics, which enjoy milder weather, average temperatures are about one or two degrees higher than on the mainland.

✦ FORMALITIES

EU regulations and Schengen visa provisions are in force. EU boats that come from another EU country do not need to report. Both EU and non-EU boats arriving from outside the EU must contact customs at the first port. The Schengen Agreement applies to visa requirements, and non-EU boats that have called first at other Schengen countries must be able to prove this.

In 2009, as a result of too many foreign boats being based permanently in marinas and hardly ever moving, a 12 per cent levy started being imposed on boats that had spent more than 183 days in Spain in any one year.

harbours, but this is compensated for by having the Balearic Islands within striking distance. Few other destinations seem to concentrate all the ingredients considered essential by cruising sailors as the Balearics: distances between places are relatively short; the weather is quite predictable during the sailing season; there is a good choice of both ports and safe anchorages; and there is a lot to see and do ashore. But regardless of where one may land in Spain, its main attraction is the relaxed way of life that can be savoured in the typical waterfront cafés and restaurants.

✦ COUNTRY PROFILE

The Iberian Peninsula was inhabited from Stone Age times, and in the first millennium BCE the Celts invaded and mingled with the native Iberians. Phoenician and Greek colonies were later established along the coasts. The Carthaginians conquered Spain in the third century BCE, but were expelled by the Romans who spread their control over the whole peninsula. After the decline of the Roman Empire, Vandals and Visigoths overran the country and in 711 the Moors invaded from North Africa. Spain was gradually reconquered and, in 1492, during the reign of Ferdinand and Isabella, the Moors were driven from their last stronghold in Granada. In the same year, Christopher Columbus sailed to the New World and claimed it for Spain. Over the next century, the Spaniards explored the Americas, establishing a vast empire in their search for gold and silver.

Spain reached the height of its power in the sixteenth century under Charles V, who inherited both the Spanish and Hapsburg thrones. After this, Spanish domination was

PORTS OF ENTRY

Mainland Spain has about three dozen so-called external border ports, also referred to as Schengen ports. Because of the large number of ports of entry as well as marinas that have customs offices where entry formalities can be completed, only the mainland ports that are commonly used by foreign yachts to clear in are listed.

La Duquesa	36°21′N 15°14′W	Puerto Banus	36°29′N 4°57′W	Málaga	36°41′N 4°26′W
Motril	36°43′N 3°31′W	Almería	36°50′N 2°30′W	Cartagena	37°35′N 0°58′W
Alicante	38°20′N 0°29′W	Denia	38°50′N 0°07′E	Valencia	39°27′N 0°18′W
Tarragona	41°06′N 1°14′E	Barcelona	41°21′N 2°10′E	Palamos	41°50′N 3°08′E

✦ FACILITIES

Although there are marinas all along Spain's coast, and each provides at least some basic services, comprehensive repair facilities are only available in the most important yachting centres. Barcelona, Valencia and Malaga are major yachting centres on the mainland, with the best quality and range of repair and other services. Spanish yacht clubs (club nautico) are almost without exception exclusive social clubs, where visitors are not particularly welcome unless advance arrangements are made via one's own club.

✦ CHARTER

A few companies operate in the mainland ports, but much of the charter activity is concentrated in the Balearics. Spain Yacht Charter offers a range of yachts based at various marinas along the south and east coasts, while Azul Yachting is based in Barcelona.

www.spain-yachtcharter.com
www.azul-sailing.com

SPANISH NORTH AFRICA

Ceuta and Melilla are Spanish enclaves on the north coast of Morocco. Their status is of autonomous cities within Spain. Ceuta and Melilla became Spanish in the fifteenth century and remained so when Morocco became independent in 1956. Visa requirements are the same as for Spain.

Ceuta (35°53.5′N 5°19.3′W): There is a new marina, which is a good base from which to explore the surrounding area.
Melilla (35°17′N 2°56′W): Lying 120 miles east along the coast from Ceuta, Melilla is not as large. It has a well-equipped marina with a travelift and there is also a yacht club where visiting sailors are welcome.

THE BALEARIC ISLANDS

Lying just 60 miles off the coast of Spain, the five islands of Mallorca, Menorca, Ibiza, Formentera and Cabrera are not only one of Europe's most popular tourist destinations, but are also among the world's most famous yachting centres. Their enduring popularity is due not only to their scenic beauty and pleasant climate, but also to a rich and varied past that has left a legacy of prehistoric sites, medieval castles, picturesque villages and colourful fishing ports.

Various civilizations have left their mark on these islands, which have been inhabited since prehistoric times, and the massive stone structures of these early inhabitants are witness to a mysterious people. In 654 BCE the Carthaginians founded a port where the modern port of Ibiza stands today. The islands were later occupied by the Romans who were chased away by the Visigoths. During the tenth century the islands were invaded by Arabs who remained there for three centuries until the islands were reconquered. The British occupied Mahon on Menorca in 1708 and kept it as a naval base until 1802. Finally, in 1833, the Balearics became a Spanish province and it took 150 years for the islands to regain their autonomy, although they continue to be part of Spain.

IBIZA

Ibiza was once renowned as the most laid-back place in Europe, a reputation that lingers even if the hippies of the 1960s have now been replaced by cohorts of party-goers attracted to the island's vibrant nightlife. Away from the hot spots, Ibiza still has many charming corners, most of them along the less developed north coast. Besides its three main harbours, Ibiza has scores of small anchorages all around its rocky shores. As in all of the other Balearics, the high cliffs are interspersed with deep fjord-like inlets called *calas*.

The old town and port of Ibiza.

Palma de Mallorca is overlooked by the medieval Castell de Bellver.

Puerto de San Antonio, on the northwest coast, is the best landfall if coming from the mainland as it offers good shelter in the wide bay as well as a marina and welcoming yacht club. The main port and capital, Puerto de Ibiza, has several marinas and is an attractive medieval city that tends to be dominated by tourists. A more tranquil atmosphere will be found in the neighbouring island of Formentera.

PORT OF ENTRY

Ibiza	38° 54′ N 1° 28′ E

Clearing into the main port is only necessary if coming from outside the EU, otherwise it is possible to go straight to any other port or marina. In Ibiza Port there are three berthing areas: Marina de Botafoch, Puerto Ibiza Nueva, and Club Nautico de Ibiza. All Port Authority pontoons are occupied by local craft.

Although Ibiza Port is the place with best repair facilities, there are some such facilities in all ports as well as in the various marinas.

Charter

The main charter base is in Marina de Botafoch, but operators, offering both power and sailing yachts, are based in other marinas as well.

www.amoyachts.com
www.ibizayachtcharter.com
www.boatbookings.com

MALLORCA

The port of Palma de Mallorca has probably a higher concentration of yachts than any other place in the world, with the entire waterfront being taken up by marinas. Palma itself is an attractive town whose centre is dominated by the large medieval cathedral, but the most impressive building is that of Castell de Bellver, a massive fortress from the fourteenth century standing in splendid isolation on a hill overlooking the city. Mallorca has an abundance of natural harbours almost unmatched elsewhere, and day sailing along its beautiful coast is both a relaxed and highly enjoyable experience. The island's interior is just as interesting and there is always a convenient port or marina to leave the boat while touring inland. One such place is Porto Cristo, best known for the nearby underground Coves del Drac (Caves of the Dragon). Reputed to have the best stalactite formations in Spain, the extensive caves include an underground lake overlooked by a natural amphitheatre where each visit is concluded by a short performance by a string quartet gliding in a boat over the still dark waters.

Close to the south of Mallorca is the island of Cabrera which has been declared a national park to protect its rich wildlife and flora. Access to the island is only allowed to those in possession of a permit issued by the Cabrera National Park Office, Plaza España 8, 07002 Palma de Mallorca.

PORTS OF ENTRY

Palma de Mallorca	39° 33′ N 2° 38′ E
Andratx	39° 33′ N 2° 24′ E
Alcudia	39° 49′ N 3° 08′ E

Palma: You should avoid arriving on the off chance of finding a place in this busy and overcrowded port, so it is strongly recommended that advance arrangements are made and then to proceed directly to the respective marina or yacht club reception dock. The documents should then be taken to the marina or club office who will contact the relevant officials. If required to visit other offices, those of customs and Capitania Maritima are located in Muelle Viejo.

Facilities in Palma de Mallorca are considered among the best in the Mediterranean, with a wide range of services. Concentrated in a relatively small area are several companies specializing in work on yachts. Repair facilities outside of Palma are more limited.

Charter

There is a multitude of operators offering a wide range of charter services – from basic bare boats to luxurious fully crewed yachts. While the latter are based in Palma, others operate out of marinas such as Puerto Portals, Pollensa and Andratx.

www.nautilus-yachting.com
www.chartermallorca.com
www.saracensailing.com
www.marinayachting.net

MENORCA

Compared to busy Mallorca, Menorca looks like a younger sister, an observation that the Romans must have made when they differentiated between the two islands by calling one 'major' and the other 'minor'. Apart from their size, the two are very different in other aspects too, as Menorca has maintained much of its rural character and in some parts appears to have been left largely untouched by the modern world. Unique to the island are the numerous prehistoric remains, large stone structures built by a mysterious people over 3,000 years ago. The two main ports of Mahon and Ciutadella are almost as old themselves, their perfectly sheltered deep inlets being used as staging posts by the Phoenician navigators who were sailing in these waters 1,000 years before Christ.

PORT OF ENTRY
Mahon 39°52´N 4°19´E

Arriving yachts should contact Club Maritimo or Ribera del Puerto (the Port Authority), both of whom monitor Channel 9. Club Maritimo has some berthing spaces on the main quay and is more convenient, while the other moorings are on one of the artificial islands administered by Ribera del Puerto. The other alternative is Port d'Hivernada, a marina at the far end of the long inlet. This is also the place with best repair and haulout facilties.

Charter
The scarcity of charter opportunity only confirms Menorca's refusal to join the fast pace of her island sisters and thus adds to her charm. Among the few operators are a couple of British companies that offer bareboat and skippered charters

Tranquil Cala Coves on Menorca's south coast.

as well as offshore sail training. Club Nautic Ciutadella has a small selection of power and sailing yachts that can be booked via the online operator Alquiler Directo, who also manages an informative website.

www.menorcayachts.co.uk
www.menorcayachts.co.uk
www.alquiler-directo.com

Cruising Guides
Islas Baleares
Mediterranean Spain, Costas del Sol and Blanca
Mediterranean Spain, Costas del Azahar, Dorada and Brava
Mediterranean Islands

Websites
www.spain.info
www.illesbalears.es
www.alquiler-directo.com (details of all Spanish marinas and charter operators)

Local time	UTC +1
	Summer time: last Sunday in March to last Sunday in October
Buoyage	IALA A
Currency	Euro (EUR)
Electricity	220/230V, 50Hz

Diplomatic missions	
UK	91 7008200
USA	91 5872200
Australia	91 3536600
Canada	91 4233250
South Africa	91 4363780
New Zealand	91 5230226

Communications	
IDD 34	IAC 00

Emergency number
112

SYRIA

THE ANCIENT MARINERS used to refer to the eastern Mediterranean as the Levant as the sun rose there. Until the First World War, Syria was called the Levant as it incorporated what is now Lebanon, Israel, Palestine and Jordan. Its capital Damascus is reputed to be the city that has been continually inhabited for the longest time. After a lengthy period of isolation, the Syrian authorities have recently become more welcoming towards foreign tourists. As a result, formalities for visiting boats are also somewhat easier, and every year a few cruising vessels call at one of the Syrian ports. The coast lacks natural harbours, but there are docking facilities for yachts in the major ports. While coastal cruising is neither feasible nor permitted, the best solution is to base your boat in a port such as Latakia or Tartous and tour the country from there. It is the interior of Syria that is of real interest – whether that be ancient sites such as Palmyra or medieval landmarks like the Crusader castle Krak des Chevaliers.

✦ COUNTRY PROFILE

Damascus has been a thriving city since 5000 BCE, being successively part of the Persian, Greek, Roman and then Ottoman empires. Liberated from the Turks in 1918 by troops led by Lawrence of Arabia, Syria was placed under French mandate until finally independence was achieved at the end of the Second World War. The country went through a long period of turmoil and military coups, until in 1970 Hafiz al-Assad seized power and brought political stability to the country. In the 1967 Arab-Israeli War, Syria lost the Golan Heights to Israel. Since then, Syria has played an active role in Lebanese affairs, and its troops stationed in Lebanon since 1976 were only withdrawn in 2005. Recently there has been a gradual rapprochement with the West and also talks with Israel aimed at resolving their long-standing conflict. The majority of the 20 million population are Muslim, although 10 per cent are Christian. Arabic is the official language.

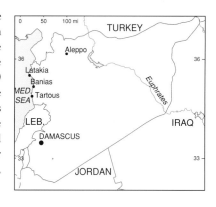

✦ FORMALITIES

PORTS OF ENTRY

Latakia	35°31´N 35°46´E	Banias	35°14´N 35°56´E
Tartous	34°54´N 35°52´E		

Latakia is the principal port for yachts entering Syria, and Latakia Radio should be contacted when 12 miles offshore, but not on a Friday, Saturday or public holiday. The Syrian Yacht Club at Latakia Marina can be contacted in advance to obtain information on the latest procedures and will also help with formalities.

Visas are necessary for all nationalities and should be obtained from the Syrian embassy in the visitor's country of nationality. Those without a visa should email the yacht club a scanned copy of the crew's passports, so the necessary arrangements are made in good time.

✦ CLIMATE

The coastal area of Syria enjoys a Mediterranean climate, with hot dry summers and mild – occasionally rainy – winters. In early and late summer the weather can be affected by spells of the hot, dry *khamsin* which sweeps in from Arabia and lasts a few days. The prevailing winds of summer are westerly. A day breeze usually comes up at noon and lasts until sunset. July and August are the warmest months with average temperatures of 23°C/73°F, but day temperatures can reach well over 30°C/90°F.

✦ FACILITIES

Latakia Marina, which is run by the Syrian Yacht Club, has the best facilities. There are also moorings for visiting yachts at Tartous and Banias, but repair facilities are more limited.

Websites
www.syriatourism.org   www.syrianyachtclub.com

Local time	UTC +2
	Summer time: late March to late October
Buoyage	IALA A
Currency	Syrian Pound (SYP) **Electricity** 220V, 50Hz

Diplomatic missions
UK	11 3391513	Canada	11 6116692
USA	11 33914444	South Africa	11 3222650

Communications	Emergency numbers
IDD 963 IAC 00	112 Ambulance 110

TUNISIA

UNIQUE AMONG NORTH AFRICAN COUNTRIES, Tunisia has approached yachting in the most systematic way. In line with the government's efforts to encourage tourism as a major source of revenue, it has also promoted the setting up of new marinas and docking facilities in old harbours conveniently spaced along Tunisia's entire coast, from Zarzis in the southeast to Tabarka in the west. All ports are within reach of interesting towns and the boat can be left in safety to visit the interior. This approach, combined with the relatively low prices of the marinas, has turned Tunisia into a popular cruising destination, especially for wintering.

With one notable exception, all marinas are on Tunisia's east coast. The oldest and best known, Sidi Bou Said, lies in the Bay of Tunis, close to the capital, Tunis, and its international airport. The marina is almost inside the ancient port of Carthage and close by are the few remains of the once grand city that Rome razed to the ground for daring to challenge its might. South of Cap Bon are several marinas, with the best repair facilities at Yasmine Hammamet. Further south, also set in the middle of tourist developments, are El Kantaoui and Cap Monastir marinas.

If one were to define any place as being the quintessence of modern Tunisia, Monastir would be a good choice. The small town is the birthplace of Habib Bourguiba, Tunisia's greatest hero and father of modern Tunisia. His mausoleum is opposite the Ribat, a fairytale citadel whose massive walls rise above the marina. On summer evenings, as the temperature starts cooling down, local people descend on the marina to walk up and down, look at boats, chat with friends, or stop for

Monastir Marina is overlooked by the medieval Ribat citadel

a coffee. It is not uncommon for an entire family to stroll along the quay, from a grandmother wearing the traditional veil, accompanied by a married daughter whose attire is usually more modern, to a teenage granddaughter who may display a bare midriff and headphones stuck to her ears.

While some of the older ports, such as Bizerte or Sousse, are quite attractive, it is the interior that makes Tunisia such an interesting country with its wealth of colourful villages and ancient sites, mostly from the times when this was one of the wealthiest colonies of the Roman Empire. As the land merges with the Sahara, a vista of golden sand dunes opens to the legendary Sea of Sand navigated by those ships of the desert, caravans of swaying camels.

The country's long association with France has left a noticeable influence on Tunisia's culture and way of life. As Tunisia is not part of the EU and the number of non-EU countries in the Mediterranean has shrunk, Tunisia is now one of the preferred destinations for non-EU flagged boats.

✦ COUNTRY PROFILE

The original inhabitants of North Africa were the Berbers, from which the name Barbary Coast derived. It is believed that the island of Djerba was the Land of the Lotus Eaters in Homer's *Odyssey*. In 814 BCE Queen Dido fled from Tyre, the Phoenician port in today's Lebanon, and founded the city of Carthage, which prospered and dominated much of the Mediterranean. This great maritime power was eclipsed by the rise of Rome, and Carthage was finally destroyed. After the Romans came the Vandals, and then Byzantium ruled over the country. The seventh century brought the Arab invasions and the spread of Islam throughout the region. Following the defeat of the Moors in Spain, many of them resettled in northern Africa and today's Tunisia.

In the nineteenth century Tunisia became a French protectorate, and many French people settled there. After the Second World War a guerrilla war was waged until independence was granted in 1957 under Habib Bourguiba.

The population is 10.5 million and is of a mixture that reflects the region's past history of Arab, Roman, Greek, Spanish, Sicilian, French, Berber and black African origins. In the south the nomadic Bedouin still follow their traditional life. The main languages are Arabic, Berber and French, the latter being used in education, commerce and administration. Tunis is the bustling modern capital.

PORTS OF ENTRY

Tabarka	36°58′N 8°45′E	Bizerte	37°16′N 9°53′E	Sidi Bou Said	36°52′N 10°21′E
Kelibia	36°50′N 11°07′E	Yasmine Hammamet	36°23.7′N 10°36.9′E	El Kantaoui	35°52′N 10°36′E
Sousse	35°50′N 10°39′E	Sfax	34°44′N 10°46′E	Gabes	33°55′N 10°06′E
Djerba (Houmt Souk)	33°53′N 10°52′E	Zarzis	33°30′N 11°07′E	Monastir	35°46.5′N 10°50′E

◆ CLIMATE

The typically Mediterranean climate of hot summers and mild winters can be influenced by the proximity of the huge Sahara Desert. August is the hottest month, with average temperatures of 27°C/81°F, although temperatures around 40°C/100°F are not uncommon. Temperatures on the coast are moderated by daily sea breezes. January is the coolest month, with average temperatures of 12°C/54°F. Westerly winds prevail along the north coast, but in summer they are usually interrupted by the daily alternating land and sea breezes. Along the east coast the prevailing winds of summer are southeasterly. The occasional sirocco, locally known as *chili*, arrives from the south with gale force winds, but is usually short lived.

◆ FORMALITIES

Arrival formalities are simplified by the fact that the various officials will visit the boat, or are often waiting on the quay when you arrive.

Visas are not required for nationals of the EU, Canada and the USA. Australian citizens can obtain a visa on arrival, while New Zealand citizens require a visa obtained in advance.

Customs may ask to see the yacht's insurance papers. A cruising permit is issued when formalities are completed. Port police must be visited before leaving for another port.

◆ FACILITIES

Yachting facilities are the best in North Africa and there are haulout facilities at Hammamet, Kantaoui, La Goulette, Monastir and Sfax, where there are also boatyards with a good range of repair facilities. The best repair facilities are at Yasmine Hammamet. Provisioning is good and there are street markets everywhere, with a very good selection of fresh produce.

Cruising Guides
North Africa
Mediterranean Almanac
Mediterranean Cruising

Website
www.tourismtunisia.com

Local time	UTC +1
	Summer time: last Sunday in March to last Sunday in October
Buoyage	IALA A
Currency	Tunisian Dinar (TND)
Electricity	230V, 50Hz

Diplomatic missions

UK	71 108700	Canada	71 104000
USA	71 107000	South Africa	71 798449

Communications

IDD 216	IAC 00

Emergency numbers

112	Ambulance 190	Police 197

TURKEY

Boasting a long coastline in the eastern Mediterranean, the Sea of Marmara and the Black Sea, Turkey is almost surrounded by water. Spanning the two shores of the Bosphorus and Dardanelles at the meeting point of Europe and Asia, Turkey cannot be labelled as either European or Asian. It is a melting pot of different cultures and civilizations, every one of which has left its indelible mark and whose remains can still be seen, from Troy to Ephesus and Byzantium. This latter city became first Constantinople as the capital of the Eastern Roman Empire, and then, as Istanbul, the centre of the vast Ottoman Empire.

Most cruising yachts sail in the southwest of the country which gets highest ratings for its scenic beauty. One of the earliest modern sailors to appreciate the uniqueness of that area was H M Denham, the author of the first cruising guide to that region: 'The scenery of Southern Turkey is unsurpassed. Here is a skyline whose sharpness of forms transcends anything elsewhere in the Mediterranean.'

Such comments, while absolutely true, should not discourage anyone from exploring other parts of Turkey such as the Sea of Marmara. The thrill of passing through the Dardanelles can then be followed by the challenge of sailing through the heart of Istanbul. Negotiating the crowded waters of the Bosphorus – weaving one's way between unyielding ferries while trying not to miss such sights as the Blue Mosque, Agia Sophia, the Topkapi Palace and other famous buildings – can be quite nerve-racking, but is an exhilarating and unforgettable experience.

The spectacular Black Sea shoreline of Turkey is lacking in natural harbours, but there are several good ports along this coast, so the scenery can be enjoyed while sailing from one port to the next. Facilities are rudimentary and some of the ports tend to be crowded with local craft, so it pays to be there during the closed fishing season, in July and August, when most trawlers are hauled out. One of the most interesting towns to visit along this coast is Trabzon. A convenient place to start a Black Sea cruise, whether along the Turkish coast or any of the other countries, is Ataköy Marina in Istanbul. Over the years, the marina has kept in contact with sailing organizations throughout that area, has been one of the sponsors of the successful Black Sea Rally, and is an invaluable source of advice to anyone heading that way.

Although lacking the profusion of islands of its Greek neighbour, there are so many bays and coves along the Aegean coast of Asia Minor all the way from the Dardanelles to the southwestern extremity of Turkey that you can almost always pick a pretty anchorage within minutes of deciding to drop the anchor. A favourite stop along this coast is Kusadasi Marina, the first international marina to open in Turkey. Located a few miles across the narrow straits from Greek Samos, the marina is also very close to Ephesus, where the temple of Artemis once stood. Little has survived of its

İçmeler Bay in Southern Turkey.

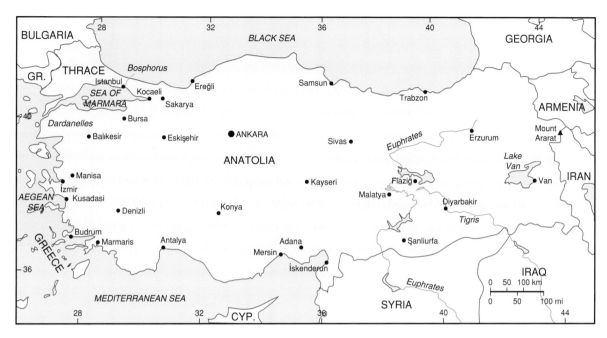

magnificent Temple of Artemis, one of the seven wonders of the ancient world, but still standing are remains of many other imposing buildings. All along the shores of Asia Minor there are other such sites from the classic period, most of them within easy reach from a port or marina, and adding a special dimension to a leisurely cruise along this coast.

Compared to the past, cruising in Turkey has seen a great improvement not least because of the upgrading and expansion of yachting facilities. Much of the emphasis in the last two decades has been put on southern Turkey, where a string of full-service marinas has been built. The policy of attracting foreign yachts has resulted in their number growing exponentially in recent years and many have made Turkey their permanent base. In spite of this, many anchorages and scenic spots are still uncrowded, especially out of the high season and particularly along the southern shore, from Marmaris to Antalya and beyond. Cruising along the Lycian coast can be a highly satisfying experience as in several places the boat can be anchored in sight of a 2,000-year-old mausoleum carved into the cliff face and a short walk ashore may lead to a well-preserved amphitheatre hidden in the hills. It is memories like these that make a cruise in Turkey an unforgettable experience.

✦ COUNTRY PROFILE

During the classical era much of the Asia Minor coast was part of the Hellenic world and the Trojan War was fought on what is now Turkish soil. Much of that area was later incorporated in the Roman Empire to be replaced by the Byzantine Empire with its capital at Constantinople. Towards the end of the thirteenth century, the Ottoman state was founded in Asia Minor and gradually expanded, eventually capturing Constantinople. The empire reached the height of its power under Suleiman the Magnificent, whose realm stretched from Hungary and the Balkans throughout Asia Minor to the Persian Gulf and across North Africa as far west as Algeria. However, after an unsuccessful siege of Vienna and the decisive defeat at Lepanto in 1571, the empire reached its limit and it started a gradual decline, although it took more than two centuries for it to disintegrate.

The nineteenth century saw states in the Balkans and Mediterranean gain independence from an empire weakened by financial difficulties and lack of reform. At home, dissatisfaction with the regime grew and in 1909 the nationalist movement of the Young Turks came to power. In 1922 Kemal Atatürk led the overthrow of the Sultanate and established a republic. Under his presidency, a modern, secular Turkey was created.

The population is 77 million, of which 90 per cent are ethnic Turks. Kurds form the largest minority in the east of the country and their campaign to form their own independent state is ongoing. Turkish is spoken by the majority. Ankara is the capital, but Istanbul is the largest city.

✦ CLIMATE

The climate is very varied, but generally can be described as Mediterranean, with hot summers and mild winters. The Black Sea has more extremes and is more humid. The Aegean coast is under the influence of the northerly meltemi wind, which blows from about June until the end of August, and at its peak can reach gale force. Lighter winds prevail along the south coast where nights are usually calm. During the rest of the year, winds are variable. Generally the sailing season comes to an end along the Aegean coast by late October, but along the south coast it is still possible to cruise to the end of November. Average temperatures vary greatly between the north and south coasts. August is the hottest month in Istanbul, with average temperatures of 24°C/75°F and peaks well over 30°C/90°F. The south coast is less extreme. January is the coldest month, with an average temperature of 4°C/39°F in the north and 6°C/43°F in the south.

The Golden Horn.

✦ FORMALITIES

Istanbul: All offices are in the same waterfront building at Karakoy. As this is a very busy area and yachts cannot berth here, it is best to head for one of the marinas (Ataköy or Fenerbahce) and visit the offices from there.

Chanakkale: Yachts that come from Greece and need to clear into Turkey ought to contact Chanakkale Yacht Harbour to see if they are allowed to dock there to complete formalities as the commercial dock is not suitable for yachts.

Formalities are completed with the harbourmaster, health, passport office, police and customs. Marinas usually act as agents and will provide both the transit log and deal with formalities. Each yacht must purchase a transit log valid for one year. A new log must be bought and completed on each arrival from another country. Changes in crew must be entered in the transit log and authorized by the harbourmaster where the change occurs.

A tourist visa, which is obtained on arrival, is valid for 90 days including the days of arrival and departure. It may be renewed by leaving the country, whether by sailing your own boat or taking the ferry for a day to a Greek island. Longer visas (up to a five-year visa) can be obtained in advance from Turkish diplomatic missions. Care must be taken to avoid exceeding the relevant date on either visa or transit log or you risk being fined, or even banished from the country for some time.

PORTS OF ENTRY

Black Sea:

Sinop	42°01´N 35°09´E	Zonguldak	41°27.6´N 31°46.8´E	Ereğli	41°17´N 31°24´E
Bartin	41°41´N 32°13´E	Inebolu	42°00´N 33°46´E	Samsun	41°18´N 36°20´E
Giresun	40°55´N 38°22´E	Trabzon	41°00´N 39°45´E	Rize	41°02´N 40°31´E
Hopa	41°05´N 41°25´E				

Sea of Marmara:

Chanakkale	40°09´N 26°25´E	Bandirma	40°21´N 27°58´E	Tekirdag	40°58´N 27°31´E
Gemlik	40°26´N 29°09´E	Mudanya	40°22.6´N 28°53.5´E	Istanbul	41°00´N 28°58´E

West coast:

Akcay	39°35´N 26°56´E	Ayvalik	39°19´N 26°41´E	Dikili	39°05´N 26°53´E
Izmir	38°26´N 27°08´E	Cesme	38°19´N 26°20´E	Kusadasi	37°52´N 27°14´E
Güllük	37°15´N 27°38´E	Turgutreis	36°59.9´N 27°15.3´W	Bodrum	37°02´N 27°25´E

South coast:

Datça	36°43´N 27°41´E	Marmaris	36°51´N 28°16´E	Fethiye	36°38´N 29°06´E
Kas	36°11´N 29°38´E	Finike	36°18´N 30°09´E	Kemer	36°35´N 30°34´E
Antalya	36°53´N 30°42´E	Alanya	36°32´N 32°01´E	Anamur	36°01´N 32°48´E
Tasucu	36°19´N 33°53´E	Mersin	36°48´N 34°38´E	Iskenderun	36°36´N 36°10´E

Procedures changed in 2009 and may be interpreted differently from place to place. Dealings with harbour-masters are likely to require the use of an agent; they are generally available in all ports. As of January 2009, a detailed inventory of all electronic equipment and removable items must be completed on arrival and stamped by customs. Special formalities must also be completed if the yacht is to be left unattended.

✦ FACILITIES

Yachting facilities have improved greatly in recent years, and as marinas are relatively new their facilities and services are of a good standard. Most marinas provide a range of repair services as well as haulout facilities, and technical support ranges from adequate to excellent. The best repair and service facilities are concentrated in the area between Bodrum and Marmaris, with the latter having a well-equipped yard with a 330-ton travelift and being used to dealing with the requirements of large yachts. Marine equipment is available in the larger marinas. All major engine manufacturers are represented in Turkey, and parts for most common makes are easily available. There are also good facilities in Istanbul, which has two marinas, of which Ataköy Marina has excellent repair facilities, a 75-ton travelift, and is a convenient base from which to visit the city or other parts of Turkey. The marina is also an excellent source of information for anyone planning to visit any of the countries in the Black Sea.

Provisioning is generally good and there are grocery shops in most marinas. Fresh produce markets are excellent everywhere in Turkey.

The Turks are very proud of their clean waters. Cruising yachts are now required to have a holding tank for toilet, shower and galley discharges. A Blue Card must be bought from marinas or port authorities in the Mugla (Bodrum to Fethiye) area to record and keep track of all discharge pump-outs.

✦ CHARTER

Most companies are located in southwestern Turkey, with the established operators having their fleets of yachts based in Bodrum, Göcek, Orhaniye, Keçi Bükü, Marmaris and Fethiye. Kiriacoulis also runs an operation in Kusadasi. A few operators also offer the popular flotilla holidays. Away from the favourite cruising sites, the choice is more limited, although privately owned skippered yachts or the typical Turkish gulets are on offer throughout Turkey.

www.sunsail.com
www.moorings.com
www.kiriacoulis.com
www.top-yacht.com
www.cosmosyachting.com
www.nautilus-yachting.com
www.seafarersailing.co.uk

Cruising Guide
Turkish Waters and Cyprus Pilot

Websites
www.tourismturkey.org
www.dmi.gov.tr (Turkish Meteorological Office daily surface charts and forecasts)

Local time	UTC +3
	Summer time: last Sunday in March to last Sunday in October
Buoyage	IALA A
Currency	Turkish Lira (TL)
Electricity	230V, 50Hz

Diplomatic missions	
UK	312 4553344
USA	312 4555555
Australia	312 4599500
Canada	312 4092700
South Africa	312 4464056
New Zealand	312 4679054

Communications	
IDD 90	IAC 00

Emergency numbers		
112	Ambulance 101	Police 100

Lycian tombs near Dalyan on Turkey's south coast.

UKRAINE

SET ON THE NORTHERN SHORES of the Black Sea, Ukraine stretches from the Danube Delta to the Azov Sea. This landlocked sea is reached through a narrow cut, the 24-mile-long Kerch Canal, on the western shores of which stands the old city of Kerch. The eastern side is Russian territory. Cruising along the 400-mile-long Ukrainian coast is restricted and foreign yachts may only stop at official ports of entry. As there are few natural harbours, this restriction is not a great impediment. All larger ports have a yacht club with adequate facilities. The spectacular Crimean coast is backed by a high range of mountains that drop precipitously into the sea. Where the imposing cliffs give way to sandy beaches the shore is lined with resorts that have developed thanks to Crimea's subtropical micro-climate engendered by the barrier created by those massive mountains. The ports along this stretch all have historic associations: Yalta, Balaclava, Sevastopol. The latter enjoys a free port status whose military facilities are shared with the Russian Navy. West of the Crimea, at the head of a wide

bay, stands Odessa. Built in the early nineteenth century in the Italian Renaissance style, it is regarded as one of the most beautiful ports in the world, with the monumental Potemkin Steps being its most famous feature. Sailing west towards Romania and the wide Danube Delta, you pass close to Moldova, Ukraine's western neighbour, which has only a token exit to the Black Sea on the right bank of the Dniester river.

✦ COUNTRY PROFILE

For much of its history Ukraine has been dominated by Russia, and in 1922 Ukraine was incorporated in the USSR. Independence was declared in 1991 after the dissolution of the Soviet Union. Democracy has remained elusive due to perpetual political infighting. A peaceful mass protest, the 'Orange Revolution', in 2004 forced the authorities to overturn a rigged presidential election, but the political situation remains unstable, the nation being torn between the temptation to join the EU and NATO, or to maintain its

The Swallow's Nest fortress near Yalta.

traditional links with Russia and thus a more reliable access to Russia's natural resources.

The population is 46 million, the majority being Ukrainian, with a large Russian minority of some 8 million. Ukrainian is the official language, but most people also speak Russian. The capital is Kiev.

✦ CLIMATE

The climate is temperate, with hot summers and cold winters. The south coast of the Crimean peninsula enjoys mild winters. Along the coast, the winds are very much influenced by the surrounding landmass and in summer there is a daily pattern of land and sea breezes. An onshore breeze comes up around midday and usually dies by dusk, to be followed by a land breeze. July is the warmest month, with average temperatures of 24°C/75°F.

✦ FORMALITIES

PORTS OF ENTRY	
Odessa	46°28′N 30°45′E
Feodosia	45°02′N 35°24′E
Sevastopol	44°37′N 33°30.8′E
Yalta	44°30′N 34°10′E
Ocadov	46°63′N 31°55′E
Izmail	45°37′N 28°87′E
Yevpatoria	45°11′N 33°22′E
Skadovsk	46°06′N 32°54′E

Yalta: When contacting the authorities by radio on arrival, you should insist on being allowed to go directly to Artek Marina and complete formalities there.

Sevastopol: Formalities must be completed at Sevastopol Free Port, 3 miles west of Sevastopol.

Odessa: Yachts should enter the harbour by the Vorontzov gateway and are normally directed to Odessa Marina (46°29.5′N 30°45′E) to complete formalities. The marina monitors Channel 73 and its call sign is Odessa Nautical Club.

Everyone should remain on board until officials have visited the yacht. The services of an agent are normally required.

All visitors must have a visa obtained in advance. It has been possible in the past to obtain visas in Istanbul with help from Ataköy Marina.

A document should be requested from customs on arrival listing all the ports to be visited. You may have to check out of Crimea when leaving that area to cruise the rest of Ukraine.

While sailing along the coast, although yachts are not allowed to stop, you should take great care never to stray outside Ukraine territorial waters (12 miles). The Ukrainian Sea Guard tracks the movement of foreign vessels on radar. It must be contacted every time a yacht changes location.

✦ FACILITIES

Facilities are comparatively good at Odessa Marina, which has moorings for visitors, fuel, electricity and some repair facilities, including a slipway. Provisioning in Odessa is quite good, with both fresh produce markets and several supermarkets. The Golden Symbol Marina at Balaclava (44°29.2′N 33°35.9′E, Tel: +38 0692 637 224) is to be preferred to the nearby naval port of Sevastopol. There are basic facilities and some repairs possible at Artek Marina, close to Yalta.

Cruising Guide
Cruise Ukraine

Local time	UTC +2
	Summer time: last Sunday in March to last Sunday in October
Buoyage	IALA A
Currency	Hryvnia (UAH)
Electricity	230V, 50Hz

Diplomatic missions
UK	44 4903660
USA	44 4904000
Canada	44 5903100
South Africa	44 2277172
New Zealand	44 537 7444

Communications
IDD 380	IAC 810

Emergency numbers
112	Ambulance 103	Police 102

NORTHERN EUROPE

THE RELATIVELY SHORT CRUISING SEASON in the North and Baltic Seas seems to discourage sailors from distant countries making the long and often demanding voyage to Northern Europe, so most visiting yachts tend to hail from neighbouring countries. For those who are prepared to face the challenge of reaching those shores, the effort is amply rewarded by the wealth of cruising opportunities. Almost equalling the Mediterranean in variety is the Baltic Sea whose traditional sailing areas in Finland and Sweden have been supplemented by the new cruising grounds in Poland, the former East Germany, the Baltic republics and Russia. The number of local yachts has greatly increased in these previously closed countries as people are now free to enjoy the pleasures of cruising whether in home waters or the favoured grounds of Finland and Sweden. Outside the Baltic, cruising opportunities in the areas that are bordering on the North Sea are almost as plentiful even if sailing conditions are more demanding as they are influenced by Atlantic weather systems. Denmark with its countless off-lying islands, southern Norway and southwestern Sweden are scenically attractive and well endowed with sheltered ports and anchorages. The North Sea shores of Germany have less appeal, while in the Netherlands and Belgium cruising is mainly limited to inland waters.

The favourable sailing season lasts from June until the end of August, although some hardy local sailors will sail virtually at any time of the year. The weather during summer is pleasant with long days and short nights, the sun hardly setting in the northern regions. Generally it is still too cold in April to enjoy cruising, especially if you are used to warm-water sailing, so cruises should not be planned to start before May at the earliest. The best weather can be expected in late June and July. Midsummer Day has a special significance to all peoples bordering on the Baltic, especially in Scandinavia where there are popular feasts held on that day. By the end of August, the sailing season is virtually over and it is time to either start sailing south or make arrangements for leaving the boat to winter in one of these countries.

Because the sailing season in the Baltic is so short, this can cause logistical problems for those who come from further away, whether Southern Europe or America. An early summer passage from mainland USA should be planned to stay within the area of the prevailing westerly winds, and ideally to sail non-stop to a North European destination. A detour via the Azores, while enjoyable, would considerably lengthen the voyage. Northbound voyages from the Mediterranean can be planned to start in late spring, and either to stay offshore from Cape St Vincent, or sail in short legs along the

The 20 mile long Schlei connects the Baltic Sea to the city of Schleswig and is a favourite sailing ground in perfectly sheltered waters.

majority of yachts sailing between those two bodies of water. Another point of access to the Baltic Sea is the Götha Canal, a system of lakes and man-made canals that crosses Southern Sweden. Both canals are free of overhead bridges and can be transited without lowering the mast. There are many other opportunities for inland cruising in Northern Europe, whether in the lakes and rivers of Poland and Sweden, or the extensive river and canal systems in Germany, the Netherlands and Belgium.

Repair facilities are generally good and each country has at least one major yachting centre where more difficult jobs can be undertaken. Facilities in the former East Germany have greatly improved, while those in Poland and the three Baltic republics are slowly getting up to Western European standards. Only Russia still has a long way to go, especially in regard to the complicated formalities to which visiting boats are still subjected.

Portuguese and Spanish coasts before crossing the Bay of Biscay to the English Channel. The alternative is to reach the Baltic or North Sea via the rivers and canals of France, Netherlands and Germany, along a route that passes through some of the most attractive areas of Western Europe. The voyage can be easily completed in six weeks and has the added attraction of being able to leave the Mediterranean as early as April and arrive at your chosen destination at the beginning of summer. There are now specialist companies transporting the masts of sailing yachts from the point of departure to the chosen port of arrival, thus making the long trip much easier.

The major waterway and convenient shortcut joining the North and Baltic Seas is the Kiel Canal, which is used by the

Yachting is well developed in the Nordic countries, Denmark, Norway, Sweden and Finland, all of which have considerable boating communities. The traditional links between these places are strong and yachts flying one of the Nordic flags enjoy many concessions when cruising in other Nordic countries. In the most popular areas, the cruising associations of the Nordic countries have laid down their own moorings, which may be used by visitors within certain limitations as there are various concessions and special arrangements that apply only to yachts from Nordic countries.

BELGIUM

SITUATED BETWEEN FRANCE and the Netherlands, Belgium has a 40 mile long coastline facing the English Channel and the North Sea. It has only four harbours along its coast: Nieuwpoort, Ostend, Blankenberge and Zeebrugge. Antwerp can be reached through the Scheldt river. The Belgian coast is fringed by sandbanks running parallel to the coast, which makes for a dangerous landfall in strong west to northwesterly winds.

Most foreign cruising yachts visit Belgian ports either as a convenient place to stop while sailing north or south through the English Channel, or are British yachts on a cross-Channel trip. The Belgian inland waterway system, which is connected to the extensive European canal network, gives access to many interesting inland destinations. One of these is the medieval town of Bruges (Brugge), which can be reached without having to lower the mast via a sea lock in the port of Zeebrugge that gives access to the city via the Boudewijnkannal.

✦ COUNTRY PROFILE

This region was originally inhabited by the Celtic Belgae, then was conquered by the Romans and later invaded by the Franks and Vikings. During the Middle Ages small independent principalities developed, while the towns became important commercial centres. Later occupied by France, it was only in 1831 that the kingdom of Belgium was recognized as an independent state. In 1948 the Benelux customs union was formed with the Netherlands and Luxembourg, and Belgium was one of the founding members of the EU. In 1993 the constitution was revised to make Belgium a federal state, with considerable autonomy given to the three regions of Flanders, Wallonia and Brussels.

The population is 10.4 million. The Flemish, who comprise the majority (60 per cent), live mainly in the north. The other 40 per cent, the French-speaking Walloons, live in the south, and there is a small German minority in the east. French, Flemish and German are spoken as official languages

Bruges

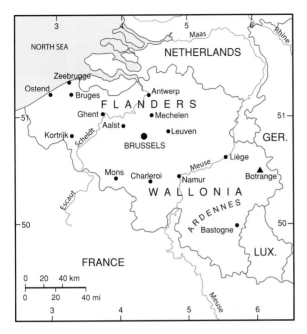

certificate of competence and insurance. If arriving by one of the canals, you should report to the first navigation tax office, usually situated in a lock. An inverted black cone must be displayed when motorsailing.

✦ FACILITIES

The best facilities are concentrated in the ports of Ostend, Antwerp, Zeebrugge and Nieuwpoort, all of which have yacht clubs and docking facilities. Most repair facilities are available, as well as chandlery, fuel and provisions.

✦ CHARTER

Sea Level is based in Antwerp and has a small fleet of both power and sailing yachts. Channel Sailing is based in Ostend, with a fleet of a dozen yachts that are available as bareboat or crewed charters.

> www.sealevel.be
> www.channelsailing.be

Cruising Guides
Inland Waterways of Belgium
Cruising Almanac
North Sea Passage Pilot

Website
www.visitbelgium.com

Local time	UTC +1
	Summer time: last Sunday in March to last Sunday in October
Buoyage	IALA A
Currency	Euro (EUR)
Electricity	230V, 50Hz

Diplomatic missions	
UK	2 2876211
USA	2 5082111
Australia	2 2860500
Canada	2 7410611
South Africa	2 2854400
New Zealand	2 5121040

Communications	
IDD 32	IAC 00

Emergency number
112

in their respective regions. The capital is Brussels, which is also the administrative centre of the EU.

✦ CLIMATE

The climate is mild, humid and wet. The prevailing summer winds are northerly. During the rest of the year winds are mostly west or southwest and most winter gales are from the southwest. The warmest month is July, with an average temperature of 17°C/63°F. The best time for sailing is early summer, which is relatively dry.

✦ FORMALITIES

PORTS OF ENTRY	
Antwerp	51°14′N 4°25′E (Channel 22)
Nieuwpoort	51°09′N 2°43′E (Channels 9, 16)
Ostend	51°14′N 2°55′E (Channel 9)
Zeebrugge	51°20′N 3°12′E (Channel 71)
Blankenberge	51°19′N 3°08′E (early April to late September)

EU and Schengen regulations apply. The maritime police should be visited on arrival if coming from a non-Schengen country. Full documentation is required, including a

DENMARK

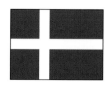

WITH ITS INDENTED SHORES bathed by both the North and Baltic Seas, Denmark is made up of the Jutland Peninsula and many islands. The Danish archipelago contains over five hundred islands that provide excellent cruising opportunities. The islands are scattered over a relatively small area, and distances between harbours are never more than a few miles. The most popular cruising destination is the archipelago south of the larger islands of Fyn and Sjaelland. In the northern part of Jutland are the perfectly sheltered waters of Limfjord, connecting the North Sea to the Kattegat. The only Danish islands lying in the Baltic Sea proper are Bornholm and tiny Christiansø, a favourite cruising ground for sailors from neighbouring Sweden and Germany.

A convenient point of access for yachts coming from the south is the Kiel Canal, which avoids a long detour around the north of Denmark and leads straight into the heart of the Danish archipelago. The capital Copenhagen is located on the east coast of Sjaelland and its closeness both to the Swedish coast and the entrance into the Baltic makes it a convenient point for starting a cruise in any direction. North of Copenhagen lies Helsingor (Elsinor), famous for Kronborg or Hamlet's Castle. The Sound between Denmark and Sweden is the main waterway between the North Sea and the Baltic, so there is very heavy shipping in this area, which explains the popularity of the Kiel Canal as an attractive alternative.

✦ COUNTRY PROFILE

Denmark has been populated since Neolithic times and was one of the most developed areas in the Bronze Age. The Vikings, who inhabited the region that is now Denmark and

Norway, were greatly feared for their raids and pillaging of the coasts of Western Europe. In 1397 the Union of Kalmar brought Denmark, Norway, Sweden, the Faeroes, Iceland and Greenland under the rule of the Danish king. The Union broke up in the sixteenth century and the next 200 years were marked by a succession of regional wars. Gradually the once extensive Danish Empire lost most of its territories, although the ties with the Faeroe Islands and Greenland have been maintained and these are now self-governing entities with weakening links to the Danish Crown. The monarchy's powers were limited in 1849, when a liberal constitution was adopted. Denmark joined the EU in 1973.

The population is 5.5 million. As well as Danish, almost everybody speaks English. The capital is Copenhagen.

✦ CLIMATE

Denmark has a temperate climate and the winters are cold. The sailing season is limited to the summer, May to September, which can be fairly wet, although enjoying long days. The prevailing winds in summer are westerly and this is also where most gales come from. The strongest winds are generated by Atlantic systems and the west coast is always quite windy. Gales may occur at any time of the year, but are less frequent and less severe in summer. July and August are the warmest months, with average day temperatures of 18°–24°C/64°–75°F.

✦ FORMALITIES

As a member of the EU and Schengen Agreement, those regulations apply. Only vessels arriving from outside the EU or the Schengen area need to contact immigration.

A certificate of competence is compulsory for the captain of any boat with a displacement of over 20 tons.

✦ TRAFFIC RESTRICTIONS

Shipping traffic between the North Sea and the Baltic is heavy and vessels must use the correct lane in traffic separation zones. These are in operation in the northern part of the Sound between Elsinore and Hälsingborg in Sweden, at the Great Belt between Korsør and Sprogoe by Hatter Barn, and the Baltic Sea south of Gedser. In Danish waters the transit route for very large vessels runs from the Skaw/Skagen to the Moen SE light vessel northeast of Gedser. In some areas larger ships on the transit route are confined by their draft to deep water routes; these are in the Great Belt east of Samsoe,

Copenhagen.

PORTS OF ENTRY

Jutland:	Esbjerg	55°28´N 8°26´E	Frederikshavn	57°26´N 10°33´E	Fredericia	55°34´N 9°45´E
	Haderslev	55°15´N 9°30´E	Holstebro (Struer)	56°30´N 8°36´E	Horsens	55°51´N 9°52´E
	Kolding	55°30´N 9°30´E	Randers	56°28´N 10°03´E	Skive	56°34´N 9°02´E
	Sonderborg	54°55´N 9°47´E	Thisted	56°57´N 8°42´E	Vejle	55°43´N 9°33´E
	Ålborg	57°03´N 9°55´E	Århus	56°09´N 10°13´E		
Funen (Fyn):	Odense	55°25´N 10°23´N	Svendborg	55°03´N 10°37´E		
Sjaelland:	Copenhagen	55°42´N 12°37´E	Elsinore	56°02´N 12°37´E	Kalundborg	55°41´N 11°05´E
	Korsør	55°20´N 11°08´E	Koge	55°27´N 12°12´E	Naestved	55°14´N 11°45´E
Lolland:	Rodbyhavn	55°39´N 11°21´E	**Bornholm:** Ronne	55°06´N 14°42´E		
Falster:	Nkobing	54°46´N 11°52´E				

along the east coast of Langeland, and northeast of Gedser. Yachts should avoid the transit and deep water routes where large vessels have little ability to manoeuvre.

✦ FACILITIES

Yachting facilities are good throughout the country, and there are either marinas or fishing harbours with moorings for yachts conveniently situated within a short distance of each other. There are good service and repair facilities close to all major harbours and marinas. The best repair facilities are concentrated in and around Copenhagen where there are several marinas, the best known of which is Langelinie, close to the centre of the capital. Also near Copenhagen is the marina at Svanemoellen. There are good facilities at Århus and Ålborg.

Harbours get very crowded in summer and it is customary to raft up extensively, often several boats deep. The Danish Yachting Association has mooring buoys (marked with 'DS' in black letters) in several harbours, but visiting sailors who are not members of DOCA, or have not made the necessary arrangements in advance, may not use such buoys.

Visiting foreign vessels are welcome to contact DOCA/ Danish Ocean Cruising Association for help and advice. Tel: +45 86182495 or email: ftlf@ftlf.dk.

In the summer, send emails to: formand@ftlf.dk.

✦ CHARTER

There are various charter operators with bases in Copenhagen, Århus, Nyborg, Øer-Ebeltoft and Bogense. Some of these work in association with Swedish or Norwegian firms, and may agree to one-way charters.

www.scancharter.dk
www.dancharter.dk
www.norseadventure.com

Cruising Guides
The Baltic Sea
Cruising Almanac
Cruising Guide to Germany and Denmark
Landsort-Skanor (includes the island of Bornholm)

Website
www.visitdenmark.com

Local time	UTC +1
	Summer time: last Sunday in March to last Sunday in October
Buoyage	IALA A
Currency	Danish Krone (DKK)
Electricity	30V, 50Hz

Diplomatic missions
UK	3544 5200	Canada	3348 3200
USA	3341 7100	South Africa	3918 0155
Australia	7026 3676	New Zealand	3337 7702

Communications
IDD 45	IAC 00

Emergency numbers
112	Police 114

ESTONIA

SITUATED BETWEEN LATVIA AND RUSSIA, Estonia is a country of low-lying land and many lakes as well as numerous offshore islands, the two largest being Saaremaa and Hiiumaa. The best cruising opportunities are along the Moon Sound that links the Gulf of Riga with the north of Estonia and the Gulf of Finland. Both the Estonian islands in the Gulf of Riga and the offshore islands provide many daysailing options. Ever since it opened its doors to foreign cruising boats, Estonia has been gaining in popularity as an attractive destination.

✦ COUNTRY PROFILE

The history of Estonia has been one of constant struggle to maintain independence and national integrity against the predatory intentions of her larger neighbours. The Vikings passed through the territory in the ninth century. Over the next few centuries, the Danes and Swedes tried to extend their influence. In 1721, Sweden ceded Estonia to Russia, but the Estonian people resisted all attempts of russification, and in 1918 declared their independence. In the Second World War Estonia was invaded by the Red Army and became part of the USSR. It was only after the collapse of communism in 1991 that Estonia gained independence from its mighty neighbour for the second time in its history. In 2004 Estonia joined the EU.

The population is 1.3 million, with Russians making up a quarter. Both Estonian and Russian are spoken. The capital is Tallinn.

✦ CLIMATE

The climate is moderate, with cool summers and mild winters thanks to the influence of the Baltic Sea, which does not freeze for prolonged periods. The warmest months are July and August, with an average temperature of 16°C/61°F.

✦ FORMALITIES

As Estonia is a member of the EU and Schengen Agreement, those regulations apply. Yachts arriving from outside the Schengen area must complete formalities at a port of entry. The authorities must be informed in advance as officials are not permanently based in some places.

✦ FACILITIES

There are many harbours and yacht clubs with good facilities, although some are only accessible by shallow draft vessels. Fuel and water are available in all major ports. The Tallinn Olympic Centre in Pirita has good facilities with water, fuel and electricity. Limited facilities are also available at Pärnu, which has a marina with spaces for visitors.

✦ CHARTER

Yacht Charter has a small fleet of sailing boats, while Bell Marine rents out small powerboats. Both companies are based in Tallinn.

www.interyachtcharter.com/estonia-tallinn.htm
www.bellmarine.ee

PORTS OF ENTRY			
Ruhnu	57° 47´N 23° 16´E	Haapsalu	58° 57´N 23° 32´E
Nasva	58°13´N 22°23´E	Lehtma	59°04´N 22°42´E
Veere	58°27´N 22°05´E	Lohusalu	59°24´N 24°12´E
Vergi	59°36´N 26°06´E	Kuressaare	58°15´N 22°30´E
Pirita	59°28´N 24°29´E	Narva-Joesuu	59°28´N 28°02´E
Pärnu	58°23´N 24°29´E	Roomassaare	58°13´N 22°31´E
Sõru	58°42´N 22°32´E	Dirhami	59°12´N 23°30´E
Heltemaa	58°52´N 23°03´E		

Cruising Guides
The Baltic Sea   Estonian Cruising Guide

Websites
www.visitestonia.com   www.marinas.nautilus.ee
www.agentuur.ee/sadamad (Estonian Marine Tourism Association)

Local time   UTC +2
Summer time: last Sunday in March to last Sunday in October
Buoyage   IALA A
Currency   Estonian Kroon (EEK)
Electricity   230V, 50Hz

Diplomatic missions
UK	6674700	Australia	6509308
USA	6688100	Canada	6273311

Communications   **Emergency numbers**
IDD 372   IAC 00   112   Police 110

FINLAND

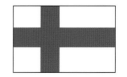

FINLAND, KNOWN AS SUOMI to its inhabitants, is situated in the northeast of Europe and is one of the largest countries on the continent. From the rolling agricultural lands of the south, the land rises towards the hills and dense forests of the north, to the peatlands and treeless fells of Lapland. Finland has some 62,000 lakes, and nearly 3,000 miles of coastline, off which lie thousands of islands, including the Åland archipelago.

Cruising opportunities in Finland are infinite, either through the many islands or on some of the lakes, the larger of which are navigable. Sailing in these sheltered and tideless waters, meandering between islands covered in trees, past little villages and tiny harbours, is a unique experience. A very special cruising ground is the Saimaa Lake and the area surrounding it, which is accessed via the Saimaa Canal. This is a huge landlocked area where you can sail in perfectly sheltered waters. Another popular area is the offlying Åland archipelago with its galaxy of over six thousand islands and islets.

Although the sailing season is rather short, from about the end of May until early September, summer days benefit from almost perpetual daylight. With a highly developed and top-quality boatbuilding industry, some foreign visitors only sample the cruising delights of Finland when they arrive to take delivery of their new craft and then sail them to warmer waters. This has changed dramatically in recent years as cruising activity has grown exponentially in the Baltic not only with sailors from neighbouring countries, but also from further afield.

✦ COUNTRY PROFILE

Little is known about the first inhabitants who arrived in Stone Age times, although the present-day Lapps are probably their descendants. Between two and three thousand years ago the Ugro-Finn tribes moved west from Asia into what is now Finland, Estonia and Hungary. In the Middle Ages Sweden was a continual aggressor, and gradually Finland came under the control of the Swedish kings. The rise of Russia as a great power led to an expansionist policy westwards, and early in the nineteenth century Finland was incorporated into the Russian Empire. The Russian Revolution was the chance the Finns had been waiting for and an independent Finland was declared in December 1917. The interwar years saw a conflict with Sweden over the possession of the Åland Islands, which were eventually awarded to Finland by the League of Nations.

In November 1939 Stalin declared war on Finland and, in spite of the Finns resisting fiercely, they had to cede much of Karelia to the Soviet Union. In the Second World War Finland fought on the side of Germany and had to pay heavy reparations to the USSR after the war. Finland joined the EU in 1995.

Finland is a sparsely inhabited country with a population of 5.3 million. There is a substantial Swedish-speaking minority. Finnish and Swedish are the two official languages and Lappish (or Saame) is a semi-official language. The majority speak Finnish, which is an Uralic language related to Hungarian and Estonian. The capital is Helsinki.

CLIMATE

Much of the country lies north of the Arctic Circle, but the influence of the Baltic Sea keeps the climate milder than on the same latitude elsewhere. The mildest part of the country in winter is the southwest coast and its off-lying islands. The weather is changeable in all seasons and sailing is limited to the summer when the winds are variable and usually light. The warmest month is July, with an average temperature of 17°C/63°F.

✦ FORMALITIES

Foreign yachts arriving in Finland must keep to the customs routes, which are channels marked on the charts that lead from the open sea to a border control station. Boats must

Islands, islands everywhere...

report to the nearest station along the channel or, if there is no station, to the nearest port of entry for customs and immigration formalities. No other routes may be taken, nor should anyone land or come aboard before customs clearance has been completed.

The relevant station should be alerted by radio on Channels 16 or 68, or by telephone, approximately one hour before arrival. Pleasure craft entering Finland from a country that is a signatory to the Schengen Agreement, or those departing from Finland for such a country, may enter and exit without calling at a border crossing point and without being subjected to border controls other than random checks. Pleasure craft sailing between Finland and a country not part of the Schengen Agreement must always visit a border crossing point for a border check.

The Finnish Coast Guard have the right to stop and search all pleasure boats in Finnish territorial waters. The code sign L is the stopping sign, which may be given visually or by sound.

✦ BORDER CONTROL STATIONS

Santio 60°28′ N 27°43′ E. Tel: +358 (0) 71 872 6110.
Haapasaari 60°17′ N 27°12′ E. Tel: +358 (0) 71 872 6139
Suomenlinna (Fairway from Helsinki lighthouse past Harmaja) 60°09′ N 24°59′ E. Tel: +358 (0) 71 872 6310
Hanko (Fairway past Russarö or fairway past Morgonlandet) 59°49′ N 22°55′ E. Tel: +358 (0) 71 872 6450
Maarianhamina/Marienhamn (Fairway past Korsö or Nyhamn) 60°06′ N 19°56′ E. Tel: +358 (0) 71 872 7230
Nuijamaa (on Saimaa Canal) 60°58′ N 28°31.6′ E

Helsinki: Clearance is done at Suomenlinna Island, southeast of Helsinki, at a special clearance station for yachts. On arrival in the Helsinki traffic control area all vessels must maintain permanent watch on Channel 71.

Schengen Agreement regulations apply to visa requirements. Although a member of the EU, Finland still imposes strict limits on the amount of alcoholic drinks or tobacco products that may be imported free of duty. Excess amounts of alcohol must be declared to customs.

According to Finnish law, lifejackets must be available for everyone on board.

There are numerous nature conservation areas where landing and anchoring are forbidden either all year round or during the bird breeding season (1 April–31 July). These restrictions are marked on the nautical charts and displayed on shore. Sailing is permitted in the national parks of the Archipelago Sea, Tammisaari archipelago, the eastern part of the Gulf of Finland, Bay of Bothnia, Linnansaari, Koli, Päijänne and Kolovesi.

All fishing (except with a handheld line or rod without a reel) requires an official licence, which may be bought from any post office or bank.

✦ THE SAIMAA CANAL

The Saimaa Lake area is now open to foreign yachts and is reached through the Saimaa Canal. As the canal is leased to Finland by Russia, transiting this canal requires passing through Russian waters. Therefore all crew must carry valid passports. Arriving from the coastal waters of Finland, an inspection is carried out at the Coast Guard stations of either Santio or Haapasaari Island. Alternatively, if arriving directly from international waters, the entry inspection is carried out at the customs quay in Nuijamaa. Vessels used to be required to have a Russian pilot between the island of Vihrevoi and Brusnitchnoe lock, but this is no longer applied as instructions are conveyed in Russian or English by VHF radio. Inspection by the Russian authorities may still be carried out

at these locations. It is possible to visit the Russian city of Vyborg if you have obtained a Russian visa in advance. The canal stretches from Lappeenranta and Imatra in the south via Savonlinna to Varkaus, Kuopio and Joensuu in the north, all of the Saimaa area being navigable. The length of the canal from Lappeenranta to the Gulf of Finland is 23 miles (43km), with eight locks.

The Saimaa Canal Authority should be contacted two weeks in advance of arrival to request permission for transit. Tel: +358 5 458 5170, Fax: +358 204 48 3110, email: saimaankanavan.hoitokunta@fma.fi.

✦ Åland Islands

These islands have an autonomous status and some of the regulations may differ from those applicable in Finland. Customs allowances for boats arriving from EU countries or from Finland itself are the same as those for arrival from non-EU countries. The islands have plenty of visitors' harbours and there are many public jetties where temporary stops can be made. Natural harbours outside of inhabited areas should only be used in emergencies and with the landowner's permission.

✦ FACILITIES

Provisioning is very good in all ports, as well as on the larger islands where there are villages or holiday resorts. Fuel is available in all ports. Most coastal towns have visitors' harbours and yacht clubs usually have a few berths reserved for those visiting. The standard of services varies and repair facilities are available only in the largest ports. With a developed boatbuilding industry, repair facilities are of a high standard. The most comprehensive range of repair services is to be found in and around Helsinki. Other yachting centres are at Turku, Hanko, Rauma, Loviisa and Pietarsaari, the latter being the home of the famous Nautor Swan yachts. Good facilities are also available in Åland, with several marinas, the largest being in the capital, Marienhamn.

✦ CHARTER

While some charter operators only cover a relatively small area, such as the south coast of Finland or the Åland Islands, some companies include Sweden and mainland Finland in their sphere of activity. Midnight Sun Sailing has a large fleet of both sail and motorboats, with bases in Taalintehdas (Finland), Marienhamn (Åland Islands) and Stockholm (Sweden). Finlandia and Fenton Sailing offer both skippered and bareboat charters.

> www.midnightsunsailing.fi
> www.finlandiasailing.fi
> www.kolumbus.fi/fenton

Cruising Guides
The Baltic Sea
Landsort-Skanor (includes Åland)
Käyntisatamat Besökshamnar A Suomen Rannikot (this is a book of harbours published by the National Board of Navigation and the Finnish Travel Association)
Finnish Cruising Club Handbook of Anchorages in Åland and the South Coast
Finnish Harbour Plans (3 volumes) (published by Turun Partio-Sissit; see publisher's website)

Websites
www.raja.fi (Finnish Border Control website with details of border control procedures)
www.fma.fi (Finnish Maritime Administration)
www.fmi.fi (Finnish Meteorological Institute – marine weather forecasts)
www.veps.fma.fi/portal/page/portal/fma_fi_en/services/fairway s_canals/the_saimaa_canal (information on the Saimaa Canal)
www.satamakirja.fi (Turun Partio-Sissit, publisher)

Local time	UTC +2
	Summer time: last Sunday in March to last Sunday in October
Buoyage	IALA A
Currency	Euro (EUR)
Electricity	230V, 50Hz

Diplomatic missions

UK	9 2286 5100	Canada	9 228530
USA	9 616250	South Africa	9 6860 3100
Australia	9 4777 6640	New Zealand	2 4701817

Communications		Emergency number
IDD 358	IAC 00	112

Sunset in the Finnish archipelago

GERMANY

GERMANY OCCUPIES A CENTRAL POSITION in Europe with coasts on both the North and Baltic Seas. Two of the most important navigable rivers in Europe, the Rhine and the Danube, flow through German territory. Although one of the most active sailing nations in Europe, Germany was not a major cruising destination, but all this changed after the reintegration of the Baltic shores and islands of former East Germany, which dramatically altered the country's cruising potential. Even so, many German sailors still seem to prefer to do their cruising away from home. One such popular area is the IJselmeer in the Netherlands, which is reputed to have more resident German yachts than locally owned ones. Sailing opportunities on the North Sea coast are rather limited and the restrictions imposed on cruising in some of the German Frisian Islands have limited the number of visiting yachts ever further.

The situation on the Baltic coast is now very different with the addition of a hitherto little-frequented corner of the Baltic to the German cruising portfolio. Although much of the coast is low lying, there are many attractive spots in the sheltered lagoons hidden behind sandbars and tree-lined spits. Picturesque hamlets nestle on the shores of placid lagoons (called Bodden in German), which are the habitat of many species of birds. A popular cruising area covers the islands of Hiddensee, Usedom, Rügen and the surrounding Greiswalder Bodden. Starting at Usedom, the Peenestrom Canal leads into Stettiner Haff (Zalev Szczecinski in Polish), an area of many inlets and small harbours shared with neighbouring Poland.

The only contact many visiting yachts have with Germany is the Kiel Canal (Nord-Ostsee Kanal in German), the convenient shortcut from the North Sea to the Baltic Sea. Formalities are completed at Brunsbüttel at its western end and at Holtenau on the Baltic side. At each end there are waiting areas for boats to moor and also temporary docking places all along the canal. Those with time in hand may be tempted to sail up the narrow estuaries that lead to the nearby Hanseatic ports of Hamburg, Bremen or Lübeck.

✦ COUNTRY PROFILE

The eastern part of Charlemagne's empire was divided in 843 when the Kingdom of the Franks became the nucleus of the German state. In the tenth century the Holy Roman Empire was formed, uniting the crowns of Germany and Italy. In 1273 a Hapsburg was elected Holy Roman Emperor, and the dynasty expanded its territories, although it was unable to establish centralized rule in a region where over three hundred and fifty small states were endlessly fighting one another. The Holy Roman Empire was finally destroyed during the Napoleonic wars, and in 1815 a German Confederation was formed, dominated by Austrian and Prussian rivalry. In 1871 the unified German state was established under the rule of Kaiser Wilhelm I. After defeat in the First World War, there followed a period of political instability, popular unrest and hyperinflation. The 1930s saw the rise of the National Socialist Party whose leader – Adolf Hitler – imposed a totalitarian regime. Defeat in the Second World

The water world of Hiddensee, a small island near Rügen.

✦ FORMALITIES

EU and Schengen visa regulations apply.

There are strict anti-pollution regulations in force throughout Germany, but particularly in the Baltic Sea, and the disposal of garbage anywhere in the Baltic is forbidden. Degradable foodstuffs can only be disposed of overboard more than 12 miles from shore.

An inverted black cone must be displayed when motor-sailing, and failure to do so can result in an instant fine. Yachts must carry on board the German collision regulations and the Kiel Canal Rules.

Kiel Canal

Laboe, at the entrance of the Kiel fjord, is the customs clearance point for yachts entering or leaving Germany via the canal. If only transiting the Kiel Canal, but not visiting Germany, the 3rd substitute pennant must be flown.

The 54-mile-long canal has strict rules, which are rigidly applied. The canal has locks at each end, there is a minimum height limit of 39.6m (129ft) and a speed limit of 8 knots. Yachts are expected to make the transit under power, and although sailing is permitted in certain parts, tacking is forbidden and the engine must be on standby.

The light signal applicable to yachts at the end locks are:

Fixed red light: entry forbidden.
Flashing white light: proceed.

Yachts approaching the Brunsbüttel lock should call Kiel Canal 1 on Channel 13. Those approaching the Kiel-Holtenau lock should call Kiel Canal 4 on Channel 12.

Boats capable of 6 knots under power can complete the transit in one day. This transit must be accomplished during daylight hours. If this is not possible, a convenient place to stop halfway is at Rendsburg, which has a yacht club. The transit fee is payable at Holtenau locks. Because of the high amount of radio traffic, the traffic control office or lock-keepers should only be called on VHF radio if absolutely necessary. Transiting vessels must monitor the correct frequencies permanently (Channel 2 between Brunsbüttel and Breiholz and Channel 3 between Breiholz and Kiel-Holtenau). When waiting at locks, yachts must stay behind commercial vessels.

War led to the country being divided by the victors into four separate zones of occupation. In 1949 the Federal Republic (West Germany) and the Democratic Republic (East Germany) were formed. In 1989 the East German Communist Party relinquished power, the infamous Berlin Wall was pulled down, and the two Germanies were officially reunited in 1990.

The German-speaking population is 82 million, with several small ethnic minorities. Bonn was the capital of the Federal Republic, but after reunification Berlin has reverted to its role as national capital.

✦ CLIMATE

Germany has a temperate climate, with warm summers and cold winters. Summers have more settled weather in the Baltic than on the North Sea coast, with more sunshine and thunderstorms on hot days. In the North Sea the predominating winds are southwest or west. The incidence of gales is low in summer, but increases in spring and autumn. Winds on the Baltic coast are variable. The warmest months are July and August, with an average temperature of 17°C/63°F.

PORTS OF ENTRY

Bremerhaven	53°33´N 8°35´E	Brunsbüttel	53°54´N 9°08´E	Cuxhaven	53°52´N 8°42´E
Emden	53°21´N 7°11´E	Flensburg	54°48´N 9°26´E	Hamburg	53°33´N 9°58´E
Laboe (Kiel)	54°24´N 10°13´E	Norddeich	53°38´N 7°10´E	Rostock	54°05´N 12°07´E
Stralsund	53°19´N 13°06´E	Travemunde	53°58´N 10°54´E	Wilhelmshaven	53°31´N 8°09´E
Wismar	53°54´N 11°28´E	Frisian Islands: Borkum	53°35´N 6°40´E	Norderney	53°42´N 7°10´E

Boats getting ready to exit the Kiel Canal.

Within the limits of the canal, yachts may moor only at the following: Brunsbüttel yacht harbour (km: 1.8), waiting area on the north side of Brunsbüttel (km: 2.7), waiting area at Dückerswisch (km: 20.5), waiting area before Gieselau lock (km: 40.5), waiting area at Obereider Lake (Rendsburg harbour) (km: 66), waiting area at Borgstedter Lake (km: 70), dock at Flemhuder Lake (km: 85.4), Holtenau yacht harbour (km: 98.5).

✦ FACILITIES

The best facilities are concentrated around the main sailing centres of Hamburg, Kiel and Bremerhaven. Good repair services are available in all these places and also a comprehensive range of marine supplies. Marinas and small boatyards are spread around the entire coastline and also in the rivers and estuaries. Facilities are also improving in the former East Germany. A marina has opened at Rügen, and this has good repair facilities. Fuel, water and LPG are easily available and so are provisions. Cuxhaven Marina, at the mouth of the Elbe, is a good place to prepare for the transit of the Kiel Canal. Kiel is the place to stop for boats transiting the canal in the opposite direction.

✦ CHARTER

There are several companies operating in both the North and Baltic Sea, the latter being more popular due to the much greater choice of cruising options. There are also several operators offering a wide range of boats to charter on the extensive inland lakes and water systems. PCO (Privat Charter Ostsee) is based in Kiel and operates a large fleet of sailing yachts. Some websites are in German only.

www.pc-ostsee.de/yachtcharter/infos/bareboat_
 charter.html
www.mare-yachtcharter.de

www.yachtcharter-dagen.de
www.aqua-yachtcharter.de

Cruising Guides
The Baltic Sea
Cruising Almanac
Cruising Guide to Germany and Denmark

Websites
www.germany-tourism.de
www.kiel-canal.org/pages_english/sport/notes_KIEL-CANAL.pdf
 (instructions for pleasure craft)

Local time	UTC +1
	Summer time: last Sunday in March to last Sunday in October
Buoyage	IALA A
Currency	Euro (EUR)
Electricity	230V, 50Hz

Diplomatic missions

UK	30 204570	Canada	30 203120
USA	30 2385174	South Africa	30 220730
Australia	30 8800880	New Zealand	30 206210

Communications

IDD 49	IAC 00

Emergency number
112

The old lighthouse at Lindau on Lake Constance.

LATVIA

LATVIA LIES BETWEEN ESTONIA, the Russia enclave of Kaliningrad, Belarus and Lithuania. The 300-mile-long coastline is made up mostly of low sandy beaches, backed by dunes and pine forests. Although it offers fewer cruising opportunities than its neighbours, Latvia's capital Riga is one of the most attractive cities in Europe. The city lies on the banks of the River Daugava and its old district from the Hanseatic era has a medieval flavour that has been surprisingly unaffected by its recent Soviet past. Eksportosta Marina is a convenient base from which to visit the city, whose old district is within walking

distance. Riga is bisected by the Daugava, and the river's mouth connects it to the Gulf of Riga to the northwest of the city. Also to the north of the city are two large lakes, Jugla and Ķīšezers, which are linked to the River Daugava. Another navigable river is the Lielupe.

✦ COUNTRY PROFILE

Baltic tribes, ancestors of today's Latvians, settled the region in around 2000 BCE, and in antiquity were known as traders in amber, which was found in large quantities on the shores of the Baltic Sea. Later the region came under the control of Germans, Poles and Swedes, and in the nineteenth century was part of the Russian Empire. Independence was finally achieved in 1918, but after the Second World War Latvia fell under Soviet control and it was only when the USSR disintegrated that the country regained its sovereignty. Latvia joined the EU in 2004. Just over half of the 2.2 million population are Latvians, nearly one-third being Russian, with various smaller minorities. The capital is Riga.

✦ CLIMATE

The climate is temperate owing to the influence of the Baltic Sea. Summers are warm and the weather in spring and autumn is mild. The warmest months are July and August, with an average temperature of 17°C/63°F. Rainfall is common throughout the year, with the heaviest rainfall in August.

✦ FORMALITIES

PORTS OF ENTRY

Riga	56°58´N 24°06´E	Ventspils	57°24´N 21°33´E
Liepāja	56°32´N 21°01´E	Roja	57°30´N 22°49´E
Salacgriva	57°45´N 24°21´E		

Latvia has no border checks for yachts arriving from the EU as it is a member of the Schengen Agreement, whose regulations apply. Boats coming from a non-EU country should proceed either to Roja or the Andrejosta Yacht Centre in Riga.

✦ FACILITIES

The capital of Riga has a number of yacht harbours along the river. The Andrejosta Yacht Centre has the best facilities and is close to the centre of town. Ventspils is an old port with many attractive medieval buildings and a designated dock for visiting yachts. The port of Roja, at the entrance to the Roja river, has a number of floating pontoons, some repair facilities, a crane and chandlery. Liepāja is a commercial harbour that has a yacht basin with reasonable facilities. There is also a yacht harbour at the resort of Jūrmala. Anchoring is not permitted in the navigation channels approaching any ports.

✦ CHARTER

The only yachts for charter are crewed, and offer tours of Riga and the surrounding area: www.latviayacht.com

---

Cruising Guide
The Baltic Sea

Websites
www.latviatourism.lv
www.jahtas.lv (information on marinas in the Riga area)
www.latviancoast.lv/en (information on Latvian coast and ports)

Local time   UTC +2
Summer time: last Sunday in March to last Sunday in October
Buoyage   IALA A
Currency   Latvian Lat (LVL)   **Electricity** 230V, 50Hz

Diplomatic missions
UK	6777 4700	Australia	6722 4251
USA	6703 6200	Canada	6781 3945

Communications   **Emergency number**
IDD 371 IAC 00   112

LITHUANIA

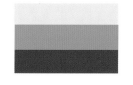

LITHUANIA IS THE LARGEST and most populous of the three Baltic Republics. Its coast is only 60 or so miles long, half of which is on the Curonian Spit (Kurši Nerija in Lithuanian, Kurskaya Kosa in Russian). This long, narrow sandbar separates the landlocked Curonian Lagoon (Kurskiy Zaliv in Russian) from the Baltic Sea. The northern half of the spit belongs to Lithuania, while the southern half is Russian. The lagoon can be entered at its northern end at Klaipéda, the country's only seaport. This medieval city was founded in the thirteenth century by the Teutonic Knights and named Memelburg, its modern name of Memer having been changed to Klaipéda.

Shallow-drafted boats can use the inland waterway that links Klaipéda with Kaliningrad in the Russian enclave wedged between Poland and Lithuania. An interesting stop is the port of Nida (Nidden) on the lagoon side of the Curonian Spit. Cruising opportunities are few, although shallow-drafted boats may explore parts of this large inland body of water fronting Kaliningrad.

◆ COUNTRY PROFILE

The original inhabitants were the Balts, who settled in the region around 2000 BCE. Through alliances and conquests, by the end of the fourteenth century Lithuania had become the largest state in medieval Europe. But gradually it diminished in importance, and by the end of the eighteenth century it had been absorbed into the Russian Empire. Occupied by the German army during the First World War, at the end of that war Lithuania proclaimed its independence from Russia. After the Second World War, Lithuania was incorporated into the Soviet Union, but in the 1980s Lithuania started to press for independence. While this was initially resisted by Russian troops, by 1991 Lithuania had become the first Baltic state to declare independence. The population numbers 3.6 million, the majority being Lithuanians, and there are Russian, Polish, Belorussian and Ukrainian minorities. The official language is Lithuanian, although minorities have the right to the official use of their language. The capital is Vilnius.

◆ CLIMATE

The climate is temperate, although considerable temperature variations are experienced. Summers are generally mild. Winters can be very cold and are dominated by cold winds sweeping in from Russia. July is the warmest month, with an average temperature of 17°C/63°F.

◆ FORMALITIES

Approaching Klaipéda seaport it is necessary to contact the State Border Guard on Channel 73. Port control should then be called on Channels 9 or 10. Yachts normally go to the Klaipéda Sailing Centre. There are no border controls for boats coming from the EU. As Lithuania is a signatory to the Schengen Agreement, those regulations apply. Occasionally yachts may be met by a police launch and escorted to the immigration dock for a random check.

◆ FACILITIES

A shallow channel leads to the Klaipéda Sailing Centre (Smiltyne Yacht Club), which has good docking and repair facilities. Visiting yachts may find a more convenient berth closer to the centre at Old Castle Marina. A small new marina, Klub Budys, is also central. Those visiting Nida may find a berth at the Nida Yacht Club.

PORT OF ENTRY	
Klaipéda	55°43′ N 21°07′ E

Cruising Guide	The Baltic Sea

Websites
www.portofklaipeda.lt/en.php/for_yacht_owners/254
www.nerija.lt/en (information on the Curonian Spit)
www.visitneringa.com   www.tourism.lt/en

Local time	UTC +2
Summer time: last Sunday in March to last Sunday in October	
Buoyage	IALA A
Currency	Lithuanian Litas (LTL)
Electricity	230V, 50Hz

Diplomatic missions
UK	5 2462900	Australia	5 2123369	USA	5 2665500

Communications	Emergency number
IDD 370 IAC 00	112

NETHERLANDS

THE NETHERLANDS, OR LOW COUNTRIES, certainly deserve the name. Much of the country is very low and parts of it are in fact under sea level, so preventing the encroaching waters has always been a battle, and over the centuries a system of dykes were built to protect the land. It is not correct to call the country 'Holland' as the Netherlands is divided into 12 provinces and this name applies to only two provinces, North Holland and South Holland.

In the Netherlands you are never far from water and the centre of the country is occupied by the IJsselmeer, formerly called Zuiderzee until it was dammed off from the sea and became a lake. Most cruising is concentrated in the IJsselmeer, Wadden Sea and Frisian Islands, an area of sand dunes, intricate channels and picturesque ports. The western part has deeper water and a keeled yacht can go everywhere, whereas a shallow-draft vessel is essential in the eastern part. At IJmuiden vessels can pass through a lock to reach the IJsselmeer and Amsterdam. Another excellent cruising ground is Zeeland, in the southwest, which can be reached via the Walcheren Canal at Vlissingen (Flushing) or through the locks on the Oosterschelde.

Cruising along the North Sea coast is more challenging on account of the strong tides, sandbanks and onshore winds. From Vlissingen in the southwest to Delfzijl in the northeast, there are several good yacht harbours in which to shelter in bad weather. The Frisian Islands have many sheltered harbours on the east side facing the Wadden Sea, which are good starting points to explore the liquid world of the Netherlands.

✦ COUNTRY PROFILE

This region was already peopled by Celtic and Germanic tribes when conquered by the Romans in 57 BCE. Later, Saxons and Franks settled in different parts. The ninth century brought Norman invasions and the country was divided into feudal duchies and earldoms. The twelfth and thirteenth centuries saw the rapid growth of the towns, their prosperity being based mainly on the cloth trade. By the fifteenth century royal marriages and inheritances led to the area being united and brought under Spanish rule. After a long struggle against Spain, the United Provinces were eventually recognized as an independent country in 1648.

The United Provinces later became known as the Netherlands and they made rapid economic progress, becoming a leading maritime power. They established a vast commercial empire in the East Indies, South Africa and parts of Brazil. However, wars with neighbouring powers weakened the state and the eighteenth century led to a decline. The Netherlands were neutral in the First World War, and occupied by Germany in the Second; after the latter, the Netherlands enjoyed an economic recovery. The country is one of the six founding members of the EU.

The population is 16.7 million. The Hague is the political capital, but Amsterdam is the commercial capital. Dutch is the official language.

✦ CLIMATE

The climate is temperate and the coastal regions have milder weather. In summer the higher midday temperatures often generate thunderstorms accompanied by heavy showers. Average temperatures in July and August are 18°C/64°F, but highs of 30°C/80°F are not uncommon. The prevailing winds are west or southwest, and most gales come from those directions.

✦ FORMALITIES

Some ports have customs only in the summer months, such as Roompot Sluis and Oost Vlieland.

Vlissingen: The port is entered through a set of lock gates and there is a marina close to the lock.
Scheveningen: The marina is located in fishing harbour number 2. The Port Authorities should be contacted on Channel 14 for permission to enter the harbour.
IJmuiden: There can be a strong tidal stream at the entrance. The Seaport Marina IJmuiden is located at the south pier.
Den Helder: Yachts can moor in the Royal Naval Yacht Harbour.
Delfzijl: The yacht harbour is 3 miles south of the old harbour entrance.

Traditional barge sailing in Zeeland.

PORTS OF ENTRY

Vlissingen (Flushing)	51°27´N 3°35´E	Breskens	51°24´N 3°34´E
Veerhaven (De Maas/Rotterdam)	51°54´N 4°29´E		
Scheveningen	52°06´N 4°16´E	IJmuiden	52°27´N 4°35´E
Den Helder	52°58´N 4°47´E	Terneuzen	51°20´N 3°49´E
Terschelling	53°22´N 5°13´E	Vlieland	53°18´N 5°06´E
Lauwersoog	53°25´N 6°12´E	Delfzijl	53°20´N 6°54´E

EU and Schengen visa regulations apply. Although an EU country, all boats arriving from overseas must report to the nearest customs office. Customs will issue a certificate of entry valid for 12 months. During this period a yacht may leave and re-enter the Netherlands, showing the certificate on each re-entry. Foreign yachts must be officially registered in their country of origin.

Any person steering a vessel endorsed for inland waterways capable of more than 9 knots or over 15m (49ft) LOA must have an international certificate of competence. There are restrictions concerning signalling pistols. Very-type flare pistols must be accompanied by a firearms certificate issued in the country of origin.

✦ INLAND WATERWAYS

Access to the inland waterways is from the ports of Veerhaven and IJmuiden. From Den Helder there are connections with Amsterdam via the Noord-Holland Canal and the River Zaan. There is access with a standing mast through Vlissingen via the canal through Walcheren with connections to Dordrecht and Rotterdam.

Yachts are required to have on board a copy of the Inland Waters Police Regulations, which are in force on most of the inland waters, the Zeeland channels (except the Western Scheldt, where its own shipping regulations apply), the IJsselmeer and Wadden Sea.

✦ FACILITIES

As can be expected in a water-based nation with a great maritime past, facilities are good everywhere. There are shops in all the small ports and fuel is available in most marinas and on the dock in harbours. Along the coast there are marinas with repair facilities at Vlissingen and Breskens, both of which are convenient if coming from the south. There are good facilities also in Zeeland, particularly at the marinas at Zierikzee and Colijnsplaat. Den Helder has good facilities, while there are smaller marinas and a limited range of repair services at Terschelling and Vlieland. Across the Wadden Sea on the mainland, Harlingen is a picturesque port with good facilities. In the north, the best facilities are at Delfzijl, which is reached by sailing up the Ems.

✦ CHARTER

While the number of companies offering yachts for charter in the North Sea is quite small, there is a wider selection of both companies and boat types operating in inland waters. Albatros Yacht Charter operates in both areas with a fleet of sailing yachts, sports fishing boats, and also some traditional flat-bottomed shallow-drafted boats ideal for the Friesland lakes. Andijk Yacht Charters has bases in the IJsselmeer and the Wadden Sea, with a fleet of fast yachts for those interested in racing.

www.yachtcharter-albatros.com
www.andijkjachtverhuur.nl

Cruising Guides
Cruising Guide to the Netherlands   North Sea Passage Pilot
Cruising Almanac   Almanac Deel 2

Website
www.holland.com

Local time   UTC +1
Summer time: last Sunday in March to last Sunday in October
Buoyage   IALA A
Currency   Euro (EUR)   **Electricity**   30V, 50Hz

Diplomatic missions
UK	70 4270427	Canada	70 3111600
USA	70 3102209	South Africa	70 3924501
Australia	70 3108200	New Zealand	70 3469324

Communications   **Emergency number**
IDD 31   IAC 00   112

NORWAY

NORWAY OCCUPIES THE WESTERN SIDE of the Scandinavian Peninsula, a mountainous, forested land, with mighty glaciers and deep dramatic fjords cutting into the coast. Much of the country is above the Arctic Circle, so summer days are very long and for a very short period the sun never sets in the country's northernmost extremity. The wild grandeur of the fjords gives Norway one of the most beautiful sceneries in the world. A chain of islands, skerries and rocks stretching parallel to the western coast and extending almost as far as the North Cape provide sheltered waters for cruising – Lofoten being the most attractive of them. The majestic fjords are less suited for cruising as the anchorages are extremely deep and the winds alternate between flat calms and violent gusts blowing almost vertically down the sides of the sheer cliffs.

Although the figure for cruising boats visiting the northern part of Norway is still low, mainly because of the short sailing season and unreliable weather, there has been a marked increase in the number of yachts attracted to cold water cruising. Svalbard is now a favourite destination for intrepid sailors attracted by the challenge of sailing as close as possible to the North Pole. More benign conditions are encountered in Southern Norway, which is easily reached from neighbouring Denmark and Sweden. In summer, the weather here can be quite pleasant and when a stationary high parks itself over the area, as happens occasionally at the height of summer, balmy temperatures, picturesque scenery and cosy anchorages provide the perfect ingredients for a leisurely cruise.

✦ COUNTRY PROFILE

From the eighth to the eleventh centuries the Vikings reigned supreme in the coastal regions of northwest Europe, often terrorizing the coasts of the British Isles, Netherlands and France. In the thirteenth century Norway expanded westwards and established control over the Faeroes, Orkneys, Shetlands, Iceland and Greenland. Intrepid Norse vessels were roaming the North Atlantic five centuries before Columbus sailed to the continent which later became known as America, but was known as Vinland by the Norse mariners.

The Union of Kalmar of 1397 brought Norway under Danish rule, and it remained under Danish control for three centuries. In the 1814 Treaty of Kiel, Denmark ceded Norway to Sweden, and in 1905 Norway gained independence. In 1972 the Norwegians voted in a referendum against Norway's entry into the EU and again in 1994. The large North Sea gas and oil deposits have brought considerable prosperity in recent years.

The population is 4.7 million. Apart from Norwegians, who form the majority, a minority of Sami (Lapps) live in the northernmost region of Finnmark. Norwegian and Lappish are the main languages. The capital is Oslo.

✦ CLIMATE

Although the interior has an Arctic climate, conditions along the west coast are milder, thanks to the Gulf Stream that reaches as far as the extreme north of Norway. The Gulf Stream stops the sea from freezing and keeps harbours open

Occasionally winds can be strong and the weather can change very suddenly.

✦ FORMALITIES

PORTS OF ENTRY

All Norwegian ports are ports of entry except those in military areas. Only the most frequently used ports are listed here.

Bergen	60°24´N 5°19´E	Haugesund	59°25´N 5°16´E
Stavanger	58°58´N 5°44´E	Egersund	58°27´N 6°00´E
Mandal	58°02´N 7°28´E	Kristiansand	58°09´N 8°00´E
Lillesand	58°15´N 8°23´E	Oslo	59°54´N 10°43´E
Fredrikstad	59°12´N 10°57´E	Tonsberg	59°16´N 10°25´E
Moss	59°26´N 10°40´E		

Although Norway is not a member of the EU, it is a member of the Schengen Agreement and therefore the Schengen visa regulations apply.

Yachts from Nordic countries do not need to make a customs declaration provided they are not carrying an excess of dutiable stores. Yachts from other countries should report immediately on arrival at a port of entry.

There are strict restrictions on the import of alcohol and a heavy tax is imposed for excess amounts. Yachts may remain for up to one year, after which VAT must be paid.

Starting in 2010, leisure craft skippers must have a certificate of competence.

A fishing licence is compulsory and foreigners may only use hand gear.

There are various conservation areas for sea birds along the coasts, access to which is prohibited between 15 April and 15 July.

Skippers of boats cruising the fjords should pay careful attention to the height restrictions caused by overhead cables.

The courtesy flag must be flown from sunrise to sunset only, but not before 0800 and not after 2100. It is considered very discourteous to leave the flag flying after sunset.

✦ FACILITIES

Provisioning is good everywhere, but the price of food is high. Fuel is available in all ports. LPG containers may be refilled only in the main centres such as Oslo, Stavanger and Bergen. There are docking or mooring provisions for visiting yachts in all ports, although occasionally a dock may be privately owned and permission to use it should be obtained first. Some yacht clubs have visitors' moorings.

The widest range of repair facilities are in the main yachting centres such as Oslo, Stavanger and Bergen, which also have the best docking facilities. A convenient marina is Her Bern Marina situated in the old Akers shipyard in the

throughout the year. Summer temperatures can be surprisingly high, with an average of 15°C/59°F – and with peaks above 30°C/90°F being not uncommon. The weather is generally rainy and changeable on the west coast, while less rainy and more predictable in the southeast. Northerly winds prevail in summer along the coast, while in winter there is a predominance of southerly winds. Winds tend to strengthen during the afternoons. Summer weather beyond the Arctic Circle, both in continental Norway and farther north, is unreliable. Visibility on most days can be poor, with low mist.

centre of Oslo. Vallo Marina is one of the biggest marinas in the Oslo area and has a good range of repair services.

Good facilities are also available at Kristiansand. There are several marinas in both Bergen and its vicinity. Askoy Seilforening in Kaggevikane near Askoy has good mooring facilities all year round, both ashore and in the water.

SVALBARD

A tempting destination beyond continental Norway is Svalbard. This is the correct name for the entire group of Norwegian islands north of 74°N among which Spitsbergen is the largest. The Spitsbergen Treaty of 1920 established full Norwegian sovereignty over the archipelago. Under the terms of the treaty, the signatory states have rights to exploit mineral deposits and other natural resources. As a result, Russian settlements grew up at Barentsburg and Pyramiden, the latter abandoned in 1998.

Svalbard now attracts around thirty yachts every year and the numbers are steadily increasing as more Scandinavian sailors head north for a summer cruise. This wild and rugged area is a spectacular cruising ground. Thanks to the Gulf Steam, Spitsbergen's west coast is mostly free of ice during summer. Conditions in Spitsbergen are most favourable at the height of summer, between early July and the middle of August, which benefits from several weeks of uninterrupted daylight, and the midnight sun becomes a constant feature. Besides its stark beauty, which is best appreciated while sailing close to the shore, Spitsbergen's great attraction is the opportunity to take long walks ashore to climb glaciers or observe the rich wildlife. There are plenty of sheltered anchorages where a boat can be left safely unattended while trekking inland. Centuries of whaling, sealing and fishing have left their mark and signs of former habitations, as well as shallow graves, can be seen in many places. Occasionally you may come across a polar bear, and the compulsory gun that visitors must carry everywhere in Svalbard may come in useful.

A distant but achievable destination is the tiny island of Moffen located at 80°01.5´N, 4°30´E, and about as close as you can sail to the North Pole – although current climate changes might soon make it possible to sail even closer to that elusive point.

Climate

Svalbard has a severe Arctic climate for most of the year, but of a milder variety during summer. The high summer can be reasonably pleasant, although – even in summer – snow rarely melts at sea level. The best time to visit is between early July and the middle of August when the average temperature is 5°C/41°F. This is also the driest period.

Formalities

PORT OF ENTRY	
Longyearbyen	78°13.68´N 15° 36.58´E

There is a pontoon for visiting yachts next to the main wharf. The Governor's office (Sysselmannen) deals with all formalities and the office is nearby. There are a number of special requirements for vessels sailing to Spitsbergen. As a safety precaution, all cruising boats must register with the authorities in Longyearbyen, which can be done by radio. Details of the special regulations for visitors can be obtained by writing to the Governor of Svalbard, 9170 Longyearbyen. Email: firmapost@sysselmannen.no.

There is also a requirement for special search and rescue insurance to be taken out by all boats going to eastern Spitsbergen. Also compulsory is having a gun to protect the crew from possible attacks by polar bears. Those who do not possess a gun can hire one locally.

The same Schengen regulations apply as in mainland Norway.

Facilities

Facilities in Longyearbyen are reasonably good. Fuel and water are available on the main dock, which is reserved for commercial shipping. Yachts must stay at anchor. Provisioning in Longyearbyen is good, as are repair facilities.

Ny Ålesund (78°55´N 11°56´E) prides itself on being the northernmost settlement in the world. Ny Ålesund is a centre for Arctic research; it has a permanent population of only about a dozen people, but their numbers are swollen each summer by scientists involved in various research programmes. There is a dock where yachts may berth. There are limited supplies, and also both water and fuel on the main quay (managed by the port captain). Rubbish can be left at the dock.

Blind Channel on the south mainland coast.

◆ CHARTER

Local operators offer a range of sailing yachts to cruise anywhere in Norway, from the relatively calm waters of Southern Norway to the spectacular fjords of the west coast and even as far north as Svalbard. Norse Adventure and Boreal Yachting offer bareboat charters in Northern Norway and also skippered voyages to Svalbard. Several privately owned yachts offer charters during summer in Svalbard, and some also operate voyages to and from the mainland.

www.swedecharter.com
www.arcticyacht.com
www.boreal-yachting.com
www.norseadventure.com

Cruising Guides
Norway
Norwegian Cruising Guide
Guest Harbours in Norway (issued by the Norwegian Tourist Board)
Cruising in Norwegian Waters (issued by the Norwegian Tourist Board)

Websites
www.visitnorway.com
www.sysselmannen.no (Governor of Svalbard)

Local time	UTC +1
	Summer time: last Sunday in March to last Sunday in October
Buoyage	IALA A
Currency	Norwegian Krone (NOK)
Electricity	230V, 50Hz

Diplomatic missions
UK	2313 2700
USA	2244 8550
Australia	6758 4848
Canada	2299 5300
South Africa	2327 3220
New Zealand	6711 0030

Communications
IDD 47	IAC 00

Emergency numbers
112

Svalbard: Satellite (Iridium and Inmarsat) phones do not support the emergency line 112; instead, the officer on duty must be called at a local number:

+ 47 79 02 43 00 (weekdays from 0830 to 1530)
after hours: +47 79 02 12 22 or +47 41 40 31 65.

Magdalene Glacier on Spitsbergen.

POLAND

FROM THE BAY OF POMERANIA in the west to the Gulf of Gdansk in the east, the low-lying Polish coastline covers some 250 miles of mostly unspoilt countryside. There are no natural harbours to speak of, but marinas are spaced at convenient distances making daysailing along the coast possible. The main cruising attractions are at the two extremes: Zalev Szczecinski, the large inland lake in the estuary of the River Odra (Oder) that takes its name from the nearby port of Szczecin, and the traditional sailing area centred on the two ports of Gdansk and Gdynia, both of which have large local sailing communities and facilities to match. Sea-going vessels can access Gdansk Bay and the Baltic Sea by way of the Vistula Lagoon and the Strait of Baltiysk. There are no height restrictions here, but other parts are only accessible to smaller sailing boats.

The attractive port of Gdansk, which in 1997 celebrated its millennium, is a medieval Hanseatic city and the marina is located right in its historic centre. The surrounding Amber Coast, so named after the large amount of amber found here, has a number of small harbours, some set in national parks. Poland is connected to the European waterways by two canal and river systems that give access to its many inland lakes as well as two routes to Berlin.

Of all the communist countries in Europe, Poland was the first to allow its sailors to cruise away from home. Although most confined their sailing to neighbouring Baltic countries, a few Polish yachts sailed as far as the Caribbean – and some even went around the world.

◆ COUNTRY PROFILE

Although Poland has been inhabited since 3000 BCE, the country's history really began in the fifth century CE when Slavs settled between the Oder and Elbe rivers. During its tumultuous early history Poland was at times a great power, and at others was partitioned and ruled by powerful neighbours. It regained independence in 1918, only to be overrun by Germany and the Soviet Union during the Second World War. Although being in the Soviet sphere of influence, following the war, its government was relatively tolerant. In the 1980s the independent trade union, Solidarity, was formed, and became a political force that by 1990 had swept through parliamentary elections and the presidency. Poland then joined NATO in 1999 and the EU in 2004.

The population is 39 million, being mainly Polish, with small Ukrainian and Belorussian minorities. Polish is spoken, and Warsaw is the capital.

◆ CLIMATE

The climate is more continental than temperate, with cold winters and moderately warm summers when the days are long and the Baltic coast can have pleasant variable breezes. The warmest month is July, with an average temperature of 17°C/63°F. Like much of Central Europe, the weather can be changeable at all times of the year.

The medieval Hanseatic port of Gdansk.

✦ FORMALITIES

As Poland is a signatory to the Schengen Agreement, these visa regulations apply. However, all foreign boats must clear in and out with customs and immigration at all major ports. Channels 10 and 12, as well as 16, are used for contacting ports.

✦ FACILITIES

The best yachting facilities are in the marinas at Gdynia, Szczecin, Trzebiez, Leba, Gdansk and Gorki Zachodnie. The best places for visitors are at Gdynia, which has four yacht clubs, each with its own docking facilities, and Gdansk Marina on Motlawa river in the city centre. Various marinas

PORTS OF ENTRY

Swinoujscie	53°55´N 14°16´E	Nowe Warpno	53°44´N 14°17´E	Trzebiez	53°40´N 14°31´E
Dziwnow	54°01´N 14°44´E	Kolobrzeg	54°11´N 15°33´E	Darlowo	54°27´N 16°23´E
Ustka	54°35´N 16°51´E	Leba	54°46´N 17°33´E	Wladyslawowo	54°48´N 18°26´E
Hel	54°36´N 18°48´E	Jastarnia	54°42´N 18°41´E	Gdynia	54°31´N 18°33´E
Gdansk	54°23´N 18°38´E	Gorki Zachodnie	54°22´N 18°47´E		
On inland waterways to/from Germany:					
Osinow Dolny (Hohensaaten) 52°52´N 14°08´E		Widuchowa	53°07´N 14°23´E	Gryfino	53°15´N 14°30´E

Peenestrom Channel: Yachts coming from Germany through the Stettiner Haff (Zalew Szczecinski in Polish) must show their papers to the Polish patrol boat stationed at the border, marked by buoys, before continuing to Nowe Warpno, Trzebiez or Swinoujscie for clearance. Continuing south on the Odra/Oder river can only be done after having completed formalities.

Gdansk: Port Control must be contacted to request permission to navigate in the port area.

There are restricted areas near Ustka and along the Hel Peninsula, where passage is occasionally prohibited. Hel fishing harbour is now open to foreign yachts.

in the Szczecin area have facilities for lowering the mast before continuing south on the Odra/Oder river to the German inland waterways.

✦ CHARTER

Several bareboat charter companies operate on the inland lakes, and there are a few privately owned yachts available for charter in the open sea that can be contacted via the yacht clubs in Gdansk or Gdynia.

Cruising Guide
The Baltic Sea

Websites
www.poland.gov.pl
www.archipelago.nu/SKARGARD/ENGELSKA/POLAND/marina. htm (marinas in Poland)

Local time	UTC +1
	Summer time: last Sunday in March to last Sunday in October
Buoyage	IALA A
Currency	Polish Zloty (PLN)
Electricity	230V, 50Hz

Diplomatic missions	
UK	22 3110000
USA	22 5042000
Australia	22 5213444
Canada	22 5843100
South Africa	22 6256228
New Zealand	22 5210500

Communications	Emergency numbers
IDD 48 IAC 00	112/999

RUSSIA

THE MAIN ATTRACTION on the relatively short Baltic coast is the historic city of St Petersburg. It is built on the banks of the River Neva and is one of the most beautiful cities in the world. Founded by Tsar Peter the Great at the beginning of the eighteenth century, it was meant to equal in splendour the cities that had impressed the young monarch during a visit to Western Europe. St Petersburg became the modern capital of Russia and also its main naval base. There are few cities in the world that match its architectural perfection.

The area between St Petersburg and Kronstadt, called the Nevskaya Guba and protected by a long sea wall, is a popular cruising ground for yachts from the many local sailing clubs.

The three main yacht clubs are the Central River Yacht Club, the St Petersburg Sea Yacht Club and the Naval Yacht Club. There are more yacht clubs in the St Petersburg area and the number of sailing aficionados, as well as that of yachts, is rapidly increasing. All this bodes well for visiting sailors as the authorities become more accommodating and yachting facilities widen in scope and quality.

The Baltic enclave of Kaliningrad (formerly Königsberg), a small region of Russia squeezed between Lithuania and Poland and separated from the rest of Russia, has also opened up to foreign visitors. Kaliningrad is the only Russian Baltic Sea port that is ice-free. It is located at the mouth of the navigable Pregolya river, which empties into the Vistula Lagoon.

An enjoyable detour on the way to or from St Petersburg can be made to the old town of Vyborg, at the southern end of the Saimaa Canal. The canal is administered by Finland and gives access to Saimaa Lake, which in the past was barred to foreign vessels.

A much longer and far more challenging detour is needed to reach the Arctic ports of Murmansk and Archangelsk as it involves a long voyage around the whole of Norway. Most sailors seem to be deterred from doing this not just by the weather conditions, but also by the need to have a special permit to visit those strategic ports. In recent years a few foreign yachts were given permission to sail along the entire Arctic coast of Russia through the NE passage all the way to the Kamchatka Peninsula in the North Pacific.

Similarly, it may soon be possible for more foreign yachts to be given access to Russia's extensive inland waterway system, which makes it feasible to take a yacht from the Baltic all the way to the Black Sea through the heart of this interesting country. A network of waterways connects the White Sea to the Baltic and the Black Seas by way of two lakes, six artificial inland seas, several rivers and man-made canals. The Russian Inland Waterways Act, passed in 1936, still prevents foreign vessels from using these inland waterways. Some exceptions have been made, and a few foreign yachts managed to sail from St Petersburg to the Black Sea or from Murmansk to St Petersburg. The Act has been amended to allow foreign vessels to transit the 30-mile canal from Vyborg to the Saimaa Lake in Finland, or to be able to reach some inland ports, such as Kaliningrad.

For Russia's Black Sea coast and general information on Russia, see page 57.

✦ CLIMATE

The climate along the Baltic coast is less harsh than in the interior, although the winters can be very cold, with freezing temperatures for several months. Summer weather in the Baltic is very pleasant, with white nights in June and good sailing breezes. The warmest month is July, with an average temperature of 17°C/63°F.

Summer evening in St Petersburg.

✦ FORMALITIES

Foreign vessels are only allowed to visit ports listed on the visa or official invitation. The most important Baltic ports of entry are listed here:

St Petersburg	59°53′N	30°13′E
Kaliningrad (Königsberg)	54°43′N	20°13′E
Kronstadt	59°59.6′N	29°42.5′E
Vyborg	60°42′N	28°45′E

Kronstadt: The territorial waters boundary is crossed by the sea channel between Gogland Island and Moshniy. At that point, the Coast Guard should be called on Channels 16 or 10. Unless instructed otherwise, yachts should proceed to the terminal at Fort Konstantin for clearance. It is forbidden to stop at any of the islands in Russian waters. The approach channel passes through the southern flood barrier. Entry formalities can also be completed at Kronstadt, although yachts have been allowed to continue to St Petersburg and complete formalities there.

St Petersburg: The 36-mile-long shipping channel is through the Kronstadt Passage and Morskoy Canal. One should call St Petersburg Radio on Channels 16 or 26 before reaching Buoy 19 and request instructions. Once in St Petersburg, the clearing dock is located near the main cruise ship terminal. After formalities have been completed, the yacht may proceed to one of the chosen yacht clubs.

Kaliningrad: Passport control and customs are located at the ferry terminal in Baltiysk on the south side of the entrance into the channel. In 2008 the Baltiysk border control post was closed and yachts were instructed to proceed to Pionerskiy Marina for clearance into Russia. A buoyed channel 22 miles long connects the sea with the city.

An alternative entry point into Russia is from Finland via the Saimaa Canal (see Finland, page 82, for further details). This route has been reported as being simpler and with easier formalities.

All nationalities must obtain a visa in advance. An official invitation is necessary and may be obtained from an accredited Russian travel company, a yacht club or from a private individual. The visa is a separate document which lists the dates and ports for which permission has been granted. It has been recommended to apply for a multiple business visa as this allows for greater flexibility in the timing of a yacht's arrival.

You need to apply for a double entry business visa to visit both Kaliningrad and St Petersburg or any other Russian port. The St Petersburg Central River Yacht Club can facilitate visas.

Yachts must clear in and out of each port, and the authorities must be notified 24 hours in advance of departure.

✦ FACILITIES

Provisioning can be quite difficult as the yacht clubs are often out of town. There is usually a good selection of fresh produce, with better quality in markets than in stores. Fuel may be difficult to obtain, so it is best to order it via a yacht club or agency.

The best facilities are at the St Petersburg Sea Yacht Club (SPYC), but access is difficult without local assistance. Facilities are also good at the Central River Yacht Club (CRYC), which is the biggest in Russia. It has easier access from the sea and is closer to the city centre. The depth limits are 2.5m (8ft) for the SPYC and 4m (12ft) for the CRYC. One other local club is the Naval Yacht Club, near the marine passenger terminal. Baltiec Yacht Club is a new marina project in St Petersburg.

Yacht building is gathering pace as there is a great demand for cruising boats. Repair facilities are good as local mechanics are used to improvising when parts are not available. Marine supplies and spares are in short supply. Ordering essential spares from abroad and clearing them through customs can take a very long time.

Visiting boats have used the services of the Kaliningrad Yacht Club located in the Kaliningrad Lagoon, about 10km (6 miles) from the city centre. Access is through the Sea Canal and the maximum depth is 1.8m (6ft) at low water, and 2.4m (8ft) at high water. Yacht Club Pionerskij has the only marina-type facility in the Kaliningrad area. There is a small marina in Vyborg.

✦ CHARTER

Sunny Sailing is the only charter company reported to operate in the St Petersburg area. Email: central4@solpar.ru. www.solpar.ru.

Cruising Guide
The Baltic Sea

Websites
www.yachtsman.spb.ru/en (St Petersburg Central River Yacht Club)
www.spyc.org (St Petersburg Yacht Club)
www.baltclub.org (Baltiec Yacht Club)
www.archipelago.nu/SKARGARD/ENGELSKA/RUSSIA/marina.htm (Russian marinas in the Baltic Sea)

SWEDEN

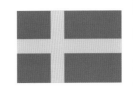

SWEDEN FORMS HALF OF THE SCANDINAVIAN PENINSULA, the tongue of Sweden dividing the Baltic from the North Sea. The country's two coastlines offer an infinite variety of cruising. On the west coast the most attractive cruising area is from the Norwegian border to Göteborg. On the east coast the most picturesque region is the Stockholm archipelago and the area to the south of it, a galaxy of tens of thousands of small islands, some barren, others verdant, and many uninhabited. These waters, peppered with challenging shallows and rocks, call for careful navigation, but the rewards of sailing in such a secluded spot with hundreds of pretty anchorages to choose from are ample. Although the area is very popular with both Swedish and visiting yachts, it is so large that it rarely feels crowded.

The most popular cruising destination on the west coast is the island of Marstrand, home of the Royal Göteborg Sailing Club, a scenic rocky island dominated by a huge stone fortress. Cars are banned from the island. Another popular cruising spot in the Stockholm archipelago is Sandhamn Island, home of the Royal Swedish Sailing Club, a relaxed place, where cars are also banned, and the famous Round Gotland Race starts and finishes here.

Besides the coastal waters and offshore islands, large areas of Sweden are broken up by many lakes, some of the large ones being linked to each other and accessible to sailing yachts. The shortcut provided by the Trollhätte and Göta Canals, a scenic route that allows a yacht to sail from one side of Sweden to the other without the necessity of dropping one's mast, provide the opportunity to amble through the picturesque Vänern and Vättern lakes. Also accessible by yacht is Lake Mälaren close inland from Stockholm, a historic area with many well-preserved buildings from days gone by. There are secluded anchorages and pretty villages throughout Southern Sweden, making it one of the most attractive cruising destinations in Europe.

Very different scenery greets those who venture north into the Gulf of Bothnia, which can be reached either through the Södra Kvarken, the straits that separate the Åland Islands (which belong to Finland) from the Swedish mainland, or through the Väddö Canal. The season is shorter in this northern area and the best time to cruise is July, as June still tends to be cold, while by late August the weather already heralds the coming winter.

✦ COUNTRY PROFILE

Inhabited from prehistoric times, from the eighth century CE onwards, the Swedish Vikings raided Russia and the surrounding region. In the Union of Kalmar in 1397, Queen Margaret I of Denmark united the Nordic countries, but Swedish opposition to Danish rule grew and in the sixteenth century Gustav Vasa expelled the Danes and was elected king, creating a strong modern state. In 1660 the Danes were forced to cede the south of Sweden, leaving Sweden to dominate the Baltic region. Sweden lost Finland to Russia in 1808, but incorporated Norway instead, which she ruled until 1905. During Gustav V's long reign, Sweden enjoyed an unprecedented prosperous period and advanced social and political legislation was implemented. Sweden remained neutral during both world wars. In 1995 the country joined the EU.

The population is 9.1 million. Besides Swedes, there are communities of Finns, Lapps and Norwegians. Due to the large inflow of refugees during the last 40 years, people of non-Swedish origin now make up 12 per cent of the population. Swedish is the main language and the capital is Stockholm.

✦ CLIMATE

The climate is temperate and the summers are pleasant. Winters are cold, with temperatures around freezing. Summer arrives only in June, and the sailing season rarely lasts beyond the end of September, but has the advantage of long summer nights. The winds in summer are variable and mostly light. The warmest month in the Baltic is July, with an average temperature of 18°C/64°F, while on the west coast temperatures are slightly lower in summer.

✦ FORMALITIES

The authorities prefer to be contacted by telephone, but Channel 16 can also be used. EU and Schengen regulations apply. If visiting Göta Älv or going through the Göta Canal, you must report to the customs office before entering.

Restricted areas are clearly marked on Swedish charts, as well as by signs on the shore. In protected and controlled areas, yachts must remain within the channels marked on the charts. In some parts of such areas anchoring or mooring is prohibited, and in others foreign yachts may not stay longer than 24 hours. Known prohibited areas are around Göteborg, the naval base at Karlskrona, and parts of the southern approaches to Stockholm. Other restricted areas are protected wildlife reserves where at certain times of the year, especially spring and early summer, access is forbidden.

Laws are strict concerning the littering of the sea and shore. Garbage, oils, petrol or harmful substances must not be discharged into the water, and in many places toilets must not be pumped out.

Scandinavians can fish for recreation on Sweden's coasts, but non-Scandinavians must have special permission. Spearfishing is not permitted.

✦ INLAND WATERWAYS

There are various canals linking rivers and lakes which give access to the interior of the country. The Göta and Trollhätte Canals are a system of lakes and canals that cuts through Southern Sweden from Göteborg in the North Sea to Mem on the Baltic Sea, a distance of some 210 miles. The 65 hydraulically operated locks raise vessels to the canal's highest point of 92m (302ft) above sea level. The canal was completed in 1832 and continues to be one of Sweden's major attractions, both with locals and visitors. In addition to private boats, the canal is plied regularly by excursion vessels, among them three original steamships. This is one of Sweden's most attractive areas of dense forests, meadows, historic towns and several freshwater lakes. As there are no fixed bridges, the canal can be navigated without dropping the mast.

There are other navigable canals such as Falsterbo, Dalslands, Arvika and Väddo, and Lake Mälaren near Stockholm, that may also be navigated. There are maximum draft as well as height restrictions on some of these canals. Maximum length: 30m (100ft), beam 6m (20ft), draft 2.82m (9ft), height 22m (71ft).

✦ FACILITIES

Facilities are of good quality everywhere; there are marinas in all major centres and moorings in all popular cruising areas. Most moorings belong to the Swedish Cruising Club, are painted red or blue, and can also be used by visitors either for short stays in daytime or for the night. Private moorings may also be used, either with permission, or if the absent owner has left a prominent green card indicating that the berth is free. The biggest marinas are in the Stockholm area (Vasahamnen, downtown Stockholm, Saltsjöbaden and Bullandö outside Stockholm) and Göteborg area (Lilla Bommen, downtown Göteborg and Långedrag, and Björlanda Kile outside Göteborg), and this is also where most repair facilities are located.

The standard of repair work is good throughout Sweden, but it may be difficult finding repair services in the more remote areas. For any major repair it is best to head for one of the larger yachting centres where almost everything is

PORTS OF ENTRY

Only the principal ports are listed below:

North Coast:	Haparanda	65°46′N 23°54′E	Tel: 0922 12949	Umeå	63°50′N 20°16′E	Tel: 090 24160
Härnösand	62°38′N 17°56′E	Tel: 0611 79082				
Stockholm archipelago:						
Furusund	59°40′N 18°55′E	Tel: 0176 8000 01	Stockholm	59°19′N 18°03′E	Tel: 08 789 76 39/789 76 40	
	Sandhamn	59°16′N 18°55′E	Tel: 08 571 532 85	Nynäshamn	58°54′N 17°57′E	Tel: 08 546 654 14
East Coast:	Gryt (Norrköping)	58°36′N 16°12′E	Tel: 0123 401 14/401 15			
Gotland:	Slite	57°42′N 18°49′E		Visby	57°39′N 18°17′E	Tel: 0498 102 45
South Coast:	Karlskrona	56°10′N 15°36′E	Tel: 0455 110 63	Malmö	55°37′N 13°00′E	Tel: 040 731 30/731 38
	Helsingborg	56°03′N 12°41′E	Tel: 042 17 08 02			
West Coast:	Göteborg	57°42′N 11°57′E	Tel: 031 63 71 50	Kungshamn	58°22′N 11°14′E	Tel: 0523 307 55

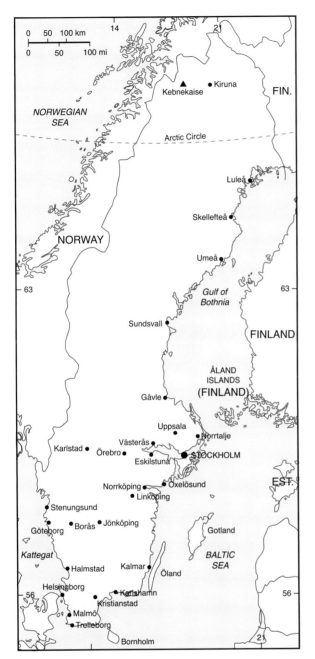

anchorages on the east and south coasts. Båtsport-kort are Swedish charts reproduced on a small scale, available in most Swedish bookshops.

✦ CHARTER

There are several charter companies operating both on the west and east coasts, in the Åland Islands, as well as in inland waters – including the Göta Canal. Both sail and motorboats are on offer and most companies allow boats to also visit neighbouring countries.

> www.swedecharter.com
> www.boatcharterstockholm.com
> www.sailmarine.com
> www.yachtcharter-sweden.com
> www.rtc.se
> www.out.se
> www.rentaboat.se

Cruising Guides

The best cruising guides are the three published by Nautiska Förlaget, of which those marked * are available in English.

Arnholma-Landsort and Gotland*
Landsort-Skanör (including the Göta Canal)*
Skanör-Strömstad (English edition in 2011)
The Baltic Sea
Norwegian Cruising Guide (includes SW Sweden)

Websites

The Swedish Yacht Club has a very useful website, and although in Swedish, it can be easily navigated. All essential features (guest and natural harbours, services, etc) are listed and the various locations can be found by clicking on Sök (seek).

www.SXK.se (Swedish Cruising Club)
www.visitsweden.com
www.visitsweden.com/sweden/Attractions/The-coastline-of-
    Sweden/Gota-Canal/
www.portfocus.com/sweden/zz_marinas/

Local time	UTC +1
	Summer time: last Sunday in March to last Sunday in October
Buoyage	IALA A
Currency	Swedish Krona (SEK)
Electricity	230V, 50Hz

Diplomatic missions

UK	8 6713000	Canada	8 4533000
USA	8 7835300	South Africa	8 243950
Australia	8 6132900	New Zealand	8 4633116

Communications		Emergency number
IDD 46	IAC 00	112

available. Provisioning is easy everywhere, with the exception of the more remote areas, and in many places it is possible to come alongside a dock close to a grocery store. Fuel is not so widely available away from the larger centres.

The Swedish Cruising Club publishes a brochure about visitors' harbours in Sweden, called *Swedish Guest Harbours*, and also *Seglarhamnar på Ostkusten*, with plans of ports and

WESTERN EUROPE AND NORTH ATLANTIC ISLANDS

THE COUNTRIES FEATURED in this section have a long maritime tradition and their sailors have played a leading role during the age of discovery and exploration when their daring voyages reached the furthest corners of the world. Similarly, the offshore island groups of the North Atlantic have a proud maritime tradition of their own and have served throughout history as welcome landfalls for weary mariners. Once used as stepping stones on voyages of discovery to remote destinations, the routes to these islands are now being retraced by modern sailors. While the northern islands of

Greenland, Iceland and Faeroes attract fewer yachts from afar, the southern islands of Bermuda, Canaries, Azores and Madeira are visited every year by hundreds of cruising yachts on their way east or west across the Atlantic. Even the Cape Verdes are slowly turning into a cruising destination in their own right, and not just a convenient stop on the way to somewhere else.

The UK, Ireland and the Channel Islands have large boating communities of their own and are also visited by many yachts from neighbouring countries. This is also the

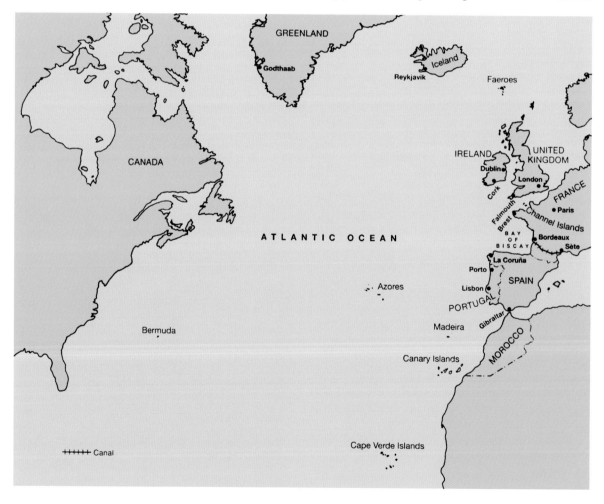

case with France and Spain, which have coastlines on both the Atlantic and Mediterranean, with countless cruising opportunities as well as good facilities on both shores. Portugal has just as much to offer, from the splendour of medieval Porto to the relaxed atmosphere of the marinas along the Algarve coast.

A favourite voyage undertaken by many European sailors is a circumnavigation of the North Atlantic that follows closely the route pioneered by Christopher Columbus on his first voyage to the New World in 1492 and his return to Europe the following year. Weather conditions have changed little in the intervening period and such a circular route can still be easily accomplished by sailing south from Northern Europe to Madeira and the Canaries with the Portuguese trades of summer, west to the Caribbean with the NE trade winds, and back to Europe with the westerlies of higher latitudes. The weather patterns, and the prevailing conditions generated by them, are due to a permanent feature of the North Atlantic, the area of atmospheric high pressure situated near the Azores, whose name it bears. Because of its influence on sailing conditions over such a large area of the North Atlantic, the position of the Azores high should be watched carefully when planning an Atlantic crossing in either direction. Furthermore, as the entire area is under the influence of Atlantic weather systems, the movement of depressions should be monitored when planning to leave on an offshore passage. This is particularly true in the Bay of Biscay where strong SW winds caused by an approaching depression can result in difficult conditions. The Bay of Biscay is usually the first and most difficult hurdle to pass for North European sailors heading south, especially those for whom this is the first offshore voyage. This is why it is so important to choose a favourable time to cross Biscay, and not to do it too early in spring, if heading for the Mediterranean; or too late in the season, if planning a transatlantic crossing from the Canaries. In this case, it is better to start the voyage earlier in the summer, when weather conditions are usually good, arrive in the Canaries in early autumn, and either cruise the islands until it is time to set off across the Atlantic, or leave the boat in a marina, fly home, and return in November for the Atlantic crossing.

North American sailors are faced with similar options, whether planning to sail to Europe in early summer, either via Bermuda, the Azores or direct, or to the Caribbean in the autumn. The prevailing westerly winds usually ensure a fast passage to Europe so, unless heading for the Mediterranean (in which case a stop in the Azores may make sense), a non-stop voyage to Northern Europe should be the logical choice.

The more remote islands of Iceland and Greenland are off the usual sailing routes, so voyages to them need to be tailored accordingly. Because of the prevailing winds, current and late ice, reaching them from the US east coast makes this a challenging undertaking, and also considerably narrows down the favourable cruising window. A summer passage from Northern Europe is, relatively speaking, somewhat easier to accomplish. In recent years, intrepid sailors have solved the problem by including those two distant destinations into a summer circuit of the North Atlantic by sailing first to Norway and Svalbard, thence to Iceland, Greenland and thus home.

The sailing season in the northern islands is strictly for the summer, whereas the southern islands benefit from an open season. Being on the transatlantic circuit they have certain peak periods, with Madeira and the Canaries being busiest between September and November when yachts prepare to cross to the Caribbean. Bermuda and the Azores are busiest in May and June, when the movement is in the opposite direction. In the entire region, only Bermuda is affected by tropical storms, with the hurricane season lasting from June to November, and September being the most dangerous month. None of the other islands fall within the hurricane zone, although on very rare occasions a hurricane may track eastwards – as happened when Hurricane Delta struck the Canaries in early December 2005.

Yachting facilities are good throughout the area, and especially in the ports visited by yachts in transit or in those with a large resident boating population. The best repair services are found in the UK and France, with equally good facilities in the main sailing centres of Spain and Portugal. In the offshore islands, Gran Canaria and Bermuda have the best facilities, although services have been steadily improving throughout the islands.

Start of the ARC (Atlantic Rally for Cruisers) in Las Pamas.

AZORES

'ONLY THOSE WHO HAVE SEEN THE AZORES from the deck of a vessel realize the beauty of the mid-ocean picture', wrote Joshua Slocum on completion of the first ever single-handed Atlantic crossing when he made landfall in Faial on 20 July 1895. Slocum was only the first of modern sailors to be enchanted by these islands, and one of his followers recently described the Azores as Europe's best kept cruising secret.

Reputed to be the fabled Atlantis, the Azores lie in mid-Atlantic 900 miles off the coast of Portugal and 1,800 miles from Bermuda. The archipelago consists of nine main islands divided into three groups: the most western islands of Flores and Corvo; the central group of Faial, Pico, São Jorge, Graciosa and Terceira; and to the southeast, São Miguel and Santa Maria. Being volcanic outbursts along the Atlantic seismic ridge, all the islands have a similarity in their rugged landscape of cones, lava fields and hot springs. Volcanic activity has often changed the face of the islands, the most recent eruption occurring at Capelinhos on Faial in 1957. The volcanic soil and moist climate support an abundant vegetation, with hedgerows of hydrangeas and vividly coloured flowers growing everywhere.

Throughout their history, the Azores have depended on the sea for their links with the outside world and sailors have always been regarded with affection by the Azoreans. There are indeed few places in the world where yachts are welcomed with such warmth as first recorded by Joshua Slocum. Reflecting this positive attitude, the authorities have made great efforts to provide adequate facilities by building marinas in most islands. With the exception of Corvo, there is at least one good port on every island. The pleasant summer weather, secluded bays, clear waters, superb scenery and protected harbours make the Azores the perfect cruising destination. Besides their natural beauty, the relaxed pace of life in the islands is for many visitors an essential ingredient of their attraction.

Horta Marina on the island of Faial.

Horta's perennial attraction is Café Sport, probably the best-known watering hole for sailors anywhere in the world. At any time of day and long into the night the blue-fronted café overlooking the port of Horta is full of sailors from the many yachts that call here. Their autographed ensigns, pennants and club burgees are displayed five and six deep on the walls or pinned to the wooden ceiling. The same Azevedo family has run this establishment for over a century and the café is now run by fourth-generation José Azevedo. According to family lore, the tradition was started when his great-grandfather greeted Joshua Slocum during the solo navigator's visit on his yacht *Spray* in 1895. Straddling the transatlantic migration routes of whales as well as yachts, the Azores have a long tradition of whaling, which is reflected in Café Sport's other attraction: a large collection of scrimshaw with hundreds of beautifully carved whale teeth displayed in glass cabinets in a large room above the café.

Because of the seasonal movement of yachts, they are regarded as migratory birds by local people, and spring in Horta is heralded every year by the arrival of the first yacht from the Caribbean. Most boats choose to stop in the Azores on their way east across the Atlantic, although a few call on their way west to the USA or when sailing from the South Atlantic towards Northern Europe. Although hundreds of yachts call every year, very few of them cruise around the islands and the majority stop only in Horta, one of the perennially favourite places of long-distance sailors. As those who take their time to spend longer in the Azores will confirm, the islands deserve more than being just a convenient landfall on the way to somewhere else, and for this reason they are visited every summer by yachts that have sailed down from Northern Europe to enjoy this attractive and unspoilt cruising destination. Some complete their round trip and sail home the same season, some continue to the Canaries and possibly across the Atlantic, while yet others leave their boats in one of the local marinas for the winter and continue the following year into the Mediterranean or south to Madeira and the Canaries.

✦ COUNTRY PROFILE

Although known in ancient times, the islands remained uninhabited until settled by the Portuguese in the fifteenth century. The Azores became an important port of call for ships, and Angra, with its natural harbour, became the leading town. Christopher Columbus stopped at Santa Maria on his first return voyage, while João Fernandez

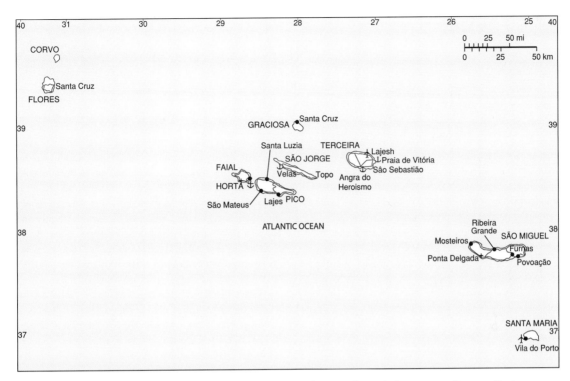

| | 40 | 31 | 30 | 29 | 28 | 27 | 26 | 25 | 40 |

CORVO
FLORES
Santa Cruz

GRACIOSA   Santa Cruz

Santa Luzia   TERCEIRA
SÃO JORGE   Lajesh
FAIAL   Velas   Topo   Praia de Vitória
HORTA   São Sebastião
São Mateus   Lajes   PICO   Angra do
Heroismo

ATLANTIC OCEAN

Ribeira
Grande   SÃO MIGUEL
Mosteiros   Furnas
Ponta Delgada   Povoação

SANTA MARIA
Vila do Porto

Labrador sailed west from here with Cabot's fleet and sighted the land that now bears his name. The islands fiercely resisted Spanish attempts to invade, but eventually Spain took control and used the islands as a stopping-off point for ships returning from South America with treasure. When Portugal regained independence in 1640, the links with the mainland were re-established. Ships remained an important source of income and employment, especially the American whalers which took on many islanders as crew, due to their whaling expertise. Later, with the laying of transatlantic cables from Faial, the islands became an important link in international communications. During both world wars the Azores were important bases for the Allies, and there is still a US base on Terceira. The Portuguese Constitution of 1976 made the Azores an autonomous region of Portugal.

The population numbers 245,000. Many Azoreans have emigrated to North America, Brazil and Bermuda. Portuguese is the main language. There is no capital, but the president of the government is based in Ponta Delgada and the Regional Assembly is in Horta.

✦ CLIMATE

The climate in the Azores is dominated by the mid-Atlantic area of high pressure that bears the islands' name. The position of the Azores high varies with the season, being more northerly in the autumn and more southerly in the spring, usually lying to the south or southwest of the islands.

The prevailing winds are generally easterlies in summer and westerlies in winter.

In winter the area can be stormy and very wet, while in summer the Azores high can be stationary with prolonged periods of calm weather. The Azores benefit from a temperate, maritime climate with mild winters (average daytime temperatures range from 12–15°C/54–59°F) and warm summers, with temperatures of 19–25°C/66–77°F.

✦ FORMALITIES

Horta Marina: On arrival, yachts should berth alongside the reception quay. The offices of immigration, maritime police and customs are next to the marina office in the same building.

Living up to its name, the island of Flores is covered in flowers. Smaller Corvo is visible in the distance.

PORTS OF ENTRY

Ponta Delgada (São Miguel)	37°44´N 25°40´W	Horta (Faial)	38°32´N 28°38´W
Santa Cruz (Flores)	39°27´N 31°07´W	Lajes (Flores)	39°23´N 31°10´W
Angra do Heroísmo (Terceira)	38°39´N 27°13´W	Praia da Vitória (Terceira)	38°44´N 27°03´W
Vila do Porto (Santa Maria)	36°56´N 25°09´W	Vila das Velas (São Jorge)	38°40´N 28°13´W
Vila da Praia (Graciosa)	39°03´N 27°58´W		

Lajes: Yachts should come to the quay or anchor in its vicinity. Formalities are completed ashore, but these must be finalised on arrival in Horta.

Ponta Delgada: There is a reception dock on the port side as one enters the marina (Channel 9), and arriving yachts are expected to stop there to be cleared and assigned a berth.

As part of Portugal, the Azores are members of the EU, with which they have a special relationship. The usual EU regulations apply, although because of their isolated position, the authorities tend to treat all arriving yachts as if coming from a non-EU country.

The Azores are part of the Schengen Agreement, whose visa requirements apply.

Yachts must show their original registration document, insurance policy and ship's radio licence. One member of the crew must have a radio operator's licence. For EU boats, proof of VAT status may also be required.

A transit log (Livrete de Transito) is issued to non-EU yachts on arrival. All subsequent movements of the yacht are recorded in this log until departure, and yachts must clear in and out of all ports. If arriving from Madeira, the same transit log may be used, but if arriving from mainland Portugal, a new log is usually issued.

✦ FACILITIES

Facilities have seen a great improvement in recent years, with marinas now being operational in almost all islands; the one in Horta has been expanded to cope with the insatiable demand during the peak arrival month of June. There are good repair facilities in all main centres, with sailmakers in Horta and Ponta Delgado. Mid Atlantic Chandlery in Horta has a reasonable supply. Provisioning in the islands is also good, with the best selection being on the islands of São Miguel, Terceira and Faial. Limited supplies are available on the smaller islands, although local fresh produce is on sale everywhere. Water and fuel is also available in all ports.

✦ CHARTER

There are only limited charter opportunities, but Azores Sailing, a local company based at Vila Campo do Franca on the island of São Miguel, is now operating a small fleet of Dufour 40 sailing yachts.

www.azoresailing.com

Cruising Guides
The Atlantic Islands
Atlantic Crossing Guide

Websites
www.marinasazores.com
www.visitazores.org
www.destinazores.com
www.visitazores.travel

Local time	UTC −1
	Summer time: last Sunday in March to last Sunday in October
Buoyage	IALA A
Currency	Euro (EUR)
Electricity	230V, 50Hz

Diplomatic missions
UK	296 628175
USA	296 282216
Australia	Lisbon 21 3101500
Canada	296 281488
South Africa	Lisbon 21 3192200

Communications
IDD 351	IAC 00

Emergency number
112

Café Sport on Horta's waterfront.

BERMUDA

BERMUDA IS AN ARCHIPELAGO of over one hundred and fifty small islands and islets, the largest linked together by causeways and bridges into a fishhook shape. The existence of coral islands so far north and only 600 miles off the east coast of the USA is explained by the warm waters of the Gulf Stream that bathe Bermuda and account for its mild climate.

One of the most popular landfalls in the North Atlantic, Bermuda has welcomed weary mariners for over three centuries. Mark Twain was one of those grateful to arrive when he stepped off the *Quaker City* in 1867 and later commented: 'Bermuda was a paradise but one had to go through hell to get there', a feeling many contemporary American sailors may well agree with.

Although it has little to offer in the way of cruising, Bermuda attracts over one thousand yachts every year, either stopping to rest and reprovision after a long passage, or simply to turn around at the finish of one of the many ocean races that run from the US east coast. Bermuda is well geared to cope with these transient sailors, most of whom arrive from the Caribbean in April and May, some on their way to Europe, others going to the USA or Canada. Later in the autumn Bermuda sees another influx as yachts make their way south from the USA to the Caribbean.

A long thin chain of linked islands form the northwestern arm of the large bay known as Great Sound. Hamilton Harbour is on its eastern side while the former Royal Naval Dockyard is located on the tip of North Ireland Island and includes a marina. The well-sheltered St George's Harbour provides a restful anchorage from which to explore this neat and tidy little country. Such exploring is best done by land, particularly by those who are short of time and treat their stop in Bermuda as a brief but enjoyable interlude. The alternative is to sail to Hamilton, but as all yachts have to clear in first at St George's, few are tempted to thread their way through the reefs to Hamilton harbour. It is easier by bus.

✦ COUNTRY PROFILE

Bermuda is reputed to be the site that inspired Shakespeare's play *The Tempest*, thus immortalizing the 1609 shipwreck of English colonists headed for Virginia, who then settled the islands. Privateers and pirates also frequented the islands in the early years. Later, Bermuda became an important base and dockyard for the British Navy. During the Second World War it was used as a US military base that only ceased operation in 1995. In 1968 a new constitution gave the country internal self-government. A referendum in 1995 decided to maintain the status of a self-governing overseas territory of the UK instead of full independence.

The population is 68,000, more than half being of African origin, with about 35 per cent being European. English is the official language, and some Portuguese is spoken. Hamilton is the capital.

St George's Harbour.

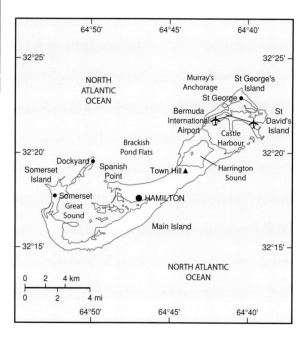

✦ CLIMATE

Thanks to the Gulf Stream, Bermuda enjoys a subtropical climate, with mild winters and warm humid summers. The Azores high dominates the summer months, bringing steady southwest winds. June to November is the hurricane season, with September the most dangerous month, although the majority of these storms pass to the west of Bermuda. The warmest month is August, with an average temperature of 27°C/81°F and peaks well above 30°/90°F. January to March are the coolest and wettest months, with an average of 17°C/63°F.

✦ FORMALITIES

PORT OF ENTRY

St George's Harbour   32°23´N 64°40´W

A radar watch is kept and unidentified vessels are usually called up. Yachts stopping elsewhere than at the port of entry will be escorted to St George's and may be fined. Bermuda Harbour Radio should be contacted on Channels 16, 27 or HF 2182, 4125 prior to arrival to give an ETA; the station will issue arrival instructions.

Visas are not required for nationals of most European countries, Australia, Canada, New Zealand, South Africa or the USA. A three-week stay is normally given on arrival, which can be extended. If visas are required for the next destination country, such as the USA, these must have been obtained previously. It is the captain's responsibility to

ensure that any crew leaving the boat also leave the island. Yachts may stay up to six months, after which a duty of 33.5 per cent on the vessel's value is imposed by customs, although there is some flexibility for delays caused by repairs, illness, weather or sometimes the hurricane season.

✦ FACILITIES

You may anchor in St George's and Hamilton harbours. In St George's there are limited pontoon berths available. Provisioning is reasonable, one supermarket being within walking distance. In Hamilton, visiting yachts may use the services of the yacht club, boatyards and marinas. Berthing for yachts at commercial docks is usually prohibited.

Although there is a boatyard, slipway and some repair facilities at St George's, comprehensive repair and service facilities are dispersed all over Bermuda. Unavailable marine supplies or essential parts can be ordered from the USA, from where there are several flights a day.

✦ CHARTER

Those who do not arrive by boat and wish to experience Bermuda and its surrounding waters in the only way that does them justice can contact one of the various operators offering bareboats for charter.

www.bermudawindsailcharters.com
www.sailbermuda.com
www.charterbermuda.com

Cruising Guide
Yachts (Private) Sailing to Bermuda (an annual information sheet published by the Bermuda Department of Tourism)

Websites
www.bermudatourism.com (Bermuda Tourism Office)
www.weather.bm (local weather reports)
www.rccbermuda.bm (Maritime Operations Centre)

Local time	UTC –4
	Summer time: second Sunday in March to first Sunday in November
Buoyage	IALA B
Currency	Bermuda Dollar (BMD)
Electricity	110V, 60Hz

Diplomatic missions	
UK	2922587
USA	2951341
Canada	2922917

Communications	
IDD 011	IAC 1441

Emergency numbers		
911	Rescue Co-ordination Centre	2971010

CANARY ISLANDS

NO OTHER ARCHIPELAGO has attracted more complimentary names than this group of eight islands that have been described at various times during their long and eventful history as the Elysian Fields, the Fortunate Isles, Garden of the Hesperides, or Islands of Eternal Spring. Called by the Romans the Enchanted Islands, the Canaries have indeed enchanted countless sailors over the centuries. These high volcanic islands resting on the Atlantic seismic ridge are very close to Africa, a combination of factors that explains the varied scenery, from sandy deserts and stark lava fields, to lush mountain valleys, pine forests and the snow-capped Mount Teide on Tenerife – a dormant volcano rising out of the ocean to a height of 3,718m (12,198ft).

The logical route for most yachts arriving from the north is to make landfall in tiny Graciosa, then visit Lanzarote and Fuerteventura before sailing to Gran Canaria. Those who wish to see more of the islands should continue to Tenerife, La Gomera, La Palma and finally El Hierro, although this route may have to be altered if planning to continue across the Atlantic, in which case it is best to take your leave from a port with good provisions such as Santa Cruz de la Palma. The alternative is to complete a circuit of the islands and return to a port with the best range of facilities, such as Las Palmas, to prepare for the forthcoming passage.

Until Christopher Columbus set off from the Canaries to discover a new world on the far side of what was then called the Ocean Sea, El Hierro was regarded as the end of the world. Rugged El Hierro still lives up to that description, a quiet place whose leisurely pace of life is its enduring charm. Neighbouring La Palma boasts the largest volcanic caldera in the world created by a now dormant volcano whose smaller offspring continue to spew forth modest amounts of fire and brimstone at the southern tip of the island. La Gomera's claim to fame is that Columbus set off from there on three of his four transatlantic voyages, and some of the buildings from that era are still standing. Across the windy straits, Tenerife's Mount Teide dominates the imposing seascape and *gomeros* rarely fail to remind visitors that *tinerfeños* might have their mountain, but the stupendous view belongs to them. Friendly rivalry between the islanders is the order of the day and as Gran Canaria cannot compete in the beauty stakes, it is the proud host of the Atlantic Rally for Cruisers (ARC) that starts from here in late November every year and, a quarter of a century after its inception, still counts as the largest transocean event in the world. Fuerteventura's very name betrays its windy nature, while neighbouring Lanzarote's stark scenery confirms the volcanic nature of the entire archipelago. A continent in miniature indeed.

Throughout history, their geographical situation has made the Canaries the logical staging post between Europe and the Americas. They continue to be the jumping-off point for yachts crossing the Atlantic to the Caribbean, and the example set by Columbus over five centuries ago is copied by over one thousand yachts every year. From late October to December the ports and marinas are abuzz with yachts and their excited crews getting ready for the Atlantic crossing. While for some the Canaries are just a quick provisioning stop, others take advantage of what the islands have to offer and leave Europe before the end of summer, so that they can spend a couple of months cruising the Canaries. Facilities for boats have greatly improved over the years and there is now at least one marina on every island. As a result, more cruising yachts are spending longer in the islands and some are permanently based there. Also on the increase is the number of yachts that sail down from Europe or the Mediterranean to spend the winter months in the Canaries' pleasant climate. There are some charter companies, but chartering has been very slow to develop, mainly because of those northeast

Brisk sailing in the lee of Tenerife's Mount Teide.

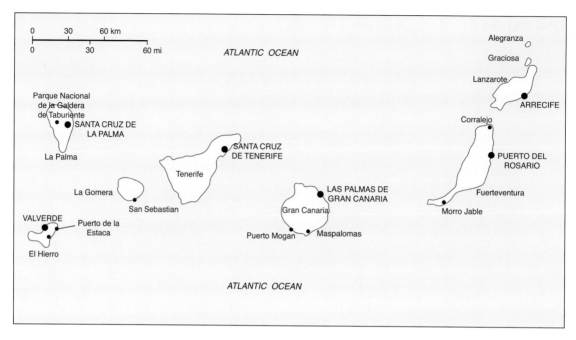

winds that make it so easy to sail among the islands from east to west, but a lot more difficult to return to base. Obviously even in the Enchanted Islands gentlemen don't like sailing to windward.

✦ COUNTRY PROFILE

The early population were called Guanches, probably descended from Berbers who came over from North Africa. The islands were known to both the Greeks and Romans, and the first recorded expedition sent by King Juba of Mauritania called here in the year 60. The Roman writer Pliny, in describing the islands, called one of them Canaria from the Latin word for dog, 'canis', due to the number of large wild dogs roaming the island. Originally applied to Gran Canaria, the name later came to be used for the whole archipelago and also for the small birds that originate from here.

After the Roman era, the Canaries were largely forgotten until several Genoese and other European expeditions started exploring the islands in the thirteenth and fourteenth centuries. The Guanches put up a fierce fight and resisted all attempts to subdue them, and only in 1495 was the last Guanche resistance crushed. Three years before that Columbus sailed to the Canaries and left on his voyage of discovery from La Gomera. The new routes pioneered by Columbus opened up the Atlantic Ocean and had a big impact on the Canaries. They developed as a repair and provisioning centre for westbound vessels and many merchants and traders settled there. Although attacked by pirates, the Dutch and the English, the islands remained under Spanish

control and in 1823 the Canaries became a full Spanish province. Thriving on trade, in the mid-nineteenth century the islands were declared a free trade area and have remained a duty-free zone ever since. The Canary Islands now form an autonomous region of Spain with their own parliament.

The resident population is 2 million, although swollen by some 10 million visitors annually. The Canary Islanders are proud of their differences from the mainland Spanish, whom they call *peninsulares*. Spanish is the official language. Due to rivalry between the two main islands, the government sits alternately in the provincial capitals of Las Palmas de Gran Canaria and Santa Cruz de Tenerife.

✦ CLIMATE

Despite their position close to the tropics, the Canaries are not too hot in summer, with temperatures in the 21–29°C/70–84°F range, and pleasantly warm in winter (15–21°C/59–70°F). The annual average temperature is 20.7°C/69.3°F, which is one of the main reasons the islands are regarded as an all-year cruising ground. The frequency of gales is low and the islands are not affected by hurricanes, although Hurricane Delta, which was the first hurricane ever recorded in the islands, and which struck in early December 2005, may herald a change in climate. The prevailing winds are northeasterly, and while these are rarely strong, the height of the land creates wind acceleration zones in some areas. They are worst in the channels between the islands and the sudden blasts are called mosquitoes by local sailors – as they are only heard when they bite.

✦ FORMALITIES

PORTS OF ENTRY	
Arrecife (Lanzarote)	28°57′N 13°33′W
Puerto del Rosario (Fuerteventura)	28°30′N 13°51′W
Las Palmas de Gran Canaria	28°09′N 15°25′W
Santa Cruz de Tenerife	28°29′N 16°14′W
Santa Cruz de la Palma	28°40′N 17°45′W

Only the above are so-called Schengen ports and yachts are not supposed to call anywhere else before clearing in at one of them. As part of Spain, the Canaries are members of the EU, with which they have a special relationship. The usual EU regulations apply, although because of their isolated position, the authorities tend to treat all arriving yachts as if coming from a non-EU country. The Schengen Agreement has complicated matters as it made provision for only five official ports of entry. On arrival, the captain should report to the Port Authority or marina office which will advise on the correct procedure and, in the case of the marinas, will contact the relevant authorities. Immigration will only stamp the passports of non-EU nationals, who should make sure that this is indeed done for otherwise those leaving the islands by air may encounter problems at the airport. The Canaries are a duty-free area, so yachts are not required to clear customs. VAT is not charged on goods or services although there is a local sales tax of 5 per cent.

Arrecife: The capital of Lanzarote has two ports used by yachts. The more northerly is the fishing harbour of Puerto Naos, where two pontoons have been installed for visiting yachts. In the old port of Arrecife, yachts tie up to the wall inside the breakwater. In the approaches to both ports attention must be paid to the outlying reefs. Formalities are completed at the Policia Nacional. As docking facilities are much better at the marinas called Puerto Calero or Marina Rubicon, it may be better to go there directly and return to Arrecife by taxi to complete formalities.

Puerto del Rosario: Fuerteventura's main commercial port is being expanded to include a marina. Until the project is completed, yachts may come alongside the dock used by local and fishing boats south of the main quay. All offices are in the port area.

Las Palmas de Gran Canaria: Arriving yachts should proceed into the marina (Muelle Deportivo) in the southwest corner of the large commercial harbour and tie up at the reception dock on the portside by the entrance. Formalities are completed at the nearby marina office.

Santa Cruz de Tenerife: Yachts berth at either Marina del Atlantico in the centre of Santa Cruz or in the fishing harbour (Darsena Pesquera) north of the city. The marina office should be contacted on arrival.

Santa Cruz de la Palma: Yachts should proceed into the new marina in the northern part of the commercial harbour. All offices are nearby.

Visa exemptions and requirements are as for Spain; however, this does not appear to be applied strictly to yachts, provided the non-EU national also leaves the islands by yacht.

Passports are not normally stamped on arrival, but if non-EU crew members wish to leave by air, it is essential to get their passports stamped, as otherwise they might be turned back from the airport.

There are no restrictions on yacht movements in the Canaries, although papers may be checked at subsequent ports.

Customs are concerned about drug trafficking, especially from North Africa, and although they appear to be easy-going, they do keep a close eye on yacht movement.

Foreign vessels under 15m (50ft) LOA are prohibited from operating commercially and are impounded by customs if not flying the Spanish flag.

Equipment and spare parts can be imported free of duty provided they are clearly marked as being for a yacht in transit. The use of an agent can speed up the extrication of these goods from the airport.

✦ FACILITIES

Yachting facilities in the Canaries are constantly improving and repair services are good, particularly on Gran Canaria. There are yacht clubs on most islands, but as they are primarily social clubs, visitors are not particularly welcome.

Gran Canaria: The widest range of facilities is concentrated in the capital of Las Palmas, which has a marina administered by the Port Authority. There are various workshops in the

Muelle Deportivo, the large marina inside the commercial harbour of Las Palmas de Gran Canaria.

Cebadal industrial estate, close to the commercial harbour. A sailmaker operates in town. There are several chandleries with a reasonable selection. There is a boatyard with a 40-ton travelift next to the marina in Las Palmas, and also a synchrolift in the commercial harbour that can handle large yachts. Provisioning in Las Palmas is the best in the Canaries, with several supermarkets and daily fresh produce markets. Fuel is available in the marina.

Gran Canaria's south coast has several good marinas at Pasito Blanco, Puerto Rico and Puerto Mogan. There are haulout facilities at all of them, as well as at the fishing harbour Arguineguin.

Tenerife: Docking facilities in the capital of Tenerife have improved dramatically with the opening of a new large marina in the very centre of the capital Santa Cruz. This Marina del Atlantico provides only docking, so for any repairs boats may still have to use the facilities of Marina Tenerife in the old fishing harbour (Darsena Pesquera), 3 miles north of the city.

Outside of Santa Cruz there are some repair facilities in the marinas at Radazul, Los Gigantes and Puerto Colon. The boatyard at Los Cristianos also has haulout and repair services. Provisioning is good everywhere, with well-stocked supermarkets close to all marinas, all of which also have fuel, except Marina del Atlantico.

Lanzarote: Most facilities are in the capital Arrecife, around the commercial Puerto Naos. A small industrial estate in the neighbourhood provides a range of services. Provisioning is good, with supermarkets and fresh produce markets. Fuel, water and LPG are available in the commercial harbour. The two private marinas, Puerto Calero, on Lanzarote's east coast, and Marina Rubicon, on the south coast, both have boatyards with travelifts and a range of services.

Fuerteventura: The small marina Puerto Castillo has a travelift and some repair facilities as well as fuel, and there are limited repair services in the capital Puerto del Rosario,

where a new marina will greatly improve matters. There is also a small marina at Morro Jable, a ferry port in the south of the island.

La Gomera: The capital San Sebastian now has its own marina, located in the commercial harbour. There are some local workshops that undertake maintenance and repairs on yachts.

There are new marinas inside the commercial harbours at Santa Cruz de la Palma and Puerto de la Estaca on El Hierro. Provisioning is good on both La Palma and El Hierro, but repair facilities are better on La Palma and almost non-existent on El Hierro.

✦ CHARTER

Club Sail is based in the new San Miguel Marina on the south coast of Tenerife, and Canary Sail, based in San Sebastian de la Gomera, offers both tuition courses and charters in sail and power boats. Nautilus Yachting, based in Santa Cruz de Tenerife, has a fleet of sailing yachts and the location of these operators is more convenient for exploring the western islands. Two operators based in Lanzarote, Catalanza in Puerto Calero, and Lanzarote Yachting in Marina Rubicon, are best placed for visiting the eastern islands. Canary Sailing is centrally located in Las Palmas de Gran Canaria.

www.clubsail.com	www.canarysail.com
www.nautilus-yachting.com	www.canarysailing.com
www.catlanza.com	
www.lanzaroteyachting.com	

Cruising Guides
Canary Islands Cruising Guide
Atlantic Islands

Websites
www.turismodecanarias.com
www.bluemoment.com/portguide-canaries.html (details of marinas in the Canaries)

Local time	UTC
	Summer time: last Sunday in March to last Sunday in October
Buoyage	IALA A
Currency	Euro (EUR)
Electricity	230V, 50Hz

Diplomatic missions	
UK	928 262508
USA	928 271259/928 222552
Australia	Madrid 91 3536600
Canada	Madrid 91 4233250
South Africa	928 265452

Communications	**Emergency number**
IDD 34 IAC 00	112

La Palma's Caldera de Taburiente betrays the island's volcanic past.

CAPE VERDE ISLANDS

CONVENIENTLY PLACED close to the traditional sailing route from the Canaries to the Caribbean or South Atlantic, ships on transatlantic voyages have always found the Cape Verdes a useful stopover, although nowadays it is modern yachts that call here instead of square riggers and steamers. Most cruising vessels are on their way to the Caribbean, a few to Brazil or to West Africa, mainly Senegal and Gambia. In the past, yachts only stopped at Mindelo on the island of São Vicente, usually in an emergency or to buy fuel, but the islands now attract an increasing number of cruising boats that take their time to explore this interesting archipelago. Yachting facilities are limited, but the opening of a marina in Mindelo has greatly improved matters and may be followed by similar projects on some of the other islands, as the authorities are making great efforts to expand the tourism industry of this country that is bereft of any reliable sources of revenue.

Although lying close to Africa, the islands' culture reflects their close historic association with Portugal rather than their geographical position. The climate tends to be very dry, the scenery is rather bleak, and they have had severe drought problems throughout their history. There are ten main islands, divided into the Windward group (Barlavento) and Leeward group (Sotavento). São Tiago is the largest island and the capital Praia is located on its south shore.

◆ COUNTRY PROFILE

Discovered by the Portuguese in the fifteenth century, the uninhabited islands were named for their proximity to Cabo Verde in neighbouring Senegal. Over the next 300 years they were gradually devastated by the introduction of goats and the steady deforestation undertaken to free land for the creation of slave plantations. With the rise in the number of liners and freighters sailing to South America or Africa, the Cape Verde archipelago became an important coaling station. The Cape Verdes declared their independence from Portugal in 1975. Until recently, the islands were one of the poorest in Africa, but the development of fishing and tourism is slowly making a beneficial contribution to the economy.

The population of 430,000 is of mixed African and Portuguese descent. Although the official language is Portuguese, among themselves Cape Verdeans usually converse in Crioulo, a local dialect closely related to Portuguese. The capital is Praia.

◆ CLIMATE

The climate is typically tropical with no cool season, although there is a small variation of temperature around the year, the coolest period being December to March. August is the hottest month, with an average of 27°C/81°F, and January the coolest, 23°C/73°F. Rainfall is limited to a few

The port of Mindelo on São Vicente Island is a popular port of call for yachts crossing the Atlantic.

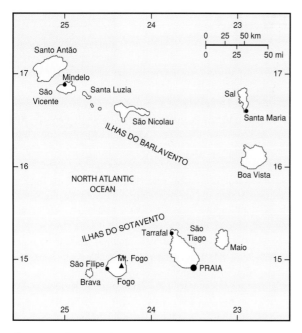

downpours between late August and October, although there are years with little or no rain. The prevailing winds are the northeast trade winds, which can be replaced inshore by a daily sea breeze.

✦ FORMALITIES

PORTS OF ENTRY	
Mindelo	16°53′N 25°00′W
Sal	16°45′N 23°00′W
Praia	14°54′N 23°31′W

The harbour of Praia, the capital of the Cape Verdes.

Mindelo: The marina should be contacted in advance (Tel: +238 2300032) so as to be able to proceed to it directly and complete formalities from there.

In Sal, clearance is usually done at the international airport, and in Praia at the immigration office in town.

Crew on yachts making a short stop are normally issued with a visa on arrival.

All except nationals of South Africa require a visa unless there is no Cape Verde representation in their country of origin, in which case they will be issued on arrival.

✦ FACILITIES

The new marina in Mindelo has good facilities, with diesel, water, electricity and wifi internet connection. Some repairs, including engineering, rigging and sail, are also available, as is a 100-ton lift. Praia is a difficult anchorage in a swell and it is best to try and come alongside another vessel, such as a harbour tug. Sal has a good anchorage in the Baia da Palmeira except in southerly winds, with some limited facilities ashore.

Theft is a general problem in the islands. If the boat is left unattended, it is recommended you employ a watchman, who may be recommended by the port captain.

Provisioning is best in Mindelo and Praia, but limited on all the other islands. There are fresh produce markets in Mindelo and Praia, which vary in variety and quality with the seasons.

Cruising Guide	
Atlantic Islands	

Websites	
www.caboverde.com	
www.marinamindelo.com	

Local time	UTC −1
Buoyage	IALA A
Currency	Cabo Verde Escudo (CVE)
Electricity	230V, 50Hz

Diplomatic missions	
UK	2323512
USA	2608900

Communications	
IDD 238	IAC 00

Emergency numbers	
Ambulance 130	Police 132

CHANNEL ISLANDS

'FRAGMENTS OF EUROPE dropped by France and picked up by England' is how Victor Hugo, in exile there, described these islands lying near to French Normandy, but being closely associated with the UK, hence their French name of Iles Anglo-Normandes. This cluster of five islands and many smaller islets is divided into two regions. The Bailiwick of Jersey comprises the largest island, Jersey, and its islets, while the Bailiwick of Guernsey includes Guernsey, Alderney, Herm and Sark. The bailiwicks have their own parliaments and are proud of their autonomy, which was granted to them by King John in 1204. In many ways the culture of the islands is closer to Normandy than the UK. Being outside the EU VAT area, the islands enjoy a special tax regime, which explains the profusion of Channel Islands registered yachts that you meet in distant waters.

The Channel Islands are a popular cruising destination both with French and British sailors, who find here some of the most challenging sailing conditions in Europe and a very special atmosphere ashore. The main hazards are strong tidal streams, concealed rocks and poor visibility. There is complete shelter in St Peter Port in Guernsey and St Helier in Jersey. There are many well-protected anchorages on all the islands, and the smaller ones provide an interesting alternative to the busy main ports.

◆ COUNTRY PROFILE

The Channel Islands are the last remnants of the medieval Dukedom of Normandy, which held sway in both France and England. After the Norman invasion of England in 1066, the islands were fought over by England and France. The French never succeeded in taking the islands and they remained loyal to Britain for hundreds of years. The islands were the only British soil occupied by German troops in the Second World War. Today they are crown dependencies, although not part

Sailing past Moulin Huet Bay on Guernsey

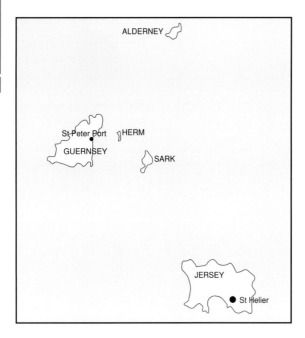

of the UK. However, the UK government is responsible for the defence and international affairs of the islands. In recent years the Channel Islands have found a new role as a leading offshore banking centre.

The population numbers 160,000. English is the official language, although French is also spoken.

✦ CLIMATE

The Channel Islands climate is temperate, with mild, damp winters and warm, drier and sunnier summers. July and August are the warmest months, with average temperatures of 19°C/66°F. January and February are the coolest, with an average of 9°C/48°F. The winds during summer alternate between northwest and northeast. At other times, southwest winds are more frequent and this is also the direction of most gales. More than strong winds, the main danger in the islands are the extremely strong tidal streams, the notorious Alderney Race reaching 8 knots on occasions.

✦ FORMALITIES

PORTS OF ENTRY

Alderney:	Braye	49°43′N 2°12′W
Guernsey:	St Peter Port	49°27′N 2°32′W
	Beaucette Marina	49°30′N 2°29′W
Jersey:	St Helier	49°11′N 2°07′W
	Gorey	49°12′N 2°01′W

✦ FACILITIES

As a favourite offshore cruising area for UK yachts as well as a traditional tax-free shopping destination for the French, the Channel Islands have good marinas. Repair and haulout facilities are generally good and there are several chandleries. The Royal Channel Islands Yacht Club and the St Helier Yacht Club are welcoming to visiting sailors. Both Guernsey and Jersey are favourite wintering places for non-EU yachts.

✦ CHARTER

Both companies listed offer both skippered and bareboat charters as well as tuition, although they stress that in view of the difficult local sailing conditions bareboats are only available to experienced sailors.

> www.seascapeyachtcharter.com
> www.jerseysailing.com

Cruising Guides
Channel Islands
Cruising Almanac
North Brittany and the Channel Islands
North Brittany and Channel Islands Cruising Companion
The Shell Channel Pilot

Websites
www.visitguernsey.com
www.jersey.com
www.herm-island.com
www.jersey-harbours.com
www.gyc.org.uk (Guernsey Yacht Club)
www.rciyc.com (Royal Channel Islands Yacht Club)
www.shyc.je (St Helier Yacht Club)

Local time	UTC
	Summer time: last Sunday in March to last Sunday in October
Buoyage	IALA A
Currency	British Pound (GBP)
Electricity	230V, 50Hz

Diplomatic missions
In London: see UK

Communications
IDD 44   IAC 00

Emergency number
999

FAEROE ISLANDS

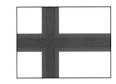

SITUATED IN THE HEART OF THE GULF STREAM, the Faeroe Islands (Føroyar in Faeroese) are a group of 18 islands that lie northwest of Scotland and halfway between Iceland and Norway.

The Faroese are descendants of the Vikings, who came mainly from Norway, sailed westwards looking for new land and reached the Faeroes, Iceland, Greenland and even Vinland in continental North America. In 2007 the country was rated as 'the most appealing destination in the world' by *National Geographic* magazine.

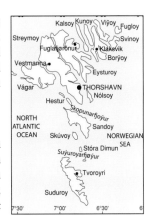

✦ COUNTRY PROFILE

The Faeroes were settled by the Vikings in the ninth century and came under Danish rule in 1380. They were granted autonomy in 1948, and in 2008 voted not to accede to the EU, even though they are dependent on Denmark for assistance. Denmark is also responsible for foreign affairs and defence. The Faeroes have close traditional ties to Iceland, Norway, Shetland, Orkney, the Outer Hebrides and Greenland. The population of 47,000 speak Faeroese, a Norse dialect akin to Icelandic, as well as Danish. English is widely understood. The capital is Thorshavn.

✦ CLIMATE

The weather is often unsettled and visibility is frequently poor, when the land may be obscured by fog or drizzle. The incidence of summer gales is similar to other places on the West European seaboard. Sudden squalls may be experienced inside the fjords. In summer months there are long daylight hours, the weather is fairly mild due to the Gulf Stream, and winds are often light.

✦ FORMALITIES

The Faeroes courtesy flag should be flown, not the Danish. Suduroy is the most convenient harbour when approaching from the south and should be contacted on Channel 23. Normally police board a yacht and give customs clearance, but if the boat is not met, the captain should go ashore to complete formalities. The Faeroes are not covered by the Schengen Agreement, but there are no border checks when travelling between the Faeroes and any Schengen country.

PORTS OF ENTRY		
Eysturoy:	Fuglafjordur	62°15´N 6°49´W
Bordoy:	Klaksvik	62°14´N 6°35´W
Streymoy (Strømø): Thorshavn (Torshavn) 62°00´N 6°45´W		
Vestmanna (Vestmanhavn)	62°09´N 7°10´W	
Suduroy: Tvoroyri 61°33´N 6°48´W Vagur 61°28´N 6°48´W		

✦ FACILITIES

There are no special facilities for yachts, but berthing is allowed at some commercial quays and there are some good anchorages. Basic repairs can be carried out using the extensive repair and shipbuilding facilities provided for the local fishing fleets. There are shops in all the main ports and a supermarket in Thorshavn. Fuel and water are available in Thorshavn, Tvoroyri, Fuglafjordur, Klaksvik and other fishing ports.

✦ CHARTER

Although there are no yachts for charter locally, some operators based in Western Scotland undertake regular voyages to the Faeroes.

> www.newhorizonsailing.com
> www.northernwanderer.co.uk
> www.beyondthebluehorizon.co.uk

Cruising Guide
Faeroe, Iceland and Greenland

Websites
www.faroeislands.com   www.streymkort.fo (online tidal maps)

Local time	UTC
Summer time: last Sunday in March to last Sunday in October	
Buoyage	IALA A
Currency	Faroese Krona, Danish Krone (DKK)
Electricity	230V, 50Hz

Diplomatic missions
UK	298 13510
USA	Copenhagen +45 3341 7100
Canada	Copenhagen +45 3348 3200
Australia	Copenhagen + 45 7026 3686
South Africa	Copenhagen + 45 3918 0155

Communications	**Emergency number**
IDD 298 IAC 00	112

FRANCE

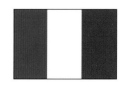

The Atlantic coast of France is more challenging than the Mediterranean in almost every respect, but brings its rewards in an abundance of natural harbours, wide tidal estuaries and snug coves. Making landfall at picturesque ports like Sauzon, Morlaix, St Malo or Lézardrieux justifies all the effort, especially if celebrated by a delicious meal in one of the restaurants that line the shore. Although spectacular, sailing along this coast can be nerve-racking as there are many offlying hazards, strong tidal streams and frequent gales. The western coast divides into four distinct areas: the northernmost includes all of Normandy, a shoreline backed by chalk cliffs leading to the port of Le Havre and the Seine estuary with the charming harbour of Honfleur. To the south, the craggy Cotentin Peninsula shelters the port of Cherbourg, an important yachting centre and nuclear submarine base. Further south is the port of Granville which has the greatest tidal range in Europe, with a difference of some 11m (35ft) at springs. Tides in this area are indeed fierce and used to pose a nail-biting challenge to mariners, who have described these waters as the most dangerous in the world – a reminder to today's sailors that we cannot be grateful enough for GPS.

The most picturesque part of the Brittany coast starts west of St Malo along the Côte de Granit Rose, the roseate granite cliffs giving this area its enticing name. This 40 mile long stretch between Paimpol and Trébeurden has many good anchorages amid dramatic scenery punctuated by towering rock formations. Rounding the rocky islands of Ushant (Ouessant) and entering the Bay of Biscay, the

Bono Harbour in Morbihan.

climate becomes milder and the odd palm tree can be spotted on the shoreline. There are several navigable rivers from here onwards as well as the Morbihan inland sea. The area between Loctudy and Concarneau is enormously popular with French sailors, many of whom may have honed their skills at the world-famous Glénan Sailing School based on Ile Cigogne in the small archipelago whose name it bears. The area abounds in sheltered harbours, making it possible to sail almost regardless of weather.

For those interested in navigating the extensive French waterway system, and are prepared to lower the mast, this can be accessed at the ports of Dunkerque, Calais, Gravelines or St Valéry-sur-Somme. Further south, the Brittany Canal runs from the English Channel to the Bay of Biscay through 63 locks from St Malo via Dinan, Rennes, Redan and the River Vilaine.

At the southern limit of Brittany, marked by the River Loire, the scenery starts to change, the rocky foreshore gradually giving way to sandy beaches. This area has several offlying islands: Noirmoutier, Ile d'Yeu, Ile de Groix, Ile de Ré and Ile d'Oléron, as well as two of France's major yachting centres, La Rochelle and Les Sables d'Olonne. Two great rivers, the Loire and the Gironde, lead into the extensive inland waterway system. The aptly called Canal des Deux Mers that links the Atlantic to the Mediterranean starts from the Gironde estuary and, via the Canal de Garonne, at Toulouse joins the Canal du Midi that ends at Sète. This route offers a tempting shortcut to the Mediterranean that takes in some of France's most beautiful countryside, passing within a stone's throw of the famous Médoc wine area with illustrious names such as Pauillac, Blaye or Bourg, and medieval gems such as Moissac, Montauban, Carcassone, Béziers and Agde.

The fourth and final section starts south of Bordeaux, a low-lying area stretching to the Spanish border. This area is less appealing as a cruising destination as the coast is a succession of wide sandy beaches backed by dunes and clumps of pine trees with only a few harbours along the way, such as the large inland tidal lagoon of Arcachon. Close to the Spanish border, the beautiful bay of St Jean de Luz contains three harbours: Ciboure, La Nivelle and Socoa.

◆ CLIMATE

The climate on the Atlantic coast of France is temperate and summers are quite pleasant, with the sailing season lasting from late spring to early autumn. August is the warmest month, with an average of 17°C/63°F, and January is the coldest (6°C/43°F) in Normandy and, on average, three degrees higher in the southwest. Winters are generally mild, frost and snow being quite infrequent. The prevailing winds of summer are northerly, becoming southwest when a system of low pressure comes in from the Atlantic. The strongest winds also come from the southwest.

✦ FORMALITIES

✦ CHARTER

There is a whole range of charter opportunities with operators offering all types of boats, both power and sailing yachts. Cap West, based in Normandy, also serves the Channel Islands, while all other listed companies operate in Brittany.

www.capwest.fr (Fleury-sur-Orne)
www.saint-malo-sailing.com (St Malo)
www.solentys.com (Port la Forêt)
www.eridan.org (Brest and Port de l'Aber Wrac'h)

PORTS OF ENTRY

Channel/North Sea:

Dunkerque	51°03′N 2°21′E	Gravelines	50°59′N 2°08′E	Calais	50°58′N 1°51′E
Boulogne	50°44′N 1°37′E	Le Touquet-Etaples	50°31′N 1°38′E	Abbeville	50°06′N 1°51′E
Dieppe	49°56′N 1°05′E	Le Havre	49°29′N 0°07′E	Caudebec-en-Caux	49°32′N 0°44′E
Le Tréport	50°04′N 1°22′E	Fécamp	49°46′N 0°22′E	Honfleur	49°25′N 0°14′E
Caen	49°11′N 0°21′W	Cherbourg	49°38′N 1°38′W	Granville	48°50′N 1°36′W
St Malo	48°39′N 2°01′W	Le Légué-St Brieuc	48°32′N 2°43′W	Paimpol	48°47′N 3°03′W
Morlaix	48°38′N 3°53′W	Roscoff	48°43′N 3°59′W		

Atlantic:

Brest	48°23′N 4°29′W	Quimper	47°58′N 4°07′W	Douarnenez	48°06′N 4°20′W
Lorient	47°45′N 3°22′W	Vannes	47°39′N 2°45′W	La Trinité-sur-Mer	47°35′N 3°01′E
Concarneau	47°52′N 3°55′W	St Nazaire	47°16′N 2°12′W	Nantes	47°14′N 1°34′W
Les Sables d'Olonne	46°30′N 1°48′W	La Rochelle	46°09′N 1°09′W	Rochefort	45°56′N 0°58′W
La Tremblade	45°46′N 1°08′W	Le Château d'Oléron	45°53′N 1°12′W	Royan	45°38′N 1°02′W
Bordeaux-Bassens	44°50′N 0°34′W	Pauillac-Trompeloup	45°12′N 0°45′W	Blaye	45°07′N 0°40′W
Le Verdon	45°33′N 1°05′W	Arcachon	44°40′N 1°10′W	Bayonne	43°30′N 1°29′W
Ciboure	43°23′N 1°41′W	Hendaye-Béhobie	43°22′N 1°46′W		

✦ FACILITIES

Chandleries and repair facilities are widely available and small jobs can be undertaken in most ports. For more complicated or specialized tasks, it is best to go to one of the major centres, where there are established boatyards and specialist companies offering a complete range of repair facilities. Some of the best-known boatbuilders are also based on this coast.

The most active sailing centres, all with good facilities, are at St Malo, Ouistreham, Cherbourg, Brest, La Trinité, Les Sables d'Olonne, La Rochelle, Le Havre, Lorient and Bordeaux. There are yacht clubs in all ports, and visiting sailors are welcome – especially if their own clubs have reciprocal arrangements.

For more background and practical information on France, see pages 31–32.

Cruising Guides

North Biscay
South Biscay
North Brittany and the Channel Islands
North Brittany and Channel Islands Cruising Companion
The Shell Channel Pilot
Cruising Almanac

Websites

www.normandie-tourisme.fr
www.brittanytourism.com
www.tourisme-aquitaine.fr
www.portfocus.com/france/zz_marinas_french_atlantic/index.html (list of Atlantic marinas)

GREENLAND

GREENLAND, KNOWN AS KALAALLIT NUNAAT in the Inuit language, is the world's largest island. Lying mostly within the Arctic Circle, much of the land is under ice and in places the ice cap is over 3 km (2 miles) deep. Greenland is undoubtedly the most challenging cruising destination in the North Atlantic and every year a few yachts brave the elements to explore this wild and beautiful island during the all too short summer season. The deeply indented coasts offer a variety of anchorages in steep-sided fjords or among the myriad islands. By June, the west coast is usually clear of ice between 63°N and 69°N and can be reached by passing well to seaward of Cape Farewell. Depending on conditions, vessels may have to pass as far as 100 miles offshore. July and August are the best months for cruising. The effects of climate change and the milder weather conditions have already brought about a steady increase in the number of cruising yachts, some of which have navigated successfully the once impenetrable North West Passage.

✦ COUNTRY PROFILE

It is believed that the Inuit population originally settled in Greenland from the west. They arrived shortly before the Vikings who sailed over from Iceland at the end of the first millennium. Most colonies were along the southwest coast and it is now believed that in the Middle Ages the climate was warmer than it is now. Colonized by the Danes from 1721 onwards, Greenland was incorporated into Denmark, but full internal self-government was agreed in 1981. In 1985 the population voted to leave the EU, which the country had previously joined as part of Denmark, mostly because of disagreements about fishing quotas. In 2008 Greenland voted to become a separate country within the Kingdom of Denmark, effective from June 2009.

The population of 58,000 is concentrated in the southwest, being a mix of Inuit and European, with a Danish minority. Both Greenlandic (Kalaallisut) and Danish are spoken, but in 2009 Greenlandic was declared the only official language. The capital is Nuuk.

✦ CLIMATE

The weather is cold all year round and the winters are particularly harsh, with some ports being icebound until well into the summer. Temperatures are low even in the summer months. July and August are the warmest months, with average temperatures of 7°C/45°F.

The prevailing winds in the southern part are south or southwest, while easterly winds predominate further north. Winds are light and variable in summer. Depending on latitude, the midnight sun is visible from the end of May until the end of July.

The port of Qaqortoq

PORTS OF ENTRY

Tasiilaq (Ammassalik)	65°35′N 37°30′W	(August to November)			
Christianshaab (Qasigiannguit)	68°49′N 51°11′W	(May to November)			
Faeringehavn	63°42′N 51°33′W	(year round)	Frederikshaab (Paamiut)	62°00′N 49°40′W	(year round)
Godthaab (Nuuk)	64°10′N 51°44′W	(year round)	Holsteinsborg (Sisimiut)	66°57′N 53°41′W	(year round)
Julianehaab (Qaqortoq)	60°43′N 46°02′W	(year round)			
Nanortalik	60°08′N 45°15′W	(August to December)			

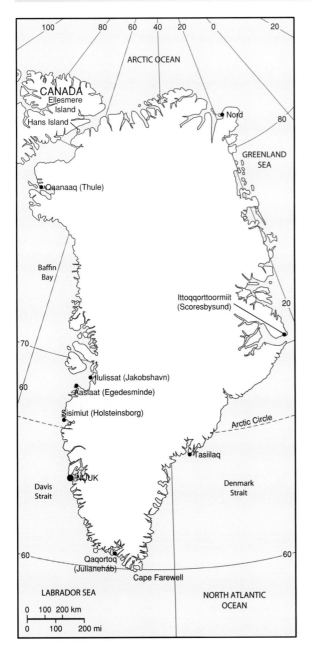

◆ FORMALITIES

The Port Authorities should be contacted on Channel 12 or 16 well in advance – 24 hours before if possible. Greenland is not a member of the EU, but is a signatory to the Schengen Agreement.

Some areas of the country may only be visited with a special permit and all military areas must be avoided. The importation of fresh food is prohibited.

◆ FACILITIES

There are no conventional marina facilities. Because of the large fishing fleets, some repair services are available. The best range is in Nuuk, and more limited repair facilities are available at Holsteinsborg and Jakobshavn, which also have slipways. Fuel and water are available in all ports. Provisions are available only in the larger settlements, with the best in Nuuk.

◆ CHARTER

Greenland has started attracting charter yachts, and there may be more as cold water sailing attracts more aficionados.

www.beyondthebluehorizon.co.uk

Cruising Guide	
Faeroe, Iceland and Greenland	
Websites	
www.greenland-guide.gl	www.greenland.com

Local time	UTC −3
	Summer time: last Saturday in March to last Saturday in October
Buoyage	IALA A
Currency	Danish Krone (DKK)
Electricity	230V, 50Hz

Diplomatic missions	
UK	24422

Communications		**Emergency number**
IDD 299	IAC 00	113

ICELAND

ISOLATED IN THE NORTH ATLANTIC with Greenland as its only neighbour, Iceland consists of one main island and numerous smaller ones. It is a country of stark beauty, of mighty glaciers, hissing geysers, boiling lakes and live volcanoes. Visited by only the most intrepid yachts during its short summer, a passage to Iceland and a cruise along its rugged coasts offers an experience difficult to match anywhere else in the North Atlantic.

✦ COUNTRY PROFILE

In the ninth century Norsemen and Irish came to settle on the island, and in the year 930 the Althing, an assembly of free men, was formed. The Althing is considered to be the oldest democratically elected assembly in the world. Norway took control of Iceland in the thirteenth century, and then itself fell under Danish rule, taking Iceland with it. Autonomy was achieved in 1903, and in 1918 the independent Kingdom of Iceland was formed, although still under the Danish Crown. In 1944 the Republic of Iceland was proclaimed. It also joined NATO and in 1958 the USA took control of Iceland's defence. After the economic crisis in 2008, Iceland applied for membership of the EU.

The population is 307,000, half of whom live in the capital, Reykjavik. The language is Icelandic, which is closer to old Norse than Norwegian is.

✦ CLIMATE

Although lying just south of the Arctic Circle, the climate is not too harsh and winters are relatively mild, due to the Gulf Stream. The average temperatures are 11°C/52°F in summer, and 0°C/32°F in winter. Because Iceland lies in the track of most Atlantic depressions, the weather is changeable. Prevailing winds are from the south or southeast. Summer winds are often light and calms are common.

✦ FORMALITIES

The captain must inform customs of a yacht's arrival. They will then give clearance to all places within Iceland. No cruising permit is required, but yachts must obtain a permit from customs to temporarily import the vessel exempt from duty. In Reykjavik Port Control should be contacted on Channel 12 for berthing instructions. Iceland is a signatory to the Schengen Agreement. Danish embassies will handle visa requests on Iceland's behalf.

✦ FACILITIES

Reykjavik is best for both facilities and provisioning. Although there are not many local yachts, repair services are relatively good, particularly in active fishing harbours such as Reykjavik, Isafjördur and Olafsvik. Keflavik is a well-protected port with some repair facilities.

A feature along the Icelandic shores are orange huts, set up as refuges for shipwrecked sailors. Every hut has some emergency supplies and a radiotelephone.

✦ CHARTER

There are a number of yachts undertaking North Atlantic voyages that also call at Iceland.

> www.beyondthebluehorizon.co.uk
> www.velvetadventuresailing.com

Cruising Guide		Website	
Faeroe, Iceland and Greenland		www.visiticeland.com	

Local time	UTC	Currency	Icelandic Krona (ISK)
Buoyage	IALA A	Electricity	230V, 50Hz

Diplomatic missions			
UK	5505100	Canada	5756500
USA	5629100	South Africa	5910355

Communications		Emergency number	
IDD 354	IAC 00	112	

PORTS OF ENTRY

Reykjavik	64°08′N 21°54′W	Keflavik	64°00′N 22°33′W	Isafjördur	66°05′N 23°06′W	Akranes	64°19′N 22°05′W
Saudarkrokur	65°45′N 19°36′W	Siglufjördur	66°12′N 18°52′W	Akureyri	65°41′N 18°03′W	Husavik	66°03′N 17°22′W
Seydisfjördur	65°15′N 13°55′W	Neskaupstadur	65°09′N 13°41′W	Eskifjördur	65°05′N 13°59′W		
Vestmannaeyjar	63°26′N 20°16′W	Hafnarfjördur	64°04′N 21°55′W				

IRELAND

THE APTLY CALLED EMERALD ISLE is made up of two political units, the independent Republic of Ireland, also known as Eire, and the smaller region of Northern Ireland, which is part of the UK and is covered on pages 133–6. Ireland has a coastline of nearly 3,000 miles, with many deep and sheltered bays. Described by some sailing authors as one of the finest cruising grounds in the world, the only missing element to put Ireland near the top of the table is better weather. At least this is more than made up for by a profusion of perfectly sheltered anchorages. Besides the country's natural beauty, a great pleasure of Irish cruising is finding a pub at the end of a day's sailing in which to enjoy the lively atmosphere and some good music.

Ireland's three coasts are very different and varied. The east coast is the most easily accessible for yachts coming from the UK, but Ireland's real beauty lies on its southern and western coasts. The most popular cruising area is between Cork's spectacular natural harbour and the Dingle Peninsula, with an abundance of snug harbours, sheer cliffs, deep estuaries and picturesque anchorages. The wilder northwest coast is more exposed and the distances between sheltered harbours are greater. Some two hundred islands lie scattered off the west coast of Ireland and only a handful are inhabited. While the east and southeastern coasts have a sizeable local boating population and also attract a number of foreign cruising yachts, the west of Ireland is less frequented.

✦ COUNTRY PROFILE

The Celts settled in Ireland in the fourth century and in the following one St Patrick brought Christianity to the island. Ireland became a flourishing cultural and religious centre and Irish monks travelled around and established important monasteries in some of the Atlantic islands and also on the mainland of Europe. Political disunity due to the rivalry between the Irish kingdoms was exploited by the Anglo-Normans, and in 1175 King Henry II imposed English rule on Ireland. In 1541 Henry VIII took the title of King of Ireland. The Catholic Irish rebelled against the Protestant king, and in retaliation lands were confiscated by the English Crown and given to English gentry, while Protestant Scots were encouraged to settle in Northern Ireland. The Act of Union united Ireland and England in 1800. The potato famine of 1846–8 plunged the island into misery and caused mass emigration. Nationalism continued to be strong; the Easter Rising of 1916 was cruelly repressed by the British

army and guerrilla warfare followed. In 1920 the six counties of Northern Ireland were incorporated into the UK, and a year later the Irish Free State was formed. In 1937 a new constitution was adopted and the name changed to Eire. Neutral during the Second World War, Eire became the Republic of Ireland in 1948.

Following two decades of civil disturbances in Northern Ireland, an agreement was reached between all parties in 1999 that resulted in peaceful relations between the two communities, Catholic and Protestant, and a gradual return to normality. Ireland joined the EU in 1972.

The population is 4.2 million. Irish (Gaelic) and English are spoken. The capital is Dublin, whose Gaelic name is Baile Átha Cliath, meaning 'The town on the hurdled ford'.

✦ CLIMATE

Ireland has a mild and humid climate that is influenced by the Gulf Stream. As a result, the weather is wet all year round, cool and cloudy in summer, and mild in winter. July and August are the warmest months, with an average temperature of 16°C/61°F. Rainfall is heavy all year on the western coast. Strong winds and gales are most frequently from the southwest and are very common in winter. The weather is generally very changeable. The prevailing winds are westerly.

✦ FORMALITIES

As Ireland is a member of the EU and Schengen Agreement, those regulations apply. Boats from non-EU countries, or EU boats arriving from a non-EU country, must notify customs. At night a red light over a white light, not more than 6ft apart, must be shown. On arrival, the customs office should be

Crosshaven near Cork in Southern Ireland.

PORTS OF ENTRY

Dublin	53°21´N 6°13´W	Dun Laoghaire	53°18´N 6°08´W	Wicklow	52°59´N 6°02´W
Dundalk	54°00´N 6°23´W	Drogheda	53°43´N 6°21´W	Carlingford	54°03´N 6°11´W
Greenore	54°02´N 6°08´W	Waterford	52°07´N 6°57´W	New Ross	52°24´N 6°57´W
Dungarvan	52°05´N 7°36´W	Wexford 52°20´N 6°27´W	Cork Harbour (Crosshaven and Cobh)			51°54´N 8°28´W
Kinsale	51°42´N 8°30´W	Baltimore (summer only)	51°27´N 9°24´W	Skibbereen	51°33´N 9°16´W
Bantry	51°42´N 9°28´W	Castletown Bere	51°39´N 9°54´W	Glengariff	51°43´N 9°33´W
Youghal	51°56´N 7°50´W	Limerick	52°40´N 8°38´W	Tralee	52°16´N 9°46´W
Galway	53°16´N 9°03´W	Westport	53°48´N 9°32´W	Sligo	54°16´N 8°28´W
Ballina	54°07´N 9°10´W	Moville	55°11´N 7°02´W	Ballyhoorisky	55°15´N 7°46´W

contacted, or if no customs officer is available, the local police (Garda). All dutiable, restricted and prohibited items must be declared to customs. The harbourmaster must also be notified.

✦ FACILITIES

There is good provisioning in all ports, but repair facilities range from excellent in such major yachting centres as Cork to virtually non-existent in some of the smaller places. The facilities at Crosshaven are the best in Ireland, with a wide range of repair services, including travelift, workshops, rigger and sailmaker. Further east, repair services are also available at Youghal and Waterford. There are several marinas and repair facilities in and around the capital, Dublin, with the best centres being at Dun Laoghaire, Howth and Malahide. The Howth Yacht Club marina has good docking facilities and its location is ideal for visiting Dublin. A useful source of help are the many yacht clubs dotted about the coasts, the

most famous among them being the Royal Cork Yacht Club in Crosshaven, founded in 1720 and considered the oldest sailing club in the world. Most yacht clubs have moorings for visitors who are generally made welcome.

✦ CHARTER

Based in Kilmore Quay in County Wexford, Sailing Ireland offers tuition, bareboat charters and also the opportunity to use such boats in local regattas. The other two companies have a wide range of boats to explore the spectacular west coast of the country.

> www.sailingireland.ie
> www.kinsaleyachtcharter.com
> www.charterireland.ie

Cruising Guides
Cruising Almanac
Cruising Cork and Kerry
Irish Sea Pilot
East and North Coast of Ireland Sailing Directions
Lundy and Irish Sea Pilot
Southern Ireland Cruising Companion
South and West Coast of Ireland Sailing Directions

Website
www.discoverireland.ie

Local time	UTC
	Summer time: last Sunday in March to last Sunday in October
Buoyage	IALA A
Currency	Euro (EUR)
Electricity	230V, 50Hz

Diplomatic missions

UK	1 2053700	Canada	1 2344000
USA	1 6688777	South Africa	1 6615553
Australia	1 6645300		

Communications		**Emergency numbers**
IDD 353	IAC 00	112/999

MADEIRA

MADEIRA LIES IN THE ATLANTIC some 300 miles off the African coast. Only two islands of this volcanic archipelago are inhabited, the largest, Madeira Grande, which gives its name to the entire group, and Porto Santo to the northeast. The smaller islands of the main group are Ilha Chao, Ilha Deserta Grande, and Ilheu de Bugio. The Ilhas Selvagem, about halfway to the Canary Islands, are a wildlife refuge administered by Madeira, and yachts wishing to visit them need permission from the Department of Fisheries in Funchal. While the outer islands are mostly dry, Madeira Grande's lush vegetation and profusion of flowers account for its enduring charm.

The Madeiran archipelago is one of those places whose geographical position means that it is always visited by yachts en route to somewhere else and rarely as a destination in its own right. This seems to have always been the case and over the centuries many famous sailors called here for fresh stores. Captain Cook stopped here in 1768 at the start of his first circumnavigation on the *Endeavour* and loaded a staggering total of 3,000 gallons of Madeira wine for the exclusive use of the officers and gentlemen on board. Visiting the old wine lodges is still a favourite pastime among visiting sailors. But sampling the distinctive wine is only one of the local attractions as the islands have much to be enjoyed and many

sailors regard Madeira with special affection. The majority of yachts arrive between September and November on their way to the Canary Islands and the Caribbean, while some leave direct from Madeira to cross the Atlantic. There has also been an increase in the number of American boats cruising the Atlantic circle of Bermuda, Azores, Madeira and Canary Islands during the summer, while Madeira has also become a popular port of call in the spring, for yachts returning to Europe after wintering in the Canaries.

✦ COUNTRY PROFILE

Legend says that Madeira was part of the lost kingdom of Atlantis and the islands were already known to the Phoenicians. The islands were uninhabited and covered in dense forest, hence the name, which means Island of Timber in Portuguese. Settled by the Portuguese in the fifteenth century, prosperity soon came with the cultivation of sugar cane and wine production. Christopher Columbus lived on Porto Santo for several years after he married the daughter of the island's governor. With the growth in the numbers of ships calling for provisions, Madeira wine rapidly became sought after in many countries. But the wine was not the only reason for trading vessels and passenger ships to stop here. The variety of fresh provisions available made it a popular

The port of Funchal.

port of call for British vessels on their voyages to all parts of the globe.

Madeira is an autonomous region of Portugal. The population is 264,000 and Portuguese is the official language, although many understand Spanish and there has been a resident British community for many years. The capital, Funchal, is a pleasant city with attractive mosaic pavements and whitewashed buildings in the Portuguese colonial style.

◆ CLIMATE

The islands have a pleasant and mild climate all year round, the air temperature rarely falling below 14°C/57°F in winter, or rising above 25°C/77°F in summer. Due to the influence of the Gulf Stream, the water temperature similarly varies only between 17° and 21°C (63–70°F). The prevailing winds are northeasterly. Only the more variable winds of winter and the passage of lows across the North Atlantic can affect the weather, otherwise Madeira can be visited all year round.

◆ FORMALITIES

PORTS OF ENTRY

Madeira: Funchal	32°38´N 16°54´W
Quinta do Lorde	32°44.5´N 16°43.3´W
Calheta	32°42.8´N 17°10.1´W
Porto Santo:	33°03´N 16°19´W

Funchal: The small boat harbour inside Funchal harbour is run as a marina, but all spaces on the pontoons are occupied by local craft, and visiting yachts are obliged to tie up alongside the harbour wall or anchor outside. Formalities are completed in the marina. Visiting yachts rarely find a free place, so it is better to stop at marina Quinta do Lorde east of Funchal.
Porto Santo: The captain should report to the port captain's office on the north side of the harbour. Even if arriving from Madeira Grande, you still have to report to all the offices.

Madeira comes under Portugal's Schengen Agreement and therefore has similar visa regulations.

Although Madeira is a member of the EU, all boats must contact the authorities on arrival, whether coming from an EU country or not. A clearance document is issued to yachts at the port of entry and must be presented to the authorities when visiting any other port. Even if possessing a transit log from mainland Portugal or the Azores, clearance must still be done on arrival in Madeira. Both marinas at Quinta do Lorde and Calheta are ports of entry and formalities can be completed there. The former is convenient for boats arriving from the north, while the latter for boats arriving from the Azores and the west.

◆ FACILITIES

Facilities have been greatly enhanced with the opening of two marinas, Quinta do Lorde and Calheta, on Madeira Grande, and the improvements to Porto Santo Marina. Docking facilities in Funchal are inadequate as the marina is always full. Repair services are good in Funchal, with various engineering shops and a travelift in the boatyard next to the marina. The new marinas are expanding their range of services. All marinas have fuel, and provisioning is good everywhere. There is an excellent fresh produce market in Funchal.

There are only basic repair facilities in Porto Santo, and for any work it is best to sail over to Madeira Grande. The islands Desertas and Selvagem are uninhabited with no facilities.

◆ CHARTER

Tamisa Boat Charters, based in Funchal, offers a range of services, from both power and sailing boats for charter, to tuition and offshore fishing trips.

www.tamisa-boat-charters.com

Cruising Guide
Atlantic Islands

Websites
www.madeiratourism.org
www.quintadolorde.com (details of Quinta do Lorde and Porto Santo marinas)

Local time	UTC
	Summer time: last Sunday in March to last Sunday in October
Buoyage	IALA A
Currency	Euro (EUR)
Electricity	230V, 50Hz

Diplomatic missions

UK	291 212860	Canada	Lisbon 21 164600
USA	Lisbon 21 7273300	South Africa	291 223521
Australia	Lisbon 21 3101500	New Zealand	Lisbon 21 3705779

Communications		**Emergency number**
IDD 351	IAC 00	112

PORTUGAL

PORTUGAL OCCUPIES the western part of the Iberian Peninsula, its exposure to the Atlantic Ocean having shaped the character and destiny of its inhabitants. A nation of seafarers, the Portuguese started the European age of discovery and exploration in the fifteenth century. Portuguese ships sailed beyond the known horizons to discover the route around Africa to India and then were the first to circumnavigate the world. Little remains of the once mighty empire except the Atlantic islands of Madeira and the Azores, which enjoy a degree of autonomy and have been dealt with separately in this book.

From the cruising point of view, mainland Portugal divides into two distinct areas, the west and the south. The ports on the west coast, which is exposed to the Atlantic, are situated mostly in estuaries or rivers, often with bars at the entrance. Among them, the most interesting landfall is the capital, Lisbon, set on the River Tagus, which can be navigated right into the centre of the city. An equally interesting foray is provided by the River Douro that leads to the medieval city of Porto. The west coast has a number of strategically placed ports where you can find shelter if necessary.

The Algarve coast in the south has better weather and easier approaches to its small picturesque ports. As you sail around Cape St Vincent, a deep bay opens to port and perched above on the high cliff is a fort. Here are the remains of a school of navigation founded by Prince Henry the Navigator in 1419, which trained the intrepid explorers whose ships reached the furthest corners of the world. An impressive monument to those outstanding sailors stands on the bank of Tagus at the entrance into Lisbon.

An interesting cruising ground is the River Guadiana, which forms the border between Portugal and Spain. The river is home to all kinds of wading birds and is also an important staging post for migratory birds commuting between Northern Europe and Africa. Migratory birds of another kind spend the winter here too: cruising sailors attracted by the mild climate and the facilities set up for their benefit by the small towns on both shores. The Guadiana is navigable by keeled yachts for some 20 miles as far as Pomarão where a small restaurant has a dock for visitors – rewarding those who have made it that far inland with a delicious lunch of freshly caught fish.

✦ COUNTRY PROFILE

Portugal was originally inhabited by Iberian tribes who came into early contact with Phoenicians, Greeks and Romans, the latter making the country part of their empire as the province of Lusitania. In the fifth century the entire Iberian Peninsula was overrun by Visigoths, and then by Moors in the eighth century. By the eleventh century the Portuguese kings had expelled the Moors and an independent kingdom was established. Portugal's borders have remained basically

The medieval city of Porto on the banks of the Douro river.

SPAIN

NORTH
ATLANTIC
OCEAN

• Viana do Castelo
• Braga
• Vila Real
Leixões
• Porto
• Aveiro • Viseu
• Coimbra • Covilhã
Figueira da Foz
• Leirla • Castelo
Branco
Tagus
• Caldas da Rainha
• Santarém
SPAIN
LISBON
• Barreiro
Setúbal
• Évora
Rio Guadiana
Sines • Beja •
Portimão
Faro
Golfo de Cádiz

influence. This was an artificial line dividing the world in two, with Spain claiming most of the Americas, and Portugal laying claim to Africa and everything to the east of this hypothetical line – which is how the Portuguese acquired Brazil. In 1580 the country was occupied by Spain and independence was only restored in 1640. By then France, England and the Netherlands were overtaking the Portuguese in maritime strength and Portugal went into decline. In 1910 the monarchy was overthrown in a revolution, but strife continued and a fascist regime was established in the 1930s. After the Second World War the colonies pushed for independence and several prolonged and costly wars were fought in Africa. In 1974 the military regime was replaced with civil government and democracy. In 1986 Portugal joined the EU.

The population numbers 10.7 million. The capital is Lisbon on the north bank of the River Tagus, which opens into the Mar de Palha (Sea of Straw). The area has been settled since the time of the Phoenicians and the town became the capital in 1260.

✦ CLIMATE

The climate of the western shores of Portugal is much influenced by the Atlantic, whereas its southern coast enjoys a Mediterranean type of climate. It is generally mild, being cooler in the north and warmer in the south. The winters are mild but rainy. The Algarve coast is the driest and warmest part of the country. The average summer temperature in the north is 20°C/68°F and 5° higher in the south. In winter the average temperature in the north is 8°C/46°F compared to 12°/54°F on the Algarve coast. The prevailing winds of summer, known as the Portuguese trades, are northerly; they commence in about April and last until September. On the Algarve the northerly winds of summer are often replaced by land and sea breezes. Most gales occur in winter, when the prevailing winds are westerly. Due to their location, some Atlantic ports are not accessible in strong onshore winds.

✦ FORMALITIES

Lisbon: The approaches to the River Tagus (Rio Tejo) are straightforward, but you should keep to the marked channel as there are shallows in the approaches. Clearing formalities can be completed at Cascais Marina, or you can proceed up the river to Doca de Alcântara, upstream of the first bridge, where all officials are based. The swing bridge at the entrance to this dock opens on request (Channel 12).

Porto: There is a bar at the entrance to the River Douro and the entrance is dangerous in strong winds or with a heavy swell. The deep-water channel is on the north side. For both mooring and clearance, it is best to use the yachting facilities in the commercial port of Leixões, which can be entered under most conditions and has a marina and three yacht clubs.

unchanged as Portugal was unified into a state earlier than most European nations. In the fifteenth century Prince Henry the Navigator initiated a series of voyages of discovery into the Atlantic, along the African coast and then to the East Indies. Vasco da Gama found the sea route to India, and prosperity came with the Portuguese monopoly of the spice trade as the country gradually established a widespread maritime empire. Rivalry with Spain was intense and the two countries eventually concluded a treaty, which laid out their spheres of

PORTS OF ENTRY

Viana do Castelo	41°41´ N 8°50´ W	Leixões (Porto)	41°11´ N 8°42´ W	Figueira da Foz	40°09´ N 8°52´ W
Nazaré	39°35.2´ N 9°04.4´ W	Peniche	39°21´ N 9°22.5´ W	Cascais	38°42´ N 9°25´ W
Sesimbra	38°26´ N 9°06´ W	Lisbon	38°44´ N 9°07´ W	Sines	37°57´ N 8°52´ W
Lagos	37°06´ N 8°40´ W	Portimão	37°08´ N 8°32´ W	Vilamoura	37°04´ N 8°07´ W
Faro	37°01´ N 7°55´ W	Vila Real de Santo Antonio	37°11´ N 7°25´ W		

Vilamoura: Vilamoura Radio monitors Channels 16 and 20. The wide entrance leads into an outer basin used mainly by local fishing boats, from which a narrower entrance leads to the marina. For clearance, yachts must come alongside the reception dock on the port side in front of the control tower.

All boats arriving from abroad must contact either a port or marina office to complete formalities. Non-EU yachts will receive a transit log (livrete de trânsito) which is stamped at the first port and must be stamped again at the last port of departure. All major marinas have been designated to deal with clearance formalities.

Visa requirements are in line with the provisions of the Schengen Agreement. The captain may be required to show a certificate of competence, and at least one crew member must have a VHF radio operator's certificate.

EU boats must clear out only if departing for a non-EU destination. Non-EU vessels must clear out and have their transit log stamped.

✦ FACILITIES

Yachting facilities are of a good standard. The best repair services are concentrated in the three areas that have a local boating community. The capital, Lisbon, has several docking facilities for yachts and the repair services are spread out. Facilities at Porto are concentrated around the marina in Leixoes. Vilamoura Marina on the Algarve coast is popular among North European sailors as it is a good place to leave the boat for long periods, especially if planning to set off

The monument to Portuguese discoveries set on the shore of the River Tagus in Lisbon.

across the Atlantic and not go into the Mediterranean. Repairs here are the best in Portugal, with a complete range of engine, sail, electrical, electronic and fibreglass services as well as a travelift. Vila Real de Santo Antonio on the west bank of the River Guadiana is a good base from which to explore this area. The bridge over the river has a reported air clearance of 20m (66ft).

✦ CHARTER

With the exception of the OnDeck charter company in Cascais, all others are based in various marinas on the Algarve coast. Portiate Charters, one of the oldest charter companies in Portugal, has a mixed fleet of power and sailing yachts at Portimão, while Sea Vision International is based in Vilamoura and offers only powerboats. Quima Yachting, with bases in Vilamoura and Portimão, is the local agent for Sunsail and the Moorings.

www.portiate.com
www.seavisioninternational.com
www.quima-yachting.com

Cruising Guides
Atlantic Spain and Portugal
Cruising Almanac

Website
www.visitportugal.com

Local time	UTC
	Summer time: last Sunday in March to last Sunday in October
Buoyage	IALA A
Currency	Euro (EUR)
Electricity	230V, 50Hz

Diplomatic missions
UK	21 3924000
USA	21 7273300
Australia	21 3101500
Canada	21 3164600
South Africa	21 3192200
New Zealand	21 3192200

Communications
| IDD 351 | IAC 00 |

Emergency number 112

SPAIN

ATLANTIC SPAIN IS DIVIDED by the bulk of Portugal into two distinct sections: the north and northwest coast bordering the Bay of Biscay, and the smaller southwest coast of Andalucia stretching from the Portuguese border to the Straits of Gibraltar. Nature has been generous along the coasts, creating many natural harbours, secluded coves and pretty anchorages. Of the four regions fronting the north coast, Pais Vasco (Euskadi), Cantabria, Asturias and Galicia, the first and last have a long seafaring tradition. Galician seamen played a major part in Spain's overseas expansion while Basque fishermen roamed the Atlantic far and wide – and there is speculation that they were fishing the cod-rich grounds off Newfoundland long before John Cabot put this corner of North America on the world map. Spain's most famous sailor, Juan Sebastian Elcano, who brought Magellan's ship safely back home in 1522 after his commander was killed in the Philippines, was the first man to circumnavigate the globe. Elcano hailed from the small Basque port of Guetaria.

The north coast is rocky and barren, with steep cliffs rising over the clear water. The coast has few indentations and natural harbours are sparse, some being at the mouths of various rivers. The background is quite spectacular, with high mountains whose peaks are covered in snow for most of the year. The rugged coastline continues all the way to Cabo Villano, then gradually the high mountain ranges give way to steep-sided fjord-like estuaries called Rias Altas. The scenery changes dramatically as the coast takes a hard turn southwards and the Rias Altas give way to the wider bays and estuaries called Rias Baixas. This is a stormy corner aptly called in Spanish Costa da Morte, Coast of Death, on account of all the ships that have met their end on this unforgiving shore. All-weather harbours are few and the large swell makes their approaches treacherous. Landfall after a crossing of the Bay of Biscay should take this into account so as to either make for the safety of La Coruña or, if in any doubt, stay well offshore. The Rias Baixas are Spain's best coastal cruising grounds, with plenty of safe harbours, nice anchorages in attractive inlets, and interesting towns with good marinas. In this country of rich culture and traditions there is much to see both in the ports along the coast as well as inland.

The Atlantic coast of Andalucia has much in common with the Mediterranean. Stretching from the River Guadiana to Gibraltar, its harbours are steeped in history, from Cadiz, the ancient Gadir founded by the Phoenicians 3,000 years ago, to the now silted-up Palos de la Frontera on the Rio Tinto from where Christopher Columbus's three caravels set off in 1492 on a voyage that ended with the discovery of a new world. Palos and the sites associated with Columbus, such as La Rabida Monastery where he was based before his history-making voyage, are within easy reach of the marina at Mazagon at the mouth of the Odiel river.

Navigable rivers are a special attraction in this corner of Andalucia, such as the Guadalquivir that allows even

La Concha Bay off San Sebastian.

freighters to sail as far inland as the medieval city of Seville. Visiting yachts can use the facilities of the friendly Seville Yacht Club and the best time to be here is during Semana Santa when the heart of this medieval city throbs in rhythm with the most spectacular Easter celebrations anywhere in Spain, if not the world. Another river that offers even better cruising opportunities is the Guadiana, which forms the border between Spain and Portugal. The river is navigable for some 20 miles as far as Pomarão, and the scenery and wildlife are well worth the detour.

✦ CLIMATE

The climate varies greatly between the shores facing the Atlantic or the Bay of Biscay, which are wet and cool, and the southern coast which has an almost Mediterranean climate. Along the north and northwest coast, July and August are the most pleasant months, with average temperatures of 19°C/66°F, whereas summers on the southern coasts can be much warmer, with temperatures well over 30°C/80°F. Winter variations are not so pronounced, with an average of 10°C/50°F in the north and, on average, only two degrees warmer in the south.

The winds are just as varied, the north and west coasts coming under the influence of Atlantic weather systems, with southwest or northwest winds predominating in winter and northerly winds in summer. Along the southern coast, prevailing winds are either easterly or westerly.

✦ FORMALITIES

EU and Schengen regulations apply. Most marinas have either been designated to deal with entry formalities or can assist in contacting the relevant officials.

✦ FACILITIES

Most marinas have haulout facilities, usually by travelift, while in many ports there are slipways dealing with fishing boats. Repair services are generally good and there is a reasonable supply of marine equipment and spares, although in smaller ports and marinas the availability is limited. There are very good facilities in Santander and the surrounding

PORTS OF ENTRY

Northwest coast:

San Sebastian	43°28´N 30°48´W	Santander	43°28´N 3°46´W	Bilbao	43°17´N 2°55´W
Gijon	43°33´N 5°40´W	El Ferrol	43°28´N 8°16´W	La Coruña	43°23´N 8°22´W
Bayona	42°57´N 9°11´W	Vigo	42°14´N 8°40´W		

Southwest coast:

Ayamonte	37°13´N 7°22´W	Huelva	37°07´N 6°49´W	Puerto Sherry	36°36´N 6°13´W
Cadiz	36°30´N 6°20´W	Algeciras	36°07´N 5°26´W	Sevilla	37°22.6´N 5°59.2´W

The city of Seville can be reached even by large ships sailing up the navigable Guadalquivir river.

Fishermen mending their nets on the bank of the Rio Tinto near Huelva.

area, which has a large resident sailing community served by several marinas. The same is true of La Coruña, Gijon, Vigo and Bayona. On the Andalucian coast the best facilities are at Cadiz and Puerto Sherry Marina. Provisioning is very good, fuel is easily available, and both Spanish and foreign sailors agree that in no other part of the world is seafood more delicious than on Spain's Atlantic coast. Most Spanish yacht clubs are exclusive social clubs, but whereas those on the Mediterranean coast are not always welcoming to visitors, the hardier Atlantic sailors tend to be much friendlier and helpful.

For more background and practical information on Spain, see page 60.

✦ CHARTER

Veleros Galicia, a company run by local sailors, operates a fleet of sailing yachts from three strategically located locations in Vigo, Arousa and La Coruña. Spain Yacht Charter offers a range of yachts based at various marinas in the Cadiz and Huelva area.

www.velerosgalicia.com
www.spain-yachtcharter.com

Cruising Guides
Atlantic Spain and Portugal
Cruising Almanac
Cruising Galicia
South Biscay

Websites
www.spain.info
www.alquiler-directo.com (an informative site that lists details of all Spanish marinas and also acts as an intermediary for yacht charter in various areas of Spain)

UNITED KINGDOM

THE UNITED KINGDOM OF GREAT BRITAIN AND NORTHERN IRELAND incorporates the three countries of England, Scotland and Wales, the six counties of Ulster in Northern Ireland, as well as several smaller island groups such as the Scillies, Orkneys, Hebrides and Shetlands. The Isle of Man, situated in the Irish Sea, has a special status and enjoys a certain degree of autonomy. The Channel Islands enjoy even greater autonomy and are treated separately (see page 115).

With hardly anywhere more than 50 miles from the sea, the British Isles has always been a maritime nation and has produced some of the greatest sailors and navigators in history. This tradition has continued into the modern age, with British yachts being among the first to sail to the furthest corners of the world. Sailing is a national pastime in the UK and the proportion of yachts per head of population is among the highest in the world.

One of the most popular cruising areas is the Solent and Isle of Wight, in the south of England, where modern yachting is reputed to have had its origin and some of the world's most famous races were started from the Royal Yacht Squadron in Cowes, and international regattas continue to be held here every summer.

Away from the busy Solent, the atmosphere in the ports and estuaries of the West Country, both on the water and on land, is much more sedate. A popular port with foreign yachts is Falmouth in the protected estuary of the River Fal, the last sheltered harbour to await favourable conditions for a voyage south across the Bay of Biscay.

Shallow estuaries with meandering rivers are the main feature of East Anglia, as are the unmistakable Thames barges, reminders of a bygone era when the river whose name they bear was the heart and lungs of the far-flung British Empire. Navigating the Thames is still possible right into the heart of London, with a couple of marinas conveniently located for those who wish to visit this exciting city on their own yacht.

Scotland's west coast is scenically the most attractive cruising area and its indented shoreline and its hundreds of

The Royal Observatory on top of Greenwich Park, on the south bank of the River Thames, marks the location of the Prime Meridian.

plenty of variety, the greatest drawback being the weather, which rarely ensures enjoyable cruising conditions for more than a few days at a time. Most visiting yachts limit their cruising to the south coast, where there is a wide availability of yachting facilities, but also an abundance of local craft, resulting in crowded harbours. There are many cruising attractions and more space to be found elsewhere, and while more challenging conditions may be encountered to reach such destinations, they should not deter any serious sailor from savouring the delights of cruising the rugged coast of Northern Ireland or Scotland's west coast and islands.

◆ COUNTRY PROFILE

The original inhabitants of the British Isles were of Iberian origin, and later the Celts settled in the islands. The Romans invaded and established the province of Britannia, with the Celts fleeing west to Wales and north to what the Romans called Caledonia, both areas resisting Roman expansion. The inhabitants of Caledonia were Picts and this area was also settled by the Scots, a Celtic tribe originating in Ireland. After the collapse of the Roman Empire, Germanic tribes, Angles, Saxons and Jutes drove the remaining Celts into Wales and Cornwall. From the eighth century the Danes were constant raiders and established settlements on the east coast. Danish kings ruled in the tenth and eleventh centuries, then a Saxon dynasty was re-established, but it fell to a Norman invasion in 1066. A strong state was finally forged in the sixteenth century under Henry VIII and Elizabeth I. Wales was united with England, and later Scotland also joined the union when the Act of Union was passed in 1707. King James VI of Scotland became James I of England and united the two kingdoms. An intense era of maritime exploration led to an expansion of Britain's influence and commercial interests, with many colonies being acquired. Despite the loss of the American colonies following the War of Independence, Britain gained Canada and India and continued to expand its empire, which peaked during the reign of Queen Victoria.

During the Second World War, when Britain was left alone to resist the German war machine, the nation suffered much deprivation and the major war effort came with a great cost to the economy. In the postwar years Britain followed a policy of granting independence to the majority of its former colonies, although most agreed to remain within the Commonwealth. Although the UK joined the EU in 1973, because of the chronic British ambivalence towards Europe, participation in European affairs is often half-hearted and lacks the genuine enthusiasm embraced by most other member nations.

The population is 60 million, of which the majority are English with large Celtic minorities, Scots, Welsh and Irish. There are sizeable West Indian and Asian communities in larger cities, and London is the most cosmopolitan city in the

islands abound in sheltered anchorages. The main attraction of Scotland's Outer Islands is their remoteness. Far to the north, the Shetlands are home to Europe's largest concentration of seabirds.

Among the least visited part of the UK is Northern Ireland and its diverse coastline, where, along the spectacular Antrim coast, are the famous polygonal columns of the Giant's Causeway, a unique natural phenomenon of volcanic rocks.

The British Isles provides a vast cruising ground with

world with well over one hundred different ethnic communities. Apart from English, Welsh is spoken in North Wales, and Gaelic in parts of Scotland and Ireland. While London is the capital of the UK, Edinburgh is the Scottish capital, Cardiff is the capital of Wales, and Belfast is the capital of Northern Ireland. In recent years, a devolution of central power has resulted in the establishment of a Scottish parliament, and Welsh and Northern Ireland assemblies.

✦ CLIMATE

The climate is mild and temperate, being greatly influenced by the benign effect of the Gulf Stream. Spring can be cool and wet, while summers can be warm. Generally the south is warmer than the north and the west wetter than the east. Average summer temperatures are 21°C/70°F, although days with temperatures well over the average are not uncommon. Average winter temperatures are 6°C/43°F. The weather is very changeable, although occasionally there are long spells of pleasant conditions when a system of high pressure remains stationary over the British Isles. Depressions tracking east across the Atlantic, to the north of Scotland, bring strong southwest winds, usually of gale force. The prevailing winds of summer in England are northeast, although southwest winds predominate throughout the year and this is also the direction of most gales.

✦ FORMALITIES

There are no official ports of entry listed, as all boats arriving from outside the EU and from the Channel Islands should contact National Yachtline by telephone on 0845 723 1110 to be given instructions. As a member of the EU, these regulations apply. EU boats arriving from another EU country do not have to fly the Q flag and need only contact customs if there are goods to declare or there are non-EU nationals on board.

As the UK is not a signatory to the Schengen Agreement, if anyone on board is a non-EU national, immigration must be contacted if arriving from outside of the UK, Isle of Man, Republic of Ireland, or Channel Islands. In most ports the customs officer also acts as the immigration officer.

Visas are not needed for nationals of the EU, while nationals of Australia, Canada, New Zealand, South Africa and the USA can get a visa on arrival, which is usually valid for six months. Nationals of countries that need visas to travel to the UK must obtain them in advance.

On departure, customs need not be informed by boats leaving the UK for another EU country, but boats going directly to a country outside the EU must inform customs. Failure to do so can result in a fine. Immigration does not have to be notified when leaving the UK if the destination port is in the EU or Channel Islands. If the first port of call will be

Traditional Thames sailing barges racing at Malden on the east coast.

outside the EU, an immigration officer need only be notified if there is someone on board who is not an EU resident.

Yachts can no longer be provisioned with duty-free goods if going to another EU country. Both non-EU and EU boats bound for non-EU destinations should contact customs in advance to make any necessary arrangement for duty-free stores. Non-EU boats may be able to get a refund on the VAT paid on goods that are being exported outside of the EU.

✦ FACILITIES

Provisioning is good throughout the country. Fuel is available in most ports. LPG containers of non-UK standard are difficult to refill, and for longer stays it is advisable to change over to UK-type tanks. Marine supplies are widely available.

Mooring facilities vary both in quality and availability. In some of the fishing and commercial harbours these can be very basic. Not all yacht clubs have their own moorings, but when they do a place can usually be found for a visiting member of an overseas club. There are some 150 purpose-built marinas scattered about the coasts of Great Britain and Northern Ireland. All marinas operate on Channel 80. Many marinas have chandleries and also repair facilities, as well as slipways or travelifts. The most comprehensive range of repair services is to be found in the area between Southampton and Portsmouth where the biggest names in the British yachting industry are concentrated. For those who wish to take their boat right into the heart of London, there are two marinas close to the centre.

The Caledonian Canal provides a convenient shortcut across Scotland. The canal is 60 miles long, has 29 locks and 10 swing bridges. The canal is entered either from Inverness on the east coast or from Corpach on the west coast, and saves the passage round the north of Scotland with the attendant weather and tidal complications. There are good facilities along its entire length as well as many attractive places to stop and explore.

Northern Ireland's spectacular Antrim coast.

✦ CHARTER

As can be expected in a country with such an interest and tradition in sailing, chartering a boat is often easier than hiring a car. There are bareboat charter operators in all popular cruising areas, so only some of the most important ones are listed here. However, it may be worth checking out some of the smaller operators as they often offer better deals and are also located in some out-of-the-way and more interesting places.

www.sunsail.com (Portsmouth)
www.yacht-charter.co.uk (Hamble)
www.solentsail.co.uk (Portsmouth)
www.britanniasailingschool.co.uk (Ipswich)
www.fy-charter.co.uk (Largs)
www.isleofskyeyachts.co.uk (Ardvasar, Isle of Skye)
www.crystalyachtcharter.com (Craobh Haven)
www.pembrokeshirecruising.co.uk (Neyland)
www.asyc.co.uk (Association of Scottish Charterers)

Cruising Guides
Bristol Channel and Severn Cruising Guide
Cruising Almanac
East Coast Pilot
Irish Sea Pilot
Isles of Scilly
Lundy and Irish Sea Pilot
North Sea Passage Pilot
Sailing directions for Scotland, Hebrides, Orkney and Shetland
    Islands (six volumes) (see www.clyde.org)
Shell Channel Pilot

Shetland Islands Pilot
The Channel Cruising Companion
The Solent Cruising Companion
West Country Cruising Companion
Yachtsman's Pilot to Scotland (several volumes)

Websites
www.bluemoment.com (directory of marinas and services)
www.visitbritain.com
www.visitwales.com
www.visitscotland.com
www.discovernorthernireland.com
www.westcoastboating.org

Local time	UTC
	Summer time: last Sunday in March to last Sunday in October
Buoyage	IALA A (not universally, as the lateral system is still used in some places)
Currency	British Pound (GBP)
Electricity	230V, 50Hz

Diplomatic missions

USA	0207 499 9000
Australia	0207 379 4334
Canada	0207 528 6600
South Africa	0207 258 6600
New Zealand	0207 930 8422

Communications

IDD 44	IAC 00

Emergency numbers
112/999

WEST AFRICA AND SOUTH ATLANTIC ISLANDS

Morocco, Senegal and Gambia are the only countries that attract cruising yachts to their shores in any numbers. The rest of West Africa is largely bypassed by yachts and only a few of them venture south of Senegal. Indeed, for a taste of Africa, no place is better suited to explore on your own vessel than what is occasionally referred to as the Senegambia, that strange geographic combination of the larger Senegal looking as if it is about to swallow its smaller neighbour. This large network of rivers and estuaries provides an attractive cruising ground without many of the dangers and difficulties associated with the countries located further south. A quite different picture awaits the sailor at the southern tip of the continent where great changes have occurred in recent years. After many years of isolation, South Africa has rejoined the international community, while its former dependency, Namibia, has joined the ranks of independent nations. Most cruising boats arrive in South Africa from the South Indian Ocean before continuing to the Caribbean with stops at St Helena and Ascension Island.

For the intrepid sailor, the islands of the South Atlantic are interesting destinations – each in its own different way. St Helena and Ascension have a long history of being welcome stops on the tradewind route to the equator, whereas the main attraction of Tristan da Cunha and the Falkland Islands is their very remoteness. It is indeed the even greater remoteness of Antarctica that some sailors find so tempting as to be undeterred by the challenges inherent in a voyage across the Southern Ocean. The seventh continent is no longer the exclusive destination of cruise ships and scientific expeditions, as sailing boats are now making their way there regularly, the majority during the short summer season, although a few have even wintered there.

Considering the vast area covered by this region, weather conditions vary greatly, from pleasant tradewind sailing to some of the roughest seas and strongest winds encountered anywhere on the planet. While the northern half is dominated by the southeast trade winds, conditions in the southern half are under the influence of systems generated in the Southern Ocean. The prevailing weather conditions have a direct bearing on the limited choice of routes that lead to this area. Hence, the countries of West Africa are best visited as part of a voyage from the Canaries to Brazil, or south towards the Falklands, Patagonia and Antarctica.

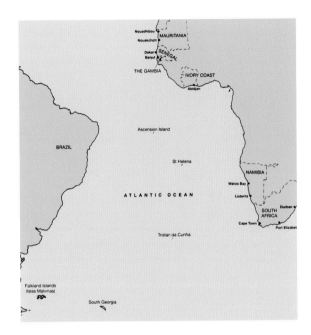

The best time to visit Antarctica is at the height of the austral summer, between late December and early March. Although other parts of Antarctica that are under the jurisdiction of Australia and New Zealand are visited by the occasional yacht, it is the Antarctic Peninsula, almost due south of Cape Horn, which is by far the most popular destination, both for cruise ships and yachts.

Most passages bound for the Antarctic Peninsula leave from Chile's Puerto Williams on the Beagle Channel. Because the prevailing winds in the Drake Passage are westerly, it is best to plan a roundabout route by sailing first to Deception Island, then to cruise along the Antarctic Peninsula as far southwest as possible, and start the return voyage north from the Melchior Islands so as to get the best sailing angle for the return to the mainland.

The best yachting facilities are to be found at the two extremes of the African continent, in South Africa and, increasingly, Morocco. Good facilities are also found in the Argentine port of Ushuaia, the main base for preparing voyages to Antarctica, while the amenities in all other places described in this section are either very limited or non-existent.

ANTARCTICA

UNTIL VERY RECENTLY the number of sailing yachts visiting the seventh continent could be counted in single figures. But the increasing popularity of Patagonia among cruising sailors has now spilled over, and every year more yachts venture south of the 60th parallel. Almost without exception, their destination is the Antarctic Peninsula, also known as Graham Land, which extends northwards for about 300 miles from the permanently frozen landmass. The western side of this peninsula is usually free of ice during the short summer, which makes it possible to find sheltered anchorages. In some milder years, the peninsula can be relatively free of ice as far south as 70°S, but this is quite rare and no cruising yacht has ever reached that far. The number of protected anchorages is very small and any boat venturing this far should be totally self-sufficient in every respect, as well as strong enough to withstand the danger of collision with floating ice, or even the possibility of being frozen in.

The first cruising yacht to visit Antarctica is believed to have been the British explorer and mountaineer Bill Tilman's *Mischief*, which called at the South Shetlands in the summer of 1966–7. The first to reach the Antarctic Peninsula were the French sailors Jérôme Poncet and Gérard Janichon on *Damien* in 1973. The numbers have increased gradually over the years, and about thirty sailing yachts visited the Peninsula in 2008, half of them private boats, the rest being engaged in charter.

The small Chilean port of Puerto Williams on the southern shore of the Beagle Channel is the starting point for small boat voyages to Antarctica. Those who prefer not to sail directly to the Peninsula can make landfall at Deception Island, a former whaling station with a perfectly protected anchorage inside the flooded crater of a still active volcano. The subsequent cruise along the Peninsula provides a unique opportunity to sail in sheltered waters amid stunning scenery of towering icebergs, past islands with teeming penguin colonies, ice floes covered in resting seals, and almost within touching distance of slowly moving humpback whales who spend the summers there gorging themselves on the rich krill. Several countries maintain research stations in the area, but these may only be visited by invitation. Anyone wishing to

visit a base should contact the base commander on Channels 12 or 16 to request permission.

✦ PROFILE

Almost the entire surface of the continental landmass of approximately 5 million square miles (14 million square km) is permanently covered by ice, the thickness of which can reach as much as 2,000m (6,000ft). In spite of the low temperatures, which rarely rise above freezing, Antarctic flora and fauna are abundant. To study and protect the Antarctic and also to carry out research in various fields, the international community has agreed to administer the territory jointly. These provisions are encompassed in the Antarctic Treaty which was signed in 1959 by Argentina, Australia, Belgium, Chile, France, Japan, New Zealand, Norway, South Africa, the USSR, UK and the USA. The Treaty came into force in 1961; since then, a total of 44 countries have acceded to it. The Treaty reserves the Antarctic area south of 60°S latitude for peaceful purposes, provides for international co-operation in scientific investigation and research, and preserves for the duration of the Treaty the status quo as regards territorial rights and claims. In 1991 a Protocol on Environmental Protection was signed and later ratified by the Treaty parties. The Protocol consists of a framework document laying out a series of principles that deal with environmental impact assessment, conservation of flora and fauna, waste disposal and management, prevention of marine pollution, and protected areas. All voyages and expeditions to Antarctica south of 60°S must obtain permission from their national Antarctic authority or relevant government department.

✦ CLIMATE

The frozen continent has extreme weather conditions during the long Antarctic winter. The Antarctic Peninsula has a more moderate climate and this fact, coupled with the relative short distance from South America, makes it the most popular Antarctic destination with both cruising yachts and passenger ships. The best weather is between late December and early March when the average temperature is slightly below freezing. During the short summer there can be spells of sunny weather with little wind, and daytime temperatures hover around freezing, making this the perfect time to visit. Prevailing winds are westerly, and while strong winds in the vicinity of the Antarctic Peninsula are relatively rare in summer, the situation can be very different in the Drake Passage where passing depressions are often accompanied by winds over 40 knots.

✦ FORMALITIES

Any vessel intending to visit Antarctica must obtain written permission from its national authority responsible for the

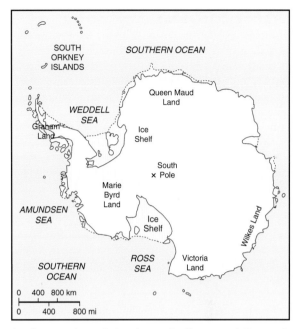

implementation of the Antarctic Treaty and Protocol. However, not all countries apply this provision strictly and boats continue to arrive without such permits. This attitude appears to be tolerated, but the situation may change. British vessels are not supposed to sail into Antarctic waters without permission from the relevant department in the Foreign and Commonwealth Office. Penalties are very severe if this ruling is not observed. The US and French authorities seem to take a more lenient view.

Although various countries claim sovereignty over parts of the Antarctic territory, the only one relevant for yachts planning to sail to the Antarctic Peninsula is Chile, which controls the area south of the Beagle Channel, including Cape Horn, and also claims much of the Antarctic Peninsula. As these are the areas where the majority of cruising boats go, it is essential to complete the necessary formalities in Puerto Williams before proceeding south. This is also a good insurance as the most likely source of help, should there be an emergency, is the Chilean Navy.

The Chilean authorities do not impose any restrictions on a vessel intending to visit the Antarctic Peninsula, but certain formalities must be completed in Puerto Williams, both before going and on your return.

Once in Antarctica there are no formalities to be completed and yachts are free to cruise, subject to various restrictions. Most of these are self-imposed and self-controlled. The success of these restrictions being observed depends entirely on the captain and crew of each individual yacht, who should do everything in their power to protect the fragile environment.

✦ RESTRICTED AREAS

There are approximately fifty Antarctic locations in five separate areas that are legally out of bounds and may not be visited without a permit. The areas are: the Antarctic Peninsula, Ross Sea Region, Greater Antarctica, South Shetland Islands, and South Orkney Islands. A few intrepid sailors have visited these locations, but the Antarctic Peninsula continues to be the most frequented among them.

Certain rules must be observed in order to comply with the Antarctic Treaty conservation provisions, such as: no killing or capturing of any wildlife (seals and birds), nor collection of eggs, minimal interference with plants, animals and soil. Visitors should keep their distance from wildlife, especially when the latter are breeding, and not touch or disturb them. Nothing should be removed, including plants and rocks, and historical evidence of human activity should be left undisturbed.

✦ FACILITIES

Neither provisions nor repair facilities are available and you should not expect to rely on outside help. The personnel of the research stations are usually far too busy to help out, and their resources are also limited, so assistance can only be expected in serious emergencies.

There are several bases along the Antarctic Peninsula and most of them are manned during the summer months. None of them should be visited without prior arrangement and they should be contacted on VHF radio before going ashore. The most accessible are the Chilean and Argentine bases in Paradise Harbour (64°53′S 62°52′W), the Ukrainian base, formerly the British Faraday base (65°15′S 64°16′W) at the Argentine Islands, and the US Palmer base on Anvers Island (64°45′S 64°03′W). The UK Antarctic Heritage Trust usually has a person on duty during the summer months at the former base, now a museum, at Port Lockroy on Wiencke Island (64°49′S 63°31′W).

Wordie House, the oldest British Antarctic station, set up during the British Graham Land Expedition in 1934–37

King George Island is the largest of the South Shetland Islands. Russia, China, Korea, Poland, Brazil, Uruguay and Argentina all maintain research stations there. Some of these stations welcome visitors, and researchers seem pleased to talk about their projects and life in the Antarctic.

✦ BRITISH ANTARCTIC TERRITORY

The British Antarctic Territory was established in 1962 and encompasses the lands and islands within the area south of 60°S lying between 20°W and 80°W. The area of approximately 1.3 million square kilometres (500,000 square miles) includes the South Orkney and South Shetland Islands and the Antarctic Peninsula (Palmer Land and Graham Land). There is no permanent population, but there are always a number of scientists and other personnel manning the various research stations.

✦ SUBANTARCTIC AND SOUTHERN OCEAN ISLANDS

These lie north of 60°S and thus outside the Antarctic Treaty Area, so they are administered by their respective governments. Most are uninhabited and often have pristine environments unspoilt by human contact. To preserve this, visits are restricted or prohibited. Yachts should exercise strict precautions to avoid introducing non-native animals or pests, which has already occurred in some places much to the detriment of the indigenous flora and fauna. It is best to follow guidelines as for Antarctica.

✦ BOUVETOYA

54°26′S 3°24′E. This is a Norwegian possession and protected nature reserve.

✦ SOUTH GEORGIA AND SOUTH SANDWICH ISLANDS

South Georgia lies 800 miles ESE of the Falkland Islands, while the South Sandwich Islands are 470 miles SE of South Georgia. Argentina made claims to the islands and in 1982 invaded South Georgia, site of a British Antarctic Survey Base; three weeks later British forces recaptured it, also expelling the Argentines who had lived on the previously uninhabited South Sandwich Islands from 1976. The British government extended its territorial jurisdiction from 12 to 200 miles offshore in 1993 to conserve fishing stocks. Argentina still maintains its claim to the islands and British naval forces patrol the area regularly. There is a permanent military base at Grytviken, the administrative centre of South Georgia. This is visited by cruise ships and occasionally by sailing yachts, and visits are only allowed with permission from the Commissioner for South Georgia and the South Sandwich Islands, based in Stanley.

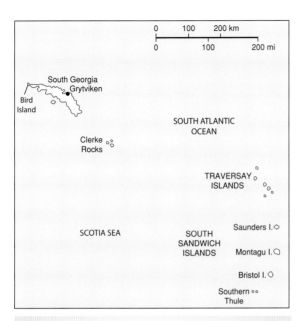

Elephant seals come to South Georgia Island during the breeding season.

Vessels should report to King Edward Point. Customs and immigration formalities will be carried out by the officer in charge or the harbourmaster.

✦ NEW ZEALAND SUBANTARCTIC ISLANDS

These islands, lying south of New Zealand, are administered as nature reserves by the New Zealand Department of Conservation (DOC). Tourism is allowed and various cruise ships visit the islands, but all visits are strictly controlled by the DOC. All indigenous flora and fauna is protected. Quarantine is strict to prevent the introduction of non-native pests; DOC officials may carry out checks at the ports of departure from New Zealand. No animals are permitted on board vessels visiting the islands.

Entry to the islands is by permit only, issued by the DOC. There is an annual quota of tourists allowed to visit each site. All visitors, including those on yachts, must be accompanied by an official DOC guide. Guided visits can be made to Campbell Island and the Auckland Islands. The Bounty Islands are restricted to small special interest groups. Visitors are not allowed to land on the Antipodes Islands or Snares Islands.

✦ AUSTRALIAN ANTARCTIC TERRITORY (AAT)

With a total land area of 5,800,000 square kilometres (2,239,383 square miles), the AAT encompasses all islands and territories south of latitude 60°S and between longitudes 45°and 160°E. Not included is the French sector of Terre

Adélie, which comprises the islands and territories south of 60°S latitude and between longitudes 136°and 142°E. The AAT is the single largest sector of the continent and covers much of east Antarctica. There are three stations, Mawson, Davis and Casey, as well as various summer bases and temporary field camps. There is a temporary population of scientists, ranging from about seventy in winter to two hundred in summer.

✦ AUSTRALIAN SUBANTARCTIC ISLANDS

The islands of Heard, McDonald and Macquarie in the South Indian Ocean are owned by Australia. All three have uniquely unspoilt environments. Access is by permit only; applications may be made to the Australian Antarctic Division. Heard and McDonald Island have only been visited by a few scientific expeditions and remain unspoilt. Macquarie Island is administered by Tasmania as a nature reserve and limited tourism is allowed. A permit for entry can be obtained from the Tasmanian Department of Parks, Wildlife and Heritage. There is a permanent research station on the island.

Storm brewing over Port Circumcision.

142

✦ FRENCH SUBANTARCTIC TERRITORY

This consists of the islands of Saint Paul, Amsterdam, Crozet and Kerguelen, all of which are French possessions. There are several protected areas that may be visited by permit only. Yachts should call first at one of the research stations.

Martin-de-Vives, Ile Amsterdam 37°50′ S 77°35′ E	
Port Alfred, Ile de Possession 46°25′ S 51°45′ E (Iles Crozet)	
Port-aux-Français, Grande Terre 48°00′ S 68°45′ E (Iles Kerguelen)	

✦ SOUTH AFRICAN SUBANTARCTIC ISLANDS

Marion and Prince Edward Island are nature reserves whose wildlife is protected. Tourism is not encouraged. A permit to visit is necessary, obtainable from the South African Scientific Committee for Antarctic Research in Pretoria.

✦ CHARTER

A number of sailing yachts based in Ushuaia or the Falkland Islands operate charter voyages to the Antarctic Peninsula, South Georgia and, by arrangement, to other locations. Among the best known are Jérôme Poncet's *Golden Fleece*, Skip Novak's *Pelagic Expeditions* and Hamish Laird's *Expedition Sail*.

  www.horizon.co.fk
  www.pelagic.co.uk
  www.expeditionsail.com
  www.magodelsur.com.ar
  www.ocean-expeditions.com

Cruising Guides
Antarctica Cruising Guide
Antarctica: An Introductory Guide (details of national institutes)
Antarctic Treaty Handbook (maps and descriptions of protected areas)
South Georgia
South Shetland Islands and Antarctica
Southern Ocean Cruising

Cruising notes on Antarctica, South Shetlands and South Georgia can be downloaded from the Royal Cruising Club website: www.rcc.org.uk.

Websites
www.discoveringantarctica.org.uk (details of the Antarctic Treaty)
www.antarcticanz.govt.nz (New Zealand Antarctica)
www.aad.gov.au (Australian Antarctic Division)
www.sanap.org.za (South African National Antarctic Programme)
www.iaato.org (International Association of Antarctic Tour Operators)
www.sgisland.gs (South Georgia)

Emergency number
McMurdo Station 911

The Chilean Eduardo Frei base on King George Island (62°21′ S 58°97′ W) has a runway with frequent links to the mainland throughout the year, and maintains a fully equipped hospital with resident doctors who have given assistance to emergency cases on cruise ships.

ASCENSION ISLAND

A MOUNTAINOUS PEAK rising from the floor of the Atlantic Ocean, Ascension is a dormant volcanic island astride the mid-Atlantic volcanic ridge – like the Azores and Tristan da Cunha. Lava flows have formed a barren twisted landscape, and its highest peak, Green Mountain, rises to 859m (2,817ft). The small island is a communications centre for the BBC, Royal Air Force, US Air Force, NASA and the European space project. As a traditional port of call for ships on the Cape of Good Hope route, the few yachts that sail this passage sometimes stop at Ascension. Short stops are normally allowed and help is always at hand in a genuine emergency.

Wideawake Airfield, named after the sooty wideawake terns that breed there, is a critical refuelling point on the air-bridge from the UK to the South Atlantic as well as between the USA and Africa. Apart from its many species of seabirds, the island is renowned for green turtles, while the surrounding ocean abounds in sailfish, marlin and other game fish.

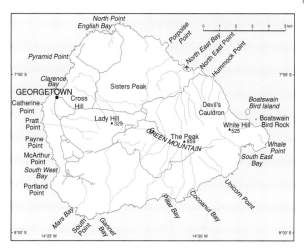

✦ COUNTRY PROFILE

Ascension was discovered in 1501, and visited occasionally by sailors who took turtles and eggs for food, and left goats that slowly destroyed most of the vegetation. Ascension became a known stopping point for ships, but was only settled in 1815, when Britain feared attempts to free Napoleon from nearby St Helena. In 1922 St Helena took over the administration from the British navy. In 1942 the Americans constructed a base and airfield to refuel planes flying between Brazil and Africa, and in the 1950s established a missile tracking station and a NASA earth station.

The resident population is approximately 1,100. Many of the workers are from St Helena. The language is English, and Georgetown is the capital.

✦ CLIMATE

The climate is tropical, hot and dry, with most rain coming from squalls. Average temperatures are stable throughout the year at 27°C/81°F. The island is under the influence of the southeast trade winds for most of the year. The weather can change rapidly.

✦ FORMALITIES

PORT OF ENTRY
Clarence Bay, Georgetown 7°56´ S   14°25´ W

Yachts should anchor to the northeast of the wharf. It is not permitted to tie to any buoy or mooring. You should avoid arriving at night as there are mooring lines all over the place. On arrival, Ascension Radio should be called on Channel 16. Crew must stay on board until the captain has cleared formalities at the police station. It is possible to clear out when clearing in if intending to leave within 24 hours or at the weekend.

All persons who wish to land must have medical insurance cover, including emergency evacuation. This is available on arrival if necessary. The crew may not stay ashore between 2300 and 0700.

✦ FACILITIES

Anchoring is permitted only in Clarence Bay. Water and fuel are available, but LPG is not. Only minor repairs can be done, although in an emergency you may be able to enlist the help of the Ascension Island Services (AIS). There is a super-market, but the selection of fresh produce is limited.

Cruising Guide	Website
South Atlantic Circuit	www.ascension-island.gov.ac

Local time	UTC	Buoyage	IALA A
Currency	Ascension Pound or British Pound (GBP)		
Electricity	240V, 50Hz		

Diplomatic mission	
UK	7000 (Administrator's Office)

Communications	Emergency numbers
IDD 247 IAC 00	Ambulance 6000 Police 6666

FALKLAND ISLANDS

THE FALKLAND ISLANDS, also known by their Spanish name of Islas Malvinas, are a British dependency in the South Atlantic. The archipelago is made up of two groups of over seven hundred islands, East Falkland and its adjacent islands, and West Falkland. Port Stanley is the main town and is where most people live. The rest of the country is called 'the camp'.

The Falklands used to be an important port of call for sailing ships on the Cape Horn route and the hulks of abandoned square riggers scattered around Port Stanley bear silent witness to that glorious era and its magnificent ships.

The Falklands' traditional role as a convenient stop for reprovisioning has been resuscitated in recent years by modern yachts, some sailing the classic Cape Horn route, but most being on their way to or from the Straits of Magellan, the Chilean Canals or Antarctica. Some of the charter boats that operate in Tierra del Fuego, South Georgia and Antarctica spend the winters here between seasons.

Only a few visiting craft have either sufficient time or the inclination to cruise these wild and windswept islands. Although access is restricted to some areas, either for military reasons or because some islands are nature reserves, most of them can be visited and a glimpse caught of their rich wildlife with large colonies of penguins, sea lions and elephant seals. The weather is the greatest impediment to cruising, as it can change rapidly and without warning, but there are many protected anchorages, so that you are never too far from shelter.

◆ COUNTRY PROFILE

While the islands were first sighted in the sixteenth century, it was not until the eighteenth century that France established a colony and named the islands Les Malouines, after the port of St Malo. In the nineteenth century the islands became a dependency of Britain, but Argentina continued to maintain a claim that culminated in the invasion of 1982. After a brief conflict, British forces recaptured the islands. Relations between the two countries have improved since then, but as Argentina has not formally given up her claim, the Falklanders treat any overtures by their neighbours with great suspicion.

The population of about 3,100 is of British origin.

Peaceful co-existence between natives and immigrants on East Falkland.

✦ CLIMATE

The climate is temperate, although very changeable. Prevailing winds are westerly, often strong, and their yearly average is 17 knots. Summer winds are more northerly in direction and this is also where the worst gales come from, usually with very little warning. Winter gales can be very violent. Another local phenomenon occurring during strong westerly winds are the willywaws, violent gusts that affect mostly the lee of the islands and the passages between them. January is the warmest month, with an average temperature of 10°C/50°F. December and January are the wettest months.

✦ FORMALITIES

PORTS OF ENTRY

Port Stanley 51°39′ S 57°43′ W

Fox Bay East 51°57′ S 60°4′ W (vessels over 50 tons only)

Port Stanley: The yacht's ETA should be reported in advance to the authorities on Channel 12. You should anchor in the inner harbour and ask permission to come alongside the public jetty or pick up a mooring buoy. The customs and immigration official will visit the yacht.

Fox Bay East: Only vessels over 50 tons may enter here and one week's notice of arrival is required. Certain restrictions apply and travel costs for officials must be paid for.

There is a £62 landing fee. Visas are not required by EU citizens, but they are needed by nationals of Australia, Canada, New Zealand, South Africa and the USA. Crews of yachts making a short stop are normally granted visas on arrival and are only allowed ashore during daylight hours. Boats may stay up to 30 days.

Minefields from the 1982 conflict are still a danger, but are clearly marked and fenced off. They are mainly around Port Stanley, Port Howard, Fox Bay and Fitzroy. A map can be obtained from the army office in Port Stanley.

✦ FACILITIES

Provisioning is good and there is some fresh produce grown locally. Port Stanley is the winter base for some of the charter boats plying the South Atlantic. As a result, repair facilities are good, with a 60-ton slip. Fuel is available at the service station, but supplies of LPG can take up to one month. Those wishing to leave their boats for longer may store them ashore. There are also some limited facilities in Fox Bay East, on West Falkland.

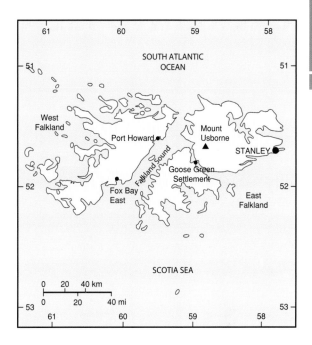

✦ CHARTER

The well-known French sailor and explorer Jérôme Poncet, who now lives in the Falklands, organizes charter voyages to South Georgia and Antarctica on his 20m (65ft) steel *Golden Fleece* (www.horizon.co.fk).

Cruising Guide	
Falkland Islands Shores	
Website	
www.falklands.gov.fk	

Local time	UTC −4
	Summer time: second Sunday in September to third Sunday in April
Buoyage	IALA A
Currency	Falkland Pound (FKP)
Electricity	240V, 50Hz
Diplomatic mission	
UK	28200
Communications	
IDD 500	IAC 00
Emergency number	
999	

GAMBIA

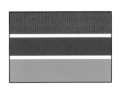

SURROUNDED ON ALL SIDES BY SENEGAL with only a narrow outlet to the Atlantic Ocean, the Gambia is a thin ribbon of land stretching along the Gambia river. The 300-mile-long river is the heart of this small country, which rarely exceeds 20 miles in width. It is navigable for 169 miles. Currents are strongest in the lower reaches, but diminish above Elephant Island – although the river continues to be tidal for almost all its navigable length. The Gambia river is only buoyed in the lower approaches. Cruising yachts regularly sail upriver without encountering serious navigational problems, but above Georgetown, rocks and the narrowing river make progress more difficult. Both the birdlife and wildlife are prolific, and there are many villages along the river where it is possible to stop for provisions.

◆ COUNTRY PROFILE

Originally part of the empire of Mali, both Britain and France established trading posts in the sixteenth and seventeenth centuries and competed for the territory. Awarded to Britain in the Treaty of Versailles, it became

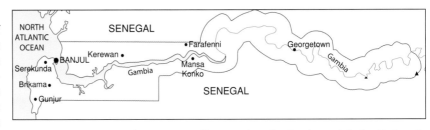

a British Crown Colony and achieved independence in 1965. There are 1.8 million people in the Gambia and the land is densely populated. The Mandinka are descendants of the rulers of the old Mali Empire and live mostly inland, while the Wolof are mainly in Banjul. There are also Fulani and ten other ethnic groups. English is the official language, but Mandinka, Fula, Wolof and other languages are also spoken. The capital, Banjul, was originally called Bathurst.

◆ CLIMATE

The climate is tropical, with two distinct seasons. The dry and more pleasant weather is from November until May, while the remainder is the wet season. The hottest months are from February to May. The winds are variable throughout the year, with the strongest winds in September and October.

◆ FORMALITIES

PORT OF ENTRY
Banjul   13°27´N 16°34´W

The average depth in the approach channel is 9m (30ft), and vessels should keep all buoys to starboard when entering. Yachts either proceed to the government wharf or anchor. The Gambia Yachting Association acts as the agent for visiting yachts and will approach those arriving to offer their services. The fee should be agreed in advance.

All yachts arriving in the Gambia are granted a one-month stay, which can be extended up to three months at the immigration office. A permit must be obtained to navigate the river. Tide tables are essential.

◆ FACILITIES

There is good provisioning in Banjul, with supermarkets and fresh produce. Fuel and LPG gas are available in the harbour. Some repairs can be made at the Port Authority shipyard, which also has a slipway. The Gambia Sailing Club in Banjul will help visitors if needed. Theft can be a problem.

Cruising Guide
Cruising Guide to West Africa (updates at www.rccpf.org.uk)

Website
www.visitthegambia.gm

Local time	UTC
Buoyage	IALA A
Currency	Gambian dalasi (GMB)
Electricity	230V, 50Hz

Diplomatic missions
UK	4495133
USA	4392856

Communications	**Emergency numbers**
IDD 220 IAC 00	Ambulance 16 Police 17

MAURITANIA

STRETCHING ALONG THE WEST COAST of Africa between Morocco and Senegal, a large part of Mauritania is the Sahara Desert. The republic is based on an Islamic socialist constitution and a traditional Muslim society that does not encourage tourism. Its long coastline has very few natural harbours and the endless sandy beaches are its most remarkable feature. For those in search of solitude, these deserted waters and uninhabited shoreline might be sufficient attraction, but otherwise the country has very little to offer the cruising sailor.

◆ COUNTRY PROFILE

Lying on the trade route between the Maghreb and West Africa, Mauritania once enjoyed great prosperity. During the nineteenth century the country was added to France's large colonial possessions, but independence was gained in 1960.

There are around 3.1 million inhabitants, with ethnic tensions between its black and Arab-Berber communities. Arabic is the official language and French is also spoken. The capital is Nouakchott.

◆ CLIMATE

Most of the land has a harsh desert climate, though conditions are better along the coast where the prevailing winds are northerly. The rainy season is from July to September, when it sometimes rains heavily. A strong swell is often felt along the coast from January to March.

◆ FORMALITIES

PORTS OF ENTRY

Nouâdhibou 20°54´ N 17°03´ W	
Nouakchott 18°02´ N 16°02´ W	

The Port Authority should be contacted on arrival for instructions as to where to berth. Nouâdhibou is the main commercial port and is a better place for yachts as Nouakchott has little protection.

The situation is changeable, but visas are required by almost all visitors except citizens of some West African countries. Visas can be obtained at the Mauritanian missions in Las Palmas de Gran Canaria and Dakar. Because of periodic conflict, travel advice should be sought before entering the country.

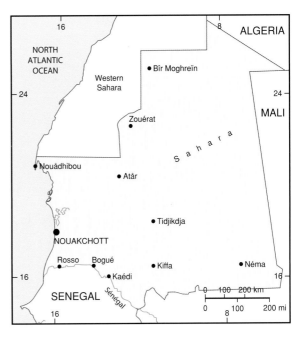

◆ FACILITIES

The only repair facilities available are at Nouakchott where there is a shipyard that may take on work on a yacht in an emergency. Fuel is available in both ports, and also some basic provisioning. Water should be treated.

Cruising Guide	
Cruising Guide to West Africa	

Local time	UTC
Buoyage	IALA A
Currency	Mauritanian Ouguiya (MRO)
Electricity	220V, 50Hz

Diplomatic missions	
USA	5252660
Canada	5292697

Communications	
IDD 222	IAC 00

Emergency number	
Police 117	

MOROCCO

SITUATED ON THE NORTHWEST shoulder of Africa, Morocco has for a long time played the role of a bridge between Africa and Europe, a symbolic situation that may turn to reality as there are plans to build a bridge close to the Straits of Gibraltar. All Morocco's main cities lie along the fertile coast, while behind Marrakesh stand the Atlas Mountains, which in ancient times were believed to hold up the heavens. The Sahara stretches to the south, while to the north are the narrow Straits of Gibraltar. The short Mediterranean coast surrounds the two Spanish enclaves of Melilla and Ceuta.

In spite of its strategic position close to the sailing routes between Europe, the Mediterranean and the Canary Islands, Morocco has done very little in the past to develop yachting facilities, but this situation is now changing as marinas have opened at several locations. Most of the large ports have a yacht club and there are a certain number of locally owned yachts, but for a long time facilities were often inadequate. Formalities were also complicated and foreign sailors used to be regarded with a certain degree of suspicion, an attitude that also shows signs of changing.

Some of the ports on the Atlantic coast have been in use since time immemorial, the small port of Asilah being founded by the Phoenicians. Its massive fortifications, erected by the Portuguese in the fifteenth century, still stand practically intact, as do those of El Jadida, Safi and Essaouira. These places, and some of the smaller fishing ports, offer an interesting insight into the traditional Moroccan way of life.

✦ COUNTRY PROFILE

The original inhabitants were Berber, and they still form the core of the population. Arabs invaded in the seventh century, and the Alaouite dynasty came to power in Morocco in the seventeenth century and still rules today. In the early twentieth century the country was divided into Spanish and French protectorates, but became independent in 1956. Despite continuing reforms, ultimate authority remains in the hands of the monarch, currently King Mohammed.

Many Moroccans have emigrated, especially to France, and their remittance money plays an important role in the economy, which is also heavily dependent on foreign tourism. The population numbers 35 million, mainly Arab in urban areas and Berber in the rural regions. Arabic is the main language, while French and Berber are widely spoken. The capital is Rabat.

✦ CLIMATE

Along the coast the climate is one of hot summers and mild winters. Westerly winds predominate on the North African coast in winter, while on the Atlantic coast most of the summer winds are northerly.

✦ FORMALITIES

Arriving yachts should contact port control and all crew must remain on board until formalities have been completed, although the captain may have to go ashore to look for officials. Marinas should be contacted on Channel 9 and they

The old port of Essaouira on Morocco's Atlantic coast.

PORTS OF ENTRY

Nador	35°17´N 2°56´W	Al Hoceima	35°15´N 3°54´W	Tangier	35°47´N 5°48´W
Kenitra	34°16´N 6°35´W	Mohammedia	33°43´N 7°22´W	Casablanca	33°37´N 7°36´W
El Jadida	33°16´N 8°31´W	Jorf Lasfar	33°07´N 8°38´W	Safi	32°18´N 9°15´W
Agadir	30°25´N 9°38´W	Asilah	35°28´N 6°02´W	Essaouira	31°30´N 9°46´W
Marina Smir	35°45´N 5°20´W	Rabat	34°03´N 6°52´W	Saidia	35°05´N 2°14´W

will assist with formalities. Yachts must check in and out with the port captain and police at each port visited. Speaking French is helpful.

Visas are not required by nationals of EU countries, Australia, Canada, New Zealand and the USA for a stay of up to three months. In an emergency, even nationals of countries that need visas may be allowed to make a short stop. There are certain areas prohibited to yachts.

✦ FACILITIES

After years of official neglect, yachting has finally caught the attention of the Moroccan authorities who have embarked on an ambitious programme of building marinas and improving facilities generally. The new Marina Smir, a few miles east of Gibraltar, is equipped to a high standard and has a good range of repair services including a boatyard with a 150-ton travelift. New marinas have opened also at Agadir and Bouregreg, the latter close to the capital, Rabat. The marina has good facilities, a chandlery and fuel. A new marina is due for completion in Casablanca, Morocco's

principal commercial port, and will greatly improve facilities for visitors. All these new developments bode well for the future of yachting, as until recently finding space to dock a yacht in places such as Casablanca was often impossible.

Provisioning is good in all major ports, although imported products are expensive. The fresh produce markets are good everywhere. Repair facilities in the larger ports and new marinas are adequate and there are some small boatyards dealing with local fishing boats.

✦ CHARTER

There are as yet no charter operators based in Morocco, but several companies in Gibraltar, the Spanish Costa del Sol or the Portuguese Algarve extend their operations to include nearby Moroccan ports. Based in Gibraltar, Alfer Sea School has a small number of both sail and power yachts that are offered for both bareboat and crewed charter. It also offers tuition and its yachts regularly visit Morocco.

www.alferseaschool.com

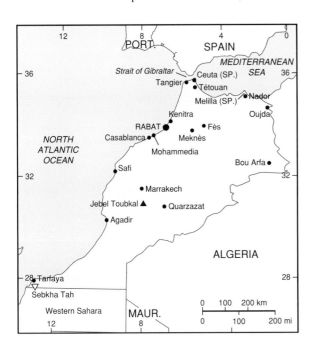

Cruising Guides	
North Africa	
Straits Sailing Handbook	
Website	
www.visitmorocco.com	

Local time	UTC
	Summer time of +1 hour varies from year to year
Buoyage	IALA A
Currency	Moroccan Dirham (MAD)
Electricity	220V, 50Hz

Diplomatic missions	
UK	37 633333
USA	37 762265
Canada	37 687400
South Africa	37 706760

Communications	
IDD 212	IAC 00

Emergency numbers	
Ambulance 15	Police 19

NAMIBIA

NAMIBIA lies on the southwest coast of the continent, and used to be known as South West Africa. The easternmost area of it is part of the Kalahari Desert, while the Namib Desert stretches along the west coast. Most of the coast is inhospitable, but inland there are many national parks and areas of dramatic scenery and great natural beauty.

Because of poor visibility in coastal mist and sandstorms, as well as inshore hazards, yachts normally stay well offshore and only close with the coast when they intend to make landfall. For northbound boats the first convenient port is Lüderitz, set in the well-protected Robert Harbour. Further north is Walvis Bay, a busy harbour with good repair facilities for the large fishing fleet. This port makes a convenient stop en route to St Helena and, if time permits, also gives a chance to visit some of the interior of this interesting country, which was for a long time in the grip of a violent guerrilla war.

◆ COUNTRY PROFILE

The Portuguese sailed along the Namibian coast as early as the fifteenth century while searching for a route to Asia. Ignored by the colonial powers because of the country's lack of natural resources, it was only in the nineteenth century that South West Africa became a German protectorate. In the aftermath of the First World War, South Africa was given a mandate to rule South West Africa and with it came a ruthless form of apartheid. In the 1950s nationalism and opposition to South African rule grew into guerrilla warfare led by the Marxist South West Africa People's Organization (SWAPO). By 1966 the United Nations changed the country's name to Namibia and cancelled the mandate, but South Africa refused to withdraw. Independence was finally obtained in 1990.

The population is 2.1 million. English is the official language, with Herero, Owambo, Afrikaans and German also spoken. The capital is Windhoek.

◆ CLIMATE

The weather is usually hot, although it is milder on the coast. Winds are mostly from the south. The cold Benguela current produces misty conditions close to the coast and up to 5 to 10 miles offshore. February is the warmest month, with an average temperature of 20°C/68°F, while August is the coolest, 14°C/57°F.

◆ FORMALITIES

PORTS OF ENTRY

Lüderitz 26°38′ S 15°09′ E   Walvis Bay 22°57′ S 14°30′ E

Lüderitz: The harbourmaster or Dias Point Lighthouse should be contacted for instructions. If arriving at night, it is best to raft up to one of the tugs until the morning. Yachts can come alongside the commercial wharf for clearance.

Walvis Bay: The port captain should be contacted on Channels 16 and 12, or the port office visited during office hours.

Visas are not needed by nationals of most European countries, Australia, Canada, New Zealand, South Africa and the USA.

◆ FACILITIES

The Lüderitz Yacht Club (Tel: 63 312754) welcomes visiting sailors. Provisions are obtainable from supermarkets, while water and diesel fuel are available in the harbour. There are some repair facilities as the port is used by fishing boats.

Walvis Bay has a small boat harbour and a yacht club (Tel: 64 209685). Repair facilities and provisioning are good.

Cruising Guides	Website
South Atlantic Circuit	www.namibiatourism.com.na
South African Nautical Almanac	

Local time	UTC +1
Summer time: first Sunday in April to first Sunday in September	
Buoyage	IALA A
Currency	Namibian Dollar, South African Rand (ZAR)
Electricity	220V, 50Hz

Diplomatic missions			
UK	61 274800	South Africa	61 224140
USA	61 2958500		

Communications	**Emergency numbers**
IDD 264 IAC 00	Ambulance 2032276 Police 1011

ST HELENA

FOR MOST SAILORS, St Helena's isolation is its main attraction, as the lack of an airport means that only determined travellers set foot on this island lost in the vastness of the South Atlantic. Its most regular visitors are cruising sailors, who stop here on the way from South Africa to Brazil, the Caribbean or Europe. The large number of yachts is in contrast to the diminishing number of passenger ships, for whom St Helena was once a favourite port of call on the Europe to South Africa run. However, all this may change as there are now plans to build an airport, and St Helena's long isolation will thus come to an end.

St Helena's 5,000 inhabitants are called 'Saints', their rainbow mix of colours and races reflecting the island's chequered history. It is always a good feeling to arrive in a place where visiting sailors are not only very welcome, but where their presence makes a visible contribution to the local economy. In this small place visitors are warmly greeted in the street, making everyone feel immediately at home.

The protected harbour off the main settlement of Jamestown gives the opportunity of getting a better feel of the island by visiting the interior. A steep winding road leads to the hilly interior that rises gradually to the island's highest point, Diana's Peak at 823m (2,685ft). The interior is surprisingly lush, with grassy meadows sprinkled with all kinds of flowers, whereas the western lee side is parched brown. The road ends at Longwood, once Napoleon Bonaparte's residence, and now a museum set in a landscaped garden. The defeated emperor spent six years of enforced exile here, spending his last days on this remote speck of land.

The island's main international event is the bi-annual Governor's Cup, a hotly contested race that starts in Cape Town in late December and is joined both by state-of-the-art racing yachts and family cruising boats on the first stage of a longer world voyage.

✦ COUNTRY PROFILE

The island was discovered on 21 May 1502, which in the Eastern Church is the feast day of St Helena, mother of the Byzantine emperor Constantine. The discoverer was a Spanish navigator in the service of Portugal. This find was kept a secret until 1588, when the English navigator Captain Thomas Cavendish of HMS *Desire* visited St Helena on his return from a voyage around the world. At that time the island had lush vegetation and fruit trees, which were slowly destroyed by wild goats left by ships. By the end of the sixteenth century, a little community was established and St Helena became known to the rest of the world. Despite Dutch efforts to claim the island, in the mid-seventeenth century the English East India Company set up a base to protect their interests against Dutch warships and Spanish privateers. A settlement grew in James Valley, plantations were cultivated, and African slaves brought in as labour.

In 1815 St Helena received its most famous visitor, when Napoleon Bonaparte was brought here as a prisoner, remaining with a mini-imperial French court until his death in 1821. It marked a period of prosperity for the island with the influx of naval and military personnel, but this faded after Napoleon's death. Slavery was abolished in 1832, and two years later St Helena became a Crown Colony. The British government used the island as a base for the campaign against the slave trade and many freed slaves settled there.

Jamestown with the main anchorage.

CLIMATE

The climate is strongly influenced by the southeast trade winds and the cold Benguela current. The southeast trades blow throughout the year. No tropical storms have been recorded in the South Atlantic, but Hurricane Katrina, which formed off Brazil in August 2005, may point to a change in climatic conditions that could affect St Helena as well. The weather is warm and occasionally humid and misty. The coastal areas are drier and hotter than the interior. In Jamestown, the warmest and also wettest month is March, with an average temperature of 25°C/77°F, while September is the coolest at 20°C/68°F.

FORMALITIES

PORT OF ENTRY
Jamestown 15°55´S 5°43´W

St Helena Port Control should be called on Channel 14 on weekdays, and St Helena Radio at weekends. There are a number of mooring buoys off West Rocks, but if they are occupied, then visiting yachts should anchor. The captain is normally instructed to visit the various offices ashore. Clearance for departure at weekends can be given by customs on the Friday before departure.

The police handle immigration, and visitors are normally issued a shore pass for a period of one month. No visas are required, but an entry fee for persons over 12 years of age is charged.

Police will ask to see a personal health insurance policy that provides for evacuation in a medical emergency. Those who do not have one and will be staying more than 48 hours must purchase insurance from a local company. British nationals do not need medical insurance.

FACILITIES

Visiting yachts should anchor west of the landing pier. Commuting ashore in your own tender is difficult due to the constant surge. There is a ferry service for local fishermen which can also be used by visiting boats. Diesel fuel can be bought by jerrycan from a fuel station in town, or arrangements can be made for it to be delivered in drums. Visiting vessels are not allowed to come alongside the dock, so all fuel has to be transported by launch or dinghy.

It is advisable to arrive in St Helena with a well-stocked boat, and only expect to buy a few fresh provisions locally. Fresh bread must be ordered in advance. Simple repairs can be carried out at a workshop dealing with local boats.

The island has no airport, but there are regular links by ship with the UK, South Africa, Namibia, Ascension, and occasionally Tristan da Cunha.

Cruising Guide	
South Atlantic Circuit	
Website	
www.sthelenatourism.com	
Local time	UTC
Summer time	UTC +1
Buoyage	IALA A
Currency	St Helenian Pound (SHP)
Electricity	240V, 50Hz
Communications	
IDD 290	IAC 00
Emergency number	
911	

The oldest 'Saint'.

SENEGAL

SENEGAL WAS ONCE THE CENTRE of French West Africa and Dakar prided itself on being one of the most sophisticated African cities. The French influence is still noticeable and the mixture of the two cultures has produced some interesting results in music, the arts and even cuisine. Today it is the West African country most visited by cruising sailors.

Senegal is mostly flat except for the mountains in the far southeast and east. There are several rivers that are navigable for some distance inland and are Senegal's main cruising attraction. The most interesting area is the River Casamance basin, a labyrinth of creeks and islets south of the Gambia, which is populated by millions of migratory birds during the dry season. The river is navigable for a long way inland, but the most difficult area to negotiate is the entrance, which has many uncharted shallow areas and navigational aids are often missing.

There has been intermittent fighting in western Casamance between government forces and separatists, and although the situation has improved, it should be checked before visiting.

◆ COUNTRY PROFILE

This area is known to have been inhabited since at least 13,000 BCE, making it one of the earliest inhabited areas in West Africa. Islam was well established by the fourteenth century. Starting in the fifteenth century with the arrival of the Portuguese, followed by the Dutch, French and British, intensive slave trading was carried out from this area until slavery was finally abolished. The French colonies of Senegal and French Sudan were merged in 1959 and granted their independence as the Mali Federation in 1960. The union broke up after only a few months. Senegal joined with the

The anchorage near Ziguinchor on the Casamance river.

Gambia to form the nominal confederation of Senegambia in 1982, but the envisaged integration of the two countries was never carried out, and the union was dissolved in 1989. There has been a separatist insurgency in southern Senegal since the 1980s, and several peace deals have failed to resolve the conflict that is still simmering.

The population is 13.7 million. Wolof, the largest ethnic group, comprises one-third, while other peoples are Serer, Diola, Fulani, Toucouleur and Mandinka. French is the official language, and the main indigenous language, Wolof, is spoken by most people. Dakar is the capital.

✦ CLIMATE

The climate is tropical with a rainy season between July and September, but hardly any rain the rest of the year. The winter months, from November to March, have more pleasant weather. The wet season winds are mostly from the southwest and west, while in the dry season the prevailing winds are northerly. Occasionally from December to May a dust-laden *harmattan* blows from across the desert. Along the coast the warmest months are September and October, with an average of 28°C/82°F, while February is the coolest, with an average 22°C/72°F.

✦ FORMALITIES

PORTS OF ENTRY

Dakar	14°41′N 17°25′W	Ziguinchor 12°35′N 16°16′W
Saint Louis	16°02′N 16°30′W	

Dakar: The Port Authority should be contacted for directions, and will send yachts to Hann Bay or the local yacht club (Cercle de Voile). The latter is the better option. Officials may not come to the boat, so all papers should be taken to the port captain's office in the commercial harbour.

Cruising yachts in Hann Bay anchorage near Dakar.

Ziguinchor: This port lies 33 miles up the Casamance river, which is well buoyed, but has many dangerous shallows so it should only be navigated in daylight. The seas occasionally break over the entrance bar, which is best negotiated on a flood tide.

Saint Louis: A breaking and dangerous bar at the entrance may pose problems to a keeled yacht in onshore winds.

Visas are not required for 90-day stays by nationals of the EU (pending for countries that joined after 2004), Canada, South Africa and the USA. Australians and New Zealanders need to obtain a visa in advance. They are not issued on arrival.

There are Senegalese missions in Cape Verde, Gambia, Rabat and Tunis, otherwise visas may be issued by French embassies.

✦ FACILITIES

Provisioning is good in Dakar, where there are several supermarkets and a fresh produce market. The capital also has reasonable repair facilities, with various workshops being located in the Medina industrial estate north of the city. Marine equipment is non-existent, and there is a limited range of spares. Duty-free diesel is available in the main harbour, and water at the yacht clubs. The Cercle de Voile is reported to be the best base for visiting yachts. Some limited provisions and fuel are also obtainable in Ziguinchor.

Cruising Guide
Cruising Guide to West Africa (latest updates available at www.rccpf.org.uk)

Website
www.senegal-tourism.com

Local time	UTC
Buoyage	IALA A
Currency	West African CFA Franc (XOF)
Electricity	230V, 50Hz

Diplomatic missions
UK	33 8237392
USA	33 8292100
Canada	33 8894700
South Africa	33 8651959

Communications
IDD 221	IAC 00

Emergency numbers
112	Ambulance 1515

SOUTH AFRICA

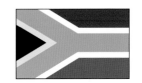

THE REPUBLIC OF SOUTH AFRICA lies at the southern tip of the African continent, its shores washed both by the Indian and Atlantic Oceans. Much of the interior is a high semi-arid plateau, called the veld. The narrow plain along the long coast is rugged and more fertile, with a subtropical climate on the eastern shore and a Mediterranean-type climate on the west coast. South Africa has been an important shipping centre since the Portuguese pioneered the route around the Cape of Good Hope to the Indies and the Spice Islands, more than five centuries ago. That classic sailing route is nowadays sailed mostly by cruising or racing yachts. Until recently, the number of cruising boats visiting South Africa was relatively low as the Red Sea route was often preferred by sailors undertaking a circumnavigation. With the return of South Africa to the international fold, more sailors are tempted to enjoy this country's many attractions. The threat of piracy in the approaches to the Red Sea has also persuaded more sailors to take the longer route around the Cape of Good Hope. South Africa's popularity, and especially that of Cape Town, is not limited to cruising sailors. Several round the world races include South Africa on their itinerary.

There is a general absence of natural protected harbours and cruising is often limited to sailing along the coast between ports during a weather window, except in Western Cape waters. Ports are conveniently spaced along the coast, and provide good shelter in adverse weather conditions, or to leave the boat unattended to visit the interior. South Africa may lack picturesque cruising grounds, but it scores high on the diversity of its land-based attractions: spectacular landscapes, well-tended vineyards, and some of the most acclaimed nature reserves in the world. The country's convenient position and good yachting facilities, in Durban and Cape Town, make it a natural stopover. There are times, however, when the weather makes the sailing conditions around the tip of Africa among the most dangerous in the world. The main cause is the southwest-setting Agulhas Current, which can cause hazardous conditions when a strong wind blows against the swift current.

✦ COUNTRY PROFILE

The oldest inhabitants of the Cape area were the Khoi-San Bushmen. By the thirteenth century several Bantu tribes had settled east of the River Kei. They had been forced to move gradually south by wars, and to find new grazing lands. The Portuguese first visited the Cape in the fifteenth century. Over the years, other Europeans arrived to colonize the land. Of note were the large influx of French Huguenots whose legacy are the wines of the Cape Region. Later, British settlers came and their efforts to gain control led to the Boer Wars. English control accelerated the migration inland of the earlier Dutch settlers, and they formed a close-knit Boer society of Afrikaans speakers.

In 1910 the Union of South Africa was established as a British colony. This continued until 1948 when the National Party won the election, with the white minority holding power and legally enforcing the policy of apartheid. The African National Congress was formed in 1923 to campaign for the rights of black South Africans and in 1961 founded a military wing, Umkhonto we Sizwe, Spear of the Nation. In the 1960s the ANC was banned and many of its leaders were imprisoned. Nelson Mandela, the best known of the imprisoned leaders, became a symbol of resistance. Democratic elections in April 1994 ended apartheid: all citizens, regardless of race or colour, gained the right to vote. The ANC had a majority in the national government led by Nelson Mandela, South Africa's first black president. Subsequently, the ANC has maintained its majority as the ruling party, Jacob Zuma becoming president in 2009. Since the end of apartheid, South Africa has undergone major changes, but it will take more than one generation to create a society with equal opportunities for all its citizens.

Dawn landfall at Cape Agulhas, Africa's southernmost point.

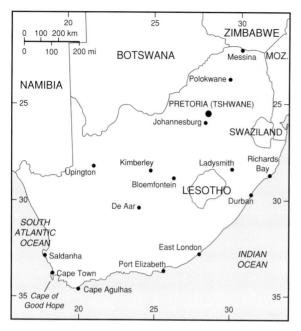

The population is 49 million; approximately 79 per cent are African, 9 per cent of mixed race and 10 per cent of European origin, with the rest made up of various small minorities.

There are 11 official languages. Afrikaans and English are most commonly spoken, with Xhosa and Zulu being the main African languages. Pretoria is the administrative capital, while Cape Town is the home of the legislative assembly.

✦ CLIMATE

The climate varies greatly between the Atlantic and Indian Ocean coasts, Mediterranean in the Cape and subtropical in the rest of the coastal areas. The prevailing winds of summer are easterly. Gales are frequent in winter. Summer depressions cross the South Atlantic and usually curve southwards by the time they reach land. In winter, the South Atlantic High moves north, allowing more depressions to reach land and resulting in westerly winds. Conditions are particularly bad when such gales blow against the southwest-flowing Agulhas Current. In Cape Town the warmest month is January, with averages of 21°C/70°F, but also many hot days with temperatures well over 30°/90°F. July is the coolest month at 12°C/54°F and also the wettest.

✦ FORMALITIES

Yachts arriving from a foreign port must proceed directly to a port of entry.

Richards Bay: Port Control should be contacted on Channels 16 or 12 before entering the harbour. If arriving from a foreign port, yachts must first proceed to the small craft harbour and await clearance at the quarantine jetty. Thereafter they can proceed to Tuzi Gazi Marina or Zululand Yacht Club.

Durban: Durban Port Control should be contacted on Channel 16 to request permission to proceed through the entrance channel. Arriving yachts may be advised to go to the marina, and they must contact the following departments within 24 hours of arrival: customs, immigration, port liaison officer and health. The marina office will advise on clearance formalities.

Cape Town: All yachts entering the port must monitor Channel 14 and proceed to the small craft basin at the Royal Cape Yacht Club (RCYC). The RCYC deals with all yacht movement within Table Bay Harbour, so the club should be contacted first, and not the Port Authority. The movement of shipping around the harbour is indicated by lights displayed on the Port Authority building: red (Ben Schoeman Dock), green (Duncan Dock) and orange (Victoria Basin). A flashing light signifies a ship is entering port, and a steady light shows that one is leaving. Yachts should keep to starboard when entering the harbour. The RCYC basin and yacht club are located at the southeast end of Duncan Dock. Berths may also be available at the Victoria and Alfred Waterfront Marina located at the eastern end of the harbour. The marina monitors Channel 14. Because of the great demand for space, this marina seems to prefer allocating any free slips to larger yachts.

The captain must report to immigration within 24 hours. Most nationalities obtain a visa for up to 90 days; extensions require a fee. Those planning to travel inland need a tourist visa if the stay extends past the original 90 days' period granted on arrival. Those who leave South Africa temporarily must inform immigration and have their passports stamped; if they don't, they may not be allowed to leave from the airport. Before departure, all crew must present themselves to immigration in person.

Yachts must check in and out with customs, immigration and port captain at each port. On approaching a port, Port

PORTS OF ENTRY
The ports of entry are listed in the order of the route from the Indian to the Atlantic Ocean:

Richards Bay	28°48′S 32°06′E	Durban	29°52′S 31°02′E	East London	33°02′S 27°55′E
Port Elizabeth	33°58′S 25°38′E	Mossel Bay	34°11′S 22°10′E	Cape Town (Table Bay)	33°55′S 18°26′E
Saldanha Bay	33°03′S 17°56′E				

Control should be called on Channel 12 for instructions. It is necessary to obtain coastal clearance to sail between ports. The authorities must be informed if a yacht goes out for a daysail and returns to the same port. This function is delegated to the yacht clubs, and yachts just sign out.

Visiting yachts can obtain a tax refund on goods bought in South Africa that are being exported. An original VAT invoice should be requested when purchasing such goods. VAT is not refundable for services.

✦ FACILITIES

Yachting facilities throughout South Africa are of a variable standard and there are yacht clubs in most ports, the clubs being the best source of information on local conditions. The yacht clubs like to be contacted in advance by those wishing to use their amenities as most slips are occupied by local yachts, and getting a space is often difficult. South Africans who live aboard their yachts are charged for doing so, but a concession may be made for visiting foreign yachts for a limited time. Some yacht clubs, such as Cape Town and Durban, have their own hauling facilities; others work closely with a local boatyard. For any major repair, Cape Town and Durban have a complete range of services: electronic, electrical, sailmaking, rigging, refrigeration, diesel and outboard engines, metal, fibreglass and woodwork. Fuel and water are easily available and provisioning in all major centres is very good. LPG containers can be filled in Durban and Cape Town.

Yacht clubs are also convenient places to leave the boat while visiting the interior. The Zululand Yacht Club in Richards Bay is a good location from which to visit the Umfoluzi, Hluhluwe and St Lucia reserves, while Kruger Park can be easily reached from Durban. The Point Yacht Club administers Durban Marina.

For those who are concerned about the passage from Durban to Cape Town, advice on the best tactics to use in these stormy waters can be found in the *South African Nautical Almanac*. Along that route there are docking facilities at East London, Port Elizabeth, Knysna and Mossel Bay. Space at the Royal Cape Yacht Club is severely limited, since the club no longer has access to the overspill area in Elliott Basin.

✦ CHARTER

There are several local operators offering crewed yachts for charter, but there are no bareboat craft to hire. The Royal Cape Yacht Club and Point Yacht Club will advise on availability in that area, while Rodman S.A., also operating in Durban, has a fleet of powerboats for charter.

www.rodmansa.co.za

Cruising Guides
South Africa Nautical Almanac
South Atlantic Circuit

Websites
www.southafrica.net (Department of Tourism)
www.pyc.co.za (Point Yacht Club)
www.rcyc.co.za (Royal Cape Yacht Club)
www.yachtclub.org.za (Zululand Yacht Club)

Local time	UTC +2
Buoyage	IALA A
Currency	South African Rand (ZAR)
Electricity	230V, 50Hz

Diplomatic missions

UK	012 4217500
USA	012 4314000
Australia	012 4236000
Canada	012 4223000
New Zealand	012 3428656

Communications

IDD 27	IAC 00

Emergency numbers
107 (Cape Town only)   Ambulance 10177   Police 10111

Waterfront Marina in Cape Town's Victoria and Alfred Dock, with Table Mountain in the background.

TRISTAN DA CUNHA

THERE ARE FEW PLACES in the world more remote than this speck of land lost in the vastness of the South Atlantic. As the island is hardly ever visited by cruise ships, the few yachts that call here are assured of a warm welcome. Tristan da Cunha is almost circular, the cone of a volcano with steep cliffs plunging into the sea. On the northwest corner, on a small habitable plateau, sits the settlement of Edinburgh overlooking the island's precarious anchorage. The volcano's summit is bleak and often snow-covered from June to October. Tristan da Cunha came to the world's attention in 1961, when a volcanic eruption forced the entire population of 241 to be evacuated to Britain, most of whom have now returned home. Nearby are the small and uninhabited Inaccessible, Nightingale, Gough, Middle and Stoltenhoff Islands. Since 1938 all the islands have been administered by St Helena, 1,500 miles to the north.

The anchorage is completely unprotected and a heavy swell is constant, worst in a northwesterly. The small boat harbour is very shallow and there is constant heavy surge. Yachts can rarely stay for very long even if they want to. Yet in spite of all the difficulties, every year this remote community is visited by a few intrepid sailors.

✦ COUNTRY PROFILE
In 1506 the Portuguese Admiral Tristão da Cunha reported the first sighting of the island. The first settlement was established in 1810 when three American sailors made their base there. A few years later, England claimed the island as part of the defence of St Helena, primarily to guard against Napoleon's unlikely escape. Deserters from ships, American whalers and castaways came and went. In 1876 the island was declared a British territory.

The population numbers around 300, most of whom can trace their descent back to the first settlers. English is the language spoken.

✦ CLIMATE
The climate is temperate, with moderate rainfall and high humidity. The wind is strong most days, and gales are frequent all year round.

✦ FORMALITIES

PORT OF ENTRY
Edinburgh 37°03´S 12°18´W

Yachts should anchor off Edinburgh settlement and contact Radio Tristan on Channel 16, which also operates on 4149/6230/8294 MHz. If possible, you should give advance notice of arrival to tdcenquiries@stratosnet.com.

Advice on anchoring can be obtained from the harbourmaster, who recommends two anchorages: 37°03.10´S 12°18.60´W or 37°03.04´S 12°17.85´W.

The yacht will be boarded by the immigration and medical officials. No visas are required.

No person may land at Nightingale, Alex or Stoltenhoff Islands without first clearing at Tristan and obtaining permission from the administrator.

Cruising Guide
South Atlantic Circuit

Websites
www.tristandc.com
www.tristandc.com/visitsships.php

Local time	UTC
Currency	Pound Sterling
Electricity	240V, 50Hz

Communications
Tristan Radio ZOE (tristan.radio@yahoo.co.uk)
Tel: +44 20 3014 2034;+44 20 3014 5024 (after hours)

Two albatrosses skim the waves in synchronized flight over the Southern Ocean.

THE CARIBBEAN

THE ISLANDS OF THE CARIBBEAN are one of the most popular cruising destinations in the world. This is particularly true of the Eastern Caribbean, an area that attracts a large number of cruising yachts and where the resident charter fleets are poised to overwhelm the former. Indeed, in some parts, such as the Virgin Islands, charter yachts are already in the majority, although in the Leeward and Windward Islands the stage still belongs largely to cruising boats. Also gaining in popularity are the islands off Venezuela, both those belonging to that country and the ABC Islands of Aruba, Bonaire and Curaçao. By contrast, the Greater Antilles are generally off the cruising track and are visited by fewer yachts, although this may change once Cuba's long isolation is finally brought to an end.

While the Eastern Caribbean continues to be associated in most people's minds with the Caribbean as a whole, the Bahamas, Turks and Caicos Islands, which are also included in this section, are cruising destinations just as exciting and diverse as the Lesser Antilles or Virgin Islands. The hundreds of islands of the Bahamas, Turks and Caicos offer a multitude of cruising opportunities quite different to those experienced farther east.

The long period of colonialism has left its mark and a patchwork of political systems – such as the bizarre situation of the French-speaking islands of Martinique and Guadeloupe being departments of France with the same status as their departmental sisters in mainland France. The Netherlands Antilles are part of the Kingdom of the Netherlands, but enjoy full internal autonomy. Politically one unit, geographically the islands form two groups. One group is in the Leeward Antilles and is made up of Sint Maarten, Saba and Sint Eustatius (Statia), and is usually referred to as the three 'S's, while the second group, Bonaire and Curaçao, lie off the Venezuelan coast. The latter, with neighbouring Aruba, which is a separate political unit within the Netherlands, are commonly called the ABC Islands. To complicate matters further, the northern half of the island of Sint Maarten is known as Saint-Martin and is a French overseas collectivity.

The long British colonial era has also left its mark, and while most former colonies have been independent for a long time, some islands have preferred to retain a closer association with the UK, such as the British Virgin Islands, Anguilla, Montserrat and the Caymans. This is similar to the situation of the US Virgins and Puerto Rico, which continue to be dependencies of the USA.

The sailing season in the Eastern Caribbean lasts from the end of November until June, which is the accepted start of the tropical storm season. The weather during the safe phase, particularly from early December until the end of April, is pleasant with steady easterly winds and not much rain. Any rain that falls is usually accompanied by sudden short squalls that also produce an increase in wind speed. The telltale black cloud that precedes the downpour and blast of wind is easily

Brisk tradewind sailing among the Grenadines on *Duen*, a converted Norwegian fishing boat.

seen in the open, so that sail can be reduced quickly, but there is no such warning when anchored in a steep-sided bay. Even experienced sailors, who are not used to sailing in tropical waters, have fallen victim to such vicious squalls by blowing sails or breaking gear. The only way to deal with them is to reduce sail as soon as a squall appears to be heading your way, and also to make sure that the crew is well aware of this phenomenon.

The prevailing winds are northeasterly at the beginning of winter, then gradually turn east; by late spring or early summer, they have normally settled in the southeast. This pattern can be used to good advantage by planning to cruise the chain of islands from north to south in winter and from south to north in spring. The direction of the prevailing winds should also be borne in mind by those chartering a yacht as it is always preferable to do the hard work first, and ideally be upwind of the charter base when the rental period is coming to its end. Bareboat customers are also well advised to choose the charter base carefully, so that it is within a convenient and easily sailed distance from the favourite cruising grounds in the area, and these should be well researched before committing to a particular company and its Caribbean base of operations.

The entire region can be affected by hurricanes, with the exception of the southern part, Trinidad and the islands off Venezuela, where tropical storms are extremely rare. After several storms of unprecedented violence, most insurance companies now stipulate that boats left in the Caribbean during the hurricane season must be laid up south of 12° 40´ N. In practice this means Trinidad, Tobago, Grenada and Venezuela, although it may be possible to obtain a dispensation and leave the boat in a well-protected marina or boatyard north of that latitude. Sailors planning to leave a yacht in one of these places during the hurricane season should book a place early as the popular boatyards and marinas tend to fill up quickly. Those who intend to continue cruising north of that critical latitude during summer should monitor the weather carefully and always have a fallback plan prepared. Finally, those who plan to return home at the end of the safe cruising season should make their way north by April or May, and be ready to leave the Eastern Caribbean by June at the latest. North American sailors have three basic route choices: sail to Florida via the islands or take an offshore route to any point on the east coast, while those heading for more northern destinations may prefer to make an intermediate stop in Bermuda. Yachts sailing to Europe

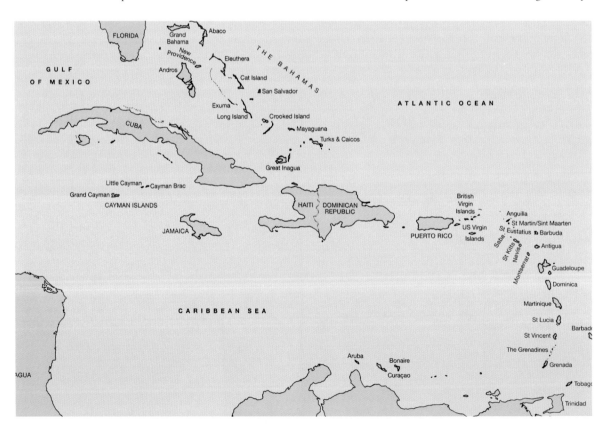

and the Mediterranean have two choices: head first for Bermuda and then stay within the prevailing westerly winds for a passage to the Azores or directly to one's destination. An alternative that has gained popularity in recent years is to set a direct course from the Caribbean to the Azores. This is indeed a shorter route, but also one that may be bedevilled by calms and light winds. Finally, there are also those yachts that are hoping to head for the Pacific Ocean, whether North or South. These passages are normally planned to start before the end of the safe season in the Caribbean and transit the Panama Canal in February or March so as to reach the desired destination at the beginning of the safe season in that part of the world.

To cope with the constant demand, amenities have greatly improved; with hundreds of yachts plying up and down the island chain, you are never too far away from a marina or boatyard with a good range of repair facilities. For any major repair work, you should head for one of the islands that has a yachting centre offering a complete range of services – such as the Virgin Islands, St Martin, Antigua, Guadeloupe, Martinique, St Lucia, Grenada or Trinidad. Although in many islands mooring is still on your own anchor, there are now purpose-built marinas throughout the area, with the highest concentration in the Virgin Islands. One aspect that has deteriorated over the years is that of personal safety, with theft, muggings and even violent robberies being reported in some countries. The worst situation is in Venezuela, which has seen several fatal incidents.

Provisioning is better in the major centres, although most islands have shops with a reasonable selection, and fresh produce is widely on offer. Although most islands have air links with the outside world, direct flights to Europe or North America are only available from some islands, so crew changes are best planned for such places as Barbados, St Lucia, Martinique, Guadeloupe, Antigua, Trinidad, St Martin or Puerto Rico.

Entry formalities have been greatly simplified in recent years as most governments recognize the importance to their economy of the revenue generated by visiting sailors. Among recent improvements being introduced by a number of islands is the Caribbean Pre-Arrival Notification system, eSeaClear™. This is a service that provides vessel operators with the ability to submit electronic notifications of arrival to participating customs offices. Registered users can access the system on the internet to enter and maintain information about their vessel and crew. Prior to arrival in a new country, the vessel operator simply ensures the information is accurate for the upcoming voyage and submits a new notification. Upon arrival, customs can access the notification information to process the boat's clearance efficiently and without the need for the captain to fill out the declaration forms. It greatly speeds up departure formalities too. If the system is successful, the following countries plan to participate: Anguilla, Aruba, British Virgin Islands, Dominica, Netherlands Antilles, St Kitts and Nevis, St Lucia, St Vincent and the Grenadines.

ANGUILLA

ANGUILLA is the northernmost of the Leeward Islands. Long and flat, this coral island was named 'eel' in Spanish. Anguilla's brief claim to fame occurred in 1969 when it was invaded by a British expeditionary force accompanied by a posse of London policemen. This is probably the only instance in which London bobbies have been used as an occupying force, and their presence on the island was greeted with delight by the Anguillans. The crisis came to a head after Anguilla decided to secede and declare its independence from St Kitts and Nevis, two other British colonies with whom it had been administered jointly. Anguilla's main attraction is its isolation, and although distances to neighbouring Caribbean islands are small, the changes that have occurred elsewhere have left Anguilla largely untouched. There are several delightful bays on the south and north coasts of the island, while those in search of solitude can do no better than anchor off Prickly Pear Cays and Dog Island, north of Anguilla.

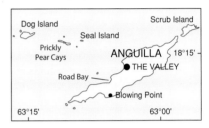

◆ COUNTRY PROFILE

Although believed to have been sighted by Columbus in 1493, Anguilla was only settled in the middle of the seventeenth century by the British. Since 1971 the island has had internal self-government, while remaining a British overseas territory.

The original inhabitants were Arawaks, and traces of their occupation of the islands have been dated to at least 1300 BCE. The current population numbers 14,500, mostly of African origin and some of European descent. The language is English.

◆ CLIMATE

The climate is semi-tropical, with an average temperature of 27°C/81°F, but cooled by the constant trade winds. The hurricane season is from June to November.

◆ FORMALITIES

PORTS OF ENTRY

Road Bay 18°12′N 63°06W	Blowing Point 18°12′N 63°06′W
Shoal Bay 18°15′N 63°2′W	

The usual port of entry for yachts is Road Bay, which is the island's main port. Visas are not required for citizens of the EU, Australia, Canada, New Zealand, South Africa and the USA. A fee is charged for yachts over 20 tons. The National Park office only has to be visited by those intending to dive. Likewise, a cruising permit, which is issued by customs, is only needed if going anywhere apart from Road Bay or Blowing Point.

Anguilla has several national park areas, is very environmentally conscious, and there are many commonsense regulations concerning waste dumping and spearfishing. There are also several areas where anchoring is prohibited, which should be checked when obtaining the cruising permit.

Anguilla's offshore islands are protected and several bays and reefs are off limits. In all sensitive areas there are mooring buoys in place for the use of yachts under 17m (55ft).

◆ FACILITIES

There are reasonably good repair facilities in the area where two local companies, Techni Marine and Rebel Marin, share a boatyard. Between them they can deal with most emergency repairs and also stock a good range of spares. For more difficult jobs, you have to go to nearby Saint-Martin. There are several supermarkets. Fuel is available, but must be taken in jerrycans.

◆ CHARTER

There are no bareboat operators based in Anguilla as most clients arrange to pick up their boats in Saint-Martin or Antigua. Footprints Charters is a local company that has a crewed boat for charter. Anguilla has strict rules on the number of crew on charter boats.

www.footprintscharters.com

Cruising Guides
Cruising Guide to the Leeward Islands   The Leeward Islands

Websites
www.anguilla-vacation.com   www.anguillaguide.com

Local time UTC −4	**Currency** East Caribbean Dollar (XCD)		
Buoyage IALA B	**Electricity** 110V, 60Hz		

Diplomatic missions
UK   4972621

Communications	**Emergency number**
IDD 1 264 IAC 011	911

ANTIGUA AND BARBUDA

ANTIGUA OCCUPIES A CENTRAL POSITION in the Lesser Antilles, and the beauty and historic significance of English Harbour made an early contribution to turning the Caribbean into a dream destination for European and American sailors alike. Antigua administers two other islands: Barbuda, 30 miles to the north, and the small uninhabited Redonda, 35 miles to the southwest.

Antigua has been blessed by nature with a beautiful coastline and by the British Admiralty with one of the most picturesque harbours in the world. English Harbour is an enclosed bay that offers protection in all kinds of weather, which is why it was used as a hurricane hole by the British West Indies fleet for nearly two centuries. English Harbour, and particularly Nelson's Dockyard, has been saved for posterity by the foresight of a British yachtsman who stopped there during a world cruise shortly after the Second World War, fell in love with the island, and never sailed on. Due to the tireless efforts of Vernon Nicholson, the derelict port with crumbling buildings underwent a gradual metamorphosis and Nelson's Dockyard is now the undisputed centre of Caribbean yachting. The old sail lofts, powder rooms, rope walks and officers' quarters have been restored and given new roles to play, while a museum housed in the former Admiral's Residence helps bring to life this harbour's fascinating history.

Several thousand yachts pass through English Harbour each year, many of them charter boats based in the area. While some of the larger charter vessels arrive from the Mediterranean at the start of the winter season, most cruising boats arrive towards the end of the season, in April and May, as they make their way home either to Europe or North America. They are joined by hundreds of racing enthusiasts who congregate in Antigua at the end of April for the annual Antigua Sailing Week, which brings together the cream of Caribbean and international yachting and signals the end of the sailing season in this part of the world.

A favourite and traditional spot that brings together visiting sailors to watch the sunset are the Shirley Heights that overlook the most picturesque vista in the Caribbean. As the sun's upper limb is about to sink below the western horizon, everyone stares – hoping to see the rare green flash, a unique experience that any sailor worth his or her salt must have witnessed at least once. It is said that the frequent sightings on Shirley Heights are in direct proportion to the amount of rum punch consumed by the observers.

Antigua's coastline is dotted with secluded coves and attractive bays, and once away from the bustle of English Harbour the solitude of some anchorages is quite surprising. Those in search of absolute peace and quiet can sail to Antigua's smaller sister, Barbuda, a coral island surrounded by a maze of reefs that over the centuries have claimed over

View over English and Falmouth Harbours.

two hundred ships. Although modern charts, GPS and good sunlight reduce the hazards, the area should be treated with caution, as coral growth has made even relatively new charts not entirely reliable.

In recent years the safety situation in both islands has been causing concern as there have been some violent attacks on foreign sailors.

◆ COUNTRY PROFILE

In the pre-Columbian era, at least as far back as 2400 BCE, Antigua was inhabited by the Amerindian Siboney, to be followed later by the Arawaks. Columbus visited the island on his second voyage in 1493, naming the island after the Church of Santa Maria de la Antigua in Seville. The English were the first to settle in 1632, and apart from a brief French occupation, the islands remained a British possession until independence. English Harbour was developed as a major naval base, and Horatio Nelson spent much time there during his command of the Leeward Islands Squadron. Antigua, Barbuda and Redonda became fully independent in 1981.

The population of 86,000 is mostly of African origin, with only 2 per cent of European descent. St John's on the west coast is the capital. English is spoken.

◆ CLIMATE

Antigua has a tropical climate, with a rainy season from September to November and relatively dry weather for the rest of the year, albeit interrupted by squalls. The tropical storm season is from June to November, with most hurricanes developing between August and October.

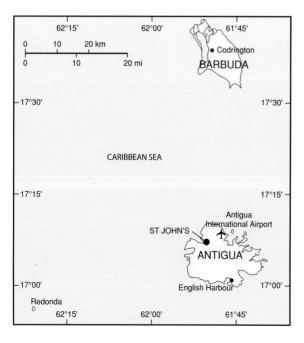

◆ FORMALITIES

PORTS OF ENTRY	
Antigua: English Harbour 17°00′N 61°46′W (this includes the Dockyard and Falmouth Harbour)	
Jolly Harbour 17°06′N 61°53′W	St John's 17°07′N 61°52′W
Barbuda: Codrington 17°38′N 61°49′W	

The Coast Guard monitors Channels 16 and 68 and may intercept, and even board, yachts coming from abroad.

English Harbour: Yachts should anchor in the bay (Freeman's Harbour) and the captain only should go ashore to clear. All offices are located in the old Officers' Quarters building, where customs, immigration and the park department have to be visited. Crew must remain on board until clearance has been completed, even when arriving after office hours. On departure from English Harbour, harbour fees must be paid at the paymaster to collect the port clearance certificate. This should then be presented to the immigration officer, with the ship's papers and passports.

Falmouth Harbour: Yachts requiring clearance should anchor or proceed to one of the marinas. The captain should then walk over to Nelson's Dockyard to complete formalities.

St John's Harbour: The port facilities are at the outer end of the peninsula running west into the middle of the harbour and its use is restricted to commercial vessels. The inner harbour, between the deepwater port and town waterfront, is used by small local craft with less than 1.8m (6ft) draft. Yachts may come alongside either the deepwater dock or, more conveniently, at the head of the Heritage Quay Dock, close to Customs House. Clearance is done at the port authority offices in the deepwater dock on the north side of the harbour.

Jolly Harbour: The marina monitors Channel 68. Customs, immigration and port authority have an office in the marina.

Barbuda: There are several anchorages on the south side of Barbuda. Customs and immigration are located in Codrington and as this is a long walk from any of the anchorages, a taxi can be called on Channel 68. Boats coming from another country cannot clear in at Barbuda and must do so first in Antigua. Vessels visiting Barbuda must have a valid cruising permit issued in Antigua.

No visas are required by nationals of EU countries, Australia, Canada, New Zealand or the USA. Immigration grants a 60-day stay on arrival and this can be extended.

Crew leaving a boat must have a valid airline ticket to a country that will accept them. This ticket must be presented to the immigration official when being signed off the vessel. Captains wishing to exchange crew members with another vessel must do so in the presence of an immigration official.

Spanish Point anchorage on Barbuda's south coast.

Immigration must be notified of any crew departures or changes.

All boats must have a cruising permit that is obtained on entry and enables you to go anywhere in Antiguan waters, including Barbuda. The permit is valid for one month or until the yacht leaves Antigua.

Spearfishing is illegal in Antigua and Barbuda waters by non-Antiguan nationals. The coastline between the Pillars of Hercules and the entrance to Mamora Bay is protected and no fishing of any type is allowed in this area.

English Harbour regulations

The navigation channel from Fort Berkeley to the inner harbour must be kept free. Yachts can either anchor off the channel, or come stern-to the quay. There is a dinghy speed limit of 5 knots, and exceeding this will lead to an instant fine. There have been several accidents caused by speeding tenders, including one fatality. Old fuel and used oil must be disposed of in the special containers provided.

✦ FACILITIES

Because of Antigua's long-standing involvement with yachting, service and repair facilities are of a high standard and almost anything can be fixed on the island. Most specialized firms are concentrated around English Harbour. Foremost among them is Antigua Slipways, which undertakes all kinds of boat repair and has a well-stocked chandlery. Electronic repair is undertaken by the Signal Locker in English Harbour, and there are also two sailmakers nearby. Seagull Yacht Service in Falmouth Harbour is a marine engineering service. Jolly Harbour Marina has a full service boatyard with its own travelift. The Map Shop in St John's has a good supply of British and US charts for the North Atlantic and South Pacific.

All companies in the English Harbour area undertaking yacht or equipment repair monitor Channel 68, and this is the quickest and surest way to obtain help if anything needs to be done on the boat.

BARBUDA

The whole population lives in Codrington, which has a post office and limited provisioning. Palaster Reef is a national park and no fishing with a speargun or rod is permitted. There are virtually no repair facilities in Barbuda, and only a limited selection of supplies can be obtained there. There are various inland areas that are wildlife sanctuaries; these can be visited, and the best way to do this is with a local guide who can be contacted on Channel 68.

Older charts of Barbuda have been reported as unreliable because of coral growth.

REDONDA

This rocky island (height: 305m/1,000ft) with sheer cliffs has only one decent anchorage on the southwest coast.

✦ CHARTER

Some of the world's most luxurious yachts are based in English Harbour during the winter and are available for hire. There are also a few bareboat charter operators based in nearby Falmouth Harbour, or at other marinas around the island. Also based in Falmouth Harbour is Ondeck, a charter company that organizes crewed trips to other islands. Its yachts also take part in various Caribbean regattas and are crewed by charter customers.

www.sunsail.com
www.nautilus-yachting.com
www.horizonyachtcharters.com
www.ondeckoceanracing.com

Cruising Guides
Cruising Guide to the Leeward Islands
Grenada to the Virgin Islands
The Leeward Islands

Websites
www.antigua-barbuda.org
www.antiguamarineguide.com
www.antiguayachtclub.com

Local time	UTC −4
Buoyage	IALA B
Currency	East Caribbean Dollar (XCD)
Electricity	230V, 60Hz

Diplomatic missions	
USA	463 6531

Communications	
IDD 1 268	IAC 011

Emergency numbers
999/911

ARUBA

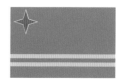

THE WESTERNMOST OF THE ABC ISLANDS, Aruba is a convenient stop for yachts heading for Panama. The most attractive part of it is the sheltered northwest coast fronted by pristine white beaches. Among the inland attractions are interesting limestone caves and stone structures called spirit houses, built by local people to elicit the support of their ancestors when they prayed for a wish to come true. One such wish may have been in the early nineteenth century when gold was discovered and brought Aruba unprecedented prosperity. When the deposits were exhausted, plantations of aloe vera took over and for a time Aruba was the largest exporter of this medicinal plant.

No longer part of the Netherlands Antilles, Aruba broke away from the other five islands in 1986 to become an autonomous member of the Kingdom of the Netherlands. The Hague is now only responsible for defence and foreign affairs.

✦ COUNTRY PROFILE

The first inhabitants were the Caquetios, an Arawak tribe that were living on this island when the Spanish first landed in 1499. Many of them were forcibly transported by the Spanish to Santo Domingo to work in the copper mines, their place being gradually filled by people originating from other parts of the world. As a result, the current population claims to be made up of 45 different ethnic strands, although there are still a number of people of pure Arawak descent – one of the few places in the Caribbean to claim this.

The Netherlands established its rule over the island in 1636 and resisted all challenges from other European powers. Aruba has maintained its close association with the Dutch nation to this day.

The population of 103,000 includes those of Spanish and Dutch origin as well as many recent immigrants. Dutch is the official language, but English and Spanish are widely spoken,

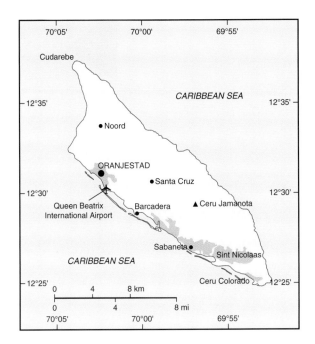

based in both harbours. On departure, yachts must also come to the dock to clear out. Oranjestad is a free port and no customs restrictions apply.

Nationals of the UK, USA, Canada and most European countries may stay 180 days without a visa. Nationals of Australia and New Zealand may stay 30 days without a visa, extendable to 180 days if they have a yacht based temporarily in Aruba. South Africans need a visa.

✦ FACILITIES

The Renaissance Marina in Oranjestad is a full service marina catering for all sizes of yachts, and electric, mechanical and electronic repairs are available. In addition to Renaissance Marina, there is the smaller Surfside Marina as well as two yacht clubs whose moorings may be used by visitors. Down the coast from Oranjestad, near Spanish Lagoon, is the Aruba Nautical Club, which has berths, fuel, water and electricity. Between Oranjestad and Spanish Lagoon is the Bucuti Yacht Club, which also has docking space for visitors. Provisioning is best done in Oranjestad, where there is a good selection of fresh produce. There are excellent supermarkets about 2km north of town.

Aruba is increasingly used by sailors as a convenient place to leave their yachts during the hurricane season.

Cruising Guide
ABC Islands

Website
www.arubatourism.com

Local time	UTC −4
Buoyage	IALA B
Currency	Aruban Florin (AWG)
Electricity	127V, 60Hz

Diplomatic missions	
UK.	Curaçao +599 9 461 390
USA	Curaçao +599 9 461 3066

Communications	
IDD 297	IAC 00

Emergency numbers
911/112

as well as the local Papiamento. This unusual local language is unique to the ABC Islands and is a mixture of Spanish, Portuguese, Dutch, English and some African and Amerindian dialects. Dating back at least to the early eighteenth century, Papiamento is in everyday use and there are both books and newspapers published in it.

✦ CLIMATE

Aruba lies outside the hurricane belt and has a relatively dry climate. Temperatures are higher from August to October, although there is not a great difference from the cooler months, which are from December to February.

✦ FORMALITIES

PORT OF ENTRY	
Oranjestad	12°30′ N 70°02′ W
Barcadera	12°28.6′ N 69°59.9′ W

Aruba Port Control should be called on Channel 11 or 16. Usually they direct yachts to the commercial dock at either Oranjestad or Barcadera. Customs and immigration are

BAHAMAS

OVER 700 ISLANDS and 2,400 uninhabited cays make up the Bahamas, its name coming from the Spanish *baja mar*, meaning the 'shallow sea' – and indeed depths on the banks throughout the archipelago are rarely more than 10m (30ft). In the world of cruising, the Bahamas stand out as a totally different experience. These low islands surrounded by clear waters of exquisite colours and unbelievable transparency have a charm all of their own. The distinctive features are the large shallow banks and coral reefs which, although a hazard to shipping, provide excellent diving and underwater scenery. The shallow depths and strong tidal currents call for very attentive navigation. To protect the fragile environment, nature reserves and underwater parks have been established in some islands, and visiting sailors are expected to do their best to cause as little damage as possible, both ashore and afloat. In particular, they should avoid anchoring in coral, which is easily destroyed by the anchor and rode. Mooring buoys have been installed at some locations, and these should be used in preference to anchoring.

Cruising opportunities are infinite and making the right decision is no easy matter, but very few sailors leave disappointed. There are strings of small islands, such as the Abaco, Berry and Exuma Cays, where it is possible to cruise in almost any weather as there is always a safe anchorage within reach. The large islands of Grand Bahama, Andros and Eleuthera call for a different approach as there is a more limited choice of safe harbours and distances are too great to explore by dinghy or on foot.

Because of their close proximity to Florida, the Northern Bahamas – and in particular the Abacos – are a perennial destination for US sailors. These islands, though, have a lot more in their favour than just being a convenient landfall, and the colour of the water, extensive sandy beaches and attractive harbours, not to mention the excellent fishing, ensure their status as the best introduction to the Bahamas.

Those with more time on their hands eventually end up in the Outer Bahamas where Great Exuma is a favourite wintering spot. The sheltered Elizabeth Harbour off George Town

A distinctive Bahamian seascape.

provides a temporary home from home to hundreds of cruising sailors, many of whom spend the entire winter anchored off Stocking Island. Regatta Week in late spring adds several more hundreds to their number during this annual feast of fun and – occasionally – some serious racing too. Great Exuma is also the venue for the Family Islands Regatta, held in the third week in April. For over half a century this popular event has attracted dozens of traditional Bahamian schooners, sloops and dinghies. The fiercely contested three-day event gives the thousands of spectators, both local and foreign, the chance to see old working boats in action.

When it was declared a national park in 1958, the Exuma Cays Land and Sea Park was not only the first national park in the Bahamas, but the first land and sea park in the world. In a nation profoundly concerned with its natural heritage, it has led to the founding of the Bahamas National Trust, which has now grown to include many nature reserves and parks. As all such parks are charitable foundations, it is good to know that visiting sailors make a considerable contribution not just to the Exuma Park, but to other such popular locations as well.

In the far corner of the Outer Bahamas lies an island with an immense significance in relation to its modest size. San Salvador, originally Guanahani, is the place where Christopher Columbus and his three caravels made landfall on 12 October 1492 and altered for ever humanity's perception of the world. A cross marks the spot in Landfall Bay where it is believed Columbus first set foot in the New World, and it is well worth a detour to visit this historic place.

Their closeness to the USA has profoundly affected the islands, but outside of the main tourist centres the Bahamas have changed little and the slow pace of life in the outer islands is their enduring charm.

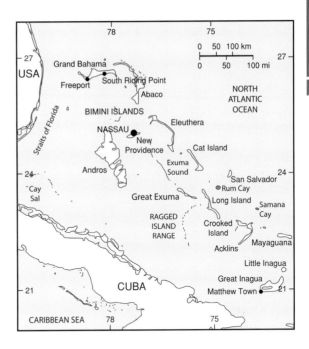

✦ COUNTRY PROFILE

When Christopher Columbus made landfall on Guanahani, the Bahamas were inhabited by the peaceful Lucayans. Within a few years of their arrival, the Spanish deported most of the population to work in the gold and silver mines in Hispaniola and Cuba, and the Lucayans disappeared as a people. Once plundered of their only valuable resource, the Spanish left the islands alone. From the time of the first settlement in 1629 by Protestant settlers from Bermuda escaping religious persecution, the Bahamas remained under British rule until 1973 when they became a fully independent nation.

Landfall Bay.

Over four million tourists visit the Bahamas every year and the majority of the population is employed in the tourist industry. The total number of people in the islands is 310,000, largely of African origin with a minority of European descent. Only 30 of the islands are inhabited and 60 per cent of the population lives on New Providence Island, location of the capital, Nassau. The outer islands are known as the Family Islands. English is the main language.

◆ CLIMATE

The climate is very pleasant, as the islands lie on the edge of the anticyclone belt. The first to comment on the weather was Christopher Columbus: 'The air is as soft as that of Seville in April, and so fragrant that it is delicious to breathe it.' The weather is particularly pleasant in summer, between June and October, when it is cooler than on the eastern seaboard of the USA or in the Eastern Caribbean islands. Unfortunately, this is also the hurricane season, which lasts from June to November. Although several years can go by without a hurricane affecting the Bahamas, occasionally they are hit by a particularly violent one. This risk should be borne in mind by those who spend the hurricane season in the Bahamas as it may be impossible to find shelter at short notice. Dreaded almost more than hurricanes, because they occur during the winter cruising season, are northers. Such winds, which can be quite violent, are caused by the arrival of a cold front. The worst situation is to be caught by such a norther while sailing in the Gulf Stream when the strong wind against the swift current can produce very rough seas.

◆ FORMALITIES

Mayaguana: Abrahams Bay is not an official port of entry, and boats that have tried to stop there on their way to or from the Bahamas have not been able to do so. Those wishing to stop there on their way out should make this clear when clearing out of the last port as yachts are not allowed to stop at Mayaguana without permission.

Entry into the Bahamas must be made at an official port of entry. Clearance must be done at the earliest opportunity, and in major ports officers are on call at all hours and there are no overtime charges. The Bahamas can be transited without clearing in until arrival at a port of entry, but during transit you cannot anchor overnight or enter a port. In the outer islands, the customs officer may handle all formalities, but in Nassau and other larger ports both customs and immigration officials must be seen. Officials are supposed to come to the yacht, but in some smaller islands the captain will have to go ashore to find them. Crew must remain on board until clearance is completed. If clearing in at a marina, the marina personnel will call customs and immigration.

PORTS OF ENTRY		
Abaco: Walker's Cay	26°32´ N	76°57´ W
Green Turtle Cay	26°45´ N	77°20´ W
Marsh Harbour	26°40´ N	75°05´ W
Sandy Point	26°01´ N	77°24´ W
Andros: Morgan's Bluff	25°10´ N	78°01´ W
San Andros	24°43´ N	77°47´ W
Fresh Creek	24°41´ N	77°50´ W
Mangrove Cay	24°13´ N	77°41´ W
Congo Town	24°09´ N	77°35´ W
Berry Islands: Great Harbour Cay	25°44´ N	77°49´ W
Chub Cay	25°25´ N	77°55´ W
North Bimini: Alice Town	25°48´ N	79°18´ W
Cat Cay: Cat Cay Club	25°33´ N	79°18´ W
Eleuthera: Harbour Island	25°34´ N	76°40´ W
Governor's Harbour	25°12´ N	76°15´ W
Rock Sound	24°53´ N	76°10´ W
Cape Eleuthera (sometimes)	25°12´ N	76°15´ W
Spanish Wells	25°33´ N	76°45´ W
Exuma: George Town	23°34´ N	75°49´ W
Grand Bahama: West End	26°42´ N	78°59´ W
Freeport Harbour	26°31´ N	78°47´ W
Lucaya Marina	26°29´ N	78°38´ W
Xanadu Marina	26°29´ N	78°42´ W
Inagua: Matthew Town	20°57´ N	73°41´ W
New Providence: Any marina in Nassau	25°04´ N	77°21´ W
Long Island: Stella Maris	23°34´ N	75°16´ W
Ragged Island: Duncan Town	22°12´ N	75°44´ W
San Salvador: Cockburn Town	24°03´ N	74°32´ W

Visas are not required by nationals of most countries, although the length of stay granted may vary depending on the country concerned, but this can be extended up to eight months. Every crew member must complete an immigration card, and at the request of the immigration officer they may have to accompany the skipper to sign the individual forms.

A cruising permit valid for one year will be issued on arrival and gives permission to visit all islands. This permit must be presented to officials if requested at any port visited. The permit must be retained until the cruise is finished and handed back at the port of exit. If for any reason you are not able to clear outbound, which is not required, the permit should be mailed back from the next destination. However, as some countries, notably the Dominican Republic, require a clearing out document, this should be obtained on departure from the Bahamas.

Dinghy jam in George Town.

can be done. Basic supplies are available and there is a daily fresh produce market. Any parts not available locally can be obtained from either Nassau or Florida from where there are frequent flights.

✦ CHARTER

With the notable exception of the two leading international companies, the Moorings and Sunsail, both based in the Abacos, no other well-known bareboat operators maintain bases in the Bahamas, although some companies located in Florida do allow their clients to take the boats across the strait. There are a few privately owned yachts, both sail and power, which are locally based and are available for charter, usually with a skipper.

www.moorings.com
www.sunsail.com
www.bahamassailing.com
www.aquacatcruises.com

Penalties are severe for not clearing customs on arrival and can lead to fines, imprisonment and even confiscation of the boat.

There is a flat fee to clear customs and immigration, which is valid for two entries within 90 days and covers a vessel with four persons or less. Also included in the fee is the cruising permit, a fishing permit, customs and immigration charges and the departure tax for up to four persons.

The movement of vessels is strictly controlled in Nassau and Freeport, where yachts are required to clear with harbour control on Channel 16 when entering, leaving and even changing position within any of the ports. The number of the ship's registration document will be requested, so this should be readily available.

No marine life at all may be captured in the national marine parks: Exuma Cays Land and Sea Park, Peterson Cay National Park (Grand Bahama) and Pelican Cays (Abaco). Elsewhere, fishing regulations are strict and a permit is issued at the time of inbound clearance.

✦ FACILITIES

Almost everything is available in Nassau, which has several marinas, chandleries and repair facilities. Fuel and other marine supplies are also obtainable, as are provisions. There is an excellent fresh produce market at Potter's Cay. *The Yachtsman's Guide to the Bahamas* gives details of facilities available not only in Nassau, but throughout the islands.

Another popular destination with good amenities is Freeport on Grand Bahama Island. The main port is geared to dealing primarily with commercial vessels, so visiting yachts might find it more convenient to clear in at nearby Lucayan or Xanadu marinas. Facilities at both are good and most repairs can be undertaken locally. In the outer islands, there is a small marina with basic facilities and fuel on San Salvador, while George Town in Great Exuma is slowly establishing itself as a yachting centre where some repairs

---

Cruising Guides
Abaco Cruising Guide
Abaco, Ports of Call and Anchorages
Cruising Guide to Abaco
The Exuma Guide
The Gentleman's Guide to Passages South
The Northern Bahamas
The Southern Bahamas
Yachtsman's Guide to the Bahamas

Websites
www.bahamas.com
www.bnt.bs (Bahamas National Trust – details of all nature reserves)
www.basra.org (Bahamas Air and Sea Rescue Association, a voluntary organization that depends on donations from mariners)

Local time	UTC –5
	Summer time: second Sunday in March to first Sunday in November
Buoyage	IALA B
Currency	Bahamian Dollar (BSD)
Electricity	120/220V, 60Hz

Diplomatic missions	
USA	3221181

Communications	
IDD 1 242	IAC 011

Emergency numbers
911
BASRA Tel: 325 8864

BARBADOS

AS THE MOST EASTERLY of the Lesser Antilles, Barbados is the nearest landfall for yachts crossing the Atlantic on the traditional tradewind route. For most sailors, this is usually the only opportunity to visit Barbados as its position to windward of all other islands in the Lesser Antilles means that few yachts attempt to beat their way against the prevailing trade winds to visit an island that has little to offer from a sailing point of view. The only cruising area is along the sheltered west coast, which is dotted with tourist resorts. The east coast, exposed to the Atlantic breakers, is wild and inaccessible, with strange rock formations along its beaches; it should be given a wide berth.

Despite having a developed tourist industry, which benefits from the island's good air links, relatively little has been done to accommodate those arriving by sea, and facilities in Carlisle Bay, the main anchorage, are basic. The only proper marine facility is Port St Charles on the northwest coast of the island. This is a deluxe development surrounding a man-made lagoon and caters primarily for superyachts, although its clearance facility may be used by any boat making landfall in Barbados.

◆ COUNTRY PROFILE

The pre-Columbian population of Barbados were probably Arawaks, but the first European settlers in the seventeenth century were British.

Due to the island's position it never changed hands, unlike its Caribbean neighbours. Barbados became independent in 1966 and has maintained its independent stance towards the rest of the Eastern Caribbean by resisting suggestions to join a federation, and insisting on having its own currency.

The population is 285,000, mainly of mixed African and European origin. There is a small white minority who descend from the original English settlers. English and Bajan, a dialect, are spoken. The capital is Bridgetown.

Carlisle Bay.

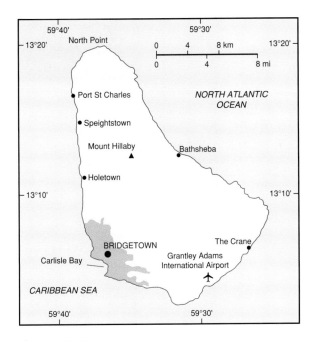

CLIMATE

Barbados has a tropical climate, with high average temperatures throughout the year but cooled by the constant tradewinds. The tropical season is from June to November, but as the island is farther south, it is rarely hit by hurricanes. June to January is the rainy and humid season.

FORMALITIES

PORTS OF ENTRY

Bridgetown	13°06′ N 59°38′ W
Port St Charles	13°15′ N 9°38′ W

The Bridgetown signal station should be contacted on Channels 12 or 16 for instructions. The yacht must be docked where instructed, and anchoring before formalities have been completed is prohibited. Clearance is done in the Deepwater Harbour north of Bridgetown. You should monitor Channel 12 while entering the harbour and watch out for cruise ships. After clearance, yachts can move to anchor in Carlisle Bay.

Clearance is also possible at Port St Charles, where the dockmaster should be contacted on Channels 16 or 77.

Visas are not required for stays of up to six months for nationals of the EU, USA, Australia, Canada, New Zealand and South Africa.

Cruising outside the port area where you cleared in requires permission from customs and the port authority. Permission to cruise along the west coast must be requested when clearing in, and a planned itinerary submitted to

customs. Marker buoys are being placed at several locations where there are sandy areas that are large enough to permit anchoring. A chart showing these authorized anchoring areas is available from the Barbados Port Authority. In any case, yachts should only anchor in sand, never coral. Heavy penalties apply to transgressors.

There are clearance charges on departure and the port authority's clearance must precede customs clearance.

FACILITIES

Barbados Yacht Club can advise on engine and sail repairs, which are available locally. There is a travelift at the Shallow Draft Harbour. Electrical, electronic, refrigeration, metal-working workshops and other facilities can be found, even if they don't primarily cater for yachts. The boatyard jetty in Carlisle Bay has some facilities for cruising boats. There are two fuel docks in the fishing harbour just north of the Careenage that should be contacted in advance on Channel 68.

Port St Charles is a luxury development catering primarily for superyachts – with prices to match. Fuel, water and electricity are available. Holding tanks are obligatory, and repairs and maintenance work are not permitted because of nearby residences.

CHARTER

There are no bareboats for charter, but several local operators offer day trips on sailing or power yachts.

www.dreamsbarbados.com

Cruising Guides	
The Atlantic Crossing Guide	
Cruising Guide to Trinidad and Tobago plus Barbados	

Websites	
www.barbados.org	
www.portstcharles.com	

Local time	UTC −4
Buoyage	IALA B
Currency	Barbadian Dollar (BBD)
Electricity	115V, 50Hz

Diplomatic missions	
UK	430 7800
USA	431 0255
Canada	429 3550

Communications	
IDD 1 246	IAC 011

Emergency number	
911	

BONAIRE

THE STUNNING UNDERWATER SCENERY is the chief attraction of this easternmost of the ABC Islands, and anyone with even the smallest interest in diving should use their stay to best advantage. Bonaire is ranked as one of the top three dive spots in the world, and as a result all waters around the island are a protected marine park. Bonaire is less densely populated and less developed than its neighbour Curaçao. The European influence is more pronounced than in other Caribbean islands and is reflected in the Dutch cottages in pastel colours that line the streets. The people of Bonaire are highly environmentally conscious and there are many protected sites both on land and at sea.

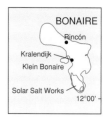

✦ COUNTRY PROFILE

The island was discovered, along with Aruba and Curaçao, in 1499 by the Spaniard Alonso de Ojeda. At that time an Arawak tribe lived there, and although only a few survived, they managed to retain their separate identity until recently. The Dutch took the island in 1636 and in 1954 the Netherlands Antilles were granted full internal autonomy.

Bonaire's population numbers over 14,000 of mixed Arawak, European and African descent. They speak Dutch, the official language, and Papiamento, a local dialect. English and Spanish are also widely spoken. The capital is Kralendijk.

✦ CLIMATE

Bonaire is blessed with one of the gentlest climates in the Caribbean, with January being the coolest month, with an average temperature of 26°C/79°F, while August and September are the warmest, with an average of 29°C/84°F. The island is cooled throughout the year by the easterly trade winds. Rainfall is low and the island lies south of the hurricane belt.

✦ FORMALITIES

PORT OF ENTRY

Kralendijk   12°09´N 68°17´W

The harbourmaster should be contacted and will usually allow a yacht to pick up a mooring controlled by the Harbour Village Marina, just north of Kralendijk. The customs and immigration offices are close by. Clearance can also be done in the marina.

Visa requirements are the same as those of the Netherlands, and Schengen rules apply. Usually yachts are granted a stay of three months, which can be extended by another three months if you leave and return to Bonaire after a minimum of four days. Due to the marine park status of the island, spearfishing is forbidden and marine life is protected. Possession of spearguns is illegal and they must be left with customs for the duration of your stay.

The authorities are very strict about the protection of the marine environment. Except in an emergency, anchoring is prohibited. Cruising boats are expected to have holding tanks and the discharge of any waste is prohibited. There are mooring buoys on all popular dive sites, and the marinas collect fees on behalf of the Bonaire National Marine Park. Cruising boats are expected to use only Channels 71, 77 and 88A. Use of other channels can lead to fines and confiscation of equipment.

✦ FACILITIES

One attraction for visiting sailors is the better than average repair and service facilities. A much needed new marina was created by dredging a channel through to a salt pond close to the capital, Kralendijk. There are three other marinas: Plaza Resort, Club Nautico and Harbour Village Marina, the latter having the best facilities. Provisioning is very good in Kralendijk, which has several supermarkets. The largest is the warehouse on the way to the airport.

✦ CHARTER

Charter opportunities are limited to daysailing on one of the locally owned boats.

www.suavesailing.com

Cruising Guides
Cruising Guide to Venezuela and Bonaire
The Bonaire Marine Park Guide

Websites
www.tourismbonaire.com   www.infobonaire.com
www.bmp.org (Bonaire Marine Park)

Local time UTC −4   **Electricity** 127V, 50Hz
Buoyage IALA B
Currency Netherlands Antillean Gulden (ANG)

Communications IDD 599 7   IAC 00

Emergency numbers 911/112
St Francis Hospital has a decompression chamber.
Tel: 8900/8445.

BRITISH VIRGIN ISLANDS

THE VIRGIN ISLANDS are an archipelago comprising hundreds of small islands and cays situated between Puerto Rico and the Leeward Islands. The western part, having some of the larger islands, is US territory, while the eastern half is a British overseas territory. The language and US currency may be shared, but the US Virgin Islands are more developed and also very different culturally. The largest British islands are Tortola, Virgin Gorda, Jost van Dyke and, slightly set apart to the north, Anegada. Most of the smaller islands are strung along the Sir Francis Drake Channel.

There are few island groups in the world that are better suited for cruising than the Virgins. They are scenically beautiful with countless bays, coves and anchorages, the waters are sheltered from the strong tradewinds and ocean swell, and navigation is never taxing. With so many convenient hideaways and access channels, it is not surprising that the islands became a favourite base for pirates and buccaneers in days gone by. It is exactly these same features that attract modern-day sailors to these shores, and the British Virgin Islands are now the largest charter area in the world. For this reason, they are somewhat less tempting to long-distance cruising sailors, who often prefer the less crowded islands found elsewhere in the Caribbean.

There are too many highlights to mention, but the few that should not be missed are the idyllic Cane Garden Bay on Tortola, considered one of the most picturesque in the Virgins; the Baths, a jumble of gigantic granite boulders on Virgin Gorda; or the Bight on Norman Island. Better known as Treasure Island, the latter was the inspiration for Robert Louis Stevenson's novel of the same name, its storyline possibly being based on a true incident as Norman himself is reputed to have been an eighteenth-century pirate whose lair this was.

Nanny Cay

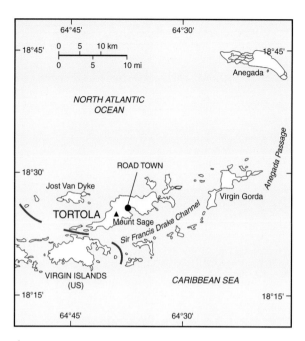

COUNTRY PROFILE

The original inhabitants were Arawaks and Caribs. Visited by Columbus on his second voyage, he named the islands after Saint Ursula and her 11,000 virgin warriors who died rather than submit to pagan assault. Soon after their discovery, the Virgin Islands' strategic position rapidly turned them into a popular stop for vessels plying between Europe and America. As Spanish power waned, several countries fought over the islands. At the end of the seventeenth century England annexed Tortola, then Virgin Gorda and Anegada. After 1956 the British Virgin Islands were administered separately and developed close links with the US Virgin Islands. Today the British Virgin Islands have internal self-government, but remain a British overseas territory.

The capital is Road Town on Tortola, the largest island, where about half the total population of 24,500 lives. The language is English.

CLIMATE

The islands have a subtropical climate, although temperatures are moderated by the trade winds. Temperatures in summer average from 26° to 31°C (79°–88°F) and between 22° and 28°C (72°–82°F) in winter. Rainfall is low and occurs mostly during squalls. The prevailing winds are from the east. The islands lie in the track of tropical hurricanes, which are most likely to develop between August and October.

FORMALITIES

Road Harbour: Customs and immigration are at the government dock at Road Town. Yachts should anchor off the dock and check in with customs and immigration.

Sopers Hole: Offices are at the ferry dock at West End. Ferries from the US Virgin Islands stop here, so formalities can take longer when a ferry has arrived.

Great Harbour: Customs and immigration offices are in the same building by the dock.

Virgin Gorda: Offices are in a new government office block by the ferry jetty.

No visas are required for nationals of most countries, and normally a 30 day stay is granted on arrival. All members of the crew must be present to clear immigration.

The British Virgin Islands and US Virgin Islands require full customs clearance in and out when sailing between them. For short stays, you may be able to clear in and out at the same time. A 30 day cruising fee is charged, based on tonnage. The large increases in fees for private vessels announced in 2008 have now been deferred indefinitely.

Non-residents must obtain a recreational fishing permit in order to fish in BVI waters. Spearfishing, lobstering and the collection of live shells is prohibited. The use of jet-skis is prohibited.

NATIONAL PARKS

A reef protection programme is in operation in an effort to limit damage caused by visiting boats. Mooring buoys have been laid in a number of sensitive areas that have suffered extensive damage due to increased anchoring activity. Cruising boats must obtain a National Parks moorings permit, and follow the regulations concerning the use and colour coding of the buoys: red buoys: non-diving, day use only; yellow buoys: commercial dive vessels only (or boats over 17m/55ft); white buoys: non-commercial vessels for dive use only, on a first come first served basis and a 90 minute time limit; blue buoys: dinghy use only. Private mooring buoys are provided by Moor Seacure Ltd at locations throughout the British Virgins and a daily fee is charged for their use.

FACILITIES

Virtually all amenities are concentrated on Tortola, particularly around Road Town, where there are several

PORTS OF ENTRY		
Tortola: Road Harbour	18°25′N	64°37′W
Sopers Hole	18°23′N	64°42′W
Jost van Dyke: Great Harbour	18°27′N	64°45′W
Virgin Gorda: Virgin Gorda Yacht Harbour	18°27′N	64°26′W

marinas and a large haulout facility at Tortola Yacht Services, with full facilities and services on site. There is a large marina at Nanny Cay with a travelift, chandlery and extensive repair facilities. A smaller marina at Sopers Hole has its own slipway, whereas nearby West End Slipways offers a wider range of repair facilities, including a 200-ton marine railway. Virgin Gorda Yacht Harbour has full marina facilities, a 60-ton lift, and good provisioning. Only limited facilities are available at Great Harbour on Jost van Dyke. On all small islands, only basic provisions can be bought, so it is best to fully provision in one of the larger centres.

The Caribbean's first walk-in weather centre, CARIBWX, is based in Road Town. Customized weather forecasts, a daily Caribbean SSB weather net, and also daily email marine forecasts are among the many services it offers.

✦ CHARTER

The ideal location and geographical make-up of the Virgin Islands have turned them into the most popular charter destination in the world, with a wide enough choice of yachts to satisfy such demand.

> www.caribbeancruisingclub.com
> www.horizonyachtcharters.com
> www.sunsail.com
> www.moorings.com
> www.conchcharters.com

Cruising Guides
Cruising the Virgin Islands
Cruising Guide to the Virgin Islands
Grenada to the Virgin Islands
Virgin Anchorages
Yachtsman's Guide to the Virgin Islands

Websites
www.bvitourism.com
www.britishvirginislands.com
www.caribwx.com
www.bareboatsbvi.com

Local time	UTC −4
Buoyage	IALA B
Currency	US Dollar (USD)
Electricity	115V, 60Hz

Diplomatic missions
UK	494 2345

Communications
IDD 1 284	IAC 011

Emergency number
999

The Baths anchorage on Virgin Gorda.

CAYMAN ISLANDS

THE CAYMAN ISLANDS LIE SOUTH OF CUBA AND WEST OF JAMAICA and are off the usual cruising track. Grand Cayman, lying some 80 miles west of its smaller sisters, has several anchorages and also a well-protected marina inside a shallow lagoon. Little Cayman and Cayman Brac ('bluff' in Gaelic) are less developed, and even less visited by cruising yachts than the main island. Grand Cayman's chief attraction is its underwater world, which has been described as a diver's paradise. The sea surrounding the island is a marine park and conservation area.

✦ COUNTRY PROFILE

The islands were first sighted by Columbus on his last voyage to the Americas. They have been a British dependency since 1670 and, although now self-governing, have chosen to continue as an overseas territory of the UK. The English-speaking population of mixed African and European descent is 49,000, most of whom live on Grand Cayman. The capital is George Town.

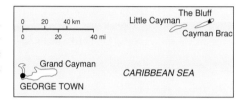

✦ CLIMATE

The island is cooled by the prevailing northeast trades, so the mean winter temperature is 24°C/75°F, and 27°C/81°F in summer. The strong winter northerlies make most anchorages untenable, and shelter must be sought either off the south coast or inside North Sound. The hurricane season is from June to November.

PORTS OF ENTRY		
Grand Cayman: George Town	19°18´N 81°23´W	
Cayman Brac: Creek	19°45´N 79°44´W	

✦ FORMALITIES

Port Security must be called on Channel 16 on entering Cayman waters. Directions as to where to go will depend on swell conditions. Officials are very strict, and visiting boats have been fined for the smallest infringement. A mosquito control officer will spray inside the boat. Boats must clear in and out of each island and all crew must be present.

Although Little Cayman is not listed as an official port of entry, the resident customs agent may allow a short stop and will deal with formalities.

No visas are required for a stay of up to six months by nationals of most European countries, Australia, Canada, New Zealand, South Africa and the USA.

✦ MARINE PARKS REGULATIONS

The Cayman Islands have a particularly rich marine life and many indigenous species are protected, including sea turtles, iguanas and orchids. In the marine parks and environmental zones, coral, sponges and all marine life are protected, spear guns may not be used without a licence, holding tanks must be used, and all dumping is prohibited.

Yachts must use the fixed moorings wherever they are available. Boats of less than 18m (60ft) may anchor in sand, as long as no grappling hook is used and no coral is touched. Anchoring is only permitted in designated anchorage areas.

The protected areas are clearly marked and patrolling officers can arrest offenders. Penalties are severe.

✦ FACILITIES

George Town has a boatyard with a travelift and some repair facilities. The new Barcadere Marina has the best amenities and is most conveniently located. Harbour House Marina has the best repair facilities. The Cayman Islands Sailing Club on Grand Cayman welcomes visiting sailors who may use the club facilities. While Cayman Brac and Little Cayman have excellent scenery and diving, they have little in the way of facilities for yachts.

✦ CHARTER

There are some local operators, such as Sail Cayman, offering daysailing or diving trips on crewed boats.

www.sailing.ky   www.sailcayman.com

Websites	Cruising Guide
www.sailcayman.com	The Northwest Caribbean, Vol 1
www.barcadere.com	
www.harbourhousemarina.com	

Local time	UTC −5	Electricity	120V, 60Hz
Buoyage	IALA B	Currency	Cayman Islands Dollar (KYD)

Diplomatic missions	UK 244 2401

Communications	Emergency number
IDD 1 345 IAC 011	911

CUBA

Largest of the Caribbean islands, Cuba has been endowed by nature with both forested mountains and a spectacular coastline of golden beaches and tropical islets. Man has added his own touches by building some of the most beautiful towns in Latin America. World-famous for its cigars and its revolution, Cuba is another example of the wide diversity of the Caribbean nations. Half a century after the revolution, political attitudes have started to change both inside Cuba as well as north of the Florida Straits, and there is hope that the end of Cuba's pariah status is only a matter of time.

In recent years the country has opened its doors to foreign tourists, and sailors have benefited from this thaw, which has seen the number of visiting yachts increase. Cuba's coastline measures well over 2,000 miles and its offshore islands are also in their thousands, so cruising opportunities are indeed vast. The diversity of the coastal waters is just as large: from long stretches of mangrove shores and sandy beaches to high mountains that march right down to the edge of the sea. The inshore waters abound in all kinds of fish and colourful coral reefs. An added attraction are the old towns spread along its shores, some dating back to the beginning of the Spanish colonization of the New World.

Because Cuba's cruising attractions are so spread out, the obvious way to do justice to this rich variety would be a complete circumnavigation of the island. Unfortunately, as the island runs in a general SE–NW direction and the prevailing winds are easterly, this may not be so easy to accomplish. Even if a more limited itinerary is envisaged,

weather conditions should be taken into account as prevailing winds and currents make an east-to-west cruise the better option. Those arriving from the east need to decide whether to cruise along the south or north coast. The south coast is less developed and more suited for those seeking tranquillity, while the north coast has the better facilities, both in Havana itself and in some of the tourist resorts farther east.

Starting from Punta Maisi, at the island's southeast extremity, is Cuba's most spectacular coast, and the scenery is of a wild and primeval beauty. An interesting port is Baracoa, an attractive sixteenth-century town and the earliest Spanish settlement in Cuba. Past Baracoa, the sheer cliffs gradually give way to long stretches of mangrove-covered shores with shallow lagoons and swampy inlets. This largely uninhabited area offers a range of cruising options, with countless cays, cosy anchorages and prolific birdlife, with several lagoons being populated by large flamingo colonies. This coast is protected by a succession of offshore reefs that make it possible to sail in sheltered waters regardless of weather conditions outside, a highly appreciated feature during the less reliable winter weather.

Approaching Havana, the coastline turns to long stretches of sandy beaches that are lined with tourist resorts where there are several marinas. Their primary role is to service those resorts, and some are full with excursion vessels and other craft, but a space for visiting boats is usually found. Marina Hemingway, just to the west of the capital, is an ideal base from which to explore the city. The marina is perfectly protected, although its approaches can be a challenge, as the

Bay of Santiago on Cuba's south coast.

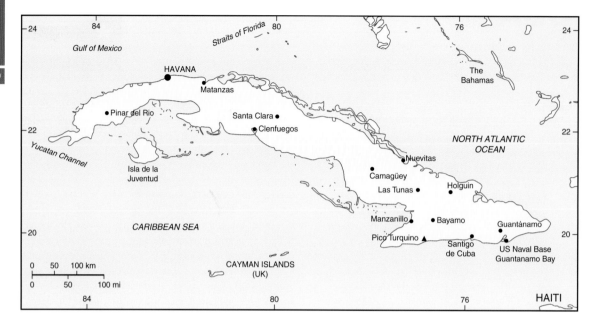

narrow opening faces north and if there is any wind from that direction, getting through the breakers can be tricky, if not outright dangerous. Havana is an attractive city, with many beautiful colonial buildings and a variety of museums, historic palaces, colourful street markets and a choice of venues with the excellent music that has made this island a household name throughout the world.

A highlight of a cruise along the south coast is a stop in Santiago, the country's oldest city and original capital, where some of the best Cuban music can be sampled. The mighty San Pedro del Morro fort marks the entrance into the Bay of Santiago, where in 1898 US troops and ships defeated the Spanish garrison, thus preparing the ground for Cuba's independence. Inside the well-protected bay, the neglected installations at Ponta Gorda hardly deserve being described as an international marina, but nearby Santiago more than makes up for this by its relaxed atmosphere and excellent music venues.

Farther along the coast, albeit a few miles inland, is Trinidad, which is best visited from Casilda where there is a small marina at Cayo Blanco. Trinidad is regarded as the most attractive town in the whole of Cuba. Founded in 1514, it has preserved some of the best Spanish colonial architecture anywhere in the Americas. The old city's cobblestone streets, pastel-coloured houses with elaborate wrought-iron grilles, as well as its imposing palaces and elegant plazas, almost give the impression of walking through a film set.

Continuing along the south coast past Cabo Cruz, Cuba's most beautiful cruising area opens into the twin bays of Golfo de Guacanayabo and Golfo de Ana Maria. This is a vast area

of about 200 miles protected from seaward by a long chain of uninhabited cays, reefs and shallows: the attractively named Jardines de la Reina (the Queen's Gardens). There are few navigable channels that cut through this labyrinth, so the choice is between exploring the area by following the inside passage or staying outside – the second alternative depending on settled weather. The inside channel north of Jardines de la Reina (Canal del Pingua) is well marked and easy to follow, but has a 3m bar at its southern end.

◆ COUNTRY PROFILE

When discovered by Columbus during his first voyage in 1492, the island was populated by Arawaks. After a long struggle for freedom from Spain and later involvement by the USA, Cuba became independent in 1901. In 1959, after three years of guerrilla warfare, the movement led by Fidel Castro replaced the corrupt government of Fulgencio Batista. Castro's programme of much needed social reform caused alarm both in the USA and among some of Cuba's neighbours. Fearing the establishment of a communist enclave on its doorstep, the USA withdrew all its support and, in the following years, actively supported several attempts to remove the Castro regime. Not surprisingly, this forced Cuba to seek help elsewhere and it ended up in the Soviet sphere of influence. The collapse of the Soviet Union, depriving Cuba of Soviet aid and an assured market for its goods, badly affected an economy already weakened by the continuing US trade embargo. Isolation led Cuba to improve relations with Western Europe, Latin America and the Caribbean. The Obama administration has made it clear that it intends to re-establish normal relations with its southern neighbour.

The capital is Havana, in which one-fifth of the 11.5 million Spanish-speaking population lives. The majority are of Spanish origin, with around 12 per cent of African descent.

◆ CLIMATE

The climate is subtropical, with November to April being the cooler dry season, and thus the most pleasant. The rest of the year is often humid, rainy and very hot. The hurricane season is from June to November. Cuba lies in the track of hurricanes and is hit by at least one such storm virtually every year. In winter and early spring, Western Cuba is occasionally affected by a wave of cold air from the interior of North America, with temperatures dropping below 10°C/50°F. In Havana the coolest month is January, with an average of 22°C/72°F, while July and August are the hottest months, with mean temperatures of 27°/81°F and highs well over 30°C/90°F.

◆ FORMALITIES

PORTS OF ENTRY

North coast:

Santa Lucía	22°41´N 83°58´W
Hemingway Marina	23°05´N 82°30´W
Acua Marina (Varadero)	23°03´N 81°12´W
Baracoa 20°21´N 74°30´W (although listed as a port of entry, some people have not been able to clear in here).	

South coast:

Punta Gorda (Santiago)	19°59´N 75°52´W
Casilda	21°45´N 79°59´W
Marina Jagua	22°08´N 80°27´W
Marina Puerto Sol, Cayo Largo	21°36´N 81°34´W
Isla de la Juventad: Colony	21°55´N 82°46´W

The requirement to contact the Border Guard on entering territorial waters is no longer enforced and yachts are expected to proceed directly to a port of entry. Channel 16 is monitored by the marinas and they will also provide assistance. In no circumstances should you attempt to arrive unannounced or anchor in a bay. Boats must clear in and out at a designated international marina.

The commercial port of Havana should not be entered as it has no provision for clearing yachts, although yachts that have been forced to enter the port in an emergency have not been turned away.

Hemingway Marina: Most visiting yachts try to enter at Hemingway Marina as the officials are used to dealing with foreign vessels. There are reefs on either side of the entrance,

which is difficult to identify until fairly close in. The GPS co-ordinates of the sea buoy are reported as 23°05.3´N, 82°30.6´W. With an onshore wind, which is the usual direction during winter months, entering the marina is not easy, and in strong winds and breaking seas it should not be attempted. The marina should be contacted if help is needed.

There is a reception dock in the entrance channel to the marina where clearance formalities are completed. Foreign boats are under 24-hour surveillance and neither the crews of other yachts, nor Cubans, are allowed to come on board.

Santiago de Cuba: Morro Santiago should be called on Channels 16 or 68. Yachts are normally instructed to proceed to the marina.

In all ports clearance must first be obtained from the Guarda Frontera, after which the yacht will be visited by immigration, customs, agriculture department, ministry of transport and health officials. A sniffer dog is sometimes used and the boat may be searched. A 30 day tourist visa is issued on arrival to all nationalities. Tourist cards are only available for one month and then renewable for one further month only. For longer stays it is advisable to arrive with a visa obtained in advance. Yachts may be left in Cuba unattended for longer periods, provided this is cleared with the authorities and all docking fees are paid in advance.

Once initial clearance has been completed, a coastwise permit must be obtained from the Guarda Frontera to proceed to the next port. Anchoring along the way is now permitted. Although the clearance allows a yacht to cruise and anchor along the coast, if any of the ports of entry are entered, one has to go through the clearance procedure again.

Strict currency rules followed the introduction of the convertible peso in November 2004 and foreign visitors are allowed to use only the 'tourist peso', but the position is likely to change as relations with the USA improve and the internal situation is relaxed as a result.

Morro Castle guards the entrance into Havana.

✦ RESTRICTIONS

It is forbidden to land at unauthorized places along the coast, and also to take any other person on board apart from those on the crew list.

Cruising boats are not allowed to fish in Cuban waters. Scuba diving can only be done through the tourist office with an official instructor. Spearfishing is prohibited and no marine life, flora, fauna or any other object may be taken from the sea.

✦ FACILITIES

Yachting is still in its infancy, and as there are very few locally owned yachts, repair facilities are limited. The situation is somewhat better in the Havana area where workshops dealing with commercial craft and fishing boats may be persuaded to work on a yacht. Hemingway Marina has a good range of services, and Yacht Services, based in the marina, is a useful source for local conditions. Boats can be hauled out by crane and it is possible to store a boat ashore. Outside Havana, mechanical repairs are available at Cienfuegos, Santiago and also, to a limited extent, in some of the marinas. Except for a few makes of diesel engines and outboard motors, spare parts are unobtainable.

Water and electricity are laid to the berths in the new marinas. Diesel fuel is generally available. General provisioning is not easy as ration books are required to buy food in most places outside of Havana. Foreigners can only buy provisions at special shops where purchases have to be made in foreign currency. These shops are located in tourist resorts and the diplomatic area of Havana. All these arrangements may well change if the internal situation alters.

✦ CHARTER

Caribbean Adventure operates from Cienfuegos and Casilda (Trinidad), both on the south coast.

www.caribbean-adventure.com

Cruising Guide
Cuba: A Cruising Guide

Website
www.cubatravel.cu

Local time	UTC −5 Summer time: second Sunday in March to last Sunday in October
Buoyage	IALA B
Currency	Cuban Convertible Peso (CUP)
Electricity	110V, 60Hz

Diplomatic missions	
UK	7 204 1771
USA	7 833 2302
Canada	7 204 2516
South Africa	7 204 9658

Communications	
IDD 53	IAC 119

Emergency number
Ambulance 26811

Hemingway Marina near Havana.

CURAÇAO

PROBABLY BEST KNOWN for the orange liqueur named after it, Curaçao is the largest of the ABC Islands. A very dry island, it has a barren landscape and an excellent natural harbour at Schottegat. Curaçao is a favourite stop for yachts en route to Panama. Most yachts who stop here arrive from Bonaire, and the contrast between the two is quite striking, particularly the capital, Willemstad, which is a true metropolis by Caribbean standards. In spite of the increasing number of modern constructions, the waterfront buildings have an Old World charm redolent of Amsterdam.

Each of the ABC Islands prides itself on having something different to its neighbours, and for Curaçao it is the spectacular Carnival, which takes over the entire island, all swaying to the beat of the tumba, a suggestive dance of African origin. During the first weeks of the year there are costume competitions, Calypso festivals, beauty pageants and street parades, climaxing in a musical street extravaganza on the weekend and Tuesday preceding Ash Wednesday.

Although it is not comfortable to linger in Willemstad after clearing in, the continual big ship movement in and out of this busy port is a sight to behold. Most yachts choose the protected anchorage at Spanish Water, while Klein Curaçao, an uninhabited island to the southeast, is a more solitary spot.

◆ COUNTRY PROFILE

The first inhabitants of the island were Arawaks, who left remains of villages and cave drawings. Although the Spanish were the first Europeans to visit, the Dutch developed the island and, despite challenges from other colonial powers, retained their rule. Since the creation of the Netherlands

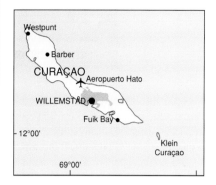

Antilles in 1954, Curaçao has enjoyed full internal autonomy and is the administrative centre of the Netherlands Antilles. There has been a move among Curaçaons to follow the example of Aruba and establish Curaçao as a separate entity in association with the Netherlands, but the decision is still pending.

The population of 225,000 is a reputed mix of 80 different nationalities, a result of the island's history as a thriving trading port. Dutch is the official language, but English, Spanish and the local Papiamento dialect are also spoken.

✦ CLIMATE

Located outside of the hurricane belt, Curaçao has a warm, sunny climate all year round with an average temperature of 27°C/81°F. Refreshing trade winds blow constantly from the east, becoming stronger in spring. The rainy season is from October to February and is marked by short showers.

✦ FORMALITIES

PORTS OF ENTRY

Willemstad	12°07′N 68°56′W
Spanish Water	12°04′N 68°51′W

Willemstad: Yachts are usually directed by the port captain to the commercial dock in St Anna Bay, near customs and immigration. Because of the heavy wash here from the constant commercial traffic, many yachts prefer to clear in at Spanish Water.
Spanish Water: The entrance is sometimes difficult to locate, even during daylight hours. On arrival, yachts can tie up to the reception dock at Seru Boca or anchor off Sarifundy's Marina but the marina itself was destroyed by fire in 2009.

Nationals of most countries do not need a visa for a period of up to 90 days. For stays exceeding 90 days, all nationals require a visa.

A cruising permit from the Harbour Authority in Willemstad is required for those who wish to anchor and to dive along the coast. All intended anchorages must be listed on the permit.

The area southeast of Willemstad, from Jan Thiel Bay to East Point, is an underwater park. Permanent moorings are provided to protect the coral from damage and anchoring is prohibited. The use of harpoons or spear guns is not allowed.

Only immigration has to be cleared on departure.

✦ FACILITIES

Most visiting boats anchor in Spanish Water Bay, which is well sheltered. There is a wide range of haulout, repair and auxiliary services available, including a 60-ton haulout facility and full service yard. The marinas Kima Kalki and Seru Boca also have good facilities.

Willemstad is more convenient than Spanish Water for provisioning and some repairs.

Cruising Guide
The ABC Islands

Websites
www.curacao.com
www.curacao-guide.info

Local time	UTC −4
Buoyage	IALA B
Currency	Netherlands Antilles Gulden (ANG)
Electricity	110V, 60Hz

Diplomatic missions

UK	461 3900
USA	461 3066
Canada	466 1115

Communications

IDD 599 9	IAC 00

Emergency numbers

112/911	Ambulance 112	Police 444444

St Elisabeth Hospital in Willemstad has a decompression chamber. Tel: 624 900.

DOMINICA

THE ISLAND OF DOMINICA, known as the Common-wealth of Dominica to distinguish it from the Dominican Republic, is one of the most mountainous of the Leeward Islands. Seen from afar, the forest-clad island presents a forbidding face with its lofty peaks brushing the rain clouds that frequently shed their load to make this the most lush island in the Caribbean. It has been said, 'if Columbus came back today, Dominica is the only island he would recognize'.

Unable to compete with the beauty of the anchorages of neighbouring islands, it is Dominica's interior that is the main attraction for visiting sailors. There are various hikes for the energetic leading into the interior. One of the most interesting trips is to Trafalgar Falls where you can bathe in a cascade of hot sulphurous water. More arduous is the hike to the Boiling Lake, which is another volcanic phenomenon. A more sedate glimpse of Dominica's varied interior can be gained by making a dinghy trip up the Indian River, which is easily reached from the sheltered anchorage in Prince Rupert Bay.

Dominica's wild interior allowed a group of the indigen-ous Carib population to escape extermination and the remaining Carib settlement on the east coast is open to visitors. The Caribs called Dominica 'Waitukubuli', meaning 'tall is her body', a fair description of this beautiful island, which is often bypassed by cruising yachts – their crews mistakenly believing that the island has little to offer.

✦ COUNTRY PROFILE

Dominica was sighted by Christopher Columbus when he reached the Caribbean on his second voyage in 1493. The island was inhabited by the indigenous Caribs, who fiercely resisted both French and English attempts to acquire their island. Eventually in 1805, Dominica became a colony of Britain, but it remained one of the least developed and stayed largely so until independence was achieved in 1978.

Of the 73,000 inhabitants, the majority are of African descent. The 3,000 Carib Amerindians still living on

Indian River.

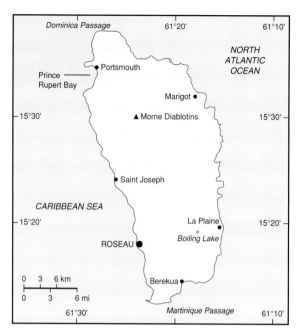

Dominica are the only pre-Columbian population surviving in the Eastern Caribbean. English and Creole French are spoken. Roseau is the capital.

✦ CLIMATE

Dominica is a rainy island, especially between June and November, which is also the hurricane season. Its lofty interior is often covered by swirling mist and its rainforest is one of the most diverse in the Caribbean. The hottest months are August and September, with a mean temperature of 28°C/82°F, and the coolest month is January (25°C/77°F).

✦ FORMALITIES

PORTS OF ENTRY

Roseau 15°17´N 61°24´W   Portsmouth 15°32´N 61°23´W

Roseau: The customs office is in the ferry terminal during office hours and also when ferries operate, or at the deepwater port north of Roseau. Yachts normally anchor or pick up a mooring just south of the ferry dock. Those who wish to anchor close to the deepwater harbour must request permission to do so from Port Control. The captain should go ashore and call at the office for clearance.

Portsmouth (Prince Rupert Bay): The captain should go ashore to obtain clearance at the dock south of the town, just north of Indian River.

Formalities have been greatly simplified and are now the easiest in the Caribbean. Yachts that do not intend to have any crew changes can check in and out at the same time for a two week period. Formalities are completed only with customs, who will hand over a copy of the yacht's crew list to immigration. Three copies of the crew list are required for clearance. No office need be visited again unless there is a crew change, and yachts are free to stop anywhere they wish, with the exception of restricted places such as marine parks. Moorings have been put down in these areas for local operators and they are not to be used by visiting yachts. No anchoring is allowed in marine reserves or on reefs.

Visas are not required for stays of up to six months for most members of the EU and the USA. They are also not required for stays of up to 21 days for nationals of Australia, Canada, New Zealand and South Africa.

A permit is required for fishing. Scuba diving is only allowed if accompanied by a licensed local operator. Spearfishing, damaging coral or taking coral or shells is forbidden.

✦ FACILITIES

In Roseau there have been moorings laid down for yachts at various locations and a fee is charged for their use. Fuel is available, but repair facilities are very basic, although there are a few diesel mechanics in Roseau. Provisioning in Roseau is reasonable, as there are supermarkets and a fresh food market.

Prince Rupert Bay is a popular anchorage among both charter and cruising yachts whose crew normally explore the nearby Indian River. This is best done in the company of a local guide, who can be contacted on Channel 16 or, more likely, will meet the yacht on arrival and offer his services. These guides also undertake various trips inland.

Cruising Guides
Cruising Guide to the Leeward Islands
Grenada to the Virgin Islands
The Leeward Islands

Website
www.visit-dominica.com

Local time	UTC −4
Buoyage	IALA B
Currency	East Caribbean Dollar (XCD)
Electricity	230V, 50Hz

Diplomatic missions	
UK	255 3116

Communications	
IDD 1 767	IAC 011

Emergency number
999

DOMINICAN REPUBLIC

ONE OF THE GREATER ANTILLES, the island of Hispaniola, of which the Dominican Republic occupies the eastern two-thirds, is a mountainous island cut by deep valleys and sometimes troubled by earthquakes. The other third of the island is Haiti, culturally very different to the Dominican Republic where Hispanic culture dominates. Described by Christopher Columbus as 'the fairest land human eyes have ever seen', the Admiral had no difficulty in choosing a name for it: 'Seeing the grandeur and beauty of this island and its resemblance to the land of Spain I named it La Isla Española.' Still being called this in Spanish, the Latin version of Hispaniola is in general use.

Until not long ago, this beauty was largely denied to cruising sailors as yachting was not encouraged by the authorities in Santo Domingo. The situation is very different now; foreign yachts are welcome, facilities are steadily improving and entry formalities have also been greatly simplified. Most yacht traffic takes place along the north coast as yachts make their way either east or west between the USA and Puerto Rico, the Virgin Islands or Lesser Antilles. Because of the prevailing northeast winds, the south coast offers more protected anchorages, although the more scenic bays are on the wild and rugged north coast. The capital Santo Domingo lies at the mouth of a heavily polluted river and although the city itself is very attractive, facilities for visiting yachts are limited. A better alternative is Boca Chica, a beach resort close to the capital, where you can use the facilities of the local yacht club.

The spectacular north coast has only a few sheltered anchorages, and as it is usually difficult to cover the distances between them in one day, cruising here needs careful planning. There is no doubt that this coast is best enjoyed if heading westwards, otherwise the continuous beating into the trades can mar the pleasure of exploring this unspoilt region. In the northwest of the country, and a pleasant first landfall, is the spectacular bay of Montecristi overlooked by the El Morro Mountain. Close by are the Cayos de los Siete Hermanos, a group of cays (the seven brothers) with several attractive anchorages. Further on, the best anchorages are to be found between Puerto Plata and Manzanillo Bay. The most attractive area is at Samana Bay, which is still largely undeveloped. Pods of humpback whales migrate here for the breeding season.

◆ COUNTRY PROFILE

Arawaks were living on the island when Columbus visited it during his first voyage. The island was settled by the Spanish until, later, the French gained control of the western

The statue of Christopher Columbus in Santo Domingo.

part. Sovereignty remained in dispute until in 1844 the Dominican Republic declared its independence.

The Spanish-speaking population is 9.6 million and is a mixture of people from Spanish and African origins. The capital, Santo Domingo, is the oldest city in the New World.

✦ CLIMATE

The Dominican Republic has a typical tropical climate with little temperature variations between summer and winter. The varied relief of the large island results in a diverse climate according to location, from warm and tropical to arid and more temperate. August is the hottest month on the coast, with a mean temperature of 29°C/84°F. December to March is the most pleasant period, with average temperatures of 25°C/77°F, this also being the dry season.

✦ FORMALITIES

PORTS OF ENTRY

North coast:

Puerto Plata	19°49´N 70°42´W
Ocean World Marina	19°50´N 70°43.8´W
Luperon (Puerto Blanco)	19°55´N 70°56´W
Samana	19°13´N 69°19´W

South coast:

Casa de Campo	18°24´N 68°55´W
Santo Domingo	18°28´N 69°53´W
Punta Cana	18°32´N 68°22´W
Las Salinas	18°16´N 71°19´W

Port control should be contacted and everyone should remain on board until officials have boarded and issued clearance. Marinas usually arrange for the officials to visit the boat to complete formalities. Formalities have been greatly simplified in 2009 with marinas now granting permits to proceed to another port. An exit paper (*despacho*) is issued by the Navy for boats leaving the country.

Visas are not required for stays of up to 30 days for nationals of most countries and a 30-day tourist card is issued on arrival for a fee.

Vessels must clear in and out of each port with both immigration and customs. Permission must also be obtained from the Port Authority to cruise outside of the port.

✦ FACILITIES

The Dominican Republic has embarked on an ambitious plan to expand its yachting facilities, with several new marinas reaching completion or being planned. There are marinas in Boca Chica, Casa de Campo, Luperon, Puerto Plata and Punta Cana. Some repair facilities are available at every

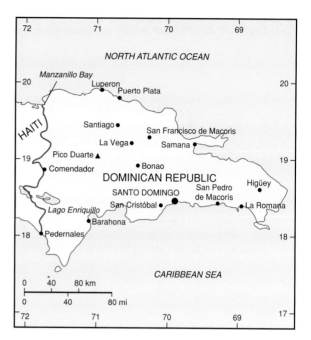

marina, but the best range is in the Santo Domingo area. Club Nautico de Santo Domingo has good repair services and administers several marinas in the immediate area. The best provisioning is in the capital.

Luperon is a popular meeting place for foreign cruising yachts on their way to or from the Eastern Caribbean and is a good base from which to visit the interior. The new marina has greatly improved the facilities, repairs and other yacht services now being available. Only basic repair services are obtainable at Samana, where there is fuel and water on the dock and a good fresh produce market.

Cruising Guides
Cruising Guide to the Dominican Republic by Frank Virgintino (free download) www.noonsite.com/PDF_Files/DRCruising Guide2009eng
The Gentleman's Guide to Passages South
Turks and Caicos and the Dominican Republic Guide

Websites
www.godominicanrepublic.com   www.clubnautico.com.do

Local time	UTC −4
Buoyage	IALA B
Currency	Dominican Peso (DOP)
Electricity	110V, 60Hz

Diplomatic missions

UK	472 7111	USA	221 2171

Communications	**Emergency number**
IDD 1 809/1 829 IAC 011	911

GRENADA

THE MOST SOUTHERLY of the Windward Islands, Grenada is a beautiful island with lush mountains and silvery beaches. Renowned for its great variety of spices such as nutmeg, cinnamon, ginger, mace and cloves, it is proud of its epithet as the Spice Island and has been taking great strides towards becoming an entirely organic island. The southern part has many deep inlets both on the eastern, windward coast, as well as on the protected western side. Several marinas are located in this area and the best facilities are also concentrated here. All installations have been restored and improved following the devastation caused by recent hurricanes. A top-range marina opened recently in the capital St George's, showing that Grenada is determined to become a leading yachting destination in the Southern Caribbean. The island is already host to a number of international sailing events, among which the most spectacular is the annual Grenada Classics Regatta, which attracts not only some of the best-known classic yachts, but also many local traditional sailing vessels.

Situated conveniently close to the Grenadines, with which it is linked by its smaller sisters, Carriacou and Petit Martinique, Grenada is the turning point for yachts cruising down the chain of the Windward Islands, some of whose skippers have fallen victim to Grenada's many temptations and made their permanent base there.

Carriacou is the largest of the Grenadines, a less developed island where customs and beliefs of African origin have been preserved, as seen in the annual Big Drum dances and Tombstone feasts. A Scottish tradition has also survived in the locally built schooners that are raced in the Carriacou Regatta each August. The regatta began in 1965 as a local boat race using traditional fishing workboats. It has become a major Caribbean event, held over the Emancipation holiday weekend, with keen competition among sailors from many of the neighbouring islands.

Petit Martinique, an island with an air of mystery due to its reputation as a smuggling centre, is less visited than the nearby Grenadines, which belong to St Vincent. In principle this means that those who wish to visit only Petit Martinique have to sail first to Carriacou to clear in and then sail back to Petit Martinique, something that many object to. As a result, some of the boats coming directly to Petit Martinique from the Grenadines usually take a chance as the authorities appear to tolerate a short stop. Boats sailing north from Grenada are allowed to clear out at Carriacou and obtain special permission to make a final stop at Petit Martinique.

◆ COUNTRY PROFILE

The Caribs who originally lived on Grenada called it Camerhogue, then the Spanish gave it first the name of Concepción, then later Granada – after the town in Spain. Carib hostility delayed the European invasion, but finally the French settled and the Caribs were exterminated. Those who survived threw themselves into the sea on the north coast at Morne des Sauteurs (Caribs' Leap). As in other parts of the Caribbean, the local population was gradually replaced by slaves transported from Africa. The country was ceded to Britain in 1763. Full independence was granted in 1974, but a military coup in 1979 brought to power the New Jewel Movement led by Maurice Bishop. The most dramatic event in the island's history occurred in October 1983 when US troops invaded it and deposed the Marxist regime. The ringleaders and their Cuban advisers were captured, while Maurice Bishop was tried and executed. Free elections were held the following year as democracy returned to the island.

The population is 91,000. English is the main language and some French patois is spoken. St George's is the capital.

◆ CLIMATE

The climate is tropical, with high average temperatures throughout the year. The hurricane season lasts from June to November, but although most hurricanes pass to the north of the island, on rare occasions Grenada has been hit by a violent hurricane, as happened in September 2004 when Hurricane Ivan destroyed much of the island's infrastructure.

◆ FORMALITIES

The authorities must be informed within two hours of arrival. A combined immigration/customs/ports authority form can be downloaded from the Board of Tourism website: www.grenadagrenadines.com/grenada_clearance_form.pdf.

St George's, the main port and capital of Grenada.

PORTS OF ENTRY

Grenada:	St George's	12°03´N 61°45´W		Prickly Bay	12°00´N 61°45´W	L'Anse aux Epines	11°59´N 61°46´W
	St David's	12°01´N 61°40´W		Grenville	12°07´N 61°37´W		
Carriacou:	Hillsborough	12°29´N 61°30´W					

St George's: Officials have been relocated to the new marina at Port Louis where formalities are completed.

Hillsborough: Yachts should anchor in the port area and report to the customs office near the jetty.

Visas are not required by nationals of the EU, Australia, Canada, New Zealand, South Africa and the USA for stays up to three months. To cruise in Grenada a cruising permit should be obtained from customs when clearing in. Marinas usually assist with formalities.

Yachts should not anchor anywhere in the Grand Anse Bay area or in the Carenage (St George's), or by the oyster beds in Harvey Vale (Carriacou), nor within 200m of any beach in Grenada, Carriacou or Petite Martinique. Taking lobsters and spearfishing is prohibited for visitors, but scuba diving is allowed. It is also prohibited to pump bilge or waste into the water, and marine toilets may not be used within 200m of beaches.

✦ FACILITIES

Grenada's facilities are generally of a good standard. In St George's, the Grenada Yacht Club operates a small marina with the usual facilities including fuel. The new marina, managed by Camper and Nicholson, will have the best range of repair facilities once it is fully operational. In Prickly Bay,

Spice Island Marine has a small dock, chandlery, fuel and a 35-ton travelift. Prickly Bay Marina has limited docking and other services. The True Blue Bay Marina has floating docks and moorings, along with other facilities. Grenada Marine in St David's has a 70-ton travelift, chandlery and full service yard and is the best on the island. Provisioning is generally good, especially in St George's, with several supermarkets and an excellent fresh produce market.

Facilities in Carriacou are far less developed, which is perhaps to be expected in a place that has been described as '…an island with over one hundred rum shops and only one gasoline station'. The situation is somewhat better at Tyrrel Bay, where the Tyrrell Bay Yacht Haul Out is a small, but well-equipped, boatyard offering a range of services including a 50 ton travelift.

✦ CHARTER

There are several operators based in the marinas on the southwest coast. Because of the difficulty in reaching the Grenadines against the prevailing northeast winds, some operators offer the option of one-way charters by starting the charter in one of the Grenadines.

www.moorings.com
www.top-yacht.com
www.definitivecaribbean.com

Cruising Guides
Cruising Guide to the Windward Islands
Grenada to the Virgin Islands
Sailor's Guide to the Windward Islands
Windward Anchorages

Websites
www.grenadagrenadines.com (Grenada Board of Tourism)
www.pagegangster.com/p/qkcDo/ (Grenada Marine Guide)

Local time	UTC −4
Buoyage	IALA B
Currency	East Caribbean Dollar (XCD)
Electricity	230V, 50Hz

Diplomatic missions	
USA	444 1173

Communications	
IDD 1 473	IAC 011

Emergency numbers	
911	Ambulance 434

GUADELOUPE

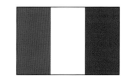

THE LARGEST OF THE LEEWARD ISLANDS, Guadeloupe is an overseas department of France and its inhabitants are French citizens. The department includes the neighbouring islands of Iles des Saintes, Marie-Galante and La Désirade. Guadeloupe is composed of two islands in the shape of a butterfly. The western island is called Basse-Terre and has impressive scenery, black beaches, gorges, waterfalls and rainforests, as well as La Soufrière, a still active volcano. One of the most spectacular sights, not just in Guadeloupe but anywhere in the Caribbean, are the Carbet Waterfalls in the south of Basse-Terre.

The eastern island is the lower Grande-Terre, more developed with white beaches and tourist resorts. The two butterfly wings are separated by the Rivière Salée, which is navigable by boats with a 1.8m (6ft) draft. Boats can get up this river even if, occasionally, they may have to plough through soft mud. The added advantage of taking this shorter route is that the sailing angle for boats continuing to Antigua is much more favourable if the winds have any north in them.

The proximity between French-speaking Guadeloupe and English-speaking Antigua invariably leads to comparisons between these two rival yachting centres. While there is not much difference in the type and quality of services offered, where Guadeloupe scores is in the blend of French sophistication and Caribbean joie de vivre that has produced a very special atmosphere. The French influence has mixed with the African heritage to form a distinctive and rich culture seen in music and cuisine – and especially in the colourful carnival.

From the cruising sailor's point of view, Guadeloupe has almost everything that a sailor wants: attractive anchorages, good marinas, excellent restaurants and an interesting interior. Les Saintes, lying some 10 miles to the south, were originally occupied by Breton fishermen, and their influence still lingers on in the charming Bourg des Saintes, the main settlement on the largest island, Terre de Haut.

South of Guadeloupe stands Marie-Galante, a quiet backwater with two reasonable anchorages where you can relax in an unspoilt environment and enjoy the tasty Creole cuisine. Guadeloupe's other sister is La Désirade, which looks like a slab of rock and has no natural harbours. The only possible refuge is a man-made inlet restricted to shallow-drafted vessels.

◆ COUNTRY PROFILE

The Caribs called the island Karukera, Island of Beautiful Waters. Arawak archaeological finds indicate they had an advanced culture, but the Caribs who followed them were fiercer and less developed. Columbus named the island Santa Maria de Guadalupe de Extremadura, but Spain showed little interest in settling it. In 1635 a French expedition of colonization had some success, despite conflict with the hostile Caribs. The island was briefly occupied by England, but the Treaty of Paris in 1763 returned Guadeloupe to France. This was one of history's strangest arrangements as, in return for Canada, Britain ceded Guadeloupe and Martinique to France.

The 453,000 inhabitants are a mixture of French, African and Amerindian descent. French is the official language, although Creole is also spoken. Basse-Terre is the administrative centre and capital, one of the oldest French colonial towns in the Caribbean, founded in 1640. In Petit Cul-de-Sac Marin, a bay to the south, lies Pointe-à-Pitre, the largest city and the economic centre of Guadeloupe.

◆ CLIMATE

The climate is tropical, and although it is under the influence of the tradewinds these are not very noticeable in the lee of this high island, which also contributes to a high rainfall. Everyday temperatures vary around an average of 27°C/81°F, with a maximum of 32°C/90°F, and only rarely descend below 20°C/68°F. Hurricanes may occur any time from June through November and, historically, the most likely time is during September.

◆ FORMALITIES

Pointe-à-Pitre: Customs and immigration are located in the harbour office.
Basse-Terre: Customs is on the main road south of the village.
Iles des Saintes: The immigration office is in the Mairie (Town Hall) at Bourg des Saintes.

The port of Deshaies on Guadeloupe's west coast.

PORTS OF ENTRY

Pointe-à-Pitre	16°13´N 61°32´W	Marina Rivière Sens	15°59´N 61°44´W	Port-Louis	16°25´N 61°32´W
Deshaies	16°18´N 61°48´W	St François	16°15´N 61°16´W		
Iles des Saintes:	Bourg des Saintes	15°52´N 61°34´W			
Marie-Galante:	Grand Bourg	15°52´N 61°19´W			

Marie-Galante: The customs office is located in the port of Grand Bourg.

A new system is being introduced with special customs computers being installed at a number of offices and outlets (chandleries, cafés, etc), where the captain enters his details, prints it out, and has it stamped by a customs officer or the owner of the establishment where the computer is. This service is available in most major anchorages around the island.

As an overseas department of France, visa requirements are similar to those of France. EU nationals do not require a visa, even for longer stays. Visas are waived for many other countries, including Australia, Canada, New Zealand and the USA for stays of up to 90 days. South Africans need a visa.

Similar rules apply as in mainland France, and a private yacht may stay in the country for 18 months before becoming liable to tax.

✦ FACILITIES

Yachting facilities in Guadeloupe are very good. There are several marinas and, as Guadeloupe has been chosen as the finish of several transatlantic races from France, repair and service facilities are of a high standard.

Pointe-à-Pitre has a protected harbour and an excellent marina complex. All services are available in the marina as well as a large selection of marine supplies in several chandleries and specialized shops. There is a 27-ton travelift in the marina and two slipways at a boatyard nearby. Provisioning is also of a very good standard.

Basse-Terre has good repair facilities, most of them concentrated around Marina Rivière Sens. There are various repair shops and a chandlery with a reasonable selection. There is a good fresh produce market in town and a large supermarket on the outskirts.

The small fishing harbour of St François has a municipal marina offering the usual services, but only a limited range of repair facilities. Only basic amenities are available in Deshaies.

The Yacht Club des Saintes has moorings, water, some facilities, and can help with repairs.

✦ CHARTER

Corail Caraïbes has a fleet of the entire range of Fountaine Pajot Lagoon catamarans. All monohulls offered by Antilles Sail are in the aluminium range of OVNI and Cigale built by Alubat. Sunsail, based in Gosier Marina in Pointe-à-Pitre, offers its usual services as well as one-way charters to its Caribbean bases.

www.corail-caraïbes.com
www.sunsail.com
www.starvoyage.com
www.antilles-sail.com
www.seaandsail.fr

Cruising Guides
Cruising Guide to the Leeward Islands
Grenada to the Virgin Islands
The Leeward Islands

Websites
www.lesilesdeguadeloupe.com/2/Home-guadeloupe.htm
   (Tourist Board site)
www.voile-en-guadeloupe.com (yachting information)
www.caribbean-direct.com (information on Guadeloupe, Iles des Saintes and Marie-Galante)

Local time	UTC −4
Buoyage	IALA B
Currency	Euro (EUR)
Electricity	230V, 50Hz

Diplomatic missions	
UK	825 757

Communications	
IDD 590	IAC 00

Emergency numbers 112   Ambulance 15   Police 17

Map of Guadeloupe showing CARIBBEAN SEA, Grande-Terre, La Désirade, Grande-Anse, Pointe-à-Pitre, Basse-Terre, Marigot, GUADELOUPE, Îles de la Petite Terre, BASSE-TERRE, Marie-Galante, Iles des Saintes, Grand-Bourg. Scale 0–20 km / 0–20 mi.

HAITI

THE ISLAND OF HISPANIOLA in the Greater Antilles is divided between Haiti and the Dominican Republic, with Haiti occupying the western third of the island. This part is very mountainous, hence the name of Haiti, which means 'high ground' in Taino, the language spoken by the original inhabitants. Current Haitian culture is a rich mixture of African and French, and Haitians are proud of being the first independent black republic in the world. The devastating earthquake that struck in January 2010 has caused untold suffering to this unfortunate country, which was already one of the poorest and least developed.

Decidedly off the cruising track, the relatively few sailors who visit Haiti find the experience either appalling or delightful. While visitors may get used to the poverty of most Haitians, it is the exasperating bureaucracy that turns most cruisers off. At least there are some compensations: one is the stunning scenery, the other the tasty cuisine, as despite nearly two centuries of separation, the French heritage still makes itself felt.

As in the case of Haiti's neighbour, the Dominican Republic, cruising is best done from east to west, because particularly during the winter the strong tradewinds make eastbound passages difficult. If sailing south from the Bahamas, the most convenient and interesting landfall is at Cap Haïtien, as it allows a glimpse into this fascinating country's turbulent past. Above the town of Milot stands the Citadelle, a huge fortress built by self-proclaimed king Henri Christophe, one of the most ruthless dictators who have ruled this unfortunate country. A contrasting glimpse into Haiti's present can be gained by visiting the daily market in Cap Haïtien, a colourful experience not to be missed.

The southern cruising route leads towards the capital, Port-au-Prince, past several attractive harbours, none of which offer all-weather protection. Port-au-Prince lies at the head of the Golfe de les Gonâve and is a city of contrasts – like the country itself. Beyond Cape Tiburon at Haiti's south-west extremity, there are several attractive anchorages, with the most scenic surroundings being in the Baie des Cayes.

◆ COUNTRY PROFILE

During his first voyage to the New World, Columbus had the bad luck to lose his largest ship, the *Santa Maria*, on the north coast of Hispaniola. With the timbers rescued from the wreck, the Spaniards laid the foundations of La Navidad, showing a weird sense of humour as their ship had been wrecked on Christmas Day. This is how the birth of the first European settlement in the New World came about. Unfortunately, it was soon destroyed by the indigenous inhabitants who fell out with their uninvited Spanish guests. Later the Tainos themselves were wiped out by disease, war and slavery. As elsewhere in the New World, the European settlers – in this case French – replaced the indigenous Tainos

Blue Bay.

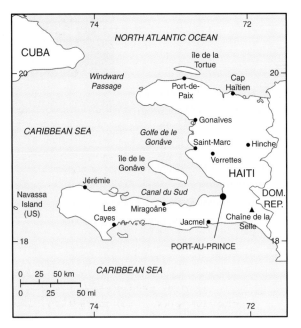

Port-au-Prince: Ibo Island Marina (Channels 16 or 70) is a convenient place to complete formalities as a bus runs to the capital, where formalities are completed in the main harbour.
Port Morgan: Clearance formalities can be carried out at Port Morgan Marina (Channels 16 or 9) on Ile à Vache, on Haiti's south coast, even though it is not officially a port of entry. Similarly, boats may proceed to Les Cayes and complete formalities there.

Visas are issued on arrival to nationals of most countries, usually for 90 days. Clearance from the last port must be shown. A cruising permit must be obtained from the port captain and allows access to all ports in Haiti. There is no limit on the time a yacht may remain in the country if contact is maintained with the authorities.

✦ FACILITIES

Facilities in Haiti are generally poor and the 2010 earthquake has made matters worse, although the coastal areas have suffered less than inland. The small marina Port Morgan on Ile à Vache offers berthing alongside a quay and also on buoys. Electricity, fuel, LPG, water and some repair facilities are available. Ibo Marina on Ibo (Carenage) Island, 9 miles north of Port-au-Prince, has a 25-ton slipway.

Spare parts are almost impossible to find locally. In most places fuel is obtained by jerrycan. Water is available everywhere, but should be treated. There is good provisioning with fresh fruit, vegetables and fish, but imported goods are scarce.

with slaves transported from Africa to work on their plantations. The new slaves did not put up with their status for long and, after several uprisings, in 1804 the rebels declared independence under the new name of Haiti. Revolutions and dictatorships have dogged the country's history, but in 2006 Haiti inaugurated a democratically elected president and parliament. The situation seems to have stabilized, but the country can only survive with massive assistance from the outside world.

Haiti is probably the poorest country in the Western hemisphere. The population is 9 million, with many of mixed French and African descent. The languages spoken are French and Creole. The capital is Port-au-Prince.

✦ CLIMATE

Haiti has a tropical climate and the weather is generally hot and humid, with sultry, warm nights. It is more pleasant and drier from December to March, when the coastal areas are cooled by sea breezes. The rainy season lasts from October to May, while the hurricane season is from June to November. The island is often hit by violent hurricanes, as happened in 2008 when several storms caused enormous hardship to this poor country's population.

✦ FORMALITIES

PORT OF ENTRY

Port-au-Prince	18°33′N 72°21′W
Cap Haïtien	19°46′N 72°12′W
Les Cayes	18°11′N 73°44′W

Cruising Guide
The Gentleman's Guide to Passages South

Websites
www.haititourisme.org
www.port-morgan.com/US/marinao.html (Port Morgan Marina)

Local time	UTC −5
Buoyage	IALA B
Currency	Haitian Gourde (HTG)
Electricity	110V, 60Hz

Diplomatic missions
UK	257 3969
USA	229 8000

Communications
IDD 509	IAC 00

Emergency numbers
112
Ambulance 118
Police 114

JAMAICA

PART OF THE GREATER ANTILLES, Jamaica is one of the largest islands in the Caribbean. Lying south of Cuba, this mountainous and scenic island is known worldwide as the birthplace of reggae music. It is stunningly beautiful, and with hundreds of miles of coastline and an abundance of natural harbours, it has all the ingredients for a perfect cruising destination. Unfortunately, reports on the high level of crime, muggings and theft have kept most sailors away. The often unfriendly stance of officials has not helped matters either, even if such attitudes can perhaps be justified by the relentless fight against the drug traffic into which cruising yachts have become unwillingly entangled. Recently the situation has seen a remarkable change for the better as the authorities are making a determined effort to improve their island's image. It is indeed regrettable that Jamaica has earned itself such a bad reputation, much of which was probably quite undeserved. In spite of all the difficulties, Jamaica continues to attract a number of visiting yachts, predominantly racing yachts taking part in the annual Pineapple Cup Race from Fort Lauderdale to Montego Bay.

From the cruising point of view, Jamaica's long coastline has many attractive spots, but most visiting sailors prefer daysailing and spending the nights in marinas or ports. The south of Jamaica is the most unspoilt part of the island, and less touched by the tourist boom so obvious elsewhere. The north coast is more exposed and only has sheltered anchorages at its western end, at Montego and Negril. Otherwise there are a number of small ports, among which colourful Ocho Rios may be of interest to Caribbean music lovers because the most famous Jamaican, Bob Marley, was born and grew up in the nearby village of Nine Mile.

One of Jamaica's hidden gems is the Morant Cays, a small group of uninhabited coral islets off Jamaica's southeast point; in fact, they are not much more than a couple of sandbanks in the middle of the ocean. As they are an important nesting ground for large numbers of seabirds, they have been designated a nature reserve, but visits by cruising yachts seem to be tolerated.

✦ COUNTRY PROFILE

The name 'Jamaica' comes from the Arawak word *Xaymaka*, meaning land of wood and water. Arawaks were the original inhabitants, but did not survive long after the first Spanish settlement in the fifteenth century. In 1525 Santiago de la Vega, now Spanish Town, was founded and was for a long time Jamaica's capital. The seventeenth century saw England stake its claim and capture the island from Spain. Jamaica declared independence in 1962.

The population is 2.8 million, of which the majority are of African descent, but there are also minorities of East Indian, Chinese, Lebanese and European origin. English is spoken and also a local patois. Kingston is the capital.

✦ CLIMATE

Jamaica has a tropical climate with high temperatures and humidity, and little seasonal variation. The wettest months are May and October. The hurricane season is between June and November. The daily high temperatures are tempered by the trade wind – known locally as the 'doctor breeze' – while the offshore breeze that occurs at night is known by the less appealing words 'undertaker breeze'. Cold northerly winds occasionally occur in winter, causing drastic drops in temperature.

Ocho Rios.

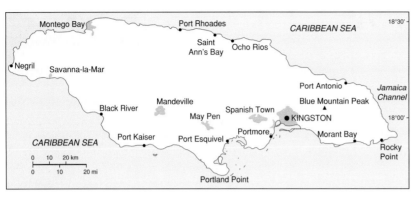

FORMALITIES

PORTS OF ENTRY

Kingston	17°58´N 76°48´W	Montego Bay	18°28´N 77°56´W
Ocho Rios	18°25´N 77°07´W	Port Antonio	18°11´N 76°27´W

Yachts clearing in from foreign ports may not be allowed to dock until given permission by customs.

Montego Bay: Yachts normally proceed to Montego Bay Yacht Club and the club office will advise on the correct procedure. Officials may come to the club, or the captain will be asked to go to the airport to complete formalities there.
Kingston: Yachts can contact Morgan's Harbour or the Royal Jamaica Yacht Club and request permission to come alongside. Both these clubs are located in the Port Royal area. Arrangements can then be made to clear in at either club.
Ocho Rios: If there is no space at the crowded dock, you have to anchor in this open harbour. The various offices are all in the port area.
Port Antonio: You can come alongside the dock at the Port Antonio Yacht Club and formalities are completed here.

No visas are required for nationals of most countries, although the length of time given may vary from one to six months depending on the nationality.

Yachts must advise the authorities if they intend to sail to another port. The captain should provide customs with a detailed itinerary and they will then issue a cruising permit. The authorities must be notified every time you move and boats must clear in and out at every port. A yacht can only go to places mentioned on the permit. Vessels are monitored and those checking in late or making unauthorized stops are fined. Foreign-registered boats that have already cleared into Jamaica must notify customs within 24 hours of arrival in another port.

Theft is a problem and no yacht should be left unattended unless docked in a marina.

FACILITIES

The best ones are at the Port Antonio Marina and at Montego Bay Yacht Club. Both have a good range of repair services as well as haulout facilities. As the host of the annual Pineapple Cup Race, the Montego Bay Yacht Club is used to dealing with visiting yachts. Both marinas in the Kingston area have good amenities, being used mainly by locally owned boats. The Royal Jamaica Yacht Club maintains a marina about 12 miles from Kingston, and visitors belonging to reputable clubs are welcome. Morgan's Harbour Club at Port Royal has similar docking facilities, as well as fuel and water. Duraes Boat Sales and Marina Supplies in Kingston is a good source for spares.

Repair services outside the marinas can only be described as adequate, and workshops willing to undertake an urgent job can only be found with local help.

Provisioning with local produce is generally good, but the range of imported goods is limited, except in tourist resorts.

CHARTER

There are no bareboat charters available, but a number of local operators offer skippered yachts based in Montego Bay, Ocho Rios and the Kingston area. They can be contacted via the local yacht clubs.

Cruising Guides
The Northwest Caribbean Vol 1
Yachtsman's Guide to Jamaica

Websites
www.visitjamaica.com
www.montegobayyachtclub.com
www.rjyc.org.jm (Royal Jamaica Yacht Club)

Local time	UTC −5
Buoyage	IALA B
Currency	Jamaican Dollar (JMD)
Electricity	110V, 50Hz

Diplomatic missions

UK	510 0700	Canada	926 1500
USA	702 6000	South Africa	978 3160

Communications
IDD 1 876   IAC 011

Emergency numbers
112   Ambulance 110   Police 119

MARTINIQUE

MARTINIQUE IS THE MAIN ISLAND of the French Antilles and its association with France was forged during a long and often tumultuous history. The island is volcanic in origin and Mount Pelée, in the northwest, is still active. The year 1902 saw the last major eruption, which completely destroyed the old capital, St Pierre, and brought Martinique to the attention of the world.

The Atlantic side of this mountainous and lush island is rugged and rough, while the west coast is more sheltered, with beaches and pleasant anchorages. Various yachting facilities are concentrated around the capital Fort-de-France, which is the largest city in the Windward Islands and has a distinctly European flavour. The main port is a busy place, so cruising boats normally head for the southern shore of the wide bay where Anse Mitan, Trou Etienne and Trois Ilets provide both anchoring and docking facilities.

The south coast is rather disappointing as it has no good anchorages, but this is made up for by the almost landlocked bay of Sainte-Anne. The pleasant small town that gave the bay its name is a popular watering spot with sailors whose boats are docked or anchored at the head of the bay in the descriptively called Cul-de-Sac du Marin. The latter is Martinique's leading yachting centre, with excellent facilities, and is also the base of a large charter fleet. Some of the best workshops in the Eastern Caribbean operate here. The east coast is mostly fronted by a fringing reef, which gives some protection from the mighty Atlantic rollers, but also makes for some tricky navigation. This part of Martinique is only visited by intrepid sailors.

Even more inaccessible is Diamond Rock, a rocky pinnacle that caused serious embarrassment to the French during the Napoleonic Wars when it was occupied briefly by a posse of British sailors, who planted a flag on its summit and declared it to be a Royal Navy ship HMS *Fort Diamond*.

◆ COUNTRY PROFILE

The origin of the name 'Martinique' is disputed, coming either from the Carib word *madinina*, island of flowers, or Saint Martin, as named by Columbus after he spotted the island in 1493. The first Europeans to settle there were the French and conflict with the fierce indigenous Caribs was resolved with a treaty in 1660, but the Caribs quickly died out. All through the seventeenth and eighteenth centuries the French and English fought over their colonial possessions, until the 1763 Treaty of Paris established French control of

Martinique and Guadeloupe in return for France relinquishing Canada. Martinique became a French department in 1946 and the inhabitants are French citizens.

The 405,000 Martiniquais are a mixture of French, African and Asian origins, speaking French, as well as Creole – a patois that combines French and African languages. The capital is Fort-de-France.

◆ CLIMATE

The island has a warm and humid tropical climate, with temperatures constant throughout the year, with an average minimum of between 21°C/70°F and 23°C/73°F, and an average maximum between 28°C/82°F and 31°C/88°F. There are two distinct seasons, the dry and more pleasant season between December and May, and the rainy, humid and hot season, between June and November, which coincides with the hurricane season.

◆ FORMALITIES

PORTS OF ENTRY	
Fort-de-France	14°38′N 61°04′W
Le Marin	14°28′N 60°53′W
St Pierre	14°44′N 61°11′W

Yachts must complete customs and immigration formalities at one of the official ports of entry. A new system is being introduced, with special customs computers being installed at a number of offices and outlets (chandleries, cafés, etc), where the captain enters his own details, prints it out, and has it stamped by a customs officer or the owner of the establishment where the computer is.

Anse Mitan with Fort-de-France in the background.

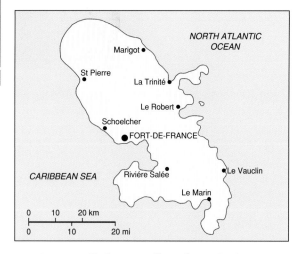

NORTH ATLANTIC OCEAN

CARIBBEAN SEA

Marigot
St Pierre
La Trinité
Le Robert
Schoelcher
FORT-DE-FRANCE
Rivière Salée
Le Vauclin
Le Marin

0   10   20 km
0   10   20 mi

Fort-de-France: Yachts normally anchor at La Savanne, an anchorage marked by buoys east of the town. Customs and immigration are at the ferry terminal, but it is now possible to also complete formalities at Sea Services, a large chandlery located on the seafront, which has the new self-service customs computers.

Anse Mitan: Formalities have been simplified and it is now possible to complete these at the fuel dock in Marian du Bakoua.

Le Marin: The joint clearance office is in the marina. Both immigration and customs formalities are done at the same time. Unless intending to use the marina, arriving boats usually anchor and take their dinghy to one of the marina pontoons.

St Pierre: Customs is close to the tourist office. Outside of working hours the completed forms may be left in the mail box.

For boats arriving from across the Atlantic, Le Marin is a more convenient port to clear in as formalities are streamlined and facilities are very good. On departure it is essential to clear out at one of the official ports so as to obtain the clearance certificate needed for other islands.

As Martinique is a department of France, EU nationals do not need visas. Visas are waived for stays of up to 90 days for many other countries, including Australia, Canada, New Zealand and the USA.

✦ FACILITIES

Although the anchorage in front of Fort-de-France, at La Savanne, gets very crowded at times, the discomfort is made up for by the fact that virtually everything is available ashore. There are good repair facilities, several well-stocked chandleries, and all major engine manufacturers are represented

locally. There are boatyards with slipways or travelifts. Also, there are several large supermarkets as well as a good fresh produce market. Those who need to have any repairs done should head for Baie des Tourelles, a narrow bay northeast of Fort-de-France where many of the workshops are located.

Anse Mitan is the main tourist centre of Martinique and a popular spot with yachts. Marina Pointe de Bout is close by and the complex surrounding this marina offers various repair facilities, chandleries and supermarkets. Marina de Cohe is a small marina north of Fort-de-France, with its own dry dock and repair facility.

Le Marin is now one of the largest yachting centres in the Caribbean, with facilities to match. There are several workshops in the marina for sail, mechanical and electronics repair, as well as a full service boatyard with a 60 ton travelift. There are two chandleries with a good selection of marine equipment.

✦ CHARTER

Le Marin is the main charter base, with several operators located there. Corail Caraibes has a fleet of Lagoon catamarans, while Antilles Sail has the aluminium OVNI and Cigale yachts. Star Voyage offers both bareboat and crewed charters in both monohulls and catamarans, as well as flotilla sailing from their base in Le Marin – as does Sunsail.

www.corail-caraïbes.com
www.sunsail.com
www.seaandsail.fr
www.antilles-sail.com
www.kiriacoulis.com
www.starvoyage.com

Cruising Guides
Cruising Guide to the Windward Islands
Grenada to the Virgin Islands
Sailors Guide to the Windward Islands

Websites
www.martinique.org
www.caribbean-direct.com/Martinique-Direct/Home Page/Martinique-Direct.html

Local time	UTC −4
Buoyage	IALA B
Currency	Euro (EUR)
Electricity	220V, 50Hz

Diplomatic missions	
UK	618 892

Communications	
IDD 596	IAC 00

Emergency numbers		
112	Ambulance 15	Police 17

MONTSERRAT

THE ISLAND OF MONTSERRAT CAME TO WORLDWIDE ATTENTION in 1995 when the dramatic eruption of the Soufrière Hills volcano caused the evacuation of the population and buried the capital Plymouth in ash and rock. The entire southern two-thirds of the island was declared an exclusion zone because of ongoing volcanic activity, but the volcano now shows signs of becoming dormant again. There is no natural harbour on Montserrat, but there are a few sheltered bays on the northwest coast, with Old Road Bay, Bunkum Bay, Little Bay and Rendezvous Bay being the major ones. Little Bay is the main port and is set in attractive countryside. The northern part of the island is lush and green – in total contrast to the moonlike aspect of the south.

Although the volcano is no longer perceived to pose a serious threat, up-to-date information on the current situation should be obtained before visiting.

✦ COUNTRY PROFILE

A few Caribs lived on the island when Columbus sighted it on his second voyage in 1493, naming it after the well-known abbey in Spain. In the first half of the seventeenth century, Montserrat was settled by Irish colonists and the island became a refuge for Catholics fleeing persecution not only in Ireland, but also in Virginia. France fought to gain control from time to time, but the island was finally ceded to Britain. In 1967 Montserrat became self-governing and today is a UK overseas territory.

Much of population fled after the Soufrière Hills volcano eruptions, which began in 1995 and recurred in 1997 with devastating effect. The volcanic activity has endured, the last eruption being in 2003. The islanders began to return to their homeland in 1998. The English-speaking population still numbers only 5,000. Half of the island is expected to remain uninhabitable for at least another decade.

✦ CLIMATE

The climate is subtropical, with the high temperatures being tempered by the trade winds. There is little climatic variation throughout the year. June to November is the hurricane season. Montserrat lies on the track of violent hurricanes, which are most likely to develop between August and October.

✦ FORMALITIES

PORT OF ENTRY
Little Bay 16°48′ N 62°12.5′ W

Yachts normally anchor in the southern part of the bay and the captain should go to customs and immigration in the Port Authority complex during office hours (0800–1515 weekdays). Overtime charges apply at all other times. A customs declaration form can be downloaded from the yachting section of the Montserrat Tourist Information website. Permission must be obtained to anchor in other bays, the granting of which may depend on volcanic conditions. No visas are required for most nationals.

✦ FACILITIES

There are few local facilities and no boatyard. There is neither fuel nor water at Little Bay, but there is one fuel station and two supermarkets located some 2km inland. As the island is connected by daily flights to Antigua and Sint Maarten, spare parts could be flown in.

Montserrat Volcano Observatory Tel: 491 5647.

✦ CHARTER

The Antiguan-based company Ondeck offers sailing trips to Montserrat on a Farr 65 racing yacht.

www.ondeckoceanracing.com

Cruising Guides
Cruising Guide to the Leeward Islands   The Leeward Islands

Websites
www.visitmontserrat.com
www.mvo.ms (Montserrat Volcano Observatory)

| **Local time** | UTC −4 | **Currency** | East Caribbean Dollar (XCD) |
| **Buoyage** | IALA B | **Electricity** | 230V, 60Hz |

Diplomatic mission
UK   491 2688

| **Communications** | **Emergency numbers** | | |
| IDD 1 664 IAC 011 | 112 Ambulance 911 Police 999 | | |

PUERTO RICO

San Felipe del Morro Castle guards the approaches to San Juan.

THE MOST EASTERLY ISLAND of the Greater Antilles, the US Commonwealth of Puerto Rico, also comprises the small islands of Mona to the west, and Vieques and Culebra to the east. From the high mountain range in the interior, the land plunges down past coastal plains into the Puerto Rico Trench north of the island to a depth of 9,200m (30,190ft). Puerto Rico has a number of harbours on each coast, those on the south coast being generally better protected. On the northern coast, only San Juan offers total protection from the prevailing northeast winds. A busy and noisy port, the capital has good facilities and Old San Juan is an attractive well-preserved city from Puerto Rico's colonial past.

Frequented mainly by US cruising boats on their way to or from the Virgin Islands and Lesser Antilles, Puerto Rico has failed to become part of the cruising circuit, whose playground remains the islands to the east. Among the few who venture past the Virgins, even fewer are tempted to go beyond Vieques and Culebra to visit the main island. The reason for this reluctance is that once committed to sailing to Puerto Rico, you have to either carry on west or fight your way back east, a prospect not relished by most cruisers.

Vieques and Culebra are similar to the Virgin Islands, and are popular spots with local sailors. Culebra was badly hit by Hurricane Hugo, when scores of boats were destroyed in the anchorage, which was previously considered to be a safe hurricane refuge.

◆ COUNTRY PROFILE

Christopher Columbus landed on the island in 1493, accompanied by Juan Ponce de León, who returned 15 years later and established the first settlement. The island lay in a prime location between Spain and her American empire, and attacks by other maritime powers were frequent. At the end of the Spanish–American war in 1898, Spain ceded Puerto Rico to the USA. In 1952 Puerto Rico's status was declared that of a state in free association with the USA. Spanish is the first language of the 4 million population, although English is widely spoken. The capital is San Juan.

◆ CLIMATE

The island has a tropical marine climate, with little seasonal variation and an average annual temperature of 26°C (80°F). The northern coastal areas have more rainfall, while the climate is more arid in the south. The hurricane season is from June to November.

◆ FORMALITIES

PORTS OF ENTRY	
Culebra 18°18´N 65°17´W	Ponce 17°58´N 66°39´W
San Juan 18°28´N 66°07´W	Mayaguez 18°12´N 67°07´W
Guanica 17°58´N 66°55´W	
Playa de Fajardo 18°20´N 65°38´W	

Yachts arriving from outside the territory should contact customs by telephone. For the correct phone number, contact the US Department of Homeland Security on +1 787 253 4538. Culebra, San Juan and Mayaguez are the most convenient ports for clearance. It has been reported that Bahia Boqueron can be used instead of Mayaguez.

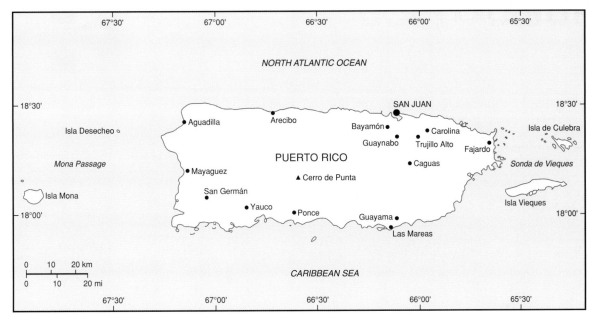

US yachts coming from the US Virgin Islands must clear customs on arrival. The US department of customs has implemented a Local Boater Option programme to expedite the arrival-reporting process for yachts that visit frequently, details of which are available from the US Department of Homeland Security. This is available for US citizens only.

Entry for non-US citizens is as for the USA and, similarly to the mainland, the visa-waiver programme is not applicable to any foreign national arriving by yacht. All nationalities (except Canadians) need to acquire a visa in advance. A multiple-entry visa should be requested if also planning to visit the US Virgin Islands or any other US territory.

A 12-month cruising permit can be obtained free in the US Virgin Islands, or you can obtain one for a fee on arrival in Puerto Rico.

Military activity occurs in some areas, so you should request details on arrival and monitor Channel 16.

Only San Juan has garbage removal facilities, otherwise garbage must be disposed of only outside of Puerto Rico. US marine regulations apply, and marine police occasionally fine yachts for not having a holding tank with the valve in the correct position.

✦ FACILITIES

With a large fleet of local craft, facilities are of a good standard and there are several marinas dotted around Puerto Rico's coastline, the best being in and around San Juan. Facilities are also of a good standard in Ponce, Mayaguez, Culebra and Fajardo. Shipyards, chandleries, haulout facilities and marine supplies are all available, and parts can be flown in easily from the mainland. Provisioning is good in all ports.

✦ CHARTER

Caribe Yacht Charters has bases in Puerto del Rey, on the main island, and Villa Sol in Culebra, operating a fleet of both power and sailing boats, monohulls and catamarans.

www.sailcaribe.com

Cruising Guides
Cruising Guide to Puerto Rico
Gentleman's Guide to Passages South

Websites
www.welcome.topuertorico.org
www.marinamate.com/m-cb-pr.html (Puerto Rico marinas)

Local time	UTC −4
Buoyage	IALA B
Currency	United States Dollar (USD)
Electricity	120V, 60Hz

| **Diplomatic missions** | |
| UK | 850 2400 |

| **Communications** | |
| IDD 1 787 | IAC 011 |

| **Emergency numbers** | |
| 911/112 | |

SABA

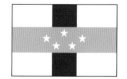

No other Caribbean island better fits the saying that 'small is beautiful' than Saba. An extinct volcano only 2 miles in diameter, the island rises sheer out of the sea to a lofty peak of 940m (3,084ft). Saba's small size does not offer much protection from the prevailing swell, but the slight discomfort at anchor is made up for by the delights experienced ashore, not to speak of the underwater scenery which is among the best in the Caribbean. There are well-protected anchorages at Well's Bay and Ladder Bay on the west coast.

Until not so long ago the interior was completely inaccessible and the sole way to reach the island's only villages, Bottom, Windwardside and Hell's Gate, was to land at Ladder Bay and negotiate the 800 steps cut into the rock. Although the building of a road was deemed an impossible task, the Sabans proved the experts wrong by building one. The road was finished in 1958 and runs almost all the way around the island. With the same determination, a small airport was built on the only flat area possessed by this rugged island. The villages perched on the side of the mountain are neat and picturesque, and visitors are treated to a view of a tranquil life that has disappeared elsewhere.

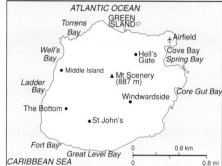

✦ COUNTRY PROFILE

Settling Saba was difficult and it was left to the hardy and adventurous. Like many other Caribbean islands, it was at various times under English, French, Spanish and Dutch rule. Peace finally came when the Dutch took possession in 1816. The population is 1,500 and reflects the mixture of nationalities that have settled here over the years. Dutch is the official language, but everyone speaks English.

✦ CLIMATE

The climate is hot, but tempered by cooling tradewinds. The annual mean temperature is 27°C (80°F), varying by only a few degrees throughout the year. The hurricane season lasts from June to November.

✦ FORMALITIES

PORT OF ENTRY
Fort Bay 17°37′ N 63°15′ W

The harbourmaster should be contacted on Channels 16 or 11. In settled weather one may pick up a mooring off Fort Bay while clearing in ashore. A more protected anchorage is in the area between Ladder Bay and Well's Bay, where several moorings have been laid for visiting yachts. One can then go to Fort Bay by dinghy for clearance during office hours. One can check in and out at the same time, even if staying a few days.

Visa requirements are the same as for the rest of the Netherlands Antilles, and visas are not required for most nationals for a stay of 90 days. Saba is a free port and there are no customs restrictions.

All waters around the island have been declared a national marine park and anchoring is restricted to sandy areas. Spear-fishing and the taking of coral or shells is prohibited. Marine park officials patrol the anchorages and welcome yachts.

✦ FACILITIES

A fee is charged for the maintenance of the marine park. Several mooring buoys are available for visiting boats, and there are also some smaller buoys for the dinghy when diving in protected areas.

Sea Saba is a diving shop based at Fort Bay. It has a small chandlery, a mechanical shop for emergency repairs, and it will order spares from Sint Maarten. Fuel can be taken in jerrycans from the fuel station at Fort Bay. Some provisioning can be done in Windwardside, which has the better shops.

Cruising Guides
Cruising Guide to the Leeward Islands
The Leeward Islands

Website
www.sabatourism.com

Local time	UTC −4	**Buoyage**	IALA B
Currency	Netherlands Antillean Gulden (ANG)		
Electricity	110V, 60Hz		

Communications		**Emergency numbers**	
IDD 599 4 IAC 00		112 Ambulance 912	

ST BARTHÉLEMY

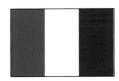

St Barthélemy, commonly known as St Barth in French and St Barts in English, is an attractive island with white sandy beaches and volcanic hills. In recent years the island has become a trendy destination, with chic boutiques and celebrity visitors. The social scene culminates at New Year when scores of superyachts congregate in the picturesque harbour of Gustavia. Winter is also the time of art exhibitions and a well-attended classical music festival. Cruising sailors are primarily attracted to Gustavia to provision their boats with duty-free goods. The island is surrounded by several bays and small islets, but it is in Gustavia where all the action is.

✦ COUNTRY PROFILE

Christopher Columbus named the island San Bartolomé after his brother's patron saint. The French were the first to settle, but it was ceded to Sweden in 1874 and bought back by France 100 years later. St Barts retained a free-port status along with various Swedish reminders such as Swedish street and town names, and the three crown symbol on the coat of arms. In 2003, the islanders voted to secede from Guadeloupe, with whom they were part of a French department, and in 2007 St Barts became a French overseas collectivity. The islanders are French citizens.

Of the 8,500 inhabitants, most are of French descent and some Swedish, with a small percentage of people of African origin. Gustavia is the capital.

✦ CLIMATE

The island has a pleasant tropical climate as the daily hot temperatures are cooled by the prevailing trade winds. The average temperature varies little throughout the year, with an annual mean of 27°C/81°F, although record highs of 35°C/95°F have been recorded. September to November are the wettest months, and June to November is the hurricane season.

✦ FORMALITIES

PORT OF ENTRY
Gustavia 17°55′ N 62°50′ W

On arrival, the port captain should be called on Channel 12, but if requesting a space on the dock, the port should be contacted one hour before arrival. The port captain's office should be visited during office hours. For stays of less than 24 hours, the clearing in and out procedure can be done at the same time. Visas are not required for those from the EU and for most other nationalities for stays of up to 90 days. Third party insurance is occasionally requested to be shown. Both

the spaces on the dock and the moorings are administered by the port captain, who will allocate a space or mooring.

Anchoring is not permitted in Baie St Jean. The speed limit is 3 knots and no water sports, fishing or diving are allowed inside Gustavia harbour. Barbecues are prohibited on boats at the quay.

✦ FACILITIES

Boats either come stern-to at the two quays, pick up a mooring in the inner harbour, or stay at anchor in the outer harbour. Water, showers, toilets and garbage disposal are available ashore. Fuel and LPG gas are available from St Barth Marine (Channel 16). St Barth Boatyard offers a limited range of repair services, and also has a hardstand. Provisioning in town is adequate, though expensive compared to other French ports.

✦ CHARTER

Because of the relatively short distance from St Martin where several operators are based, there are no bareboat charters available in St Barts. For those who aim for something more exclusive, some of the crewed yachts based in Gustavia can be privately chartered.

Cruising Guides	
Cruising Guide to the Leeward Islands	
Grenada to the Virgin Islands	The Leeward Islands

Websites
www.st-barths.com
www.caribbean-direct.com/St-Barth-Direct/Home Page/
St-Barth-Direct.html (general information)

Local time	UTC −4	Currency	Euro (EUR)
Buoyage	IALA B	Electricity	220V, 60Hz

Communications		Emergency numbers	
IDD 590 IAC 00		112 Police 18	

ST EUSTATIUS

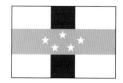

St Eustatius, affectionately known as Statia, lies north of St Kitts in the Leeward Islands chain. It is hard to believe that this small island used to be the trading capital of the West Indies, and at the peak of its commercial success in the late eighteenth century it was not unusual to have over one hundred sailing ships anchored in the roads.

Lacking safe anchorages, the island's interior of pretty villages and interesting trails fully justifies a visit. The only anchorage is off the main village of Oranjestad, in Oranje Baai, which is an open roadstead where the swell usually makes itself felt, although the bay is protected from the prevailing winds. The island holds a special attraction for scuba divers due to an impressive underwater world rich in flora and fauna, as well as several shipwrecks that lie near the coast. A national park protects the fragile underwater environment.

◆ COUNTRY PROFILE

The first inhabitants of Statia were the Saladoids, who it is believed arrived in great seagoing canoes from South America before the end of the fifteenth century. Christopher Columbus called in 1493, and during the subsequent colonial era the island changed hands at least twenty-two times. During the American War of Independence, Dutch Statia made best use of its neutrality and traded with both sides. During the first half of the eighteenth century Statia was a thriving trading centre, with thousands of ships calling at this busy port for transshipment of goods from all over the world. Statia became known as the Golden Rock, but this golden age came to an end when the UK went to war with the Netherlands, partly because of Statia trading with the rebel Americans. Statia is part of the Netherlands Antilles and continues to be a free port to this day.

The population numbers around 3,200 and is made up of some twenty different nationalities. Dutch and English are spoken, as well as the local Papiamento dialect. The capital is Oranjestad.

◆ CLIMATE

The island has a tropical climate, but with a higher rainfall than its eastern neighbours. The temperatures are also milder than in other Caribbean locations, varying by no more than 2 or 3 degrees throughout the year, with January temperatures ranging from 23°C/73°F to 27°C/81°F, and July temperatures from 25°C/77°F to 30°C/86°F.

◆ FORMALITIES

PORT OF ENTRY
Oranjestad   17°29′N 62°59′W

On arrival the captain should proceed ashore for clearance with immigration and the harbour master.

Statia is a free port, like Saba and Sint Maarten. Visas are not required for most nationals for stays up to 90 days.

Diving is only allowed if accompanied by someone from the local dive centre.

◆ FACILITIES

Facilities are quite basic. Moorings are laid for visiting yachts both in the harbour and the marine park. Golden Rock Dive Centre (Channel 11) has its own moorings and can also help with engine repairs. Fuel is available by jerrycan. There are two supermarkets in Oranjestad, with a good selection of both imported and local produce.

Cruising Guides
Cruising Guide to the Leeward Islands, The Leeward Islands

Website www.statiatourism.com

Local time	UTC −4
Buoyage	IALA B
Currency	Netherlands Antillean Gulden (ANG)
Electricity	110V, 60Hz

Communications	**Emergency numbers**
IDD 599 3 IAC 00	112/911

ST KITTS AND NEVIS

Nevis seen from St Kitts.

AFTER INDEPENDENCE from the UK in 1983, the two islands of St Christopher and Nevis joined into a federation. St Kitts, as it is commonly known, is a green, mountainous island with a low-lying peninsula to the southeast, while Nevis is smaller and circular, rising to a volcanic peak with a dramatic crater at the top. Their relative isolation – and, until recently, the absence of docking facilities – have combined to make these islands some of the least frequented in the Lesser Antilles. As the first English settlement in the Caribbean, St Kitts is of historical interest. There are old relics, ruined forts, grand plantation houses, and in Basseterre, the capital since 1727, the best-preserved colonial town in the British West Indies. A railway that ran around the entire island to transport sugar cane now carries a luxury train that takes visitors on a scenic sightseeing tour, and is the only surviving railway in the Eastern Caribbean.

The main town of Nevis, Charlestown, also retains a picturesque colonial air. For the energetic there are some challenging hikes up to the peak of the Nevis volcano at 985m (3,232ft). The summit is often covered in mist and this may explain why Columbus called the island 'Nuestra Señora de las Nieves' as it is hard to believe that he saw it covered in snow.

Both islands have a few anchorages, but the opening of two marinas will undoubtedly attract more cruising yachts and finally place St Kitts and Nevis firmly on the Lesser Antilles cruising circuit.

◆ COUNTRY PROFILE

Some archaeological remains have been found of the original inhabitants, who suffered a similar fate to those on other islands, perishing at the hands of Europeans. They called the island Liamuiga, 'fertile island'. Columbus visited the island on his second voyage and renamed it after St Christopher, the patron saint of travellers. Nevis was originally called Oualie by the native Amerindians, meaning land of beautiful water, and the name Nieves given to the island by Columbus became corrupted over the years to Nevis.

St Kitts was the first British settlement in the West Indies, although there were some French settlers and for a while the island was divided between the two colonial powers. From their base in St Kitts both the English and French colonized other Caribbean islands and the relationship was often stormy. St Kitts and Nevis are the smallest sovereign nation in the Americas in both area and population.

There are around 45,000 inhabitants, mostly of African descent, whose first language is English, although some French patois is also spoken.

◆ CLIMATE

The islands have a tropical climate with high average temperatures, but these are tempered by tradewinds through-out most of the year. The driest period is from January to April and there is increased rainfall in summer and towards the end of the year. The islands lie on the track of violent

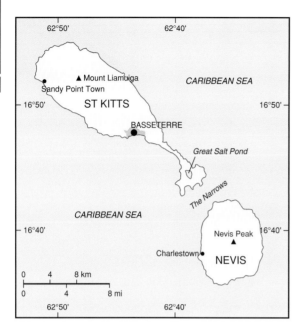

tropical hurricanes, which are most likely to develop between August and October. The hurricane season is from June to November.

✦ FORMALITIES

PORTS OF ENTRY	
Basseterre (St Kitts)	17°18′ N 62°43′ W
Charlestown (Nevis)	17°08′ N 62°38′ W

Basseterre: Customs should be contacted for information on clearance options. Zante is the official port of entry for cruise ships only. There is no customs office at Zante Marina, but yachts may dock there and then visit the relevant offices. Port Zante Marina can only be entered after having been given permission by Basseterre Port Control. Clearance formalities are completed at the customs and immigration offices on the cruise-ship dock, but once Port Zante is fully operational it will have its own clearance facility.

If you cleared in first at Basseterre, you had to clear in again at Charlestown and vice versa. This can now be avoided as formalities have been simplified so you can request coastwise clearance on arrival. This permit is valid for one week and allows the yacht to stop at any of the places listed on the permit. It must be presented to the Nevis customs on arrival. It is also possible to request permission to stop at some of the south coast anchorages when clearing out of St Kitts for another country.

Charlestown: Yachts should anchor off the pier and go first to customs, which is opposite on Main Street, and then to immigration at the police station. Formalities have been greatly simplified and for those who wish to visit both islands, coastwise clearance should be requested on arrival, as described above. The clearance paper must be presented to Basseterre customs on arrival.

Visas are not required for citizens of most European countries, Australia, New Zealand, Canada, South Africa and the USA.

There is a customs charge, but this does not have to be paid again if visiting both islands.

✦ FACILITIES

An ambitious redevelopment project in Basseterre will radically alter the situation once it is completed as it includes Port Zante, a full-service marina. Indigo Yachts is a boatbuilding firm near the deepwater harbour in Basseterre that will undertake glassfibre work and general repair, and it also has a well-stocked chandlery. There are other workshops in Basseterre offering a good range of services. There is also good provisioning, and there are several supermarkets. A fuel dock is planned, but in the meantime the marina can arrange for the delivery of larger quantities by tanker.

The Nevis Port Authority has installed 100 yacht mooring buoys, and now requires yachts to moor rather than anchor. The moorings are laid out at Pinney's Beach, Nelson's Springs, Cades Bay, Tamarind Bay and Oualie Bay.

Facilities are basic on Nevis, but there are plans to build two marinas. There is less selection in provisions than in St Kitts, but there is a good supply of fresh produce.

✦ CHARTER

There are no bareboat operators, but Nevis Yacht Charters based in Oualie Beach has a crewed yacht available.

www.sailnevis.com

Cruising Guides
Cruising Guide to the Leeward Islands
Grenada to the Virgin Islands
The Leeward Islands

Websites
www.stkittstourism.kn
www.nevisisland.com
www.portzante.com

Local time	UTC −4
Buoyage	IALA B
Currency	East Caribbean Dollar (XCD)
Electricity	230V, 60Hz

Communications		**Emergency number**
IDD 1 869	IAC 011	911

ST LUCIA

THIS VOLCANIC ISLAND boasts some of the most beautiful scenery in the region, which has earned it the name 'Helen of the Caribbean'. The spectacular mountainous interior is covered in dense rainforests that march up the steep slopes all the way to Mount Grand Magasin, which can be reached by a nature trail. The unmistakable sugarloaf cones of the Grand and Petit Pitons rise out of the sea at Soufrière Bay and there are few Caribbean anchorages to match the beauty of this spot. Not far away lies Marigot Bay, a landlocked bay that reputedly hid from sight an entire British squadron during the Napoleonic wars and now shelters a fleet of charter yachts.

The main yachting centre is at Rodney Bay close to the northern end of the island, where a full-service marina has been built in a dredged lagoon; since 1990, this has been the finishing point of the annual ARC (Atlantic Rally for Cruisers). Rodney Bay Marina is the creation of Arch Marez, a Californian who arrived here on his yacht in the early 1980s and, realizing the untapped potential of this spot, decided to build a marina. In the intervening years Rodney Bay Marina has turned into one of the most popular Caribbean landfalls for transatlantic sailors, and the once mosquito-ridden lagoon is now surrounded by boutiques, restaurants and elegant residences.

Rodney Bay, though, is known not just for its yachting facilities, as many sailors make a point of stopping by for the aptly called jump-up that takes place in nearby Gros Islet, where every Friday night the people of this small village throw open their houses. The narrow streets are packed with revellers; beer, rum and fried chicken are sold from stalls while the air throbs with the deep bass of reggae. The wild and unrestrained atmosphere strikes anyone who has just completed an Atlantic crossing that this is the kind of welcoming landfall that cannot be experienced anywhere else in the world.

In line with other Caribbean nations, several marine reservations have been established in recent years, where anchoring is prohibited. In full view of the Pitons, the

Soufriere Bay overlooked by the Petit Piton.

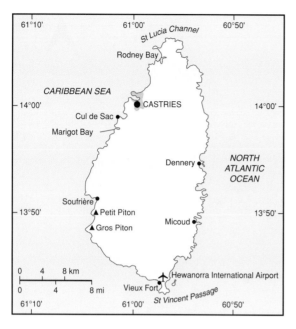

protected anchorage at Soufrière has several mooring buoys which have been laid for the use of visiting boats.

COUNTRY PROFILE

The first European sighting remains a matter of controversy and it is disputed that Columbus ever came to the island in 1502 on 13 December, which is celebrated as St Lucia's Day, the national holiday. Populated by hostile Caribs, the Europeans had little interest in settling, the island changing hands between the French and the English some fourteen times before becoming a British colony in 1814, which it remained until independence in 1979. The majority of the original settlers, however, were of French origin and the French influence remained strong, still to be seen in the French place names and the patois spoken.

The population is 160,000. The majority are of African origin, descendants of the slaves brought to work on the sugar plantations. English is the official language, but many speak a French patois. The capital is Castries.

CLIMATE

St Lucia enjoys a hot, tropical climate throughout the year, cooled by constant tradewinds with only minor temperature differences. The best weather is between January and March, which are the driest months. The coolest month is January, with an average temperature of 24°C/75°F, while the hottest, as well as wettest, are July and August, with a mean temperature of 27°C/81°F and with highs well over 30°C/90°F. The hurricane season is from June to November.

FORMALITIES

PORTS OF ENTRY	
Rodney Bay	14°04´N 60°58´W
Castries	14°00´N 60°59´W
Marigot Bay	13°58´N 61°58´W
Soufrière	13°50´N 61°04´W
Vieux Fort	13°44´N 60°57´W

Rodney Bay: Yachts should tie up at the customs dock in the marina, which is marked by yellow posts, although as this is often occupied, boats usually dock wherever they can find a space. The captain is required to report immediately to the customs and immigration office inside the marina. There is no docking charge if coming in only to clear. The channel leading into Rodney Bay Marina has a maximum reported depth of 4m (13ft), but there are plans to increase this depth.

Castries: Yachts clearing in must come straight to customs dock or, if there is no space, must anchor in the quarantine anchorage to the east of the customs dock. Customs and immigration officials are available during office hours.

Marigot Bay: The customs office is in Marina Village.

Vieux Fort: The customs office is at the head of the large dock. The immigration office is at Hewannora Airport.

On arrival, the captain should go ashore to report to customs and immigration. The crew must remain on board until clearance has been completed. Customs clearance from the last port is required. Visas are not required for nationals of most European countries, Canada, New Zealand, South Africa and the USA. Other nationals, including Australians, will be granted a visa on arrival. Normally a six-week stay is granted by the immigration officer when clearing in and a stay of up to six months can be requested on arrival.

St Lucia is piloting a scheme called eSeaClear™, which allows captains to pre-clear their yacht, crew and passengers' details online. This avoids having to complete multiple copies of lengthy documents on arrival. The scheme is also being introduced by other Caribbean countries.

A cruising permit is not obligatory, but permission is needed to move to any place other than the port of entry, so a cruising permit for sailing the coast or for visiting other places in St Lucia is best requested when clearing in. If a boat is leaving with the same crew as on arrival, it may do so without clearing out provided its stop is less than 72 hours, but this must be made clear when clearing in. After clearing out, yachts have 72 hours to depart St Lucia, or 24 hours for local or charter boats. Duty-free fuel may be purchased after clearing out. This is best done at Rodney Bay Marina where one can go directly to the fuel dock after clearing customs.

Marigot Bay

✦ FACILITIES

St Lucia is constantly improving its yachting facilities and several charter companies have their base there, which means that most repair work can be undertaken locally. Rodney Bay Marina has been rebuilt by its new owners who wish to attract more superyachts. Also, being the annual host of the ARC transatlantic rally, repair facilities at Rodney Bay Marina are of a good standard, with a well-stocked chandlery, electronics workshop, sail repair and dive shop. The boatyard has a 50-ton travelift and extensive dry storage facilities. There are two banks in the marina, as well as a small supermarket. Two large supermarkets are close by. More facilities are available at Vigie near the capital, Castries, where St Lucia Yacht Services operates a small marina and has a range of repair facilities, travelift and slipway.

The Moorings charter company maintains a base of operations in Marigot Bay. The company's employees will undertake outside work if they are not needed to work on the firm's own yachts. Fuel and water are obtainable at the dock of the Moorings and provisions can be bought at their supply store.

A few services are available at Soufrière, and fuel is available at the fishing port dock. There are only basic services available in Vieux Fort, although some engine repair work can be undertaken at the Goodwill Fishermen's Cooperative. Some supplies, as well as fresh fruit and vegetables, are available.

✦ CHARTER

The Moorings fleet of both monohull and multihull sailing yachts is based in picturesque Marigot Bay. From its base in Rodney Bay Marina, Kiriacoulis offers a choice of sailing yachts, while Free Spirit Charters has a range of small power-boats, ideal to explore the tranquil waters in the lee of St Lucia.

www.moorings.com
www.kiriacoulis.com
www.freespirit-charters.com

Cruising Guides
Cruising Guide to the Windward Islands
Grenada to the Virgin Islands
Sailor's Guide to the Windward Islands
Windward Anchorages

Websites
www.stlucia.org
www.eseaclear.com (online clearance form)

Local time	UTC −4
Buoyage	IALA B
Currency	East Caribbean Dollar (XCD)
Electricity	240V, 50Hz

Diplomatic missions
UK   452 2484

Communications	**Emergency numbers**
IDD 1 758 IAC 011	999/911

SINT MAARTEN AND ST MARTIN

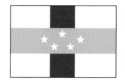

DUTCH SINT MAARTEN and French St Martin occupy the two halves of the same island. Sint Maarten forms part of the Netherlands Antilles, while St Martin is an overseas territory of France. There is an apocryphal story according to which the division came about as a result of an amicable solution to a territorial claim between a Frenchman and a Dutchman, who agreed to settle their dispute by walking in opposite directions, one armed with a bottle of wine, the other with a flask of gin, and where they met became the boundary. Apparently the French ended up with a larger slice because the gin took a more potent toll on the Dutch walker. The island is split down the middle, with the more hilly and forested French side being slightly larger to the north, and the low sandy south being Dutch.

In recent years the island has become one of the leading yachting centres in the Caribbean, with excellent docking and a wide range of repair facilities centred on Simpson Bay Lagoon in the centre of the island. Its main drawback is that it lies in an area prone to be hit by hurricanes, as has happened on several occasions in recent years.

Philipsburg and Simpson Bay are two sheltered anchorages on the southwest coast of the island. Simpson Bay is connected to the landlocked lagoon, which is shared by both sides and is reached by a channel and lifting bridge. Those who do not wish to use one of the marinas may anchor in Simpson Bay or inside the lagoon, although the recent construction of a large cruiseship dock has restricted the available space.

Sint Maarten's biggest annual event, and now one of the major regattas in the Caribbean, is the Heineken Regatta held every year during the first weekend of March. This is preceded in January by the Classic Regatta, which attracts both classic yachts, among them some famous names, and also traditional craft, previously humble workboats used by local fishermen.

French St Martin is different from its Dutch neighbour not only in culture and language, but also in terrain, as the north is more hilly than the flatter south. Marigot Bay is the main port and anchorage, a chic seaside resort that seems to have been transplanted from the Mediterranean. The anchorage is connected to Simpson Bay Lagoon via a narrow canal with an opening bridge. There are other, more tranquil anchorages on the north coast.

Both tourism and yachting have developed at a great rate in recent years. There are casinos and scores of duty-free shops, restaurants that cater for all tastes and, above all,

Marigot Bay and marina.

excellent repair facilities and technical services for yachts – and the best-stocked chandleries in the Caribbean.

✦ COUNTRY PROFILE

The Caribs were the original inhabitants of this island, which Christopher Columbus probably sighted on St Martin's Day in 1493, and claimed for Spain, who showed little interest. The French settled in the north, while the salt ponds attracted Dutch settlers to the southern coast. A treaty in 1648 divided the island between France and the Netherlands on the basis that residents of either side could be commercially active on the other side without any restrictions. This contract of peaceful coexistence is one of the oldest active, undisputed treaties on the planet. In 2003, the population of St Martin voted to secede from Guadeloupe and in 2007 St Martin became a French overseas collectivity.

The population of Sint Maarten is now over 41,000. Dutch is the official language, although most people speak English. The population of St Martin is around 29,000. Marigot is the capital of the French side, and Philipsburg is that of the Dutch side.

✦ CLIMATE

The island has a mild tropical climate, with monthly temperatures varying little throughout the year. The annual average temperature is 27°C/81°F. July to November is the rainy season, while December to June is dry, although conditions vary little between seasons. June to November is the hurricane season.

✦ FORMALITIES

PORTS OF ENTRY	
Sint Maarten:	
Philipsburg	18°02´N 63°03´W
Simpson Bay	18°02´N 63°06´W
St Martin:	
Marigot Bay	18°04´N 63°06´W
Anse Marcel	18°07´N 63°03´W
Oyster Pond	18°03´N 63°01´W

Sint Maarten: All vessels arriving in or departing from Sint Maarten must call at the immigration and port authority station on the northwest side of the entrance channel into the lagoon. It is also required to clear with the Simpson Bay Lagoon Authority and pay an anchorage fee regardless of whether you stay outside or go into the lagoon. Formalities on the Dutch side are generally more complicated and costly.

Nationals of most countries do not need a visa for stays up to 90 days.

Cruising fees are charged on a sliding scale depending on

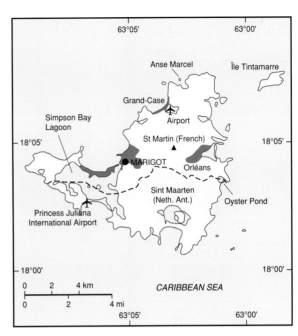

length. The bridge fees or departure fees are payable whether one uses the Simpson Bay bridge or not, and are on a similar sliding scale. A form for the waiver of liability, which must be signed before a vessel can pass through the Simpson Bay Bridge, can be obtained from the clearance office.

Outward clearance papers are necessary if sailing to another island, even another Dutch one, though not if sailing across to French St Martin.

St Martin: The immigration office is near the ferry dock. A new system is being introduced, with special computers being installed at a number of offices and outlets (chandleries, cafés, etc), where the captain enters his details, prints it out, and has it stamped by a customs officer or the owner of the establishment where the computer is.

Visas are not required by nationals of the EU. Nationals of Australia, New Zealand, Canada and the USA do not need a visa for stays of up to 90 days. South Africans require a visa.

As the airport is in the Dutch Sint Maarten, captains of crew arriving in St Martin to join a yacht should contact immigration in advance to avoid difficulties as normally a return ticket needs to be shown by all arriving passengers.

✦ FACILITIES

The entire island is duty-free and spares are not taxed on importation.

The Simpson Bay Bridge (Channel 12) opens at least three times a day. The waiver form is not necessary when leaving the lagoon, nor is it required on the French side of the bridge. The Sandy Ground Bridge, on the French side, also

Simpson Bay and marina.

opens three times a day and there is no charge. There are anchoring fees in Marigot Bay, but not if the yacht is only waiting for Sandy Ground Bridge to open.

In Sint Maarten facilities are concentrated in Philipsburg's Great Bay, Cole Bay and Simpson Bay. Simpson Bay Marina can accommodate vessels up to 55m (180ft) with a maximum draft of 4.5m (15ft) and prides itself on providing the highest-quality services and amenities. The marina is at the core of a yachting hub with a wide range of services and marine suppliers. Overall, repair facilities are somewhat better on the Dutch side of the island. Provisioning is good in Philipsburg. Near the marinas is a large selection of shops, several of which have dinghy docks.

St Martin is well supplied with marinas and boatyards and a wide variety of services are available, including haulout, repair and engineering workshops, sailmakers and riggers, metalwork, hull and GRP repair, electronics and chandleries.

In Marigot there is a good supermarket, and the large market on the waterfront has the best selection of local fresh produce. Port Lonvilliers Marina is an excellent hurricane hole, being completely enclosed and offering protection from every direction.

◆ CHARTER

Several charter companies are based on the island, with most bareboat operators being on the French side of the island. Among the most important are Sunsail in Oyster Pond, Horizon and Dream Yacht Charters in Cole Bay, Moorings and Sea and Sail in Marigot, and VPM in Anse Marcel.

www.antilles-sail.com
www.horizonyachtcharters.com
www.dreamyachtna.com
www.moorings.com

www.sunsail.com
www.seaandsail.fr
www.vpm.fr

Cruising Guides
Cruising Guide to the Leeward Islands
Grenada to the Virgin Islands
The Leeward Islands

Websites
www.stmaarten.com (Sint Maarten Tourism Office)
www.st-martin.org (St Martin Tourism Office)
www.caribbean-direct.com/St-Martin-Direct/Home Page/ St-Martin-Direct.html (general information)

Local time	UTC −4
Buoyage	IALA B
Currency	Netherlands Antillean Gulden (ANG) Euro (EUR)
Electricity	220V, 50Hz

Communications
IDD 590   IAC 00

Emergency numbers
Sint Maarten 112/911   St Martin 112

ST VINCENT AND THE GRENADINES

Tobago Cays.

THE ISLAND OF ST VINCENT and its satellites the Grenadines have always been a popular yachting destination. The long-established cruising Mecca of the Caribbean, the thirty or so islands that make up the Grenadines have not lost their appeal in spite of the steady increase of sailing pilgrims flocking there. The anchorages might be better in the Virgins, the scenery more stunning in the Leewards, but the affection of discriminate cruisers for the Grenadines remains unswayed. Why this is so is difficult to say, but the fact that the Grenadines have changed so little compared to the rest of the Caribbean is probably the main reason.

St Vincent was the first country in the Caribbean to recognize the great value, but also critical fragility, of the islands' environment and to impose strict rules for its conservation. These were initiated under the guidance of the Prime Minister James Mitchell, who grew up in Bequia, an island with a long seafaring tradition, so he was familiar with the needs of sailors. St Vincent was also the first place in the Caribbean to ban water scooters and jet skis, which have destroyed the tranquillity of many resorts around the world.

Arbitrarily divided by the British Colonial Office, the Northern Grenadines are administered by St Vincent, while the smaller southern group belongs to Grenada. Compared to its southern neighbours, St Vincent is an island of stunning scenery, both in its mountainous interior and the picturesque coastline that abounds in pretty anchorages – Blue Lagoon being foremost among them.

A warm welcome awaits sailors in neighbouring Bequia, whose Port Elizabeth in Admiralty Bay is one of the most famous watering holes on the international cruising scene. Bequia is a true island of sailors and boats. The seafaring tradition is very much alive among today's Bequians, most of whom are descendants of early Scottish settlers and whaling crews.

The other Grenadines all have their special character, from the unspoilt Tobago Cays and Mayreau to tranquil Canouan and Union, and not least exclusive Mustique, retreat of royalty and rock stars. Mustique is also the venue of a highly successful jazz festival.

◆ COUNTRY PROFILE

Caribs inhabited Hairoun, as they called the main island of St Vincent, when Columbus called here on his third voyage, and their hostility initially prevented European settlement. In 1675 a Dutch ship carrying settlers and slaves was wrecked on the island and only the slaves survived. They mixed with the Caribs, and some of their descendants are still alive today.

England and France disputed possession of the island and both occupied it at different times – St Vincent and the islands to the south eventually being incorporated into the British colony of the Windward Islands. The volcano of Soufrière erupted in 1902, two days after Mount Pelée on Martinique, killing 2,000 people. It still remains active, with the last eruption occurring in 1979. Full independence was gained the same year.

The population numbers 105,000. English is the main language, but some people also speak a Creole dialect.

◆ CLIMATE

The islands have a pleasant tropical climate all year round. The warmest month is September, with an average temperature of 27°C/81°F, while January is the coolest, with an average of 25°C/77°F. December to May is the most pleasant period, with settled weather and constant winds. The hurricane season lasts from June to November.

◆ FORMALITIES

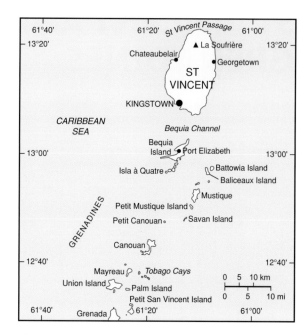

PORTS OF ENTRY

St Vincent:

Kingstown	13°09′N 61°14′W
Wallilabou Bay	13°15′N 61°17′W
Young Island Cut	13°08′N 61°12′W
Bequia: Port Elizabeth	13°00′N 61°16′W
Mustique: Grand Bay	12°53′N 61°11′W
Union Island: Clifton	12°35′N 61°25′W
Canouan: Charlestown	12°42′N 61°20′W

Yachts arriving in St Vincent territorial waters must proceed to a port of entry to clear in before stopping at any other port or anchorage. The captain only should go ashore.

Wallilabou Bay: Wallilabou Bay is the first port of entry on the western side of St Vincent, particularly for yachts arriving from St Lucia and Martinique. It is also the last port north for departing yachts.
Kingstown: Yachts should anchor near the new Kingstown cruise ship terminal. First the captain should clear in with customs and then immigration, which is in town, and finally the port authority. This can take some time. Because of the difficulty mooring in Kingstown, as well as the lengthy formalities, it is better to use the services of a local agent (Channel 68) or proceed directly to Bequia to complete formalities there.
Bequia: As Bequia is more used to yachts, clearing in at Port Elizabeth can be done more quickly. In Port Elizabeth, customs and immigration are in the same building.

Clearance must be done with the port authorities, customs and immigration. Visas are granted on arrival to all nationalities, the length of time given on arrival being from one to six months depending on the nationality. A cruising permit will be granted on clearing in, if the officials are satisfied that the voyage is for cruising only. A yacht may stay up to one year subject to immigration requirements, provided customs is satisfied that it is a genuine visiting yacht.

Yachts must clear out at one of the official ports. For southbound boats, formalities are simplest at Clifton on Union Island where customs can be cleared in the port, but for immigration you have to walk to the airport, which is very close.

The use of spear guns is not allowed. Trolling and handlining fish for your own consumption is allowed, with the exception of the Tobago Cays. The removal of coral, or even causing damage to it, is forbidden.

◆ FACILITIES

The Ottley Hall Marina and Shipyard near Kingstown provides a complete range of repair and service facilities, from a 500-ton shiplift and 40-ton travelift to covered drydocks. There are also good repair amenities at Young Island and Blue Lagoon, which has been a charter base for many years. There is a small boatyard undertaking glassfibre repair and metalwork, as well as various workshops specializing in electrical work, rigging and engine repair, both outboard and diesel. Water and fuel are available at the dock in Blue Lagoon. There is also a supermarket geared specifically towards charter clients, while other supermarkets can be found in Kingstown and near the airport.

Blue Lagoon on St Vincent's south coast.

The anchorage at Chateaubelair is not recommended as there have been several violent attacks on visiting yachts.

The range of repair facilities on neighbouring Bequia is more limited. There is a small boatyard and two chandleries, with a good selection of spares, charts and accessories. Water and fuel are available from the dock next to the slipway. The range of provisions is less varied than in Kingstown. The traditional meeting point for sailors is the Frangipani bar.

The new Gloss Bay Marina on the southwest side of Canouan will have a good range of services when it becomes fully operational. On the other Grenadines, facilities are very basic. Only essentials can be obtained in Mayreau, rather less on Petit San Vincent, and nothing at all in the Tobago Cays.

◆ CHARTER

There are various operators located in the area to serve the Southern Caribbean's main attraction: the Grenadines and the famous Tobago Cays. Both Moorings and Sunsail have local bases, Sunsail at Lagoon Marina on the south coast of St Vincent, while the Moorings is closer to the action in Charlestown Bay on the west coast of Canouan. Both Barefoot Yachts and TMM Yacht Charters operate out of Blue Lagoon on St Vincent.

www.moorings.com
www.barefootyachts.com
www.sunsail.com
www.sailtmm.com

Cruising Guides
Cruising Guide to the Windward Islands
Grenada to the Virgin Islands
Sailor's Guide to the Windward Islands
Windward Anchorages

Website
www.svgtourism.com

Local time	UTC −4
Buoyage	IALA B
Currency	East Caribbean Dollar (XCD)
Electricity	230V, 50Hz

Diplomatic mission
UK   456 5981

Communications
IDD 1 784   IAC 011

Emergency numbers
999/911   Coast Guard 457 4578/457 4554

TRINIDAD AND TOBAGO

The Trinidad and Tobago Yachting Association base at the Carenage.

THE TWIN COUNTRY of Trinidad and Tobago lies just off the Venezuelan coast and is the most southerly of the Caribbean islands, regarded by some as the most exotic of them all. Cosmopolitan Trinidad, home of calypso and steel drum, is famous for its carnival called De Mas (short for masquerade). Tobago is more sedate, and was used by Daniel Defoe as the setting for *Robinson Crusoe*, although Alexander Selkirk, on whom the story is based, was in fact marooned on Juan Fernandez Island in the South Pacific.

Until not so long ago, Trinidad and Tobago used to be far less visited by cruising boats than the islands farther north. Trinidad and Tobago were considered out of the way and did not offer many cruising opportunities. The situation changed dramatically after a series of devastating hurricanes in the mid-1990s when most insurance companies started stipulating that boats must spend the hurricane season south of latitude 12°40′ N, which is just north of Grenada, so it only includes that island as well as Trinidad and Tobago, and Venezuela.

Suddenly these places became popular destinations during the summer months, when islands farther north are threatened by tropical storms. Aware of Trinidad's newfound popularity, the authorities simplified formalities, while local businesses made great efforts to improve yachting facilities, which now are among the best in the Eastern Caribbean.

While lacking the natural bays and anchorages of its northern neighbours, Trinidad's beauty lies mostly inland. One interesting visit is to the Caroni Swamp bird sanctuary to see some of Trinidad's 400 species, making it one of the richest birding countries per square mile anywhere in the world. The original inhabitants reflected this by calling their island Iere, or land of the hummingbird.

Most yachts sail to Trinidad to be there in time for carnival, when both marinas and anchorages get very crowded. Even so, this is certainly the best time to visit, as the carnival is the most spectacular to be seen outside of Brazil or, as the locals insist, even better. What makes this carnival stand out is the music, both the locally born calypso and the inimitable steel pans, a possible by-product of the local oil industry, as the instruments are made from discarded oil drums.

After the hustle and bustle of Trinidad, Tobago is an entirely different experience because the island is largely undeveloped and unspoilt. There are several nice anchorages as well as colourful reefs to explore. As in other Caribbean islands, the interior is still covered in rainforest and Tobago is criss-crossed by many trails that lead to bird sanctuaries and waterfalls. The one drawback is the difficult passage from Trinidad as it is encumbered by shoals and a strong west-setting current. It is therefore advisable to attempt to call at Tobago first before continuing to Trinidad.

◆ COUNTRY PROFILE

The Arawaks and Caribs were the first inhabitants of the islands. Columbus spotted Trinidad on his third voyage, although no one is quite sure whether he named it after the Holy Trinity or the three distinctive peaks on the southeast of the island. Tobago's name is a corruption of tobacco, which was grown here by the Caribs.

Spain used Trinidad as a base to explore South America, and the late eighteenth century saw an influx of French settlers, but Spain ceded the islands to Britain in 1802. After the abolition of slavery, the British brought in Indian and Chinese indentured labourers to fill the labour shortage. Immigrants also came from neighbouring islands, North America, Madeira and Europe.

Tobago was first settled in 1641 when the Duke of Courland obtained a royal grant to settle on the island, until it was ceded to England in the eighteenth century. In 1888 Trinidad and Tobago were united into one Crown Colony and in 1962 the islands became independent, with the country being declared a republic in 1976.

The population of Trinidad is 1.3 million, the majority being of African or Asian origin. Chinese, Portuguese, Syrian, Jewish and Latin American minorities make up Trinidad's very cosmopolitan population. Tobago has 45,000 inhabitants. English is the main language, although Spanish, French patois and Hindi dialects are also spoken. Port of Spain is the capital of Trinidad, and Scarborough is Tobago's main town.

◆ CLIMATE

The islands have an equatorial climate within the tradewind belt. Temperatures are a little higher in Trinidad than in the islands farther north. Tobago's temperatures are cooler, being more exposed to the northeast tradewinds. There is a dry season between January and May and a wet season from June to December. Although the islands are considered to lie outside the hurricane belt – and indeed most hurricanes pass to the north – in recent years Trinidad has been affected by Hurricanes Ivan in 2004 and Gustav in 2008.

◆ FORMALITIES

PORTS OF ENTRY	
Trinidad:	
Port of Spain	10°39´N 61°31´W
Chaguaramas	10°43´N 61°40´W
San Fernando	10°17´N 61°28´W
Brighton	10°15´N 61°38´W
Pointe-à-Pierre Yacht Club	10°19´N 61°28´W
Point Gourde	10°40´N 61°38´W
Point Tembladora	10°41´N 61°36´W
Point Fortin	10°11´N 61°41´W
Tobago:	
Scarborough	11°11´N 60°44´W

Yachts entering Trinidad territorial waters should call the Coast Guard to advise of the boat's arrival and to give an ETA. The captain must proceed to clear immigration regardless of the time of day. For all nationalities, an initial visa for three months will be issued on arrival, which may be extended for another three months for a fee.

Although there are several official ports of entry, arriving yachts should clear at either Chaguaramas in Trinidad or Scarborough in Tobago. Port of Spain is geared primarily towards commercial ships, and pleasure craft should only stop there in real emergencies, otherwise they will be sent to Chaguaramas.

Chaguaramas: There is an office dedicated to clearance formalities. If the dock is not occupied, yachts may come alongside the customs dock, otherwise they should anchor nearby. A clearance certificate from the last port will be required.

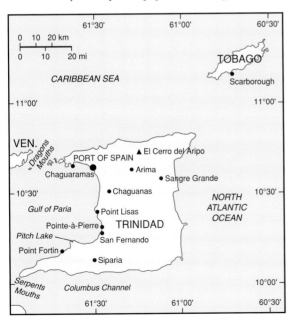

Trinidad carnival.

Scarborough: Yachts should come to the government dock to complete formalities. These have now been simplified and yachts are free to visit all the usual places without the need to inform customs of every move.

Yachts sailing from Trinidad to Tobago have to present their arrival form to the customs officer in Chaguaramas. He will endorse this form, which needs to be presented to customs on arrival in Tobago. The same procedure is necessary for the reverse voyage.

Although boats are required to clear customs again at Scarborough, with permission from the customs officer in Trinidad you can anchor elsewhere in Tobago, such as Store Bay, and go overland to Scarborough to complete the formalities.

When a new crew member arrives in Trinidad, the captain must present the crew's passport to the immigration officer at the Chaguaramas station within 24 hours in order to sign the crew on.

There are certain rules for importing spare parts duty-free for yachts in transit. Only the captain of the vessel is allowed to carry duty-free parts from the airport to Chaguaramas customs station, where they will be transferred on board.

Vessels must clear out of one of the two recommended ports. Yachts clear out with customs, immigration and the port authority.

✦ FACILITIES

Docking facilities have improved due to the opening of a number of new marinas. The closest to the capital of Port of Spain is the Trinidad and Tobago Yacht Club, which has a limited number of berths available to visitors.

A full range of repair services is available at Chaguaramas, where there are several boatyards with hauling facilities up to 200 tons, and large hardstanding areas. Many boats are stored here on the hard during the hurricane season. There are

chandleries well stocked with all essential spares and equipment. The range of repair services is comprehensive and able to deal with all requirements of the large numbers of yachts that are laid up here between seasons.

Another area with good facilities is Carenage, where the Trinidad and Tobago Yachting Association is based. The association welcomes visitors on sailing yachts and has reserved moorings for their use.

Only basic amenities are available in Tobago. Fuel can be loaded in Scarborough by contacting National Petroleum, which will send a fuel truck to the Coast Guard dock.

YSATT, the Yacht Services Association of Trinidad and Tobago, is a non-profit organization that was set up by local businesses involved with the yachting industry and whose aim is to represent and protect the interests of visiting sailors. Over the years it has done a lot to simplify formalities, improve facilities, and generally to make foreign sailors feel welcome.

The one sour note regarding Trinidad is that theft, particularly dinghies and other portable equipment, as well as armed robberies both on board and ashore, has been on the increase in recent years.

✦ CHARTER

There are no bareboat charter operators based in Trinidad. Sand Dollar Sailing, based in Store Bay in Tobago, offers both crewed and bareboat charters.

www.sanddollarsailing.com

Cruising Guides
Cruising Guide to Trinidad and Tobago
Cruising Guide to Trinidad and Tobago plus Barbados and
   Guyana

Websites
www.gotrinidadandtobago.com
www.ysatt.org (Yacht Services Association of Trinidad and
   Tobago)

Local time	UTC −4
Buoyage	IALA B
Currency	Trinidad and Tobago Dollar (TTD)
Electricity	115V, 60Hz

Diplomatic missions	
UK	622 2748
USA	622 6371
Australia	628 0695

Communications	
IDD 1 868	IAC 011

Emergency numbers
112	Ambulance 990	Police 999
Coast Guard 634 4440		

TURKS AND CAICOS

THE TURKS AND CAICOS are two groups of islands clustered in the shape of a crescent around the edge of the Caicos Bank, and include about forty low-lying cays and islands. Turks Island Passage separates the Turks from the Caicos. The windward sides of these islands of coral and limestone tend to be bare cliffs or sand dunes, while the western, leeward coasts are greener. Only a few are inhabited, the largest concentration being on the principal island, Grand Turk. The islands are a tranquil area, with stunning underwater scenery, which is strictly controlled by conservation laws. The area is an important stop for migratory birds and fulfils the same role for boats on passage to the Eastern Caribbean.

Cockburn Town is the sleepy capital of this remote British colony. Its main attraction is a small museum, which exhibits items found on a Spanish ship wrecked around 1510 on Molasses Reef. This is the earliest wreck discovered in the New World, and the well-preserved objects provide a fascinating glimpse into life on board an armed sailing vessel five centuries ago.

Across Turks Island Passage, the sparkling Caicos Bank can be compared to a 60 mile wide atoll, its perimeter being fringed by reefs. Its shallow turquoise waters, which teem with fish, have a maximum depth of 6m (20ft). Most of the bank is unsurveyed so boats transiting it should keep to the recommended tracks, which have a maximum depth of 2.40m (8ft). Passages should only be made in settled weather and with good visibility to avoid the shallow areas close to

Caicos Bank with a Turk's head cactus that has given the islands their name.

such tracks. The Turks Bank is similar to its western neighbour, but more difficult to navigate.

For the visiting sailor the main attraction is the clear unpolluted waters that give access to an underwater scenery of rare beauty and also the possibility of diving on some historic wrecks. The one drawback is the tricky navigation among the reefs, sandbanks and coral heads, with few navigational aids – and those that are in place are often unreliable.

The islands have pursued a programme of development as a tourist destination and the building of a large airport on Providenciales Island, capable of handling intercontinental jets, has thrown this little country into the modern age. The opening of a number of exclusive holiday resorts has produced a boom in tourism, and yachting facilities are rapidly catching up – with several new marinas having recently been commissioned.

Situated conveniently halfway between the Bahamas, Florida and Puerto Rico or the Virgins, the islands are an enjoyable break during the long passage and are also conveniently located in case of an emergency. With their improved facilities, they now fully deserve to be considered a cruising destination in their own right.

✦ COUNTRY PROFILE

Arawaks were probably the first inhabitants, although none were left by the mid-sixteenth century. Both Grand Turk and Caicos have been put forward as the original San Salvador where Columbus made his first landfall, though this landfall controversy is still not resolved.

During the nineteenth and twentieth centuries the Turks and Caicos were administered alternately by the British colonies of the Bahamas and Jamaica, but when they became independent, Turks and Caicos remained a British overseas territory. Since 1976 the islands have had internal self-government. The English-speaking inhabitants number around 23,000. Cockburn Town on Grand Turk is the capital.

✦ CLIMATE

The islands have a tropical climate which varies little between winter and summer. Between June and October the temperature hovers between 29°C/84°F and 32°C/90°F, dropping only a few degrees in winter. The hurricane season is from June to November. The islands are not affected by the cold northerlies of winter as in the neighbouring Bahamas.

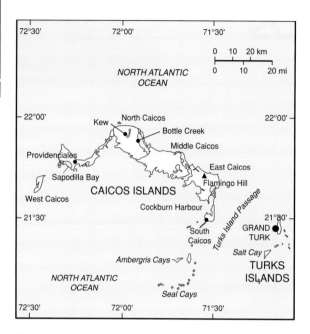

FORMALITIES

PORTS OF ENTRY

Grand Turk: Cockburn Town (Grand Turk) 21°28´N 71°06´W

Providenciales: Sapodilla Bay 21°44´N 72°17´W

Caicos Marina and Shipyard 21°44´N 72°10´W

Leeward Marina 21°47´N 72°17´W

Turtle Cove Marina 21°48.5´N 72°12.5´W

South Caicos: Cockburn Harbour 21°30´N 71°31´W

Cockburn Town: When contacted by radio, the harbourmaster usually directs boats to the commercial dock at the island's southern extremity to be met by customs and immigration officials.

Providenciales: Inward or outward clearance can be completed at the commercial dock close to Sapodilla Bay or at any of the marinas.

Clearance can be completed at any government dock or marina. Visas are not required for nationals of most countries. For stays longer than seven days, or to visit other islands, customs will issue a cruising permit valid for three months.

Sport fishing without a permit is forbidden, as are spearguns and the use of scuba gear to take any marine life. Lobster may only be taken in season (1 August to 31 March), by hand or noose.

FACILITIES

Few other places have seen such a rapid expansion of their yachting services spurred on both by the demands of an increasing number of visitors, but also as a deliberate attempt to attract more yachts. The best amenities are on Providenciales, with well-stocked supermarkets and some repair and haulout facilities. There are now several marinas, Caicos Marina, Shipyard and South Side Marina, that have good facilities, while Turtle Cove Marina, on the north coast, is used primarily by powerboats because of the difficult access through the shallow Sellar's Cut. The anchorage in Sapodilla Bay, a favourite with cruising boats, is open to the south and therefore not a safe place to leave the vessel unattended for too long.

Facilities on the other islands, including the main island of Grand Turk, are more limited. Flamingo Cove Marina on Grand Turk is small and shallow. On South Caicos, Seaview Marina has a fuel dock and some mooring spaces for visitors. Turks and Caicos Yacht Club Marina on Providenciales and West Caicos Marina are under construction.

Yachts in transit can have parts and equipment shipped duty-free via frequent flights from Florida.

CHARTER

There are no bareboat charter operators based in the islands, but several local firms have boats for rental as listed on this site:

www.turksandcaicostourism.com/sailing-boating.html

Cruising Guides
Gentleman's Guide to Passages South
Turks and Caicos and the Dominican Republic

Websites
www.turksandcaicostourism.com
www.turksandcaicos.tc/marinas

Local time	UTC −5
	Summer time: first Sunday in March to first Sunday in November
Buoyage	IALA B
Currency	United States Dollar (USD)
Electricity	10V, 60Hz

Diplomatic mission	
UK	946 2309

Communications		Emergency numbers
IDD 1 649 IAC 011		999/911

US VIRGIN ISLANDS

THE US VIRGIN ISLANDS consist of three main islands, St Thomas, St John and St Croix. Most of the other 65 islands are uninhabited. Although scenically the US Virgin Islands are on a par with their British counterpart, some of their charm has been lost by overdevelopment. Their appeal as a cruising destination, both among US and foreign sailors, has also suffered from restrictive Coast Guard regulations and reports of a high crime rate.

St Thomas is the main, although not the largest, island and the capital Charlotte Amalie is located on its south coast. This is a bustling duty-free port, always busy with cruise ships loading and offloading passengers, and yachts taking on provisions or changing crew. Charlotte Amalie provides good shelter, but a better-protected anchorage is inside the lagoon in Benner Bay, at the southeast end of the island, which provides the best hurricane shelter in the area.

Compared to the hectic pace on St Thomas, the situation is very different in the other two large islands, St John and St Croix, with many tranquil anchorages and a slow pace of life. St John is ringed with pleasant anchorages both on the north and south coasts, while Hurricane Hole, on the east coast, provides the best protection. Much of St John has been designated a national park and this wise decision has kept development in check.

St Croix, in spite of being the largest of the US Virgins, is least endowed with good anchorages. The only well-protected harbour is Christiansted, which is also the main settlement.

The one quaint feature that comes as a great surprise to first-time visitors is that traffic is on the left side of the road. This is a leftover from the days when the islands were still owned by Denmark at a time when Britain was not the only European nation to drive on that side of the road.

◆ COUNTRY PROFILE

The Spanish were the first Europeans to settle the area after Columbus called here in 1493 and named the islands after St Ursula and her virgin disciples. A number of other countries laid claim to the islands, and after several changes they became a Danish colony. The Danish West Indies were purchased by the USA in 1917 for $25 million and renamed them the US Virgin Islands. As a US unincorporated territory, the islanders are US citizens, although unable to vote in federal elections.

The population is around 110,000, mainly of African origin. English is the main language, with some Spanish and Creole.

◆ CLIMATE

The islands have a pleasant climate and do not experience significant seasonal changes. Both weather and temperatures are fairly consistent all year round, with an annual mean temperature of 26°C/79°F in winter and 28.5°C/83°F in summer. From November to April the north-facing coasts occasionally experience a high swell caused by storms in the North Atlantic. June to November is the hurricane season.

◆ FORMALITIES

PORTS OF ENTRY		
St Thomas: Charlotte Amalie	18°23′N	64°56′W
St Croix: Christiansted	17°46′N	64°41′W
St John: Cruz Bay	18°20′N	64°47′W

In their fight against drug traffic, US Virgin Islands special strike forces patrol the waters around the islands. Any yacht within territorial waters may be stopped, boarded and searched.

Yachts must go directly to a port of entry for clearance. All crew should stay on board until clearance has been completed, but it is reported that crew members must then accompany the captain to immigration and sign the entry permit.

Charlotte Amalie: The captain and all crew members should proceed to the customs office at the ferry terminal to complete formalities.

Cruz Bay: The customs office is in the northern part of the bay in the so-called Creek. If there is space on the quay, yachts clearing in may come alongside.

Charlotte Amalie on St Thomas.

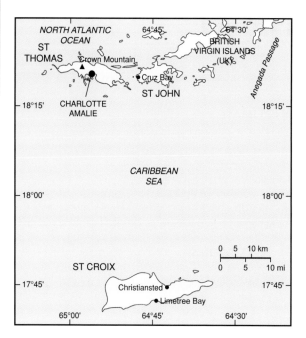

Christiansted: Yachts arriving from a foreign port must proceed to Gallows Bay harbour dock to clear customs and immigration. Those who arrive after hours, or at the weekend, must phone 340 778 0216 to report their arrival.

Immigration requirements are the same as for the US mainland. All nationalities arriving by private yacht, except for Canadians, must have a valid US visa, obtained in advance.

You must clear in with immigration every time you arrive from another island, including the British Virgin Islands, but not if coming from Puerto Rico. All yachts must clear out with customs before going to Puerto Rico.

US citizens who are frequent boat users in the area can use the Local Boater Option (LBO) to simplify the arrival procedure.

Cruising permits are not required, but those who intend to spend longer than six months must have their yachts registered locally.

Mooring permits are required in some places, but are not needed for day use on public or national park moorings. The Reef Ecological Foundation has laid down public moorings in various locations in St Thomas and St John. They are coloured white or orange and have Reef Ecology stickers on them. Any yacht under 18m (60ft) may use them; there is a three-hour limit and no charge. No anchoring is permitted in Salt Pond, Reef Bay, Great and Little Lameshur Bays, where yachts must use the white, blue-banded moorings, and in other places no anchoring is allowed on coral and all reef damage is forbidden.

Line fishing and lobster taking is permitted with some restrictions, but otherwise the taking of live or dead marine life is forbidden, as is spearfishing or tying boats to shoreline vegetation.

◆ FACILITIES

A good range of repair facilities are concentrated around Charlotte Amalie on St Thomas. There are several marinas, all with good amenities, dotted around St Thomas's indented coastline. Christiansted in St Croix has comparable facilities, including slipway and travelift, and well-stocked chandleries. Repair and general amenities on St John are more limited, although 200 moorings have been laid around the island for visitors to the St John National Park. A further 45 moorings for boats under 18m (60ft) are for public use. There are restrictions on vessels anchoring in National Park areas.

◆ CHARTER

There are several locally based companies offering crewed charters, but the choice of bareboats is limited as most such companies are based in the British Virgins. Islands Yachts Charter, based at Red Hook, St Thomas, has a fleet of Island Packet boats and has been operating in the area for over thirty years. VIP Yachts, based at Compass Point Marina, operates a fleet of both power and sailing boats. Jones Marine in St Croix and St John Yacht Charters are smaller local companies.

www.iyc.vi
www.vipyachts.com
www.jonesmaritime.com
www.stjohnyachtcharters.com

Cruising Guides
Cruising the Virgin Islands
Cruising Guide to the Virgin Islands
The Virgin Islands
Virgin Anchorages
Yachtsman's Guide to the Virgin Islands

Websites
www.usvitourism.vi
www.usvi.net

Local time	UTC −4
Buoyage	IALA B
Currency	United States Dollar (USD)
Electricity	110V, 60Hz

Diplomatic missions
UK	BVI +1 284 494 2345

Communications
IDD 1 340	IAC 011

Emergency number
911

NORTH AND CENTRAL AMERICA

FROM THE TORRID JUNGLES of Panama to the frozen wastes of Alaska, this region encompasses a vast array of cruising areas as well as some of the most famous yachting centres in the world. The coasts of Mexico and Central America are mostly visited by North American sailors, who have some of the best cruising spots on their doorstep. For west coast sailors the perennial temptation of Baja California with its star attraction of the Sea of Cortez draws flocks of migrating yachts every year.

The USA itself has enough cruising attractions to satisfy even the most demanding sailor, which can also be said of Canada, whose western coast is of a beauty rarely matched elsewhere. While the greatest allure of the northern destinations is their scenery, a major attraction of the southern destinations is the opportunity to visit the remains of some of the great civilizations that flourished in the region in pre-Columbian times. From a sailor's point of view, the main feature of Central America is the Panama Canal, one of the greatest technological achievements of modern times, and transiting the canal on your own vessel is a uniquely rewarding experience.

Besides the many opportunities provided by coastal cruising, much of North America is also accessible through an extensive network of rivers and canals. While the Intracoastal Waterway runs parallel to almost the entire east coast of the USA, a system of canals and locks link New York to the Great Lakes, which can also be reached via the St Lawrence River. The Great Lakes are the largest inland cruising area in the world and, as boating facilities are of a high standard, they provide a special destination to anyone looking for something different.

Weather conditions over such a vast region show a great variation, and both shorter and longer voyages need to be planned carefully to take into account prevailing winds and favourable seasons. The southern areas on both coasts can be affected by tropical storms between June and November, so voyages bound for the tropics from either coast, whether to Baja California and beyond, or the Bahamas and Western Caribbean, should not start earlier than November. The extreme south of the region, such as Panama, is not affected by tropical storms. Primarily due to their unpredictability, sailors seem to dread some of the violent local winds even more than hurricanes. On the Pacific coast of Mexico, *chubascos* occur mostly in summer and early autumn and affect the entire coast, but are worst in the Sea of Cortez where gusts can reach 70 knots. A *chubasco*, which actually means 'squall' in Spanish, often strikes at night. A similarly unpleasant local wind affects the Gulf of Tehuantepec, and is called by sailors a *tehuantepecer*. Such winds can occur throughout the year, with the worst period being between December and February. Winds can reach hurricane force in a relatively short time and with very little warning. On the east coast, but mainly from Florida southwards, northers are a winter phenomenon and are caused by the arrival of a cold front. The worst situation is to be caught by such a norther while sailing in the Gulf Stream when the strong wind against the swift current can produce very rough seas.

Sailors who are planning a voyage to this region have a choice of routes. Those hoping to sail from the Eastern Caribbean to ports on the east coast north of New York may be tempted by an intermediate stop in Bermuda. Ports that are further south can be reached by an interesting route that passes through Turks and Caicos as well as the Bahamas. Once there, the route can turn south towards Central America, or north all the way to Canada. Transiting the Panama Canal is only the first, and often easiest, step to reach the west coast. Cruising north along the western coasts of Central America and Mexico is relatively simple, but beyond that, the prevailing contrary winds can seriously complicate matters. The logical, if not necessarily the easiest, solution is to make a long detour to Hawaii, and possibly continue from there to Alaska, and cruise the west coast of North America on the way south.

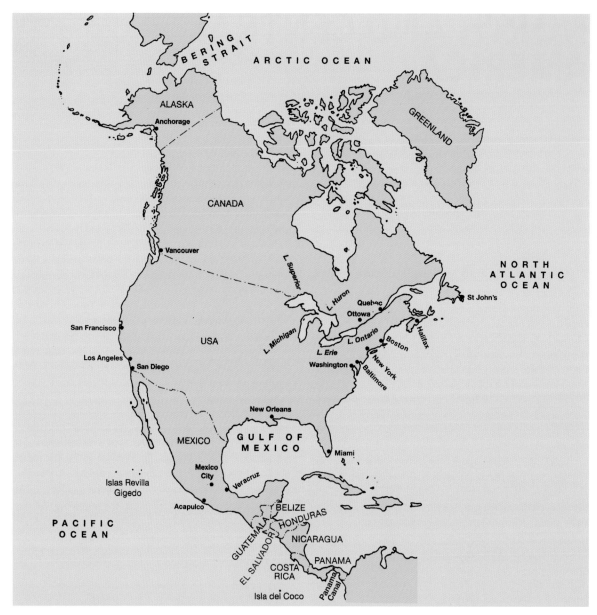

Among the European sailors who wish to explore North America, few attempt a crossing of the Atlantic by the shortest route and most prefer to do it along the classic tradewind route. This usually means a longer voyage that encompasses the islands of the Eastern Caribbean as well. Once there, mainland America is almost within reach.

The west coast of the continent is far less accessible along a southern route. Perhaps the only positive outcome of the current climate change is that, at some point in the not too distant future, sailors from Europe and the east coasts of the USA and Canada will be able to reach the Pacific not via the Panama Canal, but through the North West Passage.

Yachting facilities in the USA, Canada and much of Western Mexico are of a good standard, with well-equipped marinas, boatyards and a wide range of repair services on both coasts. Facilities in the other countries have been getting better in response to the demands of the increasing number of visiting yachts, but can still only be described as adequate. The one exception is Panama, where facilities have seen a great improvement in recent years, primarily in response to an expanding local boating community.

BELIZE

BELIZE CONCENTRATES all the tempting ingredients associated with sailing in the tropics: palm-covered cays set in clear waters, easy sailing in sheltered waters cut off from the ocean by a barrier reef, and is a true Garden of Eden for divers and fishermen alike. Belize's coastlands are low and swampy with mangroves and lagoons, while forested mountains present a contrast in the southwest of the country. Belize's main attraction lies offshore: a 175 mile long barrier reef, second only in size to the Great Barrier Reef of Australia. Between the reef and the coastal strip runs the 100 mile long Inner Channel, which provides exhilarating sailing conditions in flat water as the tradewinds blow strongly across the outer reef. Both on the outer reef and inshore there are hundreds of uninhabited islands and cays. Most of the northern cays are covered in mangroves, but further south the cays become more attractive, being surrounded by sandy beaches shaded by coconut palms. Just east of the barrier reef are three coral atolls, Turneffe, Glovers and Lighthouse, each with its own lagoon, providing a protected habitat for both aquatic creatures and seabirds.

The price to pay for this near perfection is that navigation inside the reef is not easy as the sea is shallow and there are not many navigational aids, although GPS and electronic charts have greatly simplified matters. The abundance of secluded anchorages, unsurpassed diving, excellent deep-sea fishing – as well as the many Mayan remains – continue to ensure Belize's attraction as an alternative to the crowded Eastern Caribbean.

✦ COUNTRY PROFILE

Hidden in the interior of Belize are many ruins of the ancient Mayan empire, which flourished in this region from the fourth to ninth centuries CE. In the mid-seventeenth century, the country was colonized by English settlers from Jamaica, who initially came for the logwood used for textile dyes. Both Guatemala and Mexico laid claim to the territory in the nineteenth century, but later accepted Belize as a British colony. Formerly known as British Honduras, Belize became independent in 1981.

The 308,000 inhabitants are mainly Creole and *mestizo* (mixed European and Amerindian), with smaller Maya and Garifuna minorities. The latter are descended from Caribs, who were deported from St Vincent in the eighteenth century. English is the official language, but a wide range of other languages are spoken. Belmopan is the capital.

✦ CLIMATE

The tropical climate can be hot, especially from February to May, although the prevailing wind helps to keep the coast cooler. During winter months the anchorages are rather exposed to the northers that sweep down across the Gulf of Mexico. The hurricane season lasts from June to November.

FORMALITIES

PORTS OF ENTRY	
Belize City	17°30′N 88°11′W
Punta Gorda	16°06′N 88°48′W
San Pedro	17°56′N 87°57′W
Placencia	16°31′N 88°22′W
Dangriga	16°58′N 88°13′W

Belize City: The port captain should be contacted before arrival to arrange clearance. Yachts should anchor off the commercial dock and are normally visited by customs and immigration officers, unless the captain is instructed to complete formalities ashore. The alternative is to proceed to either Cucumber Beach or Fort George Marina and make arrangements from there.
San Pedro: The entrance through the reef is rather complicated, but you can call the San Pedro Yacht Club on Channel 16 for directions. It is possible to go straight to the yacht club and complete formalities from there. This is the most convenient port for those sailing from the north as it is close to the Mexican border.
Punta Gorda: This is the southernmost port in Belize and a convenient place to clear if sailing to or from Honduras or Guatemala. The customs and immigration offices are in town.

Visas are not required for nationals of EU countries, Australia, Canada, New Zealand and the USA. If a visa is required, normally 30-day visas are issued on arrival.

Customs require four crew lists and four store lists.

Yachts may remain in Belize for up to six months.

No fresh produce can be imported and may be confiscated on arrival.

Nature conservation is a high priority and there are many national parks, wildlife sanctuaries and nature reserves, such as Half Moon Cay Natural Monument and Hol Chan Marine Reserve. There are fees for sailing in the eight marine park areas which cover most of the barrier reef. It is prohibited to damage or remove any forms of sealife, black coral or to spearfish.

FACILITIES

The best amenities are in Belize City. There are repair services, good provisioning and some hardware. Water and fuel are available and LPG tanks can be filled. The anchorage is open, often rolly and not secure, so a better solution is to use one of the two marinas – Cucumber Beach or Fort George. Both are safe places to leave the boat to visit the interior. There is good provisioning at San Pedro, on Ambergris Cay, which also has daily flights to the mainland. The San Pedro Yacht Club has good facilities, including fuel. Alistair King's is a small marina in Punta Gorda with basic amenities.

CHARTER

Both TMM Yachts and Nautilus maintain a fleet of catamarans at San Pedro on Ambergris Cay and Placencia on the mainland, and in addition offer the possibility of one-way charters. Also based in Placencia are the Moorings and Belize Sailing Charters, the latter with a mixed fleet of catamarans and monohulls.

www.moorings.com
www.sailtmm.com (TMM Yachts)
www.belize-sailing-charters.com
www.nautilus-yachting.com

Cruising Guide
Cruising Guide to Belize and Mexico's Caribbean Coast

Website
www.travelbelize.org

Local time	UTC −6	**Currency**	Belize Dollar (BZD)
Buoyage	IALA B	**Electricity**	110V, 60Hz

Diplomatic missions	
UK 822 3146	USA 822 4011

Communications	**Emergency number**
IDD 501 IAC 00	911

CANADA

SPANNING THE NORTH of the American continent, Canada has cruising grounds on both the western Pacific coast and the eastern Atlantic coast. While the west coast offers visiting yachts a rich variety of cruising opportunities, the east coast is somewhat less tempting, so foreign sailors may decide to follow the Canadian example and make their way to the Great Lakes and do some inland sailing for a change. This cruising area, popular with sailors from land-bound states from both Canada and the USA, can be reached by either sailing up the St Lawrence River from the Atlantic or by way of the Hudson River and Erie Canal. Some sailors from the US east coast have extended that tour and turned it into a complete round trip by sailing to Nova Scotia, up the St Lawrence to the Great Lakes, and then back to the US east coast through the Erie Canal. Even more intrepid sailors have further extended that voyage to complete the Great Loop by entering the St Lawrence River via the Champlain Canal, and to reach the Great Lakes via the Rideau and Trent Canals, before turning south from the Great Lakes to reach the ocean via the Illinois, Mississippi, Ohio and Tennessee rivers.

ATLANTIC COAST

The shortest way to reach Eastern Canada from Europe is the classic route across the Northern Atlantic, plied in days past by countless fishing boats working the rich grounds off New-foundland. Although the prevailing westerly winds make such a voyage a challenging undertaking at all times, summer con-ditions and a more northerly route may sometimes be more favourable. Cruising Eastern Canada is strictly for the summer months, and even then it can be cold, wet and windy. The rewards are a vast choice of anchorages in small bays, harbours and islands, and the few cruising boats sailing this far north can find complete isolation in beautiful surroundings. More often visited by foreign yachts is Nova Scotia, the first stop downeast from Maine. Halifax, the main harbour, is a large yachting centre and, like St John's in Newfoundland, a trans-atlantic springboard and landfall. An area until very recently unaccessible to cruising yachts is Northern Canada and the North West Passage. The current climate change has already had a bearing on weather conditions in the Arctic, and in the last few summers the passage has been free of ice long enough for this important waterway, which has tempted mariners for centuries, to be navigated along its entire length. A number of sailing yachts have successfully completed that still daunting passage, most of them sailing from west to east.

Climate

The climate varies considerably around the country. Atlantic Canada is very cold between November and April, while May to October is mild and generally pleasant. There are few gales in summer, but the area is affected by fog. In spring and summer up to July, icebergs can be seen in the Newfoundland area. Northern Canada has subarctic conditions during winter and the climate in the Great Lakes area is also harsher in winter.

PACIFIC COAST

British Columbia boasts one of the most beautiful and dramatic cruising grounds in the world, with its snow capped mountains, waterfalls cascading down rugged cliffs, a myriad of islands, and quiet, still fjords. The 100 mile long Vancouver Island protects most of the mainland from the Pacific Ocean and creates an inland sea dotted with islands and spiked with inlets, where the absence of swell provides great sailing conditions. The city of Vancouver is an important yachting centre and an ideal place to enjoy some urban luxuries after time spent in the wilderness.

The most popular cruising area is the Gulf Islands, with pleasant harbours and anchorages on both sides of the Strait of Georgia, which separates Vancouver Island from the mainland. Another good cruising area is to the north, where a cluster of islands border the magnificent Desolation Sound. North of this begins the inside passage to Alaska. A large tidal range and strong currents make for attentive navigation, as do the hazards of floating logs and kelp. Fog can be a danger

Sunset over Virgin Arm in Newfoundland.

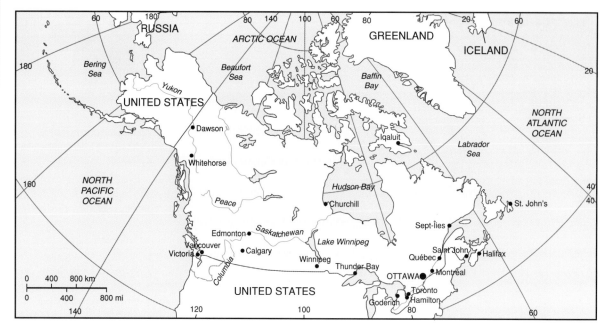

along this coast and radar is a great boon, especially as there is a lot of other traffic: logging tugs, fishing boats, fast ferries to and from the islands and, especially near Vancouver, commercial shipping. Nature's rich rewards of magnificent scenery and abundant wildlife – including superb fishing – more than make up for the need for attentive navigation.

Climate

The climate along the west coast can be described as temperate between November and April, while May to October is warm and rainy. The southern area, nicknamed the 'banana belt', is in the rain shadow of Vancouver Island, has milder winters, and therefore cruising is possible all year round, while the northern sector tends to be suitable for summer cruising only. Land breezes often dictate the sailing conditions, and calms are

Princess Louisa Inlet.

commonplace. In the summer, gales are rare and west or northwesterly winds blow most afternoons.

◆ COUNTRY PROFILE

The first inhabitants were Inuit tribes who came over from Asia thousands of years ago. The earliest European visitors were Vikings, who left traces of a settlement dated around 1000 CE. The first recorded arrival was that of John Cabot in 1497. Jacques Cartier explored the St Lawrence River in the sixteenth century, claiming it for France, and Quebec was founded in 1608. French settlement of New France, as the area was called, was slow at first, but increased in the seventeenth century. New France came into conflict with England and, after France's defeat in the Seven Years War, in 1763 the rest of Canada was ceded to England in exchange for the Caribbean islands of Guadeloupe and Martinique – probably the worst deal France has ever made.

A united Canada was created by the British government and given internal self-government in 1848. The Dominion of Canada was established in 1867, as a Confederation of the various provinces. Independence from the UK was granted in 1931. Demands for greater independence by part of the population of the French-speaking province of Quebec is an ongoing issue. In a referendum held in 1995, the population of Quebec voted by a narrow margin to remain part of Canada.

The population numbers 33.5 million, of which most are of British or French origin, with many other more recent ethnic backgrounds adding to the cosmopolitan mix. Only about 2 per cent are Native Canadians. English and French are the official languages, and the capital, Ottawa, is in Ontario province.

PORTS OF ENTRY
Only the more maritime ports are listed:

Newfoundland:	St John's 47°34′N 52°41′W		Corner Brook	48°57′N 57°56′W
	Fortune	46°54′N 55°38′W	Harbour Grace	47°41′N 53°13′W
	Argentia	47°18′N 53°59′W		
Prince Edward Island:	Charlottetown	46°13′N 63°07′W	Summerside	46°24′N 63°47′W
Nova Scotia:	Sherbourne	43°45′N 65°20′W	Yarmouth	43°50′N 66°07′W
	Le Havre	44°17′N 64°21′W	Lunenburg	44°22′N 64°18′W
	Halifax (customs Tel: 426 2071 0800 2200) 44°38′N 63°33′W			
	Parrsboro	45°23′N 64°20′W	Pictou	45°41′N 62°43′W
	Port Medway	44°08′N 64°34′W	Pugwash	45°52′N 63°40′W
	Sheet Harbour 44°51′N 62°27′W			
New Brunswick:	Caraquet	47°48′N 65°01′W	Chatham	47°02′N 65°28′W
	Dalhousie	48°04′N 66°22′W	Newcastle	47°00′N65°33′W
	St Andrews	45°04′N 67°03′W		
British Columbia:	Kitimat	54°00′N 128°42′W	Nanaimo	49°10′N 123°56′W
	Port Alberni	49°14′N 125°00′W	Woodfibre	49°40′N 123°15′W
	Prince Rupert Harbour 54°19′N 130°22′W		Vancouver	49°17′N 123°07′W
Gulf Islands:	Bedwell (South Pender Island, summer only) 49°38′N 124°03′W			
	Sidney 48°39′N 123°24′W		Nanaimo (Vancouver Island) 49°10′N 123°56′W	
	North Head Harbour (Grand Manan) 49°10′N 123°56′W			

✦ FORMALITIES

Port control should be contacted prior to entering any of the larger ports. St John's Traffic monitors Channel 11.

On arrival at a port of entry, the Canada Border Services Agency (CBSA) should be contacted at a telephone reporting site (TRS) by calling 1 888 226 7277. If the 1 888 number does not answer, the captain should call the appropriate area number:

Northern or Eastern Ontario: 613 659 4576
Central Ontario, Quebec, Atlantic coast: 905 679 2073
Southern Ontario: 519 967 4320
West coast: 250 363 0222

The CBSA officer will want to know the location of the boat, which must be docked at an approved TRS facility, boat name, registration number and last port of call. Customs may also request a list of the ports to be visited. For each person on board, you must provide full name, date of birth, citizenship, purpose of trip, and length of stay in Canada. All personal goods being imported, including firearms as well as alcohol, tobacco or animals, must be declared. All other crew apart from the person reporting must remain on board. The CBSA officer will advise if you are free to enter Canada, or if you have to wait for an officer to conduct an examination. At the conclusion of the process, a report number is given as proof of reporting. This number should be displayed in a suitable place where it can be seen.

Nationals of most European countries, Australia, New Zealand and the USA do not need a visa to enter Canada. The length of stay, up to six months, is decided by the CBSA officer at the port of entry. A visa is required by nationals of South Africa and some East European countries.

US citizens who travel frequently to Canada can register to participate in the CANPASS or NEXUS programs. Both programs provide fast customs and immigration clearance for pre-screened persons entering Canada by private pleasure boat.

The captain must have a certificate of competence if the yacht spends more than 45 days in Canada.

There are complex requirements and restrictions that apply to importing meat, dairy products, fruit and vegetables and other foodstuffs. This is best avoided by not bringing

Vancouver.

such goods into Canada. Some types of souvenirs cannot be imported into Canada under CITES (Convention on International Trade in Endangered Species).

Non-resident visitors may leave their boats in Canada during the off-season without payment of duties only if repair or maintenance work is to be undertaken by a bona fide marina or boatyard. Before leaving a boat, the owner must advise the local customs office of the details.

A fishing licence is required in British Columbia.

✦ FACILITIES

There are good facilities in all major yachting centres. Provisioning is excellent in larger ports, but only adequate in some of the smaller places.

On the Atlantic coast, Halifax, in Nova Scotia, has a wide range of repair facilities and services. There are three yacht clubs, and visitors can secure free mooring for one week at the Maritime Museum of the Atlantic in the main harbour. The Royal Nova Scotia Yacht Squadron welcomes visiting yachts and has good facilities. Best repair services are at Lunenburg, an important fishing port, which has an interesting fishing museum. The limited yachting amenities in St John's busy commercial harbour are concentrated in Long Pond, on the west side of the Avalon peninsula. This is also the home of the hospitable Royal Newfoundland Yacht Club. The only marina-type facility is at Lewisport.

On the west coast, the best stocks of chandlery and general repair services are in Vancouver and its suburb of Surrey. In Vancouver itself there are good docking facilities at the Royal Vancouver Yacht Club and the nearby Royal Vancouver Rowing Club, both of which welcome visitors and are close to the centre. Nanaimo, on Vancouver Island, is a good provisioning place used by the local fishing fleet, so docking

space is sometimes limited. There are several marinas in Pender Harbour, with stores, post office and fuel station. Similar services are available at Sullivan Bay on North Broughton Island. There are good facilities in Prince Rupert, although it gets crowded when the fishing fleet is in. North of Vancouver, grocery stores and fuelling stations are far apart.

✦ CHARTER

There are limited opportunities for chartering a bareboat to explore Newfoundland or Nova Scotia, although there are a few local operators offering shorter or longer trips on their own crewed boats. The situation is very different in British Columbia with several companies, both Canadian and US, offering every type of boat to explore those unique cruising grounds all the way to Alaska. Vancouver Island Cruising, with bases at Port Sidney and Pacific Playgrounds Marina, has a large fleet of both monohulls and catamarans as well as a few powerboats. ABC Yacht Charters, based in Anacortes, and Voyages NorthWest, based in Seattle, both offer a range of power and trawler-type yachts, some of which are based in summer in the San Juan Islands.

> www.islandcruising.com
> www.abcyachtcharters.com
> www.voyagesnw.com

Cruising Guides
Cruising Guide to Labrador
Cruising Guide to Newfoundland
Cruising Guide to the Nova Scotia Coast
Dreamspeaker Cruising Guides, Pacific Northwest, 6 vols
Exploring North British Columbia
Exploring South British Columbia
Exploring the San Juan and Gulf Islands
Exploring Vancouver Island's West Coast

Websites
www.travelcanada.com
www.cbsa-asfc.gc.ca/prog/nexus/marine-maritime-eng.html
(entry regulations)

Local time	UTC −3.5 to −8
	Summer time: first Sunday in March to first Sunday in November
Buoyage	IALA B
Currency	Canadian Dollar (CAD)
Electricity	120V, 60Hz

Diplomatic missions

UK	613 237 1530	South Africa	613 744 0330
USA	613 688 5335	New Zealand	613 238 5991
Australia	613 236 0841		

Communications		Emergency numbers
IDD 1	IAC 011	911/112

orseshoe Bay, north of Vancouver.

COSTA RICA

COSTA RICA HAS COASTLINES on both the Caribbean Sea and the Pacific Ocean, the latter being the more appealing to sailors. Compared to its northern neighbours, Costa Rica's indented coastline presents a welcome change and a pleasant cruising ground. The 300 mile west coast is indented by several sheltered bays where you can anchor in attractive surroundings. Bahia Santa Elena in the far north is well protected and there are several sheltered anchorages in the Gulf of Papagayo. The large Nicoya Gulf leads to Puntarenas, the oldest Spanish settlement in the area, now a vibrant city with a whole range of facilities for yachts. The deep bay of Golfito, the southernmost port of entry into Costa Rica, is a popular port of call, with cruising boats plying the western coast of Central America.

The sparsely inhabited Caribbean coast is far less attractive, being a narrow strip of swampy ground backed by tropical forests. Puerto Limón, halfway up the coast, is the main port of Costa Rica.

An exciting destination 300 miles offshore in the Pacific is the fabled treasure island of Coco. Hundreds of expeditions have been mounted over the years to find the various treasures reputed to have been buried there, but nothing has been found so far. The island's real treasure is its unspoilt nature, and Isla del Coco was declared a national park by the Costa Rican government. It is worth the detour to watch the birdlife and underwater scenery teeming with fish.

Protection of the environment is a high priority for the Costa Rican authorities and several areas along the coast have national park status. Although covering only 0.1 per cent of the world's landmass, Costa Rica contains 5 per cent of the world's plant and animal species. One-quarter of the country's land area is protected, which is the largest proportion of protected areas of any country in the world. The country has set itself up as an important eco-destination and there are many interesting nature reserves in the hilly interior, which can easily be reached from either Puntarenas or Puerto Limón, and also the attractive capital of San José.

✦ COUNTRY PROFILE

After Columbus's brief visit in 1502, attempts at colonizing were unsuccessful due to the combination of tropical heat, resistance by local tribes, and disease from mosquito-infested swamps. The Spanish finally settled in the highlands, and in a relatively short time most of the native population had been decimated by European diseases. Costa Rica became independent in 1821 when all Central American colonies put an end to Spanish colonial rule. The country enjoys the highest standard of living in Central America and also has the reputation of being the most stable Latin American democracy. It is one of the few countries in the world that has decided not to have an army, and the absence of armed forces has undoubtedly contributed to its stability. Costa Rica has also declared that it intends to be the first carbon neutral country in the world by 2021.

The 4.3 million inhabitants are mostly white or mestizo, and only a small number of Amerindians are left. Spanish is the main language.

✦ CLIMATE

The Pacific coast of Costa Rica is drier, while the Caribbean side has heavy rainfall. Both coasts are hot and humid. December to April are the dry months, while May to November is the wet season. The east coast is under the influence of the northeast tradewinds during the winter months, but the west coast has light winds, and often calms. Costa Rica is rarely affected by tropical storms. The worst local phenomenon is the *papagayo*, a violent north or northeast wind that affects the area from which it drew its name, and can be felt as far away as 150 miles offshore. *Papagayos* occur between October and April, with the worst period between the end of November and the end of January.

Tortuguero village in one of Costa Rica's nature reserves on the Caribbean coast.

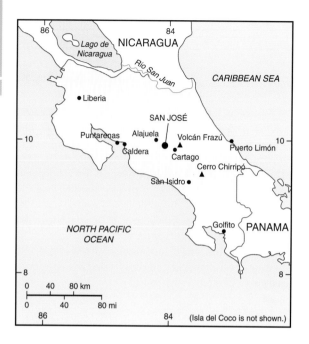

import certificate valid for three months. This limit must not be exceeded, for otherwise customs might charge import duties on the value of the yacht. The alternative is to put the boat in bond at a marina before the expiry of the three months period for a minimum of three months. After this bond period, another temporary import permit will be issued.

When visiting subsequent ports, you must go ashore and clear with the port captain and show this import permit.

The crew of yachts arriving from a yellow fever zone, especially South America, must have valid yellow fever vaccinations and certificates to prove it, or immigration may deny entry.

When leaving from the last port, an international departure certificate (*zarpe*) will be issued by the port captain.

Boats with any fishing equipment on board must obtain a fishing permit.

✦ FACILITIES

The number of marinas in Costa Rica is constantly increasing and facilities are improving at the same rate. The best repair services are at Playa del Coco, Tamarindo, Montezuma (near Bahia Ballena), Puntarenas, Quepos, Dominical, Puerto Jimenez and Golfito. In all these places there are also good supermarkets and excellent fresh produce markets. Golfito is popular with cruising sailors as a good place for repairs and reprovisioning. With four marinas and more projected, there is a good range of facilities both afloat and ashore.

Puerto Limón, on the Caribbean side, is the main port of Costa Rica. Hence there is good provisioning and adequate repair facilities there. Trains and buses run to San José.

✦ FORMALITIES

PORTS OF ENTRY

Caribbean coast:	Puerto Limón	10°00´N 83°03´W
Pacific coast:	Playa del Coco	10°35´N 85°42´W
Golfito		8°38´N 83°11´W
Puntarenas		9°59´N 84°51´W
Marina Papagayo		10°42´N 85°48´W

Yachts should not stop anywhere before arrival at a port of entry. Formalities can be lengthy everywhere. You must clear with the port authority, customs and immigration. Port officials rarely visit the yacht, and formalities are usually completed ashore.

Golfito: Formalities are completed at the various offices ashore and yachts arriving from abroad must also clear quarantine.

Playa del Coco: Formalities are not easy as there is no local customs office, so unless the customs officer comes to the boat, the captain must go to Liberia to visit customs.

Marina Papagayo: The marina has an immigration office and online clearance arrangements, but very high fees are charged for this facility, while the service is free for those who do it themselves. The docking fees are also reported to be high.

Visas are issued on arrival to nationals of most countries and either a 30 or 90 day stay will be given. Clearance from the last port, and exit stamps in the passport from the last country visited, will have to be shown. Customs will issue a temporary

Cruising Guides
Costa Rica
Explore Central America Part II – West Costa Rica (see Sarana website)

Websites
www.visitcostarica.com
www.costarica.com
www.sailsarana.com/guide

Local time	UTC –6
Buoyage	IALA B
Currency	Costa Rican Colon (CRC)
Electricity	120V, 60Hz

Diplomatic missions	
UK	258 2025
USA	519 2000
Canada	2242 4400

Communications	
IDD 506	IAC 00

Emergency numbers 911/112

EL SALVADOR

EL SALVADOR IS A SMALL, HIGHLY POPULATED, country on the Pacific side of Central America. The spectacular interior of volcanic uplands with deep craters and soaring peaks now includes several nature reserves, the rainforest marching up to the base of San Miguel volcano with its moonscape scenery. This fertile interior is also home to large coffee plantations.

Cruising boats are now welcome to stop in El Salvador and the situation has greatly improved with the opening of Barillas Marina in the beautiful Bay of Jiguilisco, parts of which are a nature reserve. The marina facilities are of a good standard and this is a safe place to make inland trips from. Another good base is Bahia del Sol, a resort with a small marina across a bar that can be difficult to negotiate.

Map showing GUATEMALA, HONDURAS, Santa Ana, Apopa, SAN SALVADOR, Acajutla, Nueva San Salvador, Rio Lempa, San Miguel, Usulután, Puerto Cutuco, Isla Conejo, Golfo de Fonseca, NORTH PACIFIC OCEAN, with coordinates 14 and 13.

✦ COUNTRY PROFILE

El Salvador remained largely isolated after the Spanish conquest, as it had no precious metals. It achieved independence from Spain in 1821. Between 1979 and 1992 instability and civil war cost the lives of tens of thousands of people. The conflict was between the government forces and an alliance of Marxist movements. Finally, negotiations between the two sides led to a peace accord and the situation has largely returned to normal, although crime is a continuing problem.

The 7.2 million inhabitants are mostly *mestizo*, with small minorities of pure Amerindians and Europeans. Spanish is the main language and the capital is San Salvador.

✦ CLIMATE

The coast is hot and humid, especially March to May, and is coolest from December to February. The tropical storm season lasts from June to November. This entire area is affected by the *papagayo*, a violent north or northeast wind whose effects can be felt as far as 150 miles offshore. *Papagayos* occur between October and April, with the worst period being between the end of November and the end of January.

✦ FORMALITIES

Boats are likely to be intercepted, and sometimes boarded, by Navy patrol boats while passing the Gulf of Fonseca. They will then be advised to proceed to a port of entry. You should maintain VHF contact with the Navy. Both Barillas Marina and Bahia del Sol Marina welcome cruising yachts and assist with clearance formalities. Acajutla is a commercial port not suitable for yachts.

Nationals of most countries do not require a visa in advance. A tourist visa card must be purchased on arrival, normally for 90 days. Under a new scheme, called the CA-4 visa, this is also valid for the neighbouring countries of Guatemala, Honduras and Nicaragua. You should request a cruising permit if planning to cruise El Salvadoran waters.

✦ FACILITIES

The marinas have a good range of the usual facilities and will assist with clearance and provisioning. Limited supplies are available in the two main ports, where simple repairs can be undertaken. The commercial port of Acajutla has a good range of workshops. There are also good workshops in San Salvador and a marine store with a small stock of equipment. They can also order parts from the USA. San Salvador is easiest to reach from Bahia del Sol.

PORTS OF ENTRY

Acajutla	13°36′N 89°50′W
Bahia del Sol Marina	13°15.9′N 88°53′W
Barillas Marina	13°15.63′N 88°28.52′W
Cutuco (La Union)	13°19′N 87°49′W

Cruising Guides
Explore Central America Part 1 (see Sarana website)
Cruiser Guide to Bahia del Sol (free from Sarana website)

Websites
www.elsalvador.travel   www.sailsarana.com/guide

Local time	UTC −6	**Electricity**	115V, 60Hz
Buoyage	IALA B		
Currency	Salvadoran Colon (SVC) US Dollar (USD)		

Diplomatic missions
UK	281 5555	Canada	2279 4655
USA	2501 2999	New Zealand	278 3372

Communications		**Emergency numbers**
IDD 503	IAC 00	911/112

GUATEMALA

Among the Central American nations, Guatemala stands out as the country that has most successfully preserved the language, customs and character of the original Maya population. The centre of Maya civilization encompassed this area, and some of the best-preserved sites are in Guatemala.

With coasts on both the Pacific and Caribbean Sea, sailors going to Guatemala find few attractions on the narrow west coast which is mostly low and featureless. It is the shorter Caribbean coast that draws most visiting yachts. There are several rivers that drain into the Caribbean Sea and are navigable for longer or shorter distances.

It is the Rio Dulce that gives sailors a chance to savour a different kind of cruising and it has been described as one of the most scenic rivers in the world. No wonder that the Rio Dulce is the ultimate destination of almost every yacht cruising this corner of the Caribbean. Boats with a draft of less than 1.8m (6ft) can negotiate the bar at the entrance to the Rio Dulce, after which the river virtually belongs to them. The impenetrable jungle comes down to the water's edge where there are small villages – almost hidden by the thick foliage – whose inhabitants, like their Maya predecessors, lead a tranquil life. The sheer cliffs of this green canyon lead into El Golfete, a small inland lake. Farther on, the river opens into Lake Izabal, whose entrance is guarded by the fort of San Felipe, now restored according to original plans found in the Spanish archives. Several marinas have been set up in these tranquil natural surroundings and they make good bases to visit some of the Mayan sites – foremost among them being Tikal. Surrounded by tropical rainforest, this is the largest site from the Maya classic period and in its heyday Tikal played a dominant role in the region.

◆ COUNTRY PROFILE

The Maya civilization developed at the beginning of the first millennium and flourished for several centuries in the area that covers present-day Guatemala, Belize, Honduras and parts of Mexico. The Mayans developed mathematics, architecture and writing, and at the height of their civilization they were equal to any developed society in the world. By the eleventh century, their advanced civilization started to disintegrate, with its total demise being hastened by the arrival of the Spanish. The Spanish colonial presence ended in 1821 when Guatemala gained full independence. Since then the history of Guatemala has been tempestuous, with a bloody conflict in the 1960s that caused the death of more than 100,000 people and made some 1 million people refugees. In recent years the situation has stabilized and life has returned to normal.

Of the 13.3 million inhabitants, more than half are Maya, with the rest of mixed origin. Spanish is the official language, with many indigenous languages and dialects being spoken. Guatemala City is the capital.

◆ CLIMATE

The climate is tropical, being hot and often humid. The Caribbean coast has a dry season in winter when it is occasionally affected by strong northers. Throughout the year the prevailing winds are easterly. The tropical storm season is June to November, with the Pacific coast being less exposed to hurricanes.

◆ FORMALITIES

PORTS OF ENTRY	
Caribbean coast: Livingston	15°39.41´N 88°59.9´W
Puerto Barrios	15°44´N 88°36´W
Santo Tomás de Castilla	15°42´N 88°37´W
Pacific coast: Champerico	14°18´N 91°55´W
Puerto Quetzal	13°55´N 90°47´W
San José	13°55´N 90°49´W

Livingston: There is a bar at the river entrance with a maximum depth of 1.80m (6ft). The reported position of the mid-channel marker is 15° 50.08´N 88° 43.89´W. Tidal information can be obtained on Channel 68. Yachts normally anchor off the commercial dock to be visited by various officials. The alternative is to go to La Marina where the office will assist with formalities.

Puerto Barrios: Yachts anchor south of the pier. Dinghies can be left at Tecno Marine. Entry formalities are completed at the nearby customs and immigration offices.

Santo Tomás: Authorities normally direct yachts to clear at nearby Puerto Barrios or Livingston.

Puerto Quetzal: Port Control should be contacted for berthing instructions. All formalities are completed at the naval basin.

Visas are not required by nationals of the EU, Australia, Canada, New Zealand, South Africa and the USA. A tourist visa card must be purchased on arrival, normally valid for 90 days. Under a new scheme, called the CA-4 visa, this is also valid for the neighbouring countries of Honduras, El Salvador and Nicaragua.

Yachts intending to spend longer than 30 days in Guatemala can be issued on arrival with a special 90-day permit that can be extended.

✦ FACILITIES

With the growth of yachting, the range of repair services is improving and there are several marinas along the Rio Dulce that cater for visiting vessels. There are three fuel docks on the Rio Dulce, and a fuel dock and marine stores in Livingston. Repair services, small boatyards and a travelift are available. All marinas stand by on Channel 68.

There is good provisioning and a fresh produce market in Puerto Barrios. Amatique Bay Resort and Marina also has a reasonable range of facilities, with repair services and marine supplies. Fuel is available from the ferry dock, but there is little depth alongside.

There have been a number of yacht boardings and robberies (and even one fatal attack) on cruising boats in the Rio Dulce area, so care should be taken by choosing a safe anchorage and preferably spending nights in marinas. The authorities have responded with a determined security enforcement programme and the situation has returned to normal.

✦ CHARTER

There are several local operators offering crewed yachts and they are best contacted via one of the marinas. Tropical Yachts has a small selection of catamarans.

www.tropicalyachts.com

Cruising Guides
The Northwest Caribbean, Vol I
Cruising Guide to Belize and Mexico's Caribbean Coast
  (includes Rio Dulce)
Explore Central America Part 1 – Guatemala (see Sarana
  website)

Websites
www.visitguatemala.com
www.mayaparadise.com (information for visiting yachts)
www.riodulce.net
www.sailsarana.com/central_american_guidebook.htm

Local time	UTC –6
Buoyage	IALA B
Currency	Guatemalan Quetzal (GTQ)
Electricity	120V, 60Hz

Diplomatic missions

UK	2380 7300
USA	2326 4000
Canada	2363 4348
New Zealand	2431 1705

Communications

IDD 502	IAC 00

Emergency numbers

1500 (bilingual operator)	Ambulance 123	Police 110

HONDURAS

HONDURAS HAS COASTLINES on both sides of Central America, while the interior is mountainous and sparsely populated. Its Pacific coast on the Gulf of Fonseca is only about 70 miles long compared to a 400-mile shoreline in the Caribbean. Although the mountainous Caribbean coast is scenically very attractive, it is not suitable for cruising as there are no protected anchorages. This is more than made up for by the Bay Islands (Islas de la Bahia), the country's prime cruising ground, whose popularity with yachts has increased steadily in recent years. Roatan, Utila and Guanaja are the main islands of this group of scattered isles, islets and cays which cover an area larger than the Virgin Islands, and with whom their scenic beauty is on a par. For those who find the Eastern Caribbean, and the Virgin Islands in particular, too crowded for their taste, the Bay Islands provide a perfect alternative. Until recently tourism has been low key, but this will probably change following the expansion of Roatan's airport. In order to visit some of the Mayan sites, such as Copan, it is best to leave the boat at the perfectly protected French Harbour Yacht Club on Roatan and fly to the mainland.

Honduras is one of the most ecologically aware nations in the Americas and has the region's largest remaining area of primeval forest. To protect this heritage, large tracts of land as well as coastal areas have been declared national parks. Much of the latter is along the Pacific coast where an interesting stop is El Tigre Island in the Gulf of Fonseca. The small archipelago surrounding the extinct volcano is part of a marine and terrestrial reserve.

Beach welcome in the Bay Islands.

✦ COUNTRY PROFILE

When the Spanish pushed east from Guatemala early in the sixteenth century, they found silver in Honduras, and it became part of Spain's vast empire in the New World. The capital, Tegucigalpa, whose name means 'silver mountain' (Taguz Galpan) in Mayan, was founded as a mining camp in 1578. Honduras became independent in 1821. The Bay Islands were only ceded to Honduras by Britain in 1859, hence their distinctly different atmosphere as their inhabitants are descendants of settlers from the Cayman Islands, Caribs deported from St Vincent, and a fair proportion of pirates, whose ships were based in these sheltered waters. Also part of Honduras is Swan Island, a naval base to which access is not permitted and therefore should be avoided.

The population numbers 7.8 million. The main language is Spanish, but English is spoken in the north and in the Bay Islands.

✦ CLIMATE

A subtropical climate, it is usually hot and humid, with an average high temperature of 32°C/90°F, and an average low of 20°C/68°F. Rain is frequent on the Caribbean coast all year round, but heaviest from September to December. The drier months are April to May, but these months are very hot.

The east and north coasts have strong northeast trade winds throughout the winter months. The best time to cruise the Bay Islands is at the end of winter or early spring when the northers of winter are no longer a problem. The hurricane season is from June to November.

✦ FORMALITIES

PORTS OF ENTRY	
Caribbean coast: Puerto Castilla	16°01´N 86°03´W
Puerto Cortés	15°51´N 87°56´W
La Ceiba	15°47´N 86°45´W
Tela	15°47´N 87°30´W
Puerto Lempira	15°16´N 83°46´W
Bay Islands: Roatan (Coxen's Hole)	16°18´N 86°35´W
Utila	16°16´N 86°40´W
Guanaja	16°28´N 85°54´W
Swan Island:	17°27´N 83°56´W
Pacific coast:	
San Lorenzo (Puerto de Henecan)	13°24´N 87°25´W
Amapala (El Tigre Island)	13°18´N 87°39´W

Roatan: Officials are used to dealing with yachts, so formalities are easier here. Sometimes the use of an agent is suggested by the authorities but it is not compulsory.

If the boat is not visited by officials, the captain and crew should report to the port captain and immigration offices, taking clearance papers from the last country visited.

Utila: Formalities are difficult to complete here and, if possible, Roatan should be preferred.

Puerto de Henecan: This has now replaced the shallow port of San Lorenzo as the country's main port. The port is reached via a long buoyed channel. Formalities are completed in the nearby town.

No visas are required for nationals of the EU, Australia, Canada, New Zealand or the USA. A tourist card must be purchased on arrival, normally valid for 90 days. Under a new scheme, called the CA-4 visa, this is also valid for the neighbouring countries of Guatemala, El Salvador and Nicaragua. Passports should be carried at all times as police do spot checks.

A cruising permit is issued by the port captain for 30 days. This can easily be extended, especially on the Pacific side, where the authorities seem happy to see more cruising yachts. Outward clearance must be obtained in each port before proceeding to the next.

On departure, exit clearance from the last port visited should be obtained and an exit stamp from immigration.

Most of the marine areas of Honduras are protected. Anchoring is prohibited in protected areas and the use of mooring buoys is free. All live and dead marine life is protected and must not be removed. Littering, spearguns, fishing nets, release of any toxic chemicals (including petroleum products) is prohibited. Protected areas are patrolled and the penalties for infringements are severe: impounding of the vessel, fines or a jail sentence.

✦ FACILITIES

Facilities have improved as more cruising boats visit Honduras. La Ceiba has two marinas, and also a range of mechanical workshops, chandleries and good provisioning.

In the Bay Islands, Roatan has fuel and the best provisioning and repair facilities. Guanaja and Utila also have a reasonable range of amenities. On the Pacific coast, Puerto de Henecan, near San Lorenzo, is a busy commercial port with some workshops. San Lorenzo itself is very well protected, even in bad weather, and is a popular stop among cruising sailors because of its good shops and friendly people. Only basic facilities are available at Amapala, and San Lorenzo is the better alternative.

✦ CHARTER

There are some crewed yachts for charter in the Bay Islands, but the nearest bareboat charter base is in Placencia, Belize.

Cruising Guide
Explore Central America Part 1 – Honduras (see Sarana website)

Websites
www.hondurastourism.com
www.roatanmarinepark.com
www.sailsarana.com/central_american_guidebook.htm

Local time	UTC –6
Buoyage	IALA B
Currency	Honduran Lempira (HNL)
Electricity	110V, 60Hz

Diplomatic missions			
UK	550 2337	Canada	232 4551
USA	236 9320		

Communications	
IDD 504	IAC 00

Emergency numbers		
112	Ambulance 195	Police 119

MEXICO

MEXICO HAS ALL THE INGREDIENTS of an ideal cruising destination: an ancient culture; a vibrant atmosphere unmatched anywhere else in America, south or north; and a landscape of varied scenery, from the high mountains of the interior to the silvery beaches lapped by the Pacific Ocean and Caribbean Sea. Mexico's principal cruising attractions are concentrated in three areas: the Yucatan Peninsula on the east coast, the Sea of Cortez, and the Mexican Riviera on the west coast. While Baja California's attractions compete between the stunning scenery and abundant wildlife that inhabits the limpid waters of the Sea of Cortez, the Yucatan's temptations lie mostly ashore, among the awe-inspiring ruins of the mighty Mayan empire.

✦ CARIBBEAN COAST

To sailors heading south from Florida, the Yucatan Peninsula and the offlying islands of Mujeres and Cozumel used to offer a sharp contrast to the urban scenery they had just left behind, but rapid tourist development has created a skyline similar to Miami on the formerly deserted beaches, bays and lagoons, where for centuries the tallest buildings were those of the Mayan temples. The 200 mile long Caribbean coast is fronted for much of its length by a fringing reef, occasionally broken by passes that lead to protected anchorages and a few marinas where the boat can be left unattended while visiting the interior. For those sailing south, Isla Mujeres is a convenient place to clear in and also a good introduction to the colourful Mexican ambience. Cozumel is a rather featureless island, but the surrounding reef offers great underwater scenery, especially the famous Palancar Reef. The best Mayan site within sailing distance is Tulum, close to which there is an anchorage that can be reached via a break in the reef. The ruins are quite impressive, but no match for the spectacular site of Chichen Itza located further inland.

✦ CLIMATE

The east coast climate is tropical, with hot dry summers and cooler pleasant winters. The Caribbean coast benefits from consistent winds, with east to southeast winds blowing between February and September, while winter winds are north to northeast. Along the Yucatan Peninsula winds tend to freshen in the afternoons and get lighter during the night. Cold weather systems occasionally reach the Yucatan during winter, and some of these northers can be quite violent. Summer coincides with the hurricane season, June to November, and it is believed that the word 'hurricane' is of Mayan origin as the ancient Quinche people of Guatemala worshipped Hurakan, a fearsome deity of torrential rainstorms and violent thunderstorms.

✦ PACIFIC COAST

For many years the Sea of Cortez has been the preferred foreign destination for Californian sailors, a place so near and yet so far from their own highly developed home. The distances on the Pacific coast are long, but prevailing northwest winds make a voyage south from the USA quite painless, in contrast to the return voyage. There are several good ports as well as a number of sheltered anchorages along the west coast of Baja California, where those who do not wish to sail non-stop can break up the voyage, provided they have cleared into Mexico first, with the conveniently located Ensenada being a favourite landfall for this very reason.

The Sea of Cortez is a world in itself, with many areas of outstanding natural beauty and cruising opportunities to match. There are scores of attractive anchorages both along the east coast of the peninsula and around the offshore islands. The beautiful Bahia de la Paz and the nearby protected islands of Isla Espiritu Santo and Isla Partida are gems that provide in a relatively small area everything you expect to find. Farther north the scenery is dominated by the powerful colours of Sierra de la Giganta, the dry-blood red so typical of Baja California. Another stunning location is Loreto, which is yet another example of why the Sea of Cortez fully deserves such superlatives.

Although it is possible to sail along the eastern side of the Sea of Cortez in daily stages, as there are anchorages and ports along the way, this section of the mainland is far less attractive than the western Baja side, and many prefer to stay offshore. One interesting stop is Topolobampo, a good base from which to visit the impressive Copper Canyon. A last opportunity to spend some time in a natural environment before reaching busy Mazatlán or Puerto Vallarta are Las Tres Marietas, three small uninhabited islands and a bird sanctuary.

Another popular offshore stop between Mazatlán and Puerto Vallarta is Isla Isabella, a national park that has been compared to the Galapagos Islands. Just as in the Galapagos, the large colonies of blue-footed boobies, frigate birds and iguanas have no fear of humans.

Past Puerto Vallarta, the Pacific Riviera shoreline is punctuated by high mountains and provides some of the most interesting cruising on Mexico's west coast, with many pretty anchorages protected from the prevailing northwest wind. South of Manzanilla the scenery becomes less attractive and there is also less choice of anchorages until one reaches Acapulco, with its spectacular harbour and tourist resorts. The notable exceptions are the popular Zihuatanejo anchorage and the nearby marina at Ixtapa. The best choices south of Acapulco are Bahia Dulce, Punta Galera, Puerto Escondido, Puerto Angel and the attractive area around Huatulco which is peppered with several calm coves.

There is a regular annual migration between the Sea of Cortez and Mexico's Pacific Riviera as sailors head south for the winter season to enjoy tropical, moderate weather and warm water. The trend is reversed in the spring, when the northwesterly winter winds lose their bite and the weather and water get warmer in the Sea of Cortez as the summer's calms or southeasterly winds become predominant.

Less than 400 miles off Mexico's western coast lie a group of islands rarely visited from the mainland, except by yachts on passage to the South Pacific. Of the four Islas de Revillagigedo, only two, Socorro and Clarión, are inhabited; Partida is just a rock, while San Benedicto was devastated by a volcanic eruption in 1952. The lack of rainfall has resulted in an arid landscape, in contrast to the rich underwater scenery. Diving here is an exhilarating experience as the waters teem with giant mantas, fish of all kinds, and also sharks – reportedly of the curious rather than aggressive kind. The islands are a protected area and in 2009 the Mexican government lifted the requirement for the expensive permit allowing yachts to anchor here.

Even more remote, and the subject of a long dispute with France, is Clipperton Atoll lying some 700 miles off the Mexican coast. The lagoon has no pass, but the few yachts that stop can shelter in the lee of the reef. Landing through the surf is sometimes difficult, but the diving on the surrounding reef makes up for it.

◆ CLIMATE

The west coast climate is tropical and it can often be very hot between May and October, which is also the hurricane season (June to November). The prevailing winds are northwesterlies that become less consistent towards the south. Summer winds are occasionally from the south. A local phenomenon is the *chubasco*, which is a violent wind that occurs mostly in summer and early autumn and affects the entire Pacific coast. It is at its worst in the Sea of Cortez where it can gust up to 70 knots. A *chubasco*, which actually means 'squall' in Spanish, often strikes at night. A similarly dreaded local wind affects the Gulf of Tehuantepec, and sailors call it the *tehuantepecer*. Such winds can occur throughout the year, with the worst period being between December and February. Winds can reach hurricane force in a relatively short time and with very little warning.

◆ COUNTRY PROFILE

In the last 4,000 years, Mexico has enjoyed a succession of civilizations and has over one thousand archaeological sites to show for it. Before the arrival of the Spanish conquistadors, several highly developed and complex civilizations had risen to power and fallen. Huge ceremonial cities were built, the centralized states being based on the autocratic rule of a small elite over a people bound by strong family and community ties. By the sixteenth century, the flourishing Aztec empire, with its capital at Tenochtitlan, had succeeded the Mayas. An estimated 20 million people populated Mexico at that time. This flourishing civilization was brought to an abrupt end by the arrival of the Spanish conquistador Hernando Cortez, whose small band of men defeated the Aztecs, took over Tenochtitlan and then slowly the rest of the country. The colony of New Spain remained under Spanish control for the next 300 years. The War of Independence brought an end to Spanish domination and in 1821 Mexico became a fully independent nation. In the following years, large tracts of territory were lost to the expanding USA, including Texas, present-day California and New Mexico. Between 1911 and 1920 revolution and civil war tore the country apart, with Pancho Villa and Emiliano Zapata being the popular heroes. The fierce conflict resulted in a federation of 31 states based on a social democratic constitution.

The population is 111 million. Mestizos, mixed Spanish and Amerindian, form the bulk of the population, while Amerindians comprise over fifty different ethnic groups. The official language is Spanish and there are various Amerindian languages. The capital is Mexico City, built on the site of the former Aztec capital, Tenochtitlan.

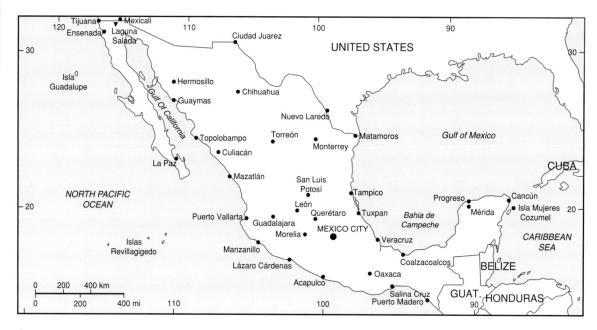

✦ FORMALITIES

On arrival in Mexico, yachts must go to the nearest port of entry. Formalities can be time-consuming, but for those who prefer to avoid this, there are agents in the major ports who will deal with the formalities for a fee, as will some of the marinas. Normally immigration must be cleared first, then customs, quarantine (not always requested), and finally the port authority. Where there is not a port authority, you may have to report to the Navy.

Caribbean coast

Isla Mujeres: The usual anchorage is south of the Mexican Navy base, but there is also an anchorage off Tiburon Island. Formalities are relatively simple as all offices are within walking distance on the main street opposite the ferry quay.

A health inspection is carried out at the local hospital. The Navy sometimes inspects vessels in the harbour.

Cozumel: Yachts anchor at San Miguel, on the north side of the commercial dock, which is used by large ferries so yachts cannot come alongside. The anchorage is uncomfortable in westerlies and strong northers. The easier alternative is to go directly to the yacht club marina which has an agent who deals with all necessary formalities.

Xcalak: There is a port captain's office but no immigration, so you should check in with the police instead. The Navy may inspect the boat.

Pacific coast

Ensenada: Boats either anchor inside the breakwater or dock at Pirates Pier marina.

PORTS OF ENTRY

Caribbean coast: Altamira	22°25´N 97°55´W	Tampico	22°13´N 97°53´W	Isla Mujeres	21°10´N 86°43´W
Progreso	21°17´N 89°40´W	Cancún	21°08´N 86°46´W	Cozumel	20°30´N 86°58´W
Campeche	19°51´N 90°33´W	Veracruz	19°12´N 96°08´W	Alvarado	18°46´N 95°46´W
Ciudad del Carmen	18°39´N 91°51´W	Frontera	18°37´N 92°41W	Chetumal	18°30´N 88°17´W
Xcalak	18°16´N 87°49´W	Coatzacoalcos	18°09´N 94°25´W		
Pacific coast: Ensenada	31°51N 116°38´W	Cedros Island	28°03´N 115°11´W	Cabo San Lucas	22°50´N 109°55´W
La Paz	24°10´N 110°19´W	Santa Rosalia	27°20´N 112°16´W	Guaymas	27°54´N 110°52´W
Topolobambo	25°32´N 109°06´W	Mazatlán	23°11´N 106°26´W	San Blas	21°32´N 105°19´W
Chacala	21°10´N 105°14´W	Puerto Vallarta	20°37´N 105°16´W	Manzanillo	19°03´N 104°20´W
Lázaro Cárdenas	17°55´N 102°11´W	Zihuatenejo	17°37´N 101°33´W	Acapulco	16°50´N 99°55´W
Puerto Escondido	15°51´N 97°06´W	Puerto Angel	15°39´N 96°31´W	Salina Cruz	16°10´N 95°11´W
Puerto Madero	14°42´N 92°27´W	**Islas de Revillagigedo:** 18°42´N 110°58´W			

Formalities are completed at a new facility that houses all officials in one office. It is highly recommended that boats coming from the USA stop here as formalities have been greatly streamlined. The office is called Centro Integral de Servicios (CIS) and includes customs, immigration, port captain, fishing licence officer, and even a bank to take care of all clearing procedures in one convenient office.

La Paz: Yachts should proceed through the buoyed channel, which is is easier to negotiate in daylight. The best anchorage is south of the municipal pier, but there is also an anchorage off Mogote beach. All offices are close to the municipal pier. Because of the precarious anchoring conditions, it may be preferable to proceed to one of the marinas and arrange formalities from there.

Mazatlán: Yachts anchor where convenient and dinghies can be left at one of the yacht agencies on the waterfront. Frequent buses go into town where the offices of immigration and port captain are situated. Boats on short stays can clear in and out at the same time.

Puerto Vallarta: Marina Vallarta is a convenient place to complete formalities.

Acapulco: Yachts can either anchor outside or arrange a berth in the Yacht Club Marina. The yacht club facilities can be used by visitors and the yacht club can arrange clearance formalities.

Salina Cruz: This commercial port is not recommended for yachts.

Puerto Madero: This is the last port on the Pacific coast for those going south. Yachts may anchor in the outer fishing harbour.

Islas de Revillagigedo: Yachts should clear with the Navy, which has a garrison on the main island of Socorro.

It is recommended to arrive with a tourist card (FMT) for every crew member, obtained in advance from a Mexican consulate or tourist office abroad. If not, you should go first to the immigration office where the FMT can be obtained. The card is valid for six months and allows multiple entries. Nationals of European countries, Australia, Canada, New Zealand and the USA are eligible for a tourist card, but some other nationalities may need a visa, preferably also obtained in advance. Particularly if coming from Belize, it is advisable to arrive in Mexico either with a tourist card or visa secured in advance. These can be obtained from the Mexican consul in Belize City.

The captain should then proceed to customs where he or she will be issued with a temporary import permit. These permits are valid for ten years, but are only issued at major ports of entry, such as Ensenada and La Paz. The permit is requested by all marinas and boatyards on the west coast.

As well as the ship's papers, the captain should have six crew lists in Spanish. Crew list forms in Spanish can be obtained before arrival from a Mexican consulate – or on arrival. Every official will stamp and sign all the crew lists and will keep a copy. You should list on the import permit as many places as you might wish to visit. This may ease the paperwork until the final exit clearance.

According to the latest regulations, once a yacht has formally cleared into Mexico at an official port of entry, the only requirement at subsequent ports is that the vessel notifies the port captain's office or an authorized marina of its arrival and departure. The information required is the vessel's name, last port of call or port of destination, changes in crew, and vessel documentation or registration number. Depending on the port, the report can be done in person or over the radio. Departure certificates are no longer needed.

After several hurricanes caused extensive damage to unattended boats that were found to be uninsured, port authorities, marinas and boatyards require all visiting yachts to have at least liability insurance.

Each person on board must have a fishing licence. Spot checks are made, and simply having fishing tackle on board is considered sufficient reason to have a licence. The licences can be obtained in advance from the Mexican Fisheries Department in San Diego, California, or on arrival from the local fisheries department.

Leaving the yacht in Mexico for over six months is possible if it is left in a marina, and if the owner is a foreign national and not resident in Mexico. The owner or his legal representative must visit the yacht at least once a year to renew the custody.

A national park pass must be purchased by all visiting yachts; this gives access to all national parks, including those in the Sea of Cortez and Islas Revillagigedo.

A permit is necessary to stop at Isla Contoy, north of Isla Mujeres, which is a nature reserve. The permit can be obtained from the office of the nature reserve, located in Rueda Medina on Isla Mujeres.

On final departure from Mexico, the port captain, customs and immigration must be visited with six copies of

The anchorage at Bahia Cobre on Isla Carmen.

the crew list, and a departure clearance form obtained from the port captain. Although this document may not be requested when clearing into the next country, it will have to be shown if stopped by a Mexican Navy boat while still in Mexican waters. If wishing to stop anywhere in Mexico after clearing out, this should be written down by the relevant official on the outward clearance. Occasionally the port authority insists on a health inspection before issuing a clearance certificate for an international destination. The tourist card must be returned on clearing out.

✦ FACILITIES

All major ports visited by cruising yachts have a reasonable range of services and the majority of routine repairs can be dealt with locally. In most places there is good provisioning, with both supermarkets and fresh produce markets. Fuel is available almost everywhere, and that bought from the Pemex docks is clean, but occasionally fuel delivered in drums can be dirty. The port captain in some ports is in charge of fuelling, and a permit may be needed either from him or from customs.

On the Caribbean side the yacht club in Cozumel is run as a marina and has fuel and water, a haulout facility, and some small workshops that can undertake simple repairs. Puerto Morelos has a good boatyard and repair facilities. There are daily air trips to the Maya ruins on the mainland, which can also be reached by taking the ferry to Playa del Carmen and thence by bus or taxi to the ruins. Isla Mujeres is another place where yachts can be left while visiting the Mayan sites on the Yucatan peninsula. Puerto Isla Mujeres Marina is in the protected Laguna Makax and has good repair facilities and a 70-ton travelift. Puerto Aventuras Marina, a new large resort near Cancun and the international airport, is also recommended as a place where a yacht can be left safely.

On the Pacific side La Paz is a major gathering point for yachts wintering in the Sea of Cortez and there are excellent repair facilities with four shipyards capable of handling all jobs, and five good marinas with several chandleries, fuel, and all the usual services. In Manzanillo, fuel and water are available on the dock, good provisioning in the neighbouring town, as well as various workshops, engine repairers and spares. Mexican charts can be bought at the Instituto Oceanigrafico in Las Brisas. At Puerto Vallarta there is a chandlery at the new marina. Opequimar offers a complete range of repair services as well as a 30-ton travelift. Acapulco's yacht club has a wide range of services for visiting yachts; there are also good facilities at La Marina in Acapulco. Other marinas on Mexico's west coast, where good facilities have been reported, are at Cabo San Lucas, Marina San Carlos, Mazatlán, Puerto Vallarta and Marina Ixtapa, north of Zihuatenejo.

Most insurance companies require boats to be out of the hurricane area between 15 May and 31 October. For this reason, the area between San Carlos and Guaymas in the Sea of Cortez has become very popular for storing boats during the summer as it is above 27°N. There are many reasonably priced dry storage locations capable of storing hundreds of boats.

✦ CHARTER

The Moorings has the largest operation from its base in La Paz, in the Sea of Cortez. There are several smaller operators, with only some of those in the Baja area listed. Also listed are some companies offering crewed yachts from their bases in Acapulco and Puerto Vallarta.

www.moorings.com
www.tourbaja.com
www.fraseryachts.com

www.seascapecharters.com
www.bajaseafaris.com
www.myursamajor.com

Cruising Guides

Cruising Guide to Belize and Mexico's Caribbean Coast
Mexico Boating Guide
MexWX – Pacific Mexico Weather for Cruisers
Sea of Cortez
Sea of Cortez Cruising Guide, Vol II
Spanish for Cruisers
Western Coast of Mexico
Crew List for Spanish Speaking Countries (on the Sarana website)

Websites

www.visitmexico.com
www.latitudemexico.com (information for visiting yachts)
www.exploringcortez.com
www.sailsarana.com/guide

Local time	Three time zones: UTC –6 , UTC –7, UTC –8
	Summer time: first Sunday in April to last Sunday in October
Buoyage	IALA B
Currency	Mexican Peso (MXN)
Electricity	127V, 60Hz

Diplomatic missions

UK	55 5242 8500
USA	55 5080 2000
Australia	55 1101 2200
Canada	55 5724 7980
South Africa	55 5282 9260
New Zealand	55 5283 9460

Communications	Emergency numbers
IDD 52 IAC 98	Ambulance 065 Police 060

NICARAGUA

NICARAGUA is the largest Central American state, lying between Costa Rica and Honduras with coasts on both the Pacific Ocean and the Caribbean Sea. For many years Nicaragua was avoided by cruising yachts, but the improved political situation is persuading more sailors to include Nicaragua in their plans. The shallow reef-encumbered Mosquito (or Miskito) coast on the Caribbean side has many attractive anchorages, but navigation is difficult, so most yachts restricted their cruising to the more accessible Corn Islands. Part of this coast is a nature reserve and a special permit is needed to visit the Miskito Cays.

✦ COUNTRY PROFILE

Nicaragua was under Guatemalan jurisdiction until it gained independence from Spain in 1838. The twentieth century was characterized by the nationalist movement, originally led by General Sandino, which gained power in 1979. The US sponsored contra-guerrillas through the 1980s, and later elections saw the Sandinistas defeated. The Sandinista President Daniel Ortega regained power in 2006.

The Miskito kingdom in the Caribbean lowlands was a British protectorate until the end of the nineteenth century. Following the Sandinista revolution, the Miskito Indians fought for self-determination, and this coastal area, including the Corn Islands, has been self-governing since 1987. English is spoken here and the African influence is noticeable. The 5.9 million inhabitants are of Amerindian, African and European origins. Spanish is the main language. The capital is Managua.

✦ CLIMATE

The climate is humid and hot, with December to May being the dry months, while June and October are the wettest. Violent northerly winds can occur in winter, particularly on the Caribbean coast. The coasts are sometimes affected by tropical storms, the season lasting from June to November. The worst local phenomenon is the *papagayo*, a violent north or northeast wind occurring between October and April and which can be felt as far as 150 miles offshore.

✦ FORMALITIES

Corinto: All offices are in the port area, and formalities, while lengthy, can be done by the captain, although there are local agents who will also do it. The alternative is to go to Marina Puesta del Sol which will arrange clearance for a fee.

San Juan del Sur: The port captain's office is located within the shipyard compound and there is now a local immigration official, so all formalities can be completed locally.

El Bluff: Yachts should dock at the customs wharf.

No visas are required for nationals of most countries. A tourist visa card must be purchased on arrival, normally for 90 days. Under a new scheme, called the CA-4 visa, this is also valid for the neighbouring countries of Guatemala, Honduras and El Salvador.

To visit the Corn Islands, Bluefields and Puerto Cabezas, a permit must be obtained in Managua.

PORTS OF ENTRY

Caribbean coast: El Bluff	12°01′N 83°44′W
Pacific coast: Corinto	12°28′N 87°11′W
Marina Puesta del Sol	12°37.5′N 87°20.5′W
Puerto Sandino	12°11′N 86°47′W
San Juan del Sur	11°15′N 85°53′W

✦ FACILITIES

The Pacific coast has seen more development, with marinas opening and others planned. Marina Puesta del Sol is part of an attractive resort. There are simple repair facilities in most ports, but the most satisfactory services are found in San Juan del Sur, which has two boatyards. Provisioning with fresh produce, and shopping in supermarkets, is best in the town of Corinto, but there are well-stocked stores in most places.

Cruising Guide
Explore Central America Part 1 – Nicaragua (see Sarana website)

Websites
www.visitnicaragua.com   www.sailsarana.com/guide

Local time UTC –6		**Currency** Nicaraguan Cordoba (NIO)	
Buoyage IALA B		**Electricity** 120V, 60Hz	

Diplomatic missions
UK 254 5454	Canada 268 0433	USA 252 7100

Communications	**Emergency numbers**
IDD 505 IAC 00	911 Ambulance 128 Police 118

PANAMA

PANAMA IS A COUNTRY that lies at the world's crossroads, a narrow isthmus dividing the Atlantic from the Pacific Ocean and linking the two halves of the American continent. The country is dominated by the Panama Canal, with Cristóbal on the Caribbean side and Balboa on the Pacific being the two main ports and gateways to the canal. The port of Cristóbal incorporates the town of Colón. The recent opening of marinas on both sides of the canal has greatly improved the docking situation and has also allowed sailors in transit to visit the little-known interior of this interesting country.

In recent years there has been a hardening of attitude towards cruising yachts caused by the canal running at full capacity and pleasure craft (or handliners in Panama Canal parlance) being regarded by the Panama Canal Authority as low priority. Although transit fees have been raised twice in recent years, according to the Authority they still do not cover the actual cost of the operation. Because the canal can barely cope with the large numbers of ships, waiting times at either end of the canal have been getting longer. At peak times (February to March) some yachts have had to wait for one month, although this can be speeded up by the use of a local agent who can book a transit time in advance.

Where Panama scores highest among visitors is on the shopping side, with very attractive prices for outboards and electronics in the duty-free area at Colón, while Panama City stands out as an excellent place to victual a boat for a long passage and, for those who have been cruising in the islands, to enjoy its wide range of excellent restaurants whose cuisine reflects the city's cosmopolitan background.

The main cruising attraction in Panama are the 365 San Blas Islands off the Caribbean coast. These islands are the home of the Kuna Indians, who have preserved a traditional way of life and their distinctive handicrafts are a popular souvenir among visiting sailors. An interesting stop on the way to the canal is Portobelo, the oldest Spanish town in Panama and once the starting point for the caravels loaded with treasure that were leaving the Spanish Main for home. Several colonial buildings have survived from that golden era, among them the old customs house and the mighty San Lorenzo fortress. The main local curiosity is the Black Christ, a wooden statue with reputed miraculous powers and which attracts pilgrims to Portobelo's cathedral.

A little visited corner of Panama is the Boca del Toro archipelago, close to the frontier with Costa Rica. Among

Looking west from Pedro Miguel lock towards Miraflores locks, the Bridge of the Americas and the Pacific Ocean.

the most interesting places to visit is Bluefield Lagoon, a large bay with several good anchorages. The name should not be confused with that of the town in Nicaragua, as both come from a notorious Dutch pirate, Abraham Blauvelt, who once roamed these waters. The local people are mostly of African origin and settled here during the building of the Panama Canal when workers arrived from all over the Caribbean. They speak English as well as the local dialect of Guariguari, related to Jamaican.

On the Pacific side, the Las Perlas Islands are another unspoilt cruising ground, making an attractive stop for boats after transiting the canal.

✦ COUNTRY PROFILE

The name 'Panama' means 'abundance of fish' in the local Amerindian dialect. The San Blas coast was discovered in 1501 by Roderigo de Bastidas, and Christopher Columbus visited the islands the following year. It was in 1513, however, that the country's fate was decided, when Vasco Nuñez de Balboa crossed the isthmus and sighted the Pacific Ocean. Panama City was founded on the Pacific side and became the starting point for Spanish conquests, which fanned out north and south along the Pacific coast. All trade from the Pacific ports had to be taken overland across the isthmus, then heavily escorted ships laden with treasure left for Spain, returning later with European goods. This route was continually being attacked, and finally in the mid-eighteenth century Spain abandoned the overland route for the one around Cape Horn.

During the Californian Gold Rush, the land route was again used for transport and a railway was built across the isthmus, completed in the mid-nineteenth century with a

great loss of life. A canal was the obvious solution and Ferdinand de Lesseps, who had successfully built the Suez Canal, started work in 1882. However, this project failed after tropical diseases killed thousands of workers. In 1903 Panama declared its independence from Colombia, and work on a canal started again under US supervision. The first canal passage was finally made in 1914. The former Canal Zone was a 10 mile wide ribbon of land under US control and included the ports of Cristóbal and Balboa. In 1979 the Canal Zone was transferred to Panamanian sovereignty, and the ownership of the Panama Canal itself was transferred to Panama on 31 December 1999.

The Panama Canal is one of the wonders of the modern world and transiting it is a unique experience. Its total length is 50 miles and runs in a northwest to southwest direction, which means that the Pacific entrance lies farther east than the Caribbean one. It requires about nine hours for the average ship to transit the canal. Coming from the east, a Pacific-bound vessel is raised 26m (85ft) in a series of three steps at Gatún Locks. Each lock chamber is 34m (110ft) wide and 305m (1,000ft) long. Gatún Lake, through which ships have to travel for 23.5 miles from Gatún Locks to the end of the Gaillard Cut, is one of the largest artificial lakes in the world. It was formed by an earth dam across the Chagres river. At the southern end of Gaillard Cut ships enter the Pedro Miguel Lock and are lowered 9.5m (31ft) in one step to Miraflores Lake, a small artificial lake that separates the two sets of Pacific locks. Finally, ships are lowered the remaining two steps to sea level at Miraflores Locks, which are slightly over 1 mile in length. The lock gates at Miraflores are the highest of any in the system because of the extreme tidal variations in the Pacific Ocean.

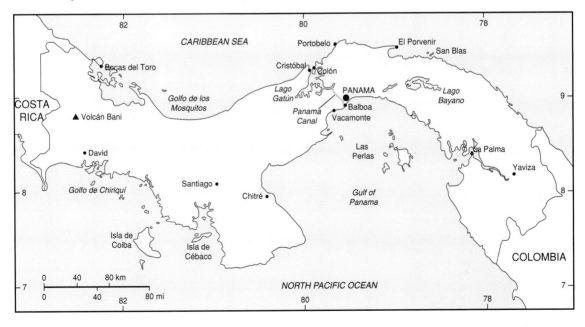

The population numbers 3.4 million. The Kuna Indians of the San Blas Islands are descendants of the Caribs, who originally peopled much of the Caribbean. The Kunas are one of the few groups to survive the arrival of the Europeans. The San Blas Islands enjoy a measure of autonomy within the state of Panama. Spanish and English are the main languages. Panama City is the capital.

◆ CLIMATE

The climate is hot and very humid, although cooled by the prevailing easterly winds. The dry season is January to April, and rain can be heavy in October and November. The Caribbean coast is twice as wet as the Pacific coast. Temperatures are high throughout the year, with an average annual temperature of 27°C/81°F. The highest average temperatures have been recorded between March and May (36°C/97°F). Panama is not affected by hurricanes.

◆ FORMALITIES

PORTS OF ENTRY	
Cristóbal 9°21´N 79°55´W	Balboa 8°57´N 79°34´W
San Blas Islands: Porvenir 9°34´N 78°57´W	
Rio Diablo 9°26.48´N 78°35.24´W	

The law concerning the pre-registration of visiting vessels is now being enforced for yachts. This requires details about the yacht and its crew to be sent to the Panamanian authorities at least 48 hours before arrival at any Panamanian port. This information may be sent by email or by filling in the online form available on the official website.

Arriving yachts should contact Cristóbal Signal Station on the Caribbean side or Flamenco Signal Station on the Pacific side. Both stations operate on Channel 12 and will give instructions on how to proceed. After clearance, the boat may anchor at a designated anchorage or move to one of the marinas. On the Caribbean side there is Shelter Bay Marina or the yacht anchorage on the Flats Area F. Since the demolition of the Panama Canal Yacht Club, boats have also

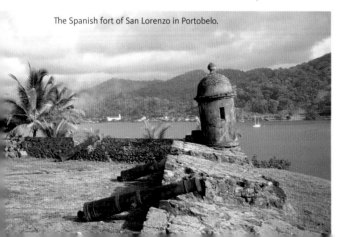

The Spanish fort of San Lorenzo in Portobelo.

been allowed to anchor behind D dock. On the Pacific side there are more choices: Flamenco Marina has a number of slips for visitors, while the Balboa Yacht Club, located close to the entrance of the canal on the east side of the channel, has swing moorings. There are also various anchorages: on the west side of the causeway between Perico and Flamenco Islands, or, depending on the wind, on the east side of the causeway. Another anchorage is south of Isla Culebra, on the west side of the causeway, called Mi Playita.

Arrangements can then be made for the transit of the canal. It is possible to complete all formalities oneself, or with the help of a local agent. If the latter is preferred, such an agent should be contacted well in advance to book a firm date for the transit.

Porvenir: The customs and immigration office is at the airport. There is a small anchorage close by.
Rio Diablo: Formalities are completed at the police station.

Visas are not required for most European countries. Nationals of Australia, Canada, Japan, New Zealand and the USA are issued a tourist card. This is valid for 30 days, but can be extended.

On arrival, the port authority will issue a cruising permit, which is needed whether transiting the Canal or not. A yacht may remain in Panama for up to 90 days, but in exceptional circumstances this can be extended. Boats that need to spend longer in Panama must obtain a supporting letter from a yacht club, marina or boatyard to present to the authorities. Yachts planning to sail to the San Blas Islands after transiting the canal should make sure that they receive a cruising permit for the islands. Yachts clearing in Cristóbal that do not intend to stop in Balboa, can clear out of Panama in Cristóbal, but they must do this one working day before transiting the canal. If intending to stop at Las Perlas, this should be mentioned on the clearance paper.

An international yellow fever vaccination certificate is sometimes requested.

PROCEDURE FOR TRANSITING THE PANAMA CANAL

After clearing into Panama, the captain must contact the Admeasures Office by calling, on the Pacific side, Flamenco Signal Station on Channel 12 or direct by telephone 272 4571, or, on the Atlantic side, Cristóbal Signal Station, or telephone 443 2293 to make an appointment for an inspection of the boat. Transit fees are based on LOA and a buffer deposit must also be made to cover any unforeseen costs, but this is usually refunded within six weeks. Fees are paid only at Citibank in either Cristóbal or Balboa, and no longer directly to the Panama Canal Commission. Payments can be made either in cash or by bank transfer. Such transfers can

Centre-locked yachts are moved in the lock with the help of a linehandler.

only be arranged after the vessel has been provided with a SIN (Ship Identification Number), which must be quoted in the transfer.

The captain must then report to the Canal Operations Captain's Office. This officer will explain the requirements needed for the transit and that the yacht should be able to maintain a minimum of 5 knots under power. If it becomes apparent at the start of the transit that the yacht is doing less than 5 knots, it will have to return to the starting point and will be charged for an aborted transit. Yachts with no engines can be towed through the canal by a PCA launch, with all towing charges to be paid by the yacht owner.

The captain will then be given a provisional time for the transit. This must be confirmed or changed by calling Marine Traffic Control, Tel: 292 4202, or VHF Channel 12. Final arrangements must be made no later than 24 hours before the scheduled transit time. Unless a yacht can sustain 8 knots, normally the transit takes two days. For a southbound (Caribbean to Pacific) transit, the adviser normally comes on board in the afternoon and the yacht spends the night in Lake Gatún. The adviser then returns early the following morning to complete the transit. For the northbound transit, the adviser arrives very early in the morning, so normally the transit is done in one day, if the boat is capable of maintaining a high enough speed to make this possible. If not, as for southbound transits, the adviser will return the following day.

The yacht will be charged a delay fee if, for whatever reason, the transit is not cancelled by the captain before the close of working hours on the day before the scheduled

transit or if the yacht is unable to commence the transit. Yachts are required to maintain their transit schedule regardless of weather conditions. Using an agent will simplify and speed up formalities considerably. The transit fee can be remitted in advance to the agent, who will make all necessary arrangements including booking a transit date.

Types of lockage

There are three different types of lockage in the canal, and all vessels must be capable of making a centre chamber lockage. Other types are sidewall or alongside a PCA tug. Whether a yacht is assigned a sidewall or centre chamber lockage is decided by the admeasurer, but the final decision will be made by the adviser, as this will depend on the situation at the time of lockage.

Centre chamber lockage: The vessel is held in the centre of the chamber by two bow and two stern lines. Yachts are sometimes rafted together.

Sidewall lockage: Only two 40m (120ft) lines are required; lots of fenders as well as suitable spring lines will be needed as the walls are rough concrete. Care should also be taken of the rigging, which may hit the walls in the turbulence that occurs mostly when uplocking.

Sidewall is acceptable for downlocking, as there is minimal turbulence and only two lines are used. This is also the only way that yachts can lock after dark, and makes it possible to complete the transit in only one day. Sidewall uplocking is not advised except alongside a tug.

Alongside a tug: Two 15m (50ft) lines will be required. This type of lockage is recommended for uplocking.

Tied alongside a tug.

Each yacht must have four linehandlers in addition to a helmsman. All lines, chocks and cleats should be inspected to ensure they are in good condition, as they will be under heavy strain during the transit. The area around the fittings must be clear of gear so that the lines can be efficiently handled.

✦ FACILITIES

The Panama Canal Yacht Club in Colón has been demolished, although its dinghy dock is still being used by yachts anchored in the harbour. This has resulted in Shelter Bay Marina often being full, with boats moored to a floating barge near the marina entrance. Docking facilities on the Pacific side are limited, although it may be possible to get a vacant slip at Flamenco Marina. There is a marina in Panama City itself, but it is tidal and has severe draft restrictions. The Balboa Yacht Club is being rebuilt but yachts can use the existing moorings and launch service. It is also possible to anchor either behind Naos Island, by the causeway, or out at Taboga Island. There are ferries from the latter into Panama City.

Provisioning is very good in both Colón and Panama City, and there are several supermarkets with a plentiful selection. There is a good range of repair facilities at both ends of the Canal, with several workshops providing a wide scope of services. Facilities in the San Blas and Las Perlas are very limited.

✦ CHARTER

There are a number of local operators offering crewed charters. San Blas Sailing has a mixed fleet of sailing monohulls and catamarans, and has been operating in San Blas for over ten years.

www.sanblassailing.com
www.theandiamo.com

Cruising Guides
Explore Central America Part II
The Panama Cruising Guide

Websites
www.panamatours.com
www.amp.gob.pa/atraque/CaptaCartaAtraqueYates.aspx
  (online arrival form)
www.pancanal.com (Panama Canal Authority). This features a
  live video feed from Miraflores locks so that it is now
  possible to view a canal transit on the internet.

Local time	UTC −5
Buoyage	IALA B
Currency	Panamanian Balboa (PAB), US Dollar (USD). The two currencies normally trade at parity and are locally interchangeable.
Electricity	110V, 60Hz

Diplomatic missions
UK	269 0866
USA	207 7000
Canada	264 9731

Communications
IDD 507	IAC 00

Emergency number
911

Typical San Blas anchorage.

UNITED STATES OF AMERICA

Fort Adams in Newport Harbour is the largest coastal fortification in the USA.

SPANNING THE NORTH AMERICAN continent between the Atlantic and Pacific Oceans, the USA is not a major cruising destination for foreign yachts and, with the exception of Canadian boats, the number who visit this great country is comparatively small. Such sailors include European yachts making a detour on the way home from the Caribbean, and occasionally a North European yacht that has braved the elements to cross the North Atlantic as part of a summer cruise. Being so remote from any sailing nation, except Canada, the west coast is even less frequented.

This is surprising as the USA has much to offer sailors, particularly the east coast, the entire length of which can be cruised from the Florida Keys to Maine. Sailing along this coast also has the added attraction of the Intracoastal Water-way, a unique system of canals, rivers and estuaries that stretches along most of the eastern seaboard, offering the chance of sailing up or down the coast in sheltered waters but often within sight of the ocean. For the foreign sailor, Florida is a perfect introduction to the USA and some of its best-known attractions are close by, such as the Kennedy Space Centre or, for the younger crew, Disney World. The waterways of the southern states wind their way through old cities, deserted estuaries and eerily silent woods to reach Chesapeake

Bay. This, the largest bay in the USA, has a shoreline of thousands of miles, and secluded anchorages and snug harbours are within striking distance of some of the USA's largest cities. A couple of days' sail up the coast, at the confluence of the Hudson and East rivers, lies New York, one of the few cities in the world where you can sail right through its centre. Having passed under the Verrazano Bridge and being greeted by the unmistakable Statue of Liberty, those planning to continue coastal cruising now head for the East River. Passing almost within touching distance of Manhattan's skyscrapers and under the many bridges, this is an experience that cannot be repeated.

New Yorkers are within easy reach of one of the best sailing grounds in the world, Long Island Sound, a sheltered body of water that can keep any sailing enthusiast happy, however demanding he or she may be. The one notable exception is the America's Cup challengers who took over one century to wrestle the Auld Mug from the clutches of the New York Yacht Club. Several rivers flow into the Sound, among them the Mystic on whose banks stand Mystic Seaport, the largest maritime museum in the world. Several classic vessels have been preserved here, thus making it a must-stop for any visiting sailors – with the added bonus that you can dock your yacht right next to the exhibits.

The historic route winds its way through the heart of New England where much of modern US history was made – past such ports as Martha's Vineyard, Newport, New Bedford and Marblehead, from which famous seafarers, whalers and explorers left in days gone by. Finally, the island world of Maine is reached, where many summers could be spent exploring the countless bays, rivers and anchorages that stretch all the way to Nova Scotia and the Canadian border.

Offering less variety, the west coast's main attractions are concentrated at its two extremes. The most popular cruising area in the Pacific Northwest is the San Juan Islands, an archipelago of some two hundred islands, many of which have been declared wildlife reserves or marine parks. Beyond these islands and through Canadian waters, the Inside Passage beckons, linking Puget Sound to Alaska, North America's ultimate cruising destination – a world of snow-clad mountains, glaciers tumbling into the sea, and cascading waterfalls. Besides swarms of boats of all shapes and sizes, summer also attracts large numbers of whales that come to feed in these nutrient-rich waters. By the side of rushing torrents, grizzly bears stand watch to grab an unfortunate salmon fighting its way upstream to lay its eggs.

For those not interested in high latitude cruising, there is all-year-round sailing in the Pacific Southwest, whether in the San Francisco Bay area or the Channel Islands, off Los Angeles. Of the eight main islands, Santa Catalina is the best known and the most popular. The others are less frequented and offer more privacy, as there are many coves around their precipitous shores.

A unique opportunity to see much more of the USA from the cockpit of your own boat is to sail the Great Loop, a round voyage made possible by the extensive inland waterway system. Most sailors do it counterclockwise to take advantage of the downstream currents on the main rivers such as the Illinois and Mississippi. The voyage can start in Florida and you can stay with the Intracoastal Waterway all the way to New York, then continue up the Hudson River and Erie Canal into the Great Lakes. From Lake Michigan, the route turns south and, via Illinois, Mississippi, Ohio and Tennessee, the loop eventually closes in Florida. To avoid summer hurricanes and winter ice, the trip starts in the spring, and the summer is spent in the Great Lakes region, before heading south to follow the sun. This is a challenging yet highly rewarding route that takes in much of the best of the continent.

◆ COUNTRY PROFILE

The original inhabitants of North America came across the Bering Straits from Asia, and spread south through the Americas. The Amerindians, or Native Americans as they became known in recent times, lived in scattered tribes. Their first contact with Europeans was not with Columbus, who only visited the off-lying islands of the Caribbean, but with an earlier expedition led by the Norseman Erik the Red, who probably landed on the eastern coast in the tenth century. European settlement began 500 years later, with the French settling in Canada, and the Spanish in Florida.

Throughout the seventeenth century it was British settlements that started to expand on the east coast, while the French lived along the Mississippi, founding Louisiana. Thirteen British colonies were established, but in the eighteenth century escalating tension with Britain resulted

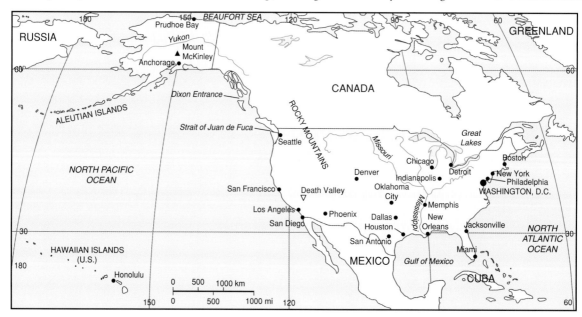

Sucia Island in the San Juan island group with Mt Baker in the background.

in the War of Independence in 1775–6. As the newly independent federal republic grew more confident, it extended its territory by conquest or acquisition and Louisiana, Florida, Alaska, Texas, New Mexico and California were incorporated. The middle of the century saw antagonism growing between the agricultural southern states and the industrializing north, with the situation being aggravated by the question of slavery. The resulting civil war in 1863 led to the north's victory and the abolition of slavery. The last three decades of the nineteenth century saw the country enjoy a golden age, with the economy growing to rival those of the European industrial powers.

After the First World War, economic growth continued until the crash of 1929 set off an unprecedented social and economic crisis. President Franklin D Roosevelt introduced a New Deal policy in an effort to combat the effects of the depression. After the Second World War, US foreign policy was dominated by opposition to the increasing influence of the Soviet Union, and to communism in general. The 1960s saw the rise of a determined civil rights movement, calling for an end to racial segregation. With the break-up of the Soviet Union and the collapse of communism in the early 1990s, the USA emerged as the world's sole superpower. In 2001 the attack on the Twin Towers in New York by Islamic extremists ushered in a period of international uncertainty that led to war in Iraq and Afghanistan. Disillusionment with the President Bush administration, and the worsening financial crisis, saw the election in 2008 of the first African-American president, Barack Obama.

The population numbers 307 million, the majority of whom are of European origin. Some 10 per cent of the population are of African origin, and there is a growing Hispanic community as well as Chinese, Japanese and many other ethnic minorities, including a small number of Native Americans. The main language is English, but Spanish is increasingly spoken, especially in some areas of Florida, California and New York.

✦ CLIMATE

Being such a large country, the climate varies considerably, from cold and temperate in the north to tropical and desert in the south. New England has a temperate climate and can experience changeable weather all year round. The southeastern states have a subtropical climate, with hot summers and mild winters. The weather in the Pacific Southwest is warm throughout the year, with most of the rainfall occurring during the winter months, and summers being very dry. Winds are mostly westerly, except for the hot dry northeast winds – the Santa Anas that come down the mountains and affect South California. The Pacific Northwest has colder and wetter weather and cruising is decidedly seasonal. Prevailing winds are northwest or west and many days are foggy.

Hurricanes occur from June to November on both the Atlantic and Pacific coasts. The Gulf of Mexico and the southeastern seaboard are particularly at risk, although hurricanes can reach as far as New York or even beyond. On the Pacific coast it is rare that a tropical storm reaches as far as California.

The Alaska climate varies widely throughout the state. Along the coast, the summer weather can be pleasant and the winters mild, while the interior has extreme weather conditions. Average summer temperatures are between 15° and 20°C/60°F and 68°F, and the winters are not as cold as they are inland or in the rest of Alaska. The prevailing winds are northwesterly. The Inside Passage benefits from the moderating influence of the warm Alaska Current.

✦ FORMALITIES

The USA has over three hundred official ports of entry, so only those normally used by foreign yachts are listed:

Alaska: Kodiak	57°47´N 152°25´W
Dutch Harbour	53°54´N 166°32´W
Sitka	57°03´N 135°20´W
California: Los Angeles	33°45´N 118°16´W
San Diego	32°42´N 117°08´W
San Francisco	37°48´N 122°25´W
Florida: Key West	24°33.4´N 81°48.2´W
Miami	25°46.5´N 80°10.3´W
Fort Lauderdale	26°08´N 80°07´W
Jacksonville	30°19´N 81°39´W
Maine: Portland	43°39´N 70°15´W
Massachusetts: Boston	42°21.8´N 71°03´W
New York: New York	40°42´N 74°01´W
North Carolina: Morehead City	34°43´N 76°42´W
Oregon: Portland	45°34´N 122°44´W
Newport	44°38´N 124°03´W
Rhode Island: Newport	41°29´N 71°18.8´W
South Carolina: Charleston	32°47´N 79°55.8´W
Virginia: Norfolk	36°51´N 76°19´W
Washington: Seattle	47°38´N 122°20´W

The US Coast Guard has the power to board any vessel within US territorial waters and it frequently does so, particularly off Florida. All vessels must fly the Q flag upon entering the 12 mile territorial limit. Yachts arriving in the USA from a foreign port must enter at a port of entry. If in doubt about whether a port is a port of entry, it is advisable to contact the US Coast Guard on Channel 16.

Formalities in the USA are strict and the authorities apply regulations to the letter, visiting sailors often falling foul of some rule or restriction, naively believing that the generally polite and pleasant officials you deal with cannot be so severe and uncompromising.

Security has increased at entry points to the USA for both US and foreign-flagged vessels. The Bureau of Customs and Border Protection (CBP) of the Department of Homeland Security now deals with entry procedures. Current regulations regarding entry clearance and cruising permits can be found on the CBP website.

Captains must announce a yacht's arrival to the CBP immediately by telephone on 1 800 432 1216 or 1 800 451 0393. Only the captain may disembark to make this report. After answering various questions about the vessel, its crew and itinerary, the captain will be told by the officer what to do next. US-registered boats are often told to proceed to their destination, but foreign yachts are normally inspected by customs. Sometimes the customs officer will also deal with health and agriculture clearance. Procedures vary slightly depending on where entry is made. A full list of locations and telephone numbers for reporting the arrival in different states can be found on the CBP website quoted below. Failure to follow the correct procedure on arrival can lead to a substantial fine, and even seizure of the offending vessel.

Although yachts can obtain customs clearance for entry into the USA by telephone, it is not valid until immigration clearance has been obtained in person at the nearest Immigration and Naturalization Service (INS) office. The captain and every other person on board, regardless of nationality, are required to report to the nearest INS office after arriving in a port of entry. If a yacht arrives after working hours, everyone must remain on board, and clear in the next morning. Clearance must be done within 24 hours of arrival. The nearest INS office might be some distance away from the port of entry, requiring a taxi or rental car to reach it. As long as this regulation remains in force, it is worthwhile selecting an entry port where an INS office is nearby.

All nationalities require a visa obtained in advance, except Canadians and Mexicans, who need only have a valid passport. Special visa regulations apply to sailors, and the visa waiver programme does not apply to persons arriving by yacht.

It is recommended to keep records of checking-in activities, such as name and serial number of any officials checked in with, email receipts of notification, as well as ensuring that the yacht's details and movement have in fact been entered onto the automated system.

All foreign-flagged yachts, including Canadians, are required to notify CBP (Homeland Security) immediately when moving to a new berth, even if it is in the same port; not complying with this may result in a $5,000 fine.

Certain countries are eligible for a cruising licence, which exempts them from having to clear in and out at any subsequent US port after entry has been made in the first port of entry. The licence can be obtained on arrival and is valid for up to one year. After expiry, another licence may only be issued after the vessel has left for a foreign port and returned from a foreign port at least 15 days since the previous licence expired.

The countries to which this applies are Argentina, Australia, Bahamas, Bermuda, Canada, Denmark, Finland, France, Germany, United Kingdom, Ireland, Italy, Netherlands, New Zealand, Norway, Sweden, Switzerland and Turkey.

The US authorities require that all vessels that have 406 MHz EPIRBs on board must have these registered and be able to show proof of such registration.

Calm evening in Chesapeake Bay.

A foreign visitor may import a pleasure boat into the USA free of duty if it is for his or her personal use. Duty must be paid if the boat is sold or offered for sale or charter in the USA.

The importing of many food and plant products is prohibited, and yachts are subject to an agricultural inspection on arrival, including those arriving in the US mainland from Hawaii, Puerto Rico and the US Virgin Islands. Meat and meat products, fresh produce and plants are among the items normally confiscated.

Licences are required for fishing by the states of Florida, Washington and Alaska.

The Washington State Pilot Board requires all foreign-flagged vessels to carry a pilot or get an exemption. Application forms for the exemption can be submitted online or by email.

All yachts in Alaskan waters must have a pilot or get an exemption. Exemptions are given for boats under 20m (65ft) in length. This should be requested when clearing in.

✦ FACILITIES

Yachting facilities throughout the USA are of a good standard. There are marinas practically everywhere and the only objection visiting sailors might have are the high docking fees. Fortunately, in almost every location there is also a place to anchor at little or no cost, and in some ports municipal marinas, docks or moorings are priced at an affordable level. Provisioning everywhere is good and marine equipment is available in most places. Repair services vary from one location to another, being best in the major yachting centres.

✦ CHARTER

As there seem to be almost as many charter companies as car rental firms, only a small number of operators based in the most popular cruising areas have been included: Florida, the Chesapeake Bay, New England, California, the Pacific Northwest and Alaska.

In South Florida, both Cruzan and Florida Yacht Charters have bases at various locations as well as the Abacos, while Miami Charters has a large fleet of both sailing craft and powerboats.

Chesapeake Charters, based near Annapolis, has a small fleet of sailing boats, while Haven Charter, based in Haven Harbour, has a wider selection. Bay Sail in Havre de Grace offers both tuition and a choice of sailing boats.

Freedom yachts are the specialty of Sail Boat Charter, based in Bristol, RI.

Hinckley Charters, based in Southwest Harbor, Maine, has been operating in this area for over seventy years and has a mixed fleet of sail and power yachts.

From their base in San Diego, Seaforth Boat Rental offers a large choice of sail or powerboats. Marina Sailing is California's largest sailing club with a wide range of sail, power and fishing boats at six locations in South California.

At its base in Marina del Rey, Blue Water Sailing offers courses in sailing, both cruising and racing, and has a fleet of Catalina yachts for charter. Based in Alameda and Sausalito, Club Nautique has a large fleet of both sail and powerboats and also offers tuition.

Close to the Canadian border, Anacortes Yacht Charters has a mixed fleet of sail and power, as does Par Yacht Charters based in Bellingham. Voyages NorthWest is a Seattle-based company with a fleet of powerboats and trawler-type yachts, some of which are based in summer in the San Juan Islands.

Alaska Boat Charter offers a variety of bareboats, both power and sail, at various bases in Southeast Alaska. All other Alaskan operators only offer crewed yachts for charter.

Florida
www.floridayacht.com
www.cruzan.com
www.miamicharters.com

Chesapeake Bay
www.havencharters.com
www.chesapeake-charters.com
www.baysail.net

Sunday exodus from Catalina Island towards the mainland.

New England
www.sailboatcharter.net
www.sailing-charter-newport-rhode-island.com
www.hinckleycharters.com

California
www.seaforthboatrental.com
www.bluewatersailing.com
www.clubnautique.net

Pacific Northwest
www.ayc.com
www.voyagesnw.com
www.paryachtcharters.com

Alaska
www.alaskacharterboat.com

Local time	UTC −5 (Eastern Standard Time)
	UTC −8 (Pacific Standard Time)
	UTC −9 (Alaska Standard Time)
	Summer time: first Sunday in March to first Sunday in November
Buoyage	IALA B
Currency	United States Dollar (USD)
Electricity	110V, 60Hz

Diplomatic missions

UK	202 588 6500
Australia	202 797 3000
Canada	202 682 1740
South Africa	202 232 4400
New Zealand	202 328 4800

Communications

IDD 1	IAC 011

Emergency number
911

Cruising Guides
Alaska Guide
Sea of Cortez
Chesapeake
Chesapeake Bay to Florida
Cruising America's Waterways: The Erie Canal
Cruising Guide to Central and Southern California
Cruising Guide to Coastal North Carolina
Cruising Guide to New England Coast
Cruising Guide to New Jersey
Cruising Guide to Puget Sound and San Juan Islands
Cruising Guide to San Francisco Bay
Cruising Guide to the Florida Keys
Cruising the Chesapeake
Cruising the Pacific Coast
East Coast of Florida
Exploring the Pacific Coast, San Diego to Seattle
Exploring the San Juan and Gulf Islands
Exploring Southeast Alaska
Florida Cruising Guide
Long Island Sound to Cape May
New England Coast
North to Alaska
Southern California Channel Islands (can be downloaded from the Royal Cruising Club website: www.rcc.org.uk)
US Pacific Coast
Intracoastal Waterway Guide

Websites
www.cbp.gov/xp/cgov/travel/pleasure_boats/ (information for visiting sailors)
www.cbp.gov/xp/cgov/travel/pleasure_boats/user_fee/user_fee_decal.xml
www.marinas.com/browse/marina/US/ (aerial views of US marinas)
www.myfwc.com/license.html (Florida fishing licence)
www.pilotage.wa.gov (Washington State Pilot exemption)
www.state.gov/www/services.html (US State Department links)
www.mysticseaport.org

Johns Hopkins Glacier in Alaska's Glacier Bay.

SOUTH AMERICA

THE SOUTH AMERICAN CONTINENT provides the extremes of cruising conditions, from the Caribbean islands of Venezuela to the remote wilderness of Tierra del Fuego and the spectacular Chilean fjords. Both mainland Venezuela and its offshore islands have been popular cruising grounds for many years, but a deteriorating security situation, with several violent incidents involving foreign sailors, has considerably reduced the number of visitors. In the past, an even greater concern for one's personal safety had kept most yachts away from neighbouring Colombia, apart from the old colonial port of Cartagena, but Columbian waters are now considered safe and the number of visiting boats is increasing.

Other parts of the continent are mostly visited by foreign yachts on their way to somewhere else. Northern Brazil has become a popular cruising destination, especially among French sailors, who stop there on their way from West Africa to the Caribbean, with a few yachts making a detour to navigate the mighty Amazon. The more frequented route is sailed by boats arriving in Brazil from South Africa, the favoured landfall being Salvador da Bahia, whose carnival continues to be its prime attraction and is considered a worthy substitute for the more famous but less spontaneous one in Rio de Janeiro. Only a few yachts venture farther south than Rio, usually on their way to Patagonia, the Chilean Canals and Antarctica. Having sailed that far south, most cruising yachts return to warmer climes by going north along the west coast of South America. No one fails to be overawed by the primeval beauty of the Chilean Canals, but their remoteness and difficulty of getting there make them accessible to only the most determined sailors. Cruising attractions north of the Chilean Canals are very limited: the desert-like coast of Peru is bare and unappealing, while Ecuador's main attraction, the unique Galapagos Islands, lies offshore.

An alternative route when visiting the west coast of South America, whether by boats going from Mexico and California, or from the Panama Canal, is to sail south along the coasts of Colombia, Ecuador and Peru all the way to Chile. An attractive detour is to the Galapagos Islands before returning to the South American coast and continuing south, either close to the coast to avoid the worst of the north-setting Humboldt Current, or further offshore. Neither the coast nor the widely spaced ports along it are attractive enough to justify this long voyage, much of it under power because of the light winds. A more rewarding alternative is not to close with the mainland coast after Galapagos, but

Cape Horn landfall.

continue offshore to Easter Island and thence to Chile. As the prevailing winds in the Chilean Canals are from northwest, once Chile is reached, either of these options will ensure better sailing conditions for the continuation of the voyage towards the tip of the continent, and possibly Antarctica.

With a few notable exceptions, sailing is not such a popular pastime in South America as in Europe or North America, although the situation is rapidly changing and there are now large boating communities in major centres such as Rio de Janeiro, Montevideo, Buenos Aires, Mar del Plata, Callao and Salinas. This is also where most repair and other yachting facilities are concentrated. As these rarely coincide with the cruising areas popular with visiting yachts, for most South American destinations you should carry essential spares and be quite self-sufficient.

ARGENTINA

ARGENTINA SHARES THE SOUTHERN TIP of South America with Chile, the soaring Cordillera of the High Andes forming a natural border between the two countries. Argentine scenery is of a rich variety, from the lofty Andes to the verdant oases in their foothills where the Spanish first settled, from the dense forests in the north and the vast central pampas, to the remote Patagonian waterways in the south. Yachts coming from the north can get a taste of Argentina in Buenos Aires and the resorts in the Rio de la Plata estuary, where most yachting facilities are concentrated. Buenos Aires, attractive as it may be, is by far not all that Argentina has to offer; to get a true and highly satisfying impression of this diverse country, you should leave the towns behind and seek out its wilder corners, of which there are still plenty. Indeed, most sailors who brave the elements to visit Argentina seldom linger in Buenos Aires or Mar del Plata, but head south, attracted by the challenging wilderness of the Magellan Straits and Tierra del Fuego. There are only a few ports along Argentina's long coastline, and there is little to see between Mar del Plata and the Straits of Magellan, with the notable exception of Puerto Madryn, in the sheltered Golfo Nuevo west of the Valdés Peninsula. The large bay is permanent home to a large pod of killer whales and is also visited by right whales for breeding, while the peninsula has the only colony of sea elephants in South America. The other ports farther south are of little interest except as convenient stops in an emergency.

In the extreme south, the port of Ushuaia, on the northern bank of the Beagle Channel, has become a major tourist centre due primarily to the relative proximity of Antarctica. Many cruise ships use it as a base, as do the yachts that plan to strike out across the Drake Passage or embark on a cruise in the Chilean Canals.

◆ COUNTRY PROFILE

When the Incas tried to push south from the Andes, the Amerindians who already lived in the area prevented them expanding any further. They were no more welcoming to the Spaniard Juan de Solis, who landed in present-day Argentina in 1516 and was killed by them. Magellan paid a brief visit in 1520, before his voyage to the Pacific through the straits that bear his name. From the mid-sixteenth century, Peru ruled over all Spanish possessions in South America. In 1816 independence from Spain was declared and José de San Martín led an Argentine army to free first Chile, and then Peru.

The 1930s saw Argentina become one of the world's wealthiest countries, a prosperity based mainly on the export of meat, and this trade made Buenos Aires one of the world's leading cities. The brief period of prosperity was brought to an end by political instability that resulted in a gradual economic decline. In 1946, General Juan Perón became president and instituted a social-democratic programme that saw many popular improvements before he became increasingly dictatorial. He ruled with one interruption until his death in 1974, and was succeeded as head of government by his wife Isabel. In 1976 she was ousted by a coup that brought to power a military junta that enforced a repressive rule during which thousands of people disappeared. Continuing economic problems and defeat in the Falklands war in 1982 brought pressure for democracy, which returned to Argentina in 1983.

The population numbers 41 million. Buenos Aires is the capital, and in that province people are mostly of European origin, while in other provinces they are a mixture of Spanish and Amerindian. Spanish is the official language, although its pronunciation and some words are different to Castilian Spanish.

The Beagle Channel.

✦ CLIMATE

The climate ranges from subtropical in the north to cold temperate in Tierra del Fuego. The central zone is temperate, while Buenos Aires is hot and humid, with the summer months of December to February being the hottest. In Rio de la Plata the prevailing winds in summer are easterly, while southwest winds are more common in winter. They are often accompanied by *pamperos*, violent southwest squalls that affect most of Argentina's coastal waters.

✦ FORMALITIES

PORTS OF ENTRY

Buenos Aires	34°36´S 58°22´W
Mar del Plata	38°02´S 57°31´W
Puerto Madryn	42°44´S 65°01´W
Puerto Deseado	47°46´S 65°50´W
Santa Cruz	50°01´S 68°30´W
Rio Gallegos	51°36´S 68°58´W
Ushuaia	54°49´S 68°17´W

The ports of entry listed above are only a selection, as foreign yachts may use any Argentine port to clear in. Boats arriving from overseas must clear with the following authorities: immigration, customs, and Coast Guard (Prefectura Naval Argentina).

Buenos Aires: Sufficient time should be allowed for the long trip up the Rio de la Plata. Smaller yachts may proceed directly to the Yacht Club Argentino (YCA) or Yacht Club Puerto Madero, which is reached via a buoyed channel. Clearance formalities are completed with the help of the marinas. Only large yachts, over 30m (100ft) LOA, need to contact port control and enter the commercial harbour. Yacht Club Puerto Madero monitors Channel 71 and will co-ordinate the opening of the bridge to the marina. Customs and immigration formalities are normally completed ashore. Quarantine inspection applies only to larger yachts.

Mar del Plata: Boats should proceed to the marina, where Yacht Club Argentino, Club Nautico and Centro Naval are located. Access to the yacht basin is barred by a footbridge that is manned 24 hours a day. The bridge operator and yacht clubs monitor Channel 71, via which boats can check on details of the docking spaces available. The clubs will assist with formalities. Those arriving from abroad may first have to see a quarantine officer.

Puerto Madryn: The local yacht club has moorings that may be used by visitors, but if none are free yachts may anchor before contacting Prefectura Naval.

Ushuaia: Port control is run by the Prefectura Naval. It only answers when hailed as 'L3P' (Lima Tres Papa) on Channels 16 or 12, and should be contacted prior to arrival in the harbour and again when moored in the harbour. Visiting boats usually moor at the ASAFYN dock on the south side of the harbour. Regulations vary from time to time, and Prefectura Naval will advise as to the current procedures. Normally all crew are required to go to the Prefectura Naval office, which also deals with immigration. The customs office is located in the commercial port area. Officials rarely visit yachts for clearance purposes.

Ushuaia in Patagonia.

No visas are required for nationals of most countries, and a 90-day visa is given on arrival.

Boats sailing from Argentina to the Falklands (Malvinas) should consider giving Chile as their destination so as to avoid complications as, in theory, as far as the Argentine authorities are concerned, the boat will not leave Argentina and therefore does not need to clear out. All boats must check in regularly with the Prefectura Naval on Channel 16 while sailing anywhere in Argentine waters. Sailing to the Falklands is no longer penalized, but on re-entering Argentine territorial waters the Coast Guard should be informed of this at the earliest opportunity.

✦ FACILITIES

Most sailing facilities are concentrated around Buenos Aires, where there are several yacht clubs in the Rio de la Plata estuary, such as San Isidro, San Fernando and Olivos. In Buenos Aires, both YCA and Yacht Club Puerto Madero have marinas conveniently located for visiting the Argentine capital. Visitors are offered one week free docking at YCA, and 24 hours at Yacht Club Puerto Madero. There are good repair services and also a reasonable range of marine supplies in Buenos Aires. A yacht club with good facilities is at San Fernando, 20 miles upriver from the capital, where there is a boatyard with a wide range of services.

Mar del Plata has a thriving sailing community with facilities to match. YCA has a base at Mar del Plata, where it shares the inner basin of the large harbour (Puerto de Yachting) with other clubs. Visiting sailors are welcome here and the facilities in this large fishing port are impressive, with excellent provisioning, good repair services – though limited haulout possibilities. This is the best place to prepare the boat for a southbound voyage, and it is also a good base from which to visit inland Argentina as it has frequent flights to Buenos

Aires and other destinations. Only basic facilities are available at Puerto Madryn and Puerto Deseado. For yachts heading south, a convenient place to reprovision is Río Gallegos.

There is good provisioning, banks, and fuel as well as LPG in Ushuaia. There are some repair facilities and fuel can be bought from the depot on the west side of the harbour. Visiting sailors are welcome at the dock belonging to ASAFYN Sailing and Diving Association, whose secretary is a good source of local information.

The excellent Cibernautica website, although only in Spanish, is relatively easy to navigate and gives a range of maritime information as well as very useful daily forecasts for every region of Argentina, including Ushuaia – and even the Argentine and Uruguayan bases in Antarctica.

✦ CHARTER

Private yachts may be available for charter in both Buenos Aires and Mar del Plata and the local yacht clubs will advise on availability. Small motorboats are available to rent in Puerto Madryn for those interested in whale watching. A number of sailing yachts based in Ushuaia operate charter voyages in the waters of Patagonia, the Chilean Canals, and to the Antarctic Peninsula.

www.pelagic.co.uk
www.expeditionsail.com
www.magodelsur.com.ar
www.ocean-expeditions.com

Cruising Guides

Havens and Anchorages	South Atlantic Circuit

Websites
www.turismo.gov.ar (Ministry of Tourism)
www.argentinaturistica.com (tourist information)
www.cibernautica.com.ar (general maritime information)

Local time	UTC −3
	Summer time: mid-October to mid-March
	(This is not observed in Patagonia.)
Buoyage	IALA B
Currency	Argentine Peso (ARS)
Electricity	220V, 50Hz

Diplomatic missions

UK	11 4808 2200	Canada	11 4808 1000
USA	11 5777 4533	South Africa	11 4317 2900
Australia	11 4779 3500	New Zealand	11 4328 0747

Communications

IDD 54	IAC 00

Emergency numbers

112	Ambulance 107	Police 101

BRABIL

BRAZIL COVERS NEARLY HALF the area of South America and shares borders with all of the countries except Chile and Ecuador. This vast and varied country is a land of plateaux and plains, huge rivers, rainforests and desert. Much of the interior is still unexplored, although the days of undiscovered Brazil are numbered and the tropical forests of the Amazon, described as the lung of the world, are slowly being cut down to make space for farming. Much of this unique world of incredible flora and fauna where a few aboriginal tribes still live a life that has not changed for thousands of years is now on the threshold of extinction.

Brazilian culture is a rich mixture of European, African and Latin American, and nowhere is this more clearly seen than at Carnival time. It is this Carnival that more than anything else brings most foreign sailors to Brazil, those who arrive from across the Atlantic normally sailing to Salvador de Bahia, while those coming from the south have the opportunity to see the greatest show of them all in Rio de Janeiro. But even without the Carnival, Rio de Janeiro's spectacular setting makes it one of the most beautiful landfalls anywhere in the world.

Brazil has many attractive places to explore on its long length of coastline, and it is a great surprise to local sailors that not more foreign yachts are seen along their shores.

Many of those who do make it to Brazil get their first taste of this fascinating country 200 miles offshore, at the Fernando de Noronha Archipelago, a nature reserve where yachts are allowed to make a brief stop at the main island. The islands are home to the largest concentration of tropical

seabirds in the South Atlantic, while Baia de Golfinhos has an exceptional population of resident dolphins.

The Brazilian mainland coast, stretching from the Uruguay border to the Amazon Delta, is of great variety, from highly developed areas to uninhabited coral islands, a scenery rich in diversity. Just as varied are the climate and weather conditions. The most attractive area is the stretch between Rio de Janeiro and São Sebastião Island (Ilhabela State Park), which has many protected anchorages and attractive scenery, parts of which are now marred by the increasing number of oil rigs. The most popular cruising ground is halfway along, on the Costa Verde (Green Coast) around Ilha Grande and Angra dos Reís. This is a sheltered area with scores of small islands set in turquoise waters, with secluded anchorages and benign weather for most of the year.

Another attractive cruising location is the Abrolhos Archipelago, which is composed of five islands of volcanic origin. Abrolhos is the largest coral and most diverse reef in the South Atlantic and, to preserve its rich flora and fauna, the area has been declared a marine national park. There are various restrictions in place, but visiting yachts are tolerated provided they observe the rules – not fishing, and avoiding anchoring among the fragile coral formations, being foremost among them. Another interesting area to explore, because it has several remains from the colonial era, is Baia de Todos Santos, close to Salvador. This is a large – almost landlocked – bay with many islands, inlets and navigable rivers.

Far to the north, the River Amazon has a special appeal as it can be navigated for well over 1,000 miles, giving an

The Bay of Botafogo in Rio de Janeiro's spectacular setting.

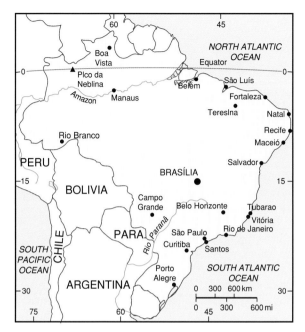

opportunity of seeing some of the interior of this huge country. Several cruising yachts have faced up to the challenge in recent years – and sailed the 900 miles as far as the legendary city of Manaus, only to realize that to get a real taste of the true Amazon they needed to penetrate even further, something that few were prepared to do, especially on a sailing yacht.

✦ COUNTRY PROFILE

Brazil's first contact with Europe was in 1500 when the Portuguese Pedro Alvares Cabral made landfall, thinking at first it was India. He called it the island of Santa Cruz, not guessing that it was part of the same continent discovered by Columbus farther north. The Portuguese established a vice-royalty in 1572. When Napoleon occupied Portugal, the Portuguese royal family fled to Brazil. After Napoleon's defeat, the King's son Dom Pedro I remained in Brazil and became emperor on the proclamation of Brazil's independence from Portugal in 1822. Emperor Dom Pedro II was

deposed in 1889 and Brazil became a republic. There followed a period of relative political instability with several monarchist rebellions, but increasing economic prosperity. There was a succession of military regimes after the Second World War until, in 1989, a new constitution brought a democratically elected president to power. The current president, Luiz Inácio Lula da Silva, came to power in 2002 on a programme of social reform.

In 2010 the population is expected to exceed 200 million. Brazilians are a rich mixture of racial and ethnic backgrounds, with 49 per cent of European origin, 8 per cent African, and the rest of mixed ancestry. The indigenous tribes of the interior number over one hundred and seventy separate groups and speak as many languages, but many are close to extinction. Portuguese is the official language, although it is slightly different to that spoken in Portugal itself. The capital of the federal republic is Brasilia.

✦ CLIMATE

Brazil's climate varies greatly. Most of the northern part of the coast is under the influence of the northeast winds, which are strongest in the summer between December and February. The rest is in the southeast tradewind belt, which predominates from March to August. During the austral winter months the southeast trades have a lot of south in them, and sailing down the coast can be difficult. The temperature range is quite wide, with average temperatures in northern Brazil around 28°C/82°F in the hottest months of January and February, dropping slightly to an annual average of 21°C/70°C in the southern coastal region.

✦ FORMALITIES

Normally yachts are not boarded and the captain has to go ashore to visit the various offices. The port captain should be visited first. The Brazilian Port Authority is called Portobras (Empresas Portos do Brasil). After that, you must go to customs and the federal police, who deal with immigration. The order of visits is important, as certain forms have to be taken from one office to another.

PORTS OF ENTRY

Belém	1°27′S 48°30′W	Macapá	1°18′S 51°01′W	São Luis	2°30′S 44°18′W
Fortaleza/Mucuripe	3°41′S 38°29′W	Manaus	3°09′S 60°01′W	Fortaleza	3°45′S 38°30.6′W
Fernando de Noronha	3°51′S 32°25′W	Natal	5°47′S 35°11′W	Cabedelo	7°02′S 34°51′W
Recife	8°04′S 34°52′W	Maceió	9°40′S 35°44′W	Salvador	12°58′S 38°30′W
Ilheus/Malhado	14°47′S 39°02′W	Vitoria	20°18′S 40°20′W	Rio de Janeiro	22°55′S 43°12′W
Angra dos Reis	23°01′S 44°19′W	Itacuruça	22°55′S 43°50′W	Macaé	22°23′S 41°46′W
São Sebastião	23°48′S 45°23′W	Santos	23°56′S 46°20′W	Paranaguá	25°30′S 48°31′W
São Francisco do Sul	26°14′S 48°38′W	Florianópolis	27°50′S 48°25′W	Rio Grande	32°10′S 52°05′W

Salvador da Bahía.

Fernando de Noronha: This is now an official port of entry and all foreign nationals must arrive with a Brazilian visa obtained in advance. Arriving yachts must clear with the port captain's office and the Guarda Territorial. There are high fees to be paid, including one to the National Park, based on the number of days you plan to stay.

Recife: Yachts should go to the Cabanga Yacht Club, which will assist with clearance formalities. The club can only be reached at high water, and even then there is a draft restriction of 2.5m (8ft).

Salvador: The most convenient place to clear in is at Bahia Marina close to the ferry terminal. Sudesb, a company formed to host international sailing events, has set up a docking facility for visiting yachts at one of the pontoons at the ferry terminal and this may also be used. All offices are close to both the marina and Sudesb.

Rio de Janeiro: All clearance formalities must be undertaken in the commercial harbour, which is not recommended to be entered by yacht. It is better to stay in one of the marinas and go to the necessary offices by taxi or public transport. Marina Gloria is the most conveniently located and the office there will help with directions to the various offices.

Santos: It is best to leave the boat at the Yate Clube de Santos on Ilha de Santo Amaro and then visit the offices in the commercial harbour.

Belém: A detailed chart is essential for the Para river, which leads to Belém 80 miles upstream. Visiting boats may use a mooring at the Belém Yacht Club, which will also help with formalities.

Visas are required by all nationals arriving by yacht and this requirement is strictly enforced.

After the initial clearance has been completed, clearance to the next port must be obtained, requesting clearance with stops (con escala) so as to be able to stop on the way. At every major port the port authority and police offices have to be visited. This is particularly important when entering a new state. This clearance is strictly enforced, and failure to do so can result in a fine.

All foreign vessels are also required to clear in and out with the health and quarantine office at every port, but this regulation appears to be rarely imposed for yachts.

In some ports the authorities insist on the use of an officially approved agent. This usually only applies to the first entry into the country and also depends on local officials.

After six months the yacht must leave the country or else it becomes liable to an import tax of about 100 per cent of its value.

✦ FACILITIES

Facilities are rapidly expanding as yachting is attracting more and more enthusiasts, especially those with powerboats. New marinas are being commissioned all over the country and repair facilities and services are improving at the same rate. There are several anchorages as well as marinas in the Rio de Janeiro area, one of the most conveniently situated being Marina Gloria, close to Rio's smaller airport. It gets very crowded with local boats, but space is usually found for visitors. The marina has some repair facilities, a fuel dock as well as a chandlery. Practically everything is available in Rio, but it can take time finding it. Niterói, across Guanabara Bay from Rio de Janeiro, has a yacht club that welcomes visitors. There are good repair services, chandlery and fuel on the club dock.

Angra dos Reis, 60 miles south of Rio, is a fast-developing yachting centre due to the popularity of the Ilha Grande area among local sailors. Angra has a large shipyard that also undertakes work on yachts and has good repair facilities. Provisioning in town is also good. Close to Angra, the marina at Porto Bracuhy has some of the best facilities in Brazil.

Santos, close to São Paolo, has a large club, Yate Clube de Santos, on Ilha de Santo Amaro, the base of a large fleet of powerboats. As a result, repair facilities are very good with all kinds of workshops and a good chandlery.

Going north, Salvador da Bahia is a first port of call for many boats arriving in Brazil. There are a number of yacht clubs, all with their own marinas, in and around Salvador, and repair facilities at some of them are very good as they cater for a large local boating community. Bahia Marina in Salvador itself is the most convenient to use as a base to visit the city. Sudesb, a government company set up to host international sailing events, has a docking facility, but no other services, at one of the pontoons at the nearby ferry terminal.

A French sailor, Philippe Fessard, has opened a yachting centre at Praia do Jacaré, on the Rio Paraiba close to the port of Cabedelo. The centre has access to a range of repair facilities and the small marina is a safe place to leave the boat to travel in the interior.

Natal is a pleasant port on the northeast tip of Brazil with a yacht club and a range of repair facilities. Similarly, at Recife, the yacht club welcomes visiting sailors and there are

good repair services locally. At Fortaleza, the Marina Park has a boatyard with some repair facilities. In the Amazon Delta, Belém is a large city 80 miles inland on the south bank of the Para river. The yacht club gives temporary membership. All services and supplies are available.

Provisioning is better in larger cities and fresh produce is plentiful in all places. Fuel and water are normally obtainable alongside at fishing docks. Diesel fuel is sometimes diluted with petrol (gasolene), but this is marked on the pump.

On the island of Fernando de Noronha only basic provisions are available. Diesel can be bought from the fuel station a short distance inland.

◆ CHARTER

There are various individual operators in the popular Ilha Grande area. One of the few to offer bareboat rentals is Angra Boats, which has a small fleet of sail and powerboats based in Angra dos Reis.

www.angracharterboats.com.br
www.sailing-brazil.com

Cruising Guides
Brazil Cruising Guide
Cruising the Coast of Brazil
Havens and Anchorages
South Atlantic Circuit

Website
www.embratur.gov.br (Ministry of Tourism)
www.marina-jacare-village.com
www.bahiamarina.com.br
www.marinadagloria.com.br

Local time	UTC −3
	Summer time: mid-October to mid-March
Buoyage	IALA B
Currency	Brazilian Real (BRL)
Electricity	110V, 60Hz

Diplomatic missions	
UK	61 3329 2300
USA	61 3312 7000
Australia	61 3226 1112
Canada	61 3424 5400
South Africa	61 3312 9500
New Zealand	61 3248 9900

Communications	
IDD 55	IAC 00

Emergency number
911

Small fishing port in the State of Parana.

CHILE

CHILE IS THE WORLD'S longest coastal country, a relatively narrow strip of land that stretches for some 2,600 miles between the Andes and the Pacific Ocean, with an average width of rarely more than 100 miles. The northern part is mostly desert, while to the south there is a vast array of lakes, rivers and dense forests, which reach down to the southern tip of South America to Tierra del Fuego, the Magellan Straits and all the way to Cape Horn.

The long and arid northern coast has few natural harbours and the commercial ports are generally not suitable for cruising yachts. Valdivia is the first port that is both attractive and has good yachting facilities. Farther south, from the large island of Chiloe commences Chile's real attraction: the magnificent cruising ground of the Patagonian waterways, generically called the Chilean Canals, although a more fitting name would be the Chilean Fjordland. A slowly increasing, but still relatively small, number of cruising yachts are attracted to this part of Chile, a vast area of islands, steep-sided fjords and narrow channels, snow-clad mountains and massive glaciers. Much of the 1,000 miles that stretch all the way to Cape Horn are uninhabited and it is not unusual to sail for many days without seeing any sign of human habitation or meeting another boat. There are few places on earth where you can experience such solitude in the midst of wild scenery that has been left mostly untouched by mankind. There are no settlements along the usual cruising route between Puerto Eden, in the north, and the Argentine port of Ushuaia, in the far south, a distance of some 600 miles, so this is an area where you have to be entirely self-sufficient. Close to Ushuaia, across the Beagle Channel, is Puerto Williams, a small Chilean military base and the southernmost settlement in the world. This is the starting point for voyages to Antarctica as this wedge of the Southern Ocean is under the jurisdiction of the Chilean authorities.

The major drawback of this unique cruising ground is the weather, as it is very changeable and the winds in the narrow channels can often blow in violent gusts – the feared williwaws. While the clearest skies are in winter, the best time for exploring this part of the world is during the southern summer, from December to March, when the weather is both more settled and warmer. Prevailing winds in the Chilean Canals are northwest, and therefore it is easier for this area to be sailed from north to south.

JUAN FERNANDEZ ISLANDS

Some 400 miles west of Chile lies a group of islands rarely visited by anyone, including yachts, although one of its early visitors was Joshua Slocum who called here in *Spray* in May 1896. The three islands, Robinson Crusoe, Alejandro Selkirk and Santa Clara, were discovered by the Spanish explorer Juan Fernández in 1574. One of the islands was the temporary home of Alexander Selkirk, a seaman who was left on the island at his own request in 1704 and lived in complete

Puerto Williams.

265

solitude for five years. It was this willingly marooned sailor whom Daniel Defoe used as the inspiration for his character Robinson Crusoe. This island now bears the fictional character's name, while Alejandro Selkirk Island lies 80 miles farther west. Only Robinson Crusoe Island (33°38´S 78° 50´W) is inhabited, most of the population of around five hundred living in San Juan Bautista village, in Cumberland Bay. The current names were given to the islands in 1935 when the group was made a national park.

Visiting sailors are always warmly welcomed and are usually en route to Easter Island, Chile's other outpost in the South Pacific, which is dealt with separately (page 311).

✦ COUNTRY PROFILE

Remains of a pre-Inca civilization have been found in the north of Chile. When the Incas expanded their empire from their base high in the Andes, they only reached as far as the centre of present-day Chile, their advance being fiercely resisted by the Araucanian tribes. In 1520 Magellan sailed through the Straits on his voyage that was to prove to all doubters that the earth was round. Tierra del Fuego was named 'Land of Fire' by his sailors who spotted the numerous cooking fires glowing on the shores, while Magellan called the people *patagones* on account of their big feet, so this southernmost part of South America has been known as Patagonia ever since.

The native population fiercely resisted Spanish encroachment but to no avail. Under the rule of the viceroyalty of Peru, a farming colony developed, although often raided by English and French pirates. A revolt against Spanish rule resulted in the declaration of an independent republic in 1818. In the War of the Pacific (1879–83), Chile defeated Peru and Bolivia, and won its present northern regions. The country, which had been relatively free of the coups and arbitrary governments that blighted the rest of the South American continent, endured a long period of military dictatorship

after the government of democratically elected socialist President Salvador Allende was forcibly removed in 1973. The ruthless dictatorship of Augusto Pinochet was replaced in 1989 by a civilian government that brought back stability to the country.

The population of 16.6 million are either of European origin or mestizo, a mixture of Spanish and Amerindian. In some rural and mountain areas, there are still a large number of Mapuche, the original inhabitants. Spanish is the main language. Santiago de Chile is the capital.

✦ CLIMATE

The Chilean climate varies considerably according to latitude, being dry and hot in the north, and wet and windy in the south. The coastal areas are cooled by the cold Humboldt Current. In the south, the most settled weather is between December and March, which is dominated by westerly winds. In this area, northerly winds usually bring rain and poor visibility, while southerlies, which occur mostly in winter, are accompanied by clear skies.

✦ FORMALITIES

Yachts are advised to contact the Chilean Navy (Armada) before entering Chilean territorial waters (which both Chile and Peru consider as extending to 200 miles offshore) either on 4146 kHz or by email: mrccchilr@directemar.cl.

Vessels arriving from a foreign port must immediately contact the port captain. No one must disembark until this has been permitted by the Naval authority whose representative will visit the boat, accompanied by immigration and quarantine. Once these formalities have been completed, the captain must visit customs.

Valdivia: The town of Valdivia, where formalities are completed, lies about 11 miles up the river. It is usually possible to clear in at the Alwoplast yard, which is halfway up the river and has a small marina. Occasionally the Navy will insist that a boat comes upriver into Valdivia itself to the dock in front of the port captain's office.

Puerto Williams: Yachts entering the Beagle Channel area should contact the Chilean Navy as Puerto Williams is a naval base. Cruising boats are usually told to proceed directly to the western basin, close to the airport, where there is a concrete dock. Shallow-drafted boats may come up on its inside, or tie up alongside the *Micalvi*, a former supply ship used as a yacht club. Officials will visit the vessel, after which the captain must go to the port captain's office to complete formalities.

Nationals of EU countries, Australia, Canada, Latin American countries, New Zealand, South Africa and the USA do not require visas. A tourist card is issued on arrival, valid for 90 days. Some other nationals may be required to get a visa in advance.

Foreign yachts should obtain a customs exemption certificate on arrival. This is valid for a limited time only and

Romance Glacier on the Beagle Channel.

must be renewed before its expiry date. Failing to insist on getting this certificate can cause serious problems when clearing out of Chile.

A cruising permit is issued to visiting yachts and must be presented to officials at every port, and is usually retained by the port captain until departure. A detailed itinerary must be submitted, listing every overnight anchorage. Yachts are normally allowed to stay up to six months, but this can be extended up to two years.

The exit permit must be requested from the port captain 24 hours before the intended departure time. On the day of departure, an official will either bring the permit to the boat or instruct the captain to collect it from the office. After this, the vessel must leave within one hour, otherwise the permit will be cancelled. Those intending to cruise northwards through the Beagle Channel may not stop at Ushuaia, but if they do, they must return to Puerto Williams to go through all the formalities again.

✦ RESTRICTIONS

Access to the Chilean Canals without a valid permit is prohibited. Boats equipped with SSB radios must report their position to the nearest radio station at 0800 and 2000 local time daily on 2182 kHz or 4146 kHz. The Navy monitors the progress of cruising boats and insists on being kept updated on a yacht's progress, primarily for the vessel's own safety.

There are restricted areas in Puerto Chacabuco and Puerto Williams. The port captain must be informed if a yacht wishes to move to another anchorage within those

PORTS OF ENTRY

Arica	18°29´S 70°26´W	Iquique	20°12´S 70°10´W	Mejillones	23°06´S 70°28´W
Antofagasta	23°38´S 70°26´W	Valparaiso	33°01´S 71°38´W	Valdivia	39°48´S 73°14´W
Puerto Montt	41°28´S 72°57´W	Castro	42°29´S 73°46´W	Puerto Natales	51°43´S 72°31´W
Punta Arenas	53°10´S 70°54´W	Puerto Williams	55°56´S 67°37´W		

harbours. Access to some parts of the Patagonian channels is prohibited.

✦ FACILITIES

There are good repair facilities and various workshops in the port area of Valparaiso, which is the port serving the capital, Santiago. There is a new marina at Algarrobo, near Valparaiso, run by the local yacht club. Because of the difficult entrance, the club launch will guide boats in. There are good facilities, including a 25-ton travelift. Valparaiso is one hour away, for provisioning, marine equipment and charts. There are also helpful yacht clubs at Arica, Antofagasta, Caldera and Coquimbo, all of which will assist with formalities, repair, and leaving the boat if wishing to travel inland.

In Valdivia, the boatyard and sail loft operated by Alwoplast, downriver from Valdivia, provide a range of repair services including metalwork, carpentry, glassfibre, rigging, as well as haulout. Yachts may also be left there while touring the interior, or stored, afloat or ashore, between seasons.

There are two marinas in the south. Marina del Sur in Puerto Montt has all services, as well as a 40-ton lifting platform. Also in Puerto Montt is Oxxean, a small marina with floating docks, fuel and basic facilities. There is a small marina in Puerto Cisne (Puyuhuapi), used as a supply base for the excursion boats going to Laguna San Rafael.

Fuel is available in all ports along the coast. In the smaller southern ports, it is available at Puerto Montt, Castro, Quellan, Chacabuco, Calbuco and Ralun, but as there are no pumps on the dock, it has to be carried in jerrycans. Fuel can also be obtained in Puerto Natales and, occasionally, in Puerto Eden. Those cruising the southern part of Chile must make adequate provision for this when planning their trip. In the south, propane is available in Puerto Montt, Puerto Chacabuco and Puerto Williams.

Provisioning in the south is variable depending on the size of town, but some supplies can be bought in Puerto Montt and Castro. In smaller ports, supplies are limited and

expensive. There are fresh produce markets in Puerto Montt and Castro. Even in more remote areas, fresh fruit and vegetables can normally be bought from local farmers, depending on the season. Fishing is excellent everywhere.

If cruising the southern channels, all essential supplies and spares must be carried, as these are impossible to obtain south of Valdivia. Repair facilities in Punta Arenas are limited and provisioning is adequate. In spite of its remoteness, provisioning is surprisingly good in Puerto Williams, where there is a bank, post office, supermarket and fuel, but no repair facilities. For any repairs, you need to sail across to Ushuaia.

Charts can be obtained from the Chilean Hydrographic Office, which also produces a comprehensive atlas comprising all national charts reduced in size.

✦ CHARTER

A number of sailing yachts based in Ushuaia operate charter voyages to the Antarctic peninsula and the southern Chilean Canals.

> www.pelagic.co.uk
> www.expeditionsail.com
> www.magodelsur.com.ar
> www.ocean-expeditions.com

Cruising Guides
Chile
Patagonia and Tierra del Fuego Nautical Guide

Websites
www.sernatur.cl (Department of Tourism)
www.directemar.cl (Chilean Navy site with weather forecasts under Meteorologia)

Local time	UTC −4
	Summer time: mid-October to mid-March
Buoyage	IALA B
Currency	Chilean Peso (CLP)
Electricity	220V, 50Hz

Diplomatic missions

UK	2 370 4100
USA	2 330 3000
Australia	2 550 3500
Canada	2 652 3800
South Africa	2 231 2860
New Zealand	2 290 9800

Communications

IDD 56	IAC 00

Emergency numbers

112	Ambulance 131	Police 133

Puerto Angusto off the Straits of Magellan.

COLOMBIA

COLOMBIA HAS A COASTLINE on both the Caribbean Sea and the Pacific Ocean. The scenery along the Caribbean coast offers more variety than either of Colombia's neighbours. From the sand dunes and arid interior of the Guajira peninsula to the dense forests of Darien, the coast shows an ever-changing face. Not far inland tower the majestic peaks of the Sierra Nevada de Santa Maria crowned by the snow-capped Mount Cristóbal Colón, the 5,762m (18,900ft) summit being visible from far offshore. The contrasts of nature are not the only attractions of this part of the Spanish Main as ashore you are forever reminded of the country's tumultuous past. The forts of Nueva Andalusia and the walled citadel of Cartagena bear witness to the once mighty Spanish Empire, the Spanish influence still being prevalent in almost every aspect of daily life.

Most cruising boats visiting Colombia do so on their way from the Eastern Caribbean to the Panama Canal, while those heading in the opposite direction use Colombia as a convenient stepping stone in their battle with contrary winds and current. The most popular landfall is the historic city of Cartagena, whose picturesque harbour is one of the most attractive ports in the New World. Safety in the area has generally improved due to a joint campaign by the US and Colombian Coast Guards, but some cases of theft and violent attacks still occur.

Also belonging to Colombia are the Caribbean islands of Providencia and San Andrés, usually visited by boats on their way north from Panama. Close to the mainland is Isla Periquito, which is a national park with several attractive anchorages. Some of the cays and reefs farther north, such as Serrana, Serranilla and Roncador, also belong to Colombia, which maintains a military presence in this area. Boats that have sought shelter there have been visited by the military, but have been allowed to stay.

The city of Cartagena.

Most people only associate Colombia with the Caribbean, but its Pacific coast is equally long and just as diverse. The Pacific side is much less developed and it alternates between mangrove lowland and tropical jungle, with few settlements, while the northern area is mountainous, intersected by rivers and some spectacular waterfalls. As a result of the improved security situation, much of the Pacific coast is considered safe, with the exception of the area around Buenaventura and the coast between Tumaco and Cabo Coriente, where it is advisable to sail well offshore. Buenaventura itself is safe and, together with Tumaco and Bahia Solano, is a convenient port of call. Isla Gorgona, previously a prison island but now converted into a nature reserve, provides an insight into Colombia's rich flora and fauna. Another protected area is Ensenada de Utria National Park, which also includes two Amerindian reserves. The park's outlet to the sea is a sheltered anchorage set amid spectacular scenery and often frequented by humpbacked whales.

✦ COUNTRY PROFILE

Long before Europeans arrived, Caribs lived along the northern coast, while the interior was inhabited by hunters, nomadic tribes, and the Chibchas – skilled goldsmiths who rolled their chief in gold dust every year. After a long period of Spanish dominance, revolts started at the beginning of the nineteenth century, and by 1819 the Republic of Gran Colombia was declared. Recent history has been characterized by long periods of political instability and guerrilla warfare, the rise of the drug barons, and the collapse of peace talks. The production of cocaine and the power of the huge drug industry is an ongoing problem for the government, which is making a determined effort to bring the continuing stalemate to an end.

The population is 45.5 million, a mixture of European, Amerindian and African origins. Spanish is the main language. Bogotá, at 2,650m (8,690ft), is the capital.

✦ CLIMATE

The climate is equatorial, with periods of high humidity and very hot days. Summer is the rainy season, although there is no specific dry season and Colombia gets even more rain than Panama. The northeast trade winds cool the Caribbean coast during the winter months, while the summer has much lighter winds. Hurricanes rarely reach as far south as Colombia, although their effects may be felt, whereas the Pacific coast is entirely hurricane free.

boat for clearance. It has been reported that electronic charts for the area have significant datum offset.

Bahia Solano: Yachts should anchor close to the Coast Guard dock and complete formalities ashore.

Visas are not required for nationals of most countries for stays up to 60 days. In its ongoing campaign against drug smuggling, the Coast Guard patrol the Colombian waters and may contact, and even board, a yacht. Inland areas are reported to be too dangerous for touring. Yachts must clear in and out with the port captain at every major port and obtain an outward clearance for the next port. A number of fees and extra charges were introduced in 2009.

✦ FACILITIES

The best facilities are in Cartagena with a good range of repair facilities, haulout, and all associated marine services. Facilities are good at San André Yacht Club, both for repair and provisioning. Facilities are more limited in Providencia, but there is fuel and water.

Provisioning is good along the Caribbean coast, particularly in larger ports, where there are both supermarkets and fresh produce markets. On the Pacific coast, Bahia Solano and Tumaco are good stops both for provisions and simple repairs. Buenaventura is also a convenient place to call as it has a good range of repair facilities.

✦ CHARTER

There are no bareboats available, only crewed yachts, and the few operators are based in Cartagena.

www.cartagenasailing.com
www.theandiamo.com

✦ FORMALITIES

PORTS OF ENTRY

Caribbean coast: San Andrés 12°33′ N 81°41′ W	
Providencia 13°23′ N 81°22′ W	
Cartagena 10°25′ N 75°32′ W	Barranquilla 10°58′ N 74°46′ W
Riohacha 11°33′ N 72°55′ W	Santa Marta 11°15′ N 74°13′ W
Pacific coast: Tumaco 1°49.04′ N 78°43.4′ W	
Buenaventura 3°54′ N 77°05′ W	
Bahia Solano 6°14′ N 77°24.6′ W	

Customs and immigration formalities are completed only in the first and last ports, and an agent must always be used. The port captain can usually recommend an agent.

Barranquilla: Yachts should dock wherever possible, then ask for a berthing assignment from the port captain. The yacht clubs have limited space and anchoring is not possible in the busy river. It has been reported that the port is not recommended for security reasons.

Cartagena: It is best to berth at either Club Nautico or Club de Pesca, and complete formalities from there. The authorities insist on the use of an agent and either club will recommend one.

Santa Marta: Yachts can anchor to the south or come alongside the eastern dock, where officials prefer to board.

Providencia: Having negotiated the buoyed channel, yachts should anchor wherever there is space. A local agent can be contacted on channel 16 and he will bring the officials to the

Cruising Guide
Pacific Colombia (can be downloaded from the Sarana website)

Websites
www.cartagenainfo.net
www.sailsarana.com/guide

Local time	UTC −5
Buoyage	IALA B
Currency	Colombian Peso (COP)
Electricity	110V, 60Hz

Diplomatic missions

UK	1 326 8300	Canada	1 657 9800
USA	1 315 0811	New Zealand	1 633 1322
Australia	1 610 9707		

Communications	**Emergency number**
IDD 57 IAC 009	112

ECUADOR

Straddling the equator on the west coast of South America, Ecuador is a country of contrasts between coastal plains and rugged mountains. The low-lying Costa is the main agricultural region and Guayaquil its principal city. Inland is the high Sierra and the western Amazon basin. In the central Sierra highlands is the capital Quito, once co-capital of the 'Tahuantinsuyo' Inca Kingdom; the Spanish conquistadors built modern Quito on the same site.

Cruising opportunities in mainland Ecuador are limited as the coast is arid and there are few natural harbours, with the notable exception of the estuary of the River Guayas. The river is navigable for the 40 miles to Guayaquil where the local yacht club welcomes visitors. The absence of other interesting places along the coast is more than made up for by the wealth of interesting things to see inland – from the isolated communities in the majestic Andes to the rich flora and fauna of the Amazon jungle, whose Ecuadorean section has hardly been touched by modern development. For nature lovers, this area is a dream destination, with exotic orchids, colourful birds and strange plants in the dripping tropical forests.

Ecuador's best-known attraction lies several hundred miles offshore in its Archipiélago de Colón, commonly known as the Galapagos Islands. As they form a separate entity, and cruising regulations also differ from mainland Ecuador, the Galapagos are described separately in the South Pacific section (page 320). For yachts heading south from Panama, a good foretaste of what the Galapagos Islands have to offer is to call at Isla de la Plata, described as 'the poor man's Galapagos'. The island lies off the Ecuadorian mainland and is a nature reserve, its rich wildlife including blue- and red-footed boobies, pelicans, petrels, terns and frigate birds. Brief stops seem to be tolerated by the resident warden.

Puerto Lucia Yacht Club.

✦ COUNTRY PROFILE

In the mid-fifteenth century the Incas of Peru expanded into Ecuador and made it part of their empire. This mighty empire was relatively short-lived and its total demise was accelerated by the arrival of the Spanish conquistadors, who incorporated it into their vast empire. After the failure of a confederation with Venezuela and Colombia, independence was finally achieved in 1830. There followed a long and bitter struggle between the religious conservatives and secular liberals, broken by periods of military rule, which did not stop until the 1978 constitution ended military rule and a more stable period ensued. The current President Rafael Correa won the 2009 elections, the first incumbent in a century to win two consecutive terms. His social policies place him firmly on the left side of the political spectrum, similar to other contemporary Latin American leaders.

The 14.5 million inhabitants are mostly Quechua or mestizo, though a small proportion of the population is of European, African or Asian origin. Spanish and Quechua are the main languages. The capital is Quito.

✦ CLIMATE

Although lying on the equator, the climate of Ecuador is pleasant, and temperatures along the coast show little difference between the seasons. Along the coast there is a humid rainy season between December and May, with March being the wettest month. December and January are the warmest months, with an average of 26°C/79°F, whereas July and August are the coolest, with an average of 24°C/75°F. The winds are mostly light southerlies, and winds over 20 knots are almost unknown.

✦ FORMALITIES

PORTS OF ENTRY	
Esmeraldas	0°58´N 79°41´W
Bahia de Caraquez (Puerto Amistad)	0°36´S 80°25´W
Manta	0°56´S 80°43´W
La Libertad (Puerto Lucia Yacht Club)	2°13´S 80°55´W
Puerto Azul (Guayaquil Yacht Club)	2°12´S 79°58´W
Guayaquil	2°17´S 79°55´W

Esmeraldas: Yachts should come to the Navy dock or anchor close to the fishing harbour, opposite the port captain's office.

Bahia de Caraquez: Puerto Amistad Marina should be called on Channel 69 from well outside the estuary and a pilot boat will be sent to escort the yacht into the marina. The marina will help deal with entry formalities.

Manta: Yachts should moor in the area reserved for the local yacht club before contacting the port captain.

Puerto Lucia: The marina should be contacted on Channel 19A (0800–1800 local time) and it will assist with entry formalities. Late arrivals should anchor outside the marina entrance.

Guayaquil: The Guayaquil Yacht Club should be called on Channel 71 as soon as within calling range.

New regulations require all arriving vessels to send an email to the maritime authorities with details of the vessel, ETA, intended port of arrival, etc (guayaquil_radio@dirnea.org).

Sending such an advance message will make it possible to complete formalities without any delays. The form can be downloaded from the DIRNEA (Direccion General de la Marina Mercantil) website by clicking first on SITRAME, and then on IAA Format English which will bring up the form.

Visas for 90 days are granted to the nationals of all countries. Citizens of the EU, USA and Canada can apply for an additional 90 days without leaving Ecuador. There are no laws stipulating how long a yacht can remain in Ecuador.

Clearance must be obtained before sailing to another Ecuadorean port. As the authorities do not give clearance to Galapagos, as by law only emergency stops are allowed there, you should indicate the Marquesas or another country as your intended destination. Stops in Galapagos are, however, normally allowed (see page 321).

✦ FACILITIES

The best facilities are in and around Salinas, where Puerto Lucia Yacht Club has a complete array of services, including all types of repairs, fuel, water and travelift. The marina is a good place to leave the boat unattended to visit the interior and also to leave for the Galapagos.

Both in Guayaquil and Puerto Azul, the Guayaquil Yacht Club has pontoons with electricity and water, good provisioning, but marine services and supplies are limited.

Esmeraldas is a small town with only basic necessities, but the new marina at Stella Maris Yacht Club (0°51.6′N 79°55.4′W), being built as part of a tourist resort a few miles south of Esmeraldas, will greatly improve matters. Located in Bahia de Caraquez, Puerto Amistad is a small marina with a limited range of facilities. Better repair services are available in the fishing port of Manta. It is possible to anchor inside the harbour and take the dinghy to the Manta Yacht Club dock.

Provisioning is adequate along the coast, but a better selection, as well as fuel, is easier to obtain in larger ports.

Cruising Guide
Ecuador Cruisers' Handbook (can be downloaded from the Sarana website)

Websites
www.ecuadortouristboard.com
www.puertolucia.com.ec
www.dirnea.org (Maritime Authority)
www.sailsarana.com/guide

Local time	UTC −5
Buoyage	IALA B
Currency	United States Dollar (USD)
Electricity	127V, 60Hz

Diplomatic missions	
UK	2 297 0800
USA	2 398 5000
Australia	4 601 7529
Canada	2 245 5449

Communications	
IDD 593	IAC 00

Emergency numbers		
911	Ambulance 131	Police 101

FRENCH GUIANA

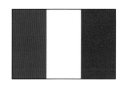

FRENCH GUIANA is an overseas department of France, sandwiched between Brazil and Suriname. The atmosphere in the country is more Caribbean and akin to Martinique than to the rest of Latin America. The low coastal regions gradually climb to the forested hills of the interior from where 20 rivers flow down to the Atlantic Ocean. Cayenne is the capital, on the island of the same name at the mouth of the Cayenne river. The Oyapok river, which borders Brazil, is navigable far into the heart of the rainforest. At the other end of the country, bordering Suriname, is the Maroni river, which is also occasionally visited by yachts.

The coast itself has few ports or anchorages worth exploring, but the off-lying Iles du Salut are a popular stop for sailors as the location of the infamous penal colony of Devil's Island. These islands can only be visited after having cleared into the country. Also interesting to visit is the Ariane Space Centre at Kourou, although an appointment has to be made in advance. River trips, usually by canoe, are another attraction of this small country, which is only visited by a small number of cruising yachts, mainly French.

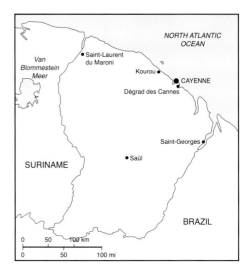

◆ COUNTRY PROFILE

Columbus was the first European visitor in 1498, to be followed by Amerigo Vespucci, Sir Walter Raleigh and many other explorers. French settlers arrived in the sixteenth century and from the French Revolution onwards, Guyane was used for many years as a penal colony for criminal and political prisoners.

The 225,000 inhabitants are Creole, Amerindian and French. French is the official language.

◆ CLIMATE

The rainy and hot season is from November to July, while August to December is the cooler, more pleasant period. Rainfall can be heavy in this tropical climate where temperatures average 27°C/80°F.

◆ FORMALITIES

PORTS OF ENTRY

Dégrad des Cannes 4°51´N 52°16´W	
Cayenne 4°56´N 52°20´W	Kourou 4°59´N 52°40´W

Dégrad des Cannes is the best place to clear in. Officials will normally come out to the boat on arrival.

Immigration and customs rules are the same as for France and for the Schengen area. A valid visa for France is also valid for French Guiana, although visitors should make it clear that they intend to visit French Guiana when applying for a visa.

Yellow fever vaccination is compulsory and an international certificate will be asked for.

It is illegal to sell any possessions to local residents and the penalties are heavy fines. As informers receive a large proportion of the fine, visitors have been set up by some of these local informers.

It is forbidden to anchor at Iles du Salut on the rare occasions when a rocket is due to be fired from the Ariane Space Centre.

◆ FACILITIES

The best repair facilities are in Kourou. There is good provisioning in all ports.

In Dégrad des Cannes there are floating pontoons on the river beyond the commercial port.

Website			
www.tourisme-guyane.com			

Local time	UTC −3	Currency	Euro (EUR)
Buoyage	IALA B	Electricity	220V, 50Hz

Diplomatic missions	
UK	311034

Communications	
IDD 594	IAC 00

Emergency numbers		
112	Ambulance 15	Police 17

GUYANA

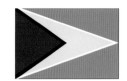

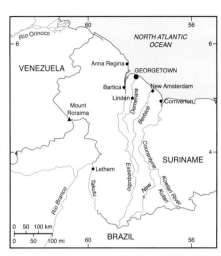

GUYANA MEANS 'LAND OF MANY WATERS' in Amerindian, which is an accurate description of this country of many swamps and rivers on the northeast coast of South America. Guyana is in many respects a spectacular country, its 215,000 sq km (83,000 sq miles) of rainforest, savannah and coastline supporting a population of barely 800,000 people. Most of them live along the narrow coastal belt, which is very low and subject to flooding. Being a difficult coast to approach, because of the shallow and muddy waters, means Guyana is not a natural cruising destination. It is possible to take keeled boats up the Rivers Pomeroon, Waini and Raima, while the River Berbice is navigable for 100 miles upstream of the port of New Amsterdam.

The capital, Georgetown, has a certain charm and the few yachts that visit Guyana rarely go anywhere else. Set on the bank of the River Demerara, the town's attractive nineteenth-century houses sit on stilts along disused Dutch canals. Those prepared to navigate the partly buoyed Essequibo river will reach, after 40 miles, the small town of Bartica, the country's second port of entry. The river is navigable for some distance inland and provides a tempting opportunity to see part of Guyana's interesting interior.

✦ COUNTRY PROFILE

Although the Spanish were the first to explore this coast, they were not too impressed by what they found. It was the Dutch who colonized the land in the sixteenth century and in 1815 the land was ceded to Britain when Essequibo, Berbice and Demerara were merged to form British Guiana. Independence from Britain was achieved in 1966.

The population is about 773,000, of which almost half are of Asian extraction, the rest African or Amerindian . English is the official language, although Creole is widely spoken.

✦ CLIMATE

The climate is hot and humid, especially from August to October. The wet seasons are from April to August, and November to January. Guyana lies outside of the hurricane belt.

✦ FORMALITIES

Georgetown: The Lighthouse Service should be called to arrange an agent, who will carry out the formalities at the customs dock. After clearance, you can proceed to the Coast Guard dock, this being the most secure docking option.
Bartica: The River Essequibo, which leads to Bartica, has a bar at its entrance that is best crossed at high water. The river shallows are marked by buoys. In Bartica, you should anchor off Roeden Rust Marina and contact the customs office (+1 592 225 4698). The marina will give help both with formalities and local information.

PORTS OF ENTRY

Georgetown 6°49′ N 58°11′ W   Bartica 6°24′ N 58°37′ W

Nationals of most European countries, Australia, Canada, New Zealand, South Africa and the USA do not require visas.

The safety situation in the whole country is uncertain and some areas are considered unsafe for travel.

✦ FACILITIES

Fresh provisions are plentiful, but prices of imported goods are high. Fuel and LPG are available, but only simple repairs are possible and there are no marine supplies obtainable. The NGEC shipyard in Georgetown operates a dry dock and slipway, and may do work on a yacht in an emergency. Some repairs are possible in Bartica.

Cruising Guide
Trinidad and Tobago plus Guyana

Websites
www.guyana-tourism.com   www.turq.com/guyana.html

| **Local time** | UTC −4 | **Currency** | Guyanese Dollar (GYD) |
| **Buoyage** | IALA B | **Electricity** | 240V, 60Hz |

Diplomatic missions
| UK | 226 5881 | Canada | 227 2081 | USA | 225 4900 |

| **Communications** | **Emergency number** |
| IDD 592 IAC 001 | 999 |

PERU

WITH ITS INCA RUINS, old Spanish colonial cities and the magnificent Andes dominating the centre of the country, Peru is one of the most fascinating places to visit in South America. In spite of all these attractions, the country is not an obvious cruising destination as there are few natural anchorages or attractive ports along its arid coast. The Atacama Desert covers a wide strip of land nearly 600 miles long down the Pacific coast. This immense desert is considered not only the driest place on earth, but possibly also includes places that have never had any rain. This dry environment has preserved thousands of ancient sites, as well as perfectly preserved mummies, many of which predate the Inca civilization.

For boats coming from the north, the ports of Ancon and Paita are convenient stops for provisions or fuel, but have little else to offer. The few yachts that call normally make their base at Callao, near the capital, Lima, whose friendly yacht club is a good place to leave the boat while touring the interior of this intriguing country.

◆ COUNTRY PROFILE

Several different cultures rose and fell in this region before the Incas came to dominate Peru and Ecuador. The Inca civilization dates from the eleventh century. Expanding outwards from the Cusco basin, by the mid-fifteenth century the Incas had conquered much of the surrounding region. All this came to an end with the arrival in 1532 of a small band of Spanish conquistadors, led by Francisco Pizarro, who defeated Emperor Atahualpa and imposed Spanish rule. Ten years later, the Spanish Crown established the viceroyalty of Peru, which included several of its South American colonies. The Inca civilization rapidly declined, its people decimated by disease, civil wars and slavery. In line with its neighbours, Peru declared independence from Spain in 1821. The nineteenth century saw the loss of some southern provinces to Chile in the War of the Pacific.

The twentieth century was marked by periods of political instability, which culminated in a military coup in 1968, but democracy was restored in 1975. There was a grave period of

Machu Picchu.

Peru claims a 200 mile territorial boundary and the authorities expect to be contacted by SSB radio as soon as a vessel enters territorial waters. If there is no answer, the call should be recorded in the log, with the position and time of attempted contact. Contact by email is: costera.callao@dicapi.mil.pe.

As soon as you are within calling distance, the marine authority (TRAMAR) should be contacted and you should then proceed directly to an official port of entry.

As few yachts visit Peru, clearance is best done with the assistance of yacht clubs in two locations: Callao and Ancon.

Callao: Yacht Club Peruano (Channel 68) will facilitate the clearing process, but does not act as an official agent. Yacht Club Peruano should be contacted in advance for assistance: yacht.operaciones@infonegocio.net.pe.

Ancon: Cruising boats should go directly to the Ancon Yacht Club dock. The club will contact the authorities for clearance.

No visas are needed by nationals of most countries for stays of up to 90 days. The crew of foreign yachts who wish to visit the interior should insist on being given a tourist card on arrival, particularly if intending to leave Peru to visit one of the neighbouring countries overland.

✦ FACILITIES

Yacht Club Peruano in Callao has the best facilities, with mooring buoys and a launch service, travelift, water, fuel and access to a good range of repair services. It welcomes visitors and is a good place to leave the yacht to travel inland. Provisioning is good and there is an excellent fresh produce market. La Punta Ancon Yacht Club is also welcoming, with moorings, fuel, water, a travelift and good security. The biggest sailing event of the year is the annual race to the Galapagos Islands and back, which is joined by many yachts from Callao's two yacht clubs.

Websites
www.visitperu.com (Peru Tourism Bureau)
www.peru.info (general information)
www.yachtclubperuano.com

Local time	UTC −5
Buoyage	IALA B
Currency	Nuevo Sol (PEN)
Electricity	220V, 60Hz

Diplomatic missions			
UK	1 617 3000	Canada	1 319 3200
USA	1 434 3000	South Africa	1 440 9996
Australia	1 222 8281	New Zealand	1 422 7491

Communications	Emergency numbers
IDD 51 IAC 00	112 Police 105

instability in the 1990s as a guerrilla war waged in the interior. The situation was eventually brought under control, and travelling in the country is now deemed to be safe.

Of the 30 million population, nearly half are Amerindian, some of mixed descent, one-third European, and the rest of African, Chinese or Japanese origin. The official languages are Spanish and Quechua. The latter is an Inca language, spoken by about half the population, many of whom speak no Spanish. The people of Southern Peru speak Aymara.

✦ CLIMATE

The climate of coastal Peru is greatly influenced by the Humboldt Current, which keeps temperatures cool throughout the year and often produces coastal fog, especially between May and November. The cold current ensures that winters are very cool, with an average August temperature of 16°C/61°F in Lima, whereas in summer the average rises to 25°C/77°F. There is very little rain along the coast. The prevailing winds are south or southeasterly and usually light.

✦ FORMALITIES

PORTS OF ENTRY	
Talara 4°34′S 81°16′W	Paita 5°05′S 81°07′W
Chimbote 9°05′S 78°38′W	Ancon 11°46′S 77°11′W
Callao 12°03′S 77°09′W	
General San Martín 13°50′S 81°16′W	
Matarani 16°59′S 72°07′W	

SURINAME

SURINAME, KNOWN AS DUTCH GUIANA BEFORE INDEPENDENCE, lies on the northeast coast of South America between Guyana and French Guiana. Spain showed little interest in it, so this area was colonized by the other European powers. As a result, the three Guyanas have always been considered more Caribbean than Latin American.

Suriname has a flat, marshy coast, where most of the population live. Uplands rise from the coast, which is indented with rivers that make the sea muddy and navigation difficult. Some of the wide rivers are navigable for a considerable distance inland, but to do this requires special permission from the authorities in Paramaribo. Many parts of the interior have been declared nature reserves, and the area of the Coppename river watershed, where the Central Suriname Nature Reserve is located, has been declared a UNESCO World Heritage Site for its unspoiled rainforest biodiversity. The capital, Paramaribo, lies on the banks of the wide Suriname river and is 8 miles from the sea.

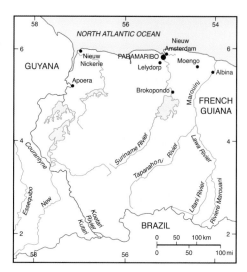

✦ COUNTRY PROFILE

The coast was first sighted by Columbus in 1498. It was in the early seventeenth century that Dutch merchants began trading along what became known as the Wild Coast. English settlers arrived and, after competing claims, Britain acknowledged the country as belonging to the Netherlands. In 1975 Suriname became independent.

The population numbers 481,000, over one-third being of Asian origin, one-third Creole, of mixed European and African ancestry, and only 10 per cent being original Amerindians. Dutch is the official language, but English and a local dialect called Sranan Tongo, of Creole origin, are also spoken.

✦ CLIMATE

The climate is tropical and humid, but not too hot due to the cooling effect of the trade winds. Average temperatures range from 23°C/73°F to 31°C/88°F. The rainy seasons are November to February and April to August.

✦ FORMALITIES

PORT OF ENTRY
Paramaribo 5°50′N 55°10′W

The maritime authority should be contacted on Channel 12 on reaching the river mouth and instructions asked for. The river is well buoyed.

On arrival, you should report to immigration. It is recommended that a visa is obtained in advance, and this can be acquired in nearby Guyana, French Guiana or Venezuela –

which may take 15 days unless extra fees are paid. If you do not have a visa, a temporary five-day stamp is issued, during which time you must obtain a visa locally. Visas are issued by the tourist police station (Vreemdelingen Politie). The crew list must be stamped as well as passports when departing, application for which must be made two days before departure.

If coming from Guyana or French Guiana, a yellow fever vaccination certificate is required.

✦ FACILITIES

The only suitable place for a longer stay is Domburg Marina, 8 miles farther upriver from Paramaribo, where there are a few moorings for visiting yachts. Otherwise, yachting facilities are very limited and only simple repairs can be done. A shipyard operates in Paramaribo harbour and they have a dry dock and lift, where yachts can be hauled out if necessary. Provisioning in Paramaribo is reasonable.

Websites	
www.surinametourism.com	www.surinametourism.net

Local time	UTC −3	Currency	Surinamese Dollar (SRD)
Buoyage	IALA B	Electricity	127V, 60Hz

Diplomatic missions			
UK	402 558	USA	472 900

Communications	
IDD 597	IAC 009, 007, 005

Emergency numbers 112/115

URUGUAY

Piriápolis.

LYING ON THE NORTHERN BANK of the Rio de la Plata, the name 'Uruguay' means 'river of birds', and it is rivers that have shaped the history of this country, which is one of the smallest in Latin America. The rivers Uruguay and Paraná meet at Nueva Palmira to become the Rio de la Plata. The Uruguay river is navigable for a long way and is used even by large ocean-going ships. An interesting side trip is up the Río Negro, a tributary of the Uruguay, which is used regularly by both Argentine and Uruguayan yachts drawing less than 1.80m (6ft).

The capital, Montevideo, has one marina, and this makes a good base from which to explore this vibrant city. Uruguay's principal yachting centre is Punta del Este, which was put on the world sailing map by the Whitbread Round the World Race (now Volvo Ocean Race) and, although the race no longer calls there, the facilities remain for yachts to use. Compared to this high-rise resort, the port of Piriápolis is on a more human scale, with a marina where visiting yachts are warmly welcomed. There are few cruising opportunities along the coast, but there are several places to leave the boat while visiting the interior of this low, undulating country.

✦ COUNTRY PROFILE

Before the Europeans arrived, this was the home of the warlike Charrúa. In 1516 the Spaniard Juan Diaz de Solis landed and claimed the land for Spain. After many years of turbulent history, the modern state of Uruguay was founded in 1825. It currently has one of the most stable political systems in South America. Agriculture, mainly cattle breeding, dominates the economy, with Uruguay being famous for its cattle-raising cowboys called gauchos.

The population is just under 3.5 million, with 50 per cent living in and around the only large city, Montevideo. Most of the population are of Spanish or Italian origin, with the original Amerindian population having virtually disappeared. Spanish is the official language.

✦ CLIMATE

The climate is temperate, but somewhat damp and windy. Winter lasts from June to September, with average temperatures ranging from 10° to 16°C/50° to 61°F, but temperatures can drop below freezing. Summer is from December to March, with an average temperature of only 23°C/73°F in the warmest month of January, although maximum temperatures of over 40°C/104°F have been recorded. The winds in the Rio de la Plata estuary are easterly in the summer months. Strong southwest winds called *pamperos* occur mostly between June and October, occasionally reaching hurricane force.

FORMALITIES

PORTS OF ENTRY

Punta del Este	34°57.5´ S 54°57´ W
Montevideo	34°54´ S 56°13´ W
Buceo	34°55´ S 56°08´ W
Piriápolis	34°52.7´ S 55°17.3´ W
La Paloma	34°39´ S 54°09´ W
Colonia	34°28´ S 57°52´ W

Before entering any port, Control Marítimo should be called on Channels 16, 11 or 9.

Montevideo: Rather than clearing in at this busy commercial harbour, it is better to head for Puerto del Buceo where Yacht Club Uruguayo has the only marina in the city and will assist with formalities.

Punta del Este: Yachts should tie up to one of the municipal marina moorings. Officials do not normally board yachts for clearance. The marina office can be contacted on Channel 71, but the captain has to go ashore and visit the offices either in the harbour (in summer) or in town.

The captain should first visit the Coast Guard office (Prefectura Naval). The officials may deal with all the entry requirements, or it may be necessary also to visit the customs and immigration offices. Visas are not required for most nationals and a tourist card valid for three months is usually issued on arrival. A 'Safety Certificate' may be asked for, and the fact that most countries do not issue such a document is not easily understood.

FACILITIES

Punta del Este: The best facilities are at Punta del Este Yacht Club Marina, which is a full service marina. Dealing with the Whitbread fleet has given local workshops a certain degree of experience, but marine supplies are limited. These are better in Buenos Aires, on the Argentine side of the river.

Montevideo: The best facilities near Montevideo are in Buceo, which is the base of the Yacht Club Uruguayo and its moorings are available for visitors. Foreign yachts normally make this their base to visit Montevideo. Good facilities include workshops and boatyard, engine repairs and maintenance.

Piriápolis: There are also good repair facilities in Piriápolis, which has the largest travelift in the country. Piriápolis is particularly popular with cruising sailors as all facilities are close by and the friendly port is a good base from which to visit the rest of Uruguay, and even neighbouring countries.

The excellent Cibernautica website, although only in Spanish, is relatively easy to navigate and gives a range of maritime information. This is mostly on Argentina, but there is also some on Uruguay, including daily weather forecasts for the Mar del Plata area and even the Uruguayan bases in Antarctica.

Cruising Guides
Havens and Anchorages
South Atlantic Circuit

Websites
www.turismo.gub.uy
www.cibernautica.com.ar
www.ycu.org.uy (Yacht Club Uruguayo)
www.ycpe.com.uy (Yacht Club Punta del Este)

Local time	UTC −3
	Winter time: second Sunday in March to first Sunday in October
Buoyage	IALA B
Currency	Uruguayan Peso (UYU)
Electricity	220V, 50Hz

Diplomatic missions
UK	2 622 3630
USA	2 418 7777
Australia	2 901 0743
Canada	2 902 2030
South Africa	2 623 0161
New Zealand	2 622 1543

Communications
IDD 598	IAC 00

Emergency number
911

VENEZUELA

VENEZUELA'S FIRST EUROPEAN VISITOR, Christopher Columbus, had an epiphany on sighting the Orinoco in 1498: 'I believe this is a very great continent, until today unknown. And reason aids me greatly because of that so great river…' He was right, and he had indeed discovered a great continent. Venezuela means 'Little Venice' in Spanish, which was the name given to this northerly country in South America by the early explorers, who found the natives living on the Sinamaica lagoon in houses built on stilts. Nature has blessed this country with great mineral wealth, with Venezuela having one of the biggest oil reserves in the world. But it is also blessed with diverse landscapes – from miles of beautiful Caribbean beaches to open plains, towering mountains, tracts of Amazon rainforest, and even a small desert. In the southeast of the country, the Gran Sabana National Park contains the spectacular Angel Falls, the world's highest waterfall.

Off Venezuela's long Caribbean coastline are scores of islands, including the popular yachting destination, Isla de Margarita. These islands abound in picturesque anchorages and diving is excellent almost everywhere, particularly among the scores of islets and cays of Los Roques. Lying on the direct route to Panama and also being rarely affected by hurricanes, the Venezuelan coast, and particularly the off-lying islands, became a popular cruising destination in the latter part of the twentieth century. This popularity was matched by a rapid improvement in yachting facilities and services.

A very different destination is the delta of the Orinoco River, much of which can be explored by keeled yachts. Those interested in the mountainous interior can leave their boats in the safety of one of the many marinas.

Recent years have seen a decline in the number of visiting yachts due to the steadily deteriorating safety situation. A spate of violent attacks on foreign yachts, several with fatal consequences, have forced sailors to change their cruising plans and avoid Venezuela for the time being. Those who intend to visit Venezuela on their own yachts are advised to find out the latest situation and avoid any critical areas, as many places are still safe and yachts continue to cruise without encountering any problems.

✦ COUNTRY PROFILE

The Carib and Arawak tribes, who lived along the coast, put up little resistance to the Spanish settlers who arrived at the start of the eighteenth century. After several uprisings against Spain's colonial rule, Simon Bolívar defeated the Spanish forces and set up the independent Gran Colombia, a union of Ecuador, Colombia, Venezuela and Panama, but in 1830 Venezuela broke away to become an independent republic. A succession of dictators ruled the country into the early twentieth century. Increasing instability led to two unsuccessful military coups in 1992. In 1999 Hugo Chavez, one of the military officers who led one of the 1992 coups, was elected president on a manifesto of economic and political reform. His long rule has brought about many radical changes, but Venezuela continues to be divided by deep conflicts of interest.

The population is 27 million, mostly of mixed Spanish and Amerindian ancestry, with pure Amerindians living in the more remote parts. The main language is Spanish. Caracas is the capital.

✦ CLIMATE

Venezuela has a tropical climate and there is little change between the seasons, although it is drier from December to April. There is little temperature variation, with an average of 27°C/81°F in the coolest month of January and 30°C/86°F in the hottest months of August and September. The northern coast and off-lying islands are under the influence of the northeast trade winds, which blow strongly between December and April. Summer winds are lighter and Venezuela is very rarely affected by tropical storms.

✦ FORMALITIES

On entry into Venezuela you must clear with customs, immigration and port captain, in that order.

Porlamar: Formalities have been simplified and the authorities no longer insist on the services of an agent. The port captain's office is close to Guardia Nacional station. This office has been expanded to include both immigration and customs.

Puerto La Cruz: Located on the mainland, boats should proceed to Xanadu Marina, where entry formalities can be completed.

Pampatar: In 2009, most yachts bypassed Pampatar as the Port Authorities were reportedly not welcoming yachts.

Los Testigos: This is not a port of entry, so theoretically you should clear into Venezuela somewhere else before going there. Boats that have not yet cleared in are normally allowed to stop for 72 hours, but extensions are usually granted. Yachts are requested to visit the Coast Guard office on Isla Iguana and also to call the office on departure. The area is occasionally patrolled by the Coast Guard, who will ask those who have overstayed to move on.

Carúpano: Boats should anchor inside the harbour. All offices are near the port.

La Guaira: This is a big commercial port and yachts cannot clear in without using an agent. It may be necessary to have an official pilot for entry into Maracaibo, La Guaira and Ciudad Bolívar. A better alternative is to stop at nearby Marina Portofino and clear from there.

Los Roques: This is not an official port of entry, but boats are usually allowed a stay of 15 days. Most yachts prolong this by taking several days to then reach Roque Grande where entry formalities are completed at various offices as well as the national park service. The park official should be informed where you intend to go as special permission is needed for some parts of the park and access to other areas is prohibited.

Most nationalities need to obtain a tourist visa in advance. There are Venezuelan consulates in Aruba, Bonaire, Martinique, Barbados, Guyana, Suriname, Trinidad and Grenada where visas are issued.

Foreign yachts may remain in Venezuela for a period of 18 months, but individuals may only stay for 90 days. Some of the agents in Puerto de la Cruz and Porlamar are able to extend this personal time allowance.

Yachts must clear in and out with customs and port captain in each state visited. Immigration clearance is only required when entering and leaving the country. As clearance is done from state to state, no cruising permit is necessary. You should be aware that the rules change often and that individual port captains often alter the rules to fit their own interpretation of the law. Visiting yachts have started being charged a tax of 1 per cent of their value. The law may be repealed as it has led to a massive exodus of cruising boats.

The captain of yachts that intend to stop at any of the Venezuelan islands between Isla de Margarita and Bonaire should mention this when clearing out of Isla de Margarita.

PORTS OF ENTRY

Carúpano	10°41´N 63°15´W	Puerto Sucre (Cumaná)	10°28´N 64°11´W	Puerto La Cruz	10°13´N 64°38´W
Carenero	10°32´N 66°07´W	La Guaira	10°36´N 66°56´W	Puerto Cabello	10°29´N 68°00´W
Maracaibo	10°39´N 71°36´W	Pampatar (Isla de Margarita)	11°00´N 63°47´W	Porlamar	10°56.5´N 63°49´W

Los Roques.

A note will be made on the clearance paper that permission had been granted to stop at 'puntos intermedios'. This may not always be acceptable to other officials, but yachts seem to be able to stop at La Blanquilla without any difficulties.

Isla Orchilla is a military base and should not be approached. Los Piedros (Punto Fijo) is also a military base and entry is prohibited.

Precautions should be taken against vampire bats on the coast from Cumaná onwards and also the Chimaná Islands, as they may carry the rabies virus. The bats will fly onto a boat at night and bite the sleeping occupants.

✦ FACILITIES

As the result of a steady increase in the number of locally owned boats as well as the large number of foreign yachts based in Venezuela, repair facilities are generally good and the prices competitive because labour costs are low. A written estimate should be obtained before embarking on any major work. The majority of cruising yachts that need work done choose Puerto La Cruz where there are haulout facilities, and spare parts are available. The Amerigo Vespucci Marina in Puerto La Cruz operates a boatyard, where yachts can be slipped and hull repair undertaken.

At Isla de Margarita, several planned marina projects have not come to fruition and there is only one marina suitable for visiting boats. A limited number of repair facilities are available. Recommended are the services of Venezuelan Marine Supplies (Vemasca) in Porlamar, which has a good range of services, does rigging work, stocks some spares, and will also order parts. Isla de Margarita is no longer a duty-free island and now has an 8 per cent sales tax, but this is still less than the mainland where the tax is 15 per cent.

Venezuela is a good place to provision, especially if continuing on to the Pacific. Prices are lower than in most areas in the Caribbean. The selection is generally good, although shortages can occur. Fuel is widely available and cheap. The 'vessel in transit' status is not recognized and getting spare parts sent in can be difficult and costly. For this reason, many sailors choose to get their repairs done in Trinidad or make sure they bring any necessary parts with them.

There are good repair facilities and several boatyards in Cumaná, but many yachts are now avoiding this area because of the rising crime rate.

Boats heading for the Orinoco will find good facilities, fuel and provisions at Puerto Ordez, at the confluence of the Orinoco and Coroni rivers. There is a yacht club, which can be used by visitors. Boats reaching the Orinoco from the south will find some supplies and fuel at Curiapo, on the Barima river.

✦ CHARTER

There are no bareboat operators, although a number of crewed yachts are available in Los Roques.

www.sailboat-obsession.com
www.sailingroques.com

Cruising Guide	
Cruising Guide to Venezuela and Bonaire	
Website	
www.venezuelatuya.com	

Local time	UTC −4.5
Buoyage	IALA B
Currency	Venezuelan Bolivar (VEF)
Electricity	120V, 60Hz

Diplomatic missions	
UK	212 267 1275
USA	212 975 6411
Canada	212 600 3000
South Africa	212 991 4622
New Zealand	212 277 7965

Communications	
IDD 58	IAC 00

Emergency numbers	
112/171	

NORTH PACIFIC ISLANDS

No OTHER REGION described in this book presents such a marked contrast as between the highly developed and fast pace of Hawaii, and the traditional lifestyle of most of the Micronesian islands lying farther west. For anyone cruising the North Pacific this way of life is the most interesting and attractive feature of these widely scattered islands, some of which are rarely visited by yachts or any other outsiders. While for most sailors the islands of the South Pacific continue to enjoy the status of a dream destination, the number of those attracted to the North Pacific is still extremely small. The few sailors who resist the temptation of the South Pacific and stay north of the equator are richly rewarded as, in the words of a well-travelled circumnavigator, 'it is in Micronesia that I found my South Seas'.

Most yacht movement is centred on Hawaii, which serves as a convenient turning point for the large number of boats sailing over from mainland North America. Hawaii is also a good platform for starting a longer cruise, whether to Alaska, Micronesia or the South Pacific. The latter is still the favourite, and Tahiti the usual destination after Hawaii. A

Palmyra Island.

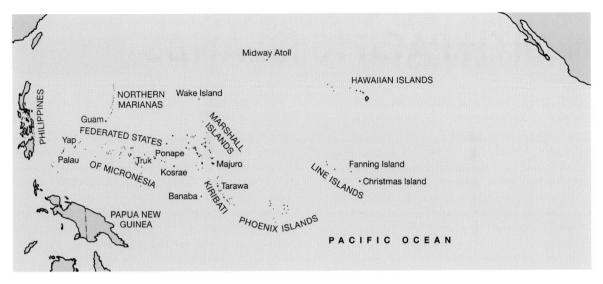

complete circumnavigation of the North Pacific, which takes advantage of prevailing conditions and calls at all island groups, follows a route that continues from Hawaii to Micronesia then turns north towards Japan at Guam or Palau. From Japan, the route turns northwest towards Alaska and British Columbia before the loop is closed.

Not all North Pacific island nations have chosen total independence. Among the former UN Trust Territories, most countries have preferred to choose only internal autonomy, while maintaining strong links with the USA, who had administered them since the Second World War. In an attempt to protect their traditional lifestyle, most Micronesian nations do not actively encourage tourism and there are certain restrictions imposed on yachts wishing to visit some of the remote islands. The western islands of Micronesia attract more visitors as yachts call there on their way to or from the South Pacific and South East Asia. The only country to have chosen to be totally independent is Kiribati.

Much of the tropical and subtropical North Pacific is under the influence of the northeast tradewinds which are most consistent during winter, from November to March. Their strength and consistency diminishes towards the equator. Those same tradewinds make planning a voyage through this area relatively easy as the logical way to do it is from east to west.

Passages from the mainland to Hawaii itself also benefit generally from the prevailing winds, whether starting from California or farther north. The ideal time to cruise the islands of Micronesia is during winter, when even in the western islands the risk of typhoons is low. Typhoons affect the area between the Carolines and Japan, with most typhoons occurring between May and December – September being the most dangerous month. In principle, west of Guam, typhoons can occur at any time of year, but the islands east of Guam are very rarely affected.

Repair and other yachting facilities are situated at the two extremes, in Hawaii and Guam, with very little in between. Anyone sailing west of Hawaii must be entirely self-sufficient and prepared to cope with any emergency.

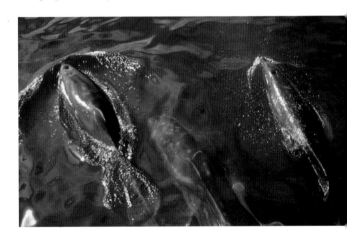

FEDERATED STATES OF MICRONESIA

Scattered over a vast expanse of Pacific Ocean just north of the equator, the Federated States of Micronesia (FSM) is composed of Kosrae, Pohnpei, Chuuk and Yap, as reflected in the four stars of its flag. The vast ocean area it occupies from Kosrae in the east to Yap in the west amounts to some 2 million sq kilometres (800,000 sq miles), while the actual land area is a mere 700 sq km (270 sq miles). Geographically, the four small states are part of the Caroline Islands, consisting between them of over six hundred islands, of which merely one-tenth are inhabited.

For the cruising sailor, the Federated States of Micronesia offers a chance to come in contact with a Micronesian society that has managed to preserve most of its traditions despite successive waves of foreign domination. Close links with the USA have brought a higher living standard, but also the social problems of modern life, which the islanders are making an effort to resist and overcome. Visitors arriving by sea, with which these seafaring islanders have a deep affinity, can be sure of a warm welcome. Famous for their sailing as well as for their navigating skills, their ancestors criss-crossed this vast ocean on their swift craft and were able to make landfall on specks of land by their observations of swell patterns, heavenly bodies and the flight of birds.

The four individual states each have their own distinct character, which adds to the attraction of sailing there. Pohnpei, formerly known as Ponape, is a lush island with eight outlying atolls. The ruins of Nan Madol, a city of nearly one hundred man-made islets dating back to the year 1200, are an impressive sight and one not to be missed. Another attraction of Pohnpei is the excellent diving, reputedly best at Ant Atoll, 10 miles southwest of Pohnpei. The atoll is privately owned and permission must be obtained from the authorities in the capital, Kolonia, before a visit.

Kosrae is a mountainous volcanic island surrounded by fringing reefs. The main port is Lelu, which used to be a meeting point for whalers who roamed the North Pacific in pursuit of their prey. Lelu Harbour and Kosrae are now quiet backwaters, mainly because the Congregationalist Church is very strong and on Sundays even leisure activities are disapproved of.

The State of Chuuk, formerly Truk, has 192 small islands, most of them uninhabited. At its centre is Chuuk Lagoon where an entire Japanese fleet was trapped and sunk by a surprise US air attack in 1944. Also part of Chuuk State are the isolated Mortlock, Hall and Western Islands, where a more traditional lifestyle is still observed.

The islands of Yap are the most isolated and also the most traditional in their way of life, and the Yapese are determined to keep it that way. Yap proper, consisting of 13 islands within a reef, is the centre of the state, while eastwards lie 134 other islands. Yap is famous for its huge stone money, which was once transported from island to island in canoes.

Many islands, especially the more isolated ones, are attempting to return to a traditional way of life by doing without Western goods and rejecting the Western way of life. Visitors are urged to respect local customs and refrain from disturbing these people's lives. Conservative dress, especially for women, is recommended.

✦ COUNTRY PROFILE

Before the arrival of Europeans, all the islands had developed civilizations based on highly stratified clan societies, and these social divisions remain strong today. Pohnpei was inhabited as early as the beginning of the first millennium and was ruled in the thirteenth century by a royal dynasty from Nan Madol. By the fifteenth century a highly developed society existed on Kosrae, with its capital on the fortified Lelu Island. On Yap, remains have been found dating back to the third century BCE, and Yap once reigned over a considerable island empire, built on the power of sorcerers.

Out of the way of the main trade routes, little attention was paid to any of the islands until the nineteenth century, when traders, whalers and missionaries arrived. New diseases wiped out many of the islanders. The surviving inhabitants saw first the Spanish, then the Germans, impose colonial rule. The Germans fled at the start of the First World War and the Japanese took over, ruling the islands on a League of Nations mandate. During the Second World War the Americans

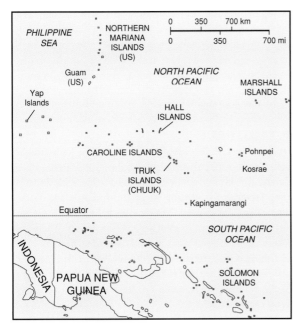

gradually pushed out the Japanese, although the worst of the fighting took place elsewhere. After the war, the USA administered the islands as part of the UN Trust Territory. In 1979 the Trust Territory voted on a common constitution, which was rejected by the Marshalls and Palau, who went their own way. The remainder formed the Federated States of Micronesia. Each state has signed a separate Compact of Free Association with the USA, with the latter keeping a military presence and the islands receiving US aid.

The population is around 107,000, with half residing in Chuuk State (Chuuk 53,500, Pohnpei 34,500, Yap 11,200, Kosrae 7,700). All are Micronesians, except for the Nukuro and Kapingamarangi islanders in Pohnpei State, who are Polynesian. Besides their own languages of Kosraen, Pohnpeian, Chuukese and Yapese, English is widely spoken. Some outer islands have their own languages.

Each state has its own centre, but the FSM capital is Palikir on Pohnpei. Colonia (the town is known locally as Donguch) is the capital of Yap, Tofol of Kosrae, and Weno of Chuuk. There is often confusion between Colonia on Yap and Kolonia on Pohnpei, because of the differing first letter.

✦ CLIMATE

The islands are under the influence of the northeast trade winds, which are most consistent between October and May. January to March is the dry season, while rainfall can be heavy in the summer months. The SW monsoon lasts from June to September when there are frequent periods of calm. Strong southwest gales can occur during August and September. They are caused by the typhoons that breed in this region, but

usually move away from the islands. Occasionally the area is affected by typhoons. Although these can occur at any time of the year, the period from early December to the end of April can be regarded as relatively safe. Some years, the typhoon season may start early or last longer than usual, so the weather should be watched carefully at all times. Guam has the best forecasts for the area.

✦ FORMALITIES

PORTS OF ENTRY		
Pohnpei:	Kolonia	6°59´N 158°13´E
Chuuk:	Weno (Chuuk Lagoon)	7°20´N 151°50´E
	Lukunor Atoll	5°30´N 153°48´E
	Satawan Atoll	5°25´N 153°35´E
Yap:	Colonia (Yap Island)	9°30´N 138°08´E
	Ulithi Atoll	9°55´N 139°30´E
	Wolaei Atoll	7°21´N 143°53´E
Kosrae:	Lele/Leluh Harbour	5°20´N 163°02´E
	Okat Harbour	5°21´N 162°57´E

All yachts must proceed directly to a port of entry. It is forbidden to stop at any islands before clearing in.

Kolonia: Port control should be contacted about two hours before arrival. The operator will advise where to come alongside. For clearing in it is best to come alongside at the commercial wharf as customs and immigration may wish to board the boat. Agriculture, police and health officials may also visit. If there is no space at the wharf, you can anchor and go ashore. Those arriving on a Sunday may anchor at buoy number 6 and clear in on Monday morning.

Weno: The government offices are on the northwest side of the island near the airport.

Colonia: Tomil Harbour, the main port, is reached through a passage in the reef. If there is space, yachts can come alongside a quay in the small boat harbour for clearance.

Stone money from Yap.

Ulithi: Clearance is made at the government dock at Falalop.

Kosrae: Lele Harbour, protected by the reef and Leluh Island, is the harbour of the capital, Tofol, located on the eastern side of the island. Marine Resources should be contacted on arrival. Customs and immigration officials will come to the anchored yacht in a launch. Occasionally the captain is asked to come ashore himself and meet the officials at the dinghy landing. Clearance is also possible at Okat Harbour on the western coast.

Entry permits for up to 30 days are granted on arrival. Yachts must clear in and out of each state, and a new entry permit of 30 days is given every time. Extensions of 30 days can be obtained, up to 90 days maximum. For stays over 90 days, a visa will be needed. US citizens can be granted an entry permit for one year.

A cruising permit must be obtained in advance of arrival. You should apply in writing to the Chief of Immigration, PO Box PS105, Palikir, Pohnpei, FSM 96941, Tel: 320 2606, Fax: 320 2234. It may take several months to receive an answer. If the permit has not arrived by the time you are ready to leave the last port, a copy of the original application should be faxed with a request to process the application immediately. An answer is normally received within 48 hours. The permit is issued for one year. Any yacht arriving without the permit may be asked to leave after three days.

Even after having cleared into one of the four member states, formalities with customs and immigration must still be completed on arrival in each individual state. Yachts sailing to another state may stop at outer islands on the way, even if they do not belong to the state that you have already cleared into, as long as a coastal clearance is obtained at the port of departure.

It is reported that the authorities in Chuuk no longer allow visiting sailors to dive on the many wrecks.

Dancers from Pohnpei.

When visiting outer islands of each state, even uninhabited islands and islets, whenever possible permission should be asked for beforehand from the owner of the land. Permission is normally granted. At all villages, the local chief should be visited first and offered a symbolic gift. On some islands, the chiefs are now legally entitled to charge visiting yachts a landing fee.

✦ FACILITIES

Facilities vary widely across the Federation, with limited repair services in the main centres and very little in the outer islands. In Sokehs Harbour in Pohnpei, Rumours Marina has some facilities for visiting yachts, including a fuel dock, dinghy dock and showers. The channel leading into the inner harbour is unmarked, so local help may be needed. There are fishery plants in several islands and, wherever there is a base for fishing boats, you can expect to find at least basic repair facilities. One of the best is Yap Fisheries, which maintains a 70-ton railway where boats can be hauled out and some repairs carried out.

Provisioning is good in all main centres, where there is a selection of imported goods. Fresh produce can be found practically everywhere. Water sources should be treated, so a watermaker is the obvious solution. Fuel can be bought in all centres, usually by jerrycan, although some fisheries have pumps or can arrange to have the fuel delivered by tanker. No fuel is available in the outer islands. Propane is usually available in Pohnpei and Chuuk, but not in Kosrae and Yap.

As in other remote cruising areas, all essential spares should be carried as the only parts that may be available locally are those used in trucks or heavy plant.

Cruising Guides
Landfalls of Paradise
Micronesia Cruising Notes

Websites
www.visit-fsm.org
www.rccpf.org.uk/ppg/pacific/pdf/route_p4.pdf (RCC Pilotage
   Foundation Notes)

Local time	UTC Yap/Chuuk +10, Pohnpei/Kosrae +11
Buoyage	IALA A
Currency	Micronesian Dollar, US Dollar (USD)
Electricity	120V, 60Hz

Diplomatic missions	
USA	320 2187
Australia	320 5448

Communications	
IDD 691	IAC 011

GUAM

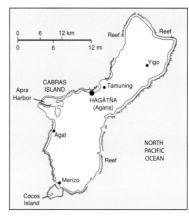

GUAM IS THE LARGEST and most populous island of Micronesia and home to an important US military base. It is the southernmost of the Mariana Islands, but forms a separate unit from the Commonwealth of the Northern Marianas. Guam is an Unincorporated Territory of the USA. Guam's close relations with the USA, and its role as a distribution centre for the rest of Micronesia, makes it rather different from the rest of the North Pacific islands.

Cruising yachts will indeed find in Guam a contrasting atmosphere to that they have experienced in other islands. The pace is faster, the buildings taller, and everything can be fixed if you are prepared to pay the price. Many American sailors make Guam their base as US citizens can work in Guam without a permit.

As a cruising destination in itself, Guam has few attractions as the only natural harbour is Apra Bay. The other anchorages are Agat, Umatac and Hagatna. Only the latter provides good protection inside its small boat harbour.

✦ COUNTRY PROFILE

The Chamorros inhabited the Marianas as early as 1500 bce, migrating east from South East Asia. A complex society developed and stone remains of this early civilization are still visible. Magellan's visit in 1521 marked the arrival of the first Europeans. In the sixteenth century Spain claimed the Marianas, which were a stopping point on the trade route between Mexico and the Philippines. At the end of the 1898 Spanish–American war, Guam was ceded to the USA. During the Second World War the Japanese occupied Guam, until US troops retook the island after some fierce fighting in 1944.

The population is 150,000. Half are Chamorro, the rest Asian and American. English is the main language and, to a lesser extent, Chamorro, which has a small Spanish influence. Hagatna, previously known as Agana, is the capital.

✦ CLIMATE

The climate is tropical, warm and humid. From January to April the northeast trades blow, while from July to November it is rainy and occasionally stormy. Typhoons can occur between July and November. For more details, see the Climate section for the Federated States of Micronesia.

✦ FORMALITIES

Visiting yachts are required to notify the US Coast Guard two weeks before their planned visit. On arrival, you should contact harbour control on Channels 13 or 12. Usually you will be directed to the Marianas Yacht Club (Channel 79A) at Drydock Point. Officials will come to the yacht.

US visa regulations are in force, and all except US citizens are required to have a visa obtained in advance. The visa waiver scheme does not apply when visiting by yacht. The inner harbour of Apra Harbor is a US naval base and yachts should not enter.

PORT OF ENTRY
Apra Harbor 13°27′ N 144°40′ E

✦ FACILITIES

Because of the high frequency of typhoons, small boats may seek shelter in Piti Channel, which has a maximum depth of 2.40m (8ft). The area is well sheltered in any kind of winds. Some moorings are available at the Marianas Yacht Club and also at Agana Boat Basin in East Hagatna.

Haulout and good repair facilities are available at Dillingham Shipyard at Cabras Island Industrial Park. There is no chandlery in Guam, but as there are regular air links with mainland USA, most parts can be airfreighted in a reasonable time. There are several supermarkets stocked with a good selection, as well as a fresh produce market. Guam is the best place to reprovision in Micronesia.

Cruising Guide	
Landfalls of Paradise	
Websites	
www.visitguam.org	www.guam-online.com
www.marianasyachtclub.org	

Local time UTC +10	**Currency** United States Dollar (USD)
Buoyage IALA A	**Electricity** 110V, 60Hz
Communications	**Emergency number**
IDD 1 671 IAC 011	911

HAWAII

HAWAII IS AN ARCHIPELAGO stretching across the North Pacific from the remote Kure and Midway atolls to the highly developed and heavily populated islands in the east. The islands are summits of an ancient volcanic mountain range with grand scenery to match. On the largest, Hawaii Island, also known as Big Island, there are the active volcanoes of Mauna Loa and Kilauea. The latter is continually releasing steam and ashes, and spewing hot lava into the ocean. The other major islands are Maui, Oahu, Kauai, Molokai, Lanai, Nihau and Kahoolawe. Hawaii is very different to the rest of Polynesia, mainly due to the strong US influence, although the old ways still survive in some places.

The most convenient landfall and start for a cruise in Hawaiian waters is the small port of Hilo on Big Island as it is upwind of the entire archipelago. Hilo is a pleasant place to unwind after the long passage and also to visit the interior of the Big Island. In most instances, only part of the sight-seeing can be done from the cockpit as many of the interesting places are either inland or difficult to reach by boat. The Big Island is a good example, and an excellent introduction to Hawaii with its magnificent volcanoes of Mauna Kea and Kilauea, orchid gardens, rainforests and scenic coastline. Mauna Kea, which in Hawaiian means 'White Mountain' because its summit is normally covered in snow, is the tallest of Hawaii's volcanoes (4,205m/13,796ft) and in fact is the tallest mountain in the world if measured from the floor of the ocean to its summit. Kilauea Volcano is one of the most active on earth and its current eruption started in 1983 and continues to this day, with red hot lava pouring relentlessly into the ocean.

A symbolic stop for any sailor is on the lee side of Big Island at Kealakekua Bay, where Captain Cook lost his life in 1779.

Captain Cook was the first European to arrive in Hawaii, which he named Sandwich Islands in honour of one of his patrons, the fourth Earl of Sandwich. A later visiting mariner, Mark Twain, perhaps had his unfortunate predecessor in mind when he declared: 'This is the most magnificent, balmy atmosphere in the world – ought to take dead men out of the grave.'

The former whaling capital of the Pacific, Lahaina on Maui Island, is a popular cruising stop, as is the marine park at Hulopoe Bay on Lanai with its superb underwater scenery. Busy Honolulu, with its wide range of facilities, has many tempting sights – which should include a visit to the Bishop Museum, especially for those planning to continue their cruise to other Pacific islands, as many of the art treasures from those islands are exhibited there. For boats heading for the mainland, a good place to leave from is the northernmost island of Kauai and its spectacular Hanalei Bay, the set for many a South Seas movie. Boats heading for the South Pacific can get an early taste of the South Seas by calling at Palmyra Island. This is now a nature reserve for which a permit is needed, obtainable in Honolulu.

◆ COUNTRY PROFILE

Hawaii is said to have been discovered three times, with the Polynesians claiming that Hawaii Loa was the first to land there over one thousand years ago. Some say that the Spanish were the first Europeans to discover the islands, but it was more likely the great navigator Captain Cook in 1778. At the end of the eighteenth century, Kamehameha the Great united all the islands under his rule. In 1893 Queen Lili'uokalani was dethroned and a republic proclaimed. Soon afterwards, the US Congress passed a resolution annexing the islands. Hawaii became a state in 1959.

Surfers at Diamond Head, Oahu

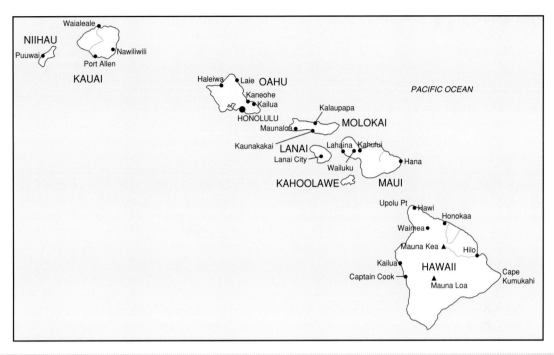

PORTS OF ENTRY

Honolulu (Oahu)	21°18´ N 157°52´ W	Hilo (Hawaii)	19°44´ N 155°04´ W	Kona (Hawaii)	19°40´ N 156°02´ W
Kahului (Maui)	20°54´ N 156°28´ W	Nawiliwili (Kauai)	21°57´ N 159°21´ W	Port Allen (Kauai)	21°54´ N 158°36´ W

Hawaii's population of 1.3 million is very mixed following the immigration of Chinese and Japanese in the nineteenth century, Portuguese, Spanish and Russian in the early twentieth century, and many mainland Americans ever since. Hawaiians of Polynesian origin now form a small minority. English is the main language, but Hawaiian is still spoken.

✦ CLIMATE

The climate is subtropical and mostly pleasant. There is no rainy season but showers, sometimes downpours, occur in winter. Occasionally a winter depression stalls over the area and will result in a spell of prolonged heavy rain. The islands are under the influence of the northeast trade winds and are only rarely affected by tropical cyclones. Wind acceleration zones occur between the islands, and should be taken into account as sudden strong gusts may strike with no warning.

✦ FORMALITIES

Hawaiian entry regulations for foreign-flagged vessels are the same as for the rest of the USA. Yachts must enter at an official port of entry. Boats stopping elsewhere may be liable for heavy fines. This rule also applies to US-registered vessels coming from foreign ports; they must call at an official port of entry before proceeding elsewhere. US captains have been fined for making landfall at minor Hawaiian ports and attempting to clear by telephone.

Hilo: Radio Bay in Hilo is now closed to visiting yachts on grounds of security. Mooring facilities are therefore even more limited, with the only places available to visitors being at the Boat Harbor and Wailoa Sampan Basin in Hilo Bay.

Kahului: Yachts should berth at the commercial wharf for clearance before anchoring in the harbour.

Honolulu: Clearance is best done at Ala Wai Yacht Harbor. Ko Olina Marina on the west coast of Oahu is another possibility.

Nawiliwili: Customs will clear yachts at the commercial wharf.

On arrival, yachts must report immediately to Customs and Border Protection (CBP) and formal clearance must be made within 48 hours of arriving. Vessels can call CBP before they arrive to minimize waiting time. CBP telephone numbers are: Honolulu: 522 8012, 861 4601 (24 hours), Hilo: 933 6975, Kona: 334 1850, Kahului: 877 6013, Nawiliwili: 237 4601 (24 hours).

No one must go ashore on arrival except for the person reporting to customs, who must afterwards return to the yacht until formalities have been completed. Violations of this rule can result in heavy penalties, even forfeiture of the boat.

All nationalities, with the exception of Canadians and Mexicans, need a visa, which must be obtained in advance. The visa waiver scheme does not apply.

Certain countries are eligible for a cruising licence, which exempts them from having to clear in and out at subsequent ports after the first port of entry. Details of this and the countries eligible are listed on page 252. The cruising licence is issued on entry by the CBP officer. It is valid for up to one year. Foreign yachts, whether or not holding a cruising permit, are still supposed to notify customs by telephone on arrival in a major port. Those not entitled to a cruising licence must obtain a permit to proceed to each subsequent port and they must complete formalities at any major port.

Quarantine must be notified if there are animals on board or if coming from any country outside the USA or Canada, in which case any fresh fruit, vegetables, eggs and other specific food items will be confiscated and destroyed. Hawaii is rabies-free, so regulations regarding animals on board yachts are stricter than on the US mainland.

US vessels arriving from a US port on the mainland who have not stopped at a foreign port en route or have had no contact with any other vessel at sea, and who have only US citizens on board, do not need to clear CBP, but must be inspected on arrival by an agricultural inspector. They must inform the agricultural department of their arrival. Having cleared into Hawaii, US boats are free to go anywhere.

On departure, all yachts, including US-registered vessels, must obtain a customs clearance for foreign destinations.

Many Hawaiian bays have been designated Marine Conservation Areas, and anchoring is prohibited in some of them. The government booklet *Marine Life Conservation Districts* gives more information on local restrictions.

Nihau Island is reserved for native Hawaiians. It can only be visited with official permission.

✦ MILITARY AREAS

Kahoolawe Island, just south of Maui, was previously used as a firing range by the US Navy, and unexploded ordnance is still being cleared. One should check with the CBP on Maui before landing at this island.

The Midway Islands, at the western extremity of the Hawaiian group, are not part of the state of Hawaii, and are administered by the US Navy. Johnston Atoll is administered by the US Air Force and is used for dumping chemical weapons as well as other military material. Part of the atoll is a wildlife refuge. The waters within a 3-mile radius of both Midway and Johnston are off limits to yachts.

✦ REMOTE ISLAND WILDLIFE REFUGES

These are administered by the US Fish and Wildlife Service in Honolulu. Permission to land will only be given for legitimate reasons. These areas include:

The northwest part of the Hawaiian archipelago from 161°W to 176°W. This includes Nihoa Island, but not Midway, Howland, Baker and Jarvis Islands, south-southwest of Hawaii. Palmyra Atoll is a nature reserve and is owned jointly by The Nature Conservancy (TNC) and the US Fish and Wildlife Department. There are permanent caretakers based on Palmyra and only one-week stops are allowed. All visits by cruising boats must be prearranged by email: Palmyra@inix.com.

Wake Island is administered by the US Air Force, but yachts can stop. The pass into the lagoon is not deep enough to enter, so one has to anchor off the reef.

✦ FACILITIES

Facilities are of a good standard and, with a few exceptions, marinas are state owned and operated. The Hawaii Yacht Club in Honolulu will allow visitors to use its facilities, usually limited to a maximum period of two weeks. Major repair work and services, such as hauling out and hull, engine and sail repair, are available at Honokohau Harbor on Big Island, at Kewalo Basin, Keehi Lagoon and at Ala Wai Boat Harbor in Honolulu. Marine supplies are good in all main centres. Ko Olina Marina, on Oahu's sheltered west coast, has good facilities and is a convenient place to prepare for a long offshore passage.

Provisioning is good everywhere and Hawaii is the best place to victual the boat, especially if planning to cruise the outer islands of Micronesia or the South Pacific.

✦ CHARTER

Because of the often challenging sailing conditions as well as the lack of natural anchorages, bareboat charters have not taken off in Hawaii. The one exception is the Honolulu Sailing Company, located in Oahu and with a fleet of both sail and powerboats. There are also a few crewed yachts based in the various islands that are available for day charters.

www.honsail.com

Cruising Guides	Website
Landfalls of Paradise	www.visit.hawaii.org
Hawaiian Islands	

Local time	UTC −10	Currency	US Dollar (USD)
Buoyage	IALA B	Electricity	110V, 60Hz

Diplomatic mission	
Australia	524 50505

Communications		Emergency number
IDD 1 808 IAC 011		911

KIRIBATI

THE REPUBLIC OF KIRIBATI (pronounced 'kiribas'), formerly the Gilbert Islands, is a group of more than thirty islands situated in the centre of the Pacific Ocean at the point where the International Dateline and the equator cross. Besides the sixteen original Gilbert Islands, Kiribati also includes Banaba (Ocean Island), the eight Phoenix Islands, and eight of the eleven Line Islands. All of these islands are low atolls enclosing lagoons, rarely more than 4m (12ft) above sea level. The notable exception is Banaba, which is volcanic. Little grows on these islands except coconut palms, and not all of them are inhabited. Kiribati is very isolated, its small islands spread out over more than 1 million square miles of ocean.

The main group, which was the original Gilbert Islands, straddles the equator north of Tuvalu and is a symbolic link between the South and North Pacific, not just geographically but also ethnically as the southern islanders are more akin to Polynesians while the northerners are closer to their Micronesian neighbours. Visiting this sprawling archipelago needs careful planning, a task not made easier by the insistence of the authorities that yachts must clear in first at the capital, Tarawa, before going anywhere else. Two interesting islands south of Tarawa are Butaritari and Abemama, which were described with much affection by Robert Louis Stevenson, who called here in 1889 and was the guest of King Tembinoka – whom he referred to as 'the Napoleon of the Gilberts'. Tarawa, the overcrowded capital of this small nation, still shows signs of the bloody battle fought here in 1943 when US forces stormed the heavily fortified beaches, resulting in heavy losses on both sides.

The Line Islands, which also straddle the equator, were likewise marred by the actions of outsiders and were used in the 1950s as testing grounds for nuclear weapons by Britain

Abemama Atoll in Southern Kiribati.

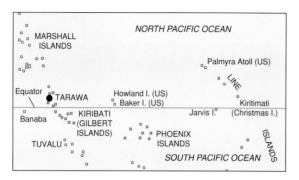

and the USA. Several islands still bear those scars, but nowhere is this more shocking than on Christmas Island, where the land is still littered with large amounts of rusting equipment half a century after the military had left. The lasting impression of anyone visiting Christmas Island, which is a convenient stopover point for boats on passage between Hawaii and French Polynesia, is of utter desolation. In contrast, Fanning Island, only 160 miles farther north, is a typical Pacific island – clean, welcoming and self-sufficient. Traditional life continues in these islands and all major decisions affecting the community are taken by consensus in meetings held in the village communal house called *maneaba*.

The local names of some of the individual Line Islands have been confused and are often wrong in nautical publications. Their correct names are Kiritimati (Christmas), Tabuaeran (Fanning) and Teraina (Washington). Although the authorities would like to see these names used more widely, sailors continue to prefer their Westernized names.

✦ COUNTRY PROFILE

The first inhabitants of these islands probably came from Australasia, with further migrations from Samoa in the thirteenth century. Although sighted by early Spanish expeditions, the first meaningful contact with Europeans only came in the mid-nineteenth century with the arrival of missionaries, whalers and slave traders. The islanders suffered greatly from new diseases brought by these visitors. At the end of that century, the Gilbert Islands, together with the Ellice Islands, now Tuvalu, willingly became a British Protectorate.

In 1890 phosphate was discovered on Ocean Island and the administrative centre shifted there from Tarawa. In 1919 Christmas Island was annexed by the British, and later also the other Line Islands. During the Second World War the Gilberts were occupied by Japan and, as the Americans advanced, the islands were the arena for fierce fighting, especially at Tarawa. Independence came to the Gilberts in 1979, under the new name of Kiribati.

The population is over 113,000, mostly Micronesians, with some Polynesians in the southern islands. I-Kiribati, a

Micronesian language, is the official one, but English is also spoken. The capital is Bairiki, one of the islands of Tarawa, a densely populated atoll where about one-third of the population live. The main port is on the neighbouring Betio islet in the same lagoon.

✦ CLIMATE

Most islands have an equatorial climate, while the islands to the extreme north of the group have a tropical climate. November to April is the rainy season, with high humidity and stronger winds. Rainfall is not reliable and drought can be a problem in all the islands. The prevailing easterlies keep the climate pleasant, although temperatures can be high, on average 27°C/81°F to 29°C/84°F.

✦ FORMALITIES

PORTS OF ENTRY	
Betio Islet (Tarawa)	1°21′N 172°55′E
Kiritimati (Christmas) Island	1°59′N 157°28′W
Tabuaerean (Fanning) Island	3°51′N 159°22′W
Ocean (Banaba) Island	0°53′S 169°32′E

Tarawa: Tarawa Radio should be called when approaching the island. The Marine Guard keeps 24-hour watch on 500, 2182 and 6215 MHz. Channel 16 is monitored only during office hours. Having been advised beforehand, officials will be waiting in Betio when the yacht arrives. All formalities are supposed to be completed alongside in the small boat harbour in Betio, but this can only take yachts under 1.80m (6ft) draft. Because of silting, the depths in the harbour are unreliable, so it may be safer for deeper-draft vessels to tie up to the commercial wharf on the way into Betio or anchor just outside the harbour entrance. An unmarked wreck, lying just below the surface, is close to the recommended anchorage and its position has been reported at 1°22.03′N 172°55.44′E. The customs office is at Betio and immigration officials will come over from Bairiki, where the government offices are based.

Nationals of most countries do not need a visa and will be issued one on arrival. Nationals of South Africa must obtain a visa in advance. A visitor's permit is normally issued on arrival, valid for one month, with extensions of one month at a time up to four months.

A cruising permit should be obtained when clearing in. This takes the form of an official letter from customs and immigration addressed to the relevant official at each island you wish to visit, stating, among other things, the duration of your allowed stop. It is therefore essential not only to obtain this letter before leaving Tarawa, but also to ensure that the visitor's permit covers the entire proposed stay.

The authorities stipulate that in order to visit any of the other islands, you must clear in first at Tarawa and also clear out there at the end of the visit. They are strict about clearance, and Tarawa must be visited first, even if coming from the south. However, on departure it may be possible to get permission to call at an island and continue on from there out of the archipelago. Due to their remoteness from Tarawa, the Line Islands are exempt from this rule.

Fanning Island (Tabuaerean): There is a wide pass on the west side, but there is always a strong outflowing current. Arrival should be timed to coincide with slack water, otherwise it is possible to anchor in the lee of the island and wait for the change of tide. Once inside, the best anchorage is southeast of the pass, close to the jetty. If no officials come out to inspect the yacht, the captain should disembark and first visit customs in the government offices just south of the jetty, then the chief of police who also acts as immigration officer.

Christmas Island: The pass into the lagoon is difficult to locate, so the recommended anchorage (1°59.08′ N 157°28.83′ W) is west of the main settlement. It is relatively easy to land on the beach there and walk to the government offices to clear in. The customs, immigration and quarantine offices are all close together. Each officer will want to inspect the boat and you normally have to transport them in your own dinghy.

Canton: This atoll in the Phoenix Islands is a former US satellite tracking station. Only a handful of people live there and only three supply ships call a year. It is not a port of entry, but if you arrive with a Kiribati visa or for emergency repairs, normally permission to stay will be granted. The local officials will request such permission by radio from Tarawa. The dredged ship pass should be entered near slack water and yachts can anchor inside the turning basin. The natural pass is not recommended. The village is 3 miles away; officials will visit the yacht.

◆ FACILITIES

Tarawa: Most facilities available in Kiribati are concentrated on this atoll, which comprises several islands. Basic services are available at Betio, including the government shipyard which has mechanical, electrical and engineering workshops capable of small repairs. They also have a slipway which can haul yachts with a maximum draft of 1.80m (6ft). Provisions are available in Betio, but a better supermarket is located at Bairiki. LPG tanks can be filled at Betio where reasonable amounts of fuel and water are also available. Drinking water should be treated.

Christmas Island: Water is available and also diesel fuel. Provisions are limited.

Fanning: The few stores only stock basic supplies. Some locally grown fruit and vegetables are usually available but not fuel.

Facilities in all other islands are basic, with few imported goods and a limited selection of locally grown fruit and vegetables, but there is plenty of fish everywhere. Water is often scarce and can be a problem in the southern and central parts of the group.

Cruising Guides	Website
Landfall of Paradise	www.visit-kiribati.com
Micronesia Cruising Notes	

Local time	Line Islands UTC +14, Tarawa UTC +12, Phoenix Islands UTC +13
Buoyage	IALA A
Currency	Kiribati Dollar at par value with Australian Dollar (AUD)
Electricity	240V, 50Hz

Diplomatic missions	
Australia	21 184
New Zealand	21 400

Communications	
IDD 686	IAC 00

Emergency number
994

Fanning Atoll

MARSHALL ISLANDS

SPREAD OUT OVER A VAST AREA of the Central Pacific north of the equator, the Marshalls comprise over a thousand small low islands, forming two chains, the eastern Ratak (towards dawn) and the western Ralik (towards sunset). It is believed that the Marshallese came from South East Asia in large sailing canoes many centuries ago. Their outstanding navigational skills have impressed Western observers, among them the writer Robert Louis Stevenson who called here in 1889 and visited Jaluit, Namorik, Ebon and Majuro, which he described as 'pearl necklace of the Pacific'. While there he was presented by King Kabua, ruler of the Marshalls, with a stick chart showing the entire archipelago. These charts made of sticks, shells and coconut fibre were used by the Marshallese sailors as maps of the ocean that helped them navigate between the islands, taking into account currents, swell, the position of heavenly bodies, as well as the flight of birds.

The USA still maintains a military presence in Kwajalein Atoll which is used for testing ballistic missiles. Nearby Bikini Atoll was used for nuclear tests between 1946 and 1958 when 23 nuclear devices were detonated over the atoll. Its small population were relocated to another atoll, but still claim that they had been affected by radiation. Having been declared safe by the US authorities in 1968, some inhabitants returned to their ancestral lands, but had to be evacuated

Humpback whales migrate to the Marshalls in winter to breed.

again when several showed signs of radiation sickness. Although the islanders have yet to return to their home island, some workers and US officials are now based permanently on the island. The excellent diving at Bikini attracts underwater enthusiasts from all over the world.

Most yachts calling at the Marshalls are on their way from Hawaii to the rest of Micronesia. The islanders welcome visiting sailors, and it is possible to stop at most islands after having cleared in at Majuro and obtained the compulsory cruising permit. Life in the outer islands continues in traditional fashion – in contrast to Majuro, which is entirely Westernised.

✦ COUNTRY PROFILE

It is not known exactly when the Micronesians first settled these islands. Marshall is the name of an English captain, who sighted the islands at the end of the eighteenth century. Germany annexed the islands at the end of the nineteenth century and developed the copra industry. During the Second World War the Japanese occupied the Marshalls, but were expelled by US forces after heavy fighting. Immediately after the war, the USA started to conduct nuclear tests on Bikini and Enewetok atolls and these became uninhabitable. Rongelap and Utirik suffered similar fates. The Marshalls became a republic in 1986 and signed a Compact of Free Association with the USA.

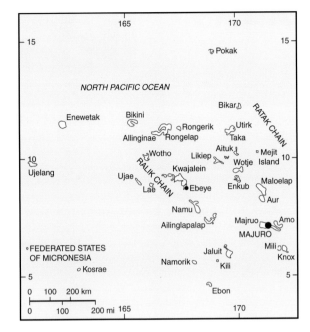

The population numbers around 64,500. Marshallese is the official language, but English is widely spoken. Majuro is the capital.

✦ CLIMATE

The climate is tropical and temperatures show little variation throughout the year. December to April is the northeast tradewind season, and even in the remaining months prevailing winds tend to be easterly. Occasionally the easterly flow is interrupted by strong southwest winds. Tropical storms are very rare in Majuro, but not unheard of and, at the turn of the nineteenth century, a typhoon killed almost everyone on Majuro. More recently, in an El Niño year, a typhoon passed close to the south of Majuro.

✦ FORMALITIES

PORTS OF ENTRY

Majuro	7°08´N 171°22´E
Ebeye Island (Kwajalein Atoll)	8°46´N 167°44´E

Majuro: Arriving yachts should call Majuro Port Control on Channel 16 and request clearance. If no answer is received, one should pick up one of the visitors' moorings, then go ashore to the government offices in Delap to clear customs, immigration and port director. Occasionally, a yacht will be directed to come alongside the commercial pier in Uliga, but that is rare and customs officials rarely board yachts

Clearing in at Majuro is strongly recommended as the US military prefer cruising boats to go straight to the capital.

Visas are not required for nationals of Australia, New Zealand, the USA and some other Pacific countries. Other nationalities must obtain a visa in advance. There are consulates in Japan, Indonesia, Fiji, Taiwan, Honolulu and the Philippines. When clearing out, the offices have to be visited in reverse order: first port director, then immigration and customs.

Entry permits are no longer required for a visit to Majuro, but are required for other atolls to be visited. Forms and a list of lagoon entry fees are available from the Ministry of Internal Affairs, and the procedure is complicated and lengthy. The permit must be presented to the mayor on each atoll and the relevant fee paid. A permit is not required for Kwajalein Atoll, but you must have a sponsor to visit.

Ebeye Island is a closed military base and the missile range includes Kwajalein and the islands up to Roi-Namur Island. Kwajalein Atoll Control should be contacted by radio beforehand if sailing within 200 miles of the atoll, which is a missile testing area.

Permission is needed to visit Bikini Atoll, Enewetak Atoll (still contaminated) and Rongelap Atoll (polluted with fallout from Bikini).

Conservative dress should be worn when visiting the outer islands. The drinking of alcohol is banned on many islands.

✦ FACILITIES

Majuro is the best for long-term provisioning as there are good supermarkets and also some local fresh fruit and vegetables. Marine supplies and repair facilities are limited, but there is a 65-ton crane in the commercial port. Fuel is available and propane tanks can be refilled. Water should not be consumed as it is contaminated. Facilities in the other islands are very limited.

Cruising Guide
Landfalls of Paradise

Websites
www.visitmarshallislands.com   www.bikiniatoll.com

Local time	UTC +12
Buoyage	IALA A
Currency	United States Dollar (USD)
Electricity	110/120V, 60Hz

Diplomatic mission
USA	247 4011

Communications
IDD 692 IAC 011

Emergency numbers
Ambulance 625 4111	Police 625 8666

NORTHERN MARIANAS

THE 14 VOLCANIC ISLANDS that stretch north to south in almost a straight line in the centre of the North Pacific are divided into a northern section of nine islands and a southern section of five islands, among which Saipan, Rota and Tinian are the largest. The Marianas may claim to be the world's highest mountains, for their bases lie in the Mariana Trench, 7 miles below the ocean surface, in the deepest part of the Pacific. Guam is geographically part of the Marianas, but politically separate. The US influence is strong, although the legacy of Spanish colonial rule is still palpable.

The islands were dominated by the military for many years and access was forbidden, but that is no longer the case and they now attract a few cruising yachts every year. Most of these come from Guam, where there is a Northern Marianas representative who can issue the necessary permit to visit the islands. The southern islands are the more developed, while some of the northern ones are wildlife reserves and cannot be visited. The entire group is subject to typhoons for most of the year – another reason why cruising boats rarely sail there.

◆ COUNTRY PROFILE

The original inhabitants of the islands were Chamorros, of Indo-Filipino origin. Magellan was the first European to visit the islands in 1521, but in the seventeenth century the islands were named Las Marianas after the Spanish Queen Mariana of Austria. Germany bought the Marianas at the end of the nineteenth century. After the First World War they were ruled by the Japanese, and by the USA after the Second World War. In 1975 the Marianas voted to become a US Commonwealth. These islands are of strategic importance to the USA, from whom they receive considerable aid. The USA controls defence and foreign policy, but the Commonwealth has internal self-government.

Ancient latte stones are found all over the Marianas, but their original purpose is unknown.

The population is 89,000, having doubled in recent years with an influx of Asian workers, so now Chamorros and Carolinians make up only about 36 per cent of the population. English is the main language, while Chamorro and Carolinian are also spoken. Saipan is the capital.

✦ CLIMATE

The islands lie in the typhoon zone and these can occur all year round, but are more frequent between June and November. It is always warm and humid. The northeast trade winds blow from January to April. As the Marianas are hit by typhoons every year, extreme caution must be exercised when cruising this area. One of the safest months is February, which has the lowest incidence. A recommended hurricane hole is in Tanapag's inner harbour (Saipan), where shelter is good from every direction.

✦ FORMALITIES

PORTS OF ENTRY

Tanapag Harbour (Saipan) 15°12´ N 145°43´ E

All boats are required to sail straight to Tanapag to complete formalities with the exception of those in possession of a special permit issued by the Northern Marianas representative in Guam that allows stops to be made in Rota and Tinian on the way to Saipan.

The port captain should be called to give your ETA. Yachts are normally directed to Smiling Cove Marina which has a berth for visiting yachts.

US citizens do not need visas, and they are not required for stays of up to 30 days for nationals of most countries. Visitors, however, must be in possession of any necessary visas for their next destination.

All yachts must possess a permit, which must be obtained beforehand from the Director of Immigration, Saipan. Alternatively, a cruising permit can be got from the Northern Marianas representative in Guam or Honolulu, which will allow a yacht to call at the islands of Tinian, Rota and Saipan. Yachts arriving without such a permit will be fined US$500.

The authorities are very concerned about the accidental introduction of diseases to local wildlife. Guguan, Asuncion and Maug islands are wildlife reserves and access to them is prohibited.

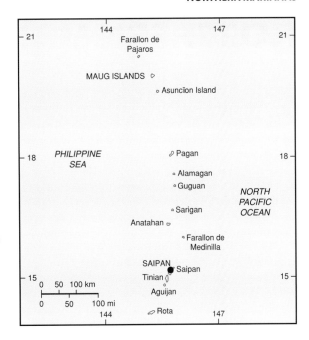

✦ FACILITIES

Most facilities are in Saipan. The inner harbour provides good shelter, but gets very crowded.

Provisioning is good, there is a reasonable selection of imported goods and a fresh produce market. Fuel can be delivered by tanker. Only simple repairs are possible, and marine supplies are limited. Provisions in the outer islands are scarce and, apart from fresh local produce, you should not expect to be able to buy more than the absolute minimum.

Cruising Guide
Landfalls of Paradise

Website
www.mymarianas.com

Local time	UTC +10
Buoyage	IALA A
Currency	Northern Mariana Dollar, US Dollar (USD)
Electricity	110/120V, 60Hz

Communications	
IDD 1 670	IAC 011

Emergency number
911

PALAU

THE REPUBLIC OF PALAU, now known as Belau, is part of the Western Caroline Islands. The richest flora and fauna in Micronesia are found here. Closely grouped together inside a barrier reef are the high islands of Babeldaob, the main island of Koror, Peleliu, and the many Rock Islands. Just outside the reef are Angaur and the atoll Kayangel, while to the south are a group of five small volcanic islands, stretching down towards Indonesia.

Conveniently situated on the route from the South Pacific to the Philippines, Palau lagoon and its many picturesque islands provide in a small area one of the most beautiful cruising grounds in the Pacific. This is slightly marred by the strict entry regulations, but this can be overcome by sorting out the necessary paperwork before your arrival and, once there, by observing the rules. The effort is entirely justified as the scenery, both above and under the surface of the sea, is rarely matched elsewhere in the Pacific. The most fascinating place to visit is the Rock Islands, which are over two hundred limestone islets covered in jungle growth. Three major ocean currents meet in this area, bringing food to nourish the rich marine life. The sea is teeming with turtles, manta rays, moray eels, fish of all descriptions, giant clams and even dugong. Occasionally you are brought back to earth by the sight of a wrecked ship from the bloody battles that were fought in these waters during the Second World War. Strict rules apply to visits to the outer islands and, because of abuses by cruising sailors in the past, the authorities treat all visitors with some suspicion.

◆ COUNTRY PROFILE

The Rock Islands were settled around 1000 BCE. There was no real contact with Europeans until 1783, but during the next couple of hundred years Palau's population was depleted by diseases from contact with traders from Britain and Spain. In the twentieth century the Germans, and then the Japanese, developed the islands, further overwhelming traditional life. After the Second World War the USA administered Palau, but the country chose independence in 1978. A Compact of Free Association with the USA came into force in 1994.

The 21,000 inhabitants are Micronesian, speaking Palauan as well as English. Sonsorolese is spoken in the southwest islands. Koror is the capital.

◆ CLIMATE

Palau lies on the edge of the typhoon belt and is only rarely affected by tropical storms. The typhoon season is from May to November. The wet season is June to September, which is the southwest monsoon. The best weather is during the northeast monsoon from December to March, when occasionally the trade winds can be quite strong.

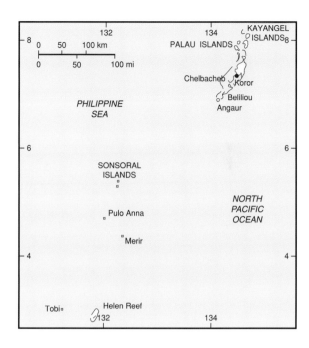

Cruising permits for anywhere outside of the harbour are now issued on arrival. US boats are entitled to an entry permit valid for one year. All other vessels receive an entry permit valid for 30 days, with the option of up to two extensions of 30 days each.

Some parts of the Rock Islands, including the Seventy Islands, are nature reserves and access by any boat is strictly prohibited.

✦ FACILITIES

Most facilities are in Koror, where the majority of the population live. There are workshops, a slipway and a small chandlery with a limited selection. Provisioning is good with two large supermarkets and locally grown produce. The Royal Belau Yacht Club welcomes visiting sailors, who have access to its facilities. Palau Super Yacht Service is based at the club and provides a range of services for visitors, including assistance with formalities and permits. It also arranges crewed charters and diving tours.

Cruising Guides
Landfalls of Paradise
Micronesian Cruising Notes

Websites
www.visit-palau.com
www.samstours.com/services-yachtclub.html (Royal Belau
  Yacht Club)

Local time	UTC +9
Buoyage	IALA A
Currency	Palauan Dollar, US Dollar (USD)
Electricity	120/240V, 60Hz

Communications	Emergency number
IDD 680 IAC 011	911

✦ FORMALITIES

PORT OF ENTRY

Malakal Harbour (Koror) 7°20´N 134°29´E

Yachts must notify the port authorities in advance of their ETA and are asked to contact Royal Belau Yacht Club for clearance assistance (rbyc@samtours.com). Palau Port Control should be called immediately on arrival. A yacht in distress forced to anchor before clearing in must immediately notify the nearest government official.

US nationals receive a one year visa on arrival. All other nationalities receive a 30 day visa, and up to two extensions of 30 days each can be requested.

SOUTH PACIFIC

A VOYAGE TO THE ISLANDS of the South Seas figures in most sailors' long-term plans, but the remoteness of the islands, which is one of their main temptations, keeps them beyond the scope of the average voyage. This is the reason why in spite of the proliferation of yachts worldwide, the number of boats cruising the South Pacific is still relatively small and is not likely to increase much in the foreseeable future. No other part of the world offers so many cruising options, nor such diverse attractions as the South Pacific – from the stupendous bays of the Marquesas to the turquoise lagoons of the Tuamotus, the giant statues of Easter Island to the traditional villages of Vanuatu, the sheltered waters of Vava'u or the remote island communities of Tokelau. The vastness of the Pacific Ocean and the great distances that separate most island groups make long passages a common feature of voyages in this part of the world. The islands' isolation and the scarcity of facilities require the yacht to be well prepared and self-sufficient.

As the safe sailing season in the South Pacific is well defined, and the weather is usually fairly benign in the eastern part of this vast ocean, for sailors arriving from the east the most critical decision concerns the time of arrival in the first tropical island group. Most boats transit the Panama Canal before the onset of the hurricane season in the Caribbean (June to November), with the busiest transit period being February and March. This is also the time when boats sailing from Mexico or Central America should start leaving for the South Pacific. Those who plan to sail in one season all the way to Australia or the Torres Straits need to reach the Marquesas not later than early April to be able to cover in only five months the considerable distances ahead of them. Those with more time on their hands may decide not to sail the classic route from Galapagos to the Marquesas, but make a detour to Easter Island and Pitcairn so as to arrive in French Polynesia via the Gambier Islands. From Tahiti, the classic tradewind route then continues west to the Cook Islands, Tonga, Fiji, Vanuatu and Australia, with countless diversions en route.

Round the world rally start in Malololailai Lagoon in Western Fiji.

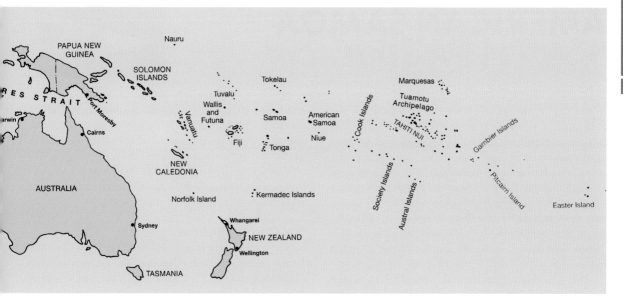

For European sailors as well as those starting from the east coast of the USA or Canada, a voyage to the South Pacific is easier to accomplish if it is planned as part of a complete circumnavigation as the prevailing conditions are then used to best advantage. Those hailing from the west coast of North America, and not tempted by a complete round the world voyage, have the choice of a shorter Pacific circumnavigation. The turning point of such a trip can be either Australia or New Zealand from where the return route must dip south to reach the area of prevailing westerlies. Having reached the Austral Islands, the route turns north to Tahiti and continues via the Line Islands to Hawaii and eventually home.

Most of the South Pacific is affected by tropical cyclones and the season lasts from December until the end of March. Most yachts leave the critical area by sailing either south to New Zealand or Australia, or north to Papua New Guinea. Those who prefer to remain in the tropics during summer can find shelter in one of the few all-weather marinas. Otherwise, the relatively small number of safe harbours considerably restricts the freedom of movement during the cyclone season. For those who wish to continue cruising, there are a few hurricane holes in Tahiti, Vava'u, Pago Pago and Suva, although in some countries, such as Tahiti, Vanuatu and the Cook Islands, the authorities insist that visiting yachts leave the country before the onset of the cyclone season. One of the advantages of spending the summer season outside the tropics is that of being able to go to a place with good repair facilities. A popular destination is New Zealand, where there are various marinas offering a wide range of services. Similar facilities are also available in some of the ports along Australia's east coast, although the more northern ones are themselves in the cyclone area. In the islands, the best repair centres are those that support their own boating community, such as Tahiti, Suva, Nouméa and Port Moresby. The establishment of charter operations in Raiatea and Vava'u has brought about a noticeable improvement in the standard of facilities there.

Most boats follow the traditional route across the South Pacific that sweeps in an arc from Panama to the Torres Strait. Favourable southeast trade winds are a usual feature of this route during the winter months. However, normal weather conditions can be affected by various factors, such as the El Niño phenomenon. Even at the height of the winter season, consistent winds are only encountered at the two extremes of this route, between Galapagos and Marquesas in the east, and in the Coral Sea, in the west. Between these two extremes, sailing conditions are often a matter of luck, with long spells of steady trade winds in some years, or an alternation of periods of several days of perfect tradewind sailing followed by a spell of unsettled weather with squalls, thunderstorms and variable winds.

A constant feature that affects weather conditions throughout the tropical South Pacific is the South Pacific Convergence Zone. The SPCZ stretches in an ESE direction from about 5°S 155°E to 20°S 150°W and can influence weather conditions all the way from Tahiti to the Solomons, although its effects are particularly felt in the central area between French Polynesia and Tonga. The location and movement of the SPCZ are monitored by the Fiji meteorological office and its co-ordinates are broadcast in its daily weather report on Inmarsat C.

AMERICAN SAMOA

WHILE SHARING BOTH NAME and ancestry, the two Samoas are very different from each other, American Samoa being a US Territory, while Western Samoa, now called simply Samoa, is an independent state. American Samoa comprises all the Samoan islands east of 171°W longitude: the main island of Tutuila, Aunuu, the Manua Group, Rose Island and Swains Island. The islands of the Manua Group – Tau, Olosega and Ofu – lie about 60 miles east of Tutuila. Swains is a privately owned atoll about 280 miles north of Tutuila, while Rose is a small uninhabited island 250 miles to the east.

This US outpost in the South Seas has been best described as the place sailors love to hate. The features that attract most cruising boats to American Samoa, such as US goods, excellent provisioning and good communications, are also those that seem to be the basis of most critical comments. The Samoans have embraced the American way of life wholeheartedly, which has led to a high standard of living compared to their neighbours, but also to a gradual loss of their traditional lifestyle, especially in the capital, Pago Pago. It is Pago Pago that beckons cruising sailors, either to reprovision in its well-stocked supermarkets, or to spend the cyclone season in this sheltered harbour. Outside of Pago Pago, life has been less affected by this kind of progress and the pace is more as you would expect to see in the Pacific.

✦ COUNTRY PROFILE

Archaeologists have ascertained that Polynesians lived on Tutuila around 600 BCE. They remained undisturbed until 1722 when the first European, the Dutch explorer Jacob Roggeveen, visited the island. Few Europeans ventured this way in the following years, especially after the 11 members of a French scientific expedition led by La Pérouse were killed here in 1787. Only in 1831 did the arrival of missionary John Williams mark a more permanent European interest, and the Samoans proved enthusiastic converts, going forth as

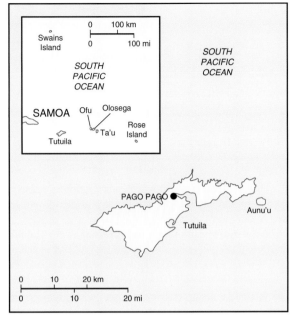

of hours, you should anchor and go ashore during office hours to visit the authorities.

US citizens need a valid passport for entry. On arrival, other nationalities are granted a 30-day stay. Entry permits are granted to all those who can provide proof of their onward passage and have adequate funds for their stay. For extensions up to a maximum of 90 days, you should apply to the immigration office. An exit permit is needed from immigration. The passport office can issue US visas. A range of high clearance fees are charged and their cost has doubled in 2009.

Rose Island, the easternmost island of the Samoan archipelago, is a National Wildlife Refuge administered by the US Fish and Wildlife Service in Honolulu. Permission from this service is needed to visit the island.

✦ FACILITIES

A wide range of repair facilities are available in Pago Pago, and in emergencies yachts have been allowed to use a slipway normally used by the fishing fleet. Provisioning is excellent both in price and range, with several supermarkets and one bulk supermarket close to the airport. Departing boats may buy spirits free of duty. Fuel is available at the fuel dock. General amenities in Pago Pago are even worse than in the past and visiting sailors do not even have a place to leave the dinghy when going ashore.

✦ CHARTER

There are no bareboat companies based here, except one local operator offering day trips.

www.pagopagomarinecharters.com

CRUISING GUIDES	
Landfalls of Paradise	South Pacific Anchorages
Polynesia	The Pacific Crossing Guide

Website
www.amsamoa.com

Local time	UTC −11
Buoyage	IALA A
Currency	US Dollar (USD)
Electricity	120V, 60Hz

Diplomatic missions		
Australia	Samoa	+685 23411
New Zealand	Samoa	+685 21711

Communications		**Emergency number**
IDD 1 684	IAC 011	911

missionaries themselves to convert other nations of the Pacific. International rivalries in the nineteenth century were settled by an 1899 treaty in which Germany and the USA divided the Samoan archipelago between themselves. Tutuila was an important base for the US Navy in the Second World War. The country is now an Unincorporated US External Territory, and since 1967 has had its own constitution.

The mainly Polynesian population is 65,000. Samoan and English are spoken. Pago Pago is the capital.

✦ CLIMATE

The climate is typically tropical with heavy rainfall all year, especially from November to April, which is the cyclone season. The temperature variations are small, with days often being hot, but cooled by day breezes or the prevailing southeast trade winds. June and July are the coolest and most pleasant months.

A tsunami triggered by an underwater earthquake caused wide destruction and loss of life in September 2009.

✦ FORMALITIES

PORT OF ENTRY
Pago Pago 14°17´S 170°41´W

Pago Pago: Harbour control should be called and, if arriving during office hours, you should tie up at the tug dock at the container wharf and then visit the authorities. If arriving out

AUSTRALIA

AUSTRALIA IS THE ONLY country that is also a continent. A land of great diversity, its centre is dominated by a vast desert plateau, separated from the narrow coastal plains by a chain of mountains, the Great Dividing Range. Its shores are bathed by both the Pacific and Indian Oceans, and running parallel to much of the eastern coast is one of the most fascinating natural phenomena in the world: the Great Barrier Reef. Also part of Australia are Tasmania and the Torres Strait Islands, while Norfolk, Cocos Keeling and Christmas Island are Australian overseas territories and are dealt with separately. Often ignored by foreign sailors, but a great favourite with locals, is Lord Howe Island, about 400 miles east of Sydney and a tempting interlude on a passage to or from New Zealand. The island's unique flora and large colony of seabirds has been recognized by the fact that it is included on the UNESCO World Heritage list.

In spite of the large number of yachts in Australia, the figures for Australian yachts cruising overseas is smaller than would be expected from such a globetrotting nation, and the only explanation for this is that Australia has such beautiful and varied cruising grounds that the inhabitants do not need to go and look for variety elsewhere. From the picturesque harbours of New South Wales to the windswept coasts of Victoria and Tasmania, the tropical islands and Great Barrier Reef of Queensland, to the deserted shores of Western Australia and the wide shallow bays of the Northern Territory, Australia has it all. This vast country is a world in itself, and even a short cruise through some of its waters will pay unexpected rewards.

Visiting yachts fall into three broad categories: those who plan to spend longer and see as much as possible, including a cruise along the Great Barrier Reef; those with less time at their disposal and who limit their cruising to the tropical north before continuing their voyage into the Indian Ocean and beyond; and the birds of passage who plan to spend the minimum of time, usually in a convenient place to reprovision and make any emergency repairs. The first group includes mostly yachts that have come to spend the tropical storm season in a safe port on the east coast and then continue north inside the Great Barrier Reef. In both the second and third group, most yachts make their base in a place such as Cairns or Darwin and visit the rest of the country by road, air, or even by train since the opening of the transcontinental rail service from Darwin to Adelaide. Sailors have heaped superlatives onto Australia's cruising opportunities, but it is the continent's unique interior that justifies the effort to tour some of

the world's natural wonders, whether it is the King's Canyon, Uluru, the Kimberleys, or at least the Kakadu National Park located so temptingly close to Darwin. Afloat or ashore, Australia can truly satisfy even the most demanding traveller.

An interesting stop for boats bound for Indonesia is the Ashmore Reef Nature Reserve, an unspoilt area and sheltered anchorage where visiting boats may stop briefly.

✦ COUNTRY PROFILE

The Aboriginal peoples of Australia probably arrived from Asia 60,000 years ago. Isolated for so long from the rest of the world, they developed a unique culture intrinsically bound up with the land. Up to the eighteenth century, Europeans believed that a great southern continent, Terra Australis Incognita, must exist to balance the land masses of the northern hemisphere. Australia was first sighted in the sixteenth century by the Portuguese and in the early seventeenth century the Spaniard Torres sailed through the strait that came to bear his name. Dutch sailors charted the north and west, and for a while Australia was called Van Diemen's Land. In 1770 Captain Cook landed on the east coast at Botany Bay. Soon afterwards Captain Phillip officially took possession of the land for Britain on the site of present-day Sydney. Britain used it as a penal colony and many convicts were deported there, often for relatively minor crimes. The continent was gradually settled and in 1901 the six colonies joined in a federation of individual states as the Commonwealth of Australia. The country was recognized as a sovereign nation by Britain in 1931. Today each state has its own capital, parliament and laws.

The population is 21 million, living mostly on the coasts and in the southeast. The majority are descendants of immigrants, and Aborigines form only 1 per cent of the population. Also indigenous to the area are the Torres Strait islanders. English is the main language. At one time there was thought to be 500 Aboriginal languages, but today there are only about four main groups still spoken. Canberra is the federal capital.

✦ CLIMATE

The climate varies from one end of the country to the other. It is mainly temperate, except for the tropical north and central desert. The hottest region is the northern two-thirds of the continent, which experiences humid and wet conditions in summer. The north has two seasons, wet from November to March, with the heaviest rainfall after January. The winter months of April to October are drier and more pleasant. In Darwin, the most pleasant month is July, with an average temperature of 25°C/77°F, while the hottest months are November and December with an average of 30°C/86°F, with many days well in excess of that. The weather is much

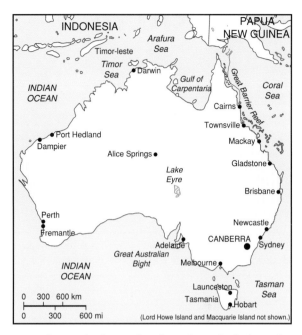

(Lord Howe Island and Macquarie Island not shown.)

more pleasant in the south and southeast. In Sydney, the warmest months are January and February, with averages of 22°C/72°F, and the coldest month is July, with an average of 12°C/54°F. The cyclone season is from December to April on both the Pacific and Indian Ocean coasts.

✦ FORMALITIES

The Australian authorities are among the strictest in the world and regulations must be observed to the letter, something that many foreign sailors do not seem to realize as shown by the numbers getting into trouble every year. Australia is a wonderful place to visit by yacht, but the price to pay for that privilege is to play everything by the book.

By law the captain must give notice of arrival not later than 96 hours before arrival. This is the minimum requirement and those who do not have long-range communications on board can report their impending arrival from the last port before Australia. This can be done by email, fax or phone to the Australian Customs National Communications Centre – tel: +61 3 9244 8973, fax: + 61 26275 5078 (yachtreport@customs.gov.au).

The information to be reported is: vessel name, country and port of registry, intended port of entry with ETA, last four ports visited, the name, date of birth, nationality and passport number of all those on board, whether any animals or firearms are on board, and if any disease has been recently experienced.

The ports of entry all have 24-hour service. There are severe penalties for stopping anywhere else before clearing in, up to an Aus$50,000 fine. The Q flag should be flown as soon as Australian territorial waters are entered.

PORTS OF ENTRY

Queensland:

Thursday Island 10°35´S 142°13´E	Weipa 12°40´S 141°55´E	Cairns 16°56´S 145°47´E
Mourilyan Harbour 17°36´S 146°07´E	Lucinda 18°31´S 146°20´E	Townsville 19°15´S 146°50´E
Abbot Point 19°51´S 148°04´E	Mackay 21°06´S 149°13´E	Hay Point (Dalrymple Bay) 21°16´S 149°18´E
Gladstone 23°50´S 151°15´E	Bundaberg 24°46´S 152°23´E	Brisbane 27°19´S 153°10´E
Rockhampton (Port Alma) 23°35´S 150°52´E		

Northern Territory:

Gove 12°10´S 136°40´E	Darwin 12°30´S 130°52´E	Groote Eylandt (Milner Bay) 13°52´S 136°28´E

Victoria:

Melbourne 37°50´S 145°55´E	Westernport 38°20´S 145°15´E	Geelong 38°07´S 144°23´E
Portland 38°21´S 141°37´E		

South Australia:

Cape Thevenard 32°09´S 133°39´E	Port Bonython 33°01´S 137°45´E	Androssan 34°26´S 137°55´E
Port Giles 35°02´S 137°45´E	Port Lincoln 34°45´S 135°53´E	Whyalla 33°02´S 137°37´E
Port Pirie 33°11´S 138°01E	Wallaroo 33°56´S 137°37´E	Port Adelaide 34°47´S 138°30´E
Port Stanvac 35°07´S 138°28´E		

New South Wales:

Yamba (Clarence River) 29°25´S 153°23´E	Coffs Harbour 30°18´S 153°09´E	Newcastle 32°56´S 151°47´E
Sydney 33°50´S 151°15´E	Port Botany and Kurnell 34°00´S 151°14´E	Port Kembla 34°28´S 150°54´E
Eden 37°04´S 149°55´E	Lord Howe Island 30°30´S 159°50´E	

Tasmania:

Port Latta 40°51´S 145°23´E	Burnie 41°03´S 145°55´E	Devonport 41°11´S 146°22´E
Launceston 41°26´S 147°08´E	Hobart 42°52´S 147°20´E	

Western Australia:

Derby 17°17´S 123°37´E	Broome 18°21´S 122°15´E	Port Hedland 20°20´S 118°37´E
Port Walcott 20°40´S 117°13´E	Dampier 20°39´S 116°43´E	Exmouth 21°54´S 114°11´E
Carnarvon 24°53´S 113°40´E	Geraldton 28°47´S 114°36´E	Fremantle 32°00´S 115°45´E
Bunbury 33°19´S 115°38´E	Albany 35°02´S 117°55´E	Esperance 33°52´S 121°53´E

Sydney: Approaching yachts should contact Sydney Maritime or Sydney Radio, who will direct them to the customs berth in Neutral Bay and advise the appropriate authorities.

Brisbane: Customs should be contacted and an ETA given at the customs dock. Occasionally, if the arrival falls outside working hours, customs may allow yachts to anchor at a certain point in the river and complete formalities the following morning.

Bundaberg: Boats must proceed for clearance to Bundaberg Port Marina, which is 3 miles upriver, as it is no longer possible to clear in at Burnett Heads Marina at the river entrance.

Cairns: On entering the Cairns shipping channel, Cairns harbour control should be contacted to give an ETA. Yachts arriving between 0830 and 1630 are normally told to go to Pier A at Marlin Marina. After 1630, the pier is used by excursion boats and yachts will be directed elsewhere, such as the main wharf. A more convenient place to clear in is at Halfmoon Bay Marina at Yorkey's Knob, a few miles north of Cairns, but permission to proceed directly there when arriving from a foreign port must be obtained from Cairns harbour control.

Thursday Island: Port Control usually directs the yacht to the customs dock. Customs, immigration and quarantine offices are all nearby. After clearance has been completed, the best place to anchor is west of the second jetty.

Darwin: Yachts are normally directed to the Fishermen's Wharf for clearance. Outside working hours, the vessel may be asked to anchor in the quarantine area. Clearance is also possible at Cullen Bay Marina, but this must be agreed with Darwin Port Control before proceeding there.

Ashmore Reef: Darwin Customs has detailed information that can be obtained when clearing out. Customs officials are based on a customs vessel at Ashmore Reef and should be contacted on Channel 16. Moorings have been laid for visitors' use.

There are particularly strict rules concerning stops in any of the islands in the Torres Strait. The area is under constant

Aboriginal rock painting in Kakadu National Park.

surveillance by customs airplanes. If an emergency stop is made at one of the islands, no one must land or have contact with any other vessel. As this is an international waterway, vessels are allowed to transit without clearing into Australia provided the above rules are observed. The nearest port of entry is at Thursday Island.

All vessels that have passed through the Torres Strait and decide to stop must contact the Australian Quarantine and Inspection Service (AQIS) to arrange a quarantine inspection, preferably at Thursday Island, before leaving the area. Alternatively, you can report to another AQIS office up to four days before making landfall on the mainland. AQIS can be contacted via phone, email, or through local harbour authorities.

At the port of entry, clearance is done by customs, immigration and quarantine (AQIS).

All nationalities, with the sole exception of New Zealanders, must obtain a visa in advance. There are Australian diplomatic missions in all neighbouring countries. It is much easier to get this done before leaving home. A multiple entry visa valid for the length of the passport's validity can be obtained. There are large fines for arriving without a visa.

Anyone who wishes to obtain a visa for a longer stay in Australia than three months, and who has spent more than three months in the previous five years in any Pacific country (New Zealand excluded) must have a chest X-ray examination for proof against tuberculosis. Visas are only granted if the result is negative.

New Zealand citizens must now obtain a visa in advance before entry to Thursday Island as the Torres Strait area has been declared a special zone.

Those travelling later to Norfolk Island, Cocos Keeling and Christmas Island should have a multiple entry visa.

A cruising permit, valid for the period of the captain's visa, is obtained from customs on arrival, being granted when the officials are satisfied that the applicant is a genuine tourist, and has proof of sufficient funds for the maintenance of the vessel and the crew. Extensions are available from customs. The permit enables foreign yachts to cruise freely between their port of entry and exit, and allows them to visit any ports and places besides official ports of entry.

The itinerary that the yacht proposes to follow while in Australia must be given to customs. Yachts are supposed to keep customs informed of their whereabouts and to notify the nearest customs office if they change their itinerary. Foreign yachts may remain in Australia for up to 12 months without paying duty or other taxes.

AQIS recommends that the hull should have been cleaned one month before arrival and antifouled at least one year before arrival. Full details are on the AQIS website. Because of infestations by the Asian green-striped mussel, yachts arriving in Darwin may be inspected by a diver. If mussels are found, the boat must be hauled out and cleaned.

The quarantine laws are strict, particularly if animals are on board, and the penalties for breaking them are severe.

Goods and Services Tax (GST): A tax of 10 per cent is included in the price of most goods, except food, alcohol, clothing and fuel. Refunds on this tax are available for visitors to Australia. A tax invoice should be obtained from retailers when purchasing goods. Full details of the Tourist Refund Scheme are on the customs website.

Clearing out from Australia can only be done at a port of entry. After clearing out, the vessel is not allowed to stop at any other places, but anchoring for the night (or in bad weather) is permitted, provided no one goes ashore.

✦ RESTRICTIONS

The coast and islands west of Gove are part of the Arnhem Land Aboriginal Reserve and a permit is needed for entry, obtainable from the Lands Office in Gove. Cotton Island is off limits as it has sacred burial sites. Coburg peninsula is a national park, but permission to enter can be obtained from

Fremantle shoreline.

the Ranger Station. Ashmore Reef is a national park where no spearfishing is allowed.

In New South Wales living aboard a yacht permanently is illegal, although foreign yachts that are cruising are considered more leniently. There are strict rules concerning the discharge of used waters in harbours, canals and marinas.

Great Barrier Reef: The Great Barrier Reef Marine Park is divided into different-coloured zones. In the Green Zones, which cover about one-third of the park, no fishing or collecting is allowed. Heavy fines, and boarding by authorities to inspect the boat freezer, are in operation. Restricted fishing is permitted in some of the other zones. For the latest information and zone maps, it is advisable to view the Marine Park Authority's website before visiting the area.

✦ FACILITIES

Facilities in Australia are generally good, and are excellent in any of the larger yachting centres. If in need of a major overhaul or repairs, it is advisable to head for a main centre, such as Sydney, Brisbane, Hobart, Melbourne, Adelaide, Fremantle, Cairns or Darwin, where repair facilities are of a high standard and spares readily available. Provisioning is very good everywhere.

✦ CHARTER

Not surprisingly, most charter activities are concentrated in the Great Barrier Reef area. Sunsail is based at Hamilton Island, while Charter Yachts Australia, Whitsunday Rent A Yacht and Queensland Yacht Charters are all based in Airlie Beach, and have large fleets of sailing monohulls and catamarans (as well as powerboats) to explore what is regarded as Australia's best cruising area. Fraser Escape Charters, based on the Fraser Coast in Urangan, Queensland, has a mixed fleet of sailing and power yachts, both monohull and catamarans. Tropic Sail offers bareboat and crewed yachts from its base in Townsville.

Team EastSail, based in Rushcutter Bay, is perfectly located for those who wish to explore Sydney Harbour in one of their sailing yachts. Based at Newport Anchorage Marina in Newport, north of Sydney, Club Sail has a fleet of sailing yachts and offers both bareboat and skippered charters as well as tuition.

On the west coast, South West Yacht Charters, based in Bunbury near Perth, has a fleet of sailing yachts, as does Yachting Holidays based in Hobart, Tasmania.

> www.clubsail.com.au
> www.sunsail.com
> www.fraserescape.com.au
> www.tropicsail.com.au
> www.eastsail.com.au
> www.charteryachtsaustralia.com.au
> www.rentayacht.com.au
> www.yachtcharters.com.au
> www.swyachtcharters.com.au
> www.yachtingholidays.com.au

Cruising Guides
Australian Cruising Guide
Cruising the Coral Coast
Cruising the New South Wales Coast
The Whitsunday Islands
Torres Strait Passage Guide
www.cruisinganchoragesaustralia.com.au (comprehensive guide that can be purchased online)

Websites
www.visitaustralia.com
www.customs.gov.au/site/page.cfm?u=4790 (clearance and reporting requirements)
www.aqis.gov.au (quarantine department)
www.gbrmpa.gov.au (Great Barrier Reef Marine Park)

Local time	Eastern Standard Time UTC +10
	Central Standard Time UTC +9.5
	Western Standard Time UTC + 8
	Summer time: first Sunday in October to first Sunday in April
	Western Australia ends last Sunday in March
	No summer time in Queensland and the Northern Territory
Buoyage	IALA A
Currency	Australian Dollar (AUD)
Electricity	240V, 50Hz

Diplomatic missions

UK	2 6270 6666	South Africa	2 6273 2424
USA	2 6214 5600	New Zealand	2 6270 4211
Canada	2 6270 4000		

Communications		**Emergency number**
IDD 61	IAC 0011	000

Hideaway Bay in the Whitsundays.

COOK ISLANDS

THE COOK ISLANDS are made up of 15 islands, spread over a large area of the South Pacific Ocean. The Southern Group, of which Rarotonga is the main island, also comprises Aitutaki, Atiu, Mitiaro, Mauke and Mangaia. These are high and fertile, and most of the inhabitants live there. Also part of the Southern Cooks are the atolls of Manuae, Takutea and Palmerston. The Northern Group are the low coral atolls of Penrhyn, Manihiki, Rakahanga, Pukapuka, Nassau and Suwarrow.

The affection that cruising sailors have for the Cooks goes back to two legendary figures who both spent a great deal of their lives on these islands. Tom Neale, a modern-day Robinson Crusoe, chose to maroon himself on Suwarrow Atoll and welcomed any sailor who called during the quarter-century he spent there. Father George Kester also ran away to the Cooks, but not in search of solitude, for his motives were altruistic. As a missionary he dedicated his life to the spiritual wellbeing of the islanders as well as the material wellbeing of all cruising sailors who happened to call at his island – first Rarotonga and then Aitutaki. Tom Neale died in 1977; Father George in the mid-1980s.

As most yachts arrive in the Cook Islands from the east, a good time to plan a passage is after the end of the annual Heiva celebrations that are held all over French Polynesia in late June and early July, a time of various events and performances that should not be missed. Leaving after Heiva is perfect timing as the first week of August is when the Cooks put on their own festivities around Independence Day. Most of the action is in Rarotonga, but the other islands can easily be visited afterwards. Aitutaki is a popular stop, and yachts are always assured of a warm welcome there. This is the case in all of the Cook Islands and, as elsewhere in the Pacific, the more remote the island the more enthusiastic the welcome. This is true of Penrhyn, or Tongareva, which lies 740 miles north of Rarotonga and whose isolated community is rarely visited by outsiders. This is even more true of Palmerston; this is an atoll without a pass into its lagoon, so visiting boats must anchor outside the reef. The 60 inhabitants are all descendants of William Marsters, an English carpenter who landed here with his two Polynesian wives in 1863 and started a dynasty that now numbers well over a thousand members, many of whom now live in New Zealand. Another atoll much favoured by sailors is uninhabited Suwarrow, which has been declared a nature reserve and has a caretaker posted there during the cruising season.

✦ COUNTRY PROFILE

Folklore says that two chiefs, one from Tahiti and the other from Samoa, arrived on Rarotonga at the same time, and divided the island peacefully between them. From here it is believed that the forefathers of the Maoris sailed to New Zealand. The timing of this is uncertain, but it could have been as early as the fifth century CE. Although this claim is disputed by some who believe those double hulled sailing canoes left from Raiatea, what is beyond doubt is that intrepid Polynesian sailors left from one of these islands in search of a new home and settled in New Zealand.

The first European to lay eyes on the islands was the Spanish explorer Álvaro de Mendaña at the end of the sixteenth century. Others soon followed, and between 1773 and 1779 Captain Cook charted and put many of these islands on the map and called them the Hervey Islands. Traders and missionaries were the next to arrive, and eventually the Cook Islands became a British colony. The islands were handed over to New Zealand in 1901 and became independent in 1965. The Cooks today have internal self-government in free association with New Zealand. There are very close ties to New Zealand and many more Cook Islanders live there than on the islands.

The capital is Avarua on Rarotonga. The 12,000 population speak Cook Islands Maori and English. Each island has its own dialect closely related to Maori, which is similar to Tahitian, while Pukapuka has a dialect that is closer to Samoan.

Anchorage Island in Suwarrow Atoll

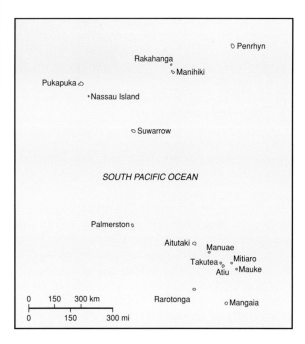

✦ CLIMATE

Generally the tropical climate is warm and sunny, with small temperature variations, but never too hot. During the winter, from May to November, the islands are under the influence of the southeast trade winds. However, sudden squalls can occur from other directions with little warning. December to April is the rainy period and also the cyclone season.

✦ FORMALITIES

PORTS OF ENTRY

Rarotonga: Avatiu 21°12´ S 159°47´ W	
Aitutaki: Arutanga 18°52´ S 159°48´ W	
Penrhyn: Omoka 9°00´ S 158°04´ W	
Sub-ports of entry are Pukapuka 10°53´ S 165°49´ W and	
Atiu (Avamutu) 19°59´ S 158°08´ W	

Rarotonga: Yachts should proceed directly to Avatiu, the commercial harbour. The harbourmaster should be contacted on Channel 12 for berthing instructions. Yachts are normally directed to the new marina-type facility. Radio Rarotonga (ZKR) monitors 2182 kHz and 4125 MHz as well as Channel 16.

Aitutaki: A shallow channel leads into the small boat harbour. Customs will come to the boat. Vessels too large for the small boat harbour should anchor outside the reef to the north of the channel. The channel has a depth of only 1.80m (6ft) and the outflowing current can reach 3 to 4 knots. If in any doubt, you can ask a local person for guidance.

Penrhyn: Yachts should anchor off Omoka village on the south side of Taruia Pass. There is also a wharf where yachts can come alongside if there is no surge.

Suwarrow: Entry formalities are not required and boats may stop here temporarily. There is a landing fee to be paid to the caretaker.

You may clear at Pukapuka and Atiu, but must pay for transporting the officials by air or sea.

At all ports of entry, a 30-day permit is given on arrival. Extensions have to be obtained in Rarotonga. For longer stays, a visa must be obtained before arrival from a New Zealand or British consulate.

Fruit and meat will be confiscated by quarantine, so it is advisable not to arrive with a large amount of fresh supplies.

Yachts may not visit any islands in the Cooks other than those mentioned as ports of entry without permission from customs and immigration.

Cruising yachts are not allowed to remain in the islands during the cyclone season.

✦ FACILITIES

Avatiu Harbour is the commercial port of Rarotonga. The harbour has been greatly improved with the addition of a small boat basin, but space for yachts is still limited. There is a good selection of fruit and vegetables on this fertile island, but repair facilities are basic. There are no marine supplies and only one chandlery, ABC Trading Company. Essential spares must be ordered from New Zealand, from where there are frequent flights. Gas bottles can be filled at an office near the harbour.

There is limited provisioning in Aitutaki. At Penrhyn, only basic provisions are available. Boats heading west and planning to stop at Palmerston should inform the authorities in Rarotonga as emergency supplies are occasionally sent with visiting yachts.

Cruising Guides	Websites
The Pacific Crossing Guide	www.cook-islands.com
South Pacific Anchorages	www.cookislands.org.uk
Landfalls of Paradise	

Local time	UTC −10
Buoyage	IALA A
Currency	Cook Islands Dollar, New Zealand Dollar (NZD)
Electricity	240V, 50Hz

Diplomatic mission	
New Zealand	22201

Communications	
IDD 682	IAC 00

Emergency numbers Ambulance 998   Police 999

EASTER ISLAND

MYSTERY SURROUNDS THIS REMOTE PLACE, the people who once lived there, and the origins of the giant statues that are scattered all over the small island. Lying at the southeastern extremity of the Polynesian triangle, only a few intrepid yachts call at this lonely outpost of Chile to whom it belongs and from which it is separated by over 2,000 miles of ocean. Isla de Pascua, also known by its Polynesian name Rapa Nui, is totally isolated and its nearest neighbour is tiny Pitcairn, 1,200 miles to the west.

For those who make the long passage, there are many rewards ashore, such as the crater of Rano Kau volcano and, above it, the sacred site of Orongo where the birdman cult was practised. At the other end of the island is the volcano Rano Raraku, where the giant statues were carved out of lava and where many still lie abandoned and unfinished.

Yachts have to be prepared to leave at short notice if the wind changes direction suddenly as there is no adequate shelter. There is some protection inside the small harbour at Hanga Piko, south of the main anchorage, but access is difficult so the port captain insists that a local pilot is employed. The open anchorage off the main settlement of Hanga Roa provides reasonable protection from the prevailing southeast winds. If the wind turns, there are three alternative anchorages: Vinapu on the southwest coast, Hotuiti on the east side, and Anakena Bay on the north side of the island. Swell is a problem in all these anchorages, but

Anakena is the best protected in southerly winds. Hotuiti anchorage is close to the Rano Raraku volcano, which can be reached by dinghy in settled weather. The port captain stipulates that a yacht must not be left unattended anywhere while at anchor.

✦ COUNTRY PROFILE

Debate over the history of Rapa Nui has been going on ever since the outside world made contact with this Polynesian outpost lost in the vastness of the Pacific Ocean. Some 600 huge abandoned lava statues, up to 9m (30ft) high, lie scattered around the island – who carved them and why remains a mystery. Easter Islanders were the only Pacific people to develop a form of writing, although no one survived who could read it.

The first European to visit the island was the Dutch explorer Jacob Roggeveen in 1722, and he seems to have arrived at a time when the inhabitants had just finished a series of internecine wars. After this first contact, the population remained stable at around 4,000 until the 1850s, when Peruvian slave traders, smallpox and emigration to Tahiti saw the number of inhabitants fall considerably. At the end of the nineteenth century Chile annexed the island. In 1955 the Norwegian Thor Heyerdahl led an expedition to Easter Island and proposed a theory that the islanders had originated in South America. This theory is no longer

312

accepted, and the islanders' Polynesian origin is beyond dispute. Today Easter Island is a dependency of Chile, with a military governor and a local mayor. In recent years, the islanders have achieved a certain level of autonomy, but relations with mainland Chile continue to be tense.

In a total population of 3,000 there are around 2,500 islanders of Polynesian origin and a few hundred Chileans. Spanish is the official language, but Polynesian, similar to Tahitian, is spoken by the islanders. Hanga Roa is the only settlement.

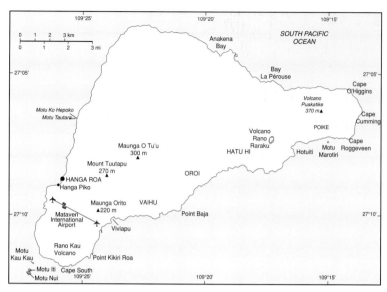

✦ CLIMATE

The southeast trades prevail from October to April. During summer, from mid-November to mid-February, the winds tend to be lighter and the seas calmer. May to September is the rainy season when westerly winds predominate. Sudden squalls can produce strong winds from a different direction to that of the prevailing one and the boat may have to be moved at short notice to a safer anchorage. The island falls outside the cyclone belt.

✦ FORMALITIES

PORT OF ENTRY
Hanga Roa 27°09´S 109°26´W

The port captain should be called on arrival. There is a black mooring buoy which can be used if vacant. Customs, immigration, health and agriculture officials will either come on board or formalities are completed at the port captain's office at Hanga Piko. Most nationalities are given a visa on arrival.

Landing the dinghy in Hanga Roa can be difficult if there is a big swell, so a local fisherman will usually ferry the officials out or the crew ashore. This can be arranged via the port captain.

Neither food products nor garbage may be taken ashore, but must be kept on board.

It is strictly prohibited to remove ancient artefacts. Around one-third of the island is a national park, for which an entry fee is charged.

Hanga Piko: The small harbour has been enlarged and dredged to about 2.40m (8ft). Boats of a maximum length of 18m (60ft) can find shelter inside. The small basin is sheltered from all wind directions, but surge causes serious problems at all times, so boats must be tied fore-and-aft to rocks ashore. The harbour should be abandoned if there is

heavy surge or as soon as the wind turns into the west, as several yachts have been damaged in such conditions.

✦ FACILITIES

All supplies are brought in from Chile by ship or air so goods in the supermarkets are quite expensive, but the selection is good. Some locally produced fruit and vegetables are available. The ATM accepts only Mastercard. Fuel is available, but must be carried in jerrycans from the fuel station. Usually this can be arranged with the same fisherman used to commute ashore. Although there are no repair facilities, there is a government workshop for maintenance purposes, and in an emergency this would undoubtedly help.

Cruising Guides	
Landfalls of Paradise	South Pacific Anchorages

Websites
www.netaxs.com/~trance/rapanui.html (Easter Island home page)
www.islandheritage.org (Easter Island Foundation)

Local time:	UTC –6
	Summer time: second Saturday in March to second Saturday in October
Buoyage	IALA B
Currency	Chilean Peso (CLP)
Electricity	220V, 50Hz

Communications
IDD 56 (Chile) 32   IAC 00

Emergency numbers	
Ambulance 100 215	Police 100 244

FIJI

FIJI IS AN ARCHIPELAGO of over three hundred islands, from coral atolls to large volcanic islands. About one hundred of them are inhabited, while many of the rest are used as temporary fishing bases or planting grounds. The two main islands are Viti Levu and Vanua Levu and the International Dateline runs through the latter. Although Fiji prides itself as being the place where yesterday becomes today, most of its islands are just west of 180°. At the crossroads of Melanesia and Polynesia, the traditional way of life is still thriving in the islands and the unthinking attitude of a few visiting sailors in the past has caused offence and animosity, which led to a strict control of cruising permits. Local etiquette should be observed and visitors are expected to pay a courtesy visit to the chief of the island or village bearing a token gift, usually yagona, a slightly intoxicating drink made from the roots of the kava plant.

For the cruising sailor, Fiji has all the ingredients of a perfect destination: beautiful islands, secluded anchorages and welcoming people. This picture of perfection is somewhat marred by a menacing array of coral reefs that almost encircle the entire archipelago. Radar and satellite navigation have significantly reduced that risk, but many a world cruise has come to a premature end on one of Fiji's reefs. The majority of visiting yachts arrive from the east, which is also where the reefs have claimed most victims. Part of the problem is that it is forbidden to stop at any of the eastern islands before clearing in and a careful watch is kept on yacht movement by the Fijian authorities. The location of the few ports of entry complicates the task of cruise planning, especially for those hoping to visit the eastern islands that lie to windward of all ports of entry. The most convenient port for those intending to cruise eastern Fiji is Savusavu on the island of Vanua Levu. A special permit is required to visit the Lau Group where the traditional way of life has remained almost unaffected by the modern world, and local chiefs have fiercely resisted any attempt at development or modernization.

South of Viti Levu, and close to the route to the Yasawas, are two other islands where traditions are still strong, Kandavu and Beqa. Traditions are not so strong in the western islands, some of which have been developed as tourist resorts, such as the picturesque Mamanuca Islands, which are a short hop from Nadi airport and very convenient for crew changes. Farther north is the Yasawa Group, a popular cruising ground due to scenic anchorages and clear waters.

Out on their own are Rotuma and several smaller islands lying approximately 200 miles NNW of Fiji. They form a distinctive group and, although administratively linked to Fiji, ethnologically they are very different as Rotumans are Polynesians. The administrative centre is at Ahau, but as Rotuma is not an official port of entry, access to it is only allowed with prior permission from the authorities in Suva.

✦ COUNTRY PROFILE

The islands were first settled by Melanesians from South East Asia around 7000–5000 BCE, while the Polynesians arrived later, around 1500 BCE. After the islands were first sighted in the mid-seventeenth century by Abel Tasman, early European contacts spread over the next 200 years. Captain Cook visited several islands in the 1770s and Captain Bligh sailed through on his epic voyage after being cast off from the *Bounty*.

During the nineteenth century, traders arrived in search of sandalwood; missionaries and land speculators also came. The introduction of firearms saw terrible tribal wars fought by a people renowned for their savagery and cannibalism. Eventually, to put an end to their exploitation and abuse by ruthless outsiders, the chiefs requested that the islands be taken under the protection of Great Britain. Labour shortages led to large numbers of Indian labourers being brought in by the British to work on the sugar plantations.

Independence came to Fiji in 1970, but racial tension remained close to the surface as the Indian population grew

Malololailai Island in Western Fiji.

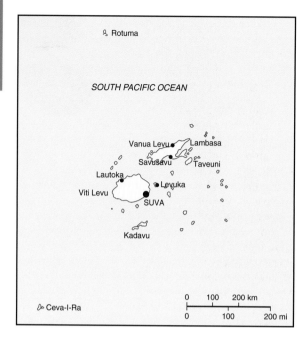

FORMALITIES

PORTS OF ENTRY

Suva 18°09´ S 178°26´ E	Levuka 17°41´ S 178°51´ E
Lautoka 17°36´ S 177°26 E	Savusavu 16°47´ S 179°21´ E

All yachts must notify Fijian customs a minimum of 48 hours before entering Fijian waters. Notification must be made using form C2C, which can be downloaded from the Fiji Inland Revenue and Customs Administration website and emailed to: yachtsreport@frca.org.fj. Any queries as to entry formalities can be sent to 'Contact Us' on the same website.

On reaching Fijian waters, yachts must go straight to a port of entry to complete customs, immigration and quarantine formalities. All vessels are required to communicate with port control on Channel 16 to request permission to proceed to the designated quarantine area.

Fiji has very strict regulations, and in 2009 these were made even more restrictive. As the authorities obviously regard yachts with suspicion, visiting sailors must do their best to act in accordance with the current rules and regulations, especially as they seem to be changing frequently.

Suva: Port control should be called at least two hours before arrival. Normally yachts are required to anchor in the quarantine area to be boarded by a quarantine official before moving to King's Wharf for the rest of formalities. It is occasionally possible to obtain radio pratique through the operator, in which case the yacht may proceed directly to King's Wharf for clearance. Immigration does not come to the boat and the captain must walk to the immigration office in town. At the same time, the health clearance fee can be paid at the health office nearby. If King's Wharf is crowded with ships, yachts may be allowed to proceed directly to the Royal Suva Yacht Club and complete formalities from there. Clearance is normally available from 0700 to sunset Monday to Friday. Yachts arriving at the weekend at Suva have been fined for not notifying the authorities and for anchoring at the yacht club until Monday.

Levuka: Yachts should anchor near the main wharf. The captain should then visit the nearby offices ashore. Occasionally officers insist on inspecting the boat. Formalities are usually simpler than in Suva, so for boats coming from the east, the detour to Levuka is probably justified as, on arriving in Suva, you can then proceed directly to the Royal Suva Yacht Club and contact the authorities from there.

Lautoka: Yachts normally anchor in the vicinity of Queen's Wharf. Arrangements are then made on VHF to meet the various officials at the dock and bring them out to the boat.

Savusavu: The marina should be contacted in advance and it will call the relevant officials.

and threatened to outnumber the native Fijians. A military coup, which followed the 1987 election, led to Fiji declaring itself a republic and being expelled from the Commonwealth. A new constitution was adopted in 1997, which enabled the country to resume membership in the Commonwealth under the new name of Fiji Islands. Another military coup in 2007 once again suspended democratic governance, and the country continues to suffer from the inability of the two ethnic groups to reach a compromise on how to live in harmony.

The population is about 945,000, of which 54 per cent are Fijian, 38 per cent Indian, and the rest of other origins. Fijian, Hindustani and English are spoken, the latter being widely used by all sections of the population. The capital is Suva, which is an important communications centre for the South Pacific. The main campus of the University of the South Pacific is in Suva.

CLIMATE

Fiji has a mild tropical climate. The southeast trade winds blow from May to November and keep the islands cooler and drier, while the summer months from November to April are wet and humid. July and August are the most pleasant months, with an average temperature in Suva of 23°C/73°F. Viti Levu and Vanua Levu can have a lot of rain and Suva is renowned for sudden torrential downpours. Cyclones occur during the period of November to April. There are very few hurricane holes in Fiji and these fill up quickly with local boats, but the situation has improved by the opening of a couple of well-protected marinas.

On arrival in a port of entry, quarantine must be cleared first. The captain should inform the quarantine officer of any food stores as well as any other articles made of plant materials. Garbage should be put in sealed plastic bags and handed over to be disposed of in the port incinerator.

A visa-free stay for up to four months is allowed for most nationals, visas being required by only a few. After four months, an extension may be obtained for up to six months.

Yachts may remain for 18 months without paying any duty.

An itinerary of places and dates where and when you are planning to cruise until departure is required for customs clearance. Once cleared into Fiji, those who intend to sail to another port of entry, either directly or via any other places, must clear out with customs from the port of entry where they cleared in first. In addition to the customs clearance, you must also obtain clearance from the Coconut Pest and Diseases Board. Prior to departing a port of entry, whether going abroad or to another Fijian destination, you should also notify port control of the intended destination. Following a ruling introduced in 2009, a cruising permit is needed to stop at any port or island outside one of the official ports of entry. Such permits are obtained from the Ministry of Fijian Affairs, 61 Carnavon St, Suva, or the Commissioner's Office in Lautoka, Levuka or Savusavu.

✦ FACILITIES

Suva has the best range of repair facilities in the Central Pacific, most of which are concentrated in the vicinity of the Royal Suva Yacht Club, which also has a dock for visiting yachts. Provisioning is good in Suva, with several supermarkets and an excellent fresh produce market. Best facilities

outside of Suva are at or near Lautoka. Two marinas on Viti Levu's west coast, Port Denarau and Vuda Point, have good amenities and are also used during the cyclone season. There are haulout and some repair services at Neisau Marina. Across Nadi Waters on Malololailai Island, a small marina at the Musket Cove Yacht Club has limited services. Copra Shed Marina at Savusavu is a good base from which to explore the eastern part of the archipelago, and there is a limited range of repair facilities locally.

Cruising Guides
Landfalls of Paradise
Pacific Crossing Guide
South Pacific Anchorages

Websites
www.frca.org.fj/docs/customs_forms/c2c.pdf (Inland Revenue and Customs)
www.bulafiji.com (Fiji Visitors Bureau)

Local time	UTC +12
Buoyage	IALA A
Currency	Fijian Dollar (FJD)
Electricity	240V, 50Hz

Diplomatic missions
UK	322 9100
USA	331 4466
Australia	338 2211
New Zealand	331 1422

Communications
IDD 679	IAC 00

Emergency number
911

Savusavu on Vanua Levu Island.

FRENCH POLYNESIA

FRENCH POLYNESIA covers an area of the South Pacific about the size of Europe. It is made up of 130 islands in five archipelagos: the Society, Marquesas, Tuamotu, Gambier and Austral Islands. So many superlatives have been bestowed on these islands since Captains Cook, Wallis and Bligh, the *Bounty* mutineers, Herman Melville, Paul Gauguin and many others visited them, that you can only repeat some of those well-worn adjectives. Robert Louis Stevenson, who stopped in the Marquesas on the schooner *Casco* in 1888, spoke for generations of sailors to come when he described what he saw in these immortal words: 'The first experience can never be repeated. The first love, the first sunrise, the first South Sea island, are memories apart and touched a virginity of sense... As the first rays of the sun displayed the needles of Ua Pou, these pricked about the line of the horizon; like the pinnacles of some ornate and monstrous church they stood there, in the sparkling brightness of the morning, the fit signboard of a world of wonders.'

As symbols of the South Seas, these islands are indeed unmatched and there are few sailors who do not dream of cruising one day among these enchanted isles. From the rugged beauty of the Marquesas to the crystal-clear waters of the Tuamotu atolls and the lofty peaks of the Society Islands, the variety in scenery and cruising opportunities is unsurpassed in the South Pacific. Most boats make their first landfall in the Marquesas having sailed along the traditional route from the Galapagos, or directly from Mexico or California. Fewer boats take the longer route to Mangareva in the Gambiers, usually after detours to Easter Island and Pitcairn. The Australs, lying south of the tropics and far from most cruising routes, are rarely visited. Remote and only administratively linked to French Polynesia is the uninhabited Clipperton atoll, some 700 miles off the Mexican coast. The lagoon of this atoll has no pass, but the few yachts that stop there can shelter in the lee of the reef. Landing through the surf is not easy, but the opportunity to visit this unspoilt gem is a worthy reward.

The spectacular scenery of the Marquesas, with their craggy soaring peaks and lush vegetation, makes them among the most beautiful islands in the world. It was not, though, their natural beauty that brought two of these islands to international attention, but the work done here by some of their famous visitors. The painter Paul Gauguin spent the final years of his life on Hiva Oa where he created some of

Fatu Hiva in the Marquesas.

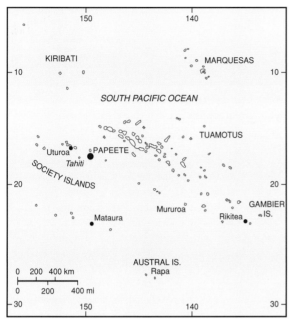

his best-known canvases depicting the beauty of his Polynesian hosts. While Hiva Oa now thrives on its association with Paul Gauguin, Nuku Hiva's claim to fame is as the setting of Herman Melville's *Typee*. Melville called at the Marquesas on the whaler *Acushnet* in 1843, where he jumped ship and spent some time in the village of Taipivae, a stay that inspired his enduring bestseller. While the story is entirely fictional, the atmosphere of days gone by depicted by Melville can still be felt in these islands where ancient stone statues and sacred sites survive in the brooding forests.

In complete contrast to the lofty Marquesas are the Tuamotus, once called the Dangerous Archipelago on account of their treacherous currents and lurking reefs. Yachts used to avoid this area, but many now stop and visit the low atolls, as the risks have diminished considerably with the advent of radar and GPS. Negotiating the passes into some of the lagoons can be a difficult operation because of the strong currents, and navigating inside the lagoons studded with coral heads can be just as daunting. This calls for careful eyeball navigation, ideally when the sun is overhead or behind the observer and the colour of the water gives an indication of its depth.

Back in the modern world, the capital Papeete is greatly enjoyed by visiting sailors as they are able to berth Mediterranean-style in the centre of this bustling town. Development, which has not affected the outer islands, has left its mark on Tahiti, but in the rest of the Society Islands life continues to proceed at a slower pace, and Moorea, Huahine, Raiatea, Tahaa and Bora Bora continue to be highly appreciated destinations for both charter and cruising boats.

In the relatively small area of the Society Islands all ingredients that make up a perfect cruising ground are concentrated: relaxed sailing inside enclosed lagoons, plenty of sheltered anchorages, a wide choice of restaurants and, for the long-term cruisers, good supplies and repair facilities in the main centres of Tahiti and Raiatea. As the ancient site of Havaiki, the island of Raiatea lies at the symbolic centre of the Polynesian triangle whose far-flung corners stretch to Easter Island, Hawaii and New Zealand. It is believed that long ago it was from here that people set off in large double-hulled canoes in search of new lands to settle. Eventually they reached New Zealand, which they called Aotearoa, the land of the long white cloud, and founded a new home there.

✦ COUNTRY PROFILE

Tahiti and the surrounding islands have been populated since time immemorial, but little is known about where the original population came from, although it is believed they migrated from South East Asia. A system of chiefdoms developed, which later became a kingdom. Remains of the past are still to be found, such as ancient stone statues and massive temple platforms.

Matai Bay in Tahiti marks the first European contact in 1767 when Captain Samuel Wallis landed there. He and his sailors found a peaceful people on a lush fertile island described thus by Captain Wallis: 'I found the country populous, and pleasant in the highest degree, and saw many canoes on the shore; but not one came to us, nor did the people seem to take the least notice of us as we passed along.' Nine months later, the French explorer Bougainville arrived and promptly claimed Tahiti for France. Next to visit was James Cook, on an expedition to observe the sun's eclipse by Venus. He made astute observations of the Tahitians and their lifestyle, including the name they gave to the island, Otaheite ('this is Tahiti'). In honour of the Royal Geographical Society, Cook named the islands Society Islands. The welcoming islanders suffered from their contacts with European sailors, as diseases hitherto unknown decimated the population.

Visitors' dock in Papeete.

Despite requests from the Tahitians, the British refused to make the islands a Protectorate, so the islands were put under French protection. The Pomaré dynasty ruled until 1880, when Tahiti became a full French colony. After the Second World War the newly named French Polynesia became a French Overseas Territory. The French maintained a military presence in the islands and used the atoll Mururoa for nuclear testing. The tests were finally stopped in 1996 as a result of international condemnation and violent demonstrations in Papeete. Although the islands enjoy a certain amount of autonomy, major decisions continue to be taken in Paris and there are increasing calls for full autonomy or even independence. In 2004, French Polynesia's status as an overseas territory of France was changed to that of a French overseas collectivity. It is expected that at some point the name may also be changed to that of Tahiti Nui (Greater Tahiti).

The population is 287,000. Polynesians form the majority, although there are a number of European settlers, mostly French, and also a Chinese minority. Papeete is the capital and is quite mixed, while the population of the outer islands is pure Polynesian. Tahitian and French are the main languages, although each island group has its own distinct Polynesian language.

✦ CLIMATE

The climate in the greater part of this vast area is tropical, with the exception of the southernmost islands of the Austral group where it borders on the temperate. July and August are the most pleasant months in Papeete, with an average temperature of 25°C/77°F. The weather between November and April is warm and rainy, while May to October is cooler and drier, when the islands are under the influence of the southeast trade winds. These winds are called *mara'amu* in Polynesian and the term also refers to the winter season, whereas the wet season is called *toerau*. Reinforced trade winds are a feature of the winter season, especially August, when they occasionally blow at 30 knots. The cyclone season is November to March, and almost every year at least one

Rally start in Bora Bora Lagoon.

cyclone affects one or more of the islands. Full cyclones rarely hit the Marquesas, but they can be affected by storms during that season.

✦ FORMALITIES

PORTS OF ENTRY

Society Islands:	Papeete (Tahiti) 17°32′S 149°35′W
Afareaitu (Moorea) 17°32′S 149°46′W	
Uturoa (Raiatea) 16°44′S 151°26′W	
Fare (Huahine) 16°43′S 151°02′W	
Vaitape (Bora Bora) 16°30′S 151°45′W	
Marquesas: Atuona (Hiva Oa) 9°51′S 139°02′W	
Taiohae (Nuku Hiva) 8°56′S 140°06′W	
Hakahau (Ua Pou) 9°21′S 140°03′W	
Austral Islands: Mataura (Tubuai) 23°22′S 149°28′W	
Moerai (Rurutu) 22°27′S 151°20′W	
Raima (Raivavae) 23°52′S 147°40′W	
Tuamotus: Tiputa (Rangiroa) 15°10′S 147°35′W	
Gambier Islands: Rikitea (Mangareva) 23°07′S 134°58′W	

Papeete: Before entering or departing Papeete harbour all yachts must contact the port captain on Channel 12 or 2683 kHz. On arrival, contact port control on Channel 12. Visiting yachts may go to the new marina off the main quay or anchor close to Taina Marina. To reach the latter, permission must be obtained from port control to cross the runway extension line. On arrival in Papeete, you must report first to immigration, then customs, followed by the port captain's office, all of which are in the Bureau des Yachts on the waterfront.

Papeete is the main port of entry and all yachts have to finalize their clearance there. Because of the long distances, the outer islands have been made informal ports of entry, where yachts may clear in initially. On arrival in one of the outer islands, you should report to the local police (Gendarmerie). Failure to report may lead to a fine. The gendarme in the first port of arrival normally issues a document, which is then stamped in subsequent ports. The yellow Q flag must be flown until clearance is completed in Papeete.

Hiva Oa: This is the most common port of entry for boats arriving from the east. No other islands should be visited before reporting to the officials in Atuona. The small harbour can get crowded and the swell is usually bad. Formalities are completed at the Gendarmerie in Atuona. Those required to deposit a bond can do this at Banque Socredo.

Nuku Hiva: If space is available, boats may come alongside the quay in the northeast corner of the harbour. Formalities are completed at the Gendarmerie in Taiohae.

Mangareva: The gendarme in Rikitea will hold passports until departure. No other formalities are needed.

Raiatea is one of the most important charter bases in the South Pacific.

must clear with customs and immigration and apply to the harbourmaster for a permit to leave.

◆ FACILITIES

The best facilities are to be found in Papeete, which has several chandleries and workshops specializing in yacht repair, as well as haulout facilities. The only other centre with extensive repair services is at Raiatea, which is a busy charter base. There are few marinas as such, and those in Tahiti are always full with local boats. Vessels can be left between seasons either in Tahiti, in the port area, or in Raiatea, either on the hard or in Marina Apoiti. In Bora Bora there are now two mooring facilities, the new marina at Vaitape or a number of visitors' mooring buoys that have been laid by the Bora Bora Yacht Club. Provisioning is best in Tahiti. The best supermarket for long-term provisioning is Carrefour in Papeete. Duty-free fuel may be purchased on departure by obtaining an exemption certificate from customs.

◆ CHARTER

Raiatea has become an important charter base because its large lagoon, which it shares with the smaller island of Taha'a, provides excellent sailing conditions, while the temptation of Bora Bora is only a few miles away.

> www.tahitiyachtcharter.com
> www.moorings.com
> www.sunsail.com

Nationals of most European countries, Australia, Canada, New Zealand, the USA and a number of other countries do not require a visa in advance and receive from 30 to 90 days depending on the country. EU citizens can extend their three-month stay by writing to the High Commissioner's office (DRCL), BP115, Papeete, at least one month before the end of the three-month period, and apply for a resident card. All non-EU nationals who intend to stay longer than three months must obtain a visa in advance from a French diplomatic mission in their own country. US and Canadian passport holders arriving without a visa are given a 30-day grace period and are expected to clear into Papeete and complete proper formalities within that period. Nationals of countries not qualifying for a visa-free entry must acquire their visas in advance.

EU citizens are no longer required to post a bond, but any person from a non-EU country on board a yacht must deposit in a local bank a sum of money equivalent to a one-way air ticket back to their home country. The bond must be deposited at Banque Socredo in Papeete, and can be paid in cash or by credit card. The bond is refunded before departure. Yachts staying only a short period may have the bond requirement waived. The bond can be avoided by buying tickets for flights back home. Crew arriving without a return ticket may be requested to post a bond on arrival. It is usually helpful if the captain meets such crew on arrival at Tahiti airport as problems with immigration by those arriving without a return ticket are not uncommon.

The movement of yachts is restricted in certain lagoons where there are pearl farms, and yachts should avoid anchoring near oyster beds (which are clearly marked).

Permission should be obtained for any cruise that takes a yacht more than 50 miles from Tahiti. On departure, yachts

Cruising Guides		
Cruising Guide to the Leeward Islands of Tahiti		
Exploring the Marquesas Islands		
Guide to Navigation in French Polynesia		
Polynesia		
South Pacific Anchorages		
The Pacific Crossing Guide		

Websites		
www.tahiti-tourisme.pf		
www.raiatea.com/carenage/index.html (Raiatea Carenage boatyard and marina)		

Local time	Gambier Islands UTC −9, Marquesas UTC −9.5, Tahiti UTC −10
Buoyage	IALA A
Currency	CFP Franc (XPF)
Electricity	220V, 60Hz

Communications	
IDD 689	IAC 00

Emergency numbers		
112	Ambulance 15	Police 17

GALAPAGOS ISLANDS

The Galapagos Archipelago, whose correct name is Archipiélago de Colón, named after Cristobal Colón (Christopher Columbus), forms a group of volcanic islands straddling the equator about 600 miles west of Ecuador. There are 13 main islands and they have both English and official Spanish names, but the latter are now in common use. The islands are famous for their unique wildlife which includes many endemic species of both land animals and birds living amid barren volcanic scenery. The way different species had evolved in isolation from the rest of the world was one of the major observations made by Charles Darwin on his visit, which led to his theory of evolution.

The Galapagos are a province of Ecuador and the Ecuadorian authorities take their custody of this unique wildlife sanctuary seriously. The bicentenary of Charles Darwin's birth in 2009 provoked a debate, both on an international level and in Ecuador itself, on the destructive impact on the islands' ecosystem of the ever-increasing number of both tourists and immigrants from the mainland. This concern by the authorities explains the difficulty of getting permission to cruise the islands on your own yacht. Cruising boats may only stop at one of the official ports, and visits to any of the protected islands are only possible on a local excursion boat. Occasionally the authorities grant permits to cruising boats following a predetermined itinerary. There is a high fee to be paid for this privilege and it is compulsory to have an official guide permanently on board. Arrangements for obtaining such a permit must be made well in advance.

The abundance of wildlife as well as its variety is truly staggering. Every island has its own resident species – giant tortoises on Isabela, sea iguanas on Santa Fé, land iguanas on Fernandina, sea lions on San Cristobal, frigate birds on Seymour, penguins on San Salvador, white-tipped sharks at Bartolomé, while Española has a large colony of blue-footed boobies whose gentle dance performed by courting couples is one of the most touching acts in the animal world. Floreana is better known for its colourful past, first as a pirates' lair, then as a convenient stopover for the crews of whalers, who visited these islands to load hundreds of the giant turtles. A leftover from those times are the post office boxes, where sailors used to leave their mail to be hopefully forwarded by some future visitor, a custom that has survived to this day.

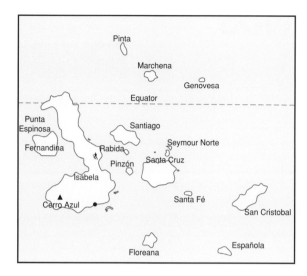

✦ COUNTRY PROFILE

The islands were found by accident early in the sixteenth century when a ship carrying the Bishop of Panama to Peru drifted off course. However, it is possible that Amerindians had earlier visited the islands from the mainland. Named by the Spaniards Las Islas Encantadas, the Enchanted Islands were not settled and in the next three centuries they were used as a base by pirates, sealers and whalers. Famous sailors such as Francis Drake, Walter Raleigh, James Cook and John Hawkins stopped there for refuge, rest and provisions. The giant tortoises, which could be kept alive in ships' holds for months on end, provided a source of fresh meat, and thousands were captured or killed. In 1835 the islands received their most famous visit, from HMS *Beagle* and Charles Darwin. The expedition stayed for five weeks and Darwin's observations of how the native wildlife had developed into unique species in response to their surroundings were central to his theory of evolution. Eventually the islands were settled by Ecuador and used for some time as a penal colony. In 1959 the Galapagos were declared a

national park, and organized tourism since the 1960s brings thousands to the islands every year.

The population has trebled in the last two decades and is now well over 20,000. Spanish is the main language, although English is widely spoken. The administrative centre is Puerto Baquerizo Moreno on San Cristobal Island, while Puerto Ayora on Santa Cruz Island is the main settlement and centre of activity.

✦ CLIMATE

The climate is equatorial, but greatly influenced by the cold Humboldt Current. December to May is the better season when the weather is pleasantly warm, with an average of 28°C/82°F, and the winds are light. From June to November the weather is overcast and cool. August, September and October are the coolest months, with an average temperature of 23°C/73°F, and with a low recorded at 14°C/57°F. The water around the islands is surprisingly cold and the meeting of the Humboldt Current and the warm air sometimes causes mist over the land. Occasionally the Humboldt Current is replaced by the warm El Niño current, a phenomenon that can affect weather conditions in the

entire South Pacific – and occasionally its effects are felt throughout the world.

✦ FORMALITIES

PORTS OF ENTRY

Puerto Baquerizo Moreno (San Cristobal) 0°54´S 89°37´W	
Puerto Ayora (Santa Cruz) 0°46´S 90°18´W	
Puerto Villamil (Isabela) 0°57´S 90°58.5´W	
Puerto Velasco Ibarra (Floreana) 1°16´S 90°29´W	

On arrival, boats must proceed directly to Baquerizo Moreno or Puerto Ayora. These are the only two ports where boats may clear in. Yachts may call at either of the other two ports only after formalities have been completed. Visiting yachts are now obliged to use an agent to complete formalities with the port caption, who usually allows stays of up to 20 days. The immigration office must be visited next and this can be done without an agent.

Puerto Ayora: The anchorage is very crowded with local excursion boats, and commuting ashore in your own tender is not advisable. There is a water taxi that can be hailed on Channel 14.

Those who wish to spend longer in the archipelago, and visit the individual islands on their own boats, must obtain a cruising permit. The procedure for obtaining a cruising permit is lengthy and carries no guarantee of success. The application should be made through the Ecuadorean embassy or consulate in the country of one's origin. In view of the concerns over protection of the environment, access to the islands may be further restricted in the coming years.

✦ FACILITIES

The anchorage at Baquerizo Moreno offers reasonable protection and is not as crowded as the one at Puerto Ayora. The latter is the base of a large fleet of local excursion boats and the anchorage is therefore very crowded. Supplies at both Puerto Ayora and Baquerizo Moreno have improved and the choice is good. Vegetables are now produced locally, so provisioning a boat for the onward passage is no longer a problem. Diesel fuel and water are occasionally difficult to obtain, so it is advisable to arrive with full tanks. There are no haulout facilities except for a drying grid in the inner harbour in Puerto Ayora.

✦ CHARTER

There are several local operators offering shorter or longer tours of the islands. Most are based in Puerto Ayora. As visiting yachts may not move outside the few designated ports, joining one of these organized tours seems to be the preferred solution for those who do not have the time or patience to obtain a cruising permit.

> www.angermeyercruises.com
> www.galapagoscharters.com

Cruising Guides
Landfalls of Paradise
The Pacific Crossing Guide
South Pacific Anchorages

Websites
www.ecuadortouristboard.com/regions/galapagos/galapagos.html
www.darwinfoundation.org
www.dirnea.org

Local time	UTC −6
Buoyage	IALA B
Currency	United States Dollar (USD)
Electricity	120V, 60Hz

Diplomatic missions
see Ecuador

Communications
IDD 5935   IAC 00

Emergency numbers
Red Cross 593 5526 129
Hospital 593 5526 10

NAURU

THE REPUBLIC OF NAURU is one of the smallest countries in the world, an 8 sq mile coral island, lying just south of the equator, west of Kiribati. An island of little attraction and just as little vegetation, but disproportionately wealthy due to its rich phosphate resources, Nauru is hardly an enticing destination for anyone cruising the South Pacific. Nevertheless, the island may be a useful stop, especially in an emergency, for boats bound for the Solomons or Papua New Guinea. There is only an open roadstead in the lee of the island, which is too deep for anchoring, and some mooring buoys have been laid for ships loading phosphate.

✦ COUNTRY PROFILE

Before the arrival of the Europeans, this isolated island had developed its own culture, but the exact origins of the Nauruans are unclear, since their language does not resemble any other in the Pacific. Annexed by Germany in 1888, and then mined for its valuable phosphate deposits by a German–British consortium, it was administered by Australia, Britain and New Zealand as a League of Nations mandate after the First World War. During the Second World War, there was a brutal occupation by the Japanese. After this war, Nauru was then administered by Australia under a UN mandate until 1968, when it became independent. Since then there has been a determined effort to ensure the country's self-sufficiency before the phosphate is totally exhausted. Reserves of phosphates may only last until 2010 at current mining rates.

The population is about 14,000. Many are immigrant workers (I-Kiribati, Chinese, Europeans and Indians). Naur-uans, who form just under 60 per cent of the population, are a mixture of Micronesian, Melanesian and Polynesian. English is spoken as well as Nauruan. Yaren is the administrative centre.

✦ CLIMATE

The climate is equatorial, 27°C/81°F being the average temperature. Rainfall is spread equally throughout the year. Prevailing winds between October and March are northeast and variable at other times. The island is not affected by tropical cyclones.

✦ FORMALITIES

The port captain should be contacted and, if a large ship's mooring is available, he may advise a yacht to tie up to it. Entry formalities are completed ashore. Yachts are not allowed to stay overnight, so if a longer visit is intended, you must stand off the island for the night.

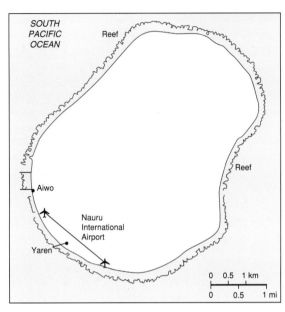

All visitors must have a visa, which can be obtained in advance from an Australian consulate, or a request may be emailed with a copy of the passport to: visa@naurugov.nr.

PORT OF ENTRY
Aiwo 0°31´S 166°56´E

✦ FACILITIES

Diesel fuel is usually available. There is a shortage of drinking water, which sometimes has to be shipped in. There is a well-stocked supermarket, where fresh provisions are usually available. Emergency repairs can be carried out at one of the workshops.

Cruising Guide
Landfalls of Paradise

Websites
www.naurugov.nr
www.discovernauru.com

Local time UTC +12	**Currency** Australian Dollar (AUD)
Buoyage IALA A	**Electricity** 240V, 50Hz

Diplomatic mission
Australia   444 3380

Communications
IDD 674   IAC 00

NEW CALEDONIA

BORDERING ON THE CORAL SEA, New Caledonia is the French Overseas Territory of Nouvelle Calédonie. The main island is the mountainous Grande Terre, whose once stunning scenery now alternates between dense forest and denuded mined slopes, for the mountains of Grande Terre are almost solid mineral deposits containing one of the biggest reserves of nickel in the world. Grande Terre also boasts one of the largest coral reefs in the world, and you can sail around much of the island inside the reef. Also part of the Territory are the off-lying islands, the Loyalty Island Group (Maré, Lifou and Ouvéa), Île des Pins (Isle of Pines), Chesterfield Islands and Belep Island.

New Caledonia, particularly the picturesque outer islands, has a lot to offer the cruising sailor. It is an interesting mixture of French and Pacific cultures. Nouméa is a busy city with several well-appointed marinas and, as expected in a French territory, good restaurants and well-stocked supermarkets. New Caledonia is occasionally visited by cyclones, but the marina offers good protection and those who wish to seek even more shelter can go to one of the nearby mangrove creeks. The best cruising is in the Baie du Prony, and also in some of the outlying islands, either the Île des Pins or the Loyalties.

✦ COUNTRY PROFILE

For centuries this land was home to a Melanesian people who practised ritualized cannibalism and headhunting. Captain Cook found them quite friendly, but when the French explorer Entrecasteaux visited a few years later he found them changed by famine, drought and tribal wars. In the nineteenth century the French claimed the islands. As in the case of neighbouring Norfolk Island, as well as Australia, the first European settlers were convicts, and France's penal colony of New Caledonia had a terrible reputation. More settlers followed to this land rich in natural resources, with a heavy influx of French colonials from North Africa after Algeria's war of independence in the 1960s. In the latter part of the last century troubles flared up as the indigenous Melanesian Kanaks saw neighbouring countries becoming independent, while they were becoming increasingly out-numbered by immigrants. A separatist movement grew, demanding independence, and a violent conflict ensued in the 1980s which eventually came to an end when the French gave the Kanaks a better deal, with improved education and health benefits, as well as the promise of a referendum on possible independence at some point in the future. In recent years the situation seems peaceful and stable.

The population is about 228,000. Melanesians make up 44 per cent of the population, living mainly on the east coast and outer islands, 34 per cent are of European descent, while most of the rest are immigrants from other French territories. French is the official language and there are some 28 indigenous languages. Nouméa on Grande Terre is the capital.

✦ CLIMATE

The islands have a subtropical climate, almost bordering on the temperate, with a hot and humid period between November and April, which is also the cyclone season. The weather is cool and dry from April to November, when the prevailing southeast trades are stronger. August is the coolest month with an average temperature of 20°C/68°F, while the warmest is February, with an average 26°C/79°F. March is the wettest month. Weather forecasts are excellent and any threatening depression is carefully monitored, so that you can count on several days' warning of an impending cyclone. Such warnings are broadcast on VHF radio throughout the islands.

✦ FORMALITIES

PORTS OF ENTRY	
Nouméa (Port Moselle)	22°16´S 166°27´E
Hienghene	20°41´S 164°56´E
Koumac	20°34´S 164°17´E
Lifou (Loyalty Islands)	20°54´S 167°12´E
Touho	20°47´S 165°14´E

Havannah Pass near Noumea.

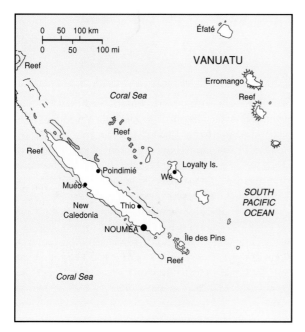

Nouméa is the only full port of entry. The other ports may only be used if you have nothing to declare to customs, such as animals, weapons or fresh food, and no crew member needs to see immigration.

On approaching Nouméa, Port Moselle Marina should be called on Channel 67. Yachts should anchor or come to the visitors' dock, for which a charge is made. The captain must visit the various offices for clearance.

No visa is required for up to three months for the nationals of most EU and other European countries, Australia and New Zealand. No visa is needed for stays of up to one month by nationals of Canada, the USA and several other countries. All others require a visa in advance.

A six-month cruising permit is granted on arrival. This relates to the boat only and crew must conform with visa requirements. The maximum period a yacht may stay before becoming eligible for import duty is six months, or one year if no visit has been made in the previous three years.

There are strict quarantine regulations. Processed, fresh and frozen meat, eggs, dairy produce, honey, fresh fruit and vegetables will be confiscated and destroyed. Other foodstuffs must remain on board.

On clearing in, you should request the special form entitling the yacht to duty-free fuel, both diesel and petrol (gasoline).

To stop at one of the Loyalty Islands or Isle of Pines after clearing out, a request needs to be registered in advance. Clearing out may also be done in one of the ports listed above, but this must be agreed before leaving Noumea. Boats leaving for Vanuatu or Fiji can request permission for an overnight stop in the Loyalty Islands.

When sailing around the Loyalty Islands or in the north of New Caledonia, the traditional call to the chief of the tribe or village should be paid. This is an important token gesture and the usual gift is a stick of tobacco, a length of cloth or, if nothing suitable is available, some money.

✦ FACILITIES

Nouméa is an excellent place to reprovision the boat, as virtually everything is available and repair facilities as well as marine supplies are very good. Specialized workshops offer engine, electrical, electronic, refrigeration, rigging and sail repair, and there are several travelifts.

There are good supermarkets and a fish and fresh produce market. Provisioning in the islands is more limited.

✦ CHARTER

Air Mer Loisirs operates out of Nouméa with a bareboat fleet of both monohulls and catamarans. Also based in Nouméa, Nirvana Charter has a small fleet of catamarans that it offers as bareboat or crewed charters.

www.aml.nc
www.nirvana-yacht-charter.com

Cruising Guides
Cruising Guide to New Caledonia
Landfalls of Paradise
Nautical Rocket Guide to New Caledonia (CD)
Pacific Crossing Guide
South Pacific Anchorages

Websites
www.newcaledoniatourism-south.com
www.cruising-newcaledonia.com (to purchase or download CD guide)

Local time	UTC +11
Buoyage	IALA A
Currency	CFP Franc (XPF)
Electricity	220V, 50Hz

Diplomatic missions
Australia   272 414   New Zealand   272 543

Communications
IDD 687   IAC 00

Emergency numbers
112   Ambulance 18   Police 17

NEW ZEALAND

THE MOST SOUTHERLY of the Pacific countries, New Zealand forms the southwestern point of the Polynesian triangle. It is made up of two large islands, North and South Island, as well as a number of smaller ones. New Zealand has many attractions, not least as a cruising ground that lies outside of the cyclone zone. It is a scenic land of high mountains, glaciers, deep fjords, sweeping sandy beaches, bubbling volcanic pools, giant ferns and unique wildlife. The North Island is rolling, green and with an equitable climate, while the South Island is mountainous, less populated and cooler.

There are more sailing yachts per head of population in New Zealand than in any other country. The beauty and variety of the coast, as well as the challenging sailing conditions that sailors grow up with, is undoubtedly the explanation why so many internationally famous sailors hail from New Zealand, a country that can be best appreciated by those who visit it by boat. From the Bay of Islands in the north to windswept Stewart Island in the south, cruising in New Zealand can fulfil the requirements of even the most fastidious. The east coasts of both islands have many harbours and anchorages, and in the summer the climate is gentle and the weather seldom threatening.

The Bay of Islands is a favourite place of entry and the cruising here is so pleasant that some visiting yachts never leave this large protected bay dotted with the many islands that gave its name. Sailing south from the Bay of Islands, Whangarei is another perennially favourite home-from-home for foreign sailors spending the summer in New Zealand. In spite of its small size, the town is a busy yachting centre with a good range of service and repair facilities. Not far offshore is one of the country's best cruising spots: the Barrier Islands, and a worthy detour before heading for the Hauraki Gulf and busy Auckland. The America's Cup has done wonders to

Auckland Harbour.

transform this once rather unimpressive port, and the town overlooking it, into a modern, vibrant centre. Auckland is the usual turning point for the majority of visiting yachts, but locals insist that in fact the best is yet to come. Highlights of a southbound trip are the capital Wellington and, across Cook Strait, picturesque Picton and the Marlborough Sound.

South Island's east coast has several attractive harbours such as Dunedin, Timaru, Lyttelton, and the scenic Marlborough Sound, but not one of them matches the wild beauty of the awe-inspiring Milford Haven. Sailing conditions around South Island are more challenging than in the benign north, and those who are short of time can enjoy its majestic scenery by cruising on four wheels. This option is often taken by those sailors who leave their yachts in a marina on North Island. Whether cruising New Zealand by yacht or car, you can easily understand why the locals call their home 'God's Own Country'.

✦ COUNTRY PROFILE

The first settlers in these islands were the Maoris, a Polynesian people, who most probably hailed from the Cook Islands and called the uninhabited lands Aotearoa, 'land of the long white cloud'. This first voyage on large double-hulled sailing canoes occurred in the tenth century, but the main wave of settlement, known simply as the 'Migration', occurred around 1350 with the arrival of what is now called 'The Great Fleet'. A warlike people, the Maoris were also fine artists, decorating their canoes and meeting houses with wooden carvings, their faces with elaborate tattoos, and wearing intricate jade ornaments. The first European to visit was Abel Tasman in 1642. The islands were then left alone until 1769 when Captain Cook claimed them for Britain. The first European settlers were whalers and sealers, who brought diseases and firearms, both of which caused a rapid decline in the Maori population. The Treaty of Waitangi in 1840 between Maori chiefs and Britain turned New Zealand into a British possession. Social reforms at the end of the nineteenth century introduced, among other things, pensions and the vote for women, making New Zealand one of the first countries in the world to do so. In the early twentieth century the country became a Dominion, and then slowly evolved into an independent nation.

The population is about 4.2 million, mostly of British descent (70 per cent), known as Pakehas by the Maoris, who number about 350,000. In Auckland there is a considerable community of other Pacific Islanders, such as Tongans, Samoans and Cook Islanders. Recent immigration has increased the number of people of Asian origin to 250,000. English and Maori are the main languages. Wellington is the capital, although Auckland is the largest city and commercial centre.

✦ CLIMATE

The climate is varied, from subtropical in the north to temperate with snow-covered mountains and glaciers in the south. The summer from November to March is the more pleasant season, while the winter is wetter and windier. South Island is cooler in both summer and winter. July is the coldest month, with an average of 11°C/52°F in Auckland, and February the warmest, with an average of 20°C/68°F, compared to Dunedin (6°C/43°F in July, 15°C/59°F in February). Although out of the tropical cyclone area, occasionally in February or March the tail of a cyclone reaches North Island. Lying in the westerly wind belt, the east coast is more sheltered and the main yachting centres are along that coast.

✦ FORMALITIES

Every yacht arriving from overseas must inform customs of the intended ETA at least 48 hours before arrival by sending a completed arrival form by email to: yachts@customs.govt.nz. The form can be downloaded from the customs website. On approaching the port of entry, an ETA should be given. This can be done on Channel 16 via Taupo Maritime Radio, which maintains repeaters along the coast. The station also keeps continuous watch on 4125 kHz and 6215 kHz. They can also be contacted on Tel: +64 9 359 6655 or +64 25 961 375 (after hours). The alternative is to call Whangarei customs on +800 428 786.

Opua: Arriving boats are directed to the quarantine dock in the new marina.
Whangarei: Harbour control should be contacted and asked to advise customs to meet the yacht on arrival. Boats should proceed to the customs wharf for clearance. A more convenient place to clear in may be the new marina at Marsden Point at the mouth of Whangarei River.
Auckland: Harbour control will direct the yacht to one of the marinas where clearance formalities can be completed.

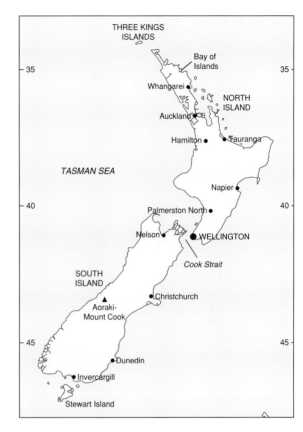

Nationals of most European countries, Australia, Canada, South Africa, the USA and several other countries do not need visas. A three-month visitors' permit is granted on arrival. Visas can be renewed through the Ministry of Immigration.

All crew are required to show evidence of funds of $400 NZ per month if living on the yacht. Anyone leaving the vessel in New Zealand may also be asked to show an onward ticket, or funds to purchase one. The owner of the yacht must show evidence of ownership and third party insurance.

New Zealand has very strict regulations on the importation of live animals, and also animal and plant products. On arrival, inspection is carried out by an agriculture quarantine officer. Nothing may be landed and

PORTS OF ENTRY

North Island: Opua 35°18´S 174°08´E	Whangarei 35°44´S 174°21´E	Marsden Point Marina 35°49.8´S 174°28.5´E
Auckland 36°51´S 174°48´E	Tauranga 37°39´S 176°10´E	Napier 39°29´S 176°55´E
New Plymouth 39°04´S 174°05´E	Wellington 41°17´S 174°46´E	Onehunga 36°56´S 174°46´E
Gisborne 38°41´S 178°02´E	Taharoa 38°10´S 174°40´E	
South Island: Nelson 42°16´S 173°19´E	Picton 41°16´S 174°00´E	Christchurch (Lyttelton) 43°37´S 172°43´E
Timaru 44°25´S 171°19´E	Dunedin 45°53´S 170°31´E	Invercargill (Bluff) 46°36´S 168°26´E
Chatham Islands: Waitangi 43°57´S 176°34´E		

all crew must remain on board until clearance has been complete. Items that must not be landed are fruit, vegetables, plant products, foodstuffs, eggs and waste from these items, pot plants, meat and animal products. All waste must be disposed of through the proper garbage disposal system, including egg containers.

All foreign yachts entering New Zealand on a temporary basis fill in a temporary import form. The maximum length of stay is 12 months. Boats that exceed the 12 months' stay must pay duty on the assessed value of the yacht. Permission to stay beyond the maximum permitted period may be granted if the vessel needs to undergo refitting or major repairs, or if crews need to wait out the South Pacific hurricane season.

Purchases made in New Zealand have duty paid on them and a refund can be claimed if the goods are exported.

On departure, notice must be given at least 24 hours prior to leaving. Once issued with a clearance certificate, yachts are required to go to sea within a reasonable time. Any delay should be reported to customs.

Kermadec Islands: These islands may only be visited with a permit from the Department of Conservation, Private Bag 8, Newton, Auckland.

✦ FACILITIES

Marine facilities are of a good standard in the North Island, particularly around such yachting centres as Auckland and Whangarei. There are several places in the North Island to carry out maintenance and repair work on long-distance cruising boats or to leave a boat unattended, whether to tour the rest of the country or fly home. Places like the Bay of Islands or Whangarei have their own charm by being more relaxed, while the marinas in the Auckland area have the benefit of being closer to where the action is.

Facilities in South Island are less extensive, although there are adequate services wherever there is a local yachting centre. As can be expected from a mainly agricultural country, provisioning is very good and New Zealand is an excellent place to stock up the boat.

✦ CHARTER

Charterlink operates out of Auckland and the Bay of Islands and has a fleet of sailing monohulls and catamarans, as well as powerboats. A similar choice of boats is offered by Compass Charters, based in Picton, to explore the Marlborough Sound and Tasman Bay.

Fair Wind Charters' fleet of sailing monohulls is based in Opua, Bay of Islands, the same as the Moorings.

> www.charterlink.co.nz
> www.compass-charters.co.nz
> www.fairwind.co.nz
> www.moorings.com
> www.tuicharters.co.nz

Cruising Guides	
Coastal Cruising Handbook	Destination New Zealand
Hauraki Gulf Boating Atlas	Northland Coast Boaties Atlas
South Pacific Anchorages	The Pacific Crossing Guide

Websites
www.newzealand.com
www.customs.govt.nz
www.customs.govt.nz/Visiting+craft/Small+Craft+
   Arrival/Arrival+Information.htm
www.nzmarine.com/shop/Dockage+and+Berthage/
   Recreational+and+Foreign+Yachts.html (list of marinas)

Local time	UTC +12
	Summer time: last Sunday in September to first Sunday in April
Buoyage	IALA A
Currency	New Zealand Dollar (NZD)
Electricity	230V, 50Hz

Diplomatic missions	
UK	4 924 2888
USA	4 462 6000
Australia	4 473 6411
Canada	4 473 9577

Communications	Emergency number
IDD 64 IAC 00	111

The spectacular Milford Sound

NIUE

THE ISLAND OF NIUE may be one of the world's smallest states, but it is the largest block of coral. Because of its unusual geological formation, Niue is riddled with underground tunnels and caves, while on the east coast, constantly battered by huge Pacific rollers, deep chasms make for apocalyptic scenery. Surrounded by sheer high cliffs, Niue has no natural harbours, and the only shelter from the prevailing winds is an indentation on the west coast where a number of moorings have been laid for the use of visiting yachts. In settled conditions this is a safe spot to leave the boat while visiting the island, although the ocean swell is forever present and the constant surge makes landing an exciting affair. There is a crane for hoisting tenders out of the water. Because of the difficult approaches and absence of lights, it is strongly advised that you arrive in daylight.

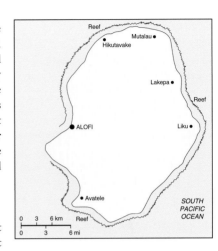

✦ COUNTRY PROFILE

Archaeological remains show that the island was inhabited by Polynesians at least 1,800 years ago. Captain Cook charted the island in 1774, and named it the Savage Island when the islanders resisted his landing. In 1900 Niue became a British Protectorate, and was later under New Zealand administration. The Niueans, not wanting total independence, chose a free association with New Zealand, which means they have New Zealand citizenship and internal self-government. As Niueans have the right to work and settle in New Zealand, there has been a steady drain so that more of the islanders now live abroad than on Niue.

The population is around 1,400. Niuean, a Polynesian language, is spoken, and also English. Alofi is the capital.

✦ CLIMATE

Niue has a tropical climate. The most pleasant weather is during the winter months when the island is cooled by the southeast trade winds. The best weather is in July, with little rain and an average temperature of 25°C/77°F. December to April is wetter, more humid and also the cyclone season.

✦ FORMALITIES

ZKN Niue Radio keeps a 24-hour watch on both VHF and HF 4125 kHz. When in range, you should contact them and they will call customs and arrange clearance. On its website, Niue Yacht Club has excellent instructions for arriving yachts. This club can also be contacted for mooring advice and other help. Yachts should proceed to the mooring area and pick up a free mooring south of the wharf, but no one should land before being instructed to do so by customs. After obtaining permission to land, formalities are completed ashore. The captain should report first to customs, then police and immigration.

Australian and New Zealand citizens do not need an entry permit and all other nationalities are granted a 30-day entry permit on arrival.

PORT OF ENTRY
Alofi 19°03´S 169°55´W

✦ FACILITIES

There is a reasonable selection of provisions in a supermarket, and there is a fresh produce market. Only basic repairs can be carried out on the island, but essential spares can be ordered from New Zealand. Niue was the first country to have a nationwide internet access service, using wireless technology (wifi). This is available to moored boats for a hook-up fee.

Cruising Guide
Landfalls of Paradise

Websites	
www.niueisland.com	www.niueyachtclub.com

Local time	UTC −11
Buoyage	IALA A
Currency	New Zealand Dollar (NZD)
Electricity	240V, 50Hz

Diplomatic mission	
New Zealand	4022

Communications	
IDD 683	IAC 00

Emergency number	999

NORFOLK ISLAND

NORFOLK ISLAND is a small volcanic island midway between Australia and New Zealand. The island is visited mainly by Australian boats on their way to the South Pacific or by those sailing from New Zealand to New Caledonia and beyond. There are anchorages at Cascade Bay and Sydney Bay near the main settlement of Kingston. Other anchorages are at Ball Bay and Headstone, but landing there is very difficult. However, none can be regarded as all-weather anchorages, therefore the boat should never be left unattended, and you should go ashore only in settled weather. Yachts have been lost at Norfolk Island through ignoring this warning. There are landing jetties at both Kingston and Cascade Bay, but landing the dinghy can sometimes be difficult. In spite of this precarious situation, the island is worth even a short visit as it is one of the earliest European settlements in the Western Pacific. There are some well-preserved historic buildings in the capital, Kingston, as well as an informative museum, and sailors are always sure of a warm welcome.

◆ COUNTRY PROFILE

Norfolk is one of the oldest British settlements in the Pacific. There is some evidence of Polynesian or Melanesian habitation on the island before Captain Cook discovered and named it in 1774. A few years later, an attempt was made to establish a colony, now known as the First Settlement. In the early nineteenth century Norfolk was uninhabited for some years, then a penal colony was set up for the worst of the Australian convicts. This period of the Second Settlement was brutal, and stone buildings built by the prisoners can still be seen. After the prison was closed, the next to arrive were a large group of Pitcairn Islanders, brought there by Britain who decided to resettle them as their tiny island home had become overcrowded. Homesick and unhappy, some returned to Pitcairn, although many remained, forming the base of the present population. Norfolk Island is an Australian territory, with its own assembly under the Norfolk Island Act of 1979.

The population is just over 2,100. English and a dialect similar to that on Pitcairn are spoken.

◆ CLIMATE

The climate is mild and subtropical, with a well-distributed rainfall. Summer winds are south to southeast, and winter winds are west to southwest. The cyclone season is December to April.

◆ FORMALITIES

PORT OF ENTRY
Kingston 29°01´S 167°59´E

Officials welcome sailors to their remote island and are helpful if contacted in advance.

You should land during daylight hours either at Cascade Jetty, on the north side, or at Kingston Jetty, on the south side. As the weather often changes quickly, it is advisable to leave a crew member on board at all times.

Visa requirements are the same as for Australia, and all nationalities, with the exception of New Zealanders, need to obtain a visa in advance. Those who wish to call at both Australia and Norfolk need to get a multiple visa, which is also required by those planning to stop at other Australian territories. Although visas can be obtained from one of the many Australian diplomatic missions in the South Pacific, it is easier to do this before leaving home. As Norfolk Island is an external territory of Australia, a valid passport is required for Australian citizens.

Landing of food, including fruit and vegetables, is prohibited.

Anchorage is prohibited in Anson Bay on the northwest corner of the island.

◆ FACILITIES

Provisioning is reasonable. Repair facilities are basic and should not be relied upon. Fuel is available.

Cruising Guide
South Pacific Anchorages

Website
www.norfolkisland.nf

Local time	UTC +11.5	Currency	Australian Dollar (AUD)
Buoyage	IALA A	Electricity	240V, 50Hz

Communications		Emergency number	
IDD 672 IAC 00		000	

PAPUA NEW GUINEA

PAPUA NEW GUINEA CONSISTS of the eastern half of the large island of New Guinea (the western half being the Indonesian province of Irian Jaya), and hundreds of islands of all shapes and sizes, from towering active volcanoes to idyllic coral atolls. One of the most fascinating countries in the world, Papua New Guinea is definitely best visited by cruising boat. This not only gives the opportunity to catch a glimpse of life in a society where people in remote villages still follow ancient ways, but also avoids the lawlessness that increasingly affects the large towns of this rich but poorly managed country. Most cruising sailors will only come in passing contact with this less attractive feature of a country in which some areas have leapt from Stone Age into the modern era in less than a century.

There is a vast difference between urban areas, where safety is now a major concern, and the rural parts of the country, where a traditional self-sufficient way of life still survives. This is particularly the case in the more remote islands that have little contact both with the local authorities and the outside world. The best cruising in Papua New Guinea is found among the many islands to the east of the main island, where islanders still live a peaceful life, tending their small gardens, going fishing in their sailing canoes, and leading an existence not much different from that of their ancestors. Remote island groups such as the Louisiades are in every respect a world apart and should be included on your itinerary even if the rest of the country is missed.

While in the past most ports were considered relatively safe to visit, and even to leave the boat unattended while exploring the interior, the situation gradually deteriorated and sailors decided to stay away. Matters seem to be improving and yachts are returning to the previously popular places. Rabaul, on New Britain Island, was always a favourite spot among cruising sailors, many of whom used to spend the cyclone season in its landlocked harbour, the crater of an active volcano whose last eruption caused great destruction. Madang, on the northern coast of New Guinea, has a well-protected harbour in an area scattered with islands, reefs and lagoons. It also has always been popular, especially for those taking the northern route – north towards Indonesia or west towards the Philippines. The capital, Port Moresby, itself has been beset by similar safety concerns, but visiting sailors can avoid this by using the services of the Royal Papua Yacht Club, whose marina and clubhouse are a welcome haven of peace and tranquillity. Port Moresby is also a convenient stop for boats heading for the Torres Straits and beyond.

Lying astride a number of popular sailing routes, Papua New Guinea, and especially its outlying islands, continues to be a major transit point for cruising yachts heading for new destinations. Some of these remote outposts present a very different picture to the mainland, such as Wuvulu, Ninigo and Hermit Islands. These are occasionally visited by boats on their way to Micronesia, Palau or the Philippines. Some are atolls and have been declared nature reserves, but brief visits by yachts on passage are tolerated.

A cruise in Papua New Guinea has been for many people the highlight of a world voyage and it is therefore sad to sound the above warnings. While visiting sailors are rightly concerned about the safety situation, particularly in the larger ports, few of those who spent time in the country recently seem to have encountered any serious problems and their experiences paint a rather different picture. While anyone

Royal Papua Yacht Club in Port Moresby.

planning to visit this highly interesting country should be aware of the risks involved, it must be stressed that all is not lost and, if you choose a safe itinerary that avoids known trouble spots, take normal precautions and use a good dose of common sense, Papua New Guinea is still a country well worth visiting.

◆ COUNTRY PROFILE

Until the 1930s, much of the highlands of Papua New Guinea and the Stone Age tribes who lived there were unknown to the rest of the outside world. Over the centuries, hundreds of tribes had lived apart, often with two neighbouring tribes separated by a hillside of impenetrable vegetation, never knowing of the other's existence. Each had its own character and its own language, proving to be an anthropologist's dream when they finally came into contact with the modern world – some as late as the latter part of the twentieth century. It is believed that even today there are still small tribes living in the heart of New Guinea that have not had any contact with the outside world.

The original inhabitants probably came from South East Asia about 20,000 to 25,000 years ago. Later there were migrations from Micronesia and Polynesia, which forced the original population into the mountains or to migrate to other islands of present-day Melanesia. Many separate cultures developed, with no larger a unit than the tribe.

In the early sixteenth century the Portuguese sighted the main island, naming it Ilhas dos Papuas, 'islands of the frizzy haired'. It was later called New Guinea by a Spanish explorer who found the people resembling those of Guinea in Africa. Traders and missionaries arrived in the nineteenth century. The Dutch claimed the western half of the main island, the Germans the northeast, and the British the southeast. At the start of the twentieth century the British sector was transferred to Australian control as Papua and, after the First World War, Australia took over the German part as well. In the Second World War Papua New Guinea was occupied by the Japanese. After the war it became the UN Territory of New Guinea and was administered by Australia. Papua remained a territory of Australia and the two entities united

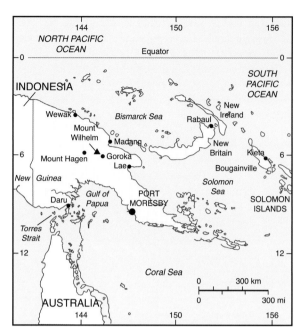

as Papua New Guinea in 1973, and gained full independence two years later. The border area with Irian Jaya is considered dangerous, as there is a secessionist movement fighting for independence from Indonesia.

The population of 6 million is mostly Melanesian, with some of the eastern islands populated by Polynesians. There are three official languages: English, Motu and Pidgin (Tok Pisin), the latter having evolved to allow the inhabitants of a country with over 800 languages to understand one another.

◆ CLIMATE

The climate is tropical. From December to March is the northwest monsoon, while the southeast monsoon is from May to December. The months June to September are the driest as well as the coolest, with an average temperature of 25°C/77°F. Only the southeast of the country is affected by tropical cyclones, which occur very rarely. The cyclone season is from December until April.

◆ FORMALITIES

PORTS OF ENTRY	
Port Moresby 9°26´S 147°06´E	Vanimo 2°41´S 141°18´E
Wewak 3°35´S 143°40´E	Samarai 10°36´S 150°39´E
Oro Bay 8°50´S 148°30´E	Rabaul 4°12´S 152°11´E
Lae 6°44´S 146°59´E	Kavieng 2°34´S 150°48´E
Daru 9°04´S 143°12´E	Alotau 10°19´S 150°27´E
Kieta 6°13´S 155°38´E	Madang 5°15´S 145°50´E
Kimbe 5°32´S 150°09´E	Lorengau 2°00´S 147°15´E

All vessels are required to give notice of impending arrival to customs, quarantine and immigration no later than 48 hours before arrival. Details and arrival forms are to be found on the customs website. Yachts must clear in and out of every port. It is an offence to depart without clearing out. Officials can often be unpleasant and one needs tact and patience when dealing with them.

No one can go ashore until clearance has been given and the yacht has been inspected by quarantine. The captain has to complete a small craft arrival report and also an incoming passenger card for each member of the crew.

It is recommended that visas are obtained in advance from one of the Papua New Guinea embassies or high commissions. If you arrive without a visa, it is possible to obtain a border visa from immigration, valid for 30 days. Although such visas are routinely being granted to tourists arriving by air, occasionally sailors coming by yacht encounter difficulties obtaining such a visa on arrival. Visa extensions can be arranged, but the passport needs to be sent to Port Moresby and it can take a long time for it to be returned.

A cruising permit is given for a period to match the captain's visa. Yachts staying longer than 60 days are required to lodge a security on the vessel, equal to the duty on its value.

All garbage must remain sealed on board. The galley stores will be inspected and suspect food destroyed. Only designated quarantine points can be used for garbage disposal.

Prescribed medicines must be declared. You must have a prescription stating that these are necessary and being used under a doctor's direction.

✦ FACILITIES

There are a large number of locally owned yachts in the capital, Port Moresby, where facilities are generally good. The Royal Papua Yacht Club has a marina with 24-hour security. Most repair services are concentrated around the yacht club. There are two careening facilities within the marina and a mobile crane can lift vessels up to 20 tons. Provisioning is good, with several supermarkets and fresh produce markets. In Rabaul, the local yacht club is very welcoming and will advise on where to find various repair services. Facilities in Madang and Lae are adequate, while those in the smaller ports and outer islands are often basic. A pontoon has now been installed by the Madang Club, for the use of yachts.

Cruising Guide
Landfalls of Paradise

Websites
www.pngtourism.org.pg
www.customs.gov.pg
http://www.pngports.com.pg/pngports_directory.html
  (directory of principal ports)

Local time	UTC +10
Buoyage	IALA A
Currency	Papua New Guinea Kina (PGK)
Electricity	240V, 50Hz

Diplomatic missions

UK	325 1677	Australia	325 9333
USA	321 1455	New Zealand	325 9444

Communications	**Emergency number**
IDD 675 IAC 05	000

Family settlement in the Louisiade Islands.

PITCAIRN ISLAND

PITCAIRN IS A SMALL ISOLATED volcanic island in the South Pacific, its closest neighbours being the Gambier Islands to the west and Easter Island to the east. A mere 3 sq miles of land, with steep cliffs all around, this remote island supports a population of only about fifty people. Pitcairn is a dependency of the UK, together with the uninhabited Henderson, Ducie and Oeno islands. These are administered by the Pitcairn Islands Office in Auckland, New Zealand, but day-to-day affairs are run by an island council. Supply ships are supposed to call three or four times a year, but there is no standard service. Other ships used to call regularly to buy fresh produce and handicrafts from the islanders, but this has declined with the cessation of passenger liners and the increase in the number of container ships on tight schedules. Nevertheless, a few ships continue to call at Pitcairn, their crews happy for an interruption in a long and monotonous ocean passage. Between 20 and 30 yachts stop at Pitcairn

every year, where a warm welcome awaits the sailors who call at this remote community, whose entire history has been intrinsically bound up with the sea. Although the anchorage in Bounty Bay is an open roadstead, by keeping an eye on the weather, you are usually able to spend some time on the island. Everyone leaves Pitcairn with unforgettable memories of having been hosted by one of the most isolated communities in the world.

◆ COUNTRY PROFILE

Pitcairn was named after a young midshipman on board HMS *Swallow* who spotted the island in 1767. Some early human remains have been discovered on Pitcairn, but who these original inhabitants were remains a mystery. When the island's most famous settlers, the *Bounty* mutineers, came here they found the island deserted. Fletcher Christian and eight of his fellow mutineers arrived here in 1790 with their

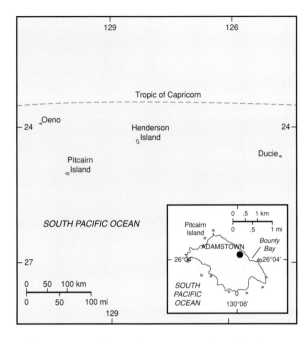

Tahitian wives and six Tahitian men on board the *Bounty*, which was then burnt and scuttled to avoid detection. Problems arose in the small community and there was much violence. When this community was rediscovered in 1808, of all the men, only the mutineer John Adams had survived – along with ten women and many children.

Less than fifty people currently live on the island, the population having dwindled as many left for New Zealand. All are descendants of the *Bounty* mutineers and their Tahitian wives, infused with some other blood from sailors and missionaries who settled on the island over the years. In 2004, several men were tried in a temporary court erected on the island for having abused under-aged girls in the past. Those who were found guilty were sentenced to prison and are serving time in a jail on the island, but are let out to lend a hand when a ship calls.

The dialect of the islanders is a blend of Tahitian and 18th-century sailors' English, but modern English is spoken by all. Adamstown is the only settlement. The islanders are all Seventh Day Adventists and Saturday is the day of rest.

✦ CLIMATE

The climate is subtropical, with the most pleasant weather being from November to March, when the winds are lighter and the seas smoother. The southeast trade winds blow mainly in the winter months, from May to October. Sudden squalls can produce strong winds from a different direction from that of the prevailing winds. Pitcairn is very rarely affected by tropical storms.

✦ FORMALITIES

PORT OF ENTRY
Bounty Bay 25°04´S 130°06´W

The islanders prefer to be informed through their powerful VHF radio of a yacht's arrival. Pitcairn is also connected to the outside world by Inmarsat satellite phone.

Yachts should anchor in Bounty Bay, but weather conditions can change very quickly. Locals will give advice as to where to find a temporarily sheltered anchorage: Tedside in easterly winds, and Down Rope in northerly ones. The islanders send out their inflatable rescue craft to advise boats where to anchor and to take the crew ashore for a USD50 fee. Landing in a dinghy, especially if there is a big swell, is often impossible.

Once ashore, you should pay a visit to the Island Magistrate to obtain permission to land. A declaration must be submitted giving health details of the crew and a brief itinerary with dates of last port. The medical officer may carry out a health inspection.

Brief visits from passing yachts are allowed and the Island Magistrate is empowered to issue written permits, and to sign and stamp your passport with the impressive Pitcairn stamp.

Landing on the islands of Henderson, Ducie and Oeno is forbidden without the permission of the Island Magistrate, in which case the landing party must be accompanied by a resident of Pitcairn.

✦ FACILITIES

Only basic imported foodstuffs are available, but there is a good choice of fresh produce. The islanders will help with emergency repairs as they have a well-equipped workshop. Communications with the outside world are by satellite telephone. Calls to Pitcairn are via Inmarsat: public telephone: +872 762 337 766; control room: +872 762 337 765.

Cruising Guides	
Landfalls of Paradise	
South Pacific Anchorages	

Website	
www.government.pn	

Local time	UTC –8
Buoyage	IALA A
Currency	New Zealand Dollar, but other major currencies accepted
Electricity	240V, 50Hz

SAMOA

The north coast of Upolu seen from Mount Vaea.

SAMOA, FORMERLY KNOWN as Western Samoa, comprises the two islands of Upolu and Savai'i, as well as several smaller ones. Savai'i is the largest, but Upolu is the more developed and the centre of government and commerce. The writer Robert Louis Stevenson was the first in a long line of famous travellers to be seduced by the Samoan way of life, and today's sailors may still experience instances of a lifestyle that has changed little since Stevenson lived there. Tusitala, the teller of tales, as he was affectionately called by the Samoans, is buried on top of Mount Vaea. The panoramic view from his tomb over the whole island and Apia Harbour is well worth the climb, and also provides an opportunity to pay one's respects to the man whose descriptions of the South Seas and its people continue to inspire sailors to follow in his wake. The moving lines of Stevenson's Requiem are carved into a bronze plate on his grave:

> Under the wide and starry sky,
> Dig the grave and let me lie.
> Glad did I live and gladly die,
> And I laid me down with a will.

> This be the verse you grave for me:
> Here he lies where he longed to be;
> Home is the sailor, home from the sea,
> And the hunter home from the hill.

Apart from Apia there are very few safe harbours on the two islands, as Fealili and Lotofaga on Upolu, and Vaialoa on Savai'i, are all on the exposed southern coast which suffered widespread devastation by the tsunami that struck the islands in September 2009. The sheltered northern coast of Savai'i is best for cruising, and the anchorage off Asau is a good place from which to explore the verdant interior with its gushing waterfalls and lush rainforests.

✦ COUNTRY PROFILE

It is said that Savai'i is the legendary Havaiki from which the first Polynesians spread out across the Pacific. Traditions have remained strong and, despite absorbing some Western influence, fa'a Samoa, the way of the ancestors, still rules the lives of Samoans. Life revolves around the extended family, with its etiquette and rituals. The first European to sight the

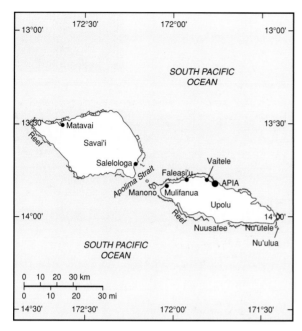

islands was Jacob Roggeveen in 1722. The arrival of the missionaries in the early nineteenth century marks the beginning of modern Samoan history. Present-day Western Samoa was administered by Germany until the First World War when the islands were taken over by New Zealand. In 1962 Western Samoa was the first Polynesian nation to regain its independence. In 1990 a referendum approved the adoption of universal suffrage, replacing the old electorate consisting exclusively of chiefs. In 1997 the official name reverted from Western Samoa to just Samoa.

The population is 220,000, the great majority being pure Polynesians. Samoan and English are spoken. Apia is the capital.

◆ CLIMATE

Samoa has a tropical climate, with the more pleasant weather being during the southeast tradewind season from April to November. During the cyclone season, from December to April, the weather is hotter and wetter. Temperature variations are very small with an average of 27°C/81°F throughout the year. As the islands are quite high, local weather conditions can be quite varied.

◆ FORMALITIES

PORT OF ENTRY
Apia (Upolu) 13°48´S 171°46´W

Yachts are requested to radio their ETA to the harbourmaster via Apia Radio at least 24 hours before arrival (SSB frequency HF 2182 or Channel 16). An ETA must be radioed to harbour control when within 40 miles. On arrival, yachts must proceed to Apia Marina for clearance. Boats are not permitted to anchor in the harbour.

Yachts are normally granted a 14-day permit. Immigration can give a 60-day entry permit to all visitors. No visa is necessary unless staying more than 60 days, in which case the visa must be obtained in advance.

All garbage must be put into sealed plastic bags and given to the quarantine office at the wharf gate for disposal.

Permission must be obtained from the Ministry of Foreign Affairs to sail to other islands in Samoa. When clearing out, it is possible to get authorization to stop in Asau on Savai'i before continuing to other destinations.

It is prohibited to enter the ferry terminal ports of Mulifanua and Salelologa, except with special permission from the Ministry of Transport.

◆ FACILITIES

The opening of Apia Marina, owned by the Samoan Port Authority, has brought a great improvement in the quality and range of facilities available. Engine repair and metalwork are available in Apia, but there are no haulout facilities for yachts. Provisioning in Apia is good. Asau is a well-protected anchorage, but only limited supplies are available.

Cruising Guides
Landfalls of Paradise
The Pacific Crossing Guide
Polynesia
South Pacific Anchorages

Website
www.samoa.travel

Local time	UTC −11
Buoyage	IALA A
Currency	Samoan Tala (WST)
Electricity	230V, 50Hz

Diplomatic missions
UK	27123
USA	21436
Australia	23411
New Zealand	21711

Communications		**Emergency number**
IDD 685	IAC 0	999

SOLOMON ISLANDS

THE SOLOMON ISLANDS are a double chain of islands in the Western Pacific stretching from Vanuatu to the eastern islands of Papua New Guinea. There are over nine hundred islands, the largest being Guadalcanal, Choiseul, Malaita, New Georgia and Santa Isabel, while remote Ontong Java is one of the largest coral atolls in the world. The Solomons' traditional culture, or 'custom', is rich and varied, from animist beliefs such as shark-worshipping to intricate woodcarving. Many islanders still live in the traditional way and the authorities are making a determined effort to preserve this. They enjoy the full support of the customary chiefs who still exert significant power and influence over village communities. This has put some restrictions on the movement of cruising yachts, but fortunately there is still a lot to see along the usual cruising route, for which special permission is not needed. Visiting yachts are welcomed in most villages, particularly by children who like to trade fruit or shells for ballpoint pens, felt-tips or balloons.

Apart from traditional village life, when cruising through the Solomons you constantly come across remains of the Second World War as some of the fiercest battles of the Pacific War were fought on these islands – Guadalcanal foremost among them. To this day, a lot of discarded military hardware is still put to good use, such as fuel tanks to catch rainwater or aircraft wings for pig enclosures. While the tropical vegetation has slowly concealed such remains, the wreckage of countless planes can still be seen resting in the clear water, their propellers encrusted with coral, their burst fuselages teeming with multi-coloured swarms of fish. Diving for a closer look, the eyes focus on the barrel of a machinegun, a mute reminder of the tragic events that once

unfolded in this remote corner of the world. Nothing explains better the irony of the Solomons springing to world attention during the Pacific War than the apocryphal story of a European man who in the late 1930s, becoming increasingly concerned about the impending war, decided to run away from that mad world to the most remote and safest place he could find. He chose Guadalcanal.

The tale of another man whose destiny was shaped by those events happened not far away, in the Blackett Strait – south of the island of Kolombangara – where on a dark night in August 1943 a Japanese destroyer rammed and sank US patrol boat *PT 109*. Its young skipper, Lieutenant John Kennedy, later to become President of the USA, and his crew made a daring escape after their boat was sunk. Plum Pudding Island, from where they were rescued with the help of two Solomon Islanders, has been renamed Kennedy Island.

Safety concerns have been raised by a number of robberies involving yachts. As in neighbouring Papua New Guinea, such incidents occur usually in or near larger ports and are unheard of in smaller communities. In contrast, the island of Malaita, particularly the Langa Langa Lagoon, is one place where you can savour village life virtually unaffected by the outside world. Another lagoon often visited by yachts for the excellent wood carvings made by the villagers is Morovo Lagoon in the New Georgia group. While the majority of Solomon Islanders are Melanesian, several islands have a Polynesian population, such as the raised atolls of Rennell and Bellona. The people who inhabit them have a way of life strikingly different to other Solomon Islanders. Also Polynesian are the few hundred who live on the two small islands that make up the Ontong Java Atoll.

✦ COUNTRY PROFILE

The first inhabitants probably came to these islands about four to five thousand years ago. But only at the end of the nineteenth century did Europeans such as traders and missionaries start arriving. Many Europeans were killed in retaliation for their abuse and cruel treatment of the islanders. Britain made the Solomon Islands a Protectorate in 1893, primarily to maintain some law and order. Independence was achieved in 1978.

Of the 596,000 inhabitants most are Melanesian, with a few Polynesians in the southern islands. English is used in schools and businesses, but there are an estimated 87 local languages. Honiara is the capital.

Junior race with palm frond sails on Roviana Island.

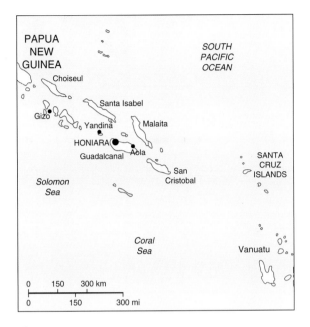

✦ CLIMATE

The Solomons have a tropical climate, with high temperatures and humidity for most of the year. January to March are the months of heaviest rainfall. April to November is the season of the southeast trade winds, while the rest of the year is the northwest monsoon, which is also the cyclone season. Long periods of calms are not uncommon around the islands.

✦ FORMALITIES

PORTS OF ENTRY

Honiara	9°25´S 159°58´E	Gizo	8°05´S 156°52´E
Noro	8°13´S 157°12´E	Yandina	9°04´S 159°13´E
Graciosa Bay	10°44´S 165°49´E		

Stopping at any island before clearing in is strictly prohibited and incurs a heavy fine. Honiara Radio should be contacted on Channel 16, HF 2182 or 6213 to give an ETA and request clearance instructions.

Honiara: Yachts should anchor in the proximity of Point Cruz Yacht Club and go ashore for clearance.

Graciosa Bay: Temporary clearance can be obtained at the police station if no officials are present, but official clearance must be finalized in Honiara.

Gizo: The Gizo Yacht Club will assist with formalities; these are reported to be easier to complete here than elsewhere although occasionally yachts have been sent to Noro to clear in there.

A visitor's permit for up to three months in any twelve is obtainable on arrival by nationals of most European countries, Australia, Canada, New Zealand and the USA. Crew arriving or departing by plane, nationals of South Africa, and other countries must get a visa in advance. This may be obtained by contacting the Director of Immigration by mail, email, phone or fax. Tel: (677) 22243, Fax: (677) 22964, PO Box G26, Honiara (immigration@commerce.gov.sb).

A yacht may stay for three months, extendable by another three months only.

All the land in the Solomons, including uninhabited areas, is someone's property, and to visit you must get permission from the relevant chief. The authorities in Honiara will advise as to where a yacht can or cannot go.

✦ FACILITIES

Honiara has the best facilities for engine and electrical repair, as well as a shipyard. There are also supermarkets and a good fresh produce market. Diesel in large quantities is only available in Honiara, Gizo and at Noro, on the island of New Georgia. Repair services in the other islands are limited, the best being at Gizo where help should be sought from the Gizo Yacht Club. The nearby island of Liapari has a repair yard with a slipway for hull repairs.

The anchorage at Honiara is not to be trusted as sudden squalls have caused several yachts to be driven ashore.

Cruising Guides
Solomon Islands Cruising Guide
The Pacific Crossing Guide
South Pacific Anchorages
Landfalls of Paradise

Websites
www.visitsolomons.com.sb
www.gizoyachtclub.com.sb

Local time	UTC +11
Buoyage	IALA A
Currency	Solomon Islands Dollar (SBD)
Electricity	240V, 50Hz

Diplomatic missions

UK	21705
Australia	21561
New Zealand	21502

Communications

IDD 677	IAC 00

Emergency number
911

TOKELAU

TOKELAU LIES JUST NORTH OF SAMOA and consists of three small low coral atolls: Atafu, Nukunonu, and Fakaofo. One of the least visited countries in the South Pacific, only a few yachts make their way to this isolated group of atolls, which lack natural harbours and for most of the year are completely cut off from the outside world. Some formalities have to be complied with before sailing for the islands, but any difficulties are justified as they give an opportunity to visit one of the most isolated communities in the Pacific.

An interesting sight is the local version of cricket, called *kilikiti*. The most popular team sport in Tokelau, it involves teams of 55 players or more. The rules were evolved locally and on Fakaofo the men and women play together, while on Atafu they play separately. Games can last from a few hours to three days and the teams often take time off to go fishing in the middle of a game, and the number of fish caught are added to each team's score.

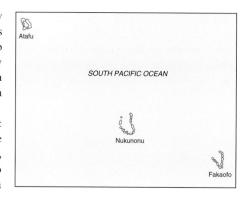

✦ COUNTRY PROFILE

Polynesian legend says that the Maui brothers pulled the three islands out of the sea while fishing. The islands were rarely visited until the 1840s. In 1889 Britain claimed jurisdiction over them, but in 1925 administration was transferred to New Zealand, an arrangement that continues to this day. There is some internal autonomy, but referenda held in 2006 and 2007 to change the status of the islands to one of free association with New Zealand failed.

About 1,400 people live in Tokelau, with many more living in New Zealand. Tokelauan and English are spoken. There is no administrative centre, with each island having a separate local government. External affairs are run by the Tokelau Liaison office in Apia, Western Samoa.

✦ CLIMATE

The climate is tropical, with little variation from the 28°C/82°F annual average temperature. From May to September the islands are under the influence of the southeast trade winds. Tokelau is at the northern edge of the main hurricane belt, but tropical storms sometimes sweep through between November and April. In recent years Tokelau has experienced three cyclones and this increase in cyclone activity seems to be related to climate change.

✦ FORMALITIES

Police, health and an administration officer normally come out to meet boats arriving at Fakaofo.

Visas are needed by all nationalities before arrival. A cruising permit is required in advance and must be authorized by the Council of Elders of each island that the yacht wishes to visit. The Office for Tokelau Affairs in Apia,

Samoa, can radio in advance for permission, and the office also issues visitor permits and visas for a one-month stay. In spite of strict regulations, boats appear to be allowed to make a short stop even if arriving without prior permission.

PORTS OF ENTRY

Fakaofo 9°23´ S 171°15´ W
Nukunonu 8°34´ S 171°49´ W
Atafu 8°34´ S 172°30´ W

✦ FACILITIES

There are no harbour facilities and you can only anchor in the lee of the reef. The anchorage due west of Fakaofo Islet is exposed to the southeast trade winds, and fairly often conditions are not suitable for anchoring. An alternative anchorage, recommended by islanders, is northwest of the island, off Fenua Fala Islet. Channels have been blasted into each lagoon and they are accessible by dinghy. There is no airport. There is one store on each island selling some staple foodstuffs, mostly imported.

Cruising Guides
Landfalls of Paradise   South Pacific Anchorages

Website
www.tokelau.org.nz

Local time UTC –10	**Currency** New Zealand Dollar (NZD)
Buoyage IALA A	**Electricity** 240V, 50Hz

Communications
IDD 690   IAC 00

TONGA

THE KINGDOM OF TONGA, situated in the heart of the South Pacific, consists of over 160 coral and volcanic islands, of which only 36 are inhabited. Best known among sailors is the northern group of Vava'u, whose maze of islets and reefs provides one of the best cruising grounds in the South Pacific. The only surviving Polynesian kingdom and the only Pacific nation to have enjoyed political independence throughout its history, Tonga is undergoing radical change as its new King, George Tupou V, is abandoning a feudal system in favour of a more modern and democratic governance. Yet even such momentous changes do not seem to have affected the unhurried pace of life in the capital, Nuku'alofa, on the main island of Tongatapu, whose small yacht harbour is a good place from which to visit this interesting island. Among the highlights are the blowholes at Houma, the mysterious trilithon at Ha'amanga, the flocks of flying foxes (fruit bats) at Kolovai, the royal tombs of the Tu'i Tonga in the ancient capital of Mu'a, or the elegant Victorian royal palace in Nuku'alofa.

Vava'u, Tonga's northern group of islands, has been a favourite cruising destination for a long time. The unique potential of its sheltered waters was recognized as far back as the 1970s when South Pacific Yacht Charters opened the first charter operation in the South Pacific. There are about one hundred islands of all sizes, sprinkled with sandy beaches, underwater caves and plenty of protected anchorages. The entire area provides an excellent opportunity for sailing in sheltered areas, its tranquil waters being the favourite destination not only of cruising yachts, but also of some travellers of a very different kind. Scores of humpback whales gather here in winter to breed and it is a great thrill to watch these gentle giants and their offspring swim slowly by, and an even greater thrill to swim in their company.

The strategic location of Vava'u at the crossroads of several sailing routes, as well as the reputation of the main anchorage, Refuge Harbour, as a safe hurricane hole, has turned it into a busy yachting centre. In total contrast is the central group of Ha'apai, an area of colourful reefs and peaceful anchorages. This calm was rudely interrupted in March 2009 when the eruption of a submarine volcano created a new island west of Ha'apai in an area where such phenomena had occurred in the past. A seismic disturbance close to that area caused a violent tsunami in September 2009, which caused wide devastation and many victims in

The islands of Vava'u

the neighbouring islands. At Tonga's northern extreme, the isolated islands of Niuatoputapu, Tafai and Niuafo'ou are located almost directly on the route from Tonga to Samoa, and these rarely visited islands make a tempting stop.

◆ COUNTRY PROFILE

Tonga was probably inhabited over two thousand years ago by migrants from Samoa. The Tu'i Tonga chiefs reigned over Tonga, and by the thirteenth century had created a Pacific empire stretching from Fiji to Niue. The first contact with Europeans was in 1616, with the arrival of the Dutch explorers Willem Schouten and Jakob Le Maire. Abel Tasman, Samuel Wallis and James Cook were subsequent visitors, the latter naming them the Friendly Islands.

In the 1820s missionaries arrived and their influence helped to end the fierce tribal wars that had been raging for 30 years. In 1845 King George Tupou I founded the present royal dynasty, which can trace its origins back to the first Tu'i Tonga. To avoid German colonization, Tonga put itself under British protection at the end of the nineteenth century. Full sovereignty was restored in 1958. The present king, George Tupou V, acceded to the throne in 2006. Two years later, following riots for more democracy, the King agreed to relinquish most of his absolute power and to surrender his role in day-to-day affairs to a prime minister and parliament to be elected in 2010.

The population numbers 121,000. Tongan is the official language, but most people also speak English. Christianity plays a leading role and, until recently, all sporting activities were banned on Sundays, which remains a day where all of Tonga is supposed to shut down, including the international airport on Tongatapu.

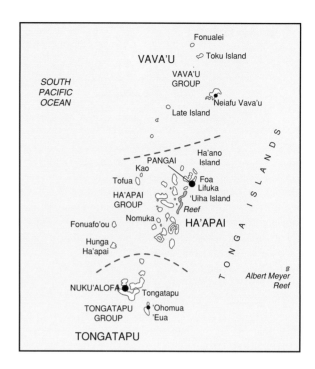

◆ CLIMATE

Tonga's subtropical climate is warm and humid, although less so than on other tropical islands. The winter average temperature is 24°C/75°F, compared to summers at 26°C/79°F. From April to November the southeast trade winds predominate, but sudden squalls can occur from other directions. December to April, which is also the cyclone season, has more rain. Recently, at least one tropical cyclone has affected the islands every year.

Neiafu anchorage

✦ FORMALITIES

PORTS OF ENTRY

Nuku'alofa (Tongatapu)	21°08′ S 175°12′ W
Lifuka (Ha'apai)	19°48′ S 174°21′ W
Neiafu (Vava'u)	18°39′ S 173°59′ W
Niuatoputapu Island	15°58′ S 173°45′ W
Niuafo'ou Island	15°35′ S 175°41′ W

Nuku'alofa: Nuku'alofa Harbour must be contacted for clearance instructions. Yachts normally clear at Queen Salote wharf or in the nearby small boat harbour at Faua, which has a depth in the entrance channel of 2.6m (8.5ft) at low tide.

Neiafu: Arriving yachts should go alongside the main wharf on the port side of Refuge Harbour. Customs and immigration offices are located nearby.

Lifuka: Yachts should anchor in front of Pangai village. The customs office is by the small dock.

Niuatoputapu: Yachts should anchor off Falehau to be inspected by the quarantine officer before completing formalities ashore.

Niuafo'ou: Yachts anchor either off the village of Angaha or northwest of the island, then proceed ashore to complete formalities.

For most nationals, including the Commonwealth, European countries and the USA, a visa free-entry permit is issued for up to 30 days. This can be extended by the immigration department. For nationals needing a visa, these can be issued locally after clearance has been completed.

Fresh fruit, vegetables and non-commercially packed eggs will be confiscated by the quarantine official, who will supervise the disposal of garbage.

A coastal clearance permit from customs is required when moving between island groups served by different customs offices. On arrival at the next group, you must contact customs. When travelling between Tongatapu and Vava'u, or vice versa, the coastal clearance can be requested to include Ha'apai. Daysailing within each group does not require clearance.

Yachts may remain in Tonga for long periods, provided the necessary arrangements are made with customs.

✦ MARINE RESERVES

There are seven marine reserves around Tongatapu: Hakaumamato Reef, Pangaimotu Reef, Malinoa Island and Reef, Ha'atafu Beach, Monuafe Island and Reef, Mounu Reef Giant Clam Reserve and Muihopohoponga Coastal Reserve near Niutoua. Three reserves are proposed for Vava'u: the wreck of the ship *Clan McWilliam* in Neiafu Harbour, the coral gardens between Nuapapu and Vaketeitu, the Giant Clam Reserves in Hunga Lagoon, Neiafu Harbour, and off Ano Beach.

Giant clams are an endangered species, and those tagged with a number printed on the shell or an aluminium tag should not be disturbed, even outside of the reserves.

A dangerous area to avoid by boats on passage to Fiji is Metis Shoal (19°11.4′ S 174°51′ W), where there has been intense volcanic activity.

✦ FACILITIES

The best facilities are in Vava'u where the Moorings maintains a workshop and can handle most types of repair. The adjacent boatyard can handle haulouts and hull repairs. Most moorings in Refuge Harbour are owned by the Moorings and Sailing Safaris. These may be used by visiting yachts and the relevant office must be visited for payment. In Nuku'alofa, there are two slipways of 100-tonnes and 15-tonnes capacity, as well as some workshops in the harbour area. Provisioning is good in both Nuku'alofa and Neiafu, and fresh produce is widely available.

✦ CHARTER

As a charter location, the Vava'u group of islands has few equals in the world and there are several international operators based in Refuge Harbour. The New Zealand company Sailing Safaris offers both bareboat and crewed yachts and also tuition, while the Moorings and Sunsail offer their usual range of yachts and services.

www.sailingsafaris.com
www.moorings.com
www.sunsail.com

Cruising Guides
Cruising Guide to the Kingdom of Tonga in Vava'u
Cruising Guide to the Vava'u Islands Group in Tonga
Landfalls of Paradise
The Pacific Crossing Guide
South Pacific Anchorages

Websites
www.tongatapu.net.to/tonga/islands/default_to.htm (information for visiting sailors)
www.tongaholiday.com (Tonga Visitors Bureau)
www.vavau.to (general information on Vava'u)

Local time	UTC +13
Buoyage	IALA A
Currency	Tongan Pa'Anga (TOP)
Electricity	240V, 50Hz

Diplomatic missions
Australia 23244	New Zealand 23122

Communications	**Emergency number**
IDD 676 IAC 00	911

TUVALU

Nukulaelae Atoll.

FORMERLY THE ELLICE ISLANDS, the name 'Tuvalu' means 'cluster of eight' although the group in fact consists of nine low-lying coral atolls. Only eight of them were inhabited when the name was chosen, but a small community now lives on previously uninhabited Niulakita, the southernmost island of the archipelago. The islands lie just below the equator and west of the International Dateline. With a total land area of only 26 sq km (11 sq miles), Tuvalu is one of the smallest countries in the world, spread out in half a million square miles of ocean. These islands are now facing the tragic prospect of being one of the first victims of the current climate change. The rising ocean level is already affecting the main island of Funafuti, which has been flooded on several recent occasions, and it is now predicted that all the islands will be submerged before the end of this century.

The small island communities still lead a traditional lifestyle and are facing the impending doom with typical Polynesian fatalism. With the exception of the island of Funafuti, yachts rarely visit the islands. Although some only have precarious anchorages in the lee of a fringing reef, the lagoon is accessible in at least two islands, at Nukufetau and

Nanumea, where visiting yachts are always warmly greeted. A similar welcome awaits sailors at any of the other islands, and although there have been plans to open passes into some of the other lagoons, this is unlikely to happen. The islands are an interesting stop for boats sailing to or from neighbouring Kiribati. Those who are heading north and intend to stop at any of the outer islands should obtain permission from the authorities in Funafuti to stop en route. Boats coming the other way may be able to make an emergency stop before clearing in at Funafuti, and ask the island chief to obtain permission by radio from the authorities in the capital.

✦ COUNTRY PROFILE

The first inhabitants arrived about two thousand years ago, mostly from Samoa, but also from Tonga and Uvea (Wallis). The northern islands, especially Nui, were populated from Micronesia. A society under the leadership of chiefs developed, and customs and traditions akin to Samoa remain today. The first European sighting of the islands was in 1765. There was little other contact until the nineteenth century when slave traders, known as blackbirders, took hundreds of

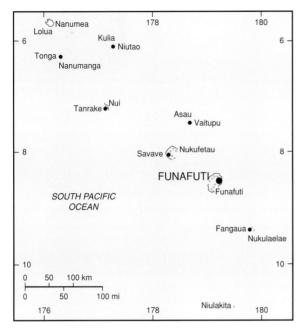

islanders to work in Peru, Fiji, Tahiti, Hawaii and Australia. The group became a British Protectorate and then part of the Gilbert and Ellice Islands colony. After a referendum in 1975, the Ellice Islands separated from the Gilberts and became Tuvalu, achieving full independence in 1978.

Welcome to Tuvalu

The population is 12,300. Tuvaluans are Polynesians, and both Tuvaluan and English are spoken. Funafuti is the capital.

✦ CLIMATE

Tuvalu lies within the tradewind zone, but on the edge of the South Pacific equatorial doldrum zone. Prevailing winds are from the easterly quarter and they occur most frequently between June and August. In most years from December to March, winds between the west and north usually exceed the easterlies in frequency. Tuvalu lies on the northern edge of the hurricane belt and occasionally severe cyclones strike the islands, as did cyclone Ofa in February 1990. Temperatures are uniformly high all year round, with the mean annual temperature of 28°C/82°F.

✦ FORMALITIES

PORT OF ENTRY
Funafuti 8°31′ S 179°12′ E

Yachts should not stop at any of the other islands before clearing in at Funafuti. Yachts should anchor close to the wharf, where the customs office is located. Officials will board the boat and it is necessary to ferry them back and forth. Entry visas for one month are granted on arrival.

Permission must be requested to visit any of the other islands. It is not normally possible to get clearance to stop at any of them on the way north to Kiribati, although in special circumstances this may be granted.

✦ FACILITIES

There is a store selling mostly imported food on all the islands. Limited amounts of fuel may sometimes be available in the outer islands, but it is only in Funafuti where you can be certain of getting fuel. There are only simple repair facilities available in Funafuti and nothing in the other islands. There are no credit card facilities or ATMs, so it is best to arrive with some Australian dollars.

Cruising Guides	Website
Landfalls of Paradise	www.timelesstuvalu.com
Micronesia Cruising Notes	
South Pacific Anchorages	

Local time	UTC +12
Buoyage	IALA A
Currency	Tuvaluan Dollar, Australian Dollar (AUD)
Electricity	220V, 50Hz

Communications	Emergency number
IDD 688 IAC 00	911

VANUATU

VANUATU, formerly called the New Hebrides, is a group of over eighty volcanic islands in the Western Pacific. Espiritu Santo, Malekula, Efate, Erromango, Ambrym and Tanna are the main ones. Ignored by Europeans for longer than other parts of the Pacific, Vanuatu leapt into the modern age quickly while remaining a place where the rich Melanesian culture is kept very much alive. It is the chance to experience some of this fascinating culture as well as the unspoilt scenery that brings most sailors to this country, which was chosen by James Michener as the setting for his *Tales of the South Pacific*. The island of Aoba was probably his Bali Hai. Nearby lies one of the permanent reminders of what happened here in the days of the Second World War: the wreck of SS *President Coolidge*. This luxurious ocean liner was used as a troop carrier during the war and, as it entered the port of Luganville in 1942, it struck two mines and sunk, the captain not having been informed of the defensive minefields. The wreck is now one of the most frequented dive sites in the Pacific.

A very different attraction is the live volcano Yasur on Tanna, where you can walk right to the edge of the crater and look into the bubbling and hissing abyss, the closest you can get to an active volcano anywhere in the world. The volcano and the area around it is the ancestral land of a small community, who have returned to a traditional way of life and enjoy a simple self-sufficient existence. The villagers tolerate visits by outsiders to the island, but access to their village is not permitted.

A thrill of a different kind is to witness a performance by the land divers of Pentecost Island. Part of a traditional tribal

Yasur Volcano.

ceremony to celebrate the start of the yam harvest (a root vegetable which is a staple food crop), the death-defying dives by young Ni-Vanuatu men from the top of an improvised tower that is at least 20m (65ft) high is believed to be the inspiration of the bungee jump. The tower has three levels and the youngest boys of nine or ten dive just from the first level, which is at 10m (33ft). It is almost impossible to describe the sheer excitement of watching diver after diver hurtling towards the ground, the impact being lessened by the lianas tied to the ankles, the green vine stretching enough to slow down the fall. Such dives take place in April and May, and occasionally also in June, and arrangements need to be made well in advance to witness one of these unique ceremonies. There are many other cultural festivals throughout Vanuatu, tribal dancing in Ambrym (July), Nalawan ceremonies in Malekula (August), a traditional sailing canoe race in Lamen Bay on Epi (also in August), and many festivals on other islands. Most of these celebrations coincide with the cruising season, and often sailors are the only outsiders to have the rare privilege to witness ancient customs that have died out elsewhere in the world.

A popular stop for boats heading north is the well-protected Double Waterfall Bay near Sasara, on the west coast of Vanua Lava. A local family have made various arrangements in this picturesque spot to make visiting sailors not only welcome and comfortable, but also to encourage them to stay longer: an airy clubhouse, trips in outrigger canoe or jungle walks, visits to the family burial cave, as well as providing meals ashore. There are now examples of such interaction between villagers and visiting sailors in other places around the world, and their success and popularity bodes well for both sailors and their hosts.

◆ COUNTRY PROFILE

The exact origins of the indigenous population are not known and it has been suggested that the Melanesians probably came from Africa thousands of years ago. They spread across the South West Pacific from Papua to New Caledonia and Vanuatu, occupying the area now called Melanesia, and developed different cultures. Isolation was broken when in 1606 the explorer Pedro Fernandez de Quiros, looking for land and gold, came across Espiritu Santo, and believed it to be the mythical southern continent. Only 150 years later did Bougainville visit Espiritu Santo and establish that it was not a continent after all. Soon afterwards Captain Cook charted the islands, naming them the New Hebrides, although they

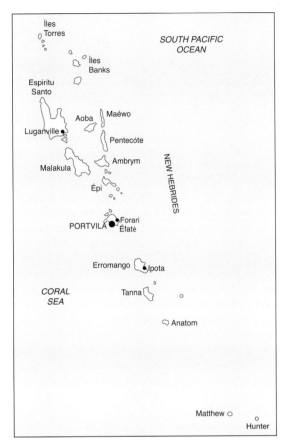

warmest, with a mean 26°C/79°F. Officially, the cyclone season lasts from December until the end of March, but in recent years cyclones have been recorded as late as June.

◆ FORMALITIES

PORTS OF ENTRY

Port Vila	17°44´S 168°18´E	Luganville	15°31´S 167°10´E
Lenakel	19°31.5´S 169°15´E	Sola	13°53´S 167°33´E

Boats must proceed directly to a port of entry. Stopping at any of the outer islands is prohibited.

Port Vila: Yachts should proceed into the harbour and anchor close to the yellow quarantine buoy. As the port rarely answers calls, it is best to contact Yachting World on Channel 16, which will then inform the authorities and also give advice on where to anchor or dock the boat. Quarantine and customs will come to the boat, and after those formalities have been completed, the caption must go into town to visit the nearby immigration office. There is an overhead power cable between the eastern side of Iririki Island and Port Vila, and no vessel whose mast height exceeds 30m (100ft) should pass under it. Yachts with taller masts can tie stern-to the quay or anchor in the quarantine area.

Land diving on the island of Pentecost.

bore little resemblance to the original Hebrides. Missionaries, whalers, sandalwood traders and blackbirders followed, as they did in so many parts of the Pacific. Later, the existence of both French and English settlements led to the creation of a Franco-British Condominium in 1906. Better known as the Pandemonium, it brought to the islands two sets of laws, education systems, as well as two languages. Until independence in 1980, yachts could choose whether to clear in with a French gendarme or a British bobby.

The 219,000 inhabitants are mainly Melanesian, calling themselves Ni-Vanuatu. The national language is Bislama, a pidgin English. The origin of the name 'Bislama' is the French *bêche-de-mer*, the sea cucumber that was exported from here in the nineteenth century. French and English are both widely spoken, and there are 115 indigenous languages. Port Vila, on Efate, is the capital.

◆ CLIMATE

The climate is sub-tropical with two distinct seasons. May to October is relatively cool and dry, while November to April is hot and humid. January to March is the rainy season. The most pleasant month tends to be August, with an average temperature of 21°C/70°F, while February and March are the

Espiritu Santo: Customs or port control should be called on Channels 16 or 12. If conditions are too rough to anchor by the old black quarantine buoy, you may pick up a mooring off Aore Resort on the south side of Segond Channel opposite Luganville. You should then cross by dinghy to the main wharf to visit the customs, quarantine and immigration offices. It is not recommended to tie up to the quarantine buoy or to the main wharf.

Lenakel: The port is not suitable for yachts. The alternative is to anchor at Black Sands Bay, north of Lenakel or, the preferred option, to use Port Resolution on the east side of Tanna as a safer base, and go to Lenakel overland. Customs in Lenakel should be called first on Tel: 68058 as occasionally they agree to send an officer over. During the cruising season, officials come every Thursday to Port Resolution so yachts can complete formalities there.

No visas are required for visits of up to 30 days for nationals of the Commonwealth, most European countries and the USA. One-month permits are issued on arrival. Extensions can be obtained from immigration, the maximum permitted stay being four months.

On arrival, the captain has to complete a declaration with yacht and crew details and also an inter-island cruising permit for yachts that lists the islands you intend to visit. Both these forms can be downloaded from the cruising yachts page of the Vanuatu tourism website. Also from this site you can download the one-way requirement form needed by any crew flying in to join a yacht.

Strict quarantine regulations are in force, and no animals, birds, reptiles, fresh meat, fruit or vegetables may be taken ashore. When clearing in, the quarantine officer will decide if some of these goods may be allowed to remain on board and will give permission to land garbage.

Yachts are considered to be temporarily imported into Vanuatu and can stay for six months in any two-year period. If the boat is used commercially, it will become liable for duty.

A taboo in Malekula forbids a male to swim under a boat with women on board. Those who break this strict taboo will have to pay a substantial fine to the village chief.

Asanwari Bay on Maewo Island.

Ipai custom village on Tanna Island.

✦ FACILITIES

Yachting World in Port Vila has expanded its facilities to provide cruising sailors with most of their immediate needs: docking, fuel, wifi, laundry and other necessary services, including a bar and restaurant on the waterfront, both greatly favoured by sailors (details on the Yachting World website). Repair facilities in Port Vila are adequate. There is a slipway, provisioning is good, and there are duty-free shops for visitors. In Santo there are a number of repair shops for electrical work, refrigeration repair, hardware, welding, hydraulics and engines. Repair services in the other islands are very limited. Local people are always welcoming to sailors and are happy to barter for fruit and vegetables in exchange for any goods that are not available in the islands.

✦ CHARTER

There are no local bareboat operators, but it is possible to charter a boat in Nouméa, in neighbouring New Caledonia. Sailaway Vanuatu, based on the main island of Efate, offers crewed charters around the islands.

www.sailawayvanuatu.com

Cruising Guides
Landfalls of Paradise
The Pacific Crossing Guide
South Pacific Anchorages
Rocket Cruising Guide of Vanuatu (CD)

Websites
www.vanuatutourism.com
www.yachtingworld-vanuatu.com
www.vanuatutourism.com/vanuatu/cms/en/activities/
   cruising_yachts.html (information for visiting yachts)
www.cruising-vanuatu.com (to purchase or download CD
   guide)

| **Local time** | UTC +11 | **Currency** | Vanuatu Vatu (VUV) |
| **Buoyage** | IALA A | **Electricity** | 220V, 50Hz |

| **Diplomatic missions** | | | |
| Australia | 22 777 | New Zealand | 22 933 |

| **Communications** | | **Emergency number** | |
| IDD 678 | IAC 00 | 112 | |

WALLIS AND FUTUNA

THESE TWO ISLAND GROUPS separated by 150 miles of ocean are a French overseas collectivity. Honikulu Pass into the lagoon at Uvéa, as the locals prefer to call their island, may be difficult to negotiate on account of the strong current, so arrival should be timed for slack water. There are several anchorages in the large lagoon, the best protected being off the village of Gahi. The anchorage off the main village of Mata-Utu is less protected from the prevailing southeast winds, but is closer to all offices and amenities. There are several small islets in the lagoon that can be used as day anchorages. Ashore, you can come in contact with a relatively unspoilt Polynesian society where the rule of the traditional Polynesian king, the Lavelua, often commands more respect than the French administration. The mellifluous Uvean singing is possibly the most beautiful in all Polynesia and this is one of the few places where traditional songs have not been affected by missionary influences.

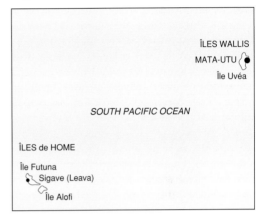

The atmosphere is similar on the smaller Futuna, which is even more isolated as it does not have a protected lagoon. The only safe anchorage is at Sigave Bay on the west coast.

◆ COUNTRY PROFILE

Futuna was the first to have a European visitor – the Dutch explorer Schouten, who called here in 1616. The island of Uvea was first sighted by Captain Wallis in 1767, who renamed it after himself. France declared the islands their protectorate in 1842 and in 2007 their status was changed from that of a French overseas territory to that of a French overseas collectivity.

The Polynesian population numbers over 9,000 on Wallis, and about 5,000 on Futuna. Uvéan, Futunan and French are spoken.

◆ CLIMATE

The islands have a tropical climate with little temperature variations and an average 28°C/82°F throughout the year. The southeast trade winds blow over the islands during the winter months from April to November. Winds are variable during summer when the weather is sometimes sultry. Westerly gales occur in summer, but the islands are rarely affected by tropical storms. The cyclone season lasts from December to late March.

◆ FORMALITIES

PORTS OF ENTRY

Mata-Utu (Wallis)	13°17′S 176°08′W
Sigave (Futuna)	14°18′S 178°10′W

You should anchor and proceed ashore to check with the gendarmerie and customs. Both offices must be visited again before departure. Yachts may stay a maximum of six months in a 12-month period.

Nationals of the EU, Australia, Canada, New Zealand and the USA do not need a visa for a stay of up to 90 days. Other nationals on a short stay are usually exempt.

◆ FACILITIES

In Wallis only simple repairs are possible, but in an emergency you may be able to enlist help from the French military. There is good provisioning in Mata-Utu, with well-stocked supermarkets, and fuel is available. In Futuna simple repairs are also possible, fuel is available, and there are also well-stocked supermarkets.

Cruising Guides
Landfalls of Paradise
South Pacific Anchorages

Website
www.tourist-office.org/wallis-and-futuna/wallis-et-futuna.htm

Local time	UTC +12
Buoyage	IALA A
Currency	CFP Franc (XPF)
Electricity	220V, 50Hz

Communications	
IDD 681	IAC 19

SOUTH EAST AND EAST ASIA

FOR SAILORS THAT HAIL FROM farther shores, what used to be called the Far East is still regarded as a remote cruising destination, but the numbers of visiting yachts that face the challenge to get there are richly rewarded for their efforts. Until not long ago, the only cruising yachts seen in this part of the world were those belonging to intrepid sailors prepared to put up with bureaucratic restrictions, safety risks, and an almost total absence of facilities. Much of this belongs firmly to the past, as yachting is now enjoyed by many of the local people; officials have learned to deal with visiting vessels; peace has come to formerly war-torn countries; and facilities have seen a huge improvement to cope with the demands of both local and visiting sailors. Thailand was among the first to identify this trend, and Phuket and the surrounding area has become the most popular cruising area in Asia. The attraction of this ideal cruising ground will increase even more once neighbouring Myanmar allows more yachts to visit its southern archipelago. Cruising opportunities are expanding throughout the region, with Malaysia, both its western mainland coast, and Sabah and Sarawak on Borneo's north coast, now firmly on the local circuit. The same can be said of the Philippines, which have the potential to eventually become one of the leading cruising destinations in the world. Indeed, the threat of piracy in the Gulf of Aden has forced many

sailors, especially from Australia and New Zealand, to reconsider their cruising plans and to make the best of the attractions lying closer to their shores, in Indonesia, the Philippines and around Borneo. This vast area has many attractions that are increasingly disappearing in other parts of the world. Tourism development, and the commercialization that goes with it, is still limited, and in rural areas people still live a traditional lifestyle and there are fewer safety concerns than in the past.

New cruising areas are gradually being added, and both Vietnam and Cambodia have started attracting visiting yachts as they are no longer closed to foreign visitors, and sailors in that part of the world have started adding them to their cruising itinerary. While China has now opened its frontiers to visitors, those arriving by yacht still have to go through a maze of formalities, both cumbersome and expensive. Always welcoming, yet far from any cruising routes, Japan is a tempting, yet challenging, destination, and everyone who has visited the land of the rising sun on his or her own boat has only words of praise for the beauty of the land and the warmth of its people.

For sailors from Europe and America much of Asia is still regarded as the 'Far East', and while the term has almost disappeared from common use, the feeling remains. Planning a cruise anywhere in that vast area entails a long-term commitment, and for many sailors the logical way to visit some of the Asian countries is to include them in a round the world voyage. Usually this means cruising the South Pacific first, then heading northwest towards the Asian mainland and, after spending some time there, completing the circumnavigation either via the North Indian Ocean, Red Sea and Mediterranean, or by sailing around the Cape of Good Hope. Sailors from the west coast of the USA have the perfect opportunity to see much of the world by limiting a circumnavigation to the Pacific Ocean.

A clockwise circuit of the Pacific benefits from favourable weather conditions along its entire length and can be joined at any point: North American sailors heading first for French Polynesia, continue west through the South Pacific, head for East Asia and Japan next, then complete the circuit with a possible detour to Alaska and finally British Columbia and the Pacific North West. Such a merry-go-round can easily be joined by yachts from New Zealand and Australia, and

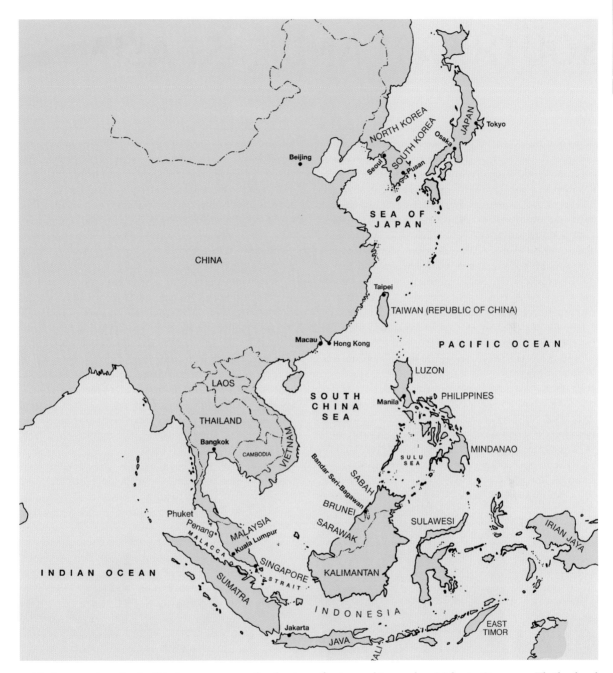

suddenly a complete circuit of the largest ocean on the planet looks like a less challenging proposition than an actual circumnavigation of the world.

Facilities vary considerably, and the countries that have their own boating communities, or that are frequented by foreign yachts – such as Malaysia, Singapore, Thailand and Hong Kong – are also those where the best repair facilities are available. In the other countries, facilities are still limited, but marinas are being built in areas favoured by cruising sailors and the situation is slowly improving throughout the region.

BRUNEI

THE SULTANATE OF Negara Brunei Darussalam, or Abode of Peace, is a small state on the north shore of the large island of Borneo, made up of two separate areas divided by the Malaysian state of Sarawak. The country is surrounded by fertile plains alternating with mangroves, rainforests and mountains. Although small, it is extremely rich because of its oil and gas reserves, and the present Sultan, one of the richest men in the world, heads a small nation with one of the highest average incomes in Asia.

Cruising along the coast is a challenge due to inshore shallows and the many offshore oil rigs that make navigation difficult, especially at night. The interior is accessible via some of the rivers, but their entrance is encumbered by bars that can only be crossed at high water. Brunei river is the country's main waterway and the deepwater port of Muara is located at its mouth. There is a good anchorage off the Royal Brunei Yacht Club at Pantai Serata and the club's main base

is upriver in the centre of the capital. The club is a good introduction to Brunei, where a formal protocol is strictly observed and correct manners are of utmost importance. The club is also a safe place to leave the boat while visiting the fascinating interior of the country. From Muara it is 16 miles up the river to the capital, Bandar Seri Bagawan. This is a modern city, but it has several interesting old buildings as well as Kampung Ayer, the world's largest village on stilts.

✦ COUNTRY PROFILE

Recent discoveries confirm that Brunei had links with the Asian continent as early as the sixth to seventh centuries. During the fourteenth to sixteenth centuries Brunei became the centre of an empire including Borneo, the Sulu Islands and the Philippines. Islam came to Brunei in the fifteenth century. After the arrival of Europeans, Brunei's empire gradually disappeared, and by the end of the nineteenth

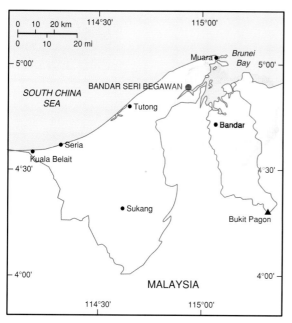

century Brunei became a British Protectorate. When oil was discovered in the 1920s, a new era of prosperity began, with full independence granted in 1984. The same family has ruled Brunei for over six centuries.

The population is 388,000, mainly Malay and Chinese, some Europeans, Indians, Filipinos and the indigenous Iban and Dusun. Malay is the official language, but English is widely spoken.

✦ CLIMATE

The climate is tropical, hot and very humid, ranging from 25°C/77°F to 35°C/95°F. There are heavy and sudden spells of rains all year round. Brunei has two monsoon seasons, with heavy rainfall from October to February and from May to June.

✦ FORMALITIES

PORTS OF ENTRY

Muara	4°53´N 114°56´E
Kuala Belait	4°35´N 114°11´E
Bandar Seri Bégawan	4°52´N 114°55´E

Muara: After contacting port control, you should anchor between the naval base and the Shell docks. Alternatively, you may anchor or take a mooring at the yacht club and go by land to clear in. The port office in the Serasa ferry terminal should be visited first, then the marine department, customs, and finally immigration.

A visa-free stay from between 14 and 90 days is given to nationals of most countries. Those requiring a visa and arriving without one may receive permission to stay 72 hours.

Muslim religious customs should be respected. Alcohol may not be consumed in public places except with discretion in some hotels and restaurants. Women are expected to dress modestly.

✦ FACILITIES

The Royal Brunei Yacht Club has premises at both Pantai Serasa (Muara) and in Bandar Seri Bégawan. The club welcomes visiting sailors, for whom it is an invaluable source of local information and who have access to its facilities such as moorings, fuel dock and free wifi. The club will also advise on any repairs. There are marine mechanics and a range of marine supplies. Provisioning is good.

Brunei Radio has been a highly popular feature among cruising sailors for many years. It provides a wide range of services to sailors and covers a vast area that comprises South East Asia, the North West Pacific, and much of the Indian Ocean.

Cruising Guides
Cruising Guide to Southeast Asia Volume I
From Yangon to Manila Bay: The Cruising Almanac 2005

Websites
www.tourismbrunei.com
www.therbyc.com (Royal Brunei Yacht Club)
www.bruneibay.net (general information)
www.bruneibay.net/bbradio/index.html (Brunei Radio)

Local time	UTC +8
Buoyage	IALA A
Currency	Brunei Dollar (BND), Singapore Dollar (SGD)
Electricity	240V, 50Hz

Diplomatic missions
UK	2 222231
USA	2 220384
Australia	2 229435
Canada	2 220043
New Zealand	2 225880

Communications
IDD 673	IAC 00

Emergency numbers
999	Ambulance 991	Police 993

CAMBODIA

ONE OF THE LATEST COUNTRIES to open its borders and welcome foreign visitors, a visit to Cambodia on your own yacht provides an opportunity to experience firsthand the many facets of this mysterious country and its long-suffering people.

Cruising options are quite limited and the thrill of navigating the long Mekong river all the way to the capital, Phnom Penh, may have to wait a few more years, but even the little cruising that is possible along the coast can make a short stay worthwhile.

A convenient place to start a cruise is near the Thai border at Koh Kong, a typical river village. Farther down the coast is Kampong Som, formerly known as Sihanoukville. This is Cambodia's principal deepwater port and is undergoing a construction boom to cope with the influx of tourists that arrive on cruise ships. The port is a good base to visit the interior, either by taking the highway to Phnom Penh or by air to Angkor, the ancient complex of Khmer temples. The boat can be left at Kampong Som – provided someone remains in charge as theft is a problem.

✦ COUNTRY PROFILE

The Khmer Empire flourished from the ninth to the fifteenth century, its centre of power being Angkor, and Angkor Wat, the famous and best preserved religious temple at the site, is a reminder of Cambodia's splendid past. During the next few centuries, the Khmer kingdom alternated as a vassal state of either the Thai or Vietnamese kings. In 1863, King Norodom sought the protection of France and Cambodia remained a French protectorate until 1963 as part of French Indochina. A turbulent period ensued exacerbated by the Vietnam War, which also claimed many Cambodian victims. In 1975 the Khmer Rouge took power and embarked on a genocide that claimed between one and two million lives. After the Vietnamese invasion of 1978 and the ousting of the Khmer Rouge, prolonged negotiations finally brought peace in 1991 and the country has been putting its tragic past behind with a slow return to normality.

The population is 14.5 million, the majority being Khmer, with Vietnamese and Chinese minorities. Khmer is the official language, but English and French are also spoken.

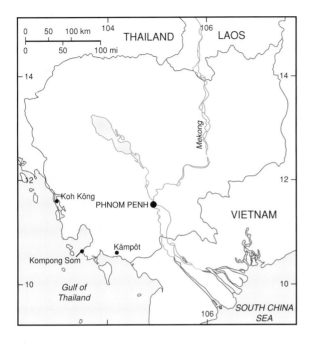

CLIMATE

The climate is tropical with high temperatures – average 27°C/80°F – on the coast all year round. The southwest monsoon, which is the rainy season, is from June to October. The northeast monsoon is the dry season, cool from November to February and hot from March to May. The typhoon season is from July to November, but such storms rarely reach Cambodia.

FORMALITIES

PORTS OF ENTRY

Kompong Som (Sihanoukville) 10°38´N 103°30´E	
Koh Kong 11°24´N 103°29.6´E	

Boats are usually met on arrival by a representative of the tourist office who will accompany the captain to the relevant offices. Visas for 30 days are issued on arrival. Two passport-sized photos are required. E-visas are also available.

FACILITIES

Facilities are limited, but some repairs are possible in Kompong Som where there is a shipyard and various work-shops. Fuel is available and provisioning is adequate. Theft is a problem everywhere. Relations with Thailand are strained and boats should avoid straying too close to the Thai border.

CHARTER

There are no locally based operators, but Gulf Charters, located in Chonburi, in the Bay of Bangkok, has a fleet of both monohulls and catamarans and is operating in Cambodia between May and September.

www.gulfchartersthailand.com

Cruising Guides
From Yangon to Manila Bay: The Cruising Almanac 2005 Southeast Asia Pilot

Website
www.tourismcambodia.com

Local time	UTC +7
Buoyage	IALA A
Currency	Cambodian Riel (KHR)
Electricity	230V, 50Hz

Diplomatic missions	
UK	23 427124
USA	23 728000
Canada	23 213470

Communications	
IDD 855	IAC 001

Emergency numbers	
Ambulance 119	Police 117

CHINA

CHINA IS A COUNTRY OF EXTREME DIVERSITY – in its climate, from the harsh north to the tropical south; its scenery, from mighty rivers to lofty mountains; and its people. A closed communist state since 1949, the opening up of this vast country that started rather timidly in the early 1980s brought many foreign tourists interested to see how the most populous nation on earth lived. Cruising yachts have also been able to take advantage of the relatively more tolerant attitude of the authorities, but the number of boats that sail to China is still very small. In most places, foreign yachts are still treated with suspicion and their freedom of movement is limited. A few yachts do visit China every year and those that sail along the coast usually find Shanghai, Fozhou and Xiamen the most convenient stops, with Fozhou being the favourite. The Chinese Yachting Association is making great efforts to develop sailing as a sport and has achieved some remarkable successes in the Olympic classes. Most sailing is done on a club basis, but ownership of small pleasure craft is rapidly expanding. The Yachting Association is keen to attract more foreign yachts to visit China, but is very much aware of the bureaucratic hurdles against which it is powerless.

The main fascination that China holds for visitors, including those on yachts, is the fact that most of the country has been forbidden territory for so long. Although there are countless interesting sites worth visiting in the interior, from the cruising point of view, China's coasts do not have much to offer. Most of the ports open to yachts are busy commercial harbours, facilities are limited and, with a few exceptions, the scenery only rarely matches that of other Asian countries.

✦ COUNTRY PROFILE

An organized state existed in China from the twenty-first century BCE, ruled by a succession of imperial dynasties. For centuries, China was a leading civilization, often outpacing the rest of the world in arts and sciences, but in modern times, in the nineteenth and early twentieth centuries, the country was beset by civil unrest, major famines, military defeats, and foreign occupation. After the Second World War, the communists under Mao Zedong established an autocratic system that, while ensuring China's sovereignty, imposed strict controls over everyday life and cost the lives of tens of millions of people. After Mao's death there was a move towards more flexibility and a pragmatic attitude to economic development was adopted. The limits of this new spirit of reform were demonstrated by the massacre of students in Tiananmen Square in 1989.

Since Mao's rule ended in 1978, his successors have focused on market-oriented economic development, and in recent years China has become the second largest economy in the world after the USA. There has been a considerable improvement in living standards, and though the room for personal choice has expanded, political control remains tight.

At 1.34 billion people, China has the largest population in the world. Approximately 90 per cent are Han, but there are a multitude of national minorities such as Mongols, Tibetans and Manchus. Mandarin is the language spoken by 70 per cent of the people, and there are several minority languages. Cantonese, spoken in southern China and Hong Kong, is in wide use.

✦ CLIMATE

The climate along the coast is mostly temperate, although there are pronounced variations between the south and the far north. The tropical areas in the south are affected by typhoons, which are most frequent between May and October. The weather in winter is cool and the coast is under the influence of the northeast monsoon from November to May. The summers are hot, humid and rainy.

✦ FORMALITIES

PORTS OF ENTRY

Shanghai	31°15´N 121°30´E
Fouzhou	26°03´N 119°18´E
Xiamen (Amoy)	24°27´N 118°04´E

The above ports have seen most foreign yachts in recent years. Only specified ports are open to foreign vessels and yachts are advised to obtain an updated list before sailing to any of them: Basuo (Hainan Island, also known as Dongfang), Beihai, Chiwan, Dalian, Dandong, Fouzhou, Guangzhou (Canton), Haikou (Hainan Island), Haimen, Huangpu, Jinshan, Jinshou, Lanshantou, Lianyungang, Longkou, Ningbo, Qingdao, Qinhuangdao, Quanzhou, Sanya (Hainan Island), Shanghai, Shantou, Tianjin, Weihai, Wenzhou, Xiamen (Amoy), Xingang (the foreign trade port of Beijing), Yangpu (Hainan Island), Yantai, Yantian, Yingkou, Zhanjiang, Zhongshan, Zhuhai (also known as Jiushou).

All ports to be visited must be notified one week in advance of ETA, and again 24 hours before arrival. There are strict regulations concerning the access and movement of all foreign vessels in Chinese territorial waters and ports.

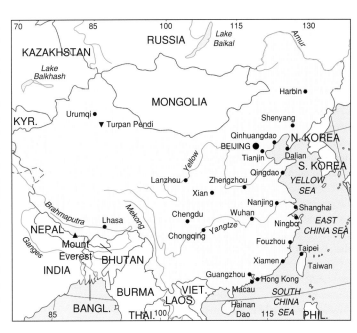

Shanghai: Vessels must call the river pilot on Channel 69 and take him on board at buoy S7 in the south channel before proceeding to the designated area. The foreign yacht berth is off the Yangtze river opposite the Oriental Tower.

All yachts must use an agent to clear customs, immigration, quarantine and harbourmaster. The China Ocean Shipping Agency (Penavico) is the only authorized agent, has branches in many ports, and should be contacted in advance. Clearance fees for all services, agent, and for berthing are expensive. Documents required include an entry report, crew list, import manifest, customs declaration, builder's certificate, captain's certificate of competence, as well as ship's registration certificate and crew passports.

A visa is required by nationals of all countries and must be obtained in advance from a Chinese diplomatic mission.

A quarantine inspection may take place.

Foreign vessels may not enter or leave ports, or change berths without permission and in the presence of a pilot. In a few recent cases, in some ports – but not Shanghai – yachts have been able to enter without a pilot or agent.

◆ FACILITIES

The number of marinas in China is increasing in line with the new affluence and interest in boating. Shanghai is excellent for provisioning and general shopping, but the strong current in the river can be a problem. Technical support is available from the Metropolitan Marina Club, where there is a dry dock and a large crane. There are other marinas in the area. Xiamen is a clean and welcoming port for yachts, with excellent and inexpensive repair facilities.

Cruising Guide
Cruising Guide to Southeast Asia Volume I

Website
www.cnto.org (China National Tourist Office)

Local time	UTC +8
Buoyage	IALA A
Currency	Chinese Yuan (CNY)
Electricity	220V, 50Hz

Diplomatic missions	
UK	10 5192 4000
USA	10 8531 3000
Australia	10 5140 4111
Canada	10 5139 4000
South Africa	10 6532 0171
New Zealand	10 8532 7000

Communications	
IDD 86	IAC 00

Emergency numbers	
110	Ambulance 999/120

EAST TIMOR

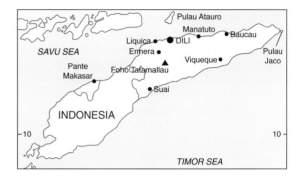

ONE OF THE LATEST COUNTRIES to join the community of independent nations, East Timor, or Timor-Leste, which is its official name since independence, is hardly a cruising destination in its own right. In recent years, its strategic location on the direct route between the South Pacific and Indian Ocean, as well as between Northern Australia and Indonesia, has seen a gradual increase in the number of yachts calling here. There are a few anchorages along the more sheltered north coast, but most yachts limit their stay to the port of Dili.

✦ COUNTRY PROFILE

The Portuguese established settlements on Timor in the early sixteenth century and Dutch traders first landed in 1613. The Portuguese and Dutch competed for influence for this corner of the Spice Islands until a series of agreements established boundaries between their territories. Dutch Timor, centred at Kupang, in the west, became part of the Republic of Indonesia in 1950. Portuguese Timor was forcibly annexed by Indonesia in late 1975 just as Portugal was going to grant the colony independence. The Indonesian occupation led to a bloody conflict in which an estimated 200,000 people lost their lives. In 1999, Portugal and Indonesia reached an agreement on a referendum for autonomy for East Timor, in which the majority of the East Timorese voted in favour of independence. A period of turbulence caused by anti-independence Timorese militias was eventually brought under control by the United Nations, and in 2002 Timor-Leste was recognized as an independent state.

The population is 1.2 million, most people being of mixed Malay, Polynesian and Papuan descent, but with a strong Portuguese influence. Portuguese is spoken, while the local language is Tetum. The capital is Dili.

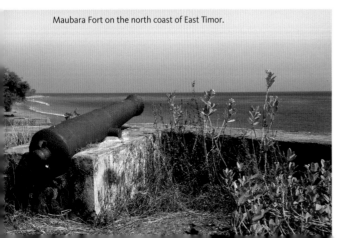
Maubara Fort on the north coast of East Timor.

✦ FORMALITIES

PORT OF ENTRY
Dili 8°32´S 125°32´E

The Port Authority should be contacted when you arrive. Formalities are straightforward. Visas are not required and an entry permit for 30 days will be issued on arrival.

The comprehensive cruising permit for Indonesia cannot be obtained in Dili.

✦ FACILITIES

Provisioning, with both local and imported produce, is good and fuel is available. The range of repair services is limited.

Website	
www.timor-leste.gov.tl	

Local time	UTC +9
Buoyage	IALA A
Currency	United States Dollar (USD)
Electricity	220V, 50Hz

Diplomatic missions	
USA	332 4684
Australia	332 2111
New Zealand	331 0087

Communications	
IDD 670	IAC 00

Emergency number	
112	

HONG KONG

IN SPITE OF ITS RELATIVELY small size, Hong Kong is one of Asia's leading yachting centres with an enthusiastic and active sailing community. Hong Kong is made up of the small Hong Kong Island, which is the administrative and business centre, and the Kowloon peninsula, the main district for shopping and entertainment. Between the two lies the well-protected Victoria Harbour. Also part of Hong Kong are the New Territories on the nearby mainland, as well as some 235 islands, many uninhabited, in the South China Sea.

Although offering limited cruising opportunities, Hong Kong is rarely bypassed by yachts in this part of the world, which are attracted both by the vibrant atmosphere of this dynamic metropolis and its excellent service and repair facilities. There are several yacht clubs where visiting boats are warmly received. A favourite outing for local sailors is to sail to a nearby bay or village for a seafood meal. It may not rate as a cruising highlight, but the quality of the food certainly does.

◆ COUNTRY PROFILE

Hong Kong was ceded to Britain in 1842 after the First Opium War, when Chinese efforts to expel the European opium traders failed. Hong Kong became an important trade centre and gateway to China, and in 1898 a 99-year lease was granted to Britain. In an agreement signed with Britain in 1984, China promised to respect Hong Kong's separate identity on expiry of the original lease. As a result, in 1997 Hong Kong reverted to Chinese sovereignty, but its special status will continue for another 50 years.

The population is over 7 million, mostly Chinese, with a small number of Europeans, Filipinos and Indonesians. Cantonese is the official language, but English is also widely used.

◆ CLIMATE

The climate is subtropical. June to September is hot, humid and rainy. October to January is cooler and less humid. The

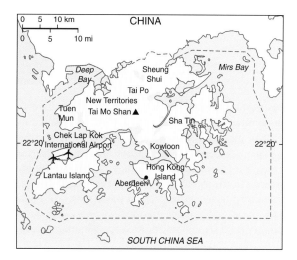

typhoon season is from May to December, with the highest frequency being between June and September.

✦ FORMALITIES

PORT OF ENTRY

Victoria Harbour 22°18´N 114°10´E

Port Operations should be called on Channel 12. Yachts may be boarded and searched in Hong Kong territorial waters, so a daylight arrival is therefore recommended. Yachts may anchor or go to a yacht club. Within 24 hours, you must report to immigration, and the marine department in the same building at the Government Pier on Hong Kong Island.

Nationals of most countries are granted a visa on arrival, the length of stay depending on the nationality – but it is normally 90 days. British citizens can receive six months. Yachts may remain up to six months, after which a pleasure vessel licence must be obtained.

The Royal Hong Kong Yacht Club

During typhoons, visiting yachts may seek refuge in an approved typhoon shelter for small craft, or secure to a Government B class mooring booked in advance.

Prohibited areas for yachts are Kai Tak Airport Area No 1, and 100m from both Green Island and Stonecutters Island.

Before departure, you must report to the port office to obtain a clearance permit, valid for 48 hours.

✦ FACILITIES

Mooring facilities for visitors are limited and it is almost impossible to find a space at the Royal Hong Kong Yacht Club, which is ideally located in the centre of Victoria Harbour. Visiting yachts usually gravitate to Hebe Haven Yacht Club, this being the safest option during the typhoon season. Most clubs have some repair and haulout facilities. Causeway Bay, where several yacht clubs and marinas are located, provides a whole range of both repair and haulout facilities in a relatively concentrated area. Several internationally known sailmakers are based in Hong Kong, and this is the place to order new sails. Marine equipment is easily available and there are several well-stocked chandleries. Provisioning in Hong Kong is good and fuel is widely available.

✦ CHARTER

There are no bareboat companies, but a number of operators offer individual yachts for charter, all of them crewed.

www.yachtchartershkg.com

Cruising Guides	
Cruising Guide to Southeast Asia Volume I	
From Yangon to Manila Bay: The Cruising Almanac 2005	
Website	
www.discoverhongkong.com	

Local time	UTC +8
Buoyage	IALA A
Currency	Hong Kong Dollar (HKD)
Electricity	220V, 50Hz

Diplomatic missions	
UK	2901 3182
USA	2523 9011
Australia	2827 8881
Canada	3719 4700
South Africa	2577 3279
New Zealand	2525 5044

Communications	
IDD 852	IAC 001

Emergency numbers	
112/999	

INDONESIA

THE INDONESIAN ARCHIPELAGO of 13,677 islands stretches from Australia to Asia and is the largest island group in the world. The main islands are Java, Sumatra, Irian Jaya (the western part of Papua New Guinea), and Kalimantan (formerly Borneo). Indonesia is a place of dense tropical forests, neat terraced rice fields and active volcanoes, the most famous being Krakatoa. The culture is rich both in traditions and relics from past civilizations as well as modern-day arts and crafts.

For many years Indonesia has been as tempting as forbidden fruit to cruising sailors because of the difficulty of obtaining a cruising permit. This is no longer the case as the permit is now only a formality, complicated but obtainable. Once in possession of this, the freedom of movement is virtually unrestricted. Yachts usually cruise the islands from east to west and, if this is planned to coincide with the southeast monsoon (May to September), this will benefit from favourable winds. A cruise along the island chain, preferably along the northern shores, offers a panoramic view of the scenic beauty of this country, each island differing from its neighbour. Just as different are the traditional sailing craft still encountered among the islands: single, double and treble hulled, from fragile one-man fishing boats to heavy schooners laden to the gunwhales with salt, copra, rice – and occasionally goats or a family's furniture – as much inter-island traffic is still done under sail.

Yachts arriving from the north should encounter more favourable winds during the northwest monsoon, from December to April, but this is not necessarily the ideal time as the weather is rainy and squally. This is also the cyclone season in the Timor and Arafura Seas, such storms occasionally affecting weather conditions in the southern islands. The tactic is to plan a voyage for the transitional period, and the best time to head south is during the spring period, from March to April, and sail north in the autumn, from September to October.

On the more remote islands you are often greeted by a crowd of curious people as such places are rarely visited by foreign yachts. Elsewhere you can come face to face with the mysterious dragons of Komodo, explore the wild interior of Kalimantan, follow a funeral procession on Bali, or visit the ancient ruins of Borobodur. For a long time Benoa Harbour in Bali has been the most popular port of call for cruising yachts. Bali is firmly on the beaten track both for sea and land tourists, but the Balinese have managed to remain generally unaffected and have retained a distinctive and rich culture, as well as being renowned for their artistic talents.

Recent political disturbances in some parts of this vast country have affected cruising boats very little, although the latest situation should be monitored carefully and uncertain areas given a wide berth. Personal safety concerns are not yet serious, but there have been a few cases of isolated incidents. Fortunately, the rich rewards of experiencing this unique country from the convenience of your own boat outweigh any intrinsic difficulties.

In a country where regulations seem to change often, and the whims of local officials can be both frustrating and unpredictable, one good solution to enjoy a hassle-free voyage through Indonesia is to join the Sail Indonesia Rally. This rally starts from Darwin in July each year and, over a period of some three months, meanders through the Indonesian archipelago, giving participants the opportunity to join in a series of cultural festivals as the fleet makes its way through the islands of Saumlaki, Alor, Lembata, Flores, Sulawesi, Bali, Java, Borneo, Belitung and finally Batam, just south of Singapore. In Batam the event joins up with the Sail Malaysia Rally, the route continuing, via Singapore, all the way to Langkawi.

◆ COUNTRY PROFILE

Some of the Indonesian islands were populated half a million years ago, as proved by the Java Man remains discovered in 1891 and now known as *Pithecanthropus erectus*. Over the years, many people migrated to Indonesia from Asia, and by the first century the Indian influence gained predominance. During the fourteenth century the expansion of Islam through Arab traders marked a new era, and only on Bali does the Hindu legacy survive. Marco Polo was the first European to arrive, landing on Sumatra in 1292, followed by the Portuguese in 1509, who in the coming years expanded their sphere of trading and eventually reaching what came to

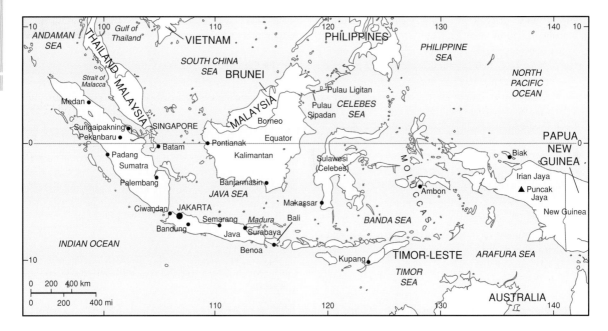

be known as the Spice Islands. At the end of the sixteenth century the Dutch arrived and for 300 years controlled the Indonesian archipelago, their widespread colony being called the Dutch East Indies. In the early twentieth century the movement for independence gathered momentum and, after the end of the Japanese occupation during the Second World War, the Republic of Indonesia was declared in 1945. A succession of dictatorships led by military leaders came to an end in 1998 and the country is now ruled by a democratically elected government.

With 240 million inhabitants, Indonesia is the fifth most populous country in the world. The Indonesians are a Malay race, but there are also Chinese and European minorities, and some aboriginal tribes in Kalimantan and Irian Jaya. Bahasa Indonesia, related to Malay, is the national language, but English is widely used. There are 250 local languages and dialects. Jakarta on Java is the capital.

✦ CLIMATE

The climate is tropical in the greater part of this vast archipelago and equatorial in the northern part. The weather is mostly hot and humid, and there are only two seasons, a wet and a dry season. July to September is the dry season, while December to January is the rainiest period. The islands are under the influence of the southeast monsoon from April to October and the northwest monsoon from November to March, although land and sea breezes predominate close to the islands. The islands are not directly affected by tropical cyclones.

✦ FORMALITIES

PORTS OF ENTRY		
Java: Tanjung Priok (Jakarta)	6°06´S 106°52´E	
Tanjung Perak (Surabaya)	7°12´S 112°44´E	
Tanjung Emas (Semarang)	6°58´S 110°25´E	
Banda Islands: Banda Neira	4°35´S 129°55´E	
Batam Island: Batu Ampar	1°10´N 104°00´E	
Nongsa Point Marina	1°11.7´N 104°5.9´E	
Riau Islands: Tanjungpinang	0°56´N 104°27´E	
Bali: Benoa 8°45´S 115°15´E	Padang Bai 8°31´S 115°35´E	
Lombok: Lembar	8°44´S 116°04´E	
Sulawesi: Bitung 1°26´N 125°11´E	Manado 1°30´N 124°50´E	
Ujung Padang	5°08.5´S 119°24´E	
Kalimantan: Banjarmasin	3°20 S 114°35´E	
Samarinda 0°30´S 117°10´E	Lingkas 3°15´N 117°40´E	
Pontianak	0°01´S 109°21´E	
Sumatra: Belawan (Medan)	3°48´N 98°43´E	
Batu Ampar (Batam)	1°10´N 104°00´E	
Teluk Bayur	0°59.5´S 100°22.3´E	
Pulau We: Sabang	5°53´N 95°19´E	
Maluku: Yos Sudarso (Ambon)	3°42´S 128°10´E	
Ternate	0°46.5´N 127°27´E	
Semarang: Tanjung Emas	6°59.5´S 110°24´E	
Timor: Kupang	10°10´S 123°34´E	

A cruising and security permit (CAIT) is required and this must be obtained in advance. Although it is possible to obtain the permit by contacting the authorities direct, it is frustrating and time-consuming, so it is better to use the services of an agent (cait@indo.net.id). The better alternative is to join one of the rallies sailing to Indonesia, the organizers of which obtain permits for all participants and deal with all formalities.

Boats possessing a cruising permit and whose crews have obtained visas in advance may enter at the first port marked on the permit even if it is not one of the above. It is wise to have a lot of photocopies of the CAIT, and the ship's papers, as officials in all the ports will want a copy.

At a port of entry, yachts should anchor and wait for the officials. If no official comes to the yacht after a reasonable time the captain should go ashore and contact the authorities. No one else must go ashore or make contact with other vessels until clearance is complete.

Usually the following offices have to be visited: quarantine, customs, immigration and port authority, in that order. Occasionally quarantine and customs officials may insist on inspecting the boat personally. In some ports local agents offer to deal with all formalities for a fee.

It is recommended to obtain a visa in advance from an Indonesian diplomatic mission. Nationals of most countries can obtain a visa on arrival, but these are only issued at a limited number of international ports, such as Kupang, Benoa (Bali) or Batam. This type of visa will only be issued for 30 days, with no extensions.

The customs, immigration and port authority offices must be visited again when clearing out.

Yachts without a cruising permit may stop in Indonesia in a serious emergency, but only for 48 hours and only at one of the ports of entry. This may be extended in the case of a genuine emergency.

In principle, a yacht can stay indefinitely in Indonesia, provided the security clearance is extended.

A new regulation introduced by the Ministry of Finance in 2007, but only starting to be applied in 2009, stipulates that on arrival in Indonesia all foreign-flagged yachts must pay an import duty to the Bank of Indonesia based on a percentage of the value of the vessel. The bond is refundable when the yacht leaves Indonesia. This bond has caused both concern and confusion, both among visiting sailors and Indonesian marinas and other operators. The regulation will probably be suspended, but if it remains in force yachts visiting Indonesia have three options: to choose a first port of entry where officials are known not to apply this rule, to go to a marina that has been contacted in advance and that will arrange for the rule to be waived or, the simplest solution, to join the Sail Indonesia Rally or a similar officially sanctioned event. Participants in such events are exempt from the requirement for the cruising permit, and also such a bond.

✦ FACILITIES

Yachting facilities are limited and only available in the few places where there is either a local yachting community, such as Java, or in those frequented by cruising boats, such as Bali Marina or Nongsa Point Marina, on Batam Island near Singapore. Spare parts and marine supplies are difficult to find and essential spares have to be ordered from Australia or Singapore. Provisioning in most islands is fairly basic, although there is a good supply of locally grown fruit and vegetables everywhere. Fuel is widely available and relatively cheap as Indonesia is an oil-producing country.

Cruising Guide	
Cruising Guide to Southeast Asia Volume II	
Websites	
www.tourism.indonesia.com	
www.balimarina.com	
www.sailindonesia.net	
Local time	Jakarta UTC +7, Bali UTC +8,
	Kupang UTC +8, Irian Jaya UTC +9,
Buoyage	IALA A
Currency	Indonesian Rupiah (IDR)
Electricity	230V, 50Hz
Diplomatic missions	
UK	21 2356 5200
USA	21 3435 9054
Australia	21 2550 5555
Canada	21 2550 7800
South Africa	21 574 0660
New Zealand	21 2995 5800
Communications	
IDD 62	IAC Indosat 001 Satelindo 008
Emergency numbers 112	Ambulance 118 Police 110

JAPAN

JAPAN IS MADE UP OF FOUR MAIN ISLANDS that stretch about 1,600 miles in a southwest to northwest direction. Central Honshu is the largest, most heavily populated and industrialized; Hokkaido to the north is forested and mountainous; Kyushu and Shikoku to the south are smaller. There are also several thousand smaller islands. Most of Japan is mountainous and volcanic, with frequent earthquakes. Mount Fuji, an almost perfectly symmetrical cone, is the highest point at 3,776m (12,400ft).

Being distant from the popular cruising routes, not many yachts visit Japan, but those that do find the Japanese very welcoming, often going out of their way to help visiting sailors. Formalities are quite strict and permission to visit some ports may have to be obtained. Until not so long ago, even local yachts were a rarity as Japan does have not have a strong sailing tradition. In the early 1990s the government decided to develop the yachting industry, more marinas were built, and international regattas were organized. One aspect that even the ingenious Japanese cannot do much about is their weather, which does not encourage cruising – as a cruise often turns into a battle against wind and current.

Fortunately, this one major disadvantage is made up for by the many attractions that Japan offers the visiting sailor. One such is the Inland Sea, Seto Naikai, a large body of water connected by three passes to the surrounding ocean, which allows a yacht access into the very heart of the country. The place abounds in pretty anchorages and picturesque fishing harbours, but there are also marinas as well as yacht clubs, which offer hospitality to visitors. There is a lot of traffic in coastal waters, both commercial and fishing vessels, but sailing at night does not present great problems as all vessels

are well lit and attentive. Typhoons are an almost constant threat, but weather forecasts are reliable and nearly every port has a typhoon shelter.

Boats on their way to Japan can sample one of Japan's most attractive areas as they sail along the Ryukyu Islands or Nansei-shoto, a long chain of small islands that stretches in an arc from Okinawa to Kyushu. These subtropical islands have many well-protected harbours and the island of Anami-o-Shima and its port of Koniya are considered the gems of this archipelago. Their drawback is that they lie astride the path often taken by typhoons, and this fact needs to be taken into account when planning a cruise through this area.

✦ COUNTRY PROFILE

The earliest inhabitants of these islands probably came from Korea and China. By the fourth century the country was already developing into a united state and a distinctive national culture emerged. At the end of the twelfth century civil wars between leading clans disrupted the country and a system of separate military chiefdoms emerged, each led by a shogun. This situation lasted into the nineteenth century, a period when Japan was largely closed to the outside world. At the end of the nineteenth century a new spirit arose, with a determined effort to modernize the country, both its political institutions and its economy, which saw a rapid process of industrialization. After its defeat in the Second World War, Japan made a spectacular recovery to become a global economic power.

The population numbers 127 million. Japanese is the official language and English is spoken in the main centres. Tokyo is the capital.

Matsushima Bay is considered one of Japan's most scenic locations.

CLIMATE

The climate is very varied, from temperate in the north to subtropical in the south. The climate is greatly influenced by the seasonal wind reversal of the two monsoons. Summer sees southerly winds and a rainy season in June and July, while winters are generally drier with predominantly northeast winds. Typhoons are most frequent, from mid-July to October, but can occur practically at any time.

FORMALITIES

PORTS OF ENTRY

Naha (Okinawa Island) 26°13′ N 127°40′ E

Aioi	34°46′ N 134°28′ E	Fukuyama	34°26′ N 133°27′ E
Kobe	34°40′ N 135°13′ E	Ishigaki	24°23.6′ N 124°12′ E
Nagasaki	32°43′ N 129°50′ E	Nagoya	35°03′ N 136°51′ E
Osaka	34°39′ N 135°24′ E	Shimonoseki	33°56′ N 130°56′ E
Tokyo	35°41′ N 139°44′ E	Yokohama	35°27′ N 139°40′ E

Although only the above are listed as official ports of entry, in practice visiting yachts can clear in at any port as all ports have the relevant offices.

Full information on requirements can be found on the Coast Guard website. The Coast Guard of the port of destination must be contacted a minimum of 24 hours before arrival to give an ETA. A form with the details required can be downloaded from the Coast Guard website and faxed or emailed to the Coast Guard office. There is a fine of $5,000 for entering without 24-hour notification.

The entry procedure is lengthy, but courteous. Inspections will be carried out by quarantine, customs and immigration, and possibly the maritime safety agency. A de-ratting certificate must be shown or the yacht will be checked. These offices are normally in the same building in the main harbour and sometimes yachts can tie up to their jetty to complete formalities. If officials do not come to the yacht, the captain should go to their offices.

Nationals of almost all countries will be given a 90-day visa on arrival.

Clearance with customs and immigration must be carried out at every port after the initial entry.

A detailed itinerary must be submitted to the Coast Guard at the first port of entry listing all possible stops, as later additions are difficult. Once approved, this will act as a cruising permit. To cruise the Inland Sea a cruising permit must be obtained from the Department of Transportation in Hiroshima.

A number of ports are closed to yachts – such as Urakawa, to the southeast of Hokkaido – and these can only be entered in an emergency.

FACILITIES

Repair facilities are generally good and there are boatyards in most ports. Marine equipment and spares are widely available. Marinas in the Inland Sea are generally expensive, but some of them offer free berthing to foreign visitors for a few days. There are no charges for tying up to a dock in a commercial or fishing harbour. There are many yacht clubs, most of whom give free membership to visiting foreign sailors and are good sources of local information.

Cruising Guide
Japan Hydrographic Department Charts

Websites
www.jnto.go.jp (Japanese Tourism Office)
www.kaiho.mlit.go.jp (Japanese Coast Guard for arrival forms and also essential charts)
www.sail-japan.info (general yachting information)

Local time	UTC +9
Buoyage	IALA B
Currency	Japanese Yen (JPY)
Electricity	100V, 50Hz

Diplomatic missions

UK	3 5211 1100	Canada	3 5412 6200
USA	3 3224 5000	South Africa	3 3265 3366
Australia	3 5232 4111	New Zealand	3 3467 2271

Communications	**Emergency numbers**
IDD 81 IAC 010	112 Ambulance 119 Police 110

MACAU

Macau occupies a peninsula on the western side of the Pearl River Delta and also includes the islands of Taipa and Coloane. Macau was the first and last colony on Chinese soil and, after nearly five centuries under Portuguese administration, Macau reverted to China at the end of 1999. Similar to Hong Kong, the government in Beijing has guaranteed the unimpeded continuation of Macau's status as a centre for international commerce. Reflecting its old trading history, the town is a mixture of old colonial styles with Chinese touches. As it has retained more of its old character and the atmosphere is also less frenetic, it may be more interesting to visit than neighbouring Hong Kong.

✦ COUNTRY PROFILE

Before the Portuguese arrived in the sixteenth century, there was only a Chinese village here and when the Portuguese sailors asked the name, the locals replied 'A-Ma-Gao', meaning the Bay of A-Ma, who was a Chinese goddess popular with seafarers and fishermen. A-Ma-Gao became corrupted into the name 'Macao' and eventually changed to 'Macau'. As China and Japan began trading with the European powers, Macau saw an increase in its prosperity. This Portuguese territory also became a base for the introduction of Christianity into China and Japan. Macau's privileged trading position ended with the establishment of Hong Kong by the British in the mid-nineteenth century, only 40 miles northeast of Macau and with a better deepwater port. Macau reverted to Chinese sovereignty at the end of 1999, and an agreement with China guarantees the continuation of Macau's current status for 50 years.

The population of 560,000 are mostly Chinese with about 3 per cent Portuguese and other Europeans. Portuguese and Cantonese are the official languages, but English is widely spoken.

✦ CLIMATE

The climate is subtropical. June to September is hot, humid and rainy. October to January is cooler and less humid. The best period is the autumn, October to December. May to September is hot and humid, with occasional typhoons.

✦ FORMALITIES

PORT OF ENTRY
Macau 22°10´N 113°33´E

Arriving yachts should contact Macau Port Control and ask for instructions on where to dock to complete formalities. You may be allowed to anchor off the Macau Sailing Club.

Visas are not required for most nationalities for stays of up to 30 or 90 days, depending on nationality.

✦ FACILITIES

Visiting boats normally anchor off the Macau Sailing Club located at Cheoc Van Beach on Coloane Island. A small marina is under construction on the northwest side of the peninsula. Repair facilities are available at a government workshop in the port area, which also has a slipway, but because of the proximity of Hong Kong, those in need of major repairs should proceed there.

Cruising Guides
Cruising Guide to Southeast Asia Volume I
From Yangon to Manila Bay: The Cruising Almanac 2005

Website
www.macautourism.gov.mo

Local time	UTC +8
Buoyage	IALA A
Currency	Pataca (M$ or MOP$)
Electricity	110/220V, 50Hz

Diplomatic missions
UK   6850886
Other countries: see Hong Kong

Communications	**Emergency numbers**
IDD 853 IAC 001	112/999

The map shows the peninsula of Macau, China, Zhujiang Kou, Breakwater, Ilha da Taipa, Lotus Bridge, Macau International Airport, Coloane, and the South China Sea, with coordinates 113°32', 113°36', 22°12', 22°08'.

MALAYSIA

THE FEDERATION OF MALAYSIA consists of 13 states: the eleven that are grouped together as Western Malaysia stretched out on the long Malay Peninsula between Thailand and Singapore; and the states of Sabah and Sarawak that constitute Eastern Malaysia, and which occupy the north coast of Borneo. Malaysia is a constitutional monarchy in which the throne is taken in rotation by each sultan of the principal states. It is a country of tropical rainforests and temperate highlands, which is fast modernizing and yet retains many traditional ways.

The west coast of the Malay Peninsula attracts most cruising yachts, being usually on their way north from Singapore to Thailand. There are several good ports to break the passage and much to see – from the attractive old city of Malacca and the fishing port of Lumut, to the islands of Penang and Langkawi. The latter is close to the border with Thailand and boasts the finest scenery anywhere in Malaysian waters. The best weather is during the northeast monsoon when Malaysia's west coast provides an excellent lee. In contrast, the east coast is less of a cruising destination as its ports are exposed during the more pleasant northeast monsoon and there is little boat movement during the sultry, humid and rainy southwest monsoon.

A very different scene unfolds for those heading for Sabah or Sarawak. Few sailors who call there miss the opportunity to visit the interior of Borneo, parts of which are still covered in primeval jungle, but whose rich flora and fauna are under serious threat of relentless deforestation and development. Sutera Harbour Marina at Kota Kinabalu in Sabah is one of the safest places to leave the boat unattended to take a trip along one of the muddy rivers that meander through the tropical forest to reach far into the interior of Borneo. Some may be even tempted to make it to the top of Mount Kinabalu, described as the most climber-friendly high mountain in the world. It is the highest peak south of the Himalayas.

An alternative way to enjoy cruising through these islands without being exposed to the unavoidable frustration of dealing with formalities is to join one of the rallies that are proving increasingly popular among yachts visiting South East Asia. The Sail Malaysia organization runs two annual events, one heading east, the other north. Sail Malaysia Passage to the East starts in Penang in May and makes its way around the peninsula to arrive in Kota Kinabalu by early August. It later joins up with the Sail Indonesia Rally that started in Darwin in July. Later in the year, the Sail Malaysia Passage to Langkawi takes over from Sail Indonesia and, after calling at various places along the western coast of the peninsula, concludes in Langkawi in late December.

The Hole in the Wall anchorage near Langkawi.

✦ COUNTRY PROFILE

From ancient times the Malay Peninsula has played an essential role in the trade routes from Asia to the rest of the world, and the influences of Indian, Chinese, Thai, Arab and European traders can still be seen in many places. Seafaring traders from India brought with them Hinduism and, after the Muslim conquest of India, the religion of Islam was spread by Muslim traders throughout South East Asia.

In 1511 the Portuguese conquered Malacca, which they held until 1641 when their Dutch rivals seized it. In 1824 the British gained possession of the city and gradually the entire peninsula came under British rule. In 1963 Malaysia came into being as the federation of the Peninsular States, Sabah, Sarawak and Singapore, the latter leaving the federation in 1965. The 26 million inhabitants are Malay, who form the majority, as well as Chinese and Indian minorities, and also the indigenous peoples of Sabah and Sarawak. Bahasa Malaysia (Malay) is the official language, but English is widely used. Kuala Lumpur is the capital, with nearby Port Kelang being its outlet to the sea.

✦ CLIMATE

The climate is tropical. November to February is the rainy season when sudden downpours are frequent. The northeast monsoon is from November to March, but on the west coast, land breezes have a major effect on sailing conditions. The southwest monsoon lasts from May to October and is the wet season. Temperatures are very stable throughout the year, ranging between an average minimum of 23°C/73°F and a maximum of 32°C/90°F.

✦ FORMALITIES

PORTS OF ENTRY

Malay Peninsula: Kuala Perlis 6°24′N 100°07′E	
Talaga Harbour 6°23′N 99°41′W	Kuah 6°19′N 99°51′E
Kuala Kedah 6°07′N 100°17′E	Penang 5°25′N 100°20′E
Lumut 4°16′N 100°39′E	Telek Intan 4°01′N 101°01′E
Port Kelang 3°00′N 101°24′E	Port Dickson 2°31′N 101°47′E
Melaka/Malacca 2°15′N 102°35′E	Muar 2°02′N 102°34′E
Johore Bahru 1°28′N 103°50′E	
Pasir Gudang/Johore Port 1°26′N 103°54′E	
Pulau Langkawi 6°18′N 99°50′E	Mersing 2°26′N 103°51′E
Kuantan 3°58′N 103°26′E	
Kemaman/Tanjong Berhala 4°15′N 103°28′E	
Kerteh 4°28′N 103°24′E	Kuala Trenganu 5°20′N 103°09′E
Tumpat 6°13′N 102°11′E	
Sarawak: Kuching 1°34′N 110°24′E	Sibu 2°17′N 111°49′E
Bintulu 3°10′N 113°02′E	Miri 4°23′N 113°59′E
Sabah: Labuan 5°16′N 115°09′E	
Kota Kinabalu 6°00′N 116°04′E	Lahad Datu 5°02′N 118°20′E
Sandakan 5°50′N 188°08′E	Tawau 4°15′N 117°53′E

Port Kelang: Yachts should proceed up the east channel to the mooring area off the Royal Selangor Yacht Club. There is a regular launch service to the club, where the office will give a map showing the location of customs, immigration and harbourmaster's offices, all of which are in the nearby commercial port area.

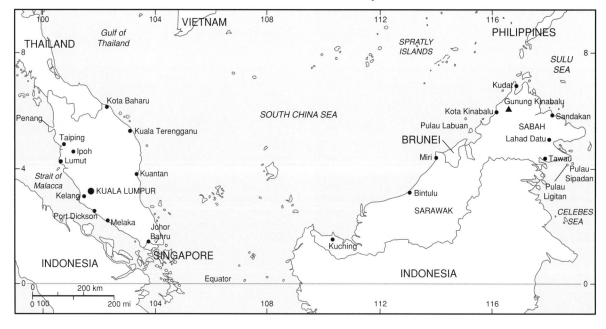

Langkawi: There are two clearance facilities: at Telaga Harbour and the Kuah ferry terminal at Jetty Point.

Sarawak: Kuching is about 20 miles up the Sungai Sarawak, which is well buoyed but has strong currents and is best negotiated one hour after low tide. There is a floating pontoon in front of the town, which visiting yachts may use. All authorities must be visited, even if coming from mainland Malaysia.

Sabah: There are a couple of marinas in Kota Kinabalu where you can moor the boat before proceeding into the commercial harbour to visit the various offices. As Labuan enjoys a certain degree of autonomy, you are supposed to clear immigration on arrival, even if coming from Sabah or another Malaysian state, but this is not always enforced.

On arrival, the captain must clear in with the marine department, immigration, customs and health. Most nationalities are given a visitor's permit on arrival, valid from 30 to 90 days depending on the nationality. Extensions are difficult to obtain and most sailors resolve that problem by going to a neighbouring country for a few days and getting a new visa on their return. There is no limit on the time yachts may stay.

The health department may require a de-ratting certificate or a de-ratting exemption certificate.

The Malaysian authorities make it very clear that trafficking in illegal drugs carries the death penalty, and that this applies also to foreign nationals. This death penalty has been carried out.

Yachts must clear in and out of each port visited. Those who have entered at one of the ports on the Malay Peninsula must obtain a new cruising permit for Sabah and Sarawak.

On departure, yachts should leave from an official port of entry, but in order to stop at a place that does not have facilities for clearance, permission may be obtained when departure clearance is requested.

Boats anchored at Telaga Marina.

◆ FACILITIES

The best facilities are in the Port Kelang area, where the Royal Selangor Yacht Club is based. Port Kelang is also a good base for trips to the capital, Kuala Lumpur, or to leave the boat for longer visits into the interior or the neighbouring countries. There are several small boatyards, often with their own slips, on both coasts of the peninsula, but as they usually only work on local craft, standards are not high. Haulout facilities are available at Pangkor, while at nearby Lumut the yacht club has a marina with limited facilities. Langkawi, now the favourite cruising destination in Malaysia, has seen a steady improvement in its facilities as a determined effort is being made to turn this area into the premier yachting centre in South East Asia. Rebak Marina has been expanded and has a range of repair facilities. The duty-free status of Langkawi makes it a good place for buying or ordering equipment.

Limited repairs are obtainable in Kuching at the Industrial and Scientific Company, but mooring facilities are poor. In Sabah there are now a number of marinas offering a range of services. Sutera Harbour Marina near Kota Kinabalu has berths for superyachts and a 70-ton travelift. Labuan Marina is reported to be under renovation.

◆ CHARTER

Langkawi is becoming a popular charter location, with Sunsail being the first international operator to be based there, along with Phuket Boat Charter. Bareboat charter has yet to take off elsewhere in Malaysia.

www.sunsail.com
www.phuket-boatcharter.com

Cruising Guides
Cruising Guide to Southeast Asia Volumes I and II
Southeast Asia Pilot

Websites
www.tourism.gov.my
www.langkawi-gazette.com
www.8north.com (marine facilities in Langkawi area)
www.sailmalaysia.net

Local time	UTC +8
Buoyage	IALA A
Currency	Malaysian Ringgit (MYR)
Electricity	240V, 50Hz

Diplomatic missions

UK	3 2170 2200	Canada	3 2718 3333
USA	3 2168 5000	South Africa	3 2170 2412
Australia	3 2146 5555	New Zealand	3 2078 2533

Communications	**Emergency number**
IDD 60 IAC 00	999

MYANMAR

Myanmar, formerly known as Burma, is a diamond-shaped country, its southern and western coasts fronting the Bay of Bengal and the Andaman Sea. Mountains surround the central fertile lowland bisected by the Irrawaddy river which ends in a wide delta, on which stands the capital and main seaport, Yangon, formerly called Rangoon.

The southern part of the country to the Thai border is a very attractive area and has the potential of becoming a perfect cruising destination. It is easily accessible from Phuket, and the Thai Similan archipelago can be visited en route before making for the well-sheltered Khawtung harbour (Victoria Point). This Myanmar port of entry is set at the mouth of Pakchan river opposite the port of Ranong in Thailand. The Mergui archipelago, which stretches north from here, offers many cruising possibilities among the hundreds of islands and cays. After being off limits for decades, in recent years the Myanmar authorities have permitted Thai dive companies to operate in this area and a few cruising boats have also benefited from this relaxation. The wildlife both on land and sea is particularly rich after being undisturbed during the long years of isolation.

✦ COUNTRY PROFILE

From around 3000 BCE successive migrations of peoples came down the Irrawaddy valley from Tibet and China. Several civilizations flourished and fell, until in the nineteenth century British dominance gradually increased and Burma was incorporated into Britain's Indian Empire. Nationalist feelings grew and independence was finally achieved in 1948. In 1990 an election was won by the National League of Democracy, led by Aung San Suu Kyi, but the military refused to yield power, put her under house arrest and, in spite of continuous international pressure, have refused to allow any expression of democracy or free elections. The military regime has announced elections for 2010.

The population is around 48 million. The majority are Myanmans, with some indigenous peoples such as Shan, Karen, Rakhine and Mon, as well as Indian and Chinese minorities. The official language is Myanmar.

✦ CLIMATE

The climate is tropical and is dominated by the two monsoons. The dry northeast monsoon lasts from November to March.

Most rain falls during the southwest monsoon, from May to October. In May 2008 Typhoon Nargis struck Myanmar, killing 140,000 and causing widespread devastation.

✦ FORMALITIES

Khawtung: Vessels should anchor off the Customs House Pier on the west shore of the harbour. The authorities must be advised of the yacht's ETA by email and the vessel must keep well away from the coast until arriving at this official port of entry (mtt.mht@mptmail.net.mm).

PORTS OF ENTRY

Yangon 16°46′ N 96°10′ E	
Khawtung (Victoria Point Harbour) 9°59′ N 98°33′ E	

Entry formalities are extensive and it is compulsory to have an official Myanmar guide on board while the vessel is in territorial waters.

A cruising permit must be obtained in advance, which can be arranged by agents in Phuket or, as has been reported, by making a personal visit to Yangon.

All nationalities require a visa, valid for a maximum of 28 days, which can be obtained in Bangkok, Kuala Lumpur or Singapore.

✦ FACILITIES

Facilities for yachts are practically non-existent. Only simple repairs are available, usually where there are fishing boats. Fuel is only obtainable in the larger ports.

✦ CHARTER

SEAL was the first charter operator to be allowed by the Myanmar government to access the Mergui archipelago. From its base in Phuket, its small fleet of crewed yachts run charters throughout the Andaman Sea, including Myanmar and the Andaman Islands.

www.seal-asia.com

Cruising Guides
Andaman Sea Pilot
Cruising Guide to Southeast Asia Volume II
From Yangon to Manila Bay: The Cruising Almanac 2005

Website
www.myanmar-tourism.com

Local time	UTC +6.5
Buoyage	IALA A
Currency	Myanmar Kyat (MMK)
Electricity	230V, 50Hz

Diplomatic missions

UK	1 370863
USA	1 536509
Australia	1 251810

Communications

IDD 95	IAC 00

Emergency number
999

PHILIPPINES

THE PHILIPPINES ARE an archipelago of over seven thousand islands that are divided into three regions: Luzon to the north, Visayas in the centre, and Mindanao in the south. The islands are mountainous and volcanic, with fertile plains and tropical rainforests. The Philippines have been a popular cruising destination for many years. Daysailing through the archipelago is undoubtedly the best way to visit this vast area and a good anchorage can be found every night. This also avoids the danger of running into one of the many unlit fishing boats, as well as their nets or traps. Cebu and the surrounding islands have some of the most attractive anchorages, while the ports of Romblon and Puerto Galera are perpetual favourites among visiting sailors. The pleasure of sailing among these islands is to drop the anchor in front of small villages where people go about their daily chores and time feels as if it is standing still. Wildlife in these largely unspoilt islands is rich and varied, and there are many endemic species of rare birds.

Facing the South China Sea on the western side of the archipelago, Palawan is another island reputed for its natural beauty. Its main attraction is a 5-mile-long underground river that can be easily reached from Puerto Princesa and is navigable by small craft for its entire length. The river winds through a spectacular cave before emptying into the South China Sea.

The most frequented area is around the capital, Manila, as its proximity to Hong Kong makes it a favourite destination both among local cruising sailors and as the finishing point for various races.

Coron Island near Palawan

All sailors who have visited the Philippines stress that people are extremely friendly everywhere and that safety has not been a real concern. In spite of rumours about the danger of piracy in the Sulu Sea, no cases involving yachts have been reported for a long time. Mindanao itself has seen some incidents involving land tourists, and while the situation in that part of the country remains uncertain, it is best avoided. Fortunately, there are plenty of other areas that can be cruised in total safety.

✦ COUNTRY PROFILE

The indigenous population came originally from the Asian mainland and developed a distinctive culture and system of government. Over the centuries, the islands have been regularly visited by Chinese, Arab and Indian traders. Ferdinand Magellan's arrival on the island of Cebu in 1521 marked the first European contact. It was here that this skilled Portuguese navigator, in the pay of the Spanish Crown, lost his life at the hands of Lapulapu, a local chief. The islands were named after King Philip II of Spain, and soon afterwards the Spaniards asserted their rule, which continued until 1898. Spain's defeat in the war with the USA sparked a revolution, but independence was brief and the USA ruled the islands until the Second World War. Independence was finally achieved in 1946. In spite of occasional abuses of power, the fragile democratic system continues to survive in a country beset by social and religious problems.

Most of the 98 million Filipinos are of Malay origin, with some inhabitants of Chinese, Spanish, Indian and American ancestry. Filipino or Tagalog is the national language. There are 87 languages and 111 dialects spoken. English is widely used and also some Spanish. The Philippines are the only Christian nation in Asia, with the exception of Mindanao, where most are Muslim. Manila is the capital on the island of Luzon.

✦ CLIMATE

The Philippines have a tropical climate. The rainy southwest monsoon season is from June to September, the dry season from October to May. The average temperature is 27°C/81°F and humidity is high. The Philippines have a high incidence of typhoons, which are most frequent between June and October. The best season for cruising is from early January to mid-May when the weather is pleasant and the danger of typhoons is lowest.

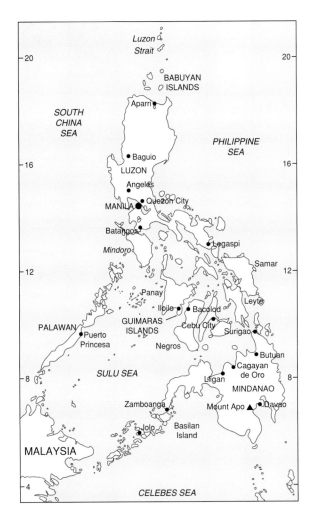

Manila: The Manila Yacht Club should be contacted on arrival and it will arrange for a team of customs, immigration and quarantine officials to visit the yacht.

Nationals of most countries are given a 21-day visa on arrival. For stays longer than 21 days, it is necessary to get a visa in advance. It is advisable that anyone planning to cruise in the Philippines should obtain a 60-day visa in advance. Extensions of this visa for a further 60 days can be obtained from immigration in Cebu or Manila only.

Yachts are allowed to remain for one year.

A bridge, which does not appear on most charts, now crosses Panaon Straits, between Leyte and Panaon. Its reported position is 10° 10´N 125° 08´E, and its height, at mean low water, is 14m (46ft).

✦ FACILITIES

General repair facilities, such as engine or electrical repair, are available in most centres, with the widest range being concentrated in and around Manila and its yacht club. There is also a good range of amenities in Subic Bay. One of the best yards dealing with yachts of all sizes is the Colorado Shipyard Corporation in Cebu City. It has a wide range of repair facilities and three slipways. There are small boatyards in various islands and the Filipinos are skilled workers, particularly in wood. Fuel is obtainable in most places; provisions and fresh produce are widely available.

✦ CHARTER

There are a small number of charter operators, but only Yacht Charter Philippines, based in Puerto Galera, offers bareboat rentals. All other companies offer crewed yachts, such as Adventure Asia Yacht Charters, based in Cebu City.

www.adventureasiacharters.com
www.yacht-charter-philippines.com

Cruising Guide
Cruising Guide to Southeast Asia Volume I

Websites
www.philtourism.com
www.sailphi.org.ph (information on yacht clubs and sailing events)

Local time	UTC +8	**Currency**	Philippine Peso (PHP)
Buoyage	IALA B	**Electricity**	220V, 60Hz

Diplomatic missions			
UK	2 858 2200	Canada	2 857 9000
USA	2 301 2000	South Africa	2 755 8826
Australia	2 757 8100	New Zealand	2 891 5358

Communications	**Emergency numbers**
IDD 63 IAC 00	112/117

✦ FORMALITIES

PORTS OF ENTRY

Luzon: Manila 14°35´N 120°58´E	Aparri 18°21´N 121°38´E
San Fernando La Union 16°37´N 120°19´E	
Subic Bay 14°48´N 120°16´E	Tabaco 13°22´N 123°44´E
Legaspi 13°09´N 123°45´E	Batangas 13°45.5´N 121°2.4´E
Cebu Island: Cebu City 10°18´N 123°54´E	
Iloilo 10°41´N 122°35´E	
Palawan: Puerto Princesa 9°44´N 118°43´E	
Mindanao: Davao 7°04´N 125°37´E	
Zamboanga 6°54´N 122°04´E	
Cagayan de Oro 8°29´N 124°39´E	

Yachts must clear in at a designated port of entry before the crew may go ashore. Overnight stops while proceeding to such a port are normally tolerated, but there should be no contact with anyone before clearance formalities have been completed.

SINGAPORE

SINGAPORE IS AN ISLAND STATE lying off the southern point of the Malay Peninsula and is linked to the Malaysian state of Johor by a long causeway. The fast-moving city and overcrowded harbour has little to recommend it as a cruising destination in itself. However, as many sailors arrive in Singapore after a lengthy cruise, often in undeveloped areas, this clean, well-organized city has its attractions, and as a convenient stop for provisioning and essential services it is difficult to beat. Virtually everything is available in Singapore, although it can take time to find it. Occasionally this can be frustrating, but chasing an elusive spare part in this cosmopolitan city is an experience in itself.

The opening of the first purpose-built marina, the luxurious Raffles Marina, in Tuas on the west side of the island, made Singapore much more attractive to those who prefer to dock in a marina. There are now several more marinas either in Singapore itself or close by in the neighbouring countries. What is in short supply to the regret of some sailors cruising on a limited budget is the steady disappearance of anchorages. The designated small boat anchorage off the East Coast Park is in an exposed and inconvenient place. Even the once favourite Changi Bay is now mostly occupied by moorings laid down by the local Changi Sailing Club. The club continues its tradition of being welcoming to visitors, as does the Republic of Singapore Yacht Club, which also has moorings for non-members. The most centrally located marina is Keppel Bay, something that cannot be said of Raffles Marina, which is far from downtown Singapore.

✦ COUNTRY PROFILE

By the seventh century Singapore was a trading centre for Sumatra's ancient Srivijaya Empire, and by the thirteenth century had become one of its three kingdoms. In 1819 Sir Thomas Stamford Raffles chose the island as a British maritime base. By his death in 1827, the Sultan of Johor had ceded full sovereignty of the island to Britain. During the Second World War the Japanese occupied Singapore by attacking this strategically important bastion not from the sea, as expected by its British defenders, but surging overland from neighbouring Malaya. With peace came demands for self-determination, and in 1959 Singapore became a self-governing state. For two years Singapore was one of the 14 States of the Malaysian Federation, but in 1965 it became an independent republic.

The population of 4.6 million are mostly Chinese (77 per cent), also Malay (14 per cent), Indian (8 per cent) and there are some European minorities. Mandarin Chinese, English,

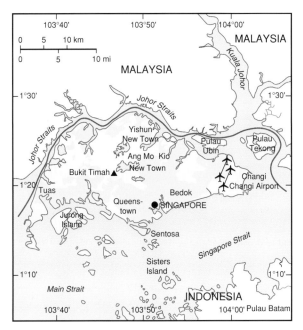

Malay and Tamil are the four official languages spoken in this diverse cosmopolitan community.

✦ CLIMATE

The climate is hot and humid all year round with heavy rainfall, especially from November to January. There is little temperature variation from an average minimum of 24°C/75°F to an average maximum of 31°C/88°F. Singapore is not affected by tropical storms and the only violent winds are the *sumatras*, which are strong, short-lived thunderstorms that form over the neighbouring island that gave them their name, and occur between April and November. Throughout the year the winds are light and there are frequent calms.

✦ FORMALITIES

PORTS OF ENTRY

Port of Singapore 1°16´ N 103°50´ E	
Raffles Marina 1°21´ N 103°38´ E	
Republic of Singapore Yacht Club 1°18´ N 103°46´ E	
Keppel Bay 1°16´ N 103°49´ E	
Changi Sailing Club 1°23´ N 103°58.7´ E	

All approaches are well buoyed and lit, but due to the large amount of shipping, night arrivals should be avoided. The immigration vessel should be contacted on Channel 74. Yachts are instructed to proceed to one of two clearance anchorages: the Western Quarantine & Immigration Anchorage, just to the north of the Sisters Island, or Changi

General Purpose Anchorage, in Changi Bay. At either location, immigration will board and check passports. Customs and immigration clearance may also be possible at Raffles Marina or the Republic of Singapore Yacht Club.

Within 24 hours the captain should report to the One Stop Document Centre at the Maritime Port Authority to complete the clearance.

Most nationalities do not require a visa, and 14 to 90 days are given depending on nationality. Nationals of countries that need a visa, but arrive without one, are given leave to stay for two weeks, which may be renewed for one week at a time up to a maximum of six months.

Customs do not normally inspect a boat but do random spot checks. The Singapore authorities have a very strict policy regarding illegal drugs and there is a death penalty for drug trafficking.

Visiting yachts must obtain a permit to move within the Port of Singapore, even between marinas. This permit must be obtained from the port master six hours in advance and to qualify a yacht must be fitted with an AIS transponder, which can be rented from the marinas or yacht clubs. This permit is not required on arrival or when departing the country.

Before departure, the yacht must proceed to one of the two arrival anchorages to clear immigration.

✦ FACILITIES

Repair facilities in Singapore are among the best in Asia, with a complete range of specialists as well as travelifts and several chandleries. Provisioning is excellent with many well-stocked supermarkets. Fuel is available at marinas and from a fuel barge opposite the Changi Sailing Club.

Cruising Guides
Cruising Guide to Southeast Asia Volumes I and II
From Yangon to Manila Bay: The Cruising Almanac 2005
Southeast Asia Pilot

Website
www.visitsingapore.com

Local time	UTC +8
Buoyage	IALA A
Currency	Singapore Dollar (SGD)
Electricity	230V, 50Hz

Diplomatic missions

UK	6424 4200	Canada	6854 5900
USA	6426 9100	New Zealand	6235 9966
Australia	6836 4100		

Communications	**Emergency numbers**
IDD 65 IAC 001	112/999

SOUTH KOREA

THE KOREAN PENINSULA IS ONE OF RUGGED MOUNTAINS AND DRAMATIC SCENERY that has been divided artificially for over half a century by the 38th parallel, with the Democratic People's Republic of Korea occupying its northern half and the Republic of Korea its southern part. Neither country is particularly welcoming to cruising yachts, but while in the north the discouragement of foreign visitors is undisguised, in the south, time-consuming formalities convey a similar message.

The most attractive cruising is along the south coast, roughly between the ports of Kunsan and Pusan, where the coastline is indented with countless coves, anchorages and hundreds of small islands. Pusan gained temporary fame as the world's sailing centre during the Seoul Olympics in 1988, and the marina built for that occasion is now used by cruising yachts. Pusan is Korea's principal port and second largest city. It is the gateway to the Hallyo Sudo Waterway, a national sea park comprising hundreds of picturesque islands along the coast west of Pusan. Cheju Island, off the southern tip of the peninsula, is a useful stop for southbound yachts or those who wish to break the passage from Japan towards the Asian mainland or vice versa.

✦ COUNTRY PROFILE

The Korean Peninsula was settled in prehistoric times by tribes from Central Asia, and from the seventh century there was a flourishing Korean culture. Over the centuries Korea suffered repeated invasions by Mongols, Manchus and Japanese. Japan annexed the peninsula in 1910. The Japanese defeat in 1945 saw Korea divided into Soviet and American occupation zones. The Korean War, which erupted in 1950, was the first serious conflict of the Cold War, and its consequences are still unresolved.

The 48 million inhabitants are Koreans of Mongol origin. There is a small Chinese minority. Seoul is the capital.

✦ CLIMATE

The country has a temperate climate, with rainy, hot summers and dry, cold winters. In summer the winds are mainly from the east and south. Typhoons can affect the coastal areas at any time, particularly from May to October.

✦ FACILITIES

Provisioning is good everywhere and fuel is easily available. The best repair facilities are in the Pusan area, with marina-type docking in the Olympic Basin, but generally there are adequate repair facilities in all fishing ports.

Website
www.visitkorea.or.kr

| **Local time** UTC +9 | **Currency** South Korean Won (KRW) |
| **Buoyage** IALA B | **Electricity** 220V, 60Hz |

Diplomatic missions			
UK	2 3210 5500	Canada	2 3783 6000
USA	2 397 4114	South Africa	2 792 4855
Australia	2 2003 0100	New Zealand	2 3701 7700

Communications		**Emergency numbers**	
IDD 82	IAC 001	112	Ambulance 119

✦ FORMALITIES

PORTS OF ENTRY
Cheju 33°31´N 126°33´E Inchon 28°28´N 126°36´E
Kunsan (Gunsan) 36°00´N 126°43´E
Pusan (Busan) 35°06´N 129°04´E Uban 35°29´N 129°24´E
Yosu 34°45´N 127°47´E

Sailing in territorial waters is forbidden at night, so arriving during daylight hours is advisable. You must clear in and out of every port and a yacht may be stopped en route by naval or police patrol boats. Port Control must be called on Channels 12 or 16 to request permission to enter a harbour.

Visas are not required by most nationalities and usually 90 days is given on arrival.

NORTH KOREA

North Korea occupies the northern half of the Korean Peninsula and its capital is Pyongyang. All foreign visitors require visas, which must be applied for well in advance. Visiting yachts are not welcome and the country is best avoided.

TAIWAN

TAIWAN, officially called the Republic of China, is a large island straddling the Tropic of Cancer, about 120 miles off the Chinese mainland. In spite of being highly industrialized, Taiwan has retained much of its natural beauty. It was this beauty that struck Portuguese sailors who called here at the end of the sixteenth century and named the island Ilha Formosa, meaning 'beautiful island'.

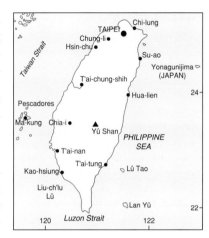

Known all over the sailing world for its yacht-building industry, Taiwan was the first Asian country to mass produce fibreglass boats. Unfortunately, this beautiful island is not geared up for cruising and very few foreign yachts call.

✦ COUNTRY PROFILE

Evidence of human settlement in Taiwan dates back 30,000 years. About four thousand years ago, ancestors of current Taiwanese Aborigines settled in Taiwan. These Aborigines are genetically related to the Malays. It is now thought likely that Polynesian ancestry may be traceable to Taiwan and that it was these people who migrated to the South Pacific.

In 1544, a Portuguese ship sighted the island. After a brief period of Dutch rule, it was settled by Chinese and eventually incorporated into the Chinese Empire. In 1895, at the end of the Sino-Japanese war, Taiwan was ceded to Japan, but after the Second World War, the island reverted to China. In 1949 Chinese nationalists led by Chiang Kai-shek fled to the island and established the Republic of China, severing all links with the mainland. This separation continues to this day, although there has been recent contact between the two governments.

The majority of the 23 million inhabitants are of Chinese origin, although some indigenous peoples still live in the mountains. Mandarin Chinese is the official language, but Taiwanese and Hakka are also spoken. Taipei is the capital.

✦ CLIMATE

The climate is subtropical, with temperatures that vary from an average 15°C/59°F in February, to the hot and humid months of July and August, with an average of 29°C/84°F and sometimes well over 35°C/94°F. The summer is also the rainy season. Typhoons are most frequent from June to September.

✦ FORMALITIES

PORTS OF ENTRY

Kao-hsiung 22°37´N 120°15´E	Keelung 25°09´N 121°44´E
T'ai-chung-shih 24°15´N 120°30´E	Hualien 23°59´N 121°38´E
Su-ao 24°36´N 121°52´E	Anping 22°58´N 120°09´E
Ken-ting 21°57´N 120°48´E	

No other harbour apart from ports of entry can be visited and the authorities should be informed by email of your arrival (tbroc@tbroc.gov.tu). Yachts over 20 tons must have a pilot to enter or exit commerical ports.

Boats should tie up to the security dock where they will be inspected by the Coast Guard. They will call customs, immigration and quarantine officials to the dock.

All nationalities must obtain a visa before arrival from a Republic of China mission abroad. Short stays may be allowed for those arriving without a visa.

✦ FACILITIES

There are now three marinas: Shaochuantou in Kao-hsiung, Houbihu in Ken-ting, and Kang-tzu-liao near Keelung. Repair facilities at any of these places are reasonable.

Website
www.eng.taiwan.net.tw

Local time UTC +8
Buoyage IALA A
Currency New Taiwan Dollar (TWD)
Electricity 110V, 60Hz

Diplomatic missions
UK	2 8722 1000	Canada	2 2544 3000
Australia	2 8725 4100	New Zealand	2 2757 6725

Communications	**Emergency numbers**
IDD 886 IAC 002	112 Ambulance 119 Police 110

THAILAND

THAILAND, PREVIOUSLY KNOWN AS SIAM, has over 1,000 miles of mainland coastline as well as thousands of islands. Its two coasts are bordered on the east by the Gulf of Siam and on the west by the Andaman Sea. The many secluded harbours, picturesque islands, clear waters and colourful coral reefs have turned Thailand into Asia's foremost cruising destination. A relatively late addition to the international cruising circuit, Thailand is now visited every year by a large number of yachts and is a major charter hub. The large island of Phuket off Thailand's west coast has jumped in a short time from a sleepy backwater to an international tourist resort with high-rise hotels, bars, night clubs and crowded beaches. The highly successful King's Cup Regatta is held here every year and attracts yachts from all over Asia and beyond. Some of Phuket's charm has been lost in the rapid process of development, but fortunately cruising yachts have the ability to seek out the less crowded places, which abound around Phuket Island and its many offshore islets.

To the northeast of Phuket, the wide Phang Nga Bay, whose stunning mountains rise vertically out of the turquoise water, has been described as a cruiser's paradise, with scores of rocky islands scattered about like confetti. There are plenty of safe anchorages from which winding mangrove channels lead to traditional fishing villages that can be easily reached by dinghy. Sailing south, the rocky pinnacles of the spectacu-lar Phi Phi Islands rise like gigantic stalagmites out of the sea.

Another favourite group of islands are the Similans, northwest of Phuket. They have a very different aspect to the other islands as they are low and covered in dense forest. Thailand's northernmost islands have started to attract more cruising boats, some of which stop here on their way to Myanmar, which in recent years has started allowing access to foreign yachts. There are also many secluded anchorages south towards Malaysia. In this corner of Thailand the choices are indeed infinite.

The Gulf of Siam is a very different story as much of the shoreline is flat and uninteresting although there are a number of attractive islands in the northern part of the gulf. One of these is the island of Ko Samui and the many smaller islands that surround it. Several rivers empty into the gulf and some of them are navigable by shallow-drafted craft, such as the Pranburi river with the Phatra Yacht Club located at its mouth. At the head of the gulf, on the banks of the Chao Praya River, lies the capital, Bangkok (Krung Thep). Nearby is the resort of Pattaya, the principal yachting centre in the area. Farther east, close to the Cambodian border, are the islands of Ko Chang and Ko Kut, with many attractive well-protected anchorages. Although much less visited than the shores and islands of the Andaman Sea, this part of Thailand is slowly being discovered by cruising yachts attracted to this

Ko Phi Phi Island.

area both by what Thailand itself has to offer as well as its two neighbours, Cambodia and Vietnam, where visiting yachts are now also welcome.

◆ COUNTRY PROFILE

Thailand is the only country in South East Asia never to have been under colonial rule and Thai people often proudly refer to their nation as The Land of the Free. The original Thai tribes were pushed out of Southeast China and slowly

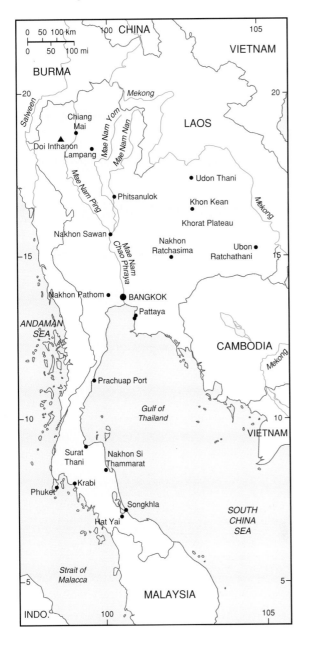

populated the land in the seventh to eighth centuries, establishing small independent states in the north of present Thailand. Thai culture and the Buddhist religion flourished and, prior to the fall of the Khmer Empire in the thirteeenth century, various states thrived here. The current Rattanakosin era of Thai history began in 1782, following the establishment of Bangkok as capital of the Chakri dynasty under King Rama I the Great. An army coup in 1932 ended the absolute power of the monarchy and the army continues to play an important role in Thai politics. The current King Bhumibol Adulyadej acceded to the throne in 1946 and is the world's longest-serving monarch.

The population is 66 million, of whom more than 5 million live in the capital, Bangkok. As well as Thais, there are also some hill tribes in the northeast and Malays in the south. Thai is the national language, but English is widely spoken. All young men are expected to spend a minimum of three months in a Buddhist monastery.

◆ CLIMATE

The tropical climate can be very humid. March to May is the hottest period, while from November to February the weather is drier and cooler. June to October is the rainy season and the southwest monsoon, while November to May is the period of the northeast monsoon. The latter is the more pleasant season on account of its weather, but also because it ensures better sailing conditions along the sheltered west coast, most of whose ports are untenable during the southwest monsoon. The South China Sea is the breeding ground of cyclones that strike the Philippines and Vietnam every year, but rarely affect Thailand's east coast. By the time such systems have crossed the Malay Peninsula, they have lost all their bite and arrive in the Andaman Sea as brisk winds that make for exhilarating sailing in the lee of the coast.

◆ FORMALITIES

PORTS OF ENTRY	
Bangkok 13°26´N 100°36´E	Phuket 7°55´N 98°24´E
Krabi 8°04´N 98°55´E	Satun 6°03´N 100°05´E
Pattaya 12°55´N 100°52´E	
Laem Chabang 13°05´N 100°53´E	

Customs very rarely visit yachts. Within 24 hours of arrival, except at weekends, the captain must go ashore to complete entry formalities.

Phuket: The pier at Ao Chalong is a one-stop check-in/check-out facility. Customs, immigration and harbourmaster offices are located there.

Boat Lagoon Marina in Phuket.

Krabi: Yachts should anchor at Ao Nang Beach and the skipper should go into Krabi Town to clear immigration, customs and harbourmaster. All these offices must be visited even if coming from Phuket.

Those arriving without a visa will be granted 30 days' stay. Obtaining visa extensions locally is very difficult, with the possible exception of serious emergencies or grave health problems. One way to solve this is to pay a bond and leave for a neighbouring country and obtain a new visa on arrival. The officially given reason for the bond is that it allows the person to leave Thailand by other means than the boat he or she arrived on. The bond is given back on return to Thailand. Obtaining a visa in advance from a Thai diplomatic mission does make it easier to stay for longer, but even with such visas, extensions are not granted easily.

Yachts are allowed to stay for one year, six months being given initially with a further extension of six months being possible.

Regulations seem to change often and are differently interpreted and applied by local officials, so it is always advisable to check the latest situation before arrival.

There are various marine parks in Thai waters, for which varying charges are made for anchoring.

✦ FACILITIES

Both repair and docking facilities have greatly improved in recent years. There are four marinas in Phuket: Yacht Haven, Royal Phuket, Ao Por and Boat Lagoon. The latter has a travelift and the best repair facilities are concentrated in this area. Provisioning is good in Phuket Town, with a good fresh produce market and several supermarkets. Fuel is available at the Yacht Haven and Boat Lagoon, and also from a barge in Chalong Bay. Facilities in the other ports are more limited. More repair facilities are available at the Royal Varuna Yacht Club in Pattaya.

✦ CHARTER

Charter has seen a rapid development, with a large charter fleet being based in the area around Phuket, and a smaller one at Pattaya, in the Gulf of Siam. Sunsail has bases in Phuket, Koh Samui and Koh Chang. YachtPro (Sailing Thailand) is based at Yacht Haven in Phuket and offers both bareboat and crewed charters as well as tuition. YachtPro also operates out of Pattaya (Sailing Pattaya).

Located in Chonburi, in the Bay of Bangkok, Gulf Charters has a fleet of both monohulls and catamarans, and now also operates in Cambodia.

Far Away is a general information site that also operates a fleet of catamarans that can be chartered both bare and crewed, as does Catamaran Sailing.

> www.far-away.net
> www.sailing-thailand.com
> www.sunsail.com
> www.gulfchartersthailand.com
> www.sailing-pattaya.com
> www.catamaransailingphuket.com

Cruising Guides
Cruising Guide to Southeast Asia Volumes I and II
Sail Thailand
Southeast Asia Pilot

Website
www.tourismthailand.org
www.8north.com (yachting information on Phuket)

Local time	UTC +7
Buoyage	IALA A
Currency	Thai Baht (THB)
Electricity	220V, 50Hz

Diplomatic missions

UK	2 305 8333
USA	2 205 4000
Australia	2 344 6300
Canada	2 636 0540
South Africa	2 253 8473
New Zealand	2 254 2530

Communications

IDD 66	IAC 001

Emergency numbers

112	Ambulance 1699	Police 191

VIETNAM

VIETNAM LIES BETWEEN CHINA and Laos, with its coastline on the South China Sea. After years of isolation, foreign tourists now enjoy a remarkable amount of freedom to go to this interesting country, which is also being visited by an increasing number of cruising yachts. Although there are more restrictions for cruising yachts than for land tourists, foreign boats can visit the main ports. The sprawling Mekong Delta in the extreme south of the country is a fascinating world of meandering waterways backed by hills covered in dense vegetation. Some 40 miles up the Sai Gon River, which empties into the Mekong Delta, is Ho Chi Minh City, formerly Saigon. This is the largest city and main commercial centre of Southern Vietnam, where evidence of the new climate of free enterprise is very apparent. Haiphong lies in the delta of the Red River and is the main port serving the capital, Hanoi. West of the Mekong Delta is spectacular Halong Bay, where some 3,000 limestone islands form strange shapes and grottoes in a place that equals – or may even surpass – the beauty of the area around Phuket. The offshore islands of Con Dao and Phu Duoc are now open to visiting yachts, with cruising opportunities steadily widening.

✦ COUNTRY PROFILE

A Bronze Age civilization was developed around the Red River Delta by the first century BCE when Chinese forces invaded. In the eleventh century Vietnam emerged as an independent force, gradually expanding south as far as the Mekong Delta. The conquest of Vietnam by France was completed in 1877 when Vietnam became part of French Indochina. France continued to rule until its defeat by communist forces in 1954. Under the Geneva Accords of 1954, Vietnam was divided into North and South. Hostilities soon flared between the two, and in 1965 the USA sent in troops to prevent the collapse of South Vietnam. The resulting war caused widespread devastation and the US forces withdrew in 1973. Two years later, North Vietnamese forces overran the South, reuniting the country under communist rule. Since 1986 there has been a gradual liberalization process, accompanied by an opening to the outside world.

The population is 87 million. The majority are Vietnamese, with several small minorities. Vietnamese is the official language. The capital is Hanoi.

Ha Long Bay.

✦ CLIMATE

The north has a subtropical climate with dry winters and wet summers, while the southeast has a tropical monsoon climate with the rainy season from May to October. The typhoon season lasts from July through to November, with the most severe storms occurring along the central coast. The frequency of typhoons is high, and the country is affected by at least one violent typhoon every year.

✦ FORMALITIES

PORTS OF ENTRY

Ben Dam	8°39′N 106°34′E
Duong Don	10°12.8′N 103°57.3′E
Vung Tau	10°23.6′N 107°06′E
Ho Chi Minh City (Saigon)	10°47′N 106°42′E
Da Nang	16°06′N 108°18′E
Pan Thiet	10°55.4′N 108°06.3′E
Qui Nhon	13°45.7′N 109°14.8′E
Nha Trang	12°16′N 109°12′E
Haiphong	20°52N 106°40′E

Ho Chi Minh City: The Coast Guard may intercept the vessel as it enters territorial waters and an attempt should be made to advise them on HF radio of your destination and ETA. The port authority must be contacted before entering to receive directions as to where to proceed. Anchoring in the river is prohibited in the area close to the city.

Nha Trang: Officials here are more used to foreign boats as this port is the finish of an annual race from Hong Kong. Due to the shallowness of the waters, visiting vessels are normally asked to anchor, the anchorage area being nearly 1 mile offshore.

Vung Tau: Yachts should proceed up the Saigon river past the shipyard and other installations to a barge flying a large Vietnamese flag where all officials are located and formalities are completed.

Permission to visit any port must be obtained in advance, and can be done at the same time as applying for a visa. In practice, foreign yachts seem to be welcome everywhere and formalities in individual ports are easily dealt with.

All nationals (with very few exceptions) require visas, normally valid for one month, obtained in advance.

Photography is not allowed in ports, airports and harbours. Because of the continuing tension between Vietnam and Cambodia, the border between the two countries is a sensitive area and yachts should keep well away from it.

✦ FACILITIES

Repair facilities are limited, although boatyards or workshops dealing with local fishing vessels might be able to deal with emergency repairs. Provisioning with fresh produce is good, and fuel is available in all ports.

Cruising Guides
Cruising Guide to Southeast Asia Volume I
Southeast Asia Pilot
From Yangon to Manila Bay: The Cruising Almanac 2005

Website
www.vietnamtourism.com

Local time	UTC +7
Buoyage	IALA A
Currency	Vietnamese Dong (DHD)
Electricity	220V, 50Hz

Diplomatic missions

UK	4 3936 0500	Canada	4 3734 5000
USA	4 3850 5000	South Africa	4 936 2000
Australia	4 3831 7755	New Zealand	4 3824 1481

Communications
IDD 84   IAC 00

Emergency numbers
112 Ambulance 05/115 Police 03/113

NORTH INDIAN OCEAN AND RED SEA

The uncertain safety situation in the Gulf of Aden and around the Horn of Africa, the prolonged conflict in Sri Lanka, the absence of facilities in India and the Maldives, the more attractive cruising destinations in the South Indian Ocean, have resulted in a considerable reduction in the number of cruising yachts visiting this area. Those that do normally pass through as quickly as possible and only make brief stops on their way from South East Asia to the Mediterranean, with even fewer attempting to sail the other way. Countries bordering on the Persian Gulf, which have started attracting some visiting yachts, such as Abu Dhabi and Dubai, have embarked on an ambitious programme of developing their yachting facilities. The future depends very much on the piracy situation and, if that situation is resolved, there is no doubt that there will be an immediate upsurge in the number of boats sailing in the North Indian Ocean, an area that has a large potential for both cruising and racing.

Piracy has been an ongoing phenomenon in the Gulf of Aden and around the Horn of Africa since time immemorial, but it has flared up considerably since the collapse of Somalia's central government. Anyone planning to sail through that area should monitor the situation carefully and visit the website of international organizations involved in piracy control such as the International Maritime Organization. The British Royal Navy operates out of Dubai and can be contacted by email (ukmtodubai@eim.ae) for an update on the situation.

In recent years, the main movement has been from east to west, mainly by yachts heading from South East Asia to the Mediterranean. Therefore most sailors plan to do this during the northeast monsoon when sailing conditions in the North Indian Ocean are the most favourable. Those leaving from Thailand or Malaysia normally plan their departure for the beginning of the year so as to have enough time to visit some of the many interesting places on the way and still arrive in the Mediterranean at the start of the sailing season in late April or May. Lying astride the main route, Sri Lanka, and its conveniently located port of Galle, continues to be a favourite port of call. From there, most boats sail either to the Maldives or Cochin in India before continuing west. In recent years many yachts have stopped in Oman, especially those that

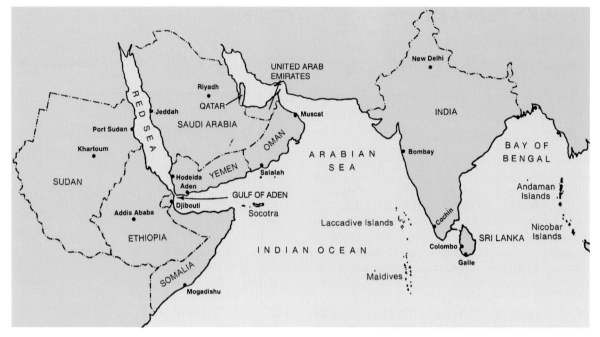

intended to join a convoy to pass through the critical area in the Gulf of Aden. But even without this consideration, Oman makes an interesting and convenient stop on this long transocean passage. Before entering the Red Sea, there is the choice between making a last stop at Aden or at Djibouti, with the latter normally being the preferred option.

Once through the Strait of Bab el Mandeb, yachts heading north through the Red Sea usually take their time to cruise the coasts of Eritrea, Sudan and Egypt, as most only aim to reach the Mediterranean by late spring. Along the eastern shores, Yemen is slowly adopting a more tolerant attitude towards yachts, but Saudi Arabia still does not allow cruising in their waters. The above route has the advantage that it takes in virtually all interesting places in the North Indian Ocean and also benefits from the best sailing conditions.

The opposite route, sailed by those who wish to reach South East Asia from the Mediterranean is similarly dictated by seasons, and therefore should be planned to take place during the southwest monsoon. A spring departure from the Mediterranean would benefit from more favourable weather in the Red Sea, as would an April crossing of the North Indian Ocean. The timing of such eastbound passages must be carefully planned to take into account the risk of cyclones in the Arabian Sea and Bay of Bengal.

While the number of cruising yachts has seen a drop in the North Indian Ocean generally, the opposite is happening in the northern part of the Red Sea which is now visited by an increasing number of yachts that come south through the Suez Canal to spend the winter in the Red Sea, whether in Southern Egypt or the Gulf of Aqaba, and to return to the Mediterranean in the spring.

Yachting facilities throughout the region are still relatively limited, and having any repair done in most places is difficult. The exception is some of the Gulf States, a few ports in India that have a local sailing community, and the new marinas in Southern Egypt. In all other places, local workshops may be able to undertake some repair even if they are not used to dealing with yachts. Marine equipment and spares are generally difficult or impossible to obtain, so anyone planning to cruise in this region should be as self-sufficient as possible.

Sailing in the North Indian Ocean has always been dictated by the monsoons and, as Arab traders in their dhows discovered hundreds of years ago, only fools try to sail against them. The northeast monsoon lasts from November to March, while the southwest monsoon is from June to September. Tropical cyclones can occur in the Arabian Sea and Bay of Bengal, particularly at the changeover of monsoons, May to June and October to November.

BAHRAIN

BAHRAIN IS AN ARCHIPELAGO in the southern Persian Gulf made up of 36 islands, most of which are small uninhabited coral reefs. Bahrain Island is the largest, and makes up 85 per cent of the country's land area. Potentially the most interesting cruising area is the Hawar archipelago, a small group of islands lying close to Qatar's west coast. The islands are a nature reserve to protect a number of endangered species, and special permission is needed to visit them. Sailing vessels have been in use here since earliest times, and while no longer used commercially, interest in sailing has survived. The Bahrain Yacht Club has an active membership of owners of both sail and power yachts.

◆ COUNTRY PROFILE

Bahrain's strategic position has made it an important trading centre since ancient times. In 1783, the Al-Khalifa family captured Bahrain from the Persians. In order to secure the territory, it entered into a series of treaties with Britain during the nineteenth century that made Bahrain a British Protectorate in 1861. The archipelago attained its independence in 1971. Facing declining oil reserves, Bahrain turned to petroleum refining and has transformed itself into an international banking centre. The Al-Khalifa dynasty has ruled the country since 1783. The current King Hamad bin Isa al-Khalifa acceded to the throne in 1999.

The population is approximately 730,000, of which over 63 per cent are Bahraini Arabs, the rest being made up of recent immigrants from East Asia, Iran and other Arab countries. Arabic is the official language, but English, Farsi and Urdu are also spoken widely. The capital is Manama.

◆ CLIMATE

The climate ranges between two extremes – cool winters with sparse rainfall and hot summers with high humidity. Daytime summer temperatures range between 38°C/100°F and 42°C/108°F. The dry northwest wind, known locally as *Al Barah*, keeps humidity down and creates more pleasant conditions.

◆ FORMALITIES

PORT OF ENTRY
Mina Sulman 26°14´N 50°35´E

This is the main port and is reached through a one mile long dredged channel between Sitra and Muharraq islands.

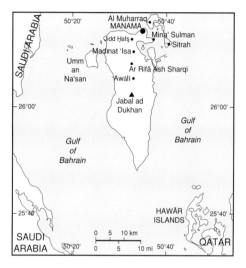

Port control should be contacted when 3 miles offshore. Pilotage is compulsory, but may be waived for small craft in daytime.

On arrival, nationals of most countries will be granted a visa for a stay of 14 days. Alternatively, an e-visa can be obtained.

◆ FACILITIES

There are three marinas: Bahrain Yacht Club, Marina Club for larger yachts, and Al Bandar Resort. Facilities are good and there is a 50 ton travelift at Marina Club.

Websites
www.bahrainguide.org
www.evisa.gov.bh/VisaBhr1En.html (Bahrain electronic
  visa service)
www.thebahrainyachtclub.com

Local time	UTC +3
Buoyage	IALA A
Currency	Bahraini Dinar (BHD)
Electricity	230V, 50Hz

Diplomatic missions	
UK	1757 4100
USA	1724 2700

Communications	
IDD 973	IAC 00

Emergency number 999

DJIBOUTI

THE REPUBLIC OF DJIBOUTI is a small country in the Horn of Africa, little more than the port of Djibouti and the surrounding semi-desert hinterland. Djibouti's strategic position between the Red Sea and Indian Ocean has always played an important role in the country's destiny and Djibouti is an important base in the international campaign against piracy. The country is also a convenient port of call for both eastbound and northbound yachts. The majority are heading for the Mediterranean and arrive in Djibouti during the northeast monsoon, mainly between February and April.

✦ COUNTRY PROFILE

The history of Djibouti is recorded in the poetry and songs of its nomadic people and goes back thousands of years to the time when this was an important trading post between the Mediterranean, Africa and Asia. The French presence expanded in the nineteenth century and the colony of French Somaliland was created in 1862, later to be renamed the French Territory of the Afars and Issas. Continuing internal unrest led France to give independence to the last French colony on the African mainland in 1977. Djibouti maintains a strong relationship with France and also hosts the only US military base in Eastern Africa.

The population of 516,000 are mainly Afars and Issas, both being Muslim peoples. Arabic and French are the official languages, but Afar and Somali are also spoken.

✦ CLIMATE

The climate is tropical, but due to Djibouti's location it can reach extremes in summer when it can be very hot, especially from June to August, when temperatures can reach 45°C/112°F. Occasionally the *khamsin* wind blows from the desert, bringing dust and reducing visibility. The weather from October to April is cooler and the winds are mostly easterly.

✦ FORMALITIES

PORT OF ENTRY

Djibouti 11°36´N 43°09´E

The port captain should be called on Channel 12. Arriving yachts may use one of the floating pontoons in front of the former yacht club building, south of the main wharf, or anchor nearby. Formalities are usually completed in the commercial harbour.

Short-term visas are issued to nationals of most countries

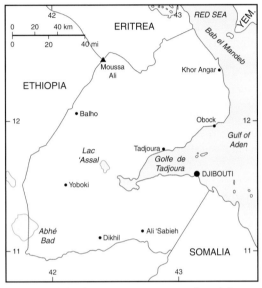

on arrival and the ship's papers are retained until departure. For stays of longer than ten days, a visa should be obtained in advance. For northbound boats, Djibouti is a convenient place to obtain an Egyptian visa at the Egyptian consulate. Eastbound boats can get information here on the latest security situation in the waters surrounding neighbouring Somalia.

✦ FACILITIES

Repair facilities for yachts are limited, although there are a few workshops capable of carrying out some jobs. Provisioning is good due to the military presence. There is a lively market in the town centre. Fuel is available in the commercial harbour.

Cruising Guide	
Red Sea Pilot	

Local time	UTC +3
Buoyage	IALA A
Currency	Djiboutian Franc (DJF)
Electricity	220V, 50Hz

Diplomatic missions			
UK	3 85007	USA	3 353995

Communications	
IDD 253	IAC 00

Emergency numbers		
112	Ambulance 351	Police 17

EGYPT

WHILE CRUISING OPPORTUNITIES along Egypt's Mediterranean shores are limited to port-hopping along the featureless coast, the Egyptian section of the Red Sea offers a wide variety of choices. Whether arriving by way of the Suez Canal or after a battle against contrary winds up the Red Sea, any sailor with time on his or her hands will greatly appreciate the only area of the country that is worth cruising – the bays and reefs that stretch all the way from the Sudanese border to the Gulf of Suez and into the Gulf of Aqaba. Daysailing along this coast is the more pleasant way to make progress against the prevailing northerlies.

Those interested in Ancient Egypt will find along the banks of the Upper Nile some of mankind's most outstanding treasures: the temple complex of Karnak at Luxor, the royal tombs in the Valleys of Kings and Queens at Thebes, and the Abu Simbel rock temples at Aswan. These sites are easily accessible from one of the marinas in the Hurghada area.

The Gulf of Aqaba and the east coast of the Sinai Peninsula have many cruising opportunities and winter weather here is much more pleasant than in the Mediterranean, making this a tempting between seasons alternative. As the northern Red Sea is slowly becoming a sailing destination in its own right, this part of Egypt has seen a rapid improvement in yachting facilities, with several marinas being opened as part of expanding tourist resorts.

✦ CLIMATE

The summers are very hot, with extremely high temperatures. Winters are mild with little rain. The hottest months are July and August, with average temperatures of 27°C/81°F and day temperatures that often reach 42°C/108°F in July and August. January is the coolest month with an average temperature of 17°C/63°F in the northern part of the Red Sea. The prevailing winds are northerly. Occasionally the *khamsin*, a hot dry wind, blows off the land; it is laden with dust and sand, reducing visibility. The prevailing winds in the Red Sea are northerly.

✦ FORMALITIES

PORTS OF ENTRY

Suez 29°58´N 32°33´N	Hurghada 27°13.30´N 33°50´E
Port Ghalib 25°32´N 34°38´E	Abu Tig 27°24.60´N 33°41´E
Safaga 26°44´N 33°56´E	Sharm el Sheik 27°51´N 34°17´E
Taba Heights 29°22.30´N 34°47.40´E	

Port Ghalib: Arriving yachts should contact the marina on Channels 16 or 10, then proceed to the end of the entrance channel and tie up at the reception dock. The marina will assist with formalities.

Hurghada: Yachts may proceed directly to the new marina to complete formalities there, but the marina should be contacted in advance on Channel 71 to make the necessary arrangements.

El Gouna (Abu Tig Marina): The marina should be contacted on Channels 16 or 73.

Taba Heights: The marina deals with all formalities and monitors Channels 16 and 73.

Safaga: Port Control should be called when approaching the port. The port captain insists that yachts come alongside the main dock, although this is sometimes unsuitable. The recommended anchorage (26°47.59´N 33°56.33´E) is in front of Paradise Hotel.

Suez: Yachts are usually met in the approaches by an agent's boat, who will offer his services, sometimes quite forcefully. It is therefore advisable to have made arrangements with an agent in advance, who will then meet the yacht on arrival in a launch. The agent will obtain permission from the Suez Port Authority for the yacht to proceed directly to the Suez Yacht Club. Otherwise yachts should anchor in the waiting area in Port Ibrahim and contact Port Control for permission to go to Suez Yacht Club, which is located on the west side of the canal, just beyond the Suez Canal Authority buildings.

At all points of entry visas valid for one month are granted on arrival. These can be extended by the local immigration

The Suez Yacht Club overlooks the Suez Canal.

office or the police. Visas are not needed by anyone on a yacht transiting the Suez Canal and remaining in the port area.

Foreign-flagged boats may stay up to one year from the date of arrival. After one year, vessels need to be bonded for four months or leave the country for the same period. It is imperative to obtain on arrival the maximum period permitted as extending the initially given time is very difficult or even impossible.

Coast Guard cruising permits are no longer issued; the only permits issued are those at the private marinas at Port Ghalib and Taba. These are monthly cruising permits, which are valid for all marinas. Yachts coming from Sudan and sheltering from strong winds, or making overnight stops without going ashore, are normally allowed to stay in Egyptian waters before clearing in at an official port of entry. Those intending to make such stops should attempt to secure a visa in advance.

✦ FACILITIES

The opening of several new marinas has greatly improved both docking and repair facilities, although major repairs may still be beyond local capabilities. Provisions and fuel are available at all marinas. The latest marina is Taba Heights, set within a tourist resort on the shore of the Gulf of Aqaba. The new marinas are a welcome sight, especially for sailors who arrive from a passage up the Red Sea. Port Ghalib Marina is part of a huge resort complex and town development, and is a most convenient place to clear into Egypt if arriving from the south. Abu Tig Marina in El Gouna is the most popular, with the best facilities. All new marinas have good facilities, with fuel, water, wifi and a range of repair services.

For those transiting the Suez Canal, Ismailia is a convenient place to leave the boat while visiting Cairo or other places in the interior. The yacht club is well run, the staff are helpful and friendly, and the town itself is well worth a visit.

Fresco of boy prince from a tomb in the Valley of the Kings.

✦ SUEZ CANAL

Transit formalities are complicated and more time-consuming than in Port Said, so using the services of a local agent is highly recommended. Those who wish to do it themselves need to visit the Small Craft Department in the main building of the Canal Authority where they will be instructed as to the various formalities to be carried out and payments to be made. These payments include the transiting fee, insurance policy, ports and lights fee. The captain must then arrange for a technical inspection of the yacht. Following this, a transit permit will be issued and a time arranged for the pilot to come on board. On the day of the transit the pilot will arrive early in the morning to guide the yacht as far as Ismailia in the northwest corner of Lake Timsah, where the vessel must spend the night as yachts are not allowed to transit at night. Those who are only transiting the Suez Canal and have not completed entry formalities are not allowed to go ashore.

Early the following morning, either the same pilot or another one will continue the transit to Port Said. Yachts are normally met by a launch that collects the pilot and directs the yacht to the Port Fouad Yacht Club on the eastern side of the harbour. If transiting the Canal, and not stopping anywhere after the transit, the outward clearance can be obtained while doing the transit formalities. Yachts may then proceed as soon as they have completed the transit and dropped the pilot. Once outward clearance has been obtained, yachts must leave within 24 hours, or obtain another clearance.

✦ RESTRICTIONS

All military zones are prohibited areas.

Egypt is very environmentally conscious and many sensitive areas in the Red Sea are protected. Spearfishing, the taking of reef fish, collecting of coral, shells and marine animals, are all forbidden. There are now national park boundaries on most islands and reefs, and anchoring in coral is prohibited. Mooring buoys are provided on most dive sites.

✦ CHARTER

Foreign-flagged vessels are not allowed to charter in Egyptian waters, so currently there are neither foreign nor local charter operators.

Cruising Guide
Red Sea Pilot

Websites
www.suezcanal.gov.eg
www.egypt.travel

For general information, see the Egypt (Mediterranean) section on page 28.

ERITREA

ERITREA HAS A LONG COASTLINE of over 600 miles along the west of the Red Sea. The coastal plain is narrow and arid, rising to highlands in the north and centre. The opening of Eritrea to foreign yachts has radically altered the sailing picture in the Red Sea as it is now possible to cruise along the entire Eritrean coast in easy stages by exploring countless anchorages and offshore islands. With its two ports of entry, Massawa and Assab, strategically located near the extremities of the country, boats sailing in either direction can clear into Eritrea at one of the ports, daysail along the coast, and then clear out at the other end.

In the Bay of Massawa lies the Dahlek archipelago, with hundreds of islets, reefs and cays, a protected marine park which provides many cruising opportunities. The relatively protected inner channel between the islands and the mainland makes it possible to sail to or from Sudan in sheltered waters.

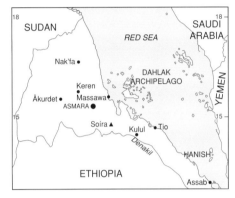

◆ COUNTRY PROFILE

Nomads and traders migrated to this area from the north thousands of years ago. The Land of Punt, visited by Egyptian ships in Pharaonic times, was believed to be located here, although present-day Somalia is the more likely location. Eritrea existed as an independent state until its annexation by the Ottoman Empire in the sixteenth century. In 1952 the United Nations sanctioned the setting up of a federation with Ethiopia, but after the Ethiopian Emperor Haile Selassie was overthrown in 1974, the federation disintegrated. In 1993 Eritrea declared independence, but a state of instability persists as Ethiopia continues to claim some territory.

Eritrea's population numbers 5.7 million. Tigrinya and Arabic are the official languages. Asmara is the capital.

◆ CLIMATE

The dry subtropical climate ensures temperatures remain high on the coast; in July and August they often reach 40°C/104°F. The northern coast has a rainy season from December to February, but little rain falls in the south.

◆ FACILITIES

Docking at the commercial dock in Massawa is reported to be bad as the quay is rough and exposed to the swell. Anchoring in Taulud Bay is not recommended because of theft by both local and foreign fishermen. Provisioning and repair facilities are limited; fuel is not always available in Massawa, but is obtainable in Assab. In both places there is some fresh produce. There are no ATMs or credit card facilities.

Local time	UTC +3
Buoyage	IALA A
Currency	Eritrean Nakfa (ERN)
Electricity	230V, 50Hz

Diplomatic missions			
UK	1 202 838	USA	1 120 004

Communications	
IDD 291	IAC 00

◆ FORMALITIES

PORTS OF ENTRY	
Massawa 15°37´ N 39°29´ E	Assab 13°00´ N 42°44´ E

Massawa: After contacting the port captain by radio, yachts should either come alongside the rough wharf or anchor off. After clearance, vessels may be allowed to proceed into the inner harbour if there is space, or anchor in the outer harbour.

Assab: Because of the constant surge, coming alongside the dock can be dangerous, so it is advisable to anchor in the lee of the sea wall. Formalities are completed ashore. There is little protection from strong southerlies, and under such conditions it is better to continue to Massawa.

A 48-hour shore pass is issued on arrival, after which a visa must be purchased. An additional fee needs to be paid if one intends to go inland. Entry formalities have to be completed at each port. After clearing out, the yacht must leave within one hour.

When in Eritrean waters yachts should expect to be approached by the military, often not wearing uniforms especially close to islands that have military posts – such as Difnein.

INDIA

KNOWN AS BHARAT IN HINDI, India is a country of infinite variety. For many years it had been avoided by most yachts cruising the North Indian Ocean mainly because of the complexity of entry formalities. In places frequented by foreign yachts, this is no longer the case as formalities have been simplified and officials are getting used to dealing with visiting sailors. The most satisfactory situation is in some of the larger ports where customs and port organizations have their own sailing clubs and welcome visiting yachts.

The best time to visit is during the pleasant northeast monsoon, between November and March. Most yachts call at Cochin (Kochi), conveniently placed close to the Red Sea route. Farther up the west coast, the old Portuguese trading port of Goa (Mormugao) provides a fascinating and colourful interlude. An even more interesting stop is Mumbai, especially as some of the local customs officials are keen sailors. The Royal Bombay Yacht Club, founded in 1846 and one of India's most prestigious clubs, welcomes visiting sailors. Mumbai is a good place from which to travel inland to experience India's rich culture. Few yachts visit the east coast, although Chennai, formerly Madras, is a port of entry with one of the oldest yacht clubs in India.

Yachts can now visit the Andaman Islands, but must be in possession of an official permit as well as a valid Indian visa.

An easy way to visit these interesting islands is to join the annual rally from Phuket, whose organizers deal with all formalities. The Nicobar Islands, which lie astride the rhumb line from Phuket to Sri Lanka, are occasionally visited by yachts on passage, but you need to have an Indian visa, unless you can claim that the stop was necessitated by an emergency.

India's coastal waters are teeming with small craft and, especially when sailing at night, you need to be extremely careful as most of them do not carry lights and collisions are a frequent occurrence.

✦ COUNTRY PROFILE

India has been inhabited since prehistoric times, and Neolithic man originated from the Indus basin. Around 2000 BCE Aryan tribes from Central Asia colonized North India, bringing with them the Sanskrit language and the caste system. Many empires rose and fell until contact with Europe developed, and by the early nineteenth century Britain controlled most of India. Full independence came in 1947 when the subcontinent was divided into the secular state of India and the Muslim state of Pakistan.

With a population of 1.17 billion, this second largest nation in the world is made up of many ethnic minorities, with Hindu the largest at 41 per cent. Hindi is the official and most widespread language and there are 250 regional dialects. English is also an official language and is spoken by many. New Delhi is the capital.

✦ CLIMATE

The coastal regions can be very hot and humid and the best time to visit is during the northeast monsoon from November to April, when it is dry and sunny and the southwest coast has the benefit of more protected harbours. In the southwest monsoon period, the west coast is mostly unprotected, there being rain and heavy swell from June to October.

✦ FORMALITIES

PORTS OF ENTRY	
Port Blair (Andaman Islands)	11°40´N 92°45´E
Mumbai (Bombay)	18°54´N 72°49´E
Mormugao (Goa)	15°25´N 73°48´E
Kochi (Cochin)	9°58´N 76°14´E
Chennai (Madras)	13°05´N 80°17´E

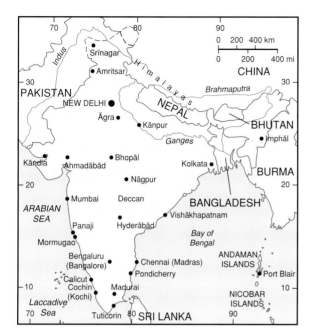

When approximately 12 miles from a port, the Coast Guard should be called, giving the yacht's details. Port control should be called on arrival to ask for permission to enter the harbour.

Andaman Islands: Yachts should proceed directly to Port Blair without stopping at any other island and come alongside the main quay. All formalities are completed ashore and they are lengthy. A detailed itinerary must be submitted and a twice-daily radio report observed while in Andaman waters.

Kochi (Cochin): Clearance normally occurs at Willingdon Island off the Malabar Hotel. Authorities will come in a launch and formalities are completed ashore.

Mormugao (Goa): The main port is busy with commercial ships, but yachts that have attempted to clear in at the smaller port of Panaji (formerly Panjim) have encountered difficulties.

Mumbai (Bombay): Yachts arriving from outside the country must advise the authorities at least 72 hours in advance. This can be done via the Royal Bombay Yacht Club.

Nationals of all countries must obtain a tourist visa in advance. On arrival, sailors are given a shore pass, so permission must be granted to travel inland. Prior permission is needed to visit the Andaman Islands. An easy way to obtain the Indian visa and have the itinerary approved to visit these islands is via Emotion Travel in Phuket (Tel. +76 222 320).

Formalities are still complicated and lengthy. Customs require a specific list of all portable items, laptops, cameras, binoculars and any foreign currency. Items not mentioned can be confiscated.

Normally a yacht can remain in India for six months.

✦ FACILITIES

The yachting infrastructure is growing rapidly, with several new marinas. Being the most visited port by foreign yachts and a port of call for the Volvo Ocean Race in 2008, Kochi has improved its facilities and a new marina was commissioned. It is possible to haul out at the Malabar Yacht Club, which has a limited range of facilities and there is a small boatyard close by. In Mumbai, the Royal Bombay Yacht Club gives honorary membership to visiting sailors and allows them to use its facilities, as well as assisting with repair advice. Spare parts are generally unobtainable, but there are workshops capable of simple repairs.

✦ CHARTER

The Malabar Yacht Club in Kochi has a crewed sailing vessel for charter, while Sea Time Yacht Charters (Rent A Boat) has a small fleet of powerboats in Mumbai.

www.malabar-yacht-club.org
www.rentaboat.in

Cruising Guides
Indian Ocean Cruising Guide
Andaman Sea Pilot

Websites
www.incredibleindia.org
www.royalbombayyachtclub.com

Local time	UTC +5.5
Buoyage	IALA A
Currency	Indian Rupee (INR)
Electricity	240V, 50Hz

Diplomatic missions

UK	11 2687 2161
USA	11 2419 8000
Australia	11 4139 9900
Canada	11 4178 2000
South Africa	11 2614 9411
New Zealand	11 2688 3170

Communications

IDD 91	IAC 00

Emergency numbers

100	Ambulance 102

JORDAN

THE HASHEMITE KINGDOM OF JORDAN has a mere 13 miles of coastline on the Gulf of Aqaba, at the head of which is Aqaba, Jordan's only seaport. Most of Jordan is desert, with a dry raised plateau stretching down the centre of the country. The valley of the River Jordan includes the Dead Sea depression which, at 400m (1,300ft) below sea level, is the lowest point on the surface of the earth.

More cruising yachts are now visiting this interesting country and although the coastline itself has little to offer, this is more than made up for by the attractions of the interior, such as the Rose Red city at Petra, the stunning rock formations at Wadi Rum, or the Dead Sea. The one notable exception is the Aqaba Marine Park, where several mooring buoys have been laid down for boats visiting the park. Tala Bay is located nearby and a new marina is now operational there.

✦ COUNTRY PROFILE

The region that is present-day Jordan has been settled from the earliest days of history, ruled over by many empires until the Ottomans' defeat by British and Arab forces during the First World War. In 1946 Jordan achieved full independence under the rule of Abdullah ibn Hussein, of the Hashemite dynasty. His grandson, King Abdullah II, acceded to the throne in 1999.

The population numbers 6.4 million and includes a considerable number of Palestinian refugees. Arabic is the official language, but English and French are also used. Amman is the capital.

✦ CLIMATE

The climate can be described as Mediterranean, with hot dry summers and cool rainy winters. For a month or so before and after the summer, hot, dry air from the desert, drawn by low pressure, produces the strong wind called *khamsin* from the south or southeast. Another local wind, the *shammal*, comes from the north or northwest, usually between June and September.

✦ FORMALITIES

PORTS OF ENTRY
Aqaba 29°31´N 34°59´E, Tala Bay Marina 29°24.54´N 34°58.14´E

The port authorities should be contacted on Channels 16 or 12 on arrival in Jordanian waters. They normally visit the yacht by patrol boat and advise where to complete formalities.
Aqaba: Yachts are either directed into the commercial harbour or to the Royal Yacht Club of Jordan.
Tala Bay Marina: On arrival, the marina should be contacted on Channel 77. Entry formalities can be completed at this new marina. A crew list, copies of passports and details of the yacht should be sent three days in advance by email to the marina.

Shore passes are issued on arrival. For travel inland, a visa is required. Most nationals can obtain visas on arrival, valid from one to three months depending on nationality.

Spearfishing and the removal of shells or coral are prohibited. If cruising the Gulf of Aqaba it has been advised that it is better to visit Jordan before Israel, and not the other way around. Some yachts coming from Eilat have been refused entry.

✦ FACILITIES

There are two well-equipped marinas, the new Tala Bay Marina and the Royal Yacht Club of Jordan. Either is a safe place to leave the boat while visiting the interior. Fuel, travelift and simple repairs are available. Provisioning is good.

Cruising Guide	Websites
Red Sea Pilot	www.mota.gov.jo (Ministry of Tourism)
	www.talabay.jo/Marina.shtm

Local time	UTC +2
	Summer time: last Friday in March to last Friday in October
Buoyage	IALA A
Currency	Jordanian Dinar (JOD)
Electricity	230V, 50Hz

Diplomatic missions			
UK	6 590 9200	Canada	6 520 3300
USA	6 590 6000	South Africa	6 592 1194
Australia	6 580 7000		

Communications	Emergency numbers
IDD 962 IAC 00	Ambulance 191 Police 192

KUWAIT

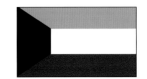

KUWAIT lies on the northwest coast of the Persian Gulf and has boundaries with Iraq and Saudi Arabia. The land is mainly desert with a more fertile narrow coastal belt. About 15 to 20 per cent of the world's known oil reserves lie under Kuwaiti soil.

There are a number of locally owned yachts, mainly power, and two marinas, one near the capital, the other in the south of the country. The northern area of the Bay of Kuwait is shallow and characterized by mud flats, whereas the southern coast along the Arabian Gulf is deeper and has sandy beaches. Most ports are on the southern shores and there are several good anchorages. Although tourism is discouraged by the authorities, the few cruising boats that have visited Kuwait have been allowed to stay for a limited period.

✦ COUNTRY PROFILE

The island of Failaka, at the mouth of Kuwait Bay, was a trading centre from ancient times, but the mainland was only settled in the eighteenth century. Ancestors of Kuwait's present rulers, the Al-Sabah family, established their rule over the emirate, which became a British protectorate in 1899. In the 1930s the exploitation of oil was begun, and British protection formally ended in 1961. Iraq's invasion of Kuwait in 1990 led to the First Gulf War that ended with the liberation of Kuwait and the defeat of Iraq.

The population is 2.7 million. The official language is Arabic, but English is widely spoken. The capital is Kuwait City.

✦ CLIMATE

The climate is subtropical with cool winters and hot dry summers when temperatures range from 29°C/84°F in the morning to more than 49°C/120°F in the shade at noon. The prevailing northwest wind called *shamal* is a cooling breeze in summer. Most rainfall occurs between October and April in the form of showers or sudden violent cloudbursts.

✦ FORMALITIES

PORTS OF ENTRY

Shuwaikh (Kuwait City) 29°21′N 47°56′E

Shuaiba 29°02′N 48°10′E Umm Al Maradim 28°40′N 48°39′E

Port Control should be called for instructions.

Shuwaikh: This is the main port, and after clearance yachts are directed to the Kuwait Yacht Club Marina.
Umm Al Maradim: Entry formalities can be completed in the port on this island, which is uninhabited except for the officials.

Nationals of most EU countries, Australia, Canada, New Zealand and the USA may obtain a visa on arrival, usually for one month. Other nationalities must obtain one in advance. Alcohol is prohibited. Other banned imports are pork products, shellfish, unsealed milk products, fresh vegetables, and items of Israeli origin. Books and DVDs may be subject to censorship.

Islamic law should be respected, both men and women should dress conservatively and, during the month of Ramadan, not eat, drink or smoke in public.

✦ FACILITIES

There are two marinas, one near Kuwait City, referred to as the Yacht Club, while Khiran Marina is near the Saudi border. Amenities at the Yacht Club Marina are good, with a range of repair and haulout facilities up to 40 tons. There is a fuel dock and good provisioning.

Khiran Marina is part of a large resort and has the usual facilities. Yachts should ask for assistance before entering as the entrance is reported to be difficult and should only be attempted with local help.

Website		
www.kuwaitiah.net (tourism information)		

Local time	UTC +3	
Buoyage	IALA A	
Currency	Kuwaiti Dinar (KWD)	
Electricity	240V, 50Hz	

Diplomatic missions			
UK	2259 4320	Canada	2256 3025
USA	2259 1001	South Africa	561 7988
Australia	232 2422		

Communications	Emergency number
IDD 965 IAC 00	777

MALDIVES

THE MALDIVES are low-lying coral islands grouped into 26 atolls protected by surrounding reefs. All the atolls are north of the equator, with the exception of Addu Atoll. The word 'atoll' is derived from *atholhu* in the Dhivehi language of the Maldives. Rarely exceeding a few feet above sea level, the Maldives are among the first countries threatened to be submerged by the rising ocean levels as a result of climate change.

From the cruising sailor's point of view, the Maldives have many attractions, but one major disadvantage is the lack of all-weather anchorages. Although there are plenty of islands to visit, in most lagoons the anchorages are very deep and exposed. This is the reason for the popularity of islands such as Thulusdhoo and Himmafushi, which have shallow well-protected anchorages. Apart from this shortcoming, the Maldives are an interesting cruising ground and the diving in some atolls is excellent.

◆ COUNTRY PROFILE

The origin of the Maldive islanders is not known, although it is thought that they probably came from India and Sri Lanka. Until 1153 the Maldivians were ruled by Buddhist kings, then an Islamic sultanate was established. The islands resisted all attempts to colonize them, although by agreement they were a British protectorate from 1887 until 1965. In 1968 the country became a republic.

Malé, the capital, is the only urban settlement. Of the 396,000 inhabitants of the Maldives, over a quarter live in Malé. The population is a mixture of Sri Lankan, Indian, Indonesian, Malay, Arab, African and European. Dhivehi is the main language, although English is also spoken. It is a Muslim country, which means certain customs must be respected. Alcohol is only available on the tourist islands.

◆ CLIMATE

Lying close to the equator, the winds are mild and calms are common. The southwest monsoon blows from May to October, bringing more rain and stronger winds, especially in June and July. The northeast monsoon lasts from November to April. This is the more pleasant season, when average temperatures range between 25°C and 31°C (77°C and 88°F).

◆ FORMALITIES

PORTS OF ENTRY	
Malé (North Malé Atoll)	4°10′ N 73°30′ E
Uligamu (Haa Alifu Atoll)	7°5′ N 72°56′ E
Gan (Addu Atoll)	0°42′ S 73°09′ E

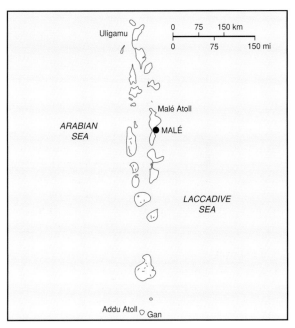

Malé: On arrival, you should contact the Coast Guard to be advised as to where to proceed. Yachts that have secured the services of an agent are normally asked to go direct to Hulhumale anchorage to await inspection. Although you may be able to clear in unaided, the authorities usually insist on the use of an agent. The anchorage near the port in Malé Atoll is difficult because of the great depth. A shallower area is reported at 4° 10.40′ N 73° 29.80′ E. Access into Malé Atoll between 2300 and 0600 is prohibited.

Uligamu: Boats en route to the Red Sea often stop at this northernmost island of the Maldives. This is now an official port of entry and there are officials located there who will deal with formalities. There are strict restrictions when going ashore: visitors may not stay ashore after 2200 hours, nor any alcohol be taken there; women must be properly dressed; and no islanders may come on board.

Gan: Visiting yachts normally anchor in the small boat harbour. Officials are reported to prefer an agent to be used to complete formalities. A local agent answers on Channel 16.

The requirement for yachts to only clear in and out at Malé has been lifted and in recent years boats have been able to stop at Uligamu in Haa Alifu Atoll and Gan in Addu Atoll. As the Maldives authorities have made it very clear that they do not particularly welcome cruising yachts as their contribution to the tourism industry is negligible, stops in these two places are only tolerated if they are short and no other islands are visited. Those who intend to call at other islands are asked to proceed to Malé and complete formalities there.

All visitors are given a 30-day permit on arrival. A cruising permit must be obtained to sail to any other atolls besides Malé Atoll. This has to be arranged via an agent and costs US$500.

✦ FACILITIES

The few available facilities are almost all at Malé, which has some small workshops capable of simple repairs. Hulhumale anchorage, which is close to the airport, is sheltered and the capital can be reached by ferry. As most food has to be imported, provisions are expensive. Fuel is only available in Malé, being scarce in the outer islands. A few basic provisions are available at Uligamu and Gan, and when fuel is obtainable you should be prepared to pay a high price for it. Some repair facilities as well as diesel are available at Gan. A marina now operates at Dhonakulhi Island in Haa Alifu Atoll, but it is part of an exclusive resort and arrangements must be made in advance if intending to call there. Some of the tourist resorts welcome visiting yachts, but others prohibit anchoring in their atolls.

✦ CHARTER

There are no bareboat operators, only a small number of companies offering crewed charters: Dream Yacht Charter, based at Thilafushi in North Malé, and Indian Ocean Charters. Both have a small fleet of catamarans, while South Asian Charters operates monohulls.

> www.dreamyachtcharter.com
> www.indianoceancharters.com
> www.sacharter.com

Cruising Guides
Atlas of the Maldives
Indian Ocean Cruising Guide
Maldives Cruising Guide

Website
www.visitmaldives.com

Local time	UTC +5
Buoyage	IALA A
Currency	Maldivian Rufiyaa (MVR)
Electricity	230V, 50Hz

Diplomatic missions
New Zealand	322 432

Communications
IDD 960	IAC 00

Emergency numbers
Ambulance 102	Police 119

OMAN

OMAN IS A SULTANATE on the eastern side of the Arabian Peninsula. For many years tourism was not encouraged, and virtually all the foreigners allowed into the country were on business. Sailors seem to have fared better as yachts were allowed to stop for a few days at Mina Raysut, near the town of Salalah, close to the Yemeni border. Although stopping along the coast is forbidden, boats are also allowed to call at Mina Qaboos (Muscat), where there is now a small marina. Practically all boats that call in at Oman are bound for the Red Sea, and although a detour is necessary if coming from Sri Lanka, the route from India, particularly Mumbai, passes very close to Raysut.

✦ COUNTRY PROFILE

During the first millennium, the northern coastal districts were dominated by the Persians. By the seventh century, Sohar, the ancient Omani capital, was one of the most important ports in the Indian Ocean. In spite of the arrival of Portuguese traders in the North Indian Ocean, Oman's maritime power continued to dominate the Gulf and surrounding waters until it was eroded by the growth of British influence in the Indian Ocean. The present dynasty began with Ahmad ibn Said in 1749. The current Sultan Qaboos bin Said has made great efforts to modernise Oman. The discovery of oil in the 1960s has radically altered the fortunes of this once poor country.

The population of over 3.4 million consists of two main tribes, the Yemeni and the Nizanis. A considerable number of Omanis still lead a nomadic life. Arabic is the official language, while English is spoken in business. The capital is Muscat.

✦ CLIMATE

April to October is very hot, with high humidity along the coasts. In summer, the temperatures can reach up to 50°C (122°F) in the shade. During November to March, the period of the northeast monsoon, the climate is more pleasant, with occasional rain.

✦ FORMALITIES

PORTS OF ENTRY

Mina Raysut (Salalah)	16°56´N 54°00´E
Mina al Fahal	23°39´N 58°32´E
Marina Bander al-Rowdha (Muscat)	23°35´N 58°37´E

Salalah: Port Control should be called half an hour before arrival for instructions on where to go.
Muscat: Marina Bander al-Rowdha should be contacted and asked to call the relevant officials for clearance.

Quarantine, customs, immigration and port officials will all come to the boat. No one may go ashore until clearance has been completed. A 30-day visa will be issued to all nationals – except Israelis, and those with Israeli stamps in their passports. A cruising permit can be obtained from the Royal Oman Police.

Clearing out can take some time as all offices have to be visited: police first, and finishing with the port authority.

✦ FACILITIES

There is good provisioning and a fresh produce market in the town of Salalah. Some repair facilities are located in the port area, together with a crane for haulout. Oasis Club near the harbour gates at Salalah is reported to welcome visiting sailors. Marina Bander al-Rowdha has good repair facilities and a travelift.

Cruising Guides	Website
Indian Ocean Cruising Guide	www.destinationoman.com
Red Sea Pilot	

Local time	UTC +4
Buoyage	IALA A
Currency	Omani Rial (OMR)
Electricity	240V, 50Hz

Diplomatic missions		
UK	24 609 000	South Africa 694 791
USA	24 643 400	

Communications	**Emergency number**
IDD 968 IAC 00	999

QATAR

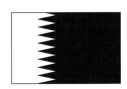

QATAR OCCUPIES A FLAT PENINSULA jutting into the oil-rich area of the Persian Gulf. Due to its large reserves, Qatar is one of the richest per capita countries in the world. Its capital, Doha, has become the region's leading cultural and communications centre. This rapid development has turned Qatar into a fully modernized country, although an effort is being made to maintain a close link to its Islamic heritage in art and architecture. Cruising opportunities as such are limited to a few small offshore islands. Not to be outdone by its neighbours, who seem to be guided by the principle that if you don't have it you make it, Qatar decided to create some of its own islands from scratch. The result is Pearl-Qatar, a vast development created on a previous pearl-diving site and consisting of a large resort built on an artificial island that surrounds a circular harbour. In its centre is a smaller island and floating pontoons are spread around the perimeter, making this the largest marina in the Middle East, if not the world.

✦ COUNTRY PROFILE

From the early nineteenth century until the present day, the Thani dynasty has ruled Qatar, although from 1916 until 1971 the country was a British Protectorate. Qatar has transformed itself from a poor country noted mainly for pearling into a rich state with significant oil and natural gas revenues.

Its population numbers about 830,000, about half of which are foreign workers. The official language is Arabic, although English is widely used. The capital is Doha.

✦ CLIMATE

Qatar has a very dry climate with almost non-existent rainfall, averaging about 80mm (3in) a year, this falling only in winter. Summer days are extremely hot, with temperatures often reaching 40°C/104°F or above. Winters are cooler by day and can be quite chilly at night.

✦ FORMALITIES

PORT OF ENTRY
Doha   25°17´N 51°32´E

Doha Port Authority may give permission to proceed directly to Doha Marina.

Nationals of the UK do not need a visa for a stay of up to 30 days. Nationals of Australia, Canada, New Zealand and the USA can apply for a visa on arrival. Other nationalities must apply for a visa in advance with the assistance of a sponsor, which can be a hotel or marina.

✦ FACILITIES

Facilities are good, with several marinas catering for a large yachting community of mostly powerboat owners.

Website
www.qatartourism.com

Local time	UTC +3
Buoyage	IALA A
Currency	Qatari Riyal (QAR)
Electricity	240V, 50Hz

Diplomatic missions

UK	496 2000
USA	488 4101
South Africa	485 7111

Communications

IDD 974	IAC 00

Emergency number 999

SAUDI ARABIA

SAUDI ARABIA IS A VAST DESERT COUNTRY on the Arabian Peninsula. Mecca, the holiest place of Islam, is situated here. This is a very conservative Muslim country, difficult to visit by foreigners, except Muslims on pilgrimage to Mecca. In order to preserve religious purity, tourism is actively discouraged. This also includes cruising yachts. A few yachts that have been forced to call at a Saudi port have been treated courteously, once the authorities have ascertained that the stop has been caused by a genuine emergency. Boats that have either strayed into Saudi waters, or been apprehended cruising the off-lying Farasan Islands without permission, have been escorted into port and detained for a few days before being allowed to continue on their way. Anyone intending to sail to Saudi Arabia must approach the authorities in advance to obtain the necessary permissions, otherwise it is better to avoid its waters, unless forced to make an emergency stop.

✦ COUNTRY PROFILE

From Saudi Arabia's holy cities of Mecca and Medina, the Islamic faith was disseminated to the rest of the world. After centuries of having been under Ottoman rule, Saudi Arabia came into being as a result of the collapse of the Ottoman Empire after the First World War. King Ibn Saud, ruling from 1932 to 1953, modernized the country and succeeding members of his family have ruled since. King Abdullah bin Abdul Aziz Al Saud has been the ruler since 2005.

Of the 28 million inhabitants, more than half are foreign workers. Arabic is the official language, but English is widely spoken in business circles. Riyadh is the capital.

✦ CLIMATE

Saudi Arabia has a desert climate. In Jeddah, on the Red Sea, it is warm for most of the year and the summers are usually very hot. Winters are cooler and the weather is quite pleasant. The prevailing winds are light northwesterly.

✦ FORMALITIES

PORTS OF ENTRY

Yanbu	24°06´N 38°03´E
Jeddah	21°28´N 39°10´E

Yachts are allowed to enter the above ports only in an emergency. Port Control should be contacted before arrival. Only the captain is allowed ashore to complete formalities. Both the yacht and crew are normally restricted to the port area, but if allowed ashore everyone must be back on board before sundown. Travel inland is not permitted and cruising along the coast is strictly forbidden. In an emergency the captain should immediately contact a coastal radio station and insist on being treated according to international maritime law.

While there have been some recent signs of relaxation, tourism is not encouraged. Visas can only be obtained by sponsorship, commercial or individual, and are only rarely granted to sailors.

Fishing, swimming and the consumption of alcohol is strictly prohibited while in harbour.

✦ FACILITIES

Jeddah has fuel, repair yards, slipways as well as electrical and electronic workshops. Yanbu also has some workshops. Jeddah has excellent medical facilities, including a decompression chamber, which has been used by sailors who suffered diving accidents in the Red Sea and were rushed to Jeddah for emergency treatment.

Cruising Guide	
Red Sea Pilot	

Local time	UTC +3
Buoyage	IALA A
Currency	Saudi Riyal (SAR)
Electricity	127V, 60Hz

Diplomatic missions			
UK	1 488 0077	Canada	1 488 2288
USA	1 488 3800	South Africa	1 442 9719
Australia	1 488 7788	New Zealand	1 488 7988

Communications	**Emergency numbers**
IDD 966 IAC 00	999 Ambulance 997

SOMALIA

SOMALIA OCCUPIES MOST OF the northeast shoulder of the African continent. With nearly 2,000 miles of coast around the Horn of Africa, Somalia has the second longest coastline on the continent. The interior is mostly desert, with mountains to the north and plains to the south. With the exception of a few man-made ports, there are no natural harbours and even at the best of times there is little to attract cruising yachts to this country. Violent crime is common, especially in Mogadishu, while many other areas of Somalia are suffering from armed conflict. There is no functioning national government and parts of the country have seceded. Three separate entities were functioning independently of each other in 2009: Puntland, Somaliland and Somalia.

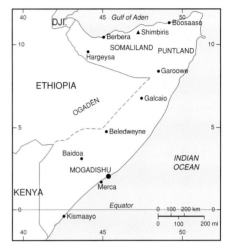

The Gulf of Aden and the waters surrounding the Horn of Africa have been plied by pirates since time immemorial, but the current situation is worse than ever with Somali pirates being so bold as to attack any vessel regardless of size – from cruise ships to supertankers, and even, to their own chagrin, naval ships. The international community has taken urgent measures to remedy the situation after pirates attacked a number of United Nations vessels carrying relief supplies. The waters around Somalia are patrolled by naval ships of various nations under the aegis of the United Nations, and a corridor has been designated that transiting vessels are advised to adhere to. Cruising boats have always been at risk when transiting this area and there have been a number of incidents involving yachts whose crews were abducted and eventually freed on payment of a large ransom. Two incidents involving French yachts in 2008 were brought to an end by commando attacks, resulting in the freeing of the captive sailors. Unfortunately, the skipper of a yacht lost his life during such an attack that also saw his captors killed.

✦ COUNTRY PROFILE

The Somalis have inhabited and traded in this area for many thousands of years. Greek and Arab writers called these people the Black Berbers, and the Egyptians called Mogadishu the Land of Punt. Following a period of colonial domination, Somalia became independent in 1960. After the regime collapsed in the 1990s, the nation descended into factional fighting and anarchy, including piracy.

The population of around 9.5 million is concentrated in the coastal towns. Somali is the official language, with Arabic, English and Italian also spoken by some. The capital is Mogadishu.

✦ CLIMATE

The climate is dictated by the two monsoons. It is hot all year round and also humid in the rainy seasons. The temperatures are very high in summer and can reach up to 42°C/108°F. At the height of the southwest monsoon, May to October, winds often reach gale force. The current along the Somali coast can be very strong, particularly during the southwest monsoon. The set changes in accordance with the direction of the monsoon.

✦ FORMALITIES

PORTS OF ENTRY

Mogadishu	2°01´N 4°21´E
Berbera	10°27´N 45°01´E

Somalia is regarded as a failed state and while the chaotic situation continues, both its waters and the country itself should be avoided.

Cruising Guide
Indian Ocean Cruising Guide

Website
www.somaligovernment.org

Local time	UTC +3
Buoyage	IALA A
Currency	Somali Shilling (SOS)
Electricity	220V, 50Hz

Communications
IDD 252   IAC 00

SRI LANKA

Known as Taprobane in antiquity and Ceylon in colonial times, this large island that looks like a tear dropping off the tip of the Indian subcontinent is one of the oldest civilizations in the world. An island of fertile coastal plains and central highlands covered in forests, its interior abounds in ancient temples and palaces.

For many years Sri Lanka was a popular stopping point for yachts on their way to the Red Sea or the South Indian Ocean. Most came from South East Asia or the Pacific and only a few from the West. The troubles that have befallen the island recently have almost destroyed the tourist industry, and many sailors decided to keep away. Hopefully the end of the prolonged war in 2009 should change that.

Virtually all yachts that call at Sri Lanka do so at the old port of Galle, conveniently located on the island's southern tip. Very few boats cruise outside of Galle. The harbour of Trincomalee was out of bounds during the internal conflict, while Colombo's commercial harbour has no provisions for yachts.

◆ COUNTRY PROFILE

The rule by Sinhalese kings that lasted for 21 centuries came to an end with the arrival of the European colonial powers: Portuguese, Dutch and British. Early in the nineteenth century the island became a British colony. Gaining independence as Ceylon in 1948, the country changed its name to Sri Lanka in 1972. Increasingly violent clashes between the Sinhalese army and Tamil separatists, known as Tamil Tigers, descended into war. The Tigers' attempt to set up an independent Tamil state in the north was fiercely resisted by the government. In 2009 the government forces finally defeated the insurgents, but the deep wounds caused by the prolonged war will take a long time to heal.

The population of over 21 million is made up of a Sinhalese majority and Tamil minority. Sinhalese, Tamil and English are spoken. Colombo is the capital.

◆ CLIMATE

The climate is tropical, with two distinct monsoon seasons. Heavy rainfall along the western coast occurs during the southwest monsoon, particularly between May and September. The temperatures on the coast are usually high, while in the hills it is pleasant all year round. The island is occasionally affected by tropical cyclones, which develop in the Bay of Bengal – the worst months being November and December.

◆ FORMALITIES

PORTS OF ENTRY

Galle 6°01´ N 80°13´ E	Colombo 6°57´ N 79°51´ E

Galle: Arriving yachts must contact Port Control before proceeding to anchor outside the harbour. During daylight hours Port Control usually allows yachts to proceed into the inner harbour and tie up to one of the new pontoons. As all vessels must use an agent to complete formalities, it is easier if one of the local agents is contacted one hour before one's ETA on Channels 69 or 71 as he will then deal with all officials and meet the yacht at the anchorage. Access into the harbour is not allowed during the hours of darkness.

All nationalities arriving on a yacht are granted a one-month visa on arrival.

◆ FACILITIES

A marina is under construction in Galle harbour, which will greatly improve the docking situation. Mechanical, electrical, engine, sail and glassfibre repair are available in Galle. There is fuel, but few marine supplies. Provisioning is limited, but good fresh produce is available.

Cruising Guide	Website
Indian Ocean Cruising Guide	www.srilankatourism.org

Local time	UTC +5.5
Buoyage	IALA A
Currency	Sri Lankan Rupee (LKR)
Electricity	230V, 50Hz

Diplomatic missions

UK	11 539 0639	Canada	11 522 6232
USA	11 249 8500	South Africa	11 268 9926
Australia	11 246 3200		

Communications	Emergency numbers
IDD 94 IAC 00	Ambulance 110 Police 118/119

SUDAN

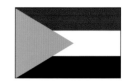

THE LARGEST COUNTRY IN AFRICA, bisected by the River Nile, Sudan is a land of contrasts: from the arid desert of the north to the tropical south. Sudan is the point where Arab and black African cultures meet and recent history has been beset by the grave tensions that underscore this.

Most sailors only come in contact with Port Sudan, the country's main port on the Red Sea. It is a convenient stop for yachts sailing up or down the Red Sea, although the harbour is dirty, crowded and has poor facilities. Boats coming from the south can find better conditions in Suakin, just south of Port Sudan. In the fifteenth century this was a major port and huge camel caravans brought copper, ivory, hides and slaves from the interior, returning with cotton, spices, silks and carpets. By the sixteenth century the harbour could hold 600 ships, but later Suakin proved too small for large ocean steamers. Today it is deserted, a sad ghost town of ruined buildings.

Port Sudan's position at the halfway mark of the Red Sea also marks the point where the winds change from prevailing southerlies to northerlies. Northbound yachts face an uphill beat from here all the way to Suez, while southbound boats usually have to fight contrary winds as far as Bab el Mandeb. If not in a hurry, the best tactic for northbound boats is to daysail inside the reefs, which extend parallel to the shore along most of the coastline. This makes life easier and also more pleasant, as the reef anchorages offer perfect shelter and the diving and fishing are superb.

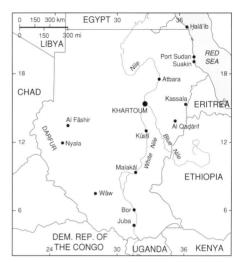

◆ COUNTRY PROFILE

The ancient Egyptians called the lands to their south 'lands of the blacks', and they made occasional forays into them for ivory, ebony and slaves. In the nineteenth century Sudan was part of the Ottoman Empire and became an Anglo-Egyptian condominium in 1916. Since independence in 1956, an ongoing conflict between the Islamic north and non-Muslim rebels in the south has cost the lives of an estimated 2 million people. The latest crisis has resulted in millions of refugees seeking sanctuary in the Darfur enclave.

The population is 41 million. Northerners are mainly Arab Muslims, while the southerners are African Christians. Arabic is the official language, with many others in use. Khartoum is the capital.

◆ CLIMATE

The climate is tropical, and on the coast summers are very hot and winds mostly northerly. The winter months are very pleasant and the prevailing winds are from the south.

◆ FORMALITIES

On arrival, port control should be called on Channels 14 or 16. Officials speak little English and often demand an agent be used. All persons should remain on board until given shore passes. These should always be carried. A travel permit must be obtained to visit the interior. When clearing out, a permit for cruising the coastline should be requested. Formalities have been reported to be simpler if one arrives with a Sudanese visa.

◆ FACILITIES

Provisioning with fresh produce is very good in both ports. In Port Sudan there are also grocery shops and fuel is available. There is no bank in Suakin, only in Port Sudan. There are only limited repair facilities in Port Sudan, and none in Suakin.

PORTS OF ENTRY

Port Sudan 19°37´ N 37°14´ E   Suakin 19°06´ N 37°20´ E

Cruising Guide		
Red Sea Pilot		

Local time	UTC +3	Currency	Sudanese Pound (SDG)
Buoyage	IALA A	Electricity	230V, 50Hz

Diplomatic missions			
UK	183 777 105	USA	183 774 701
Canada	183 563 670	South Africa	183 585 301

Communications	Emergency number
IDD 249 IAC 00	112

UNITED ARAB EMIRATES

THE UNITED ARAB EMIRATES is a federation of seven independent states, with coastlines on the Persian Gulf and the Gulf of Oman. Abu Dhabi is the largest, while Dubai, Ajman, Fujairah, Ras al-Khaimah, Sharjah, and Umm al-Qaiwain are known as the Northern States. The interior is mainly desert, but some areas of the coast are quite attractive and there is a growing interest in yachting, albeit mostly power. Although cruising opportunities are limited, a small number of foreign yachts venture into the area every year.

✦ COUNTRY PROFILE

There is evidence that the region was settled in the third millennium BCE, and was populated by nomadic herders and fishermen. Very little is known about the pre-Islamic period except that this was an important trading centre between the eastern and western worlds. A tribal confederation developed in Abu Dhabi in the late eighteenth century. In the early nineteenth century the Al Maktoum dynasty took control of Dubai. Formerly known as the Trucial States, the Emirates were under the military protection of Britain from 1853 to 1971, when six of the states became independent and known as the United Arab Emirates (UAE).

Arabic is the official language, but English is widely spoken. Islamic law should be observed by foreign visitors, but all the states except Sharjah allow the consumption of alcohol in private by non-Muslims. During Ramadan it is illegal to eat, drink or smoke in public.

The combined population is 4.8 million, although only one-fifth are Emirati, the majority being foreign workers. Dubai is the most populous of the Emirates, with almost 2.3 million inhabitants. Approximately 860,000 people live in Abu Dhabi, yet only 420,000 are native born and UAE citizens. Abu Dhabi is the federal capital, while the port of Dubai is the commercial centre.

✦ CLIMATE

Dubai: Dubai has an arid subtropical climate, with very hot summers and somewhat cooler winters. The hottest months are between June and September when temperatures can reach 45°C/113°F during the day and humidity levels are very high. Even the sea temperature touches on 40°C/104°F during the summer months. Temperatures are only slightly more moderate for the rest of the year, the coolest time being between December and March.

Abu Dhabi: Straddling the Tropic of Cancer, Abu Dhabi's climate is subtropical, with temperatures that vary from warm in the winter months to hot in the summer. The most pleasant month is December, with an average temperature of 20°C/68°F, while the hottest month is August, with an average temperature of 35°C/95°F.

Traditional dhows race in front of Dubai's Burj Al Arab.

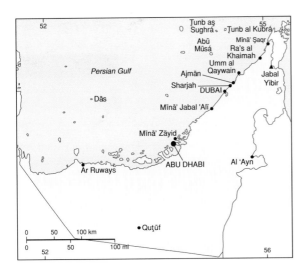

✦ FORMALITIES

PORTS OF ENTRY

Dubai: Port Rashid 25°16N 55°17′ E   Jebel Ali 25°02′ N 55°08′ E

Abu Dhabi: Mina Zayed 24°29′ N 54°22E

Sharjah: Khalid 25°22′ N 55°23′ E

Ras al-Khaimah: Mina Saqr 25°59′ N 56°03′ E

Fujairah: Port Fujairah 25°10′ N 56°22′ E

Ajman: Ajman Port 25°25′ N 55°26′ E

Umm al-Qaiwain: Ahmed Bin Rashid 25°35′ N 55°35′ E

Dubai: Yachts should call Dubai Port Control to obtain permission to proceed inside the creek to complete formalities. Nationalities of most countries can enter Dubai without a visa.

Dubai Marina.

Abu Dhabi: Formalities are very simple and no visa is necessary for nationals of the UK, while nationals of most EU countries, Australia, Canada, New Zealand and the USA are issued visas on arrival.

✦ FACILITIES

As there are a high number of locally owned yachts, facilities are of a good standard.

Dubai: There are several marinas, which are geared more for superyachts than cruising yachts. The Dubai Offshore Sailing Club is the most welcoming and offers free berthing to visiting vessels for one week. Repair facilities are very good, with workshops specializing in electrics, electronics, sail repairs and rigging.

Abu Dhabi: Port Zayed is in the process of an ambitious development plan, and is more used to commercial shipping and superyachts than smaller cruising yachts. There are three marinas: Abu Dhabi Marina, Abu Dhabi International Marine sports club, and Inter-Continental Marina. Repair facilities, as well as provisioning, are good.

✦ CHARTER

Based in Dubai, both Dusail and Duboats have a mixed fleet of sailing and power yachts for charter. Also operating in Dubai is Exclusive Yachts.

www.dusail.com
www.duboats.com
www.xclusiveyachts.com

Websites
www.dubaitourism.ae
www.visitabudhabi.ae
www.dosc.ae (Dubai Offshore Sailing Club)

Local time	UTC +4
Buoyage	IALA A
Currency	United Arab Emirates Dirham (AED)
Electricity	220V, 50Hz

Diplomatic missions

UK	Dubai 309 4444	Abu Dhabi 610 1100
USA	Dubai 311 6000	Abu Dhabi 414 2200
Australia	Dubai 508 7100	Abu Dhabi 634 6100
Canada	Dubai 314 5555	Abu Dhabi 694 0300
South Africa	Dubai 397 5222	Abu Dhabi 447 3446
New Zealand	Dubai 331 7500	

Communications

IDD Dubai 971 4	Abu Dhabi 971 2	IAC 00

Emergency numbers
998/999

403

YEMEN

YEMEN HAS COASTS ON BOTH THE GULF OF ADEN AND RED SEA. In the past, the only port accessible to yachts was Aden. The situation seems to be improving and boats have been allowed to stop at ports on the Red Sea coast. Occasionally yachts also stop at the Jabal Zugar and Hamish Islands, mainly to shelter from the weather. This practice seems to be tolerated, although one should not go ashore. Socotra, lying off the Horn of Africa also belongs to Yemen. Its inhabitants have a fierce reputation, and mariners have always been advised to give the island a wide berth.

Aden has been an important port since ancient times and is still a useful stop on the way to or from the Red Sea. It is a busy commercial port, with little attraction for cruising yachts, mostly because of complicated formalities and the restriction of movements imposed on sailors. For these reasons, many yachts prefer to stop at Djibouti.

✦ COUNTRY PROFILE

The best known of the ancient kingdoms that ruled in Yemen was that of Queen Sheba. The fabled Queen travelled north to visit King Solomon, taking gifts of myrrh and frankincense, much prized luxuries in the ancient world which occurred naturally in Yemen. It was known to the Romans as Arabia Felix, because of the riches that its trade generated. During the nineteenth century the area was controlled by the Ottomans in the north and Britain in the south. Independence was achieved in 1962. After two decades of hostilities, the reunification of the People's Democratic Republic (South Yemen) and the Yemen Arab Republic (North Yemen) occurred in May 1990.

The Arab population is 24 million. Arabic is the official language, but English is spoken in Aden. The capital is Sana'a.

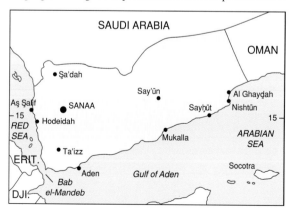

✦ CLIMATE

Yemen has a subtropical climate. May to September is the period of the southwest monsoon, when it is humid and rainy. October to February is drier and cooler, with easterly winds predominating.

✦ FORMALITIES

PORTS OF ENTRY		
Aden	12°48′N 44°58′E	Hodeidah 14°50′N 42°56′E
Mukalla	14°31′N 49°08′E	

The Coast Guard usually contacts vessels to identify them and is engaged in the campaign against Somali pirates.

Aden: Port Control should be contacted when outside the harbour entrance to find out where to anchor.

No visas are required for a short stay in the port area and shore passes are issued. If intending to go inland, a visa is required by all nationalities. In Aden it may be possible to obtain a cruising permit for the South Yemeni coast.

Hodeidah: Port Control should be contacted in advance to advise ETA, name of vessel and other details, otherwise the yacht may not be allowed into the port. The port is approached through a 10-mile-long channel.

Mukalla: Yachts have stopped at this port and been allowed to stay after obtaining shore passes through an agent.

✦ FACILITIES

In Aden only the National Dockyard has some repair facilities. Fuel is available. There are ATMs, supermarkets and good fresh produce markets in both Aden and Mukalla. The latter also has a range of repair facilities in the port area.

Cruising Guide	Website
Red Sea Pilot	www.yementourism.com

Local time	UTC +3
Buoyage	IALA A
Currency	Yemeni Rial (YER)
Electricity	230V, 50Hz

Diplomatic missions			
UK	1 308 100	South Africa	1 224 051
USA	1 755 2000		

Communications	Emergency numbers
IDD 967 IAC 00	Ambulance 191 Police 194

SOUTH INDIAN OCEAN

SCATTERED ALONG the tradewind route from the South Pacific to the Cape of Good Hope, the islands of the South Indian Ocean used to be visited by a relatively small number of yachts, but the increasing popularity of Madagascar and South Africa as cruising destinations, as well as the risk of piracy in the Gulf of Aden, has persuaded more sailors to choose this southern route.

The region is under the influence of the southeast trade winds for most of the year, which provide good and occasionally boisterous sailing conditions. The cyclone season lasts from December to the end of March and affects Mauritius, Runion and Madagascar. The more northerly islands, such as the Seychelles and Chagos, as well as most of the African coast, can be cruised safely all year round. While some yachts reach this area by sailing from South Africa, the majority of boats call at these islands as part of a longer, often round the world, voyage. The prospect of a tough windward leg from Chagos to Mauritius has resulted in the majority of boats crossing the South Indian Ocean taking one of two routes: either the traditional route from Cocos Keeling to Mauritius, Reunion and on to South Africa, thus forsaking a stop in Chagos altogether, or a more northerly route that calls at Chagos and then continues to Madagascar and on to South

Africa via the Mozambique Channel. The former route is shorter and usually quicker, whereas the latter is more attractive from the cruising point of view as it offers several alternatives – including a possible detour to the Seychelles. However, such a detour will entail a tough leg against prevailing winds and current from the Seychelles to Madagascar.

Repair facilities for yachts are available only in the few locations that have either a resident boating population, such as Mauritius and Reunion, or charter operations, such as the Seychelles. In all other places only basic repairs are possible. Provisioning follows the same pattern, with only basic supplies available in the smaller places and a somewhat better selection in the larger centres. Spares and marine supplies are not easily obtainable, so all essential spares should be carried on board.

The UK authorities, who administer Chagos, have imposed strict rules for visiting the islands and a cruising permit must be applied for and obtained before visiting. There are serious safety concerns for the islands of Comoro and Mayotte and they should only be visited if the situation is deemed to be safe. On the positive side, Mozambique is now attracting more cruising yachts, as formalities are being eased and the authorities recognize the importance of visiting boats as a source of revenue.

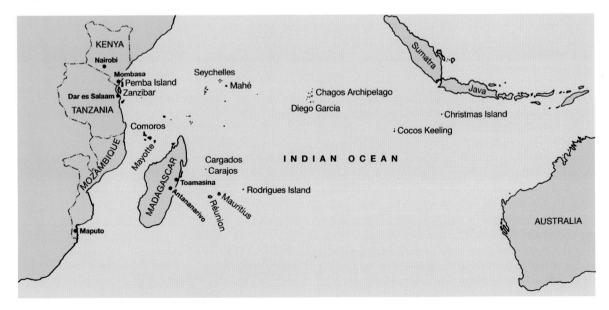

CHAGOS

Anchorage off Fouquet Island in Salomon Atoll.

THE BRITISH INDIAN OCEAN TERRITORY, commonly known as Chagos, is a collection of atolls, reefs and shoals in the South Indian Ocean and continues to be one of the most dreamed-of cruising destinations in the world due both to the remoteness of these uninhabited islands and the beauty of their tropical anchorages. The group has been a British colony since 1814, but has only been run separately since 1966 when, for strategic reasons, the native population was relocated to Mauritius and the largest island, Diego Garcia, was leased to the USA as a military base. The agreement expires in 2016.

After many years of a tolerant attitude towards visiting yachts by the UK authorities, regulations were hardened in 2007 and yachts are no longer as welcome as in the past. The archipelago has the largest expanse of undisturbed coral reefs in the Indian Ocean as well as rare and endangered species of birds, turtles and other wildlife. There are strict conservation rules, which must be observed in order to preserve this unique sanctuary in its present state. Fortunately yachts are still allowed to visit the islands, but as a few sailors have behaved irresponsibly in the past, it is in the best interests of all mariners not to upset the status quo by abusing this tolerance.

✦ COUNTRY PROFILE

Early Portuguese navigators searching for a direct route to the Spice Islands discovered these islands in the sixteenth

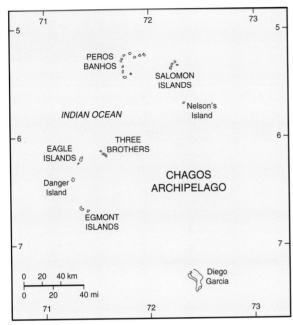

century and painted a picture of a dangerous reef-strewn area. A French settlement was established in the eighteenth century, but the archipelago was ceded to Britain in 1814 along with Mauritius and the Seychelles. After emancipation, some former slaves remained on the islands and settled there permanently. These people, a mixture of African and Tamil, became known as Ilois, sometimes also referred to as Chagossians. In 1965 the archipelago was separated from Mauritius, and the British Indian Ocean Territory (BIOT) was created. An agreement was reached between the UK and the USA in 1966 to make the territory available for defence purposes. In 1967 the inhabitants were resettled in Mauritius and the UK paid the Mauritius government £4 million on behalf of the 1,200 resettled people, of which the Ilois received £1 million. Ever since then, the Ilois have led a campaign to be allowed to return, but a final decision reached in 2008 by the highest UK court dashed any hopes of a successful outcome. It is estimated that approximately 1,200 Ilois still live in Mauritius.

The islands are uninhabited except for Diego Garcia which has about 3,000 military and civilian personnel stationed there. The commanding naval officer on Diego Garcia is the British representative, and is in charge of customs and immigration.

◆ CLIMATE

The archipelago has a tropical oceanic climate, the islands being under the influence of the southeast trade winds for much of the year. December through to February is the rainy season when prevailing winds are light west-northwesterlies. This is also the cyclone season, but such storms very rarely pass directly over the islands, although their distant effects can be felt. One cyclone did strike the archipelago in 1993, so although Chagos is considered to be outside the cyclone belt, it should be treated with great caution during the cyclone season. June to October is the dry season, with moderate southeast winds and cooler temperatures.

◆ FORMALITIES

Yachts wishing to visit Chagos must apply for a permit in advance. Full details are on the British Foreign Office website or can be requested by email (BIOTadmin@fco.gov.uk). There are a limited number of permitted anchorages at Salomon and Peros Banhos Islands. The GPS locations of the permitted anchorages are indicated on the cruising permit. Anchoring at Egmont Island is no longer permitted. BIOT customs and immigration officials visit the approved mooring sites to check permits and passports. Penalties for infringement of the regulations are severe.

Diego Garcia may only be entered in a serious emergency. Yachts trying to enter will be stopped outside the main pass and searched by the Royal Navy. If an emergency occurs, it is best to contact the authorities while approaching the island, and advise them of the nature of the problem. In the past, the authorities have done their best to render assistance to yachts with genuine emergencies.

The islands are a conservation area, and all flora and fauna, such as turtles, coconut crabs, live coral and shells, are protected. Scuba diving and spearfishing are not allowed, nor should the heart of palm be taken. People on visiting yachts are not allowed to spend the night ashore and the authorities expect boats to spend no longer than one month in the islands. Yachts are strictly prohibited from anchoring at any of the protected islands and reefs in the Chagos Banks, Peros Banhos and Salomon Islands. There are strict rules concerning the disposal of garbage.

Cruising Guide
Indian Ocean Cruising Guide

Website
www.fco.gov.uk/en/about-the-fco/country-profiles/asia-oceania/
british-indian-ocean-territory (British Foreign Office)

Local time	UTC+6
Currency:	British pound (GBP)

CHRISTMAS ISLAND

CHRISTMAS ISLAND is an Australian territory and a favourite port of call for yachts on passage to Cocos Keeling or other destinations in the South Indian Ocean. The island is the tip of an extinct volcano and steep cliffs are almost continuous around its coast. Because of its long isolation, Christmas Island has great scientific value as many unique species of flora and fauna have developed independently in the same way as they have on Galapagos, unusual flora, land crabs and seabirds being the most noticeable. The annual mass migration of an estimated 100 million red crabs to the sea to spawn is one of the wonders of the natural world and takes place each year around November and in synchronization with the cycle of the moon.

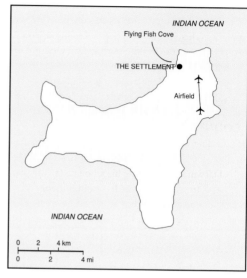

✦ COUNTRY PROFILE

While navigators knew of the island early in the seventeenth century, it was named Christmas Island by a British captain, William Mynors, who called here on 25 December 1643. Phosphate was discovered by an expedition in the 1870s, which led to Britain taking control of the island. In 1957 administration was transferred to Australia, who continued to extract the rich phosphate deposits until the mine was closed down in 1987.

The 1,400 inhabitants are Malay, Chinese and Australian. English is the main language.

✦ CLIMATE

The island has a typical tropical, equatorial climate with a wet and a dry season. The wet season is from December to April when the northwest monsoon blows. For the rest of the year southeast trade winds bring lower temperatures, humidity and some rain. The tropical storm season is from November to April when the island can be affected by cyclones. There is no safe anchorage here during this season.

✦ FORMALITIES

PORT OF ENTRY

Flying Fish Cove   10°25′ S 105°43′ E

The harbourmaster should be called on arrival. Night arrivals are discouraged for safety reasons. There are several buoys available for visiting yachts in Flying Fish Cove, where using a mooring is mandatory to protect the coral.

Australian visa requirements are in force, and everyone other than New Zealanders needs an Australian visa. Yachts travelling to Christmas Island from the mainland of Australia are deemed not to have left Australia if their trip is within 30 days of departure from the mainland. They should ensure that their visas cover the entire period of their stay including travel time. Otherwise, a multiple-entry visa is recommended for people wishing to stop at both Christmas Island and mainland Australia.

The same strict quarantine regulations apply as in mainland Australia.

✦ FACILITIES

Fuel, provisions and some repair facilities are all available. The Boat Club welcomes visitors.

Cruising Guide	
Indian Ocean Cruising Guide	

Website	
www.christmas.net.au	

Local time	UTC +7
Buoyage	IALA A
Currency	Australian Dollar (AUD)
Electricity	240V, 50Hz

Communications	
IDD 61 891	IAC 0011

Emergency number	
000	

COCOS KEELING ISLANDS

THE COCOS KEELING ISLANDS consist of two atolls, North Keeling and South Keeling, comprising 27 low coral islands, most of them clustered around South Keeling lagoon. Most of the smaller ones are uninhabited. South Keeling is a favourite stop for westbound yachts in the South Indian Ocean. Direction Island, which is the designated anchorage for yachts in transit, is unique in that it feels as if it belongs to cruising sailors. The authorities have installed a barbecue pit, rainwater tanks for showers or laundry, toilets, and built an open-sided hut with tables and benches. This clubhouse is adorned with hundreds of mementos of boats that have visited – carved name boards, inscribed fishing floats, signed country or club flags, even some paintings.

◆ COUNTRY PROFILE

North Keeling was first sighted by Captain William Keeling in 1609, and two Englishmen, Alexander Hare and John Clunies-Ross, settled on South Keeling in 1826. In 1836 Charles Darwin visited during his renowned voyage on HMS *Beagle* and the observations made during this stop were the basis of his theory of atoll formation. By 1857 the islands were considered as belonging to Britain, and George Clunies-Ross was granted all the land by Queen Victoria. In 1955 the islands became a dependency of Australia.

The population is about 600, the majority being ethnic Malays living on Home Island. Mostly Australians live on West Island. English and Malay are spoken.

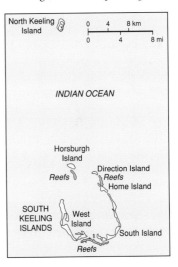

◆ CLIMATE

The islands are under the influence of the southeast trade winds for most of the year. The winds are strongest in August. During the cyclone season, from November to April, the winds are lighter. The islands are rarely affected by tropical storms. Temperatures are fairly consistent throughout the year at around 29°C/84°F, with minimum temperatures rarely dropping below 20°C/68°F.

◆ FORMALITIES

PORT OF ENTRY
Direction Island (South Keeling) 12°05´S 96°53´E

When approaching the 12 mile limit, the marine officer should be contacted on Channel 20. Yachts should proceed to the anchorage in the lee of Direction Island and anchor by the yellow quarantine buoys. All crew should remain on board until clearance has been completed. A police officer will come over from West Island to carry out the formalities.

Everyone except New Zealanders must obtain an Australian visa in advance. Yachts travelling to Cocos Keeling from the mainland of Australia are deemed not to have left Australia if their trip is within 30 days of departure from the mainland. They should ensure their visas cover the entire period of their stay, including travel time. A multiple-entry visa is recommended for people wishing to stop at both Cocos Keeling and mainland Australia.

The same quarantine rules apply as in mainland Australia, but occasionally yachts in transit have been allowed to keep some fresh produce provided it was not taken ashore.

◆ FACILITIES

All facilities are on either Home Island, which can be reached by dinghy from Direction Island, or on West Island, which is reached by the regular ferry from Home Island. Fuel and provisions are available on Home Island, but there is a better selection on West Island, where there are also some electrical and mechanical services available.

Cruising Guide	Website
Indian Ocean Cruising Guide	www.cocos-tourism.cc

Local time	UTC +6
Buoyage	IALA A
Currency	Australian Dollar (AUD)
Electricity	240V, 50Hz

Communications	Emergency number
IDD 61 IAC 0011	000

COMORO ISLANDS

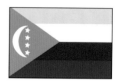

THIS SMALL ARCHIPELAGO lying between the northern tip of Madagascar and the African mainland consists of four main islands: Grande Comore (N'gazidja), Mohéli (Mwali), Anjouan (Ndzuwani) and Mayotte (Maore). Formerly a French colony, the islands are now independent, except for Mayotte, which separated from the other Comoros and is an overseas territory of France. The islands are volcanic and Mount Kartala on Grande Comore is still active. The area is mostly protected by coral reefs and the surrounding seas are rich in marine life. The coelacanth, a 350 million year old species of fish believed to be extinct, was rediscovered recently in Comoran waters.

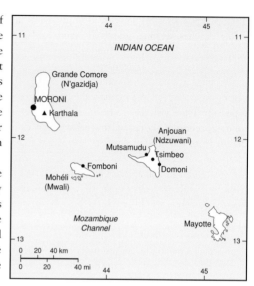

Most yachts who visit the Comoros are on their way to East Africa, the islands being conveniently located on that route. The underwater scenery is their prime attraction and the south side of the island of Mohéli is particularly beautiful, with good snorkelling, although the anchorage at the main town of Fomboni is only an open roadstead. The anchorage is not good at the capital, Moroni, either. The main port of Mutsamudu provides the best protection. A deteriorating safety situation has greatly reduced the number of visiting yachts.

COUNTRY PROFILE

The islands were originally settled by Malays, Africans and Arabs, then by prosperous refugees from Persia who created their own sultanates. In the seventeenth century pirates used the islands as a base, but during the nineteenth century France's influence increased until in 1912 Comoros was declared a French colony. This lasted until 1975, when the islands gained independence.

The population of over 750,000 is a mixture of Arab, African, Malay, Malagasy and French. Comoran (Shikomor), French and Arabic are the official languages.

CLIMATE

The islands have a tropical climate with a hot, humid and wet season from November to April, and a cool, drier season between May and October. The latter is the best time to visit as the average temperature is 24°C/75°F. November to April is the rainy season, when temperatures range from 27°C to 35°C/81°F to 95°F. This is the northeast monsoon period and coincides with the cyclone season.

FORMALITIES

PORTS OF ENTRY

Mutsamudu (Anjouan)	12°10´S 44°24´E
Moroni (Grande Comore)	11°42´S 43°15´E

Arriving yachts should contact the port captain when in VHF range.

Vessels will be boarded by various officials and advance notification is advised. Visas are required by all nationalities, but can be obtained on arrival. A two-week visa is usually given.

FACILITIES

Mutsamudu is the main commercial port and has a small boatyard, some workshops and fuel. Provisioning is good. Because of safety concerns and the volatile political situation, those planning to visit the Comoros should attempt to obtain an update before sailing there. Theft is prevalent.

Cruising Guides
Indian Ocean Cruising Guide
East Africa Pilot

Website
www.comores-online.com

Local time	UTC +3
Buoyage	IALA A
Currency	Comoran Franc (KMF)
Electricity	220V, 50Hz

Communications
IDD 269   IAC 00

KENYA

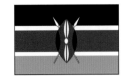

THIS SCENIC COUNTRY is the most popular tourist destination in Africa, with its golden beaches, savannah grasslands, safari parks, and spectacular mountains. Kenya has a 300 mile long coastline made up of beaches, mangrove swamps and lagoons. Much of the coast is protected by coral reefs, which provide excellent diving. Kenya's many cruising possibilities would attract more yachts were it not for the difficulty of getting there. The sailors who make the effort are rewarded with a true taste of Africa, especially if they visit the interior. Having been under the influence of Arab traders for many centuries, the coastal towns have a very different character and a few trading dhows from the Persian Gulf still ply these waters, arriving with the northeast monsoon at the end of the year and leaving with the southeast monsoon. They can be seen at Mombasa and also at Lamu, the island of the legendary Sinbad the Sailor. Mombasa is Kenya's chief port, its cosmopolitan atmosphere reflecting the port's history as an important Persian, Arab and Portuguese trading centre.

✦ COUNTRY PROFILE

Remains of some of the earliest human beings were found in Kenya. The Portuguese were the first Europeans to explore the region, with Vasco da Gama having called at Mombasa in 1498. They established trading stations along the coast and were followed by Omani Arabs, who continued this trading tradition and founded various settlements. In the interior, people lived in compact tribes whose ethnic divisions are still visible today. By the end of the nineteenth century Kenya became a British protectorate, gaining independence in 1963.

The population of 39 million includes many different minorities. The largest ethnic groupings are the Kikuyu, Luhya and Luo. Official languages are Swahili and English. Nairobi is the capital.

✦ CLIMATE

The climate on the coast is tropical and hot. April to June is called the season of long rains, and October to November the season of short rains. The weather is under the influence of the monsoons, which also dictate the direction of the currents. This must be borne in mind when planning a cruise along this coast as the best period for southbound voyages is during the northwest monsoon, and for northbound voyages it is during the southeast monsoon.

✦ FORMALITIES

PORTS OF ENTRY

Lamu	2°18´S 40°55´E	Malindi	3°13´S 40°07´E
Mombasa	4°04´S 39°41´E	Wasini Island	4°40´S 39°23´E

Mombasa: Formalities can be completed preferably at the Old Port on the northern side of Mombasa Island or also at Kilindini Harbour, which is the main commercial port.

Lamu: On arrival, after anchoring in the port area, yachts are boarded by quarantine and customs.

Most nationals can obtain a visa for three months on arrival. A transit log is necessary for any cruising in Kenyan waters and can be obtained from customs on arrival.

✦ FACILITIES

Fuel, supermarkets as well as workshops are available in Mombasa, where the Mombasa Yacht Club welcomes yachts and has some moorings. Kilifi is preferred by most yachts as it has a boatyard with good repair facilities.

Cruising Guides	Website
Indian Ocean Cruising Guide	www.kenyatourism.org
East Africa Pilot	

Local time	UTC +3
Buoyage	IALA A
Currency	Kenyan Shilling (KES)
Electricity	240V, 50Hz

Diplomatic missions			
UK	20 284 4000	Canada	20 366 3000
USA	20 363 6000	South Africa	20 282 7100
Australia	20 444 5034	New Zealand	20 601 074

Communications	**Emergency number**
IDD 254 IAC 00	999

MADAGASCAR

THIS LARGE ISLAND off the coast of Africa is very different from its continental neighbours, since the majority of its inhabitants are descended from Malay and Asian migrants, mixed with Africans and Europeans. The Malagasy language shares some of its basic vocabulary with the Maanyan language in southern Borneo and also has some resemblance to Polynesian. Having been isolated from neighbouring Africa for millions of years, Madagascar's flora and fauna are unlike anywhere else. Hundreds of species of plants and animals are unique to the island, perhaps none more distinctive than the lemur, a primate of which several species survive. A rugged mountain chain runs down the centre of the island, dividing the narrow tropical eastern coast from the savannah and forests of the west.

Thanks to its convenient location as well as its many cruising attractions, Madagascar is slowly turning into one of the favourite destinations in the South Indian Ocean. The most appealing port is Antseranana, formerly known as Diego Suarez, which occupies a beautiful natural harbour close to the island's northern tip. The most attractive bays are on the sheltered northwest coast, among them Madagascar's prime cruising feature: the picturesque Nossi Be. The island's main anchorage is the scenic Crater Bay, which is also the base for a budding charter operation. This is a most attractive area with small islands, such as Nossi Mitsio or Nossi Sakatia, with peaceful anchorages and tiny fishing villages.

Most yachts continue their voyage along the west coast,

where a convenient last stop is the colourful port of Toliara, before heading into the Mozambique Channel for the voyage south. For those whose route takes them along the east coast, an interesting stop for southbound yachts is at Taolanaro, formerly Port Dauphin, site of the first French settlement. Also betraying its French origins is Sainte Marie, also known as Nossi Boraha, an island off the east coast and once an important base for the pirates who used to ambush vessels plying the busy trading routes that passed close by.

✦ COUNTRY PROFILE

The earliest inhabitants are thought to have arrived by sea from present-day Indonesia. The migrants brought crops from South East Asia, an influence that can still be seen in Malagasy agriculture. Later, Arabs and Swahilis established towns on the coast, and from the sixteenth century the Europeans used the island as a stopping point for ships on the Cape of Good Hope route. France annexed Madagascar in 1896 and remained in control until 1960 when independence was granted. The country has experienced a turbulent time since independence, with several military coups and changes of government. In recent years foreign tourism has been encouraged and cruising yachts have also benefited from the relaxation of the previous restrictive regulations.

The 20 million inhabitants are a mixture of Malay and African. Malagasy and French are the main languages. The capital is Antananarivo.

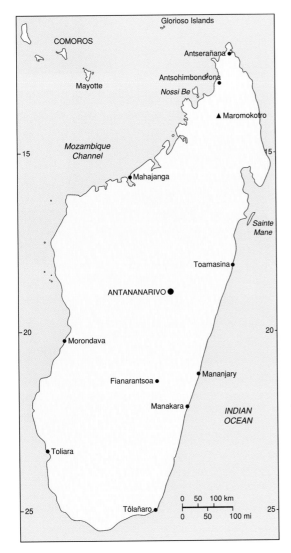

Hell-Ville: Yachts should anchor off the main dock and call the port captain. Port captain, police, immigration, customs and health offices should all be visited for clearance. Payments must be made at various offices and a receipt should be demanded as it may have to be shown later. Speaking French is an advantage. Yachts must clear in and out of every province.

Visas are required by all nationalities. They can be obtained in advance from the Madagascar consulate in Mauritius, Reunion, the Seychelles or Tanzania. Visas for three months can also be obtained on arrival. Extensions are occasionally given, otherwise those who wish to stay longer need to sail to another country, such as Mayotte, and obtain a new visa on their return.

✦ FACILITIES

In spite of the increasing number of visiting yachts, only minor repairs are available in Hell-Ville. There is a boatyard with a good diesel mechanic in Crater Bay. The best repair services are at Mahajanga, which is used by foreign shrimping boats as a base of operations. There is a boatyard with a slipway where hull and engine repair are possible. Similar facilities are also available in Toamasina, where a boatyard with some workshops is operated by the Port Authority. The same is the case in Toliara, which is a commercial harbour, with a limited range of repair services. Diesel is only available in jerrycans from roadside fuel stations.

✦ CHARTER

Dream Yacht Charter, which now has bases in several South Indian Ocean locations, is operating out of Crater Bay on Nossi Be. Other charter operations are planned.

www.dreamyachtcharter.com

✦ CLIMATE

The climate is tropical, with a rainy season between November and March. The southeast tradewind season lasts until the end of October and winds can be very strong at times, occasionally being accompanied by violent thunderstorms. The cyclone season lasts from November to April, and the island is often affected by these storms.

✦ FORMALITIES

PORTS OF ENTRY

Nossi Be (Hell-Ville) 13°24′S 48°17′E	
Toamasina 18°09′S 49°25′E	Antseranana 12°16′S 49°18′E
Mahajanga 15°43′S 46°19′E	Toliara 23°22′S 43°40′E
Sainte Marie (Nossi Boraha) 17°00′S 49°55′E	

Cruising Guides
East Africa Pilot
Indian Ocean Cruising Guide

Website
www.madagascar-tourisme.com

Local time	UTC +3
Buoyage	IALA A
Currency	Malagasy Ariary (MGA)
Electricity	220V, 50Hz

Diplomatic missions

UK	20 533 2548	South Africa	20 224 3350
USA	20 222 1257		

Communications	**Emergency number**
IDD 261 IAC 00	117

MAURITIUS

Caudan Marina in Port Louis.

A VOLCANIC OUTCROP of the land bridge that once connected Africa and Asia, Mauritius lies in the centre of the South Indian Ocean. Part of the Mascarene archipelago, Mauritius also includes the islands of Rodrigues, Agalega and the Cargados Carajos archipelago. Yachts calling at Mauritius are usually on passage westwards across the South Indian Ocean, and in a hurry to leave before mid-November because of the number of early cyclones that have hit the island in the past. Yet those who take their time to stop for longer can enjoy the beauty of Mauritius and the exotic mixture of its cultures and peoples.

The waterfront in Port Louis has been dramatically transformed by the Caudan development, which turned the once dirty harbour into an attractive complex, with shops, restaurants, hotel and a new marina. There are few cruising opportunities around the island, with the exception of the small isles off the north coast. The best anchorage is in Grand Baie on the northwest coast, a favourite spot for locals and visitors alike.

Some yachts break the passage at the smaller island of Rodrigues, which is a pleasant stop due to easier formalities and a warm welcome. The inner harbour in Mathurin Bay is well protected and the yacht can be left there while exploring the interior, particularly the caves on the windward side of the island. Occasionally boats stop at the Cargados Carajos Shoals, a large reef area lying some 200 miles northeast of Mauritius. Over fifty islets and cays make up this small archipelago which abounds in marine life.

✦ COUNTRY PROFILE

Mauritius was uninhabited until the end of the sixteenth century, although often visited by Arab and Malay sailors. The Portuguese were the first Europeans to arrive at what they called Ilha do Cirne, Isle of the Swan, early in the sixteenth century. The swan was in fact the unfortunate dodo, a flightless bird that was hunted to extinction by the crews of passing ships. In 1598 the Dutch took possession of the island, naming it after Prince Maurice of Nassau. Because of its strategic position on the Cape of Good Hope route, rivalry for the island between the Dutch, French and English was considerable. In 1715 the French gained control, renaming it Ile de France, and their influence is still visible today. A century later the Treaty of Paris ceded Mauritius, as well as the Seychelles and Rodrigues, to Britain, who reverted to the previous Dutch name. Independence from the UK came in 1968.

The history of the island is reflected in its 1.3 million inhabitants, a mixture of Indian, French, English, African

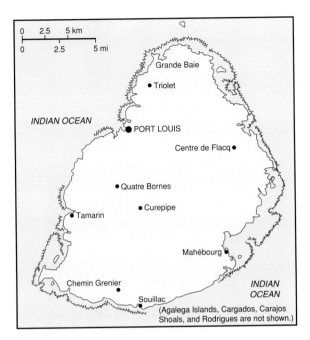

0   2.5   5 km
0   2.5   5 mi

Grande Baie

• Triolet

INDIAN OCEAN

• PORT LOUIS

Centre de Flacq •

• Quatre Bornes

• Curepipe

• Tamarin

Mahébourg •

INDIAN
OCEAN

Chemin Grenier

Souillac

(Agalega Islands, Cargados, Carajos
Shoals, and Rodrigues are not shown.)

and Chinese. English is the official language, but French, Creole, Hindi and Bhojpuri are also spoken.

◆ CLIMATE

Mauritius has a subtropical climate, with a high humidity and maximum average temperature of 33°C/91°F. The cyclone season is from mid-November to April, which is also the rainy season. September, October and early November are the most pleasant months.

◆ FORMALITIES

PORTS OF ENTRY	
Port Louis (Mauritius)	20°09´S 57°29´E
Port Mathurin (Rodrigues)	19°41´S 63°25´E

The yacht's ETA should be radioed to the Port Authority which keeps a 24-hour watch on Channel 16. Port Louis Harbour Radio should be contacted on arrival. Authorities require yachts to come alongside the customs dock to clear customs and immigration before being allowed to move to Caudan Marina. The new Cap Malheureux Marina in the very north of the island is not yet an official port of entry.

Vessels stopping first at Rodrigues must complete formalities there and then clear in again on arrival in Mauritius. The Cargados Carajos Shoals and Agalega should not be visited without prior permission from the Ministry of External Affairs in Port Louis. Emergency stops appear to be tolerated, in which case permission to anchor should be

requested from local fishermen who are temporarily based on one of the four islands.

Most nationalities do not require a visa in advance. A three-month stay is normally granted to crews arriving on a yacht.

◆ CHARTER

The new marina at Cap Malheureux forms part of a tourist development. This is the base of a growing charter fleet, with both bare and crewed yachts available. Interyacht Charter has a small fleet of catamarans and monohulls based in the new marina. Dream Yacht Charters operates a skippered catamaran out of Caudan Marina in Port Louis.

www.interyachtcharter.com/mauritius.htm
www.dreamyachtcharter.com

◆ FACILITIES

Caudan Marina has good docking facilities alongside a quay. Provisioning in Port Louis is very good, with well-stocked supermarkets and a colourful fresh produce market. There is a fuel dock in the commercial port, but marine supplies are not available. Repair facilities are limited, although there is a dry dock in Port Louis that undertakes some general repair work. There is a good anchorage in front of the Grand Baie Yacht Club, but there is a 2.5m (8ft) draft restriction in the channel leading into the bay. The club offers temporary membership to visiting sailors, who may use its facilities. It is expected that facilities at Cap Malheureux Marina will improve in time.

Cruising Guide
Indian Ocean Cruising Guide

Websites
www.tourism-mauritius.mu
www.gbyc.info (Grand Baie Yacht Club)

Local time	UTC +4		
	Summer time: last Sunday in October to last Sunday in March		
Buoyage	IALA A		
Currency	Mauritian Rupee (MUR)		
Electricity	230V, 50Hz		
Diplomatic missions			
UK	202 9400	South Africa	212 6925
USA	202 4400	New Zealand	286 4920
Australia	202 0160		
Communications		**Emergency number**	
IDD 230	IAC 020	999	

MAYOTTE

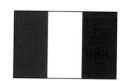

MAYOTTE, ALSO KNOWN AS MAHORÉ, is geographic-ally part of the Comoros archipelago, a small group of islands lying between the northern tip of Madagascar and the African mainland. The other three islands in the group, Grande Comore, Moheli and Anjouan, now form an independent republic. Mayotte is an overseas territory of France. It is surrounded by reefs and the main harbour at Dzaoudzi is very well protected. There are many anchorages inside the reef and diving is excellent.

✦ COUNTRY PROFILE

Mayotte and the neighbouring islands in the Comoros archipelago were originally settled by Africans and Arabs, then by prosperous refugees from Persia who created their own sultanates. In the eighteenth century the French influ-ence increased and the Comoros group was ceded to France in 1843. The other islands opted for independence in 1974, but Mayotte decided to forgo independence and maintain its links with France. In a referendum held in 2009, the population voted overwhelmingly in favour of strengthening its ties with France, as a result of which Mayotte will become a French overseas collectivity in 2011.

The population of nearly 224,000 are a mixture of African, Arab, Malagasy and French. The official language is French, but Mahorian, a Swahili dialect, is also spoken. The capital is Mamoudzou.

✦ CLIMATE

The climate is tropical, with two seasons – the dry season lasting from May to October, with an average temperature of 24°C/75°F, and the rainy season being from November to April, when both temperature and humidity are higher. The cyclone season is from November to April.

✦ FORMALITIES

PORT OF ENTRY
Dzaoudzi   12°47′S 45°15′E

Visiting yachts must use the Zamboro Pass, contact the Capitainerie du Port on Channel 9, and proceed to the anchorage off Dzaoudzi. All formalities are completed ashore. Officials have little knowledge of English so French is useful. No visas are required for stays of less than one month. The same immigration regulations apply as for other French

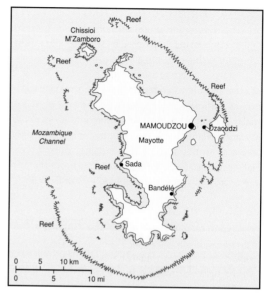

overseas territories. Personal safety is a serious concern, with several violent robberies having been reported by visiting sailors.

✦ FACILITIES

Visiting yachts may use the facilities of the Pomanzi Yacht Club, which is also a good source of local information. Some repairs are possible in workshops based in the industrial zone located out of town. Fuel and some marine supplies are available. Provisioning is very good, both with local produce and from the supermarkets.

Cruising Guide
Indian Ocean Cruising Guide

Website
www.mayotte-tourisme.com (Mayotte Tourism Office (in French only))

Local time	UTC +3
Buoyage	IALA A
Currency	Euro (EUR)
Electricity	240V, 50Hz

Communications	Emergency number
IDD 269 IAC 00	15

MOZAMBIQUE

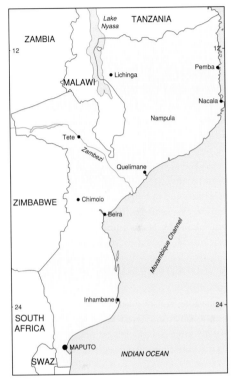

MOZAMBIQUE STRETCHES ALONG THE EASTERN COAST OF AFRICA, its 1,400 mile long shores offering many cruising opportunities, which are slowly being discovered by foreign sailors. The real attraction of Mozambique is that of being a largely unexplored country as shown by the lack of development along much of the coastline. One of the most attractive areas is the Quirimbas archipelago, with its many islands that make up the Quirimbas National Park. The wildlife along the coast is prolific and it is not unusual to see elephants and lions come right down to the water's edge. For many years cruising yachts only stopped in the two main ports of Maputo and Beira as stopping elsewhere was not permitted. Those rules have gradually been eased and foreign yachts, many of them from neighbouring South Africa, now enjoy Mozambique's natural beauty.

✦ COUNTRY PROFILE

There were several independent kingdoms thriving in this region before the Portuguese established trading posts along the coast. After almost five centuries of Portuguese dominance, independence came in 1975. The ensuing civil war brought enormous suffering to all sides in the conflict, which only ended in 1992. Since then, the country has undergone a modest programme of development as the situation has become more peaceful.

The population numbers 21.6 million. Portuguese is the official language, but many African languages are spoken. The capital is Maputo.

✦ CLIMATE

The climate is tropical, hot and humid. The prevailing winds are southeast to southwest. Much of the coast is under the influence of sea breezes, with strong onshore winds in the afternoons. In the northern part of the coast, the southeast trade winds blow during the winter months, while northeast winds prevail in summer. The tropical storm season is from November to April, with the worst months being January to March when the country is often struck by cyclones.

✦ FORMALITIES

PORTS OF ENTRY

Maputo	25°59´S 32°36´E	Beira	19°50´S 34°50´E
Nacala	14°32´S 40°40´E		

Maputo: Port Control usually instructs arriving yachts to come alongside one of the wharves to complete formalities.
Beira: The port is at the mouth of the River Pungue and is reached through Maputi Channel.

Visiting sailors are issued shore passes valid for 30 days in lieu of visas. These can be extended.

✦ FACILITIES

There is a small marina in Maputo. In Nacala, the Bay Diving Company welcomes visiting yachts and allows them to use its moorings. Provisioning is limited. Repair facilities are available in Beira and Maputo, both of which are fishing ports.

Cruising Guides	
Indian Ocean Cruising Guide	East Africa Pilot

Website
www.mozambique.embassyhomepage.com/index.htm (tourist information on London embassy site)

Local time	UTC +2
Buoyage	IALA A
Currency	Mozambican Metical (MZN)
Electricity	220V, 50Hz

Diplomatic missions			
UK	21 356 000	Canada	21 492 623
USA	21 492 797	South Africa	21 491 614

Communications	**Emergency numbers**
IDD 258 IAC 00	112 Ambulance 117 Police 119

REUNION

REUNION (LA RÉUNION) IS A SMALL FRENCH TERRITORY in the South Indian Ocean and a useful stop for yachts en route to South Africa. The lush interior of this volcanic island has some stunning mountain scenery that is dominated by the remains of huge craters called 'cirques' whose sheer walls rise to well over 2,000m (6,562ft). The volcanic scenery is breathtaking and the best way to appreciate it is to go on one of the many walks. In the southeast of the island the Piton de la Fournaise is an active volcano that has recently altered the landscape with an eruption of black lava.

With a large resident sailing community, Reunion has the best yachting facilities of any island in the Indian Ocean, but its main attraction is the French atmosphere. This is best sampled in Saint-Pierre, a small town on the south coast, whose harbour is overlooked by a promenade lined with bistros, cafés and bars with live music. Cruising around its coast holds few attractions.

The Reunion Commissioner also extends his jurisdiction over the uninhabited islands of Juan de Nova, Europa, Bassas da India, Iles Glorieuses and Tromelin that lie near Madagascar and remained French after Madagascar's independence.

✦ COUNTRY PROFILE

Reunion was discovered by the Portuguese Pedro de Masca-renhas in 1513. The island was uninhabited, although visited occasionally by Malay, Arab and European sailors. In the seventeenth century France settled the island and in 1946 Reunion became an overseas department of France.

The population is around 800,000. Most Reunionais are of French origin and there are small African and Indian minorities. French and Créole are the main languages. Saint-Dénis on the north coast is the capital.

✦ CLIMATE

Reunion has a tropical climate. The cyclone season, November to April, is hot and rainy, while the rest of the year it is slightly cooler and drier. The island is divided by a high mountain range into the rainier windward side and the drier leeward side to the south and west. Prevailing winds are from the southeast. The island is sometimes affected by cyclones.

✦ FORMALITIES

PORTS OF ENTRY

Pointe des Galets 20°55′S 55°18′E	
Saint-Pierre 21°20′S 55°29′E	

Pointe des Galets: Yachts may either tie up alongside the fisherman's wharf south of the entrance or proceed into the marina. Deep-drafted boats should not proceed beyond the main wharf, where the depth is 4.5m (14ft). The port captain will advise on the correct clearance procedure.

Saint-Pierre: Entrance into the port can be difficult due to the current caused by an outflowing river, especially after heavy rains. Having contacted the port captain, yachts are directed to a slip in the marina. Formalities are completed ashore.

The same immigration rules apply as in metropolitan France. EU nationals as well as those of Australia, Canada, New Zealand and the USA do not need visas for stays not exceeding three months.

✦ FACILITIES

Pointe des Galets is an artificial harbour on the west coast. It is both a commercial port and marina. Repair facilities are reasonable and provisioning is good both in the local supermarkets and the fresh produce market in Saint-Dénis.

Saint-Pierre has an active racing community and repair services are good. The marina has a 40 ton travelift. Essential spares can be flown in from France.

Cruising Guide	Website
Indian Ocean Cruising Guide	www.la-reunion-tourisme.com

Local time	UTC +4	Buoyage	IALA A
Currency	Euro (EUR)	Electricity	230V, 50Hz

Communications	Emergency numbers
IDD 262 IAC 00	112 Ambulance 15 Police 17

SEYCHELLES

THE SEYCHELLES COMPRISE over one hundred islands – some granite, others coral atolls, including Aldabra, one of the world's largest atolls. Having been uninhabited until two centuries ago, the islands are rich in unique wildlife, such as giant land tortoises, strange plants and many species of birds. With the reputation of being the site of the Garden of Eden, it is not surprising that the Seychelles have held such a fascination for sailors, who are forever searching for paradise on earth.

The anchorages at La Digue and Prasin Islands are particularly striking and one of the chief attractions on the latter is Baie St Anne, with its thousands of Coco de Mer palms, some of them reputedly 800 years old. Their gigantic nuts have a suggestive female shape, and when they were first discovered washed up on distant shores, mystical qualities were attributed to them. As their origins remained a mystery for many hundreds of years, they were believed to grow under the sea.

The main islands of Mahé, La Digue and Praslin (the Inner Islands) have seen a degree of tourism development, but there are still many other islands virtually untouched by mankind. Some of them may only be visited with special permission, such as Aldabra, which is a World Heritage site. The Outer Islands of Amirantes, Farquhar and a host of smaller islands and atolls lie farther southwest of Mahé, and the reefs surrounding them are among the most beautiful in the Indian Ocean. While a permit is needed to visit them, elsewhere the strict controls imposed on cruising yachts in the past have been gradually lifted and those that have been retained are only meant to protect this unique environment.

✦ COUNTRY PROFILE

Vasco da Gama sighted the Seychelles in the sixteenth century, but they were only occasionally visited until the French settled in the mid-eighteenth century. During the Napoleonic Wars the control of the islands was disputed, and they came under British control in 1814. In 1903 the Seychelles were detached to form a separate Crown Colony. The Seychelles have been independent since 1976.

The 88,000 Seychellois are a mixture of African, Asian and European origins. French and English are the official languages, but Creole is spoken by most people. Victoria, on Mahé, is the capital.

✦ CLIMATE

The climate is tropical, but as the islands lie outside of the cyclone belt, they are very rarely affected by such storms. Temperature variations are minimal throughout the year, with a minimum average of 24°C/75°F and a maximum average of 28°C/82°F. The northwest monsoon lasts from November to April, while from March onwards it is hotter and the winds are lighter until the southeast monsoon sets in from May to October.

Double rainbow over St Anne Bay on Praslin Island.

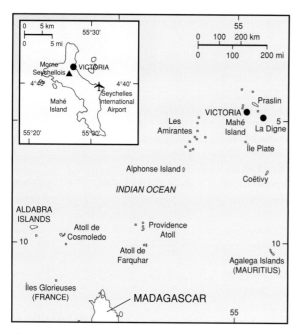

Mahé. Spearfishing is prohibited and collecting shells or coral in protected areas is forbidden.

✦ FACILITIES

With the increase in the number of cruising yachts visiting the Seychelles, and also because some charter boats are based there, facilities are steadily improving. All repair services are concentrated in Victoria, where there are several boatyards with slipways. The largest is Naval Services, which undertakes electrical, engine and transmission repair as well as metal work. There are other companies dealing with electronics, sails, rigging, glassfibre and refrigeration work. Only a limited amount of marine supplies are available locally. Yachts may use the facilities of the Seychelles Yacht Club in Port Victoria's inner harbour. The anchorage in front of the club is well protected. Two new marinas, Wharf Hotel and Eden Island, have opened as part of luxury hotel resorts. Both have good docking facilities and other services.

✦ CHARTER

The Seychelles are the most popular charter destination in the South Indian Ocean and several companies are based in Mahé, among them the Moorings, Sunsail, Dream Yacht Charter and Best Sail (VPM). Each offers a selection of monohulls or catamarans.

www.sunsail.com www.vpm.fr
www.moorings.com www.dreamyachtcharter.com

Cruising Guides	Website
Indian Ocean Cruising Guide	www.seychelles.travel
Seychelles Nautical Pilot	

Local time	UTC +4
Buoyage	IALA A
Currency	Seychellois Rupee (SCR)
Electricity	240V, 50Hz

Diplomatic missions	
UK	283 666

Communications	Emergency number
IDD 248 IAC 00	999

✦ FORMALITIES

PORT OF ENTRY

Port Victoria (Mahé)   4°37´S 55°27 E

All yachts must call at Port Victoria both on arrival to complete clearance formalities, and on departure. This rule is strictly enforced.

Mahé: Yachts must display the Q flag and contact port control to be advised as to where to anchor. Customs and immigration officials will inspect the boat, but formalities must be completed ashore within 24 hours of arrival. After the initial inspection, yachts may proceed into the inner harbour to anchor as directed by the port authority, or move to one of the marinas.

Normally a visitor's permit for two weeks is given on arrival. This can be extended for up to three months.

There are various restrictions as to which anchorages can be used and a list should be obtained from the port captain in

La Digue Island.

TANZANIA

THE UNITED REPUBLIC OF TANZANIA came into existence as the result of political union between mainland Tanganyika and the offshore islands of Zanzibar and Pemba. The largest country in East Africa, Tanzania boasts some fine scenery, the volcanic Rift Valley with its many lakes, and the high savannahs rising from the coast to Mount Kilimanjaro, which at 5,892m (19,330ft) is Africa's highest mountain. A concerted effort is being made to protect the environment, and large parts of the country have been declared national parks and reserves.

In line with a general opening up of Tanzania to tourism, cruising yachts are now welcome, even areas that were closed in the past such as Pemba Island. The underwater scenery and marine life are of comparable beauty to the spectacular interior of the country. The spice island of Zanzibar is the main offshore attraction, while inland are famous game parks, such as the Serengeti or Ngorongoro, which can be visited by leaving the yacht in the care of one of the yacht clubs.

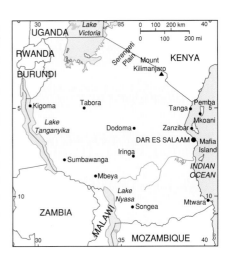

✦ COUNTRY PROFILE

Ancient remains of early human habitation were discovered in the Rift Valley. In medieval times the land thrived on trade in slaves, gold and ivory. German, and later British, colonialism came to an end in 1964 when Tanganyika and Zanzibar merged to form independent Tanzania.

The population is 41 million, made up of over one hundred tribal groups. Swahili is the official language and English is widely spoken. Dar es Salaam is the capital.

✦ CLIMATE

The climate is tropical. The rainy months are April, May, November and December. The coast is very hot and humid, especially during the northwest monsoon which lasts from December to April. The southeast monsoon is from May to October. July to September is the most pleasant time, with an average temperature of 25°C/77°F. The tropical storm season is from November to April, and Tanzania has been affected by cyclones on several occasions over the years.

✦ FORMALITIES

Dar es Salaam: The port captain usually instructs arriving yachts to anchor in the inner harbour. Formalities are completed ashore. Nationals of all countries require a visa, obtainable for a fee on arrival.

Zanzibar and Pemba Island: A cruising permit must be obtained in Dar es Salaam to visit these islands. Visitors to both islands have raised personal safety concerns. On Pemba there have been reports of officials demanding a substantial sum of money for a boat levy in an intimidating fashion.

Yachts do not have to pay such a levy and any demands for money should be resisted as they have no legal basis.

PORTS OF ENTRY

Dar es Salaam	6°49´S 39°19´E	Tanga	5°04´S 39°06´E
Mtwara	10°15´S 40°12´E	Zanzibar	6°10´S 39°11´E
Pemba Island	5°10´S 39°48´E		

✦ FACILITIES

Visiting yachts may use the facilities of two clubs: the Dar es Salaam Yacht Club and the Tanga Yacht Club. Both have small workshops and have been reported to be safe places to leave the boat unattended to visit the interior.

Cruising Guides
Indian Ocean Cruising Guide   East Africa Pilot

Websites
www.tanzaniatouristboard.com
www.daryachtclub.com (Dar es Salaam Yacht Club)
www.tangayachtclub.com (Tanga Yacht Club)

Local time	UTC +3	**Currency**	Tanzanian Shilling (TZS)
Buoyage	IALA A	**Electricity**	220V, 50Hz

Diplomatic missions
UK	22 211 0101	Canada	22 216 3300
USA	22 266 8460	South Africa	22 260 1800

Communications	**Emergency numbers**
IDD 255 IAC 000	112/999

CRUISING GUIDES

✦ MEDITERRANEAN, ADRIATIC, IONIAN, AEGEAN AND BLACK SEA

Adriatic Pilot, T and D Thompson, Imray

Corsica and North Sardinia, J Marchment, Imray

Croatia Cruising Companion, J Cody and J Nash, Wiley Nautical

Croatia, Slovenia and Montenegro, 777 Harbours and Anchorages, Anna and Rod Bailey, Sailing Books Ltd

Cruise Ukraine, Doreen and Archie Annan, Ataköy Marina

Cruising Bulgaria and Romania, Nicky Allardice, Imray

Dove Navigare Bolina, Incontri Nautici

East Aegean, Rod Heikell, Imray

Greek Waters Pilot, Rod Heikell, Imray

Ionian, Rod Heikell, Imray

Ionian Cruising Companion, Vanessa Bird, Wiley Nautical

Islas Baleares, G Hutt, RCC Imray

Italian Waters Pilot, Rod Heikell, Imray

Mediterranean Almanac, ed Rod Heikell, Imray

Mediterranean Cruising, The Adlard Coles Book of, Rod Heikell, Imray

Mediterranean France and Corsica, Rod Heikell, Imray

Mediterranean Islands, Charles Arnold

Mediterranean Spain, Costas del Sol and Blanca, John Marchment, RCC Imray

Mediterranean Spain, Costas del Azahar, Dorada and Brava, John Marchment, RCC Imray

North Africa, G Hutt, Imray

RYA Foreign Cruising Vol 2. Mediterranean and Black Sea, RYA

Straits Sailing Handbook, Colin Thomas, Straits Sailing

Turkish Waters and Cyprus Pilot, Rod Heikell, Imray

West Aegean, Rod Heikell, Imray

West Aegean Cruising Companion, Robert Buttress, Wiley Nautical

✦ EASTERN NORTH ATLANTIC AND BALTIC SEA

Arholma-Landsort and Gotland (Stockholm Archipelago) English edn, Lars Hassler and Lars Granath, Nautiska Förlaget

Atlantic Crossing Guide, A Hammick and J Lawson, Adlard Coles Nautical

Atlantic Islands, A Hammick, Imray

Atlantic Pilot Atlas, James Clarke, Adlard Coles Nautical

Atlantic Spain and Portugal, Martin Walker and A Hammick, Imray

Baltic Sea, The, RCC Pilotage Foundation, Imray

Bristol Channel and Severn Cruising Guide, P Cumberlidge, Imray

Canary Islands Cruising Guide, World Cruising Publications

Channel Islands, P Carnegie, RCC Imray

Cruising Almanac, Cruising Association, Imray

Cruising Cork and Kerry, Graham Swanson, Imray

Cruising Galicia, Carlos Rojas and Robert Bailey

Cruising Guide to West Africa, Steven Jones, RCC Imray

Cruising Guide to the Netherlands, Brian Navin, Imray

Cruising Guide to Germany and Denmark, Brian Navin, Imray

East Coast Pilot, C Jarmin et al, Imray

East and North Coasts of Ireland Sailing Directions, Irish Cruising Club, Imray

Estonian Cruising Guide, Hillar Kukk and Martsaarso, Imray

Faroe, Iceland and Greenland, Willy Ker, RCC Imray

Inland Waterways of France, David Edwards-May, Imray

Inland Waterways of Belgium, Jacqueline Jones, Imray

Isles of Scilly, Mike Lewin-Harris, Imray

Irish Sea Pilot, David Rainsbury, Imray

Labrador and Greenland, Notes on, A Hill, RCC weblink

Landsort-Skanor, English edn includes Åland, Gota Canal and Bornholm Is, Catharina Soderbergh, Nautiska Förlaget

Lundy and Irish Sea Pilot, David Taylor, Imray

North Biscay, Mike and Gill Barron, RCC Imray

North Brittany and the Channel Islands, John Lawson, RCC Imray

North Brittany and Channel Islands Cruising Companion, Peter Cumberlidge, Wiley Nautical

North France and Belgium Cruising Companion, N Featherstone, Wiley Nautical

North Sea Passage Pilot, Brian Navin, Imray

Norway, Judy Lomax, RCC Imray

Norwegian Cruising Guide, including Spitsbergen and SW Sweden, P Nickel and J Harries, e-book

RYA Foreign Cruising Vol 1. Atlantic Coasts and Baltic, RYA

Sea Sailing Directories for Scotland, Hebrides, Orkney and Shetlands, Clyde Cruising Club

Shell Channel Pilot, John Cuncliffe, Imray

Shetland Islands Pilot, Gordon Buchanan, Imray

Skanör-Strömstad, J Lannek, J Sannel, D Macfie and L Granath, Nautiska Förlaget (English edition in 2011)

South and West Coast of Ireland Sailing Directions, Irish Cruising Club

South Biscay, John Lawson, RCC Imray

Southern Ireland Cruising Companion, Robert Wilcox, Wiley Nautical

The Channel Cruising Companion, N Featherstone et al, Wiley Nautical

The Solent Cruising Companion, Derek Azlett, Wiley Nautical

Through the French Canals, David Jefferson, Adlard Coles Nautical

Wateralmanac, ANWB Almanac Deel 2, ANWB
West Country Cruising Companion, Mark Fishwick, Wiley Nautical
West France Cruising Companion, Wiley Nautical
Yachtsman's Pilot to North and East Scotland, Martin Lawrence, Imray
Yachtsman's Pilot to Skye and Northwest Scotland, Martin Lawrence, Imray
Yachtsman's Pilot to the Isle of Mull, Martin Lawrence, Imray
Yachtsman's Pilot to the Western Isles, Martin Lawrence, Imray

✦ WESTERN NORTH ATLANTIC AND CARIBBEAN

Abaco Cruising Guide, Stephen Pavlidis, Seaworthy Publications
Abaco, Ports of Call and Anchorages, Tom Henschel, Cruising Guide Publications
ABC Islands, The, D Waterson and D van der Reijden, Gotto Go Cruising
Chesapeake, Tom Henschel, Cruising Guide Publications
Chesapeake Bay to Florida, Maptech Embassy
Cruising America's Waterways: The Erie Canal, D Stack et al
Cruising Guide to Abaco, Steve Dodge, Cruising Guide Publications
Cruising Guide to Belize and Mexico's Caribbean Coast, Freya Rauscher, Windmill Hill Books
Cruising Guide to Caribbean Marinas and Services, A and N Scott, Cruising Guide Publications
Cruising Guide to Coastal North Carolina, Claiborne Young
Cruising Guide to Labrador, Cruising Club of America
Cruising Guide to the Leeward Islands, Chris Doyle, Cruising Guide Publications
Cruising Guide to the New England Coast, Robert Duncan, W W Norton
Cruising Guide to New Jersey Waters, Donald Laurer
Cruising Guide to Newfoundland, Cruising Club of America
Cruising Guide to the Nova Scotia Coast, Cruising Club of America
Cruising Guide to Puerto Rico, Stephen Pavlidis, Seaworthy Publications
Cruising Guide to Trinidad and Tobago, Stephen Pavlidis, Seaworthy Publications
Cruising Guide to Trinidad, and Tobago, Barbados and Guyana, Chris Doyle, Cruising Guide Publications
Cruising Guide to Venezuela and Bonaire, Chris Doyle and Jeff Fisher, Cruising Guide Publications
Cruising Guide to the Virgin Islands, Simon and Nancy Scott, Cruising Guide Publications
Cruising Guide to the Virgin Islands, Stephen Pavlidis, Imray
Cruising Guide to the Windward Islands, Stephen Pavlidis, Seaworthy Publications
Cruising the Chesapeake, William Shellenburger
Cuba: A Cruising Guide, Nigel Calder, Imray
East Coast of Florida, Tom Henshel, Cruising Guide Publications
Explore Central America Part I, Guatemala, El Salvador, Honduras, Nicaragua, www.sailsarana.com

Exuma Guide, Stephen Pavlidis, Seaworthy Publications
Florida Cruising Guide, Maptech Embassy
Cruising Guide to the Florida Keys, Frank Papy
Cruising the Virgin Islands, Joe Russel, Fine Edge
Gentleman's Guide to Passages South, Bruce van Sant, Cruising Guide Publications
Georgia Coast, Tom and Nancy Zydler, Seaworthy Publications
Grenada to the Virgin Islands, Jacques Patuelli, Imray
Intracoastal Waterway Guide, Waterway Guide Publications
Leeward Islands, The, Stephen Pavlidis, Seaworthy Publications
Long Island Sound to Cape May, Maptech Embassy
New England Coast, Maptech Embassy
Northwest Caribbean, The, Vol I: Jamaica, Cayman Is. Honduras, Bay Is, Guatemala and Rio Dulce, Seaworthy Publications
Northern Bahamas, The, Stephen Pavlidis, Seaworthy Publications
Panama Cruising Guide, Eric Bauhaus, Sailors Publications
Sailors Guide to the Windward Islands, Chris Doyle, Cruising Guide Publications
Southern Bahamas, The, Stephen Pavlidis, Seaworthy Publications
Turks and Caicos and the Dominican Republic Guide, Stephen Pavlidis, Seaworthy Publications
Virgin Anchorages, Cruising Guide Publications
Windward Anchorages, Cruising Guide Publications
Yachting Guide to the Atlantic Coast of Nova Scotia, Arthur Dechman
Yachtsman's Guide to the Bahamas, Tropic Isle Publishers
Yachtsman's Guide to the Virgin Islands, Tropic Isle Publishers
Yachtsman's Guide to Jamaica, John Lethbridge, Zone Publishing

✦ SOUTH ATLANTIC AND SOUTHERN OCEAN

Antarctica Cruising Guide, P Carey and C Franklin
Argentina, C Bibby, RCC Pilotage Foundation
Brazil Cruising Guide, Michel Balette, Imray
Cruising the Coast of Brazil, Marçal Ceccon, Moana Livros
Cruising Guide to West Africa, Steven Jones, RCC Imray
Cruising Guide to South Orkney, P and A Hill, RCC Pilotage Foundation
Falkland Islands Shores and Supplement, P and A Hill, Imray
Havens and Anchorages, Tom Morgan, Onboard Publications
South Africa Nautical Almanac, Tom Morgan, Onboard Publications
South Atlantic Circuit, Tom Morgan, Onboard Publications
South Georgia, A O'Grady, RCC Pilotage Foundation
South Shetland Islands and Antarctic, P Hill, RCC Pilotage Foundation
Southern Ocean Cruising, Sally and Gerome Poncet

✦ NORTH PACIFIC

Alaska Guide, Linda Lewis, Fine Edge
Costa Rica, Charlie's Charts
Cruising Guide to Central and Southern California, Brian Fagan, Bluewater Books

Cruising Guide to Puget Sound and San Juan Is, Migael Scherer, International Marine

Cruising Guide to San Francisco Bay, C and B Mehaffy

Dreamspeaker Cruising Guides, series, A and L Yeardon-Jones, Fine Edge Publications

Ecuador Cruising Guide, www.sailsarana.com

Explore Central America Part II, West Costa Rica and Panama, www.sailsarana.com

Exploring North British Columbia, D and R Douglass, Fine Edge Publications

Exploring the Pacific Coast, San Diego to Seattle, D and R Douglass, Fine Edge Publications

Exploring the San Juan and Gulf Is, D and R Douglass, Fine Edge Publications

Exploring South British Columbia, D and R Douglass, Fine Edge Publications

Exploring Southeast Alaska, D and R Douglass, Fine Edge Publications

Exploring Vancouver Island's West Coast, D and R Douglass, Fine Edge Publications

Hawaiian Islands, Charlie's Charts

Landfalls of Paradise, Earl Hines, Marine Enterprises

Mexico Boating Guide, John and Pat Rains, Point Loma Publishing

MexWX – Pacific Mexico Weather for Cruisers, Pat Rains, Point Loma Publishing

Micronesia Cruising Notes, series, Phil Cregeen, Migrant

North to Alaska, Charlie's Charts

Pacific Colombia, www.sailsarana.com

Panama Cruising Guide, Eric Bauhaus, Sailors Publications

Sea of Cortez, Shawn Breeding and Heather Bansmer, Blue Latitude Press

Sea of Cortez Cruising Guide, Vol II. Middle Gulf, Gerry Cunningham

Southern California Channel Islands, F Hawkings, RCC Pilotage Foundation

US Pacific Coast, Charlie's Charts

Western Coast of Mexico, Charlie's Charts

✦ SOUTH PACIFIC

Australian Cruising Guide, Alan Lucas, Imray

Polynesia, Charlie's Charts

Chile, A O'Grady, Imray

Coastal Cruising Handbook, Royal Arakana Yacht Club, Boat Books NZ

Cruising Guide to New Caledonia, Joel Marc et al

Cruising Guide to the Kingdom of Tonga, Ken Hellewell, Imray

Cruising Guide to the Vava'u Islands Group in Tonga, The Moorings

Cruising Guide to the Leeward Islands of Tahiti in French Polynesia, The Moorings

Cruising the Coral Coast, Alan Lucas, Alan Lucas Cruising Guides

Cruising the New South Wales Coast, Alan Lucas, Alan Lucas Cruising Guides

Destination New Zealand, Graham Brice, Bluewater

Exploring the Marquesas Islands, Joe Russell, Fine Edge Publications

Guide to Navigation in French Polynesia, P Bonnette and E Deschamps, Editions A Barthelemy

Hauraki Gulf Boating Atlas, David Thatcher, Captain Teach Press

Landfalls of Paradise, Earl Hines and J Howard, University of Hawaii Press

Micronesia Cruising Notes, Tuvalu, Phil Cregeen, Migrant

Nautical Rocket Guide to New Caledonia (CD)

Northland Coast Boaties Atlas, David Thatcher

Pacific Crossing Guide, revised R Hogbin, Adlard Coles Nautical

Patagonia and Tierra del Fuego Nautical Guide, M Rolfo and G Ardrizzi, Editrice Incontri Nautici

Rocket Cruising Guide of Vanuatu (CD)

Solomon Islands Cruising Guide, Dirk Sieling

South Pacific Anchorages, Warwick Clay, Imray

The Whitsunday Islands: 100 Magic Miles, David Colfelt, Windward Publications

Torres Strait Passage Guide, Ken Hellewell, Cevennes Productions

✦ SOUTHEAST ASIA, INDIAN OCEAN AND RED SEA

Andaman Sea Pilot, Andy Dowden, Image Asia

Atlas of the Maldives, Atoll Editions

Cruising Guide to Southeast Asia, Stephen Davies and Elaine Morgan, Imray

    Volume I: South China Sea, Philippines, Gulf of Thailand to Singapore

    Volume II: Papua New Guinea, Indonesia, Singapore, Malacca Strait to Phuket

East Africa Pilot, Delwyn McPhun, Imray

From Yangon to Manila Bay: The Cruising Almanac 2005, Joanna Greenfield, Select Books

Indian Ocean Cruising Guide, Rod Heikell, RCC Imray

Maldives Cruising Guide, Max Molteni, Edizioni il Frangente

Red Sea Pilot, Elaine Morgan and Stephen Davis, Imray

Sail Thailand, Artasia Press

Seychelles Nautical Pilot, Alain Rondeau, Praxys Diffusion

South Africa Nautical Almanac, Tom Morgan, Onboard Publications

Southeast Asia Pilot, Andy Dowden and Bill O'Leary, Image Asia

✦ GENERAL BOOKS

French for Cruisers, Kathy Parsons, Aventuras Publishing Company

Spanish for Cruisers, Kathy Parsons, Aventuras Publishing Company

World Cruising Essentials, Jimmy Cornell, McGraw Hill, International Marine

World Cruising Routes, Jimmy Cornell, Adlard Coles Nautical

World Cruising Survey, Jimmy Cornell, Adlard Coles Nautical

ACKNOWLEDGEMENTS

Many of my sailing friends have helped in various ways with this book by providing updates or supplying photographs of specific countries and I am very grateful to every one of them for their generous support: Michel Alcon on French Polynesia, Eric Baicy and Sherrell Watson on Central America and Colombia, Heather Bansmer and Shawn Breeding on Mexico and the USA, Arthur Beiser on Croatia, Erick Bouteleux on France, Terence Brownrigg on the United Kingdom, Luc Callebaut on Vanuatu and New Caledonia, Paul Ewing on New Zealand, Philippe Fessard and Fionn McKee on Brazil, João Carlos Fraga on the Azores, Phillip Gibbins on the Seychelles and Madagascar, Lars Hässler on Sweden, Bill Kimley on China and Hong Kong, Antti Louhija on Finland, Juan Francisco Martin on the Canary Islands and Spain, Italo Masotti on Italy, Mirek Misayat on Poland, Bob Mott on Thailand and Myanmar, Galo Ortiz on Ecuador, Kathy Parsons and Roxanna Diaz on Argentina, Kathy Parsons and Alberto García Scheitler on Uruguay, Karsten Pennov on Denmark, Nancy Scott on the Virgin Islands, René Tiemessen on India, Nick Wardle on the Bahamas, Martin Walker on Turkey, Dave Wilson on Panama. A special mention is due to Nancy Knudsen and Ted Nobbs who researched some of the practical information that accompanies each country.

My most grateful thanks are due to my daughter Doina who helped me research the material for *World Cruising Handbook* and later managed our website *www.noonsite.com*, both of which laid the foundations for this book.

I owe a great debt of gratitude to my editor Liz Multon whose professional and diplomatic skills have worked wonders in nursing this difficult undertaking to its end. *World Cruising Destinations* would have never come to fruition without the vision and determination of my publisher Janet Murphy who has been a most loyal supporter of the many projects that we have successfully completed over the years.

PHOTO CREDITS

Although the bulk of the photographs featured in this book are my own, I am very grateful to the following authors for allowing me to use their photographs: Klaus Bartels, publisher of Mareteam Books (pages 74 and 84), Lars Hässler, author of *Occupation Circumnavigator* (page 99), Chris Doyle, the author of the excellent Caribbean cruising guides (pages 161, 191, 197, 210, 213 and 216), photographer Jeff Fisher for the photo on page 281 featured in *Cruising Guide to Venezuela and Bonaire*, Kathy Parsons, author of *Spanish for Cruisers* and *French for Cruisers* (pages 259 and 277), Heather Bansmer, author of the *Sea of Cortez* (pages 241 and 251), Gary 'Fatty' Goodlander, author of *Cruising World Yarns* (page 285) and Tere Batham, author of *Cruising Japan to New Zealand: The Voyage of the Sea Quest* (pages 367, 369 and 372).

My thanks are also due to my sailing friends: Liviu Petri (page 56), Kari Myyrinmaa (page 83), David Sadler (page 135), Henning Blåby (page 185) and Luc Callebaut (Maewo Island, page 348).

I am also indebted to the generosity of the following professional photographers who gave me permission to use their photographs: the Finnish artist Erik Bruun (page 81), Renaud Boniech-Orsoni (pages 153 and 154), Captain Paul Harding, Safari Seaplanes of Exuma Cays Land and Sea Park (page 168), Kay Wilson of Indigo Watersports St Vincent (page 215) and Simon James, whose work is featured in the South Asia Pilot (www.southeastpilot.com) (pages 350 and 378).

I am also grateful to various organisations for providing the following photographs: the Guatemala Tourist Board (pages 7 and 234), Associação de Turismo dos Açores (page 104), Autoridad Portuaria de Las Palmas (page 111), Nanny Cay Marina (page 175), the Ministry of Tourism of the Dominican Republic (page 187), IGY Marinas – Simpson Bay Marina (page 212), the Belize Tourism Board © 2008 Tony Rath/tonyrath.com (page 225), Instituto Hondureño de Turismo (page 236) and Puerto Lucia Yacht Club (page 270).

The photographs on the following pages were supplied by BigStockPhoto.com: iii, 8, 26, 28, 42, 47, 55, 57, 60, 62, 68, 70, 71, 72, 76, 86 (Lindau lighthouse), 95, 97, 113, 115, 118, 120, 130, 131, 136, 148, 166, 183, 193, 195, 200, 205, 221, 227, 229, 230, 231, 249, 253, 260, 263, 268, 279, 284, 288, 294, 296, 298, 299, 302, 304, 307 (Fremantle), 308, 313, 328, 346, 354, 355, 358, 364, 370, 374, 381, 383, 390, 394, 402, 403, 412, 419, 420.

Photos by Jimmy Cornell on pages: iii, 1, 2, 3, 4, 10, 12, 15, 17, 18, 22, 23, 24, 25, 30, 31, 33, 34, 36, 37, 38, 40, 41, 44, 46, 50, 53, 63, 64, 66, 78, 86 (Kiel Canal), 89, 91, 93, 94, 103, 105, 106, 107, 109, 112, 114, 123, 125, 127, 129, 132, 133, 138, 140, 141, 142, 144, 151, 152, 155, 157, 158, 159, 163, 165, 169, 171, 172, 177, 179, 181, 182, 189, 207, 209, 218, 219, 223, 228, 238, 244, 246, 247, 248, 254, 255, 257, 262, 264, 265, 266, 267, 274, 282, 283, 286, 291, 293, 300, 307 (rock painting), 309, 311, 315, 316, 317, 318, 319, 320, 321, 322, 324, 326, 331, 332, 333, 334, 336, 338, 341, 342, 344, 345, 347, 348 (Tanna), 352, 356, 359, 360, 361, 363, 380, 387, 388, 406, 414.

INDEX OF COUNTRIES